I0611493

GAMESMANSHIP

A Novel

DAVID D WILLIAMS

SANDLINE  PRESS

Published By
SandLine Press, LLC
www.sandlinepress.com

The characters, companies,
and occurrences in this book are fictitious.
Any similarity to actual persons, entities,
events, or litigation is purely coincidental.

Library of Congress Control Number: 2014901768
Williams, David D
Gamesmanship / David D Williams

ISBN 978-0-9914987-2-7 (Hardcover)
ISBN 978-0-9914987-0-3 (Trade Paperback)
ISBN 978-0-9914987-1-0 (eBook)
1. FICTION 2. Thriller 3. Legal

© 2014 David D Williams
All Rights Reserved

Cover Design by Kit Foster

Printed in the United States of America

For Family, and Honest Lawyers

Contents

PROLOGUE 1

PART I   AVARICE AND ALCHEMY
1   Verdict Friday   7
2   Monday Mornings   14
3   Pick and Shovel   36
4   Spirals   45
5   News Cycle   65
6   Case Running   80
7   Own Devices   87

PART II   METHODS AND MACHINATIONS
8   First Steps   97
9   Compatibility   119
10   Cause and Effect   135
11   Teams   157
12   Crossing Lines   192

PART III   FICTIONS AND FACTS
13   Questions   221
14   Hide and Seek   240
15   Discussions   274
16   Election Day   296
17   Adverse Parties   314
18   Forms of Discovery   338
19   Thrust and Parry   360

PART IV   REMEDY AND REWARD
20   Emergency Landing   395
21   Dispositions   412
22   Recovery   429
23   Rat Trap   446
24   Reverberations   470

EPILOGUE 477

Author Note and Acknowledgements 481
About the Author 483

Lawless are they that make their wills their law.

— William Shakespeare

Prologue

The highway patrolman returned to his cruiser parked along the shoulder of the freeway, its red and blue roof lights still flashing a pattern of alarm through the darkness. His legwork was done, the scene had been cleared, and it was now time to confront the tedium of any wreck investigation — the paperwork. Switching on the cabin dome light, he placed his field notes on the dashboard and reached across the seat for the familiar two-page form, then began filling in the blanks, correctly noting the date and time of the wreck: October 25th, 1:20 a.m. Victims and vehicles were properly identified. Detailed scene measurements were placed in the appropriate sections.

The official report was meticulous but it was also badly mistaken. Not that it was the cop's fault. The document was *wrong* before he even pulled out his pen. The form's preprinted title read "Vehicle Accident Record" and that was *not* what happened. An accident, by definition, is an unplanned event. Here, every careful detail had played out perfectly.

Almost.

The intent was for first responders to discover a lifeless body. That part had gone as expected. He was found entombed inside the crushed remains of a car that lost control at freeway speed. The planners had been careful in their execution. They were confident any routine investigation would conclude it was just another wreck.

Those who knew the victim might speculate that a fatal lack of attention was to blame. He was, after all, an exhausted professional, filled with such heavy burdens, alone in his car. But that would be the end of any talk about what happened or why. The planners were sure of it. Even those who loved him would ultimately accept that it was simply an accident that took his life, quickly and tragically, on a late-night highway that was completely deserted.

Almost.

The woman inside the other car was, by definition, an accident victim. No one else was supposed to die. The time had been carefully chosen to avoid such a complication. At that hour, few cars were anywhere on the cross-town freeway. What an incalculable misfortune it had been that a rusting Buick would be traveling in the far right lane at that precise moment. Had it been five-seconds later, the aging Regal would have been safely past the doomed vehicle. She *almost* made it.

Almost.

As she approached in the adjacent lane, the right front tire of the car driven by the planners' target sprayed off its wheel hub. The instantly disabled Ford Taurus jerked then swerved, tilting off axis, its sparking metal wheel hub unable to act in concert with the steering and sudden change in direction. The left side of the Ford became slightly airborne, providing just enough angle to throw thirty-two hundred pounds of automobile onto its side and into the other lane at high speed. Its vulnerable top was quickly impaled by the woman's Buick trailing only a few feet behind, the impact tearing and grabbing the thinner roof of the Ford with the efficiency of a fish hook.

The changing geometry of metal caused the Taurus to break free from its attacker and pirouette. But once that initial spin was completed, the front end of the Buick was again upon it, its momentum persistent like a crazed fighter delivering a deadly combination to an opponent's head. The Ford twirled just halfway after the second hit, its flattened roof leading the way down the pavement.

Only physics now controlled the vehicles as they performed a death dance, grinding their way down the asphalt, traveling over four hundred feet awash in a sea of sparks, a gruesome fireworks show at ground level, before they finally came to a rest. Rest! Such a soft word. In truth, they were halted in the most violent way by a metal pillar elevating a green highway sign, its reflective characters declaring: "Exit 183 - 1/2 mile." The sign now bent downward from the structurally weakened pylon as if to stare at the confused scene below.

The sunroof section of the Ford had struck the sign post dead center causing the hood and rear quarter panels to partially deform upward around the pylon. The car's shape had been reforged by the combination of a fixed object and velocity, a physical testament to Newton's first law of motion. It looked like an angry giant force had thrown a ringer with a horseshoe. The unusual curvature, together with the Buick's ninety-degree position at the center of the Ford's undercarriage, made the final locations of the two vehicles resemble the Greek letter Psi. Traces of smoke and steam wept from both like smoldering solder. The force of that final impact seemed to permanently fuse the metal between them.

Almost.

It took nearly an hour for emergency and wrecker crews to completely separate the vehicles. The human carnage had since been taken away but only after firefighters worked for twenty-five minutes to get to the victims. It had been necessary to use the Jaws of Life, a rescue tool hopelessly misnamed in this instance. Long before the side-panels were finally cut away, there were no lives to save. The *intended* victim died of a broken neck; the *accident* victim from massive internal hemorrhage.

Death had come quickly. Not that it made any difference. For the planners, it was the need for the wreck, not the cause of death, that mattered most.

Almost.

A bigger concern was not getting caught.

Part I

Avarice & Alchemy

Chapter 1
Verdict Friday

"No emotion, not even a smile if the numbers come back big." Paul Ravich looked sternly at his once difficult but now dutiful client. "Let them see this is not some lottery to us; that we expect to receive all we deserve."

The importance of such small details, even now that it was almost over, remained lost on Bud Clayton. He was the man with a mangled leg, not his lawyer, and if this jury saw fit to award the money his attorney sued for, well, what harm could there possibly be in smiling? Still, he nodded quietly in assent as the seven women and five men of the jury filed slowly back into the jury box from their deliberations. They had last sat in their swivel chairs two days earlier.

Five days in court — the last two just waiting — over something he had caused but that his attorney had expertly blamed on someone else. Now that the verdict was about to be read, Clayton reasoned it was no time to start deviating from his lawyer's false but careful scripting of both him and the facts. He adjusted in his seat, trying to find the position that made his slightly disfigured right leg feel less heavy. It hurt only occasionally now and he could easily walk with only a slight limp. Truth be told, he now considered it a minor nuisance, although those were not the kind of truths his lawyer let him share under oath. The jury had heard something else:

"I miss walking my dog. Going for a run. Just being able to go somewhere without pain." Recalling his performance on the stand, Bud Clayton found it hard not to smile. "I feel a stabbing pain if I stand for more than twenty minutes or if I try to walk a block."

His attorney, though, had come up with the biggest lie for him to use: "I can't even take my mother shopping anymore or carry her groceries in." That one was truly deserving of a big grin. Clayton hated his mother and rarely saw her before or after his injury, but his lawyer assured him that defense investigators never check so minor a thing, making it a safe and smart fib to offer up on the witness stand. He had delivered the line with a slow sadness in his voice. The jury ate it up.

So he would show no emotion when the verdict was read even if it made no sense. After all, his lawyer clearly knew what he was doing. The evidence had been so craftily managed even he almost believed it wasn't his fault that he crashed into the construction company's road grader left along the shoulder of the road.

Paul Ravich expected the jury would see it that way as well, since almost all the liability evidence had been about safe clear distances and the proper way to warn of parked equipment. Not one word had been uttered by his client in court about the singular act that explained it all: Clayton had briefly fallen asleep, allowing his car to drift just enough to catch the outer blade of the fifteen-ton machine left barely a foot off the two-lane rural highway.

The plaintiff, of course, was asked both at trial and in his pretrial deposition why he hadn't seen the bright yellow piece of equipment. "Obviously, other cars had safely passed this alleged negligent hazard," mocked the defense. Both times, Clayton carefully followed his lawyer's advice. Both times, he lied:

"It was nighttime and the road was poorly lit to begin with, sir. The bright lights of that oncoming car prevented me from making out anything to my right or left until it was too late. When the lights passed, the blade of that thing was sticking out in my lane right in front of me."

"And this other car, this *phantom* car, why did it not stop and render aid after the crash?"

Ravich had told his client to expect the question on cross-examination and they had practiced the response.

"Sir, I don't know. That car was going the opposite way. Maybe he didn't see or want to stop. I don't know. The only thing I was aware of at that point was that my leg was crushed and I couldn't get out of my vehicle."

"Could it be there was no oncoming car? That you just weren't paying attention, or looked down at your radio, and came off the roadway and onto the shoulder?"

"No, sir. I was alert and trying hard not to be blinded by the lights of the other car. I tried even harder to stop in time but it was too late."

The "sir" business had been silly. Clayton never in real life said "sir" to anyone. Why bother in cross-examination, especially if it meant being respectful to a defense lawyer trying to deprive him of a windfall? But

Ravich had insisted: "A polite plaintiff is more likely perceived as an honest one. If the defense gets mean while you stay sweet, your status as a victim is reinforced and the jury will subconsciously come to your aid."

Amazed that he might be minutes away from pulling the whole thing off, Clayton permitted himself a gleeful but purposefully inward huff. He looked at his counsel. Paul Ravich was more than a good trial attorney. He was a courtroom *director*, eyes focused on every nuance he thought necessary to make his case — his story — seem more compelling. It didn't matter, it seemed, if any of it was honest. If a Ravich screenplay called for an untrue fact or a little faked politeness, that was the movie his jury saw.

As the twelve jurors took their seats, Clayton felt surprisingly relaxed as he looked directly at them. His story had been good, even when challenged by the very competent defense lawyer, Ben Argent.

Argent, seated one table over, was also staring the jury down, attempting to make eye contact with any member, seeking a friendly signal to indicate his defense had somehow worked. But he caught no glances. Not that he expected to. This plaintiff had been more credible sounding than most and his injury, although Argent had seen far worse, was not one to easily minimize.

The defense had been a technical case of accident reconstruction, involving the best expert he could find given the budget of the construction company's insurer. Dr. Lewis Paulston, of Failure Investigations Inc., sketched a forensic story to establish that the point of initial impact had taken place *off* the main traveled lane. The defense expert spent three hours on the stand teaching a science class to twelve quickly bored students. All that Argent wanted the jury to recall, and hopefully believe, was that the defendant's equipment had been parked on the shoulder and thus Clayton was where he shouldn't have been.

But experts can say anything and Ravich had one too. Dr. Ralph Bentson, well known to defense attorneys as a plaintiff's whore — an expert who formed opinions based upon what was needed rather than what was true — had also analyzed the same physical facts. No big surprise, he came to the opposite conclusion. He was equally adamant in his testimony that the point of impact was almost nine inches *into* the main lane of travel.

Expert opinions in a courtroom are like drugs on the street. You can find whatever you want provided you know where to look and can pay.

By the time the science war was over, the jurors would be hopelessly confused by the conflicting readings of gouge marks and metal scrapes. The only expert detail they would likely remember was that each Ph.D. had billed their respective sides over twenty-thousand dollars for their "unbiased" scientific opinions.

Ben Argent had seen it all before. He knew he would lose the case without a reconstruction expert. Hiring one to rebut the other side, however, meant at best a draw; a tie on only one aspect of the case: the physical evidence. That meant this lawsuit, like virtually every other, would be decided by the quality of the people involved and on that score Argent did not feel good.

The plaintiff Clayton was certainly no saint but the grader operator had both a surly attitude and a prior criminal record for passing bad checks. Neither particularly helped sell his testimony:

"Are you certain you parked your equipment completely off the road?" Ravich had asked on cross-examination.

The plaintiff lawyer knew what the answer would be but didn't care. He asked the question for a different reason. He was simply looking for a smug response from the worker; or better, an angry condescension that would foul the jury's senses, like irritating smoke from a nearby cigarette. He got both.

"Ab-So-Lutely!"

The grader operator crossed his arms dramatically and held his chin upright, staring straight ahead as he slowly barked the word, perhaps thinking it made him appear more certain. Instead, Ravich thought the bellicose tone and arrogant posture made the man resemble an old newsreel of Mussolini and an instant mental note was made to say something along those lines during his closing argument.

"How can you be so sure of yourself?" Ravich had taunted. "After all, it had been a long day and was getting dark."

"I've been an operator for six years, that's why, and I ain't no idiot neither."

Once again, the worker failed to speak calmly, correctly, or look at the jury. "Classic signs of deception," Ravich would remind everyone when the time came.

Paul Ravich vilified the bearded and tattooed operator in closing argument, calling him a callously mean man whose contempt for honesty was exceeded only by his employer's lack of regard for public safety. The defendant's four-year-old bad check conviction also got mentioned as if it somehow explained everything. Ravich could follow courtroom rules as adroitly as he could break them and a clear rule of evidence made such a seemingly irrelevant conviction admissible to attack the witness's character for truthfulness. He loved bringing it up. "Dishonesty is something you don't unlearn," Ravich told the jury during his final summation, sounding like a Sunday school teacher reminding children that bad habits, like lying and stealing, will get you nowhere.

It was all bullshit, of course. The fact that the worker sported a tattoo and beard, spoke poorly, or even that he got busted once for passing a few checks from an overdrawn account didn't mean he was any more likely to lie than a man who stood to make millions if the jury believed his fairy story. In fact, it had always seemed to Ben Argent that the most obvious liar in any civil suit was the person who could gain the most and yet had the least to lose.

That was Clayton. If the jury believed the plaintiff, he would be rich. If not, he would owe his lawyer nothing, having signed a contingent fee agreement. Of course, either way he would still have only one good leg, but that was a consequence of accident dynamics, not the legal system.

The road grader operator, on the other hand, had no good reason to lie. Shortly after the incident he had taken a better job with a different company and owed no loyalty to his prior employer. He also had no fear of a money judgment against him since his former employer's insurance company was providing the defense and would be paying any award if he were found at fault. Sure, he was gruff, but what construction worker wasn't? But a liar? No. Of that Argent was sure. The plaintiff would clearly be the most likely to lie. Ben Argent always felt that way. He was, after all, a defense lawyer.

"Have you, Madam Foreperson, reached a verdict?" bellowed Judge Peterson in a strong voice that belied his lack of judicial experience. This was only his fifth jury verdict since taking the bench. Peterson had been an emergency appointment after the death of Judge Lenar, who had been the county's longest serving jurist. The appointment was actually more of a gift from an old law school buddy, now the Governor. The joke among the civil bar was the Governor picked Peterson because any lawyer who still made less than fifty-thousand a year after thirty years of practice was ideally incompetent and well suited for the bench. But Peterson did look the part. His deep baritone voice and silver-white hair matched perfectly with the black robe costume.

"We have, Your Honor," replied Juror Number Eight, a school teacher elected by the others to serve as the Presiding Juror. Her tone was crisp and decisive, lacking any of the uncertainty one would expect after two arduous days of jury deliberations. Twelve people, whose service each day earned them barely enough from the county to buy a sandwich at lunch and pay for downtown parking, had just spent almost fourteen hours together in a drab and windowless room sorting out a simple crash case.

What were they doing back there? Argent briefly shook his head. After twenty-four years of practice, he knew that the thought processes of jurors could never be rationally explained.

The bailiff ceremoniously collected the verdict form and handed it up to the bench.

Judge Peterson leafed through the pages, silently reading the handwritten answers that appeared in blanks below the questions the jury had been required to consider. He sat the papers down and looked up over his rectangular reading glasses, making an effort to display a poker face.

But Paul Ravich knew better. The Judge seemed to fix his gaze a second or two longer towards the plaintiff's table and that was all the experienced lawyer needed to see. The words spoken from the bench were just a formality for the benefit of everyone else.

"The jury has found that the negligence of Brent Westerly, of Lomac Construction Company, proximately caused the incident; that Bud Clayton was not negligent; and that the sum of three-million dollars would fairly and reasonably compensate the plaintiff for his injuries." Judge Peterson flipped to the last page of the form and saw the twelve signatures. "Signed this eleventh day of October. The verdict is unanimous."

Argent closed his trial notebook and stared coldly at the jury. *Stupid, gullible fools.* Ravich had intentionally argued for a half-million more than they awarded, fully expecting the jury to compromise some on the damages if they voted his way on liability. Juries almost always did such things to signal they were no one's rubber stamp. *Morons,* Argent groused silently. Instead, they had given the plaintiff exactly what Ravich predicted he would recover.

"I'll get three at trial," the plaintiff lawyer had boasted two weeks earlier, declining the insurance company's last offer of one-million dollars. Argent closed his eyes and pictured again the smart-ass smirk that Ravich had used to punctuate the end of their settlement negotiations.

Even as euphoria welled inside him, Clayton heeded his counsel's advice and showed no reaction while the Judge made some remark about accepting the verdict and entering it of record. Clayton looked blankly at the jury. It appeared they were proud of themselves and happy for him.

Ravich also noticed the jury's sense of relief but was certain that civic pride or empathy for his client had little to do with it. *Hell, they simply did what I told them to do.* He glanced at his watch: three forty-five. Juries always seemed to reach verdicts in time to beat the rush hour traffic on a Friday afternoon. The fact that they wouldn't have to return the following Monday was the main reason he thought they looked pleased.

Another case had been won through charm and twisted facts. Paul Ravich knew how to game the system. *The rules don't apply to me.*

Seated at the counsel table closest to the jury box, he turned slowly away from his twelve gift-givers to squarely face his client. The back of the lawyer's well-groomed head was now all that any of the jurors could possibly see.

It was then that Ravich smiled — a large, beaming, toothy grin. A Cheshire-cat face for the benefit of his client and his defeated foes at the adjacent table. A look that said he could make people believe *anything*.

Ben Argent and the construction company representative shook their heads in disgust.

Clayton appreciated the performance but quickly recalled he was still on stage, his face still towards his audience, the jury. He returned his lawyer's smile with a brief nod but remembered what he had been told.

It was a solemn and expressionless nod.

Chapter 2
Monday Mornings

———⧫⧫⧫———

"If you don't leave now you'll be late again," Kate yelled, as she hurriedly threw an apple into a bark-brown lunch sack. In her haste, the hard toss crushed the already packed potato chips and they shattered in protest. *What the hell,* she thought. Her husband wouldn't care whether they are broken any more than he would likely eat the fruit. But he couldn't afford to punch in late again this month. The plant was pushing overtime double-shifts to fill an unusually large order and Dan had already been warned twice about his tardiness.

She looked at her watch with distress, then shouted: "It's almost seven!"

It wasn't the first morning she had to goad her husband, although this time he had a good excuse for being tired. The day before, he had worked a second job helping in a neighbor's house-painting business. For a hundred-fifty dollars cash, he sacrificed both a Sunday of watching football and a nice pair of jeans that now sat crumpled in the laundry basket, covered with brown latex splashes. His sleep had been fitful after a day of climbing up and down ladders and he now faced a double-shift at a job he also didn't care for but where the money was far better. Kate understood his reluctance to get moving but knew his employer wouldn't care.

"Breakfast is getting cold!"

"I'm ready! Christ, quit screaming."

Dan Crouch seemed to be speaking to his naval, busying himself with the button on his pants, as he stumbled into the small kitchen. Although Kate had tried to get him out of bed an hour earlier, he lingered there for most of that time. He now quickly tucked in his shirttail and grabbed the keys, plunging them deep inside his pocket. He reached for the slice of toast sitting on the counter. It was cold, having been made some time before along with a couple of scrambled eggs in the hope he would make time, this time, to sit down for a quick breakfast.

Kate felt foolish. His reach made her glance down at the breakfast plate, now just an unappreciated waste. The ignored eggs and her marriage of six years seemed to share the same fate. She said nothing but he noticed the strained look.

"I'm sorry, babe, but I can't get used to working this extra shift, especially after the shit-Sunday I had. I didn't fall sound asleep until two hours ago."

Maybe if he had more time he would have said something else, maybe how it would get better soon. Or maybe he would have promised that once this order was filled, they could use the overtime money and take one of those seven-day cruises where everyone in the commercial seemed happy somewhere far away. But he was too tired to know that she wanted — no, needed — to hear something like that. Instead of saying anything, he took a small bite of the toast.

What the hell. The same words came to her again. Her silent mantra. If this was all the time she would have with him today she saw no point in discussing either her disappointment over their relationship or the cold eggs. She feigned a smile, just as she had done on many previous mornings, and patted him on the back. His needs were so easy compared to hers.

"I know the hours are hard," she started, "but the pay is too good to pass up and it's only for a couple more weeks. Then it'll be back to straight eight-hour shifts, five days a week."

"And everything will be perfect again, right?" The question sounded as if it contained a hint of concern. But with Dan you could never tell for sure.

"It'll be all right," she replied, wishing he had enough time or insight to offer her a similar assurance. But of course he had neither. "You just can't be late again and expect them to keep you on."

He looked at her and felt the need to explain. "I hate my job," was all he managed to say, while plucking his lunch sack off the counter.

She shrugged her shoulders to suggest there was nothing she could do.

Satisfied that she wasn't upset, he quickly pecked her on the cheek — an expedient but almost meaningless act of affection — then turned to go. Taking one last bite of toast, he carelessly dropped the rest on the end of the counter and disappeared out the back door.

As she heard his pickup engine start, Kate walked over and grabbed the remnant of bread. She threw it, along with the untouched eggs, into the sink. The sound of the truck leaving the driveway dissolved seamlessly into the whirling grind of the garbage disposal's blades.

Closing her eyes, she basked in the flimsy comfort of darkness for a moment. She found herself doing that frequently now. With eyes shut, she could pretend not to be alone in some cheap tiny house, doing mundane chores for a husband she rarely saw. The escape felt good although she felt silly if she kept them closed for very long.

Kate Crouch was, above all else, a realist. Try as she might, she could never conjure up, behind closed lids, any image of them cavorting on the Lido deck while the Caribbean danced below. She sighed and reopened her eyes.

At precisely the same moment, the obnoxious appliance in front of her finished chewing away the last item she would ever see her husband hold.

———— ∞∞ ————

Doug Stevens disliked Mondays for reasons different from those who mourn the death of another weekend. It wasn't the job. He still looked forward to the practice of law. At thirty-three, he was decades away from disillusion. Monday mornings were bad simply because they meant motion docket and today he had two hearings scheduled at the same time in different courtrooms.

If jury trials are the grand circuses of law, then pretrial motion hearings are the equivalent of elephant shit shoveling: necessary activity to assure the circus runs right but hardly the stuff people want to see. It was boring work and no one becomes a trial lawyer because they crave the undramatic.

Doug entered Judge Thompkins' crowded courtroom to find all five spectator rows behind the rail packed with lawyers, and the overflow of suits filled every chair in both the jury box and at the counsel tables. Another fifteen attorneys stood in line at the clerk's desk situated left of the Judge's currently vacant bench. A county employee, hidden from view by the human morass, was busy taking the names of those lawyers who, like Doug, also had hearings elsewhere and needed to be excused to make similar announcements in other courts. A smaller pack of attorneys huddled around the stenographer's table where the clerk had put out an extra copy of the morning's docket sheet. Lawyers passed it around, each hoping to see their case listed first or at least on the front pages of the eleven-page schedule. Being an early up meant a prompt ruling on your motion without having to sit, sometimes for hours, forced to endure the repetitive arguments of other counsel in cases in which you have no interest.

Doug reached the hive of lawyers buzzing around the docket sheet and attempted to stare over the shoulder of another attorney who was frantically flipping through the document, having failed to find his case on the first eight pages.

"Morning, counsel," a familiar twangy voice announced to his left.

Doug turned and saw Bill Gaston, an awkwardly lanky man, who stood balancing an accordion file under each arm. The brown folders were bursting at their seams with paper that bore testament to both the age of the case file and the volume of work that Gaston had already billed to some poor soul.

"Sorry, Bill, I didn't even see you standing there."

"Son, you better wake up before ole Terrible Thompkins takes the bench. You know how he likes to catch the sleepy not paying sufficient attention to his pomposity."

Bill Gaston always dispensed advice, even the casual kind, with the folksiness of Will Rodgers. Trouble was, he looked more like Ichabod Crane. As a result, his wit was often mistaken for goofiness.

Doug knew better. They had gone to law school together. Like the rest of the class, Doug initially equated Bill's corn-pone demeanor with an inferior legal mind. Then first semester grades got posted. Gaston was top of the class in four out of five courses. By mid-term second semester, when a professor called upon Bill to recite on a case, his slow drawl was a Pavlovian cue for the rest of the class to resume note-taking.

"What a day," Doug said, slapping his friend on the back. "I've got to be in two places at once this morning, both on routine motions the other side won't agree to."

"It's always Heaven or Hell, son. Hell just has more rooms."

Doug laughed, as he almost always did at Bill's stupid sayings. He regretted he hadn't found some free time to see his odd classmate in front of a jury. He could only imagine the entertainment value of a Bill Gaston closing argument. But free time was in scarce supply for a young solo practitioner. Since his law school graduation, now eight years distant, Doug found himself with little time to kill.

Gaston sat one of his files on the floor as another lawyer dejectedly handed the docket sheet his way. Bill immediately spotted his case on page two. "You're looking at a lucky man here, boy," he said gleefully. "I'll be free of this torture chamber by ten o'clock."

Gaston was in such good spirits owing to his docket position that he performed the favor of finding Doug's case much further down the list. "Uh-oh, son, looks like you have plenty of time to figure out the relief you seek from His *Horrible*," placing emphasis on the substituted word for "Honor" to make more biting the insult directed at the Judge. "You're number thirty-eight on the docket," chuckled Bill. "Welcome to the Honeymoon Suite of Hell!"

Doug shook his head in resignation. "The only time I've ever been at the top of this docket is when I have absolutely no other place to be. Fucking figures," he spat, a bit too loudly.

The court clerk heard the remark and the rebuke was swift. "Counsel, this *is* a courtroom, please."

Doug rolled his eyes skyward, looking to curse the spirit that imbued him with the talent to say the wrong thing at just the right time. Turning to face the clerk with an apologetic smile, he breathed an instant sigh of relief.

"Sarah! What are you doing up here pushing Thompkins' paper?"

Sarah Ash sat primly behind a computer terminal, her only shield against the disheveled stacks of court files that surrounded her. The last time Doug saw her she was assigned as Judge Lewis' clerk, three floors below.

"You really want to know why I'm now up here?"

She unceremoniously pushed aside a pile of official paper and motioned for Doug to stick his head in the newly formed crack of space. Whatever the secret, it was obviously not to be shared.

"The County calls it a lateral transfer," she began in hushed tones. "Actually, it was a different kind of move, you know, the type that old weasels think they have the right to make if you've been a loyal employee."

"Oh, tell me more, humble civil servant," coaxed Doug, trying to feign a comical interest. He was always game for courthouse gossip. He was also pleased he had developed a sufficient friendship with Sarah to get the scandal report directly from her.

"This is just between us, okay?" she prefaced.

She grabbed Doug by the lapel and pulled him close; an effort to shield her confidences from the rest of the crowd. She especially did not want Bill Gaston to hear. He was now standing close by picking his teeth with a folded business card. Sarah disliked Gaston as much as Doug admired him. She made friends of lawyers she thought were smart or cute and, in her eyes, Gaston fit neither category.

"Seems Judge Lewis forgot to give me my ten-year pin, so instead he ran his hand up my dress as a gift."

Anger caused a slight rise in her voice and those standing nearby glanced over. Like preschoolers, trial lawyers enjoy hearing someone else get bawled out. They assumed Doug was getting a lecture on decorum from court personnel.

"Shhh," counseled Doug quietly. "Tell me more."

"The fat bastard thought it was his right. He said he assumed I wanted it by the way I treated him over the years."

"Well, Sarah, you are the only person who would eat lunch with the asshole. You can't blame him for mistaking that for love," teased Doug.

"Then maybe you can represent him when I decide to sue," she snapped. "In the meantime, we thought this transfer might be the best way to avoid future judicial interventions."

"I see; an out-of-his-court settlement."

Sarah smiled awkwardly, the way people sometimes do when their problems have been trivialized by a friend in whom they have confided. Doug caught the signal and smartly switched subjects.

"So, can you do anything to help me out on this docket? I've got another hearing before Judge Hinojosa this morning and that one is really important to me."

"Aren't they all, counsel?" Her sarcasm indicated some slightly hurt feelings but she immediately betrayed them with a resigning smile. "Let me see what I can do."

As Doug watched her deftly mark up the list of cases and juggle files at her desk, he thought about how little things change. Sarah certainly hadn't. On this Monday morning she was still very much in control and still very selective about the lawyers who might receive a favor from her.

She was the same way seven and a half years ago when, as a new lawyer, Doug stupidly failed to call in his announcement of ready on the Friday before the trial date as required by local court rules. His first decent paying client had been at his side the following Monday afternoon, growing flush with anger, when they were advised their case was no longer on that week's docket. Too inexperienced back then to even rely on the old lawyer standby of blaming someone else for his own oversight, Doug had simply turned away and hung his head in shame before her voice called out as if from heaven itself:

"Oh wait, Mr. Stevens. I'm sorry, there's a note here from the bailiff that your legal assistant phoned in your announcement. I must have been at lunch when the call came in. I'll get your case worked onto the docket somehow this week."

Neither Sarah nor the fuming client knew that Doug had no legal assistant. Hell, at that early point in his career, he could barely afford his part-time receptionist. But Doug knew the second she flashed a little smile that he had received his first legal rescue from an angel named Sarah Ash. Less than a year after that first encounter, Sarah again did him a favor, maneuvering one of his cases into a preferential setting. Only eight months ago, she had accepted a late filing to cover a missed deadline.

Lawyers often use friendly clerks to cut corners when possible. But Sarah was more than just a helpful county employee. She was a person; a good person. Now, as she flipped skillfully through today's docket list, the nostalgia of her past good deeds led Doug's mind astray. He briefly pictured her sexually; a thought, curiously, he never had before Judge Lewis' prurient interest piqued his own.

Sarah had a pretty face, pleasant smile, and whatever body she possessed was always amply concealed beneath the uninspired wardrobe shared by court clerks and librarians. But she seemed especially attractive to him this morning and Doug felt ashamed that he never thought of her as anything more than just a workplace ally; a friend who had, inexplicably, saved him from some tough spots.

I'm such an ass, Doug thought. He started to say something about his gratitude and to make clear he was willing to listen more seriously about Judge Lewis' actionable harassment if she wanted to talk. But, like always, her efficiency was faster than his thoughts.

"You're now number eighteen after passes. It will be at least 10:30 before you're reached and that's the best guess I can give. Go get finished with your other hearing. You should have plenty of time to get back here."

"I'll represent you for free when the time comes," was all he fumbled to say. Embarrassed by the stupid and insincere-sounding comment, Doug hastily adjusted the files under his arm and turned toward the exit while silently scolding himself again. *What an ass.*

"Make sure you're back before your case is called," she called out, as he started to walk away. "If not, Judge Thompkins will put you at the end of the list."

Hurry up or wait. It seemed those were the only options on Motion Mondays.

———— ✦ ————

For Ken Slator, the alarm clock barely won its Monday race with the sun. A harsh buzz shrilled through the small and unkept apartment. He instinctively slapped it off. Staring at the pulsing blue numbers he wondered: *Why use the damn thing anyway?* He knew the night before that his workweek would begin at daylight. Yet he had pulled the drapes, thin as they were, tightly shut in an effort to deny nature the privilege of bearing him a more tranquil awakening.

At fifty-six, the slightly balding man was simply used to unerring patterns of behavior. What he did before going to work, and the order in which he did them, seemed not just habit but the product of some strong genetic code. Rote tasks that never wavered, even though he couldn't honestly tell you why he always shaved, then showered, or why socks went on after the undershirt and never before.

Except for his marriage, now failed after twenty-three years, constancy was the single thing that defined everything in his life. Alone in his monthly rental apartment, where cheap furniture comprised the post-divorce decorating scheme, he busied himself through a standard morning script of readying himself for work. It was just another day, although this particular Monday was, he supposed, a milestone of sorts. He had been employed with SeaCoast Chemical Corporation for exactly twenty-two years; hardly the kind of anniversary to cause any change in his behavior. No one else would make a fuss so neither would he.

Had it really been that long? The thought passed quickly as he shaved the right cheek, always first. Looking at his sagging face in the mirror he found it impossible to see the same young man who had been recruited by a then new and innovative company. Switching to the stubble on his left cheek, he recalled being coaxed away from his chemical engineering doctoral studies by the promise that true science was also the economic kind. The job offer had sounded so intoxicating to a young husband with a baby on the way.

That choice, now so distant, made him a decent living over the years and some of his work certainly contributed to the company's rise in industry market share. Among its many products, SeaCoast was a leading manufacturer of synthetic fertilizer that it produced under the trade-name *Ceres,* after the Roman goddess of earth and harvest. Slator was now head of process engineering at the company's primary agrochemical plant, SeaCoast's largest facility.

Unfortunately, the high profits generated by the company's fertilizer business got harvested by management, not the scientists. All that Slator gained from his long tenure was a growing bitterness toward his work and his life. As he stepped into the shower, he realized that his employer had already delivered a lasting anniversary gift: *I'm both unhappy and alone.* He slowly dismissed the thought and began lathering his legs, then arms, ending with a little soap on the face — the order precise and always the same. The towel, when he finished with it, was returned to the left hook on the wall. The right hook, pattern dictated, was for a bathrobe he seldom wore. No one was there to care if he walked around naked.

His hands soon groped in the small closet which was more than adequate for a man who cared little about fashion. It held five business suits, the same number of button-down shirts, along with a few pair of jeans and a small handful of casual shirts that, maybe, had been in style long ago. Without thinking he retrieved the navy suit with light blue pinstripes. None of his coworkers ever called to his attention that he wore it every Monday.

Ken Slator was capable of considering the little things, he just didn't want to. A lifetime of big things — a stagnant job, a failed marriage, a daughter who recently spent her second year of college in drug rehab instead — had all coalesced to stifle any impulse for him to *stop and smell the fucking roses*. That was his obscene variation of the line his wife had used to explain why she wanted a divorce. He had surrendered himself, long before this particular Monday morning, to the notion that he would have to get by without a spouse, a responsible daughter, or any true friends. At least his company was still there for him. *The Pricks.*

In a literal way, work consumed him even when he was home alone. Tired of receiving calls from a plant worker every time a pressure reading spiked or a gauge report looked funny, he had, a year earlier, designed a simple software program. It automatically transferred to his home laptop, via the Internet, all the critical plant operation data as it constantly updated on the control system monitors at work. Nobody asked him to do it and nobody apparently cared that he had. But as process engineering manager, he was expected to be on top of things at all times. Having that kind of data in real time meant he could quickly detect and explain things to his less astute assistants who, in usually unreasonable panics, occasionally called him at home during their shift hours.

His habit, yet another, was to always look at the night shift plant data before driving to work. He thought it important to understand where things stood before he walked on the plant floor, especially at times like these when the plant was being pushed as hard as it had been this past month.

He walked out the apartment door at seven-twenty on the dot, never once questioning why he double locked a door that secured nothing of real value to him.

Ten minutes later, the blue mid-size was making its way through sluggish freeway traffic. He drove the type of car purchased only by rental companies or by people who couldn't care less. Fighting the boredom that comes with commuting, he tuned the radio to what turned out to be the closing spot on a morning news program. The polished announcer, a voice like a game show host, was completing his segment, ending with *"other items of interest."*

"The Mayor yesterday claimed her November reelection chances were strong as she thanked supporters at a luncheon hosted by a donor group calling itself 'Republicans for Better Business.'"

"And local famed tort attorney, Paul Ravich, recorded his thirty-second straight multimillion dollar verdict on Friday. The jury awarded three million for a man whose leg was injured in a nighttime driving accident."

"And now, a traffic update from Sky-Copter One high atop...."

Slator turned down the volume knob. He didn't need a glib description of the very bog he was both victim of and partly responsible for, and he didn't care to listen to a fast-speaking voice that surely found its perkiness in the exhilaration of unencumbered movement. It was better with the damn thing off.

Without the noise, and looking blankly ahead at the swath of commuters before him, Slator's mind had little to do. Instead of permitting a peaceful contemplation of the sun's beauty, now fully above the horizon and bathing the city in the warm glow of a pleasant autumn morning, his thoughts focused instead on what he had to do at work that day. Any solace which nature was trying to offer quickly disappeared.

The plant had been running at full capacity for twenty-eight straight days, producing in that amount of time more metric tons of *Ceres* than had been created in the entire prior quarter. The storage bays were already overwhelmed and pallets of finished product were now being loaded into leased railroad cars and lined up along the plant's sidetrack. *What had management been thinking?* Making money was one thing. Making a contractual commitment to deliver amounts that strain the safe working condition of equipment, to say nothing of the stress on plant operators, was too high a price for the profit. But then again, he wasn't in the loop of those who would get to keep the windfall.

A white Toyota quickly darted into his lane, filling the safety gap he had allowed to form ahead of him. An irritant, but not by far his worse.

Do they think we are making sausages? Slator doubted that the slick boys in the sales department of SeaCoast, much less the executives at the parent company, had any idea how technical it was to mass produce a pellet that was 95% concentrated ammonium nitrate. From the comfort of their offices it was just fertilizer, a nice little bag of man-made something to help plants grow. *They don't care what's in the shit, just how much can we sell?* From their viewpoint, it was sausage.

Meanwhile, somebody had to care and be careful. So it seemed fitting that such a no-win job would fall in his lap. If he met the production goal on schedule, Slator knew he would hear nothing, not even so much as an "attaboy." But if, as he expected, the automated safety system shut down a process line or system vessel after sensing that a component had been taxed to its rated capacity, then he would be the one getting the phone call from the plant's business office next door: "Why are things shut down now, Ken?

It couldn't be a worse time." As he drove past the downtown area, still twelve miles from work, Slator resolved that if such a call came he would simply say they had run out of meat and casings, then slam the receiver down.

Entering the refinery district, where a maze of cooling towers and flare stacks lined both sides of the freeway like so many reeds protruding from a stagnant pond, he finally approached his exit a mile away. Slator realized then he would have the entire day to revile his employer so he chose to spend the last few minutes of the drive thinking about something else. But the radio was still off, and the sun's beauty was now obscured by the sight of silver tubed factories on both his left and right, belching the stench of their exhaust into the sky. The ugliness and tedium of the surroundings left little for mental stimulation. His mind wandered back to the news summaries he had heard minutes before.

As for the mayor, she probably deserved reelection. Slator remembered reading in the paper that she had talked Charles Thornton, the head of SeaCoast's parent company, into giving up some of his after-tax wealth as a big donation. In exchange, he probably got to be chief of that tribe labeling themselves "Republicans for Better Business." *They deserve each other*, Ken thought. Company management had even arrogantly tried to solicit a small donation from him, not realizing their prey was both apolitical and largely broke after the divorce. It was yet another example of how little they really knew about the people who actually made them rich.

And that lawyer crap? As Slator made his way down the freeway exit ramp, he considered that as haughty as Charles Thornton might be, he certainly had nothing on some attorney who thinks his courtroom winning streak is newsworthy. *What kind of ego motivates a lawyer to promote his achievements on radio and disguise it as news?* Slator curled his lip in disgust. It took gall for some ambulance-chaser to think his job was infinitely more important than those of the thousands of other commuters, just like himself, who were slowly pulling into parking lots to start a week of honest toil.

But that's the way things are, he reasoned. Those who actually work for something real, rather than for fame, only get themselves mentioned amorphously, as a collective and lumbering mass, by an obnoxious voice coming from Sky-Copter One.

Cynicism — the Monday morning traffic kind — was just another habit that, for Ken Slator, had become deeply entrenched.

———∞∞∞———

Charles Thornton loved to tell the story.

The emergency caesarean had gone badly for his mother. She died at the very best hospital while he fought, instinctively, the placental abruption that should have also claimed his life before it even got started. Despite an alarming lack of oxygen, and defying all medical odds, he had willed himself to live. In his first life-test, he faced and defeated the very thing that makes for dead or brain-damaged babies. The heroics of the delivery room personnel and the subsequent care rendered by the neonatal intensive care specialists never got mentioned in his survival story. To hear him tell it, Charles Thornton had done it all by himself.

"Starting on Day One," as he liked to say. And he liked to say it often. To him, the story of his traumatic birth conveyed destiny and strength. His gargantuan ego blinded him to the fact that most people found such an emotionless description of a mother's death to be particularly odious, especially considering it was spoken of simply to illustrate he was someone to be reckoned with when it came to a business deal.

Had he known the story made others uncomfortable around him, he most certainly would have started every negotiation with it. Even so, the story got told often enough and always the same: *I survive today because I survived then.* The intended message was that anyone foolish enough to get in his way would lose everything and become just another prop, like his long-dead mother, in his continuing success saga. The birth story was no different from the downtown office tower that bore his name, or the framed covers of *Fortune* and *Forbes* that depicted his confident pose and which flanked the entrance to his massive fifty-second floor office. All of it was intended to impress. Failing that, it was goddamn sure meant to intimidate.

"Good morning, Mr. Thornton."

His assistant, Marlene, greeted him with such predictability he had stopped bothering to acknowledge her words. She stood before his office door holding forth a cup of coffee and a one-page itinerary of the day's meetings, both of which he abruptly snapped away while passing into his office without comment. She quickly closed the ornate walnut doors that were now already well behind him as he stomped toward his desk.

Marlene had been with Thornton Industries for eighteen-years, the personal assistant to its Chairman and CEO for the last seven, and she knew better than to expect any morning pleasantries from her boss. He had his patterns; so did she. Each weekday morning she was in her office forty-five minutes before the security desk phoned to say: "The big man is on his way up." His elevator ride timed exactly to the seconds required to pour the coffee, straighten her dress, grab the daily agenda, and post to attention beneath the *Forbes* cover of her boss that read: *"America's Best Tycoon?"* She had always been amused by that question mark. If the punctuation was intended as a sly expression of doubt by the magazine's editorial board, it certainly was not a sentiment allowed to be shared by anyone who worked inside a building that had "One Thornton Plaza" emblazoned in granite above every entrance.

"Get Bruce up here!" Even behind the five-inch thick doors, his shout could be easily heard. Men like Charles Thornton were not accustomed to using intercoms.

Marlene, now back at her desk, picked up the phone and dialed Bruce Waltman's extension. She passed along the directive. The company's legal department was five floors down but its General Counsel came bounding into the Chairman's reception area in a mere minute. Men like Charles Thornton were also not accustomed to waiting. You become the General Counsel for a holding company this big by being smart and responsive. Bruce Waltman knew that when his boss said "Jump" you were to appear quickly and say nothing other than "How high?" Waltman raced past Marlene's desk. He would give his morning greetings to her on the way out. Without knocking, he entered Thornton's office. If there was any room left in Charles Thornton's ego for an inner circle, Waltman was certainly part of it.

"Bruce, it says here the closing on the Bangalore facility purchase has been postponed for thirty days."

"Yes, sir, some last minute diligence."

Thornton, irritated, tossed aside the daily schedule memo.

"Well, I don't mind an extra forty-five minutes of free time today but I would've appreciated a hell of a lot more seeing revenues from that site appear on our books *now* rather than next month."

The tone was somewhat hostile but Waltman was unfazed. Almost nothing Thornton said ever sounded pleasant.

"Of course, sir, we understand the importance of closing as soon as possible but the Indian government has taken longer than we expected to certify the continuation of the permits after the transfer of ownership."

"Little fuckers! Do I need to pull connections or do you simply open a money bag in front of a bureaucrat over there?"

Men like Charles Thornton were accustomed to speaking crudely and employing special remedies when needed.

"I'll see if we can't light some fires and will give you a strictly verbal update by tomorrow."

Strictly verbal. Lawyer-speak for not putting anything in writing that might smack of the sinister. Thornton smiled for the first time this morning. His GC was a clever son-of-a-bitch. No Charles Thornton, of course, but clever nonetheless.

"I want you back up here in my office at one. We need to address the financial service division's numbers and I'd like to go over the strategy with the Chinese on that upcoming SeaCoast contract renewal."

"Yes, sir. The CFO of Thornton Financial will be back here with me and I'll have our latest SeaCoast production numbers for you."

Waltman rose to exit. He knew that men like Charles Thornton were not accustomed to post-meeting chitchat. Thornton, however, chose to issue a parting comment on the game ahead with his SeaCoast foreign buyers.

"Those crazy Chinamen want to buy more N2 fertilizer than we can manufacture," Thornton said laughing. "If they think they paid too much last year, wait and see. I'm gonna screw `em like a tied-up goat."

Bruce Waltman was certain of that. He didn't have to say anything, so he didn't.

"You give me ten more years of selling to those commie bastards and I'll single-handedly restore the balance of trade. I'll make them suffer for running roughshod over our dollar."

The General Counsel nodded and walked toward the walnut doors. While every Chairman or CEO could and usually did brag about their business prowess, Waltman knew his boss was doing something more concrete. Thornton was crudely announcing another deliverable promise. If you do what you say, it isn't false bravado. The Chinese stood no chance. The fact that Thornton could speak of a four-hundred million dollar customer in disparaging, even racist, terms was part of who he was. For him, it was never enough to simply win in business. The other guy had to lose. If he could make them feel bitter when they wrote their checks, so much the better.

Having entered the world in distress, Charles Thornton had a certain affinity for bringing it upon others. Starting on Day One.

—❧—

Doug knew that the Honorable Robert Hinojosa didn't care about other people's schedules. Few recalled he was the first Latino elected judge in the county. Instead, he was best known for his error-filled preoccupation with punctuality. If a fifteen-minute recess were called, you could not be heard in defense that you had been gone only ten if the Judge believed otherwise. Trouble was, neither his wrist watch nor the clock above his bench kept the same or accurate time. Litigators, litigants, even jurors were thus subjected to constant yet unpredictable harangues about lateness which Hinojosa was certain revealed a lack of respect for his Court.

In his second year of practice, Doug had witnessed a seasoned trial lawyer being held in contempt for returning late from an hour lunch break that had inexplicably lasted only forty minutes. Since then, Doug always arrived early to Hinojosa's court. If in trial there, he spent all breaks, lunch or otherwise, in the hallway within easy view of the crazed timekeeper's return.

Pressing his luck this morning, Doug ran agilely down the poorly lit stairwell of the courthouse. The stairs provided the quickest route between Judge Thompkins' court and Hinojosa's two floors below. He could leisurely take the elevator back up when he was finished, secure in the knowledge that Sarah had given him an accurate time to be back in their court. But right now he was in a hurry. Slipping around the paint-chipped and worn handrails, Doug thought with regret of his tactless handling of Sarah's troubling confidences. He would try, soon, to find a way to be a real friend.

As he arrived at the courtroom entrance he glanced at his watch, taking no comfort in the fact that it read two minutes before nine.

He was in luck. The bench was empty when he walked in. The crowd was also relatively small compared to the lawyer-cattle being herded above in Thompkins' court. With time to review the docket sheet, he happily discovered he had Hinojosa's number two setting. It meant he wouldn't have to wait too long to present his motion to a man who can't tell time. Although important, it was a straightforward request to alter the discovery schedule. Doug returned to a gallery bench, sat down, and glanced at his file.

At precisely twelve minutes after nine, His Honor strode quickly through the door of his chambers and ascended to the ceremonial throne.

"Good morning, ladies and gentlemen. It's good to see you all here right on time at nine o'clock sharp. Let's begin." Reading from his copy of the docket sheet, he said: "The first case is *Flowers vs. Motor-Freight*. Counsel, please approach."

Two lawyers rose from their seats. Although Doug knew neither, and cared less about their particular case conflict, he couldn't help but notice the stark contrast they projected. One attorney was young, female, and dressed in the well-tailored navy blue suit-dress that seemed *de rigueur* for any woman litigator. The other lawyer was an out-of-shape and age-weathered man whose non-matching pants and sports coat were accented perfectly by his stained and unfashionably wide brown tie.

The woman walked deliberately toward the bench, her short heels clicking smartly on the county's thirty-year old linoleum. Her elder and disheveled opponent followed meekly behind in his scuffed hushpuppy loafers, one hand pulling an errant coattail out from where it had become lodged inside his unbelted baggy pants.

A novice defense lawyer from a Big Three firm going up against a burned-out plaintiff's counsel, guessed Doug.

"Good morning, Your Honor. I'm with the firm of Fenwald & Bayer. My name is Delynda Collins, and we are here on Defendant's Motion to Compel."

Doug was right on the first count. Fenwald & Bayer was the second largest firm in the city and its litigation section consisted of over a hundred lawyers. Three hundred-eighty more attorneys served in the firm's corporate, real estate, energy, labor, and environmental sections. Clients were constantly being funneled to the firm's litigators as business deals crafted by the non-courtroom partners invariably led to nasty disputes over the meaning of documents or the exchange of money.

The novice aspect of Delynda Collins revealed itself not merely in her youthful appearance but also by the consistent way all F&B new hires invariably introduced themselves. Doug was always amused by how they placed primary emphasis on the firm's name rather than their own. It was an attempt, he supposed, to inform courts and opposing counsel that behind any transparent inexperience lurked a legal mind that had garnered the attention and big salary of a prestigious downtown law firm. After all, such firms hired only the best and brightest law graduates. The subconscious message the big firm rookies were trying to send was they should be feared or respected simply because of their letterhead instead of by more objective standards, like actual courtroom accomplishment.

"Mornin', Judge, I'm just here because this fine young lawyer doesn't believe me when I say I ain't got what she wants me to turn over."

Such casual language by a bum-like lawyer who didn't bother to introduce himself implied that Ms. Collins' rumpled adversary had likely stood in front of this bench before.

"Maybe she's heard that Harry Greenbaum doesn't look very hard for information that could be detrimental to his client's interests," Judge Hinojosa said, smiling at the old lawyer.

They broke into simultaneous laughter as the dour Ms. Collins stood by, uncomfortably watching the obvious familiarity.

Doug suddenly grew more interested. *So that's Harry Greenbaum*, he said to himself, taking in the colorful image of a man who had achieved legendary status among the local trial bar. Doug had heard wonderful stories about Harry but had never actually seen him in action. His Monday was suddenly getting better. The descriptions of an unkept, amiable man who spoke simply and dressed down were not saloon embellishment after all. There he stood with a Bic ballpoint pen tucked atop his ear and a Big Chief writing tablet in his hand. Doug hadn't seen one of those since elementary school. Lawyers were supposed to write on yellow "legal" pads. They were standard issue although no one knew why. Greenbaum, however, clutched what third-graders once used to practice making cursive letters. The big red pad was made even more conspicuous by the absence of anything else resembling a case file.

Doug recalled his laughter, several years ago, when Bill Gaston swore that an old trial horse named Harry Greenbaum would carry no other props into a courtroom regardless of a case's complexity. He purposefully did it, Bill had explained, to make it easy for the jury to see that Greenbaum's side had only limited means and commonsense whereas the enemy had sneaky little laptop computers, thick Mount Blanc pens, and file boxes filled with legal loopholes.

So the story was real. The unicorn lived. There he stood, making just that contrast to the starched Ms. Collins who was, at that precise moment, flipping through her neatly index-tabbed file folder, one of several thick volumes she had carried to the bench. Eager to locate and quote from her motion, she was oblivious to the comical shrugs of innocence directed from the kindly old plaintiff lawyer to the irascible Judge Hinojosa.

"Counsel, what specific relief do you seek from this Court? We don't have all day you know."

The comment drew quiet laughter among the small gallery of waiting lawyers who knew of the Judge's Mad Hatter-like penchant for time and its usage.

"I'm sorry, Your Honor, here it is," the beleaguered Ms. Collins began. "On August 23, as verified by certified-mail green card receipt, Motors-Freight, Inc. served upon Mr. Greenbaum a Request for Production calling for delivery, within thirty days..."

"I know the Rules, ma'am," interrupted the Judge, "just tell me what you asked for that he hasn't produced."

"Certainly, Your Honor. Items 14 and 27 specifically state..."

Hinojosa held up his authoritarian hand like a school-crossing guard. Doug recognized the rookie mistake. When a court asks you to cut to the chase, never simply quote from your pleadings.

"Don't read to me, little lady, just tell me what you say he did wrong."

Her flushed look revealed resentment at the Judge's interference with her neatly rehearsed presentation.

"I'm trying, if you'll please listen," blurted the neophyte. Her tone was more than a little scolding. The sexist comment had pushed her over the mark. *A very big mistake*, thought Doug, almost as bad as trying to correct Hinojosa on the time.

Harry Greenbaum also sensed there was going to be blood on the water. Befitting his carefully crafted good-guy image, he spoke up, seemingly in her defense, but really he was just grabbing the reins for his own benefit.

"Judge, she's new at this so let me take over."

The Judge's visible anger shifted to amazement at Greenbaum's offer of sportsmanship.

"See, she asked my client for copies of doctor bills and tax returns, and Judge, he just didn't keep things like that. I mean maybe if he was a finely organized individual, like this nice lawyer here, he could have gathered up such items in a timely manner, but he isn't, and he's been too busy being hurt to run all over the place getting records she can just as easily subpoena directly from the medicine men and the tax people."

Hinojosa, like everyone within earshot, was smiling — except, of course, for Delynda Collins.

"Now I have offered to have my client, Bobby Flowers, sign some proper authorizations to make it easier for her to get ahold of these things she wants, but darned if she didn't file this motion instead, accusing poor ole Bobby of discovery abuse and requiring that we take up this Court's precious time over such a trifling matter."

The less than oblique reference to the importance of time provoked audible laughs from the gallery of attorneys waiting for their cases to be called. The Judge banged his gavel and glared. Before he could scold them, Delynda Collins spoke.

"It's considerably more than that, Your Honor," injected the F&B plebe, trying vainly to regain control of how her own motion was being presented.

"Well, then, Bobby and me plead not guilty to all other charges as well," replied Greenbaum, forever stealing the spotlight from the frustrated lawyer who was, at that moment, the only person in the courtroom not laughing.

Judge Hinojosa again slammed his gavel to restore some decorum. Then he turned steely and looked at the thoroughly exasperated Ms Collins.

"Counsel, this Court is not in the business of policing routine discovery tasks. You have already wasted a half hour of my time."

In actuality, the flustered Ms. Collins had only been at the bench for a mere five minutes but she had been warned in advance by her senior partners to never challenge Judge Hinojosa on matters of the clock. So she said nothing. It was probably the only thing that saved her.

"Now, Harry, I order you to provide her those authorizations today, and I don't expect to see you two back on this matter unless it's to pick a jury or announce your settlement. Next case!"

Doug rose to his feet and made his way through the swinging door of the rail to approach the bench. Delynda Collins beat a hasty retreat in the opposite direction, no doubt trying to sort in her mind why the relief she got was so completely different from what she had been seeking. As Harry Greenbaum slowly shuffled by he made eye contact with Doug.

And winked.

———— ✳ ————

"Who the hell made that decision?"

Paul Ravich screamed the question at his assistant, Jan, but his voice carried throughout the entire law office as intended. He wanted the staff member who placed or handled the media call to know, if he or she was within earshot, that their job was in serious jeopardy.

While being driven to work, Ravich had heard the same radio blurb that irritated Ken Slator's commute. The tort attorney had expected a pleasant Monday morning ride into downtown, relaxing in the back seat of his Bentley sedan while his driver and general errand man, Carter, steered through traffic. Now that he was out of trial, Ravich could dispense with the charade of driving his paralegal's beat up Explorer. Ravich hated to drive, especially a piece of junk like that, but one never knew when or if a juror might see you pull up in the courthouse parking lot. A good *director* realized that a hard working lawyer and his poor injured client could never risk being seen coming to court in an expensive and chauffeured car.

Ravich had been reading the paper when he heard his name broadcast. He listened intently, then threw the Wall Street Journal in disgust. A thick section flew by Carter's right cheek before striking the front dash. Alarmed by the unexpected missile, his driver stepped hard on the brakes, causing Ravich to spill his venti latte that Carter had fetched for him at Starbucks. Milky-brown coffee now stained his Armani pants. Ravich fumed under his breath.

His mood did not calm much during the sixty-three story elevator ride to the penthouse offices of Paul Ravich & Associates. He stormed through the sweeping entrance of tall glass doors above which the firm's name was emblazoned in elegant bronze raised letters. His name was displayed in a markedly larger font than the rest of the title. Most law firms identify themselves by a shared listing of key partner names but Ravich believed no lawyer was worthy of being treated as his equal, so the eight attorneys he employed were relegated to an anonymous and smaller presence on the letterhead. His remaining staff of twenty paralegals, twelve assistants, two receptionists, three investigators, a couple of bookkeepers, one IT and database expert, and three other employees — about which he had no idea what they did for the firm — received even less recognition from him. Ravich figured he paid everyone extraordinarily well and they were all lucky to toil next to his shadow. That should be enough.

He blew past the front desk receptionist and continued menacingly down the long hall of other offices where he stopped abruptly just outside his own which was, of course, also substantially larger than any other at the firm. It was there that he found Jan, dutifully at her desk, and decided his first words would be something other than: "How was your weekend?"

"What decision?" ventured his shocked and worried assistant.

Jan knew if her Monday began with a shouted question, it was going to be a long day if not a long week.

"The goddamned decision to publicize a piss-ant verdict in a car wreck case! The idiot from this office who thought it would be a good idea to tell the entire city that I'm still available for fender-benders, or that a few million is a big deal to me, had better be in my office in the next two minutes!"

Wincing, Jan picked up the phone and pressed the intercom.

"I'll get Trey in your office and we can sort it all out."

Trey Galloway had been the associate most involved in the *Clayton* case.

"You do that."

At which point, the ire-filled lawyer unbuckled his belt, kicked off his shoes, and summarily removed his pants. Jan's eyes widened at the image of her crazed boss now standing half naked in the hallway before her. She was used to his unusual behavior but this was a first.

"And get these to the dry cleaners. Now! I need them back before noon."

He tossed the stained wool pants her way. He glared, then retreated into his office, his suit coat not completely draping the back of his underwear.

Jan rolled her eyes. It *was* going to be a bad week.

Trey Galloway was soon sheepishly making his way past the other associates' offices, noticing that several of his peers had stuck their heads, turtle-like, out of their doors and were staring down the hall in the direction where the volcano had erupted. They had all, on some other occasion, been summoned to Mount Vesuvius for a perceived misdeed and each was wise enough to keep their as yet unscarred bodies partially concealed within the fragile sanctuary of their own offices. Everyone liked

Trey but each was glad it was his turn, not theirs.

Trey carried the proposed Final Judgment from last Friday's *Clayton* verdict, which he had drafted early that morning. It needed to be filed today and he had learned to have things done before Ravich asked for them. Trey fervently hoped his quick work would help soothe the savage beast. When he handed it to his boss, he found out it wasn't enough.

"Close the door."

Trey stepped off the seven paces to comply. It felt like a condemned man's last walk. He turned around to face the executioner.

"Did you talk to the press over the weekend?"

Perhaps Ravich would not have looked so stern had his bare legs been visible. But they were now safely hidden behind his desk, a ridiculously massive piece of finely tooled cherry wood, yet another expensive prop of power.

"A reporter called up on Saturday asking about the case. I was here over the weekend working on the *Snyder* brief, so they gave the call to me since I had worked up *Clayton*."

Ravich just stared.

So far, so good, thought Trey. After all, he had said nothing factually incorrect to the reporter. And he had been the lawyer most knowledgeable about the case. Like any Ravich associate, he had filed the suit, interviewed all the witnesses, took every deposition. That was his job, to do all the pretrial work-up. Ravich met with the clients, sometimes for the first time, the day before trial. His job was to grab the glory at the courthouse.

"I know you like to handle all press inquiries directly but you were out of town and I thought it would do no harm."

Ravich had indeed been gone, having left Friday evening aboard his Falcon jet for a weekend at one of his three vacation homes scattered around the country, this time to Aspen. He didn't want to stick around for the *Clayton* verdict-celebration party. To him, it had been a nuisance case. He agreed to take it on and try it if necessary as a favor to a longtime referring lawyer who had funneled much bigger cases his way over the years. In Ravich's view, his personal injury practice had long since grown too big for elementary traffic cases. Like his airplane, he performed best in higher altitudes. His current docket and the only cases he wanted to brag about anymore involved mass torts, class-action litigation, and disasters that made the front page.

"No harm?" Ravich began, as he abruptly stood, revealing to Trey that he was wearing no pants. He pointed a finger at the young lawyer and shouted: "Did you hear the fucking report?"

The sight of his top-suited boss standing before him in boxer shorts might have otherwise been funny but the circumstances deprived the moment of any humor. Trey confessed he had not.

"Well, let me give you the version I heard, okay? These weren't the exact words but the message the whole goddamn city got was that the man you all thought was the best, richest, and most selective trial lawyer in the state was down at the courthouse last week, like some rookie turd, scraping around for sore back fees in a chicken-shit hurt leg case!"

Ravich's rising voice could clearly be heard through his closed office door. Out of concern for Trey's safety, Jan got up and opened it, hoping her presence in the threshold might somehow calm her boss down. He never looked her way.

"And then you had to tell the guy that it's thirty-two straight or some such crap. Now every potential juror, to say nothing of mediators and defense lawyers, will think that we consider crossing the million-dollar mark to be a big success when it's not shit to me. Let me tell you, son, that's my bar bill at the club."

Trey knew that defending his position, or any position contrary to Paul Ravich, was a waste of time.

"I'm sorry, it won't happen again."

"You're right about that, Mr. Press Secretary. You're fired. Be gone by noon. Jan will have Accounting mail your last check." Ravich pointed an accusatory finger. "And don't even think about fucking with me or the only legal job you'll ever be able to get and keep in this town is shelving books at the county law library. Now get out!"

Ravich's attack skills, honed by years of intimidating others, often ended with some veiled threat. Trey never thought he would be on the receiving end of one.

The defeated associate turned and walked past a stunned Jan who was genuinely saddened by the whole ugly scene. Not that she hadn't witnessed other firings in her fourteen years with the man-tempest but it was still hard to watch. She closed the door, leaving her boss alone to decompress. She turned to watch the verbally eviscerated young man make his way back past the turtle heads and into his office, where she heard his door slam.

She liked Trey and knew he was talented, hard working, and, most of all, that he dreamed of one day being a rich and famous plaintiff lawyer himself. Although Ravich had been a bastard, she couldn't help but think her boss had probably done the kid a favor today, in a perverse way, by assuring that he would never make that mistake.

Chapter 3
Pick and Shovel

From the control room, two stories above a sprawling grid of constantly running plant equipment, it was an expansive view. Through a wall of thick glass panels that angled out over the floor below, Ken Slator could survey the entire manufacturing process like an air traffic controller perched in a tower above busy runways. That which he could not see — the volumes inside the mixing vessels, the rates of flow, the internal temperatures and pressures — marched before him in numeric form on an array of monitors, the figures constantly updating as electronic sensors throughout the plant relayed their critical readings.

A chemical plant process manager, like a pilot, needs a certain skill. You have to be situationally aware of multiple things in concert. What is happening outside the windows and on computer displays tell the full story only when viewed and interpreted simultaneously. You have to be good at watching both to get things safely from point A to point B. The plant's main control board, which resembled an airline cockpit, contained a dizzying array of buttons and switches, each with a specific purpose that ranged from the mundane to the critical. Some could start or stop pumps and compressors. Valves the size of a car tire could be opened or closed by turning dials no larger than the volume knob on a radio.

When SeaCoast Chemical built the plant twenty years ago, Slator had been there helping to design the phalanx of tubes, storage tanks, vessels, pipes and pumps that stretched the length of two football fields. To the untrained eye, it was both visually intimidating and as confusing as a complex corn maze. Steel lines in varying diameters winded above, below, in, out, and even around large metal tanks that ranged in shape from bullet-shaped silos to round flattops that looked like small town water towers.

Smaller steel hulks, their functions critical but not readily apparent, were scattered around the plant floor. Some were the size of a refrigerator while others resembled the bell-shaped bottoms of a Saturn Five rocket.

If you didn't grow dizzy tracing the routes of stacked and bisecting lines, you might decipher where the end of a bending metal snake disappeared through massive pumps or valves that, in turn, delivered or discharged the line's contents to the next stage of production. But there were so many snakes, some of which actually hissed. Company executives being given tours would often cringe as hot vapor spat through relief valves located along the steam lines, not realizing that such bursts were normal. In such a perplexing environment they could hardly be blamed for mistaking the harmless escaping water for an expanding leak of something toxic that might swallow them whole.

The morass of interconnected equipment played tricks on the eyes, like a real-life M.C. Escher lithograph, where images and perspective collide to form a thing of beauty that is, at first glance, hard to understand. But to Ken Slator — having been involved in the design and construction process, and seeing it all efficiently operate for so many years — the complex facility was a relatively plain canvas. He knew where every brush stroke lay and the reason it was put there.

Producing synthetic fertilizer is chemically simple. It involves nothing more than mixing concentrated nitric acid with ammonia gas. But that's like saying neurosurgery is easy because it requires only a scalpel and a steady hand. The devil was indeed in the details and, like brain surgery, the process is highly complex.

When ammonia and nitric acid are blended, a ferocious exothermic reaction takes place. The alchemy inside the plant's massive steel neutralizer tank results in a boiling cauldron of liquid-concentrated ammonium nitrate, or "AN" in industrial chemistry shorthand. The solution then flows into rundown tanks before arriving at the forty-five foot tall evaporator where excess liquid is removed, increasing the chemical concentration. Finally, the "melt," as the AN run is now referred to, reaches the granulators where injected air and large rotating drums dry and shape it to become inorganic fertilizer, a nitrogen rich drug that crops around the world thirst for like street addicts crave crack. The tiny, white crystals of AN even resemble that illicit substance, at least before they are machine-molded into tapioca-size prills and bagged for distribution and sale.

Described in its simplest terms — which Slator often did for the benefit of the sales or management staff that periodically came through the plant — it sounded as if SeaCoast was making something as benign as candy and that he was Willy Wonka. But Slator knew better.

Ammonium nitrate in its lower-concentrated form had been used to blowup the federal building in Oklahoma City, killing 168 people. Foreign terrorists, like the homegrown variety, are also aware that AN, when combined with fuel oil or other combustible material, can be detonated with lethal consequences. Ammonium nitrate fuel oil, ANFO, is a common explosive used commercially in mining but, tragically, also with regularity in most of the improvised explosive devices, IEDs, that killed or maimed troops in Iraq and Afghanistan.

Even though highly concentrated AN — the type that SeaCoast made — was far less explosive than the low-grade variety used in ANFO, the manufacture of the company's trademarked *Ceres* brand fertilizer was still a very hazardous activity. Which is why Ken Slator insisted that his plant workers understand the meaning and utility of yet another acronym: DCSS. The Digital Control Safety System provided sophisticated and automated monitoring of the plant and its processes. Slator had urged the company to purchase the system after a near-catastrophic event during a production run four years earlier. A faulty Ph monitor had failed to detect an unusually high-acid condition as the AN was being formed. Five-thousand gallons of increasingly volatile chemical solution decomposed to a point that it became almost as unstable and explosive as ANFO. Luckily, there had been no outside source of detonation and before the mix could spiral out of control, the emergency was detected by a dumb-luck, but timely, gauge reading conducted by a plant-worker on the floor. The crisis, once discovered, was brought to an end by shutting down the acid feed and slowly bleeding the bad batch through the bypass valve. But not before five men, including Slator, anxiously contemplated the very real possibility of their own violent deaths.

Chemical engineers are trained not to rely on luck and that near-miss convinced Slator that placing future bets on non-redundant gauges or a chance discovery by an overworked human was as foolish as a gambler believing his hometown team will always cover the spread. Corporate, however, was far less risk-averse, especially when they learned the cost of the proposed new safety system was going to be $1.2 million. Someone at the parent company initially decided such price tag was too high even for something that might easily save their much larger investment of $340 million in plant equipment from going up in flames. Slator doubted that anyone at Thornton Industries or SeaCoast even bothered to consider the cost-benefits of keeping its workers alive. The approval, however, finally came two years after Slator first made the purchase request and, not so coincidentally, within weeks following the explosion of a small competitor's AN plant in another state that killed two workers and put that company out of business.

The safety system was purchased from Integrated Sentry Inc., a profitable division of the massively huge VyStream Corporation. It was custom-designed by ISI after Slator furnished them plant schematics, detailed inventories of components with their rated capacities, and a comprehensive explanation of all fluids, gases, and processes that would require monitoring. Given both his engineering conservatism and memories of disaster narrowly averted, Slator had instructed Integrated Sentry to not cut any corners. They were told the system should err on the side of multiple alerts and fail-safe automatic responses.

They delivered on time but way over budget. Once their technicians completed the system's installation and testing, the billings from ISI had grown to $2.3 million. But Slator received no heat from the home office. He surmised the bean-counters at Corporate were too busy making other stupid decisions and simply failed to notice the cost overrun.

The important thing was the control system worked. For the past eighteen months, the DCSS had accurately monitored and recorded data while alerting Slator to any deviation from process parameters. Four months after the system went online, a small gasket on a nitric acid pump cracked, leading to an almost imperceptible leak. A DCSS sensor immediately registered it and initiated an electronic control that promptly closed the feed-line valve, turned off the pump, and sent an alert to the control room. It was a minor thing, but Slator was comforted by the performance. Something even more reliable than his own fastidiousness was now keeping vigil over production.

As Slator looked down from his control room perch this particular Monday, he was glad things were in order. They needed to be, especially after the production schedule was increased the month before from two eight-hour shifts, five days per week, to a 24/7 operation. They had manufactured sixty-thousand metric tons of *Ceres* in those past four weeks, with twenty-thousand more needed to complete the current order. Most was going to China thanks to a lucrative contract Thornton Industries had secured for SeaCoast.

It had been necessary to hire six new workers. Schedules were also rearranged, creating three eight-hour shifts in place of the former two. Plant workers were now assigned "days," "evenings," or "deep nights," and most were pulling double-shifts when they could. They liked the overtime pay. Slator figured that some of the newest hires could be kept on after the workload returned to normal, bringing with it a resumption of more reasonable shift times for everyone. He preferred normal, although he heard the Director of Sales mention the possibility that the Chinese contract might be renewed the following year. But Slator had learned after two decades to never trust anything a company salesman said. If it happened, he would deal with it then.

Right now, he needed to watch his crew who were only into the second hour of the day shift. He could see Robert Johnson atop the ammonia scrubber assembly, changing out a lead that registered the air-quality as it vented to atmosphere. Ed Simon and Wally Brinkman were at the loading station, palletizing the bagged end-product and moving it by forklift to storage. Dan Crouch was hosing down the plant floor; a menial task but it had to be done. Bill Evans had been sent to the nitric acid tank to double-check the volume level that the DCSS system had just recorded as normal.

The metal door to the control room opened and the remaining shift worker, Dave Phillips, entered holding a clipboard. "It's going to be a bitch of a day," he announced.

Dave was a burly, avuncular man and an assistant operating manager. Like Slator, he knew that the plant running at full-bore was like a crying baby demanding constant attention. Phillips sat down and flipped to his second clipped page which listed the evening shift personnel for the day.

"We'll still be at near full flow capacity at eight o'clock tonight."

Slator knew that already and made no reply. Phillips traced the employee names with his index finger.

"Dan, Bill, and I are pulling doubles today. Three of the regular evening guys also signed on for the deep night shift, so that's six full overtimes. Other than that, it'll be the same three crews as last Monday. The rest of the boys wanted the OT but I told 'em it was better if they collapsed in their bed for a change instead of on the plant floor. They whined, but I promised that bunch they could take the gravy next week."

Slator grinned briefly. He appreciated an assistant who could run things and knew how to get along with the men.

Dave Phillips stood and walked over to the glass panels. He saw Dan coiling up the water hose. "I guess your little talk with Crouch about tardiness scared the sense into him. He came running through the locker room this morning and clocked in with an entire minute to spare."

Phillips laughed while his boss simply nodded. Slator assumed that a threat of termination was all it would take. Few high-school grads were making the kind of money Dan Crouch was pocketing right now, considering his union wage and overtime pay.

Dave Phillips liked to talk as much as Slator hated to. It made for a lot of one-sided conversations.

"You're the lucky one, hoss," Dave said, switching his subject to Slator in an effort to engage him. "You get to leave at four, just like a banker.

Can't says I blame you. If I were on salary like you, instead of by-the-hour, I wouldn't give these fools an extra minute of my time."

Again, Slator said nothing. But the comment made him ponder just how much of his off-time during the past eighteen months had been spent checking the DCSS data relay on his home computer while men like Dave Phillips sat in this control room chair, thinking they alone knew what was happening. In turn, the thought also sourly reminded him that today was still a work anniversary. He squeezed his lips tightly and thought to himself: *I've done worse than give them minutes. I've given them twenty-two wasted years.*

———⊂≈⊃———

The sign was as unimpressive as the door beside it. Three rows of stenciled black letters on a two-foot square of beige plastic, secured to the dull-white painted hallway wall by four small pieces of unseen double-sided tape. It read:

Suite 302

Law Offices Of

Douglas H. Stevens

The landlord thought it was a clever signage system. Whenever a tenant vacated — as they often did in his building — he could simply move the tiny adhesive strips around to the printed side of the plastic, then use the blank side to apply a new occupant's name, forever banishing the identity of the most recent insurance agent, chiropractor, accountant, or startup that had run out of money and broken their lease. That way, he got two uses out of a flimsy chunk of plastic that had been purchased for a buck-fifty at Office Depot.

The building owner's frugality was also evident in the thinness of the doors that lined the narrow corridors and marked the entrances to the falsely advertised "deluxe executive suites." The cheap doors were yellow pine and unadorned with panels or a fancy knob that would have cost extra. Like everything else in the building, they telegraphed that tenants would have to make do with the bare minimum.

Doug had been on the top floor of the three-story, brown-brick building since getting his license. Eight years of on-time rent payments had earned him the respect of the owner who demonstrated his gratitude and lack of alphabetical organization by putting Doug's name at the top of the lobby directory, a glass encased piece of black grooved felt-board where white plastic letters, unevenly pressed into the rows, spelled each tenant's name and provided a suite number.

Doug liked the space and didn't mind its unsophisticated

appearance. The old building was located practically along a direct line between his townhouse and the courthouse. A busy solo practice made his life three stops along a straight track with little time to veer off the rails for outside distractions. He was single but went out only occasionally. Short vacations were even more rare than dates. He knew there was more to life than the law. But he was still young enough to believe that life could wait.

He glanced at his watch as he entered his office. It was already 11:30. His motion hearings had consumed the entire morning. It made him feel strangely behind in a work week before it even got started.

"How'd it go?"

Bonnie Rogers managed to compress both a greeting and inquiry into three short words. Her voice was quirky yet strong and she used it efficiently, always directly saying what was on her mind regardless of whether she was speaking to his clients, other counsel, or to him. Doug liked that. He was more than willing to trade the fawning hesitancy of a typical employee for the spunk of someone like Bonnie who he considered his peer.

"Two for two," Doug replied. "Thompkins granted the trial setting request in the *Jenkins* case and Judge Hinojosa gave us an additional thirty days to conclude depositions in the *Hartley* matter."

"Be careful. That dumb bastard could later rule that a month meant three days."

Doug laughed. He knew Bonnie was right. It also reminded him why she was so valuable to him. She knew a lot of things.

Bonnie called herself a legal secretary because that was the title everyone used when she first started working for lawyers thirty years ago. She saw no reason to change, especially since "assistant" sounded to her like someone who ran errands for movie stars. Doug was glad she wasn't hung up on titles since Bonnie also served as his receptionist, bookkeeper, paralegal, and case consultant. She was very good in all her roles and simply amazing in the last two.

She had worked her first ten years for a senior litigation partner in a large firm, then spent the next fifteen with a smaller group of wildly successful tort lawyers. Typing pleadings, summarizing depositions, preparing trial notebooks, and just listening to lawyers strategize their cases provided her with an education that was arguably better than the traditional learning methods employed by law schools, where case study slowly teaches how legal theories evolve but not much else. Bonnie didn't need to know why the wheel was made. She knew something more important: how to turn it.

Through interest and osmosis, Bonnie absorbed everything worth knowing about a trial practice. She understood more law than most lawyers. She recalled which expert witnesses did the best job and what they charged. She could tell you the lawyers in town who could be trusted and, more importantly, which ones could not. She also remembered the attorneys who were afraid of the courtroom and those who, to use her phrase: "don't know their ass from a hole in the ground." That kind of intel was priceless but she dispensed it all like it was common knowledge.

After her last firm broke up in a partner dispute over money, Bonnie decided she wanted the relative calm of working with a young but competent solo practitioner. A friend told Doug she was looking for work and he called her to come in for an interview. Doug's part-time assistant had just given notice; she wanted to go back to school and he needed full-time help anyway.

He instantly clicked with Bonnie. Her resume was flawless and her casual demeanor and encyclopedic knowledge of the local bar was made evident during a job interview that lasted over an hour. But after only three years of practice, Doug lacked the cash flow to pay the kind of salary that someone with Bonnie's experience commanded. Still, he was so impressed with her credentials and willingness to wear all hats in a small office that he impulsively offered to beat any other employment offer she received.

Bonnie was savvy enough to tell from the crappy office and single stack of file cabinets that Doug didn't have much money or many clients and would probably have to secure a line of credit with his practice or take a second on his house to honor such a salary commitment. She liked that. It indicated that he respected her accomplishments and was confident enough of his own talents to make a futures bet with empty pockets.

Bonnie knew, from decades in the arena, the qualities of a good trial lawyer. They needed to be smart, fair, and bold. Thinking he was a diamond in the rough she took the job on the spot, telling Doug she would be happy starting out at the same pay as her last job even though both knew she was taking on far more office responsibilities.

That job interview was five years ago. Doug's practice had grown exponentially since then and in recognition that she had a lot to do with it, so did Bonnie's salary. He was now earning more than enough to move to a nicer building but thought it was smarter to save any surplus after making sure Bonnie got paid what she deserved. She liked that too. Turned out that they both had a good eye for talent.

Dropping his court files on the corner of a large table that served as both Bonnie's work station and the office reception desk, he realized it was almost lunchtime.

"You want to get out of here for a while? Let's go grab a burger."

"No time for that, hotshot. You have the Arnolds coming in at noon for depo prep." She reached below the table and produced a bag with two sandwiches from the Subway down the street. "We'll have to eat at home."

Doug had forgotten. The *Arnold* case was no big deal and typical of his current caseload. A nice couple had been sold a tract house with mold problems the seller didn't disclose. They spent thirty-grand on remediation and the resale value of the place was diminished by the taint of past problems that would have to be revealed when it came their time to move. The seller claimed he told his listing agent to include the issue on the property-condition-form and it was the broker's fault that such a material fact didn't get disclosed. The agent, of course, was contending that nothing was ever said and that it wasn't her responsibility to complete the form in any event. The Arnolds had to sue both to resolve the defendants' squabble since neither was willing to accept any responsibility.

His clients would give their depositions at one o'clock in Doug's tiny conference room where they would be questioned, ad nauseam, by the lawyers for both the seller and broker about the one thing that wasn't in dispute: that the plaintiffs were damaged through no fault of their own. Doug liked to meet with his clients at least an hour before they gave their testimony. He needed to explain the deposition process and, most importantly, to calm their fears about being cross-examined.

Doug knew he would make a recovery for these clients eventually but he also understood the defense lawyers were going to drag their feet until they racked up some fees. He, however, was working under a contingent fee agreement and would get paid only when the Arnolds collected the money that was owed. That method of compensation made him intolerant of delay and he pushed his cases hard to arrive at a settlement or trial. But there was only so much you could do. Today, he and his clients were going to have to endure seeing their time, and the defendants' money, wasted in an afternoon of repetitive questions from hourly billing counsel; money that would be far better spent by the defendants righting the wrong instead of paying their lawyers for needlessly long depositions. But Doug always felt that way. He was, after all, a plaintiff's lawyer.

He took the last bite of his six-inch sub, grabbed the *Arnold* file that Bonnie had placed before him, and retreated to his conference room to look a few things over before his clients arrived.

"Send them in when they get here," he said walking away. "And thanks for the lunch."

"Will do and you're welcome," replied Bonnie, tossing the sandwich bag into the trash can at her feet. After thirty years, she knew how to efficiently speak to, and handle, a lawyer.

Chapter 4
Spirals

"I'm out of here."

Ken Slator placed his initials beside the shift-end notations in the operations log and stood to give the binder to Dave Phillips. It was 4:15, and the assistant operations manager was now officially in charge of the evening shift. Phillips, having already completed eight hours alongside his boss, was now facing the second half of an exhausting but lucrative double-header day. His usual chattiness was now gone. He needed to preserve his energy and attention for the task ahead.

Slator grabbed the blue pinstripe jacket that had been draped since morning across the back of the control room chair. He never wore his suit coat except to enter and leave the plant. Were he not such a creature of habit, he might have asked himself why he chose business attire for an environment in which everyone else wore industrial jumpsuits. But he had worn a suit on that long-ago first day with SeaCoast and a pattern — for a man that lived only patterns — was established.

Dave Phillips settled into the control chair, the relief pilot taking the stick. The day had been manic and the evening shift would be more of the same. Batch after batch of AN had been created without any slowing of activity. The plant was now an aerobic runner trying to reach the finish line and it demanded a steady flow of energy through its arteries. The readings flashing across the DCSS panels were constantly updating, keeping pace with the roaring production activity below. At times, the numbers scrolled so quickly that only very experienced eyes could make sense of them as they raced across the screen.

"Keep a close watch on volume levels in the neutralizer," Slator warned, as he took one last glance at the monitors. "The temps and pressures are nearing maximums and we don't have any time for shutdowns."

Dave, his back towards his superior, rolled his eyes like a teenage driving student being unnecessarily coached to look both ways before entering an intersection. Dave had been at the plant for nine years. He already knew how to safely drive.

"We got it covered," Phillips replied, without turning around.

The quick and dismissive comment initially struck Slator as insubordinate but then he reconsidered. Maybe Dave was just busy focusing on the output data, as he should be, and that explained his curtness.

"Call if you need me," Slator said, as he opened the metal door of the control room to exit.

Dave Phillips raised his right hand in a backward wave, saying nothing. But the gesture's meaning was clear: *I'm busy here. Just go.*

Ken Slator descended the metal stairs, passed through the locker room, and exited through the employee entrance door. Once outside, free from the drone of the plant's interior, he appreciated the calm silence. Pausing on the sidewalk, he took in the randomness of the clouds in the late-afternoon sky. They were full of movement and message. Soft white billows were slowly being pushed away by larger ominous-looking gray ones. The sky's changing palette caused him no concern. It had been a dry fall. They needed the rain and the idle pace of the darker clouds meant he would make it home well before the showers came. He looked back down and began walking across the parking lot, retracing steps made thousands of times before. More than two decades had now been spent in a routine that changed far less than the heavens above him. The frenetic pace of production in the past month had been unusual, sure, but in a few weeks that would be gone just as the approaching thunderstorm would soon pass and return an untroubled sky.

Reaching his car and contemplating a return to an apartment that had never really been a home, he took a deep breath in resignation. The fall air, hinted with moisture, felt crisp but smelled faintly of bleach. The plant's ammonia scrubber, ordinarily capable but now taxed to capacity, could not completely wash away all traces of the noxious fumes before they were vented outside. The job was following him, it seemed, even as he breathed.

———— ⚬⚬⚬ ————

The cell phone rang at eight-twenty that night. He was half expecting the call. An hour earlier, while repeating a meal routine of another frozen dinner, Ken Slator had opened his laptop to glance at the DCSS data

46

streaming from the plant. It was a poor substitute for companionship when dining alone, like the way some read books in restaurants while others watch TV as they eat. He preferred staring at sensor readings on his computer. Not that he found it entertaining. It was, again, simply a habit.

The data had been borderline alarming. At 6:45, the neutralizer's contents were ten percent over the standard fill level: evidence that the system was being pushed hard but still easily within rated capacities. Although the mixing vessel was physically capable of holding over eight thousand gallons of ammonium nitrate, the chemical dangers rose when the fluid level climbed above a 65% fill.

He looked for and noted the latest temperature readings. The slightly increased confinement of such a volatile mass of AN had raised the heat inside the neutralizer. Again, higher than it should be but not so elevated as to trigger an auto-response from the safety system.

As he swallowed the last bite of his microwaved chicken, the numbers told Slator that Dave Phillips had been driving the family sedan like it was a Maserati. But sooner or later, if he kept going too fast, the DCSS would put the brakes on. The plant would kick into programmed shutdowns until safer balances were restored.

If it were any other evening he would have called the control room and offered advice. But tonight was the end of an uncelebrated anniversary and he decided the company had received enough of his under-appreciated attention for the day. He cleared the table, then surrendered himself to the numbing activity of watching a cable news channel repeat stories of questionable importance. Within minutes he drifted asleep on the sofa while the news carousel continued to flicker. Thirty minutes later his brief rest and an offensive story about the size of investment banker bonuses were interrupted by the chime of his cell phone. He answered on the third ring without looking at the caller ID, assuming that things at the plant had spiraled to the point of confusion for his assistant supervisor. He also doubted that anyone else would be calling him this time of night.

"Hello, Dave, what's happening now?"

"Ken, its me, Joan."

The voice of his ex-wife, a voice he had not heard in almost seven months, sounded strangely overwhelmed and exhausted. Or perhaps he was just groggy from the unplanned nap and his ears were not yet fully attentive. "It's Melissa, Ken, she's overdosed. Oh God! They've taken her to County General. I'm almost at the hospital now. The ER lady said it…was…bad."

Her last words stumbled hesitatingly through the phone's tiny earpiece and became incomprehensible as they faded into a plaintive moan. Slator wasn't certain if she had said "it was bad" or "she is dead." He sprang from the couch.

"I'll meet you there. I'm leaving now."

"Hurry" was all he made out as she tried to communicate something more between sobs. He hung up and dropped the phone on the sofa. In his haste and her shock, the badly needed clarification of his daughter's condition was denied him.

Reaching for his keys and running towards the door, he tried to make sense of the insane notion that his daughter had relapsed. *How could this be? She beat it in rehab.* He had seen her infrequently since the divorce — she was much closer to her mother — but they talked by phone occasionally. In the last call, only a week earlier, Melissa sounded upbeat. She had started a job at a local bookstore and was considering a return to college. They were small steps but given where she had been, they were optimistic ones.

Slator first learned about his daughter's drug use the way most working and uninvolved fathers do: his wife told him. She had found some pot and pills while cleaning Melissa's room. He was never much of a disciplinarian and it seemed useless to ground a seventeen-year-old with the cunning to secure her own drugs while hiding its use from parents for who-knows-how-long. The lecture he gave her on the dangers of substance abuse had little effect. Words coming from a largely absentee father carried the same credence as the corny anti-drug commercials that were being aired at the time.

By the time she graduated, barely, from high school, her disaffection with life and lack of future plans were obvious signs to Slator that her drug habit had, if anything, escalated. But she denied it and her mother took comfort in denials of her own. Melissa continued to live at home, worked an occasional minimum-wage job, and dabbled in the odd repertoire of lost kids: dying her hair blue, wearing Goth fashion, and piercing her nose. Maintaining an odd appearance took work though and she soon enough fell out of love with the physical trappings of an alternative lifestyle. But her affair with drugs continued. It was a committed relationship.

The thunderstorm finally arrived and Slator drove at speeds on the rain-slicked freeway that would have made him uneasy were his mind on safety rather than his daughter. His thoughts also raced during the twenty-five minute drive. *This can't be happening. What will we do now?*

He reached for his cell phone to let his ex-wife know he was almost there. The phone wasn't in the cup holder where, habit again, he always put it. He frantically patted his right hand around the passenger seat while trying to keep his eyes on the road. Then it dawned on him. In his rush to leave he had failed to pick it back up from the sofa. He was now much closer to the hospital than to his apartment. Circumstances wouldn't justify turning around in any event. It was no big deal, he reasoned, and his thoughts quickly shifted to all the *Whys*.

Why had they thought college would help? Melissa had promised she was done with her "experimentation." She had assured them she was ready to grow up and was determined to apply her addictive personality to a passion for the arts. Addicts want to believe, and parents of addicts need to believe, that darkness can be left behind in a bright change of scenery. So they helped her find an apartment near the art school where she planned to study graphic design. They helped her with tuition and living expenses. *They helped her, damn it, they tried.* But acquired habits are hard to break. He knew that better than anyone. By the end of her first semester, the cocaine use was so regular that it consumed all her money and most of the time intended for study. In her second semester, she discovered that crack was cheaper and began doing God-knows-what to secure it.

He grimaced at such thoughts as he saw the exit for the hospital through the lashing swipes of wiper blades trying to keep up with the rain. *Why had they not seen the continuing slide?* Slator knew too well the answer. It wasn't that she had concealed it so effectively. It was because both he and his wife chose not to look too closely.

Their marriage had grown further apart after Melissa moved out. The child with whom he had so little in common turned out to be the last remaining thing that he and his wife still shared. They both knew that their relationship — so fragile a thread — would tear quickly if Melissa didn't do well. Maybe that was why they both accepted their daughter's less than credible explanations for her weight loss and increasingly disheveled appearance. Perhaps that was the reason they delighted in, rather than question, her stories about how great school was going. They needed to believe she was not at risk because they knew they were.

Slator parked in the lot closest to the emergency room. Running through the downpour toward the entrance, the dread that pervaded him was familiar. It was the same feeling he had when the art school called to inform that Melissa had not attended class in weeks. His chest was pounding as it did when they discovered her apartment furniture had been traded for highs. It was the same fear and confusion that tore at him when they checked her into the rehab facility. The uncertainty he felt as he passed through the hospital's sliding glass doors was as stabbing as the night his wife announced she was filing for divorce.

He was growing used to all these terrible sensations. It was how overwhelming hopelessness felt.

He had pushed things too far. Dave Phillips pounded his fist against the steel surface of the control room desk. He had allowed the neutralizer tank level to rise to 94% capacity and the lack of space caused the elevating temperatures inside to reach the point where the DCSS controls took over. The electronic safety system immediately closed the flow valves, stopping any more nitric acid or ammonia from entering the overcharged tank. It then triggered the outflow valve to begin dumping the AN concentrate into the overrun tanks. Phillips, cussing himself, could only stand and watch the damn thing make its programmed corrections. In his effort to get to a destination faster, he had flown too close to dangerous peaks and the autopilot decided he could no longer be in charge.

On the plant floor, Tom Benson and Dan Crouch heard the alarms and looked up to see their assistant manager staring down at them through the control room panels. Tom was the evening shift second-in-command and pulled out his radio.

"Boss, we've gone into auto-shutdown."

Phillips angrily jerked up his handset. "No shit, Sherlock. Get over there and monitor the vapor flow."

The DCSS display in front of Phillips informed him that the automated system was now commencing an emergency drenching of the neutralizer. To reduce the temperatures inside the tank, inlet valves were being automatically opened to inject large amounts of cooler steam vapor into the overheated tank as its AN contents were simultaneously being drained. It was like hosing down a boiling car radiator and it meant that production would be stopped until things cooled off. Worse, the ammonium nitrate being drained had not reached sufficient concentration to be sent on to the evaporator for finishing, meaning the whole batch would have to be rerun.

Dan Crouch, bone-tired with three hours to go in his second shift, squatted down and leaned his head against the now stopped acid pump, realizing the screw-up would give them an unexpected break. Bill Evans, who had also worked the day shift, quickly joined him. Ordinarily, the sight of his men looking like they were ready to take a nap would have infuriated Dave Phillips. But his anger was too directed at the inanimate safety system that was showing him up for trying to do too much at once. He sat back down to watch the DCSS record his mistake and make its corrections.

Within an hour, they were ready to go back online. The system was reset, the pumps were restarted. Phillips intended to recirculate less than half of the AN from the overflow tanks back into the neutralizer. He would then add enough fresh acid and ammonia to restart the exothermic reaction. But he too had already put in long hours and, in either his fatigue or frustration, instead allowed almost all the previously discharged AN fluid to return. Within thirty minutes the temperatures in the overfilled tank again soared to dangerous levels and the automatic shutdown, drain, and drench sequence repeated itself.

"Son-of-a-Bitch!"

Phillips hurled the operations log book across the control room. He knew now he would have to call Slator. A train that stops itself repeatedly is no longer an express and he had been given orders to keep things moving.

He dialed the number and stood. He could see his entire crew assembled in front of the pumps looking up at the man who couldn't control his equipment. In an empty apartment twenty miles away, a cell phone chimed and vibrated against a sofa cushion. Phillips' embarrassment and anxiety grew with each unanswered ring.

Where the hell is he? Many times before, Dave had called Slator with operation questions, usually receiving an answer so obvious it embarrassed him for bothering his boss at home. But Slator was always available and never seemed to mind. It was also good "C.Y.A." Including the boss in any issue or decision was always the best way, Phillips reasoned, to "cover your ass."

Phillips picked up the radio and directed Tom Benson to prepare for another restart. He couldn't make out what the crew was saying due to the glass panels and distance between them, but their shaking heads spoke loudly enough. *They think I don't have a clue.* He pressed the reset button on the DSCC and flipped the switches to repeat the startup sequence. The system followed his commands while it also sent a copy of all that had transpired to Slator's home computer.

Phillips phoned his boss again, this time leaving a voicemail. He asked Slator to call back but was careful not to communicate any distress in his voice. He hung up the phone and turned his attention back to the controls.

This time he carefully monitored the filling of the neutralizer tank. The easiest thing to do, he realized, was to half fill it and eliminate any risk of excess heat due to confinement. But he was now way behind schedule and making AN a half pot at a time would only make matters worse. A compromise had to be struck. He decided to fill the tank to 80% capacity. That was only 15% higher than a normal fill and almost 15% below the levels that had triggered the earlier shutdowns. "Splitting the difference" worked in other negotiations and he figured it would be no different in chemistry. However, even with the lower percentages, the temperatures soon began to spike again and the alerts from the DCSS started to dance once more across the screen as if taunting their human master.

What is going on? Dave was not a chemical engineer. He was a floor hand who had stayed around long enough to be promoted to assistant operations manager. But he had seen tons of AN made over his career and had never seen anything like this. They had made product at 80% fill before; he was almost certain they had. Yet the tank was acting as if it were about to burst and the thermal conditions inside were spiraling upward.

He tried Slator a third time. No answer. The emergency operations manual was equally unhelpful. The only relevant language read: *"Unreasonably high temperatures are ordinarily due to excessive acid levels which require close monitoring."* He knew that already, and the acid readings were normal. Something else was making the current AN mix unstable but no book or boss could tell him why. The temperature reports were creeping towards another shutdown and he didn't know what to do. It was time for some serious C.Y.A.

He called Rob Finnegan, the President of SeaCoast Chemical, whose home and cell phone numbers appeared at the top of the *"Control Contacts"* list on the first page of the emergency ops manual. The pole position on the call sheet was due only to Finnegan's rank in the corporate pecking order and not in recognition of his operational or chemical engineering skills, of which he had absolutely none. He was a suit; a man who — when he wasn't downtown bowing before the parent company executives — spent most of his time in the air-conditioned office building on the far east-end of the plant grounds. But he was Slator's boss and since Ken couldn't be found it seemed the logical call to make. Phillips looked at his watch. It was 9:45 p.m. He hoped Finnegan had not gone to bed early.

"Yell-O."

The voice on the other end of the phone was crisp and alert. A good sign. He had not been asleep.

"Mr. Finnegan, this is Dave Phillips down at the plant. We've got some equipment trouble and…"

"Well, call Ken for Christ's sake. What do you expect me to do?"

The interruption came quick. Finnegan was, after all, an executive being bothered at home by his minions.

"I understand, sir. I've tried, but he doesn't answer his phone."

"Try again."

"I've made three attempts. Maybe his cell is dead."

"Goddamnit!" A short pause of uncomfortable silence followed before Finnegan added: "All right, give me some details."

Phillips outlined the temperature problems and the past two shutdowns. He took time to explain that the third attempt to restart the plant was fairly routine but that abnormalities were still being reported by the safety system and it was on the verge of shutting things down once again. He needed directions but the man he was speaking to was the wrong person to ask. Finnegan's mind operated as a one-way street to sales, not safety.

"Look, Dave, we can't afford to have the plant shut down. This Chinese order has to be fulfilled within fourteen days and the inventory reports I got today make clear we don't have time to take a shit, much less turn everything off while we go looking for a malfunctioning alarm."

"I realize that, sir, but I don't think the problem is with the DCSS."

"The what?"

Phillips knew at that moment that asking Rob Finnegan for technical advice was no different from asking a four-year old how to safely land an airplane. Still, he made an effort to explain how the safety system worked.

"Are you talking about that expensive upgrade thing we did? When was it? Last year?"

"It was almost eighteen months ago, yes, sir."

"Well, look, Dave, if you're telling me that the steps you've taken in this third attempt are the same ones we've used without incident for the past twenty years, then that high-priced new monitoring system is acting up, it seems to me."

Phillips didn't have an alternative explanation and knew enough about job security to not argue the point too strongly.

"Yes, sir, that's probably it. But the system is automatic. I don't know what I can…"

"Override it, for God's sake. There's got to be a manual override. Find it, use it, and then keep your eyes glued to our analog gauges, the way we used to before turning things over to some malfunctioning robot."

"But what if these system alerts are accurate?"

"Dave, did you call me at home to play a game of 'ifs and buts' or for a decision? Now listen, if we let some faulty electronic sensor shut down this plant for tonight or for who knows how long, neither you nor I will have ourselves a job when I have to explain to the home office at Thornton our failure to deliver on-time product."

"I understand, but…"

"No buts, just get it done."

"Well, sure, except this is…"

"This is *business*, Dave. That's what it is. And the clock on my nightstand says it's now my bedtime. So override that alert thing that's on the fritz and we'll get it fixed in the morning."

As the SeaCoast President continued to speak, Phillips reached over to the adjacent wall shelf and grabbed the DCSS manual. Integrated Sentry provided it at the time of their system's installation but he had never read it. He didn't think he would ever have to. Slator had trained him on the system and the system had always worked.

"Keep trying to reach Ken and when you do, tell him I said to get his ass down there right away and take a look at the damn thing. Meantime, make fertilizer."

Clutching the phone's receiver between his shoulder and ear, Phillips flipped to the manual's index and saw: *"Operating Modes - Automatic, Cascade, Manual."* He was thumbing to the referenced chapter when Rob Finnegan grew weary of the silence on the other end and shouted in his ear.

"Are we clear?"

"Yes, sir, I'm on it."

Phillips heard the line go dead and returned the phone to its cradle. He looked up and saw the abnormal DCSS readings continue across the screen. Maybe Finnegan was right. Nothing transpired in this third startup that should prompt any valid alert. Except for a slightly overfilled tank, everything about it was absolutely routine. Maybe it was just a faulty sensor that shouldn't be entrusted with the power to shut everything down. He looked to the plant floor below where everything seemed right and he could see his men milling around with no apprehension.

He had covered his ass with the call to the President but decided a little extra insurance never hurt. He tried to reach Slator again. Still no answer. He left a second voicemail then turned his attention back to the book in front of him, found the section titled *"Manual Control"* and began reading.

The nurse escorted him down the hall to an open area occupied with patients on gurneys or in hospital beds, their only privacy being thin white drapes suspended from beaded tracks mounted into the ceilings above. Some curtains were pulled half-closed and Slator could make out injuries that, while severe enough looking to justify a trip to the hospital, were obviously not so bad they required a rush to surgery. *It's a good sign if Melissa is in here*, he thought, as he continued to follow the nurse. They reached the last station on the left where the drapes were tightly drawn.

"Right here." The nurse parted them open. "I'm sorry," she said quietly, as she turned to walk away.

Melissa appeared to be sleeping, her head to one side. A breathing tube taped securely to her mouth ran to a steadily pumping device nearby. Wires crawled from under the blanket wrapped tightly around her and the multicolored lines led to a vitals monitor affixed to a nearby stand. His ex-wife sat slumped in a chair, her face buried in her hands. She was so lost in thought or exhaustion, or both, that he had to touch her shoulder to make his presence known.

"Oh God, Ken!"

She looked up at him with eyes that communicated fear louder than any scream. Before he could say anything she stood and was in his arms, embracing him with a closeness they had both long forgot. He felt her weight collapse onto him as her head sank into his shoulder, only slightly muffling the sobs that began flowing.

"Shhh," he whispered, as he began softly stroking her hair.

He could feel her shaking as she pressed harder against him. The intimacy was profound which startled him to a conclusion: *It must be bad.* He looked over at the EKG monitor. It was pulsing slowly and the blue lines formed small crests across the screen, appearing like gentle waves and equally assuring.

He reached down and cupped Joan's face in his hands, coaxing her gaze to his. It was an act of comfort toward her that warmed him as well. Such a strange yet distantly familiar closeness.

"It's going to be all right. She's going to be all right."

As he spoke the words, her eyes remained fixed, revealing no sign other than shock. The corners of her lips began to quiver and soon those small tremors convulsed her mouth oddly agape, her lower jaw shaking. It seemed she lacked the muscle control to speak. Tears traced down her cheeks as if slowly providing the lubricant necessary for words to be formed. He waited.

"It was heroin this time," she chokingly managed to say. "We've lost her."

He squeezed her tightly as she returned her head to his shoulder, crying uncontrollably.

"No, don't say that, Joan. We'll get her back." He stroked her hair once more. "She will, this time, make it back. I promise."

She grabbed him closer, her arms tightening around him. She was not his ex at this moment. She was a wife, a mother. They were a family. She must have felt something similar because she managed the strength to raise her head and lift a hand to his cheek. Their eyes again met but it gave him no comfort. Hers were filled with the heavily burdened look of someone with bad news. She started to speak but the sudden sound of metal beads moving above them startled them both. They turned to see that the privacy drape had been pulled slightly apart and a solemn-looking woman holding a medical file stood in the opening. Joan gently pushed away and retreated back to the bedside chair, leaning her head down against her raised right hand in an effort to shield her eyes. All of her movements were saying: *You deal with this. I've already heard the news.*

"Are you the father?" the woman asked.

Ken nodded yes.

"I'm Doctor Thomas. Perhaps you and I could step out in the hall for a moment."

Whatever the doctor needed to say was clearly something that, in her professional opinion, would only further wound the lady in the chair. Slator followed her the short distance to the brightly lit hallway.

"Your daughter was found unconscious and not breathing by the paramedics. While passed out on her back she aspirated vomitus; that is, she inhaled her own throw-up. Apparently, she had earlier overdosed on what preliminary toxicology is showing to be a combination of heroin and speed."

Slator leaned back against the wall. He needed something stronger than his buckling legs to keep him standing.

"Someone anonymously called for an ambulance. The front door of this house, which the EMTs said was a known shooting-gallery for addicts, had been left open and no one else was present by the time the paramedics arrived. They got her intubated on the ride over."

Slator nodded to acknowledge that he was listening but by then his eyes were clinched tightly closed. He struggled to open them and stared at the young physician whose otherwise pleasant face seemed slightly contorted by the ugliness of the words she had just spoken.

"But she will be okay?" he asked.

He felt the touch of the doctor's hand against his arm. "She almost drowned in her own fluids. We don't know how long she was without respiration but severe brain damage has resulted. She's in a deep coma and I'm sorry to be the one telling you this, the prognosis is not good."

He stared up at the white ceiling tiles and fluorescent lights. Everything was so stark and sterile, like the words the doctor just spoke.

"We have her on full assisted ventilation. She can't breath on her own. The next twelve to twenty-four hours will be critical. While we have no signs to indicate any acceptable brain function, we don't give up easily." She took his hand in hers. "And we ask that you don't either, okay?"

Slator nodded, then withdrew his hand. "Thank you, Doctor. I know you're doing all you can." Tears welled up as he thought of equally optimistic yet ultimately failed efforts in the past to help Melissa. "I just wish we had done more," he added.

"I know," she replied. "Sometimes things get beyond our control."

The doctor turned to leave. As Slator began the slow walk back toward his destroyed precious daughter and his devastated ex-wife, he thought about the last thing the doctor had said, when her empathy had not been diluted by medicine.

It was a simple human truth: no matter how hard you work, no matter how closely you watch, no matter how much you care, circumstances can still combine to defeat you and shatter your world. As he walked back through the flimsy drape and saw the two of them, both helpless, he realized he was a man who could do nothing but concede that the truly important part of his life, the part he had neglected most — his family, already distant — could soon be gone forever.

He was not aware of the parallels occurring at the place where he had squandered away his family's love and sacrificed so much of himself. Had he known, he would not have cared. Not this night. Maybe never again. But he had no reason to think about the plant. And, for the first time in twenty years, he didn't.

———◦∞◦———

Puzzling contradictions result when man manipulates nature. Ammonium Nitrate, a man-made cocktail blending natural elements, is a prime example. It becomes less volatile, not more, when you increase its potency. It does not burn but it can ferociously feed a fire with its released gases. It is born of a chemical reaction that generates heat but it gets weaker the hotter it becomes.

The human element, like nature, can similarly become confused when things get mixed. Processing information is critical to sound decision-making but an avalanche of competing thoughts is prone to produce bad judgments. The desire to reach a goal sometimes consumes the logic that says to proceed slowly. Perceived pressure often percolates into a real force that makes matters worse.

Something as insignificant as a lazy lecture from a superior can remarkably trump something as paramount as safety.

It looked like useless boilerplate to him. C.Y.A. from the lawyers. The kind of crap they stamped these days on a car visor, reminding you if you drive with the thing folded down it could block part of your vision. Plus, he was in a hurry. Dave Phillips skipped over the all-caps text in the DCSS operating manual that read:

WARNING

MANUAL MODE OPERATION AFFECTS PERFORMANCE OF SYSTEM REDUNDANCY. USE ONLY FOR MAINTENANCE OR TESTING OF DCSS COMPONENTS AND NEVER DURING PROCESS OPERATIONS.

He turned several pages and located the computer sequence instructions that triggered the switch from automatic to manual. He briefly considered the middle option, which was described by ISI as *"Cascade Operation."* In that mode, according to the manual, the system made precise programmed reactions once a manual input or override was directed to a specific component. He decided against such a hybrid solution of man and machine working together. After all, he wasn't sure which actual sensor was returning the false readings and he didn't have time to turn each one off separately then wait for the system to respond. He needed the plant to keep running. The system was preventing that for no good reason. They could use Cascade Mode later to troubleshoot and repair the DCSS. Right now he just wanted the damn thing turned off.

Immediately after typing in the command string, the monitor returned a dialog box asking: *"Automatic to Manual Operation - Are you sure?"* He mouse-clicked the *"Yes"* button. The same warning he had skipped in the manual instantly appeared on the screen and required yet another mouse-click confirmation that it had been read. *Integrated Sentry must have compulsive lawyers*, he thought, as he summarily dismissed the verbiage.

The screen refreshed and read *"Manual Mode"* across the top. Beside the title a time counter began to run. Below the recorded time appeared a list of every sensor in the system. He scrolled down only to discover two more pages of device listings. Although each had an on/off radio button toggle, he realized it would take time he didn't have to click them all individually. On the plant floor, the neutralizer was continuing to mix the AN and the past two auto-shutdowns made him suspect they were quickly nearing the third.

Then he saw what he needed. Tacked at the bottom of the third page, making them purposefully inconvenient options, were two rectangular buttons. One read: *"Select All."* The second was labeled: *"Restart."* He clicked *"Select All"* and each of the toggle buttons beside the individual sensors became highlighted. He clicked *"Off"* on the last sensor listed and the software immediately made the same change to the rest. He then selected the *"Restart"* button and received another: *"Are you sure?"* dialog box. He grimaced and thought: *Whoever designed this program must have once worked for Microsoft.* He clicked *"Yes"* and the screen went dark. Within a minute, a splash screen popped up that read: *"Integrated Sentry Inc - Digital Control Safety System, Version 3.1."* That screen was quickly followed by another that read only: *"Manual Mode - ON. Activate System Components."* Below those words, there was a single button labeled *"Continue."* He took his hand off the computer mouse.

He had done it. He was through clicking buttons. The sensors were off and he was satisfied they could stay that way until the guys from Integrated Sentry came in to find and fix their faulty component that had made him look bad.

Unfortunately, chemistry was also changing things around. While Dave Phillips busied himself closing off the plant's electronic eyes, ears, and noses, the mix inside the neutralizer tank was vigorously transforming itself. As the nitric acid and ammonia swirled together, forming AN and releasing heat, the temperatures inside the tank that had inched then climbed were now starting to run madly higher.

When highly concentrated ammonium nitrate gets too hot it decomposes into harmless gases: carbon dioxide and oxygen. The product you are trying to make just goes up in smoke, simply and safely, no different from boiling the water out of a pot left too long over a stovetop burner. You don't intend that to happen — it's an inefficient way to cook — but the only thing hurt is your pride and you start over. SeaCoast's recipe made only highly concentrated AN. It was stable, non-explosive, and resulted in exceedingly rich fertilizer. If you botched things in the neutralizer pot the worst that should happen is the product gets boiled away, like water disappearing before an inattentive cook.

But highly concentrated AN was not what was bubbling inside the tank at the time Dave Phillips bypassed the safety sensors. The previous two shutdowns, where mass quantities of steam vapor had been used to drench and cool down the neutralizer, had introduced a wild card into a normal-appearing deck.

The plant's water source for the steam generators contained chlorides: harmless salts that find their way into all water. If chloride levels get too high in a glass of drinking water, it tastes salty. You toss it out or run it through a filter. But when chlorides find their way into a metal tank where ammonium nitrate is being made, they become a catalyst, sensitizing the fluid and reducing the amount of energy necessary to start a thermal decomposition of the AN. Inorganic salts, left behind by the evaporated cooling water, had become a dangerous contaminant. The contents inside the neutralizer were degrading rapidly and what started out to be relatively safe highly-concentrated AN was chemically metamorphosing into dangerously unstable low-concentrate ammonium nitrate: the kind used in explosives.

Dave Phillips didn't know it but he made matters worse when he allowed the tank to be filled to 80%. What he thought was a safe compromise to get operations back up was yet another weakening straw and the camel's back was already buckling. When sensitizing material, like chloride, is present in the AN mix, the level of confinement necessary to start a deadly decomposition is further reduced. The steam's salty residue more than negated any margin of safety that Phillips had intended by filling the tank less full than the previous two failed efforts.

You can't build a campfire without fuel, oxygen, and a source of ignition. There has to be wood, air, and a match. That same trio, in different forms, is used to blow up rock in a mine or a federal building filled with innocents. Low-concentrate ammonium nitrate is mixed with fuel oil and then detonated. The volatile triangle is complete. But if AN decomposes too quickly in a sealed and confined space it becomes rabidly unhinged and can form the triangle all by itself. It's called a self-sustaining decomposition. No match or diesel needed.

With the DCSS monitoring systems bypassed, there was no way to diagnose that both chloride contamination and excessive confinement of fluid inside the neutralizer had started this spiraling thermal decomposition. Temperatures were rising out of control as the AN broke down and released its gases in the form of heat. The increasing heat made the remaining fluid decompose even faster. One hand washed the other as the tank's contents became more explosive, racing toward self-ignition.

The DCSS sensors and auto shutdowns were designed to stop such chemical madness long before a self-sustaining decomposition could occur. But they weren't available now when they were needed most. The fear of losing a job — equally shared by an overworked assistant manager and a sales oriented company president — had created an unseen nightmare where loss of life was imminent. And no one was going to get any advance warning.

Except for Dan Crouch.

Dave Phillips radioed down to his number-two and directed Tom Benson to have someone check the analog temperature gauge that sat atop a six-rung metal ladder on the right side of the neutralizer tank. Phillips was confident the reading would be within parameters. In his mind, the problems had been solved by not overfilling the tank and by cleverly taking a faulty sensor out of play.

Benson looked around. Two other crewmen were back in the ammonia farm, switching flow from one tank to another. Another was at the loading docks. Dan Crouch was standing by the overflow-tanks ready to monitor flow if another shutdown began.

"Crouch, go take a temp reading up on the N-tank."

Dan gave Tom Benson a puzzled look. His job with SeaCoast began after the electronic monitoring system was installed. He had never before taken a manual reading from the inconveniently placed gauge that he knew existed but thought they no longer used. He figured the order must have come from the control room where he supposed Dave Phillips, still fuming over his screw-ups, wanted to make others suffer with unnecessary work. Dan shrugged. It seemed petty to ask someone to scale a ladder to report a number that was already available, right in front of him, on a computer monitor. Phillips wouldn't even have to lean forward in that big leather chair of his. *That ain't like Dave,* he thought at first, but then remembered that even good guys become a pain when you make them the boss. Here he was being told to take his tired legs, now fifteen hours on the job, and scramble up a tank like a circus monkey. He rolled his eyes in resignation.

"Aye-aye, Captain," Dan said acerbically, as he passed Tom Benson on his way to the neutralizer. With only an hour to go in a two-shift day, he decided not to turn the stupid request into a bigger deal. *I hate this job,* Dan said to himself, echoing the last words he spoke to his wife.

As he climbed the ladder, he felt the intense heat radiating from the tank's stainless steel walls. He knew things got hot in there; that was how the stuff got made. Even though the tank had a thick layer of interior insulation, the grab rails on the ladder burned against his work gloves. Since he wasn't used to having his body a bare eight inches away from the neutralizer's outside surface, he just assumed it was always that hot when you got this close.

When he reached the top of the ladder he saw the temperature dial. It reminded him of an ordinary oven thermometer only twice as big. The gauge indicated degrees in Celsius.

Dan had never really paid attention in his high-school science class but vaguely recalled that Celsius numbers were a lot lower than their Fahrenheit counterpart for a given temperature. He saw that the gauge needle was pounding against the right side peg where the numbers stopped at 260 degrees-Celsius. He also noted that every mark higher than 180 degrees-Celsius was printed atop a bright red arc that broadened as it neared the right-side peg. He might not have known his temperature conversions but Dan knew what a redlining tachometer meant on a car. It wasn't normal, and it signaled that an engine was being pushed too hard. His lack of knowledge, of both the Celsius scale and the chemical properties of AN, meant his final thoughts would be ones of perplexed concern and not outright terror.

The ravaging contents of the tank now contained spiraling masses of superheated nitrous oxide, more sensitive than dynamite. The confined and incendiary tornado of AN had passed the point of no return. A bomb, not a campfire, was six-seconds away from lighting itself.

Dan, ignorantly unaware, shouted to Tom Benson something that sounded like: "Hey, there's a problem." Benson took two steps toward the ladder. They were the last movements he would make.

The deafening explosion rocked the plant, disintegrating the neutralizer tank and the overflow vessels nearby. A massive crater opened up through the cement floor, marking the point of ignition. The force of the blast shattered and hurled heavy stainless steel shards as easily as it completely shredded and flung the fragile bodies of the two men at its epicenter. Eighty yards away from the blast crater, a piece of jaw with a loosened tooth would be all they would ever find of Tom Benson. Time records, not dental, would end up being the only proof that Dan Crouch was dead.

Dave Phillips had only a millisecond to look up and see the angry ball of fire and shrapnel charging through the glass panels of the control room. He was far enough away from the blast center that his lifeless body would be found more or less intact in the charred upstairs chamber.

The manuals, operations log, and hard drives of the control room computers — including the DCSS — became mere ashes. The critical sequence of events and the fatal decision to bypass the safety system melted away along with the leather chair and plastic frames of the LED monitors in the control room.

The explosion's lethal discharge and the closely following fire rode through the plant like two horsemen of the apocalypse seeking their missing brethren. The third appeared when the concussion and flames reached the tank farm, as the silos collapsed and the methane lines used to make the stored ammonia severed and ignited. The crewmen that were standing nearby, Bill Evans and Hector Ruiz, were trapped in the blazing maelstrom. Their burned-black bodies were found lying with up-stretched arms, both corpses resembling the ghastly figures of the victims of Pompeii. The final deadly horseman, the stacks of palletized *Cerus* that filled the plant's storage bays, assured that the inferno would find its second wind as the melting pellets of bagged fertilizer discharged fuel-feeding nitrogen that was intended to make something other than flames grow.

The only crew member of the evening shift to survive the initial blast and flames was Derron Lucas. He had been operating a forklift on the east side of the plant when the firestorm surrounded him and inflicted second and third degree burns over 85% of his body. He managed to stumble, afire, to a backdoor bay of the plant where first responders would find him immediately upon their arrival.

The sound and vibrations of the explosions rippled out to the surrounding area. A bright orange vortex of fire lit the night sky, unaffected by what was now only dwindling rain. Fire and rescue dispatch recorded the first alert at 11:17 p.m. Over thirty more calls to 911 soon followed. The disaster could be heard, felt, or seen four miles away from the now destroyed SeaCoast facility.

Rob Finnegan, comfortably asleep in his bed, thirty miles distant in a neighborhood too nice to be anywhere near a chemical plant, was blissfully unaware that he was now the President of Hell.

⸎

An ambulance arrived at the emergency room parking bay of County General just before midnight and the horrifically bleeding and blistered body of Derron Lucas was raced into surgery, his chances of survival slim.

Ken Slator heard a commotion over the sounds of the ventilator machine and the soft snore of his now lightly tranquilized ex-wife, sitting collapsed in the chair beside their daughter's bed. He thought nothing of the noise outside their solemn cocoon and could never have suspected that the shouts of doctors and the clacking wheels of a fast-moving gurney passing through the adjacent hall were also closely connected to his life. He was concerned only with the family tragedy that quietly lay before him.

Fourteen minutes later, as a fellow employee was being administered anesthesia in an operating room forty yards away, his daughter went into full cardiac arrest. New shouts were made, followed by the havoc of a crash-cart being rushed through the thin curtain that now defined the boundary of Ken Slator's sad world. The small space was soon filled with the agonizing sounds of the hospital staff's futile attempts to resuscitate the comatose victim.

The cacophony was loud enough to wake Joan from her valium-induced sleep. She stood and leaned into her ex-husband's arms, unsure of what was happening. The blips across the vitals monitor were now flat-lined. The tenuous waves that had a short time before evidenced a hope of survival were now gone from the screen. In her groggy state and in his fully aware horror, the parents watched their daughter, at the age of twenty-one, inflict her last living punishment on their hearts.

Twin spirals had now merged, in seemingly malicious concert, to change things forever for Ken Slator. One he wasn't even aware of yet. But the other was more than enough to obliterate the already broken life of a now inconsolable man. He stood shaking, his ex collapsed in his grasp, and he broke down for the first time in his adult life. His unstoppable tears were not that of a disciplined engineer. He had ceased being a creature of habit. He was no longer a man in control.

He would never forget the cyclone that just hit him. And he would

63

learn of another soon enough. Such wholly separate storms, both sadly preventable and each carrying such grave consequences, would tomorrow feel as unrelated as their timing would seem surreal.

And they were. At least until a lawyer got involved.

Chapter 5
News Cycle

The nightshift workers, on their way to a midnight clock-in, arrived trailing the third fleet of dispatched fire trucks. A quarter mile from the plant entrance, two patrol cars with flashing roof lights partially barricaded the two-lane road, the center gap between their bumpers just wide enough for the giant hook-and-ladder engines to pass through.

Al Harris, the assistant manager scheduled to relieve Dave Phillips, was first to be flagged down. He pulled to the shoulder as directed by the waving flashlight of a state trooper. Rolling his window down, he could feel the heat from the distant inferno even in the dying mist of the now depleted thunderstorm. Gone was the singular globe of fire that had encapsulated the plant at the time of the initial explosion. There were now four distinct geysers of flame pumping skyward from different areas of what had been his place of work. Harris knew every inch of the SeaCoast facility. Even from afar, he could tell by the locations of the pulsing towers of fire that the gas lines at the west end, and the product storage areas on the east side and back of the plant, were putting up stiff resistance to the fire suppression efforts.

The hulking mass of the collapsed roof in the distance also told him that the evening crew if not all dead were likely hurt bad. He clinched his jaw at the thought of Dave and Bill, both close friends. He knew for sure they had been on duty. *Maybe they made it out somehow.* He was trying to recall who else had been scheduled on that shift when the patrolman approached.

"You might as well turn around, sir. Nobody allowed past this point except ER."

"I'm the nightshift foreman at that plant. I need to get up there. I know where the fuel sources are."

"Hold on." The trooper stepped back toward his patrol car and keyed his body radio, speaking into the small mike clipped to his shoulder epaulette. "This is Unit 104 at roadblock. I have a company rep here that knows the layout and what's burning."

The radio crackled back.

"Send him through. Tell him to find Ladder Three at the main entrance and ask for Captain Edwards."

"Roger that."

Al Harris received his instructions and was waved through as two other cars pulled up. The nightshift floor workers were starting to arrive. The police allowed those two men to wait on the shoulder near the barricade. They soon stood outside their cars talking, shaking their heads and speculating over what had happened.

Harris quickly found the red ladder truck with a gold "3" decal on its front doors. He parked a good distance away, then scrambled toward the man wearing a white captain's helmet standing near the fire truck. The intensity of the heat was now searing and his lungs caught the acrid smoke of burning ammonia and acid. As he ran, he counted five ladder cranes raised high above the plant's crushed superstructure, torrents of high-pressure water spraying down from each as the firefighters struggled to gain the upper hand.

The sooted captain lifted his fresh-air mask and reached for another that was hanging on the truck's side mirror.

"Tell me where the gas shutoff valves are located, then put this on," he shouted. "I know this is a fertilizer plant. I saw the chemical ID signs at the entry fence. Is there any more of this product that's confined?"

The fire captain obviously knew his chemical hazards. The ammonia silos had already exploded. Both he and Al Harris realized that any residual ammonia gas was being transformed to flaming hydrogen by the fire's heat. The same would happen with the nitric acid. Those were not the main source of concern. The captain also wasn't worried about the visible stacks of *Cerus* that, with sections of the roof gone, were now exposed to the night air. They were helping to keep the fires alive but they weren't going to explode.

"There's about eight sealed railroad cars along the plant sidetrack on the north side," Harris yelled back, making himself heard over the roar of both the fire and water pumps. "They're filled to the max."

That was all the captain needed to hear. He barked into his hand-held.

"Units 6 and 14. Get water on those rail cars. Now! Ladder hoses only. Maximum distance." His face tightened. He was clearly angry. "Attention all units. No one within four-hundred feet of the north side rail tracks. Repeat. Stand clear of rail cars. Explosive risk - Class 1."

Even a rookie firefighter knew that ammonium nitrate fertilizer packed in such tight spaces could detonate if an ignition source and enough heat got to it. Like the Great Chicago Fire, most firemen had heard of the historic fire that nearly destroyed the port town of Texas City back in the forties, when an overfilled and non-ventilated cargo hold aboard a fertilizer transport ship exploded.

"What the hell were you guys doing here?" the fire captain shouted.

"We were going 24/7," Al Harris replied, shrugging to convey he was not a decision-maker. "I don't know what they were thinking."

"Stay by this engine," he snapped. "And put that goddamn mask on."

The captain started to turn away.

"Wait, you wanted to know about the remote shutoff valves for the gas."

He listened attentively as Al Harris outlined their locations. The fire captain then shook his head in frustration and disgust before stomping off, shouting something else into his radio.

The phone rang loudly beside Rob Finnegan's bed. His sleeping wife groaned at the sound and rolled over, trying to smother the ringing with a pillow over her head. He looked at the bedside clock radio: 12:27 a.m. He stretched out an arm and grabbed the receiver to his ear.

"Uh, hello," he mumbled.

"Is this Robert Finnegan?"

"Yeah, who's calling?"

"This is Fire Department Central Dispatch. Your name is listed as the emergency contact for the SeaCoast Chemical facility on Platt Road."

Even had he been wide awake, Finnegan would not have recalled that all industrial plants are required to provide a management contact in the event of fire or other major emergency. *How did they find me?* he thought, in his hazy state. He sat up in bed and listened to the voice on the other end, something about explosions and fire. His mind drifted back to the call from more than two hours before. *What had Dave Phillips done?*

"Sir, can you hear me?"

"Oh, yeah, I'm sorry. I was just…I was just asleep is all."

"You need to get to the location as soon as possible to assist responders with facility logistics. Do you understand?"

He thought to ask how bad it was.

"Sir, I don't have those details. We have reports of a major event. You need to get down there."

"All right. I can be there in about a half-hour."

He was startled, tense, and hung up the phone clumsily. As he got out of bed, his wife raised her head slightly.

"What is it, dear?"

He glanced at her quickly, hoping she would not see the guilt in his eyes.

"Those damn union guys started a fire down at the plant. I've got to go."

He disappeared into their spacious walk-in closet, a room half as large as the tiny house where Kate Crouch lay sleeping across town, unaware that her husband no longer existed. Pulling on his pants, the anxious executive began to hurry his pace. He thought of something that made his heart race even faster.

I need to get Dave straight on our story before he says anything.

He would soon learn that was no longer a worry.

There were ominous signs long before the Mercedes reached the turn at Platt Road. Clouds of black smoke were continuously staining the moonlit and lighter night sky. An eerie glow seemed alive in the distance as orange and yellow light pulsed at specific points on the horizon. The windows in his car were tightly shut but the fresh air vents no longer discharged cool night air scented with freshly fallen rain. The smell was now like lighter fluid smoldering atop wet coals — pungent and not natural.

He reached the turn and accelerated down the straight strip of asphalt that led to the plant. By the time he saw the flashing lights of the police cars he knew that others needed waking up. He grabbed his mobile phone in one hand and scrolled deftly through the contact list as he drove. Taking a deep breath, he activated the call. He was about to go upstairs and this time it wasn't to tell everyone what a great job he was doing.

"Who is this?" the voice on the other end barked.

"Bruce, it's Rob Finnegan. The plant's on fire. I'm almost there. It's bad."

"Shit!" A pause. "Jesus CHRIST! What happened?"

"I don't know."

Bruce Waltman's surprised voice quickly regained control and he began, in a calm and opposite tone, to provide explicit instructions. "Okay, listen. When you get there, identify yourself to the authorities as the company man in charge. Then gather all the plant workers, make clear they are to make *no* statements to anyone, and instruct them to go down to their union hall and wait for further word from you. Call whoever knows best how that plant actually operates, because I know that isn't you, and have him down there when I arrive so I can be briefed on what may have caused this. If any press shows up before I get there, just tell them we'll have something to say once the situation is under control. And for God's sake, Rob, don't you go speculating to anybody about what happened. Got it?"

The General Counsel of Thornton Industries could sound like a lawyer even when woken from a dead sleep. Waltman had issued his commands in such a staccato and certain manner it made Finnegan suspect the words had been rehearsed. "Got it," he replied.

By the time the call ended, Finnegan had pulled his sleek SEL sedan onto the shoulder behind two junky cars that, unlike his, did not appear out of place along a dark industrial road beside a couple of flashing squad cars.

The two workmen, wearing their SeaCoast ID badges, approached and tapped on the driver-side window. From behind the glass, Finnegan gave them a "give-me-a-second" gesture with his left hand as he searched his phone with the other, finding Ken Slator's name in his list of company contacts. He dialed the number and after four rings it went to voicemail. He remembered what Dave Phillips had said about not being able to reach Ken earlier. The message Finnegan left was not pleasant and made clear that Slator's presence was being demanded, not requested.

"Thornton residence."

The house manager answered the phone at three in the morning. His businesslike voice at that hour was evidence that Charles Thornton ran a tight ship even at home.

Bruce Waltman was not surprised. He had been to Thornton's riverside mansion on many occasions — usually fundraisers for one of his wife's charities — and knew the Thorntons employed a large staff of servants that would make a country club jealous. He pictured the voice on the other end, a manservant in black suit and tie, ready to obey in the rare event that Mr. or Mrs. Thornton got up in the middle of the night.

"This is Bruce Waltman, head of Legal at Thornton Industries. I need to speak to Mr. Thornton. It's a serious emergency."

"Oh, I see….Right away, sir….Please hold."

The man's voice now carried a hint of trepidation. Waltman understood. He dreaded the upcoming conversation as much as the fellow on the other end of the phone was fearing the prospect of waking up the bear.

An anxious two minutes passed as the General Counsel stood outside the scorched remains of the plant, his cell phone pressed against his cheek. The fire department had gotten the fires extinguished but remained busy dousing the still-smoking scene with water. The area looked like the site of Armageddon and the stench of wet ash and chemical gas would have been the most obnoxious physical irritant to the now sooted General Counsel except that the press had now arrived. Satellite trucks were lining up at the police barricade waiting to broadcast the ground-level scene to the world.

There was going to be overkill coverage. He knew that much. Waltman had seen news helicopters in the sky as he was driving up to the plant. The first choppers got there before the fires were out and undoubtedly had sensational footage of the flagship facility going up in flames. It was the kind of video that would be all over the local morning programs. The story would likely go national, especially considering the probable body count.

Thornton's voice finally came on the line. "What is it, Bruce?" He sounded angry and alert. But then again, Thornton always sounded that way.

"Sir, the SeaCoast fertilizer plant has blown up. Our best guess right now is it happened sometime after eleven. There were massive fires that are just now under control. We have some confirmed fatalities and there have been chemical discharges that might affect surrounding areas."

"And what about the product? Was the inventory saved?"

"No, sir, there's nothing left but carbon and crumpled steel."

"Damn it! Well, then, you spearhead the damage-control down there. I'll head to the office."

"I'm on it. I've got Rob Finnegan, the President of SeaCoast, with me and the company is setting up a field tent to handle logistics and press inquiries."

"Those fucking vultures are already there?"

"I'm afraid so. You'll see it on the morning broadcasts."

"Look, Bruce, you make sure this is all SeaCoast. You understand? You present yourself as *their* lawyer right now, not as the General Counsel of Thornton Industries. Put that buffoon Finnegan in front of the camera to look forlorn and worried for his company. But you do all the talking and keep the parent company's name off the radar. I don't want press people showing up downtown."

"Yes, sir."

"Call me at the office with hourly updates. I'll be there."

He heard the phone hang up. Bruce Waltman pocketed his cell phone, thinking about his boss's first concerns: *Do I still have product to sell? Keep my name out of the mud.* It was classic Charles Thornton. He didn't even ask how many men had died.

SeaCoast Chemical was a union shop. Charles Thornton hated that fact but even though he tried, he couldn't dictate everything. The regional office of the Industrial Chemical & Refinery Workers Union had been unlocked at 2:30 a.m. as Stu Mitchell began setting up a disaster response center in the union's meeting hall.

Mitchell had been the local union head for the past ten years and this was not the first occasion where he had been called at home with news that an industrial accident had killed or injured his union brothers. There were dozens of oil refineries and chemical plants in his district, most of which were huddled together along an eight-mile swath of land on the eastern perimeter of the city. The SeaCoast facility was about in the middle and Stu was surprised, given the magnitude of the destruction he was learning about, that neighboring plants had not been affected. He always thought these combustible factories, lined up like so many dominoes, would one day topple over each other in a similar chain reaction. But not tonight. That was the only good news.

The two nightshift workers who had stood on Platt Road as their plant and friends burned, now sat outside Stu's office waiting for word. Al Harris got to the union hall thirty minutes after they did, having been sent away from the scene by a flustered Rob Finnegan. Al and the two floor workers were fairly certain they had pieced together who worked the evening-shift but were waiting for Finnegan to arrive with confirmation of the employee schedule.

The small executive office building at the far east end of the ravaged plant grounds was the only structure left relatively intact. It's nonattached remoteness to the actual manufacturing equipment had always been a metaphor for how things worked at SeaCoast, but now its physical disconnect also explained why business records survived when workers had not. Once the fire captain had given permission, Waltman dispatched Finnegan inside the smoke-stained building to locate shift schedules and personnel records so that contacts could be made. It took awhile but he found them. Waltman instructed that they be taken to the union hall.

Finnegan's now ash-covered Mercedes made its way along the short distance to the union's regional office, the names of the dead and missing in files atop the passenger seat. Notifying the families was not a job anyone wanted and it fell to Rob Finnegan. Bruce Waltman was too busy coordinating damage control at the scene. Besides, it would be unseemly to have the legal department calling folks to say your loved one was either missing or dead on the job. Finnegan had at least met all the men. Even so, as he continued driving past the refineries, he couldn't place their faces.

Except for one. His mind kept picturing Dave Phillips, talking anxiously into a phone.

Dave was gone, and so was their discussion about bypassing safety systems. Finnegan replayed the events in his head. His wife had been in the bathroom getting ready for bed when he took that call. She hadn't heard anything. Even if she did, she would probably lie for him. She liked the things that come with being the wife of a company president. Finnegan had no idea what had gone so horribly wrong but any attempt to rationalize away his shared responsibility failed when he recalled what he had said: *"Override it for God's sake.... We'll get it fixed in the morning.... Make fertilizer."* Those words would haunt him forever but at least no one else would ever hear them.

He parked in front of the union building and walked inside with the records tucked under his arm. He was Management. This place represented adversity to him. But negotiating union contracts, however difficult, was nothing compared to the task that faced him now: to summon the families of men he had helped to kill, to ask them to come and sit with him, to pray and hold hands until they all knew for sure, and to pledge that he would do everything in his power to get to the truth — that would be the hardest thing he would ever have to do.

———— ∞∞∞ ————

There were forms to fill out. The body had been rolled away. The mother was given another valium and was now asleep in a nearby hospital bed. The father had somehow regained some composure. The confusion, the panic, the screams, the tears, had all been replaced in the intervening four hours by the need for paperwork.

The hospital administrator — probably the least experienced considering the late shift she was working — sat and stared at the man she had escorted to her office. He had followed her from the downstairs ward, walking as if he were somnambulate, his head never looking up. He now sat across the desk with the same downward fixed gaze. She waited a respectful length of time but could tell he was not, on his own, going to leave that painful place where his mind had taken him.

"Mr. Slator, do you think you could provide me some details about your daughter?"

"Sure," he replied quietly, without looking up.

He answered her questions about Melissa's date and place of birth, her address, occupation. He knew the information was needed for the death certificate. He didn't know how much it would hurt to recite the details of his daughter's short life.

The clearly uncomfortable administrator kept saying she was sorry as she explained that state law would require an autopsy to be performed and as she asked if he had any preference of a funeral home to contact once the body was ready to be released.

"I understand," and "No, I haven't thought about that," were his only responses.

"Is there anyone that I can call for you? Maybe to help drive you and your wife home?"

Your wife. The last time he heard that phrase spoken was at the divorce hearing when the judge approved their agreed decree. The power of those words were enough to raise his head.

"No, no...I'll be fine. We'll be fine. I'll take her home as soon as she wakes up."

"Take your time, Mr. Slator," she said, as she stood to indicate their business was finished.

He took her cue and rose to exit. "Thank everyone here for their help, for what they tried to do," he managed to say.

"I will; I promise," the woman answered. "I'm just so sorry it wasn't enough."

He walked alone down the fourth floor hall, thinking how the administrator's last words seemed to bookend what he had said to the young doctor only hours before. *It wasn't enough* and *I wish we had done more* would be, he knew, the words that would plague him forever.

He took the elevator back down to the first floor and headed for the waiting room outside the ER. He would give his wife — his *ex*-wife — a little more time to hide in her drug-induced peace. He sat down in one of the uncomfortable-style chairs that find their way into waiting rooms everywhere. The area was empty, the only sound coming from a ceiling-mounted television in one corner. It was airing the end of an infomercial for what some crazed woman was calling a kitchen miracle.

He thought of phoning the plant to let them know he wouldn't be in today but remembered he didn't have his cell phone. He could have used the hospital's phone but his job was no longer a priority to him. They could wait.

He sat torturing himself with memories of his daughter before fatigue finally overtook him. He was half-asleep, his head again facing down, when the loud theme song of the early morning news came on. He lifted his chin trying to stir himself awake when he heard it.

"Breaking news. A chemical plant explosion has claimed the lives of at least three workers at a fertilizer manufacturing plant owned by SeaCoast Chemical Corporation. Channel 7's Eye-in-the-Sky files this live report...."

Slator looked up to see the smoking ruins of the plant being televised from a helicopter. He stood and walked closer to the set as the reporter relayed the obvious fact that some terrible disaster had struck. Slator's body began shaking as the live video transitioned to earlier footage that the news helicopter had captured, and he covered his mouth in shock as he watched the recorded flames leap upward from the site as if trying to lash-out and bring down the hovering witness.

It can't be, he said to himself, knowing full well that neither the reporter nor his eyes had deceived him. It was his plant. He could plainly see the toppled silo tanks, the collapsed but still recognizable roof, and the parking lot of charred cars belonging to men he knew. Men who could not have survived the devastation being shown on the screen. The towering ammonia scrubber had crumpled onto itself like an accordion squeezed tight, and a crater was visible where the neutralizer had been. From the air, the hole in the earth made it appear that a meteor had struck. Slator knew that only a massive explosion could have caused such a caldera and that only an overworked or abused mixing tank would explode.

He heard the reporter say something about the weather, how company officials at the scene suspected a possible lightening strike from last night's thunderstorm might be responsible. Slator knew better. The aerial images presented a clear picture to him, not just of the carnage, but of the cause. The plant blew itself up. Greed, not God, was responsible.

Her news came just before 4:00 a.m. She was sound asleep, dreaming of something she would never remember. The noise brought her to that strange state between sleep and awareness, when something as basic as a ringing phone confuses the mind. It took a moment to process what was happening.

He was choosing to ignore the damn thing.

Understandably exhausted — having worked so long — he deserved his rest. She didn't remember him coming in. She must have been really tired herself or perhaps he had been unusually considerate by slipping quietly under the sheets without waking her. But the phone kept ringing and it was on his side of the bed. She reached over to gently nudge her husband awake. Her arm found only mattress.

What time is it? It has to be after one. She raised her upper body in bed, an elbow for support, and saw no lights outside the bedroom door. There were no sounds of someone in the bathroom. *What's going on?* The cobwebs of slumber had not fully cleared as she rolled over and picked up the phone. She tried to speak clearly but her voice was cluttered with the gravel of night and her "hello" sounded coughing and veiled.

"Mrs. Crouch, this is Rob Finnegan from down at the plant. I'm sorry, but we've had an accident and we're looking for Dan."

"Wh…what? Ah…he's not here."

"No, ma'am, I understand. What I mean is that he's missing. We had a pretty bad fire down here. Everything's kinda confused and we're trying, but we haven't located him yet."

She bolted upright. The force of the words struck. The cobwebs blew away.

"He's missing? MISSING! In a fire?"

Her voice rose in panic as a tsunami of anguish overtook her. "No,…no, Oh, God, NO!"

He could hear the hurt. The other calls had been just the same. He should have been ready with words of calm, something that might help buffer the news. But, as in the previous notifications, he stumbled at the heart-wrenching sounds of someone starting to realize that a loved one had just been lost.

"Mrs. Crouch, I…, uh, we…want you to know we are doing everything we can to find and…help Dan. We, uh…we really are."

"Wh…wh…en?" The word, so short, sounded long and complex as it mewled out between sobs.

"We think it happened near the end of his shift. We don't know what caused it but a lot of people got hurt."

She looked at the time. *Four hours ago?*

"Please, please just tell me," she entreated in short, almost breathless words. "He's dead, isn't he?"

"No, don't say that. We'll find him. We *will* find him."

He tried to sound strong and positive but wasn't sure if she had even heard. Soft groans on the other end had punctuated every word he spoke.

Notifying families like this would be punishing to anyone. But for a person who also felt the victim's blood on his hands, it was unbearable. The company president leaned forward across the union hall table, the phone pressed tightly against his ear, his furrowed brow buried deeply in his other trembling hand. He had to end this call.

"Mrs. Crouch, the union is sending one of its people to your house. He should be there any minute. His name is Jesse and he's going to bring you down here to the union hall so that all of us, the other families and the company, can get through this together. Okay?"

He heard something amid the crying that sounded like "I'll get ready" but he wasn't sure.

"Hopefully, by the time you get here, we will have found Dan to give him the help he needs."

All he heard before the line disconnected was a painful expulsion of choking air — the piteous sound made when someone is punched, hard, in the stomach.

—— ∞∞∞ ——

He was done with sit-ups and about to get on the treadmill. It was a home gym but it was no ordinary home. The exercise room resembled an elegant health club, filled with the latest expensive equipment designed to tone the bodies of the rich or narcissistic. The man reaching for the remote control was both.

Paul Ravich turned on the gym's flat-screen TV. It was affixed to a mirrored wall. If the programming got boring, he could stare at his shrewdly maintained self. It was 5:30 a.m., the start of another day. A long morning workout five times a week had become a necessary ritual for the fifty-eight year-old trial lawyer. He liked to remind his younger attorneys that while Shakespeare's Caesar mistrusted Cassius for having a "lean and hungry look," juries saw litigators in the exact opposite way. A fat plaintiff lawyer was already too rich and content, they might speculate. He probably doesn't need the money so maybe his client doesn't either. Ravich was determined to stay in shape: it was good for the heart as well as his con in the courtroom.

Who could argue the point? The gym, like his equally oversized and ostentatious home, was a material testament to his instincts. He had made more money in courtrooms than almost anyone in the country and he attributed his success in no small measure to an ability to factor in all the little things, including how an attorney's body shape might be perceived by those writing dollar figures into verdict forms.

He was alone in the room. He liked it that way. Fitness trainers were for those who needed outside motivation or folks who didn't know what they were doing. They were for people who were the antithesis of him. He started the belt on his eleven-thousand dollar StarWalker treadmill and thumbed the TV remote to CNN. Talking heads appeared. Like him, they had to look good too.

He was thirty minutes into his run when the initial coverage of the local plant explosion aired. A chemical plant in his own town had gone up in flames and claimed victims. It was already a breaking national story. It needed to be his case.

He slapped the treadmill's stop button and leapt off. He toweled himself as he walked to retrieve his iPhone that had been tossed on the weight bench. He quickly scrolled through his neatly organized Group

Contacts. He tapped the entry labeled "Unions" and flicked until he found the name he wanted.

He was still a little out-of-breath, both from the exercise and the excitement of chasing another front-page disaster, when a voice answered and said:

"ICRW, Region 6, this is Stu."

———⊗⊗⊗———

Ken Slator stood frozen, his mind struggling to process this latest blow. *What is happening?* He should have been home in bed with another half-hour to sleep before starting a routine Tuesday. Yet here he was, in the moments before night yielded to morning, numbed stiff in a stark hospital trying to absorb another tragedy that seemed thrown, with animus, specifically at him.

He needed to go and take his forever-wounded wife out of this place. For now, and for who knew how long, the qualifier "ex" would have to be shelved if they were to have any chance of surviving Melissa's death.

He needed to flee this building where a young and troubled life had ended, and where a corpse that was once his daughter was now being shelved for autopsy, awaiting its final scars.

He needed to call his employer. They were, he was certain, trying to find him. They would want him to explain why the plant — his other and now so obviously far less important child — had suddenly destroyed itself, taking lives with it.

He needed to do all those things but couldn't summon the strength to do any. At that moment he just stood, motionless, in the middle of the room. He was the eye of a hurricane, silent and surrounded, unable to change any of the incredible destruction that revolved around him.

"Excuse me, can I help you?"

The voice came from behind the nearby information desk where a hospital volunteer was now seated. In his transfixed state he had not seen her arrive. He turned in her direction and tried to appear normal. Her look of concern was proof he had failed in the effort.

"Are you here to see someone?" the woman asked, trying to elicit a response from the strange man who now seemed to be staring directly past her.

"I'm here to get my wife. I need to take my wife home."

The words were spoken in slow monotone and Slator never made eye contact with his questioner. It was unsettling to the volunteer. *This man isn't acting normally.*

"Are you okay, sir?"

"No, I'm...fine," he lied, finally looking at her. "She's back there resting. I was told we could leave when we want."

"Let me see if I can help," she said, reaching for the phone at her station. "The patient's name?"

"Joan Slator," he replied, after an uncomfortable pause. He began staring again at the adjacent wall then said: "Or Melissa. I don't know which."

The volunteer, alone with the peculiar-acting man, was now concerned about her own well-being and spoke something hurriedly into the phone.

A male nurse soon came bounding through the automatic doors that separated the waiting room from the interior of the ER. He rushed over to Slator and intentionally invaded the personal space that is normally maintained between two strangers. He wanted to assert his authority in case the man in the waiting room was thinking of becoming a problem.

That sudden movement, followed by a few direct and pointed questions, somehow restored a temporary balance to Slator. He managed to explain the situation involving his family to the eventual satisfaction of the nurse and to the relief of the listening volunteer, who now seemed crushed herself by the sadness of the circumstances.

The nurse escorted him back to the small area where Joan had been allowed to rest in an empty bed. He found her semi-awake, her heavy lids rising occasionally. He watched her unsure eyes gaze briefly at the ceiling before the combined weight of the sedative and sadness closed them again. He took her hand and held it, then stood by the bed to wait for her lucid return.

For over thirty minutes, as she struggled to regain full consciousness, his mind fought with the enormity of the events. *What's done is done,* he finally tried to convince himself in an attempt to stop the crushing pain. He was still enough of an engineer to realize that agonizing retrospection brought only more doubts and greater remorse. What required his full attention now was how best to respond to these overwhelming horrors. Neither his daughter nor his dead coworkers were coming back. He could understandably retreat into the abyss and compound those tragedies or he could take affirmative steps to salvage his life, Joan's life, and the truth about the explosion.

Finally, she stayed awake, less disoriented, her hand still in his. He watched as she regained awareness and when he saw tears form he knew she was back. She realized where she was and remembered why. He helped her up from the bed.

"Let's go home," he said, and she nodded weakly.

After a few minutes, they walked slowly out of the hospital, his arm around her for both physical and emotional support. They left her car in the lot and, in his, headed toward *her* place, the house that had been *their* home only a year ago. While driving, he looked at her, surrendered and softly crying, her head leaned against the window. He vowed to himself that she, and they, were his main priority now.

As Tuesday's sun cast first light on the now dry pavement, Ken Slator made one additional silent vow. While the company no longer deserved his primary attention, he would also not ignore what they had done. A misspent career had imploded his life in a single day. His family, his work, his workers were each decimated by SeaCoast Chemical: the first indirectly, and the latter two in the most direct way imaginable. He promised himself that he would, if there was a way, see the bastards suffer for all the suffering they had caused.

Chapter 6
Case Running

His driver could overhear just one side of the conversations taking place in the backseat of the Bentley. Carter sat behind the wheel, shaking his head in amazement. Paul Ravich had been on his mobile phone nonstop since walking out his front door. It was only seven when they left the house, a full hour earlier than usual. Whatever was happening, it sure had his boss acting eager-beaver.

He listened as Ravich barked orders into the phone. Sounded like he was talking to one of his young lawyers. Something about gathering up their scene photographer and to get in touch with a doctor somebody; he didn't quite catch the name. Whatever kind of doctor he was, it must not be the medical kind. He heard Ravich say: "Have him at my office by nine, dressed like going to court, but tell him to bring along work clothes because he might get dirty later." In another call, he told someone they were in charge of "getting the paperwork together," reminding them that meant firm brochures, contracts, and business cards. Carter didn't even hear him say goodbye on that one. The next thing he overheard was Ravich talking to his assistant, Jan, telling her to come in early and to start clearing his calendar for the day.

That man talks more in twenty minutes than I do in a day. Carter figured he would get a headache for sure if he had to sit in court all day, listening to someone who barely takes a breath between sentences. *How he does it, I don't know.* The phone calls finally stopped as they entered downtown. A few seconds later he heard something really strange. *Not like Mr. Ravich at all.* His boss started whistling some tune. Carter glanced in the rear view mirror and saw his passenger's head tilting side-to-side with the song's rhythm.

Ravich was filled with self-satisfaction as he whistled a few bars of *Viva Las Vegas*. The song had sprung into his head as he pondered the dividends that particular city had paid him over the years and again today.

Personal injury lawyers compete for business, just like car dealers and banks. The big difference, of course, is that those enterprises and most others advertise but most trial lawyers don't. Sure, there are television commercials from a few attorneys promising big money results to folks that can't afford a lawyer. They like to air such ads especially during midday and late-night. But those lawyers, for the most part, aren't heavy hitters like Ravich. The cream of the crop doesn't depend on market saturation and clever catch-phrases to get cases.

Referrals from other lawyers, including the TV commercial kind with a case beyond their talents, is where most of Paul Ravich's docket came from. Such referrals also came at a price. It was routine for Ravich to pay his referring lawyers a third of any fee he ultimately earned on their case. It was custom and practice, and it made a lot of lesser lawyers very rich for doing nothing other than signing up a case and lateraling it over.

Ravich once delivered a check for over a million dollars to a young attorney who had the good fortune to sign up a neighbor's huge malpractice case and, more importantly, the good sense to then refer the case to Paul Ravich & Associates. The kid, just out of law school, made a cool mil off a ten-minute phone call. Ravich, of course, made two million but he had to work hard for his, scaring the hell out of some insurance company to obtain the nine-million dollar gross settlement.

A "direct" case was much more coveted because it came from a source other than another lawyer. That meant Ravich could keep the entire fee. It's illegal to share fees with a non-lawyer and you can lose your license for doing so. A client who got referred to him by a civilian, as opposed to an attorney, therefore meant more to his bottom line. Ravich, like any other businessperson, preferred a bigger bottom line. Of course, little acts of kindness and outward signs of generosity are not the same as paying fees. Lots of laypersons received fancy watches or some other high-priced gift for having thought of Paul Ravich when they recommended a lawyer. Such presents were always paid for out of his after-tax pockets and never through the firm. A gift is just a gift that way, and it was always delivered *after* the case was completed. No grievance committee of any state bar could ever make the claim that it was improper to give such a small token of appreciation to someone after all was said and done. *What would you expect a decent person to do in response to someone's flattering act of recommending your services to a desperate friend in need?* Human nature, though, is a funny thing. Sometimes those gift recipients became walking billboards for Ravich after receiving their expensive surprise. A few actually hustled to find new cases to send his way. Ravich knew how to motivate others. Good things happen when you are nice to people.

The same theory applied to the annual holiday party that Ravich threw for all court personnel. The colorful invitation always made clear that no judges were allowed. This was to be *their* party and his thank you to *them* for their tireless and often under-appreciated work. In the over-puffed words of the individually addressed invites, the event was strictly for "the unsung heroes truly responsible for the administration of justice." The parties were glorious affairs with plenty of free booze and great food. Courthouse employees filled a hotel ballroom each year where they were treated like royalty and where Paul Ravich received standing ovations.

He even had one of his investigators play Santa and draw, from out of a festive bowl, the name of one lucky clerk, bailiff, or court reporter in attendance, with the winner receiving a new car. More often than not the contest was rigged, especially if a willing bailiff from a recent trial had secretly told Ravich what the jury had already written on their not yet complete verdict form. Bailiffs are the only court personnel allowed to enter a jury room during deliberations and if one takes a peek at the verdict in progress while the jury was at lunch — perhaps while innocently refilling their water pitcher — well, that kind of inside information might just give a lawyer some remarkable insight. It's easier to know whether you should accept an at-trial settlement offer when you have some advance notice of what the jury is going to do. More than once, such espionage caused Ravich to suddenly change his mind and accept the latest offer he had summarily turned down after closing arguments. No one was ever the wiser. It was just sheer coincidence, of course, when the co-conspirator bailiff ended up with the Christmas car.

Some years, when there was no big favor to repay, it really was a random pick at the party. After all, making lifelong friends of clerks and court reporters comes in handy too. Ravich was seldom turned down when he asked any of them for a courtroom favor. The whole shebang cost him about ninety-grand each year; chump-change when considering the amazing number of cases that came through his door after a courthouse employee told a neighbor or friend what a great lawyer and generous man he was. Unlike the secret gifts to non-lawyers, he even had his accountants expense the annual party as "business development" under the theory he was only promoting the successful nature of his firm and furthering its already valuable goodwill. The IRS seemed content enough with the other millions he paid in taxes to not question the deduction.

The favorable press he got for the really big cases was another inspired marketing tool. It's good to know when to toot your own horn, and Ravich employed a high-priced public relations firm that could sound his name like a brass band. His talented PR specialists knew how to secure newspaper, magazine, and television special-interest features about his courtroom exploits. They told him which key charities he should support as a banner sponsor. In whatever form his name got out there, it was all intended as a certification to the public that he was the best and the baddest.

Who knew how many cases came to him as a result of media efforts? Then again, who knows how much more beer Budweiser sells by airing commercials during sporting events? The proof was in the success of their business, and in his. Smart advertising worked. For Ravich, that meant not directly pandering for clients through schlocky commercials or billboards touting "no fee unless we win for you." He preferred the more indirect and subliminal messages that he was the only one to call when major disaster struck. That strategy was working just fine, thank you. That was why he had been upset enough to fire Trey the day before. Promoting that little *Clayton* verdict was like taking the Rothschild name and using it to sell Thunderbird.

Ravich also got business by using professional case hustlers, "runners" in the vernacular of the trial bar. These were handsomely paid independent contractors who could, depending on their con, pose as a police investigator, an independent adjuster, a reporter, a social service worker, or some other type professional who might reasonably come in contact with a victim during the early stages following a bad accident. Access to police accident reports and hospital admissions lists — which were easy to get with cash and a willing records clerk — were all that a runner needed to identify potential targets. They would then lie to the accident victim to establish their bona fides and make up a legitimate-sounding reason for needing to visit with them soon after the event. Once credibility was falsely established, they would inevitably let slip a helpful observation about how badly the deck was stacked against hurt people who had done nothing wrong. Sooner or later, the notion that an attorney might be a good idea would come up. Not surprisingly, the role-playing runner could never recall a single time that anyone was ever treated right without an attorney on their side. A good runner knew how to set the hook. He never told the victim what to do. They would just plant seeds and wait for the victim to affirmatively ask them if they knew of any decent lawyers in town.

Ravich had three runners on his unofficial payroll and had never met any of them. His most trusted investigator, Ron Carroll, ran the operation as both trainer and bagman. Ron was a former Delta Force commando who, after the military, had a distinguished twenty-year career as a police detective before joining the firm. He was smart, mean, and discreet. He was also extremely loyal to his boss, who paid him more than any starting lawyer made. No one else at the office knew anything about the case-running program.

Ron trained each runner to never recommend only their man. Instead, they must say: "Here are three names I've heard are the best around." They never handed out cards or wrote anything in their own hand. But they would stand or sit and patiently wait while the victim scribbled down the lawyer names mentioned. Paul Ravich was always the first. For some reason, his name was pronounced perfectly and spelled out exactly, while the names of the other two lawyers were always phonetically confusing and any guess at spelling was always incorrect. After the runner left, a phonebook or Google search by the victim inevitably ended with a call to the office of Paul Ravich & Associates.

These became "semi-direct" cases for Ravich. There were no fees to split with another lawyer but a good runner could not be expected to live on just a nice watch. Ravich, through Ron, paid these con men handsomely in laundered cash when the case settled. The amount the runner received depended on the size of the fee Ravich earned.

Case-running is as illegal as cocaine. Barratry laws expressly prohibit the direct and uninvited solicitation of cases by a lawyer, either in-person or through paid agents. Honest lawyers don't engage in the practice. Dishonest, dumb ones get caught by writing law firm checks to runners or by sending them out with business cards and contracts. Ravich was too smart to generate any documentary evidence like that. If an inquiry was ever made — and there had been none yet — he could testify in response to the facts that the victim was clearly given a list of names by someone he didn't know, had never met, and who was only responding to a victim's affirmative request for information. How could that be interpreted as a violation *by him* of anti-solicitation laws?

Ravich's only real risk came if one of the runners — admittedly sleazy types — tried to blackmail him for more money in exchange for not exposing the scheme. He handled that contingency at the outset. The first time Ron put cash in a runner's hands he made clear that Ravich would have them killed if they ever did or said anything that could trace the transaction back to him. Con men know when other people are bluffing. An unblinking threat from a man like Ron was as real to them as the currency he tendered.

But *the Vegas trips*, as a tool to obtain cases, was by far the most unique business-getting concept to come from Ravich's deviously clever mind.

After all, it wasn't the socialite or white-collar professional who routinely got maimed or killed by corporate neglect. More often than not, it was the blue-collar, Joe-Six-Pack worker, toiling away in factories, plants, mines, and oil fields that got hurt the worst. Many of those people were union members. Most had never needed or employed a lawyer before their accidents. But they paid their union dues for something important: for someone to protect and look after their self-interest. That's exactly the same thing a plaintiff's lawyer is supposed to do for his client. It made perfect sense to Paul Ravich that he and the unions should work closely together.

Shop foremen and union regional directors got listened to in times of crisis. Whether it was the status of wage negotiations or hiring the best lawyer to right a wrong, the rank-and-file looked to union management for advice. Ravich had spent years developing personal relationships with those "go-to" guys. He now had an intricate network of union leaders who needed to be constantly reminded that Paul Ravich was the "go-to" guy when it came to a lawyer for dead or injured union employees.

That's where the Vegas junkets came in. All expense paid trips to Sin City were just magically offered to union bosses on the sole condition that "this is just between us." No *quid pro quo* was ever discussed. It was simply understood. Eventually, so many invitations were accepted that Ravich sometimes felt he was running a travel agency instead of a law firm. All of it was off the books, of course. The details of these union splurges were also intentionally kept far away from his staff.

Although Ravich could technically deny that this man held such status, there was only one "employee" in charge of arranging the use of Ravich's private jet, securing the hotel rooms, and chaperoning his guests once they arrived on the Strip. Diamonds may be a girl's best friend, but to the union boys, Dewey P. Smith was a diamond's equivalent when it came time for a weekend in Vegas. With Ravich's full knowledge, but never his actual participation, Dewey would make sure his VIPs had big chips to gamble with, large steaks to eat, lots of whiskey, and as many hookers as their hedonistic appetites could handle. The only thing Dewey was specifically instructed to say was: "You having a good time?" However, he occasionally got off-script, especially when he got too drunk, and would raise a glass to shout: "That Ravich is a good sum-bitch, ain't he?"

The whole Vegas enterprise cost well over a million dollars per year. The necessary capital to fund such debauchery came in the form of investments to a Nevada corporation named Bright Light City Tours which was chaired by one Dewey P. Smith. The payments came from an offshore shell company to further distance Ravich's involvement. Not once did any of these expenses appear on the balance sheet of Paul Ravich & Associates.

Unlike indirect advertising methods, where the efficacy of newspaper stories and charitable sponsorships could not easily be quantified into case loads, Ravich knew exactly how many cases these union junkets brought in each year. He knew because appreciative and fully sated union bosses would call him up to say: "I'm sending this one over to you." Most were simple workers compensation cases that offered no opportunity for riches, and some of the other type cases were just too small to keep. Those he referred to lesser tort lawyers around town, who in turn paid Ravich a referral fee on the small-fry stuff. But occasionally a whopper multi-party disaster or product liability case came in from the union pipelines. It took only a couple of big ones each year to more than justify the time and expense of running the Vegas operation.

Stu Mitchell, the regional head of the Industrial Chemical & Refinery Workers Union, had been to Vegas on Ravich's carefully laundered nickel plenty of times. Once, he got on a lucky streak and brought home twenty-grand in winnings. From that point on, any union member who asked Stu for the name of a good lawyer got only one. Ravich fully expected Stu Mitchell to steer the SeaCoast explosion plaintiffs to him eventually. But this was too big a case to rely on mere expectations. It would carry too much publicity to let things just take their usual course.

That was why he made the early morning call to Stu from his home gym. And that call was why he now had an appointment in three hours to meet with the families that Stu promised would be waiting for him at the union hall. And those all-expense paid trips were why he would be introduced to them as a good friend of the union and a champion for the rights of its victims. And that opportunity was why he had been on the phone all morning, busily assembling an investigative team and making preparations for his compelling in-person offer to come to the aid of those poor distraught family members. And his skill at talking people into anything was why he was confident that, by the end of the day, he would be the attorney-of-record for a bunch of grievers with multi-million dollar claims to collect, and from which he would take a big cut as his fee.

And *all* those reasons were why Paul Ravich was smugly content in the back seat of his chauffeured car on a Tuesday morning, whistling an old Elvis song whose title — especially today — seemed so perfectly apropos: *Viva Las Vegas!*

Chapter 7
Own Devices

It would have felt strange under the best of circumstances and these were the worst imaginable: To step over the same threshold he once crossed with a new baby girl just home from the hospital, a daughter now lying cold and lifeless inside another. To walk through a door, holding the hand of a woman who not so long ago stood in this very house and declared she didn't love him anymore. To enter a place that, twenty-two years before, the two of them had so excitedly bought with the starting salary from a company he now detested.

Ken Slator was returning to *their* home even though the divorce decree stated it was now Joan's "sole and separate property." That had been a surrendering concession, an attempt to satisfy a guilt-debt owed to a wife he knew had been neglected. The law may see it differently but in his soul, this place, this house, was still part his. A piece of paper could terminate a marriage or transfer title, but documents couldn't erase his sense of belonging. As he helped her inside, all he felt was an overwhelming commitment to his family, now half gone, the other half broken.

They didn't speak as he led her back to the master-bedroom and helped her crawl under the covers. No words were shared as he sat at the edge of their old bed, rubbing Joan's forehead softly as if that could somehow excise the painful thoughts she was feeling. Her crying gradually became light whimpers, then stopped altogether as sheer fatigue finally allowed her to fall back asleep.

As he was comforting her, he stared at three framed pictures of Melissa that sat atop the nearby dresser. Her first grade photo, a sweet-sixteen birthday, and a high-school graduation pose were clustered neatly together. Yesterday morning they had been just warm accent pieces, something that occasionally brought a smile to Joan, perhaps reminders that her married life had not been completely wasted. Now they would forever be a shrine that would bring only sadness when she looked at them. In the photos, his daughter's eyes seemed filled with innocence and hope. His were now filled with guilt and hopelessness. He tried but couldn't avert his gaze from those 5 x 7 memories that were now all they had left.

He finally rose gently from the bed and walked quietly into the small study that used to be his home office. Joan had redecorated it after the split. It was now a much lighter room. Floral fabrics covered the previous tartan-patterned sofa. His engineering treatises and historical biographies were boxed away somewhere, replaced with gardening and self-help books, along with a small stack of romance novels. A vase of autumn flowers sat beside an iMac computer on the small desk where his collection of carved ducks once rested alongside stacks of reports from the plant. This room was like the house: familiar but changed and not really his.

He found some paper and scribbled a note to leave beside her bed. He hadn't mentioned the plant explosion on the drive back from the hospital and saw no reason to now. Instead, he simply wrote that he needed to take care of an emergency at work and make arrangements to be away from the office for a while. He added he would return as quickly as he could and that she should call him when she woke up and found the note. He ended with five words he knew might be false, then penned three more below he knew were true:

"We will get through this."
"I love you."

⸺⸻★⸻⸺

The drive back to his apartment took twenty minutes. It was much-needed time to begin an uneasy transition from deep family mourning to businesslike purposefulness. He still had not spoken to anyone at SeaCoast. He knew that the answers he needed, and which they would be seeking, were sitting on top of his kitchen table. He would contact them only after he knew more than they did about what happened.

The television was still on when he unlocked his apartment door and reentered his post-divorce world. The news station, which the night before had put him to sleep in the moments before Joan's panicked call, was still squawking in predictable circles about peace talks, the upcoming elections, and various human interest stories that rarely interested anyone. But this morning there was something far more personal in the rotation. Every thirty minutes since dawn, the cable network had been rebroadcasting footage of the SeaCoast plant disaster amid speculation as to its cause. As

Slator walked over to turn off the set, the images of his burning plant reappeared as if on cue. He stood mesmerized.

A soundbite followed in which a tired fire captain looked into the camera saying it had been a difficult and dangerous fire to control; that three bodies had been located; that two men were still missing and presumed dead; and one survivor was believed to be in very critical condition.

Slator briefly wondered who had made it out. He knew from the rubble it couldn't have been anyone in the main section of the plant and that included Dave Phillips up in the control room.

The coverage continued. Standing outside the destroyed plant, beneath a hastily erected tent canopy in front of dozens of microphones, was a serious-looking man identified by a banner at the bottom of the screen that read: *"SeaCoast Attorney Bruce Waltman."* Slator had never seen nor met the man but he spotted a familiar face standing behind him. It was Rob Finnegan, his hands clasped and head bowed, somberly posed as if he were praying in church.

"We are obviously in the difficult and painful first steps of trying to determine what caused this catastrophe and claimed the lives of our beloved and valuable employees."

The lawyer spoke with the polish of a political candidate.

A reporter's voice interrupted from off camera: *"Did lightning cause the explosion?"*

"We don't know that. What we do know is this plant has been safely operated for twenty-years and was being safely operated last night. We do know there was severe weather in the area briefly. We will cooperate with authorities to get to the bottom of this tragedy but right now our main concerns are with the victims' families."

Slator's blood began to boil as the edited portion of the company's press conference came to an end. The news anchor's face reappeared.

"Officials from the EPA and OSHA are expected to arrive at the scene as early as tomorrow to commence an investigation." The anchor's voice-over continued as his face was replaced with footage of the floor of the House of Representatives. *"In the nation's capitol, House Members prepare today for the upcoming vote on a continuing budget resolution that...."*

Slator pressed the set off. Turning away, he saw his mobile phone on the sofa and reached down to grab it. Carrying it to the kitchen, he glanced at the home screen which showed a count of nine missed calls and four voicemails. They were indeed looking for him. He imagined the initial messages would be ones of panic followed by those of escalating anger at his lack of prompt reply. *Screw them,* he thought, as he sat down to review the calls. *My daughter just died.*

He saw that the first missed call had come from the plant's number at 8:43 p.m. The caller left no message but it must have been Dave Phillips. Slator thought back and recalled that was about the time he first arrived at the hospital. The next call, from the same number, had come in at 8:55. This time, there was a voicemail. He clicked to play it.

"Yeah, Ken. Dave here. Listen, we've had some temp elevations that caused auto-shutdowns on the N-Tank. I'm starting a third fill and gonna try and keep her at or below 80%. I'm sure we were running just a little too full on the others. Give me a call back when you get this if you think of something different."

There was another call from Dave at 9:40, but no message. At 10:05, he again left a voicemail. This time his voice sounded strained and the message sent a jolt down Slator's spine.

"Hey, it's me again. Look, something's not right. The DCSS is giving me numbers showing another shutdown might be coming and I need your advice. I just got off the phone with Finnegan — since I couldn't get ahold of you — and he thinks it's just a faulty sensor jacking things up. He told me to override the DCSS and keep the plant going; that we don't have time to stop. I think everything's all right doing that and we'll keep a close eye but maybe you've got a better idea. Call me ASAP and, hey buddy, sorry to bother you this late."

Slator placed the cell phone down. With trembling hands, he lifted the lid on his laptop. It felt like opening a crypt. He had just heard a dead man relate orders that amounted to his own death sentence and now he was about to see the details of that execution carried out in recorded real-time.

Fifteen minutes later, a dumbfounded Ken Slator closed the computer shut, his hands pressing tightly down on its top as though sheer pressure might help protect its secrets.

There were now three survivors of the plant explosion. The man in critical condition, if he lived, might recall the blast but wouldn't be able to explain it. The voicemail of a ghost survived to provide, briefly and damningly, the human context. But the third survivor was a detailed, all-knowing, non-human witness. And he was resting his still shaking hands on top of it.

The DCSS data relays were clear and unimpeachable. An over-stressed factory was pushed beyond its limits. Things had started to grow very bad around the time he was summoned to the hospital and they rapidly grew worse. The recorded temperatures, pressures, and flow readings documented the unstable and deadly ominous conditions inside the plant. The automatic safety system that would have prevented the disaster was incongruously switched over to manual operation at 10:18 p.m. allowing the sensors to be electronically turned off less than two minutes later. They were still bypassed at 11:16 when the DCSS relayed its last reading.

Ken Slator knew, better than anyone, what the recorded data meant. He understood that the file inside the laptop's hard drive was more incriminating than testimony from any eyewitness. It didn't blink and could tell its story without embellishment or contradiction. The plant had been flying fast and blind in its last hour. Anyone with an advanced understanding of chemistry would be able to see from those final recorded numbers and events that a crash landing was inevitable.

He picked the phone up again to see if the remaining calls held more clues. The next voicemail came in at 1:07 a.m. He didn't recognize the number but there was no mistaking the screaming voice of Rob Finnegan.

"Ken, goddamnit, where are you? The plant's blown up. It's on fire. People have been trying to reach you all night. Do you think your 8-to-4 ass could return my call? I need you down here NOW! When you get this, call me back to let me know you're on the way. And that better be soon! We don't know what happened, but it looks bad."

Ken felt his anger rise. *I know what happened, you bastard. And so do you.* There were two more call attempts from that same number, with no messages, at 2:15 and again at 4:10. An hour and a half later, Finnegan left another angry message:

"Slator, the only other reasons I can think of for why you haven't gotten back to me is either your damn phone's dead or you are. Either way, you're no help. You get this message, you get down here. I got the press and Thornton's lawyer hounding me."

It sounded as if Finnegan had become unhinged. That was understandable, but Slator knew his boss's agitated state wasn't really due to any unexplained absence. It was because guilt eats at you like acid. He had learned that all too well himself in the corridors of a hospital only a few hours before.

He laid the phone back down. He had gotten to the end of the list. There were no more calls. Finnegan had given up. Or maybe he was now too busy covering up.

Ken Slator sat in his kitchen chair staring at two ordinary electronic devices that extraordinarily revealed everything. They translated an indecipherable mystery into clearly documented acts of gross negligence and greed. His cell phone and laptop were, together, the Rosetta Stone necessary to understand the explosion and its causes.

Avarice on the part of SeaCoast Chemical and its parent corporation created the potential for controllable chemistry to lose control. A deadly human alchemy resulted when the company's insatiable desire for gain got mixed with the incredibly stupid and pressured decisions of both Slator's superior and his assistant.

It was all crystal clear: not only what happened but also why. Ken Slator, and no one else, knew the *complete* story. He had the proof before him and no one else knew that either.

The events of the past twelve hours had been swift and monumental. Death and destruction had transformed him as suddenly as chemistry had morphed a safe product into a bomb. He was done being a company man. He would not disclose his evidence until he had more time to think, until he could figure out the best way it could be used. He needed to right the wrongs of SeaCoast Chemical and Thornton Industries. He owed that much to his fellow workers who were dead. His employer had already demonstrated the folly of moving too fast. He would take his time and, unlike them, make his moves much more cautiously.

His daughter's death also fueled his commitment to see his company pay. SeaCoast didn't kill her, at least not directly. But in his anger and sadness he could see a connection that others would not. The company had taken him away from her during all those years when he could have — no, *would have* — made a difference in her life. He saw a causal link between the time he wasted on them and the time now forever lost with Melissa. It was no different from what the job had done to his marriage.

He was complicit, of course. No man who loses love through neglect can fairly blame someone else entirely for the loss. But without the excessive demands of his company, and but for his stupid willingness to put them first, he was certain, *absolutely certain*, that he would still have his family today. He didn't need that as a reason to get back at SeaCoast. He had more than enough already. But it gave him a deeper emotional impetus to do what he felt he had to do.

For now, there were just two things:

First, he would call his boss and quit. He would say that his daughter's sudden death required his full attention and they could surely get by without him, especially with no plant to run. He would inform them he could make himself available in a few days but not until after the funeral. He would no longer be their employee but he would affirm his willingness to assist the investigators in their search for answers. He would be careful not to say or suggest that he had all the answers already. He would give no hint that the cause of the explosion was something other than weather. If he were pressed, he would tell them — for the first time ever — that his family came first. If they pressed too hard, he would tell them to go to hell.

Second, he would take some clothes, his computer, and a few other things over to his old house. He would ask Joan if he could stay there, at least for a few days or for as long as they needed each other to deal with their shared sadness.

That was his plan. That was as far as he had gotten in his thinking.

But unbeknown to him, avarice and alchemy were still swirling around him. There were men whose giant egos and relentless greed would soon interact to form different dangers. There were good people who would become mixed with bad as new storms formed. Justice, not chemistry, would be tested this time. Gamesmanship, not science, would determine the outcome.

Ken Slator was not aware of the next hurricane looming. But once again, he would be at its eye.

Part II

Methods & Machinations

Chapter 8
First Steps

Fifteen people sat in a makeshift semicircle of hard aluminum chairs. Two talked calmly, while a group of four held hands and mumbled prayers. An older couple flanked a young woman, their arms around her, as they rocked heavy heads silently, eyes closed. The sadness frozen on their faces said more than enough. One older man, a victim's father, was telling anyone who would listen that he "retired from factory work after thirty years and these things don't just happen." There were nine women in the group. Five would be the widows of the dead. The rest would be mothers, or perhaps one or two were just close friends there for support. Of the six men, half were too young to be fathers of victims. They were most likely brothers.

The calls that first brought the horrible news had been hours ago. As the assembled waited tortuously in the union hall, the last remnants of hope dissolved into grief and anger.

Stu Mitchell first stood before them to say the union was part of their family and that it too had been rocked by the explosion. He promised there would be no rest until all the answers were known. He assured them that the ICRW's main priority was to take care of the families. He asked them to wait with him for more word. He offered them prayer along with donuts and coffee.

He came back an hour later to say the only survivor was Derron Lucas, who was barely clinging to life. He asked everyone to stay, to support each other, and to await further news about what was happening and where the remains of their loved ones would be taken.

The third time Stu appeared in front of the group, Rob Finnegan was at his side. The SeaCoast President had just returned from the morning press conference at the accident site, where his presence had been demanded and where he had been told by his General Counsel to say nothing and to look sad for the cameras. That had been easy. Now he was back at the union hall for the much harder task of standing before the victim's families to offer condolences on behalf of the company.

Wholly shaken, he introduced himself and began speaking haltingly. He was quickly interrupted by outbursts of "Where's my husband?" and "What did you do?" As president of the company, he expected some anger would be directed at him. He also knew better than to engage any hostility, especially not now, particularly not here. So he just stood before them, trembling and waiting for relative silence. He thought maybe they would see his obvious unease as a sign of empathy, not contrition, but when he resumed speaking he could hear culpability in his voice. He hoped they would mistake it for sorrow.

"We don't know yet what caused this. We all know it...shouldn't have happened. We all wish to God it hadn't. But we...."

"You were pushing them too hard," interrupted the retiree who had earlier been offering opinions to the group.

His accusation found receptive ears. There were a few: "Yeahs," and one loud: "That's right."

"We were all...working hard," Finnegan replied. "But we...we were trying to be...I mean, we were also working safe."

Doubtful moans from the group derailed his train of thought.

"I promise you that SeaCoast will get answers for you. For us, for everybody. Right now, all I can give is our pledge that we will, uh...make things right."

"Then find Dan," Kate Crouch spoke up.

"We will ma'am. We know that he and Tom are in there. We know they didn't make it out."

A loud sob came from across the semicircle of chairs. Tom Benson's wife was still struggling to accept that she was now a widow.

Rob Finnegan realized he wasn't doing anyone any good. Stu Mitchell knew it too and stepped in closer to signal that Finnegan should stop talking.

"I'm just...so sorry; I mean, the Company is...so sorry. I don't know what else to...."

"Okay, Rob, we appreciate your being here," Stu interjected.

Finnegan was clearly spent. He hung his head and expelled a rush of air. It was a sigh of resignation. The President of SeaCoast Chemical had only made matters worse — again.

"Now, Rob, I think it best if you went back to the plant or you can use my office to make some calls. Let's try to get these folks some real information."

Finnegan nodded and turned to walk away. He welcomed the chance to flee his confronters. He kept his head down and exited the union hall where he could face his demons alone.

Stu Mitchell then got down to important business, at least for him.

"Everybody, I know the main thing right now is your family. Of course, we also want answers about why this happened but company management always tells us that can wait. Look, I've been running this district for a long time and the one thing I've learned is that plant owners count on the families to do nothing right away other than mourn. They pat us on the back while they get real busy covering their tracks. By the time we're ready to search for the truth they've already got their story together. And guess what? They always end up blaming us, or somebody or something else."

"I know that's true," blurted the non-shy and opinionated father.

"Because the union has sadly been through this before, we know the best thing we can do for you right now, other than simply being at your side, is to even the playing field and get good people started right away, working for all of us, to find out what happened and who is responsible."

Stu feigned an apologetic tone.

"I hope nobody here gets mad at me for doing this, but I've asked the best lawyer in the state to come down here this morning to talk to us. He's a man that represents families, not companies, and he's willing to work for y'all on his nickel to get at the truth. He knows, like I do, the importance of not letting SeaCoast get ahead of us on this. So while we wait to hear where they're taking your loved ones, I would like to ask everybody if you'd be willing to stay and listen to what this man has to say?"

Kate Crouch sat with her arms crossed as the rest of the group lodged no protest. She thought it oddly inappropriate to be thinking about lawyers before her husband's body was even located. But she said nothing, especially since everyone else appeared to think it was a good idea.

Stu Mitchell's *"just trying to help"* speech had worked.

"He'll be here at ten." Stu looked up at the wall clock. "That's in fifteen minutes. If anyone wants or needs to speak with me about anything else, I'll be in my office until he comes."

He took a step away before a sudden question startled him.

"Do all of us have to hire this lawyer?"

He turned and identified the questioner. "No, ma'am, of course not. Mrs. Crouch, you're free to do as you like. I just thought we should all hear some good advice is all." He smiled weakly to indicate his sincerity. It convinced everyone except the intended target. "Again, let me know if anyone needs anything. I'm going to go call the fire department and see when they'll let us up there."

Stu Mitchell walked the short distance to his office and closed the door. *I hope she's not going to be a problem,* he thought, as he sat down to dial Paul Ravich's cell number. He would call the fire department later. Right now, he needed to tell his buddy that the skids had been greased.

The mid-morning meeting started without the SeaCoast President. Finnegan was nonessential anyway. Bruce Waltman arrived at One Thornton Plaza shortly after ten and went straight to the Chairman's office. His ash-covered suit looked like he felt.

Waltman had been orchestrating damage control at the plant site since two in the morning. He delegated family contacts to Finnegan. He summoned company employees to make sure that firefighters and police got plenty of water, refreshments, and thanks for their efforts. The plant's head process engineer was nowhere to be found, so Waltman decided to blame the weather until they got a handle on things. A couple of in-house lawyers were ordered to show up and help manage press and any official inquiries. His directive to them was clear: say nothing substantive and deny access to everyone unless he was present. He performed admirably at the dawn press conference. Both sides got what they wanted. The press took pictures of the destroyed plant and SeaCoast got to deliver images of grieving and concerned management. He then fielded an early morning call from the regional office of the EPA and another from an OSHA compliance officer. He told both regulatory agencies that SeaCoast would cooperate fully with any investigation. On top of all that, he made his hourly calls to Charles Thornton, as instructed. The General Counsel had done all those things on less than four hours sleep and knew the day ahead would be even more arduous. There would be no time for a nap, shower, or change of clothes.

He walked up to Marlene, who was at her desk piled with mounds of paper. Thornton had obviously been busy himself with a different kind of damage control. With no exchange of words, she pointed to the closed doors of Thornton's office, indicating that he was waiting. Bruce Waltman brushed off his jacket and entered.

"There you are. Get in here, we've got a lot to talk about."

Charles Thornton sat behind his desk, spreadsheets before him. Waltman took a seat. The Chairman, as always, got right down to business.

"Using depreciated numbers, the market value of the plant and equipment was $190 million. Accounting will have to confirm, but I can estimate the actual rebuild and replacement costs at damn near twice that.

Assuming a total loss of inventory, we also had $5.7 million dollars in contracted product go up in smoke, and the failure to complete the current Chinese contract will cost us over $12 million in lost revenue. On top of all that, we can't perform for the foreseeable future. The loss of that upcoming contract renewal means at least $60 million more off our books for next year fiscal, and that's assuming I couldn't hijack the Chinese for a price increase, which you know I would have."

He spat the numbers as if reporting a robbery. Waltman was not surprised that Thornton's primary concern was economic or that he had been penciling damages since arriving at his office at four that morning. He knew his boss well. The soot stains his suit might be leaving on the silk-covered office chair were probably a greater concern to Thornton than the number of dead.

"So, Bruce, how much of all that is covered by our insurance?"

Thornton was as predictable as a sunrise. Losers calculated losses. Winners looked for ways to recoup.

Waltman instantly recalled the decisions made by his boss, three years earlier, as part of a rabid cost-cutting program intended to increase profits from SeaCoast's operations. He surmised that Thornton remembered those decisions as well but wanted someone else to state the current consequences as if that would somehow shift the blame. Waltman cleared his throat and began.

"As you may recall, we elected to drop the standard property damage and business interruption coverage on all SeaCoast facilities, including the main AN plant. Instead, we secured a much cheaper 'excess of self-insured' policy with substantially reduced coverages and very high triggering limits."

"How high?"

"I'll have to confirm, but I believe the insurance kicks in only after our first $250 million out-of-pocket, and coverage applies only to market value physical damage."

"That's a goddamn high deductible for shit we depreciate on an accelerated basis."

"Yes, sir."

Waltman wanted to say more. He could have pointed out how the legal department made that same observation three years ago in a detailed memo only to have Thornton disregard their coverage advice in order to save a few hundred-thousand dollars in annual premiums. But Waltman knew better than to bring that up. You don't remain General Counsel by saying "I told you so" to your boss in times of crisis.

"Well, what about the liability coverage?" Thornton hated lawsuits. "I imagine there will be all kinds of frivolous claims by surrounding property owners alleging our smoke was toxic and is going to cause cancer. You know, crap like that."

"Again, we elected to self-insure our general liability up to the first $100 million in claims," Waltman explained. "Beyond that, we have coverage with American-Casualty of an additional $200 million. I believe we also hold an excess policy of $750 million that kicks in only after that first combined $300 million dollars is exhausted. We will have to notify the carriers, of course, but it's doubtful that such claims will come anywhere close to that first hundred-million, which is strictly our money."

Thornton became increasingly irritated with answers that were taking from, rather than adding to, his bottom line.

"And what about the dead employee claims? You know those greedy families will sue."

Thornton's comment about the victims was off-putting, even to a corporate lawyer who was no fan of tort plaintiffs. *You heartless bastard,* thought Waltman, as he carefully hid his disgust behind a lack of expression. At least this time he had some news that Thornton would be happy to hear.

"Their recovery against us is limited to workers' compensation death benefits. Those amounts are relatively small. All employers are required by law to carry comp coverage and SeaCoast's policy will handle those claims. The comp statute makes a very favorable trade for us: in exchange for getting token benefits automatically, the employee's family is barred from suing us directly for full damages. So, from a money standpoint, they're the least of our worries."

"Then why do I read in the paper all the time about these employees getting millions for some accident?" asked Thornton, questioning his lawyer's statement of the law.

"Victims have a right to sue and claim that some other company caused the accident," Waltman replied. "We lawyers call such suits 'third-party actions' because they can't and don't involve suing the employer. The only way our victims could ever get around the comp bar and recover a windfall directly from us is if they can prove gross negligence on our part."

"Which means what?"

"Well, thanks to recent tort reform legislation, it means the families would basically have to prove that SeaCoast intended to kill them or that we consciously and knowingly disregarded safety. It's a near impossible burden of proof for them. I wouldn't worry about it."

Thornton smiled for the first time since the meeting started. "Well, I guess our sizable donation to that anti-lawsuit lobby paid off then, didn't it?"

"Yes, they were very effective in getting our message out and influencing some key statutory reforms."

"What was that stupid group called again?"

"The Economic Council Against Lawsuit Abuse."

"That's right, I remember now." Thornton chuckled. "They pitched the whole damn thing as a jobs-saving initiative. Pissed off those tort lawyers good."

"Yes, sir."

"All right. Are we going to have to fade any heat from the government over this?"

"The Environmental Protection Agency has jurisdiction along with the Occupational Safety & Health Administration. They will conduct investigations but both agencies are badly understaffed. We should be able to control the outcome. Worst that would happen might be some small regulatory fines."

Thornton nodded as Marlene's voice came over the desk intercom.

"Mr. Thornton, Rob Finnegan from SeaCoast has arrived for the meeting."

"Send him in," Thornton barked loudly.

The haggard subsidiary president entered the office suite and sat down meekly after an exchange of tepid handshakes. Finnegan had attended numerous meetings at the parent company's headquarters building but had never been included in a private session with the Big Man. On the drive downtown, the SeaCoast President mistakenly assumed his morning ordeal at the union hall would be the worst part of his day. He was as unaware of his precarious fate as a cow facing slaughter. Until Thornton began shouting.

"Do you have any fucking clue how much your operation down there cost us today?"

Finnegan was caught off guard by the steely tone of the question.

"Well, sir, I don't know…"

Thornton cut him off.

"That's right Finnegan, you don't know *shit!* Because if you did, I'd still have a fertilizer plant making money instead of news."

Rob Finnegan lowered his head and said nothing. Both he and Bruce Waltman could tell that Thornton had only begun his tirade.

"I've been going over some numbers and it might end up being as high as a half-billion." Thornton paused to let the figure float around the room. Rob Finnegan bit his lip. "So tell me, Finnegan, what did SeaCoast pay you in salary and bonus last year?"

"I really don't recall the exact number, sir."

"Hazard a guess. If you're off by a hundred-thousand, that's no big deal. Today, that would just be a drop in my massively leaking bucket."

"I think it was around four hundred-fifty thousand."

Charles Thornton roughly calculated the math.

"Okay then, that means if you work for free the rest of your life, I'd still be in the hole more than $480 million when your stupid ass dies, all because you couldn't keep a goddamn fertilizer plant from blowing up. Do you understand me?"

Finnegan gave a shameful nod, the kind a remorseful kid gives when a parent catches them doing something bad.

"If Thornton Industries didn't have other and bigger business interests, this little disaster could have bankrupted us. As it stands, the other SeaCoast facilities are barely enough to keep that company afloat. And none of them can mass produce the fertilizer I need for those Chinese bastards."

"Yes, sir," was all Finnegan managed to say.

"Now, let me ask you: Do you think it's unreasonable for me to be upset about all that?"

"No, sir." Finnegan then decided to attempt some defense. "Except I don't know what happened; I mean, what caused the explosion."

"Well, if that's the case, then what Bruce and I want to find out is: Who the fuck does?"

Thornton shouted his operative question and Finnegan winced.

"Mr. Thornton, sir, we've been trying to reach the plant's process manager since it happened. That man helped design the plant. He would know best what could have gone wrong."

"Well, unless he got blown up himself, why haven't you talked to him?"

"Believe me, I've been trying. I've left voicemails and made numerous calls. He's usually a pretty reliable guy, but…"

"Give me his name and number. We'll call him right now."

"His name is Ken Slator. He's been with us for years."

Finnegan fumbled with his cell phone, then called out the number. Thornton switched the telephone on his desk to speakerphone. The number tones echoed throughout the room as his stubby fingers angrily punched the keypad. The ringing began. Rob Finnegan swallowed hard. He feared Slator would be caught off-guard, just as he had been.

For the first time, he actually hoped there would be no answer.

———— ∞ ————

They were tired of speeches. The union leader had sounded like a meddlesome priest, speaking of unity while offering them prayerful condolences and a lawyer in the same breath. The SeaCoast President had been even worse. "We're sorry" is something you say when arriving late to a dinner party, not when you kill someone. Of course, no one could say anything that would bring life back to their dead. But still, not one word of explanation had been given for why it happened. They had been sitting for hours and were in no mood for more talk.

It was not an audience for a first-time performer. You had to be a pro.

The doors of the union hall opened and five people were immediately welcomed by Stu Mitchell, who had been pacing by the entrance for the last several minutes waiting for their arrival. The families turned to see the union leader enthusiastically shake hands with one man wearing a finely tailored suit. They watched as that tall, fit person now marched confidently toward the front of the room. The rest of the entourage followed. Even Stu Mitchell walked a few steps behind the purposeful-striding man. It appeared like General Patton in a pinstripe suit had mustered his troops and was now leading them into battle. When the man got to the front, he turned to face the families. His expression was somber and imposing. He tipped his head slightly as he made eye contact with each person seated, attempting to establish a small personal connection.

Stu Mitchell put his hand on the man's shoulder. The other new arrivals assembled themselves stage left. The union head then began an introduction worthy of any carnival shill:

"Folks, I'd like to introduce you to Paul Ravich, the most successful plaintiff's lawyer in this state if not the entire country. Paul has represented only workers and their families since he began his practice and has sued companies like SeaCoast for years. He damn sure gets the attention of the other side. He will get answers for you like he has in the past for many of our other union brothers and sisters. He has collected hundreds of millions for his clients. In fact, he once handled a case where…"

Ravich politely interrupted his host. "All right, Stu, I appreciate the kind words but this isn't about me." He patted the union rep on the back, then looked directly at the people seated before him.

"This is about *you* and the person you lost last night." He paused for emphasis. "I'm not here to sell you something and I've been around enough tragedy to know I can't possibly say anything this morning that will bring you any comfort, much less begin any healing."

Years of jury argument had convinced Ravich that the trick was to sound as if you were talking one-on-one when addressing a group. His piercing eyes wandered slowly from one face to another as he spoke.

"You have other, more important things to deal with right now besides law and lawyers. So I will be brief. Unlike what you've probably already heard from SeaCoast, what I'm about to say to you is genuine."

He made certain his next three sentences had an appropriate slow cadence. He made sure the right words were emphasized in a strong and sincere voice.

"I'm *sorry* to intrude on your grief. I *apologize* for asking for even a few minutes of your time right now. I know how *hard* it is to think about anything else when you have *suffered* so deep a loss."

Ravich paused to wait for the looks he knew would come. He resumed talking only when he saw the expressions of the anguished people change, indicating they were thankful someone was finally treating them with dignity.

"If I didn't know how critically important it was, I would say 'this can wait' and come back later, when and if any of you wanted to talk. But sadly, I do know how the other side works and I can absolutely assure you they have already started to inflict more harm by making plans to hide their responsibility. And so I ask that you please forgive me for talking about what needs to be done right now. If you will permit me to offer some advice, I promise I will thereafter respect your need to be alone with your memories and your family. Is that all right with everyone?"

Ravich paused again and surveyed his audience. He had their attention. Body language and head gestures evidenced their assent and interest. Only one woman kept her head held down but she said nothing.

"Stu called me early this morning to ask if I would come down. I guess he remembered my involvement in other refinery explosions, or maybe my representation of those families whose sons and husbands were killed in that deep ocean drilling rig disaster a few years back. In all those cases, it was our ability to commence an investigation before documents and evidence could be lost or destroyed that made the difference. We got justice for those people because we got to work fast and because the defendant companies knew that I knew what needed to be done."

Ravich motioned towards his team.

"I have brought with me this morning Dr. Norman Clark, who is a preeminent industrial safety and chemical process engineer. He has the expertise to determine exactly what happened out there last night. His years in the industry allow him to piece together the truth from the physical evidence and records even as the other side tries to conceal the facts. I've worked with Dr. Clark before and took it upon myself to wake him up very early this morning. I told him there were families that needed answers. I said to him that if you folks were willing to authorize me to act on your behalf, I wanted to get him out to the scene right away and begin a thorough and responsible examination of this tragedy."

Ravich looked at his expert as if he were a guardian angel rather than a hired witness.

"He said he would help. For that, Dr. Clark, I want to thank you on behalf of everyone."

Ravich didn't need to heap false gratitude on his soon to be well-paid expert. Instead, he was using the moment to convey a message to the victims that he was now speaking for them. It was a critical first step.

"I also brought along Jeff Eastman, who is a professional photographer and videographer. If you authorize me to act, I will see to it that he gets access to that plant today so that we can completely document the scene. I know from over two-hundred successful jury trials how important it is to preserve the evidence, especially when the guilty own the property."

Nothing Paul Ravich ever said was wasted air. He had used the introduction of Eastman as a chance to reference his own impressive resume while reinforcing his theme of "Us versus Them."

"These other two folks are lawyers at my firm: Dustin Kirkland and Melanie Egan. They are young talented attorneys who could have gone to work for big corporations like SeaCoast but chose instead to work with me because they believe, as I do, that victims need justice more than some fat-cat company needs another in-house lawyer in their army."

You find a theme, you stay with it. Ask any politician. Like a good salesman, Ravich was now ready to ask for the business.

"If you will permit me, I am ready to get this team working for you so that you can focus, as I know you need to, on helping your family through this unbearable pain."

The vocal old-timer in the audience was clearly impressed but not afraid to ask the question on everyone's mind.

"And what's all this gonna cost us?"

Ravich loved getting tossed a softball.

"Yes, sir, that's a good question. You are?"

"Roy Evans. I'm Bill's daddy. He worked for them bastards for over eight years. I put in over thirty with Arlon Chemical myself."

"Well, then, you probably know as well as me how these outfits operate after they screw up and hurt somebody."

"I sure do."

Ravich nodded appreciatively. The old coot's comment was better than a church member jumping up to shout that the Lord had entered them. It made things so much easier for the preacher.

"Roy, you and the others will never receive a bill from me for anything. I consider it an honor to work for innocent victims and I believe if I don't do them any good they should pay me nothing. That's why I'm willing to front all the expenses necessary to see that justice is done. My time and effort only gets compensated when I'm able to make a recovery for you."

He shifted his gaze to another family.

"Lawyers call that a contingency fee. I call it a real promise, in writing, that I won't take advantage of you the way that SeaCoast and others felt they could. If I don't do my job protecting you, then I will get what I deserve, which is nothing. But when I hold them accountable, and I promise you I will, I get paid a third of any money that we are able to wrestle away from the companies found to be responsible."

Ravich loved the next part of his tried-and-true "hire me" presentation and always had to fight himself not to smile.

"Now, there are hundreds of other lawyers in this town who will tell you they charge the same fee. And technically, that's right. But practically speaking, it's not the whole truth. Not one of them has my record of making a defendant pay every last cent that is owed. So if you hire someone with lesser experience it usually comes down to paying the same fee percentage but with a much, much smaller net amount to you."

He gave his self-serving math a few seconds to sink in.

"I know that sounds like big talk and I don't want to stand up here, especially at a time like this, and brag. So before you hire me, ask people you trust, people like Stu here, whether it makes any difference which lawyer you hire. I hope it counts for something that your union invited me to be here for you. I hope it matters some that I came with people who are ready to go to work right now."

An older woman, a victim's mother, spoke up.

"So, who do you sue? I got hurt on my job once and was told I couldn't sue my company."

"That's unfortunately true, ma'am. Employers in this state owe only workers compensation benefits to the employees they hurt or kill. It's not fair and the payments — as you probably found out in your accident — are pitifully small compared to what is deserved. You see, big corporations like SeaCoast have friends at the state capitol and they all got together to make sure the law protects business more than it does the worker. The comp law says you can't sue your employer except in cases of intentional acts or gross negligence, which is a very hard thing to prove. So what does all that mean? Employers get off easy. They pay only the small set amounts that their pals in the legislature settled on after being told what to do by corporate lobbyists. The statute should have been called 'The Employer Protection Act.' And if all that weren't bad enough, some lawyers even charge a fee on those piddling amounts when they process a workers' comp claim for their clients."

Ravich lingered to let everyone think he was about to make a grand concession.

"Let me tell you all something about me. I don't think it's fair to charge people for that. I know it's legal, but I've been around long enough to know that legal and fair aren't always synonymous. If I become the lawyer for you folks, my office will make certain that all the workers compensation death benefits, every penny, goes directly to your family. I won't charge any fee for processing those claims even if they make us fight for it, which sometimes they do."

Ravich knew he would have no trouble collecting the clearly owed death benefits. It was a simple matter of his paralegal submitting a few forms. The only condition for payment was proof that the workers died on the job. Hard to dispute something like that when a chemical plant blows up with men inside. Most decent lawyers didn't charge for such simple administrative tasks. But truly decent lawyers also didn't pretend like it was some big deal.

Kate Crouch had heard enough. The others may have been captivated by Ravich's smooth talk of altruism and expertise but she was not convinced.

"So, you're saying you will do all this work for free?"

"No, ma'am. What I'm saying is I won't charge for helping to collect your comp benefits. You see, the law might unfairly protect employers from lawsuits, but very often in these type of disasters there are other parties, other companies, that bear some of the responsibility. That's why people like Dr. Clark are so important. Their investigation can reveal if someone sold SeaCoast a defective product that was being used in production. It might turn out that another corporation helped design a faulty plant. Our expertise can dig deep to discover if there are other unclean hands in this tragedy. The law only grants immunity to the actual employer of the victims. Any other corporation that might be responsible for this, to use a phrase my old country dad might say, is 'gonna get got.' By me, for you. The fee I charge would come out of money those other companies owe."

He looked at his questioner and noticed her suspicious expression had not disappeared. "Did that answer your question, Mrs..?"

"Crouch. My name is Kate Crouch. They haven't even found my husband's body yet. I don't care right now about lawyers, lawsuits, or who owes what. I just want Dan."

Ravich took a step toward her and lowered his voice. It was time to sound like a friend. He knew how to play the role.

"Believe me, Mrs. Crouch, I understand that. I know that everyone else here feels that way too. The only reason I can stand before you at a time like this is because I know too well that you *need* someone taking care of those other, less important things so that you can dedicate your thoughts to the only thing that really matters, which is your loss. I know because I've had the privilege of helping many families like yours. I'm not asking *you* to focus on responsibility right now. I'm simply asking for your permission to allow me to focus on that *for* you."

He continued to speak as he shot a glance back over to Roy Evans, expecting the helpful father would come to his defense. "Whoever caused this will try, at all costs, to minimize or avoid their liability. I will make sure they don't get away with that if you'll let me."

"Sign me up," the old man blurted out.

The other families seemed to agree. Ravich had convinced another jury.

"Thank you, sir, and the rest of you for your confidence in me. I will not let any of you down. Now my associates have a one-page document that gives me the authority to act as your lawyer. That document confirms everything I have just said about my fee and not charging for my help on the workers comp. The wives and parents of the victims will need to sign these forms. The wives can also sign on behalf of any minor children. Each of you have a legitimate claim."

Ravich glanced back over to his team.

"Dr. Clark, Jeff, and I will leave now and get to work. I'll be on the phone letting the SeaCoast lawyers know that we are on our way and that I want access to the accident site now. They will argue with me but they won't win. Dustin and Melanie are going to stay here to answer any other questions you might have and to help in any other way possible. If you need a ride somewhere or calls to be made, they are happy to do it. Please make sure they get all your contact information. I will personally call each of you no later than tomorrow with any news that I can find out today."

Stu Mitchell recognized his cue.

"Thank you, Paul, for being here for us."

"Again, it is my honor."

As he made his exit, Ravich worked the crowd like a presidential candidate. He shook hands with a steady confidence. He made comforting eye contact and placed reassuring hands on shoulders. He even gave one mother a warm hug. And he made a point to speak privately to Kate.

"Mrs. Crouch, I can't bring Dan back. But I will make sure they pay for what they have done to him, and to you."

"Thank you for your time," was all she quietly said in reply.

Ravich's instincts told him she might need more convincing but he wasn't worried. Like a lone doubting juror, the weight of opinion from the others would be enough to sway her his way. If not, he could always make another closing argument to her. No one had ever resisted his charms more than once.

Getting the case was the one skill most often overlooked by lesser lawyers. You had to be swift and smooth. The big ones don't just fall in your lap. You had to make it happen. To Paul Ravich's callous thinking, tort clients were the same as lottery tickets: You can't win anything if you don't hurry up and get them in hand.

———— ∞ ————

He was back at the house when the phone rang.

Joan had gotten out of bed and they were talking — between tears and cups of tea — about plans no parent believes they will ever have to make. Discussing a funeral for their young daughter was the last thing either wanted to do and it was hard. But it had to be done.

Ken Slator looked at the incoming call on his mobile phone. The screen read "Thornton Industries." He glanced at his watch. It was 10:40 a.m. and he had not yet called his employer. Joan needed him more and he was honoring his earlier pledge to make her his priority. Still, he owed a response. And he had important news to give them.

"I'm sorry, but I really need to take this," he said, as he excused himself and walked toward the home study for privacy.

Joan smiled faintly, then stared absently out the living room window, her thoughts again on her daughter.

He partially closed the study door and pressed the button to answer the call. "This is Ken."

"And this is Charles Thornton. Where the hell are you?"

Slator was stunned. He was too far down the pecking order to receive a direct call from the head of the parent company.

"Well, I'm with my wife right now. We had a, uh, serious emergency last night."

"No shit. You know, I have a TV too. Look, Slator, I've got your boss Finnegan in here with me. He's on speaker along with our General Counsel, Bruce Waltman. And all of us would like to know why you haven't returned the calls made to you?"

"I've been tied up."

"You'd better mean that literally because that's the only excuse that will save your ass with me."

"I'm sorry, what?"

Finnegan spoke up. "Ken, it's me, Rob. I left you numerous messages. The plant; we need you at the plant. We're trying to determine what happened."

The comment stung as Slator thought back to the damning things he had heard and seen in his apartment.

"Well, Rob, I think you probably already know."

Bruce Waltman and Charles exchanged quizzical glances while Rob Finnegan's face flushed like a nervous teenager.

"Mr. Slator, this is Bruce Waltman. I don't know what you mean by that but your presence down there today is essential. Do you understand? The plant has been completely destroyed, a number of lives have been lost, and investigations need to begin."

"I won't be in today, I'm sorry."

Rob Finnegan sat frozen and amazed by the insubordination he was hearing. It wasn't like Ken. He had always seemed overly cautious and milquetoast around management.

Thornton exploded. "Listen to me, you little pick-and-shovel smart-ass. Who do you think you're talking to?"

Bruce Waltman didn't wait for Slator to reply. "I have to warn you, Mr. Slator, that your attitude is quite suspicious. We had a plant blow up last night that you helped design and which you actively managed. Your failure to cooperate might be interpreted as evidencing some culpability on your part."

"My daughter died last night."

Several seconds of silence followed.

"What?" Thornton finally huffed. "There were no reports of women in that plant."

"No, Mr. Thornton," Slator corrected. "She died in another accident. I've been at the hospital all night and now I have to be with her mother. I would think even you might understand that."

Men like Charles Thornton were not accustomed to being insulted.

"I don't give a good goddamn about your personal problems," he blurted, in total disregard of basic human decency. "I've got bigger ones and so do you. If you expect to have a job tomorrow, you will get your ass to that plant today. Now!"

"Then I quit. Good day, gentlemen."

A steady dial tone filled the office. Things weren't supposed to work that way. Charles Thornton could hang up on people but not the other way around. He glared at Rob Finnegan with coal-hot eyes.

"Finnegan, you better get that prick on board or you can join him in the unemployment line. Now get the hell out of here."

Ken Slator placed his cell phone on the study desk and returned to the living room sofa. Joan had evidently overheard part of what he said but, thankfully, she had been spared listening to Thornton's cold-hearted diatribe.

"Is everything all right at work?" There was worry in her voice as she asked.

He embraced her and replied: "It doesn't matter anymore."

"What the hell was that?"

Rob Finnegan had left, and Bruce Waltman wasn't sure how to answer the question his boss posed, as the two men sat dumbfounded by the strange and abruptly ended phone call to Slator. Waltman shrugged as he looked at Charles Thornton, who genuinely seemed to be smarting from the notion that someone so insignificant had stood up to him.

The intercom broke the uncomfortable silence.

"Mr. Thornton, I'm sorry to interrupt but the Legal Department is calling to say that Mr. Waltman has to take this call. I have it on hold, your Line 2."

"Thank you, Marlene," Thornton said, as he handed the receiver across the desk while pressing the blinking button. Waltman stood up beside the desk to take the phone.

"This is Bruce Waltman."

"And this is Paul Ravich. Good morning."

Waltman cringed. He knew the name. Every corporate lawyer did. It would be bad enough taking this call in the privacy of his own office. Standing across from a still-fuming Charles Thornton wasn't going to help.

"Look, I realize that as General Counsel, you have a lot on your plate today so let me get straight to the point. I now represent the victims' families."

Waltman sputtered. "Already? How did you do that so fast?"

"Like you probably did, I got a very early call this morning. Anyway, I'm on my way to your plant entrance with my photographer and consultant and would appreciate your clearing me onto the site."

"Absolutely not. We haven't even begun our own investigation."

"Now, let's be reasonable here, Mr. Waltman. I realize you don't get down to the courthouse much yourself, being a transactional lawyer and all, but if you refuse this request I will have no alternative than to seek an emergency order. I've already got a hearing scheduled at one this afternoon."

"What!"

"And someone from my office is right now standing at the reception desk of your legal department to serve Thornton Industries and SeaCoast with notice and a copy of the emergency application."

"On what grounds?"

"Preservation of evidence. We are only seeking an immediate opportunity to photo-document the scene and to allow our consultant to walk the premises. No testing of any kind will be conducted by us nor will any interviews with your people be attempted."

"This is ridiculous. There hasn't even been a suit filed yet."

"That's true, but my accompanying affidavit makes clear there will be, and my expert will testify at the hearing about the high incidence of early evidence spoliation at disaster scenes like yours. Not saying you folks would try to hide or destroy things, only that you could."

Charles Thornton noticed the harried look of his General Counsel and gave him a "what's up" gesture. It was the last thing Waltman needed right now. He held up his index finger to his boss indicating he needed to concentrate on what was being said.

"I just don't see the need for rush here," Waltman replied.

"Well, then, you need to rush right down to the courthouse because in less than a couple of hours Judge Roberts is going to grant my motion. Especially if you say something that lame to him. You might also want to be there in case the press decides to show up. They too are about to get notice of the hearing. I'm sure you wouldn't care for them listening only to my side of the story, which is along the lines of: Why does this company want to make it so difficult for the victims to find answers?"

"This is outrageous. Surely the Judge will allow the actual smoke to settle first."

"Not Judge Roberts. Let's just say my past experiences with him gives me some certitude that I will receive a favorable ruling on my motion. It was just pure luck on my part that he agreed to hear the matter. So your call, counselor. I will get access today the easy or hard way."

Waltman had heard enough rumors about Ravich's deep tentacles and close ties with judges to assume this was no bluff.

"All right, I will permit access for the limited purposes you just stated, provided you are accompanied at all times by one of my staff lawyers. There are a couple on site now. I need to call them. The hearing won't be necessary."

"Good. It's always better if we cooperate. We will be waiting at the gate. Just send your boys out to fetch us. By the way, nice job with that press conference this morning. I'll be holding my own tomorrow. Bye now."

Waltman handed the phone back, trying to steady his slightly trembling arm. Anger or fear, perhaps both, had disrupted his ordinarily calm demeanor.

"So what was that all about?" Thornton asked.

Waltman gritted his teeth. A very bad day was a long way from over.

———⦿⦿⦿———

"I'd like to schedule an appointment, please."

"Sure, may I ask what this is regarding?"

"There was a plant explosion last night. My husband was killed."

Bonnie's jaw dropped. It was a good thing she had thirty years experience or she might have dropped the phone as well.

"You mean that SeaCoast plant? I saw it on the news this morning."

"Yes, ma'am. I think I need to talk to a good lawyer."

Shit, thought Bonnie. Potentially the biggest case of his life was on the phone and Douglas H. Stevens, Esq. was driving back from a deposition in a stupidly minor slip-and-fall case. An inexperienced receptionist might have dumbly said: "He's not in right now, can I have him call you back?" But Bonnie was not dumb. You don't let calls like this get away.

"Of course. Mr. Stevens is due back from a court proceeding any minute now. Are you available to meet with him today?"

"I guess so. Maybe around four."

"That will be fine, or if it's more convenient I'm sure he would be willing to come to your home, especially under the difficult circumstances."

"No, we will come to his office. Is it all right if I bring my mother?"

"Certainly. Just give me your name and I'll make sure he's ready to meet with you."

"Kate Crouch. My mom's name is Jackie Baker. Mr. Stevens represented her once."

"Sure," Bonnie responded, vaguely recalling the name. "I know that Mr. Stevens will be able to help you."

"That's what my mom said. Are you Bonnie?"

"Why yes, ma'am, I am," she replied, surprised by the familiarity.

"My mom said you were also very nice to her. So we'll see you at four then?"

"We'll be waiting. Do you need directions?"

"No, mom remembers how to get there."

"All right then, Mrs. Crouch, and I'm very sorry for your loss."

"Thank you. Goodbye."

"Bye."

Bonnie hung up and immediately hit the speed-dial button for Doug's mobile number. Her heart raced as the phone rang. *Pick up, son, this call is big,* she mumbled to herself, while tapping her fingers on the desk anxiously. He answered on the third ring.

"Hey Bonnie, what's up?"

"Get your lucky ass in this office as fast as you can."

"Okay," Doug replied, laughing. Bonnie was a spitfire at times.

"I'm not kidding here. You know that plant explosion that's been on the news? One of the claimants wants to meet with you."

"Wow! Really? Well, set up a time and …"

"Four o'clock today. Here. Hurry up. We need to straighten things a little and look like a big-time plaintiff's shop."

"Did she say how she came to choose us?"

"Yeah. Said something about you representing her mother awhile back. Lady named Jackie Baker; said her momma thought we were both nice. Name rings a bell but I don't recall the case."

"Oh, my God! That's because we made no money on the file. She was that middle-aged lady who got rear-ended by an idiot with no insurance. She was hurt but not too bad, and without much hassle I got her insurance company to pay the small amount of uninsured motorist coverage she had. It only took a couple of letters and a few phone calls. I felt sorry for her so didn't charge her a fee."

"That's right. I remember the case now," Bonnie replied.

"You should. You got pissed at me and said we weren't running an eleemosynary institution."

They both started laughing.

"I had to ask you what that meant, remember?"

"I sure do," she said, still giggling. "I told you it means a charity."

"Well, I guess good deeds sometimes do get rewarded, huh?"

"I guess so, Father Flanagan. Now get your tail back up to this office."

"On my way."

Doug hung up and felt a rush of excitement. Signing up a newsworthy death case was not an everyday event in his practice. In fact, it had never happened before. He felt good about himself as he mashed down on the accelerator.

The Golden Rule was about to change his life.

———◦◦◦———

By early afternoon, Rob Finnegan had called six more times. He was not going to give up. Ken Slator had long ago placed his cell phone on vibrate. He didn't want it disturbing Joan. She had now gone into the kitchen to make a late lunch, so Slator decided it was time. He went outside into the small but neatly manicured backyard and pressed the number to initiate a redial.

Finnegan had returned to the plant's largely undamaged business building and was assisting in the boxing of ash-covered records. He saw the caller ID and answered with an anxious voice.

"Ken, why haven't you called me back?"

"I thought I said everything I needed to say. You were in that room. You participated in the call."

"I know, I know. Look, I'm really sorry about your daughter. What happened? Was it a car wreck?"

"No, just a sudden collapse. It's pretty tough on us right now."

"Sure, yes. I mean, I'm really sorry for you."

"Thanks."

"But Ken, you can't be serious about quitting. Especially not now. If Thornton will allow it after what you said to him, I still need you to help us get through this plant thing."

"You don't want me involved, Rob. Trust me."

"What are you saying? Of course we do. You're the only one who knows how that plant worked. There's going to be investigations and lawsuits. The company has to come up with an explanation for why this happened. Nobody but you can figure that out."

"You have a pretty good idea don't you, Rob?"

"What's that supposed to mean?"

"Let's just say I know what you know."

Rob Finnegan felt a rush of cold overtake him. His mouth went dry. He felt like throwing up but managed to regain control. He told himself he was being paranoid, that's all.

"Well, I know we were working round the clock and I'm sure we were taxing both the men and equipment. You figure that was it?"

Finnegan was fishing and Slator would not take the bait.

"I'm sure it will all come out eventually, Rob."

Slator's voice sounded almost accusatory. *Maybe he knows more than he's letting on,* thought the now twitching SeaCoast president.

"Look, Ken, I'm your boss. If you know what happened out here, tell me."

Slator paused to think. He wanted Finnegan off his back but also wanted to keep him scared. He owed that much to his dead coworkers.

"Like you, Rob, I didn't have to be at the plant last night to know what happened out there."

Finnegan reached for a smoke-stained chair nearby and fell into it. He tried to respond but no words came out. Slator waited, but could hear only fast breathing on the other end.

"So the best thing you could do now, Rob, is leave me alone. I have more important things to deal with than SeaCoast and your problems. And you need to remember you're no longer my boss."

"Okay," Finnegan managed to mutter, before thinking of one last way to hopefully preserve some alliance. "But you heard Thornton's lawyer.

They might try to blame you for this if you don't … I mean, if we can't cooperate on this."

"All I can say is, Rob, it's in your best interest to see that I'm kept out of the fray. Are we clear on that?"

Slator's last words were delivered with a menacing tone.

"I don't deserve a threat if that's what that was, Ken."

"No, you deserve worse. Now if you'll excuse me, I have a daughter I need to bury."

Slator hung up and returned to the house. He didn't expect any more calls from Rob Finnegan.

The President of SeaCoast Chemical sat in the dirty chair staring at his phone, waiting for his heart to stop pounding. *Did Dave Phillips speak to Slator after I did?* He struggled to think. *No, Phillips said he couldn't reach him. Nobody could reach him. I tried.* Nothing made any sense. Slator was acting as if he knew everything. *If it wasn't a call from Dave, then how could he possibly know anything?* He hadn't even been back to the plant and, from the sound of things, probably never would again.

Finnegan spent several more minutes trying to convince himself that his operations manager had just been venting frustration up the chain of command for an accident they both regretted. *But what if there was more to it?* He rose from the chair, still thinking. He needed a way to be sure.

He walked over to a heat-cracked window on one side of the business building. From there, he could look out and see the rubble of the plant in the distance. He saw a group of men walking around, peering under the debris, surveying the damage. One was taking photos while another held a video camera. They seemed to be talking. Clues were being looked for. *Probably asking questions.*

It gave him an idea.

Chapter 9
Compatibility

I told them I'd think about it."

Summarizing Ravich's morning speech at the union hall, Kate Crouch concluded with what she had said to the two associates left behind to sign up clients.

Doug listened attentively while Bonnie, now wearing her paralegal hat, took notes as they sat across the conference table from Kate and her mother.

"It was a high pressure sales job if you ask me," said Kate's mother, shaking her head in disgust.

Although she hadn't been at the union hall meeting, Jackie Baker got the full report from her daughter on their drive home. The union offered to drive Kate back but she had grown leery of their motives and declined. Instead, Kate phoned her mom to pick her up. It was during that ride that Jackie recommended her former lawyer.

Doug thought briefly about the best way to deal with the criticism of Ravich. He decided not to say anything negative or engage in any of the shameless self-marketing that had so offended Kate.

"I understand, but he certainly does have an excellent track record."

"It doesn't matter," Kate said. "I wouldn't hire him if he were the only attorney in town. He walked into that hall like he was Christ sent down to save us and spoke like we were helpless children. He's only after the money."

Bonnie admired the young woman's instincts and added her two cents. "He's probably kicking some of that money back to the union to get access to you folks that fast."

Like anyone in town with vast experience in tort litigation, Bonnie had heard plenty of stories about Paul Ravich's hardball tactics and questionable practices. He was, for better and worse, a celebrity of his own-making. Many considered the rumors of Ravich's sleazy side to be nothing more than the product of professional jealousy. But Bonnie had been around long enough to suspect where there's smoke, there's fire.

Doug, however, decided to take the high road and directed the discussion back to the merits of Kate's case and the important decision she was facing.

"Mrs. Crouch, you don't have to retain any lawyer this quickly if you don't feel comfortable. The law gives you plenty of time to decide who to hire and when to sue. While it's true that an early jump on the claim investigation is good, there's no requirement that things get started the day after the accident; in fact, that's not usually the case."

Kate nodded, but was already thinking about something else.

"SeaCoast called me a couple of hours ago to say they now suspect Dan was near the first blast site and there may be no body left to recover."

The terrible thought caused her to start crying and Bonnie slid over a box of tissues.

"Thank you," she said, as she reached for one. "I just can't believe he's... gone."

As Kate tried to regain her composure, her mother spoke for her.

"Mr. Stevens, we talked about this on the drive to your office. Kate needs a good lawyer and an honest one. You proved through your deeds, not words, that you're both. You could have charged me a fee back when you handled my little case. I was surprised when you didn't. What that showed me was that you actually care about the people you represent and that's exactly the kind of person I want representing my daughter."

Doug looked over at Kate who was nodding her head in agreement as she wiped her eyes.

"Well, I appreciate those words and your confidence in me. I will do my best for you."

"That other lawyer said we couldn't sue SeaCoast unless they did this on purpose or something like that," Kate said, still confused by the nuances of workers' compensation law.

"The law does make it very difficult to sue and win against them," Doug affirmed.

"He also told us he could find other companies to blame it on," she then added.

"Perhaps a better way to say it and what I will do is to investigate whether other companies played a role in causing the explosion. If they did, they are and should be accountable. If not, then we are faced with evaluating whether the conduct of Dan's employer rises to the level of gross negligence."

"I bet you find it does. I mean, I don't know anything about the law but I do know they were working him like a dog. He was putting in another sixteen hour day when it happened."

Bonnie raised an eyebrow and made a note.

"I have just one concern and hope you aren't offended by it," Kate's mother interjected. "We realize it's just you and Bonnie here. Is this case something you two can handle? My daughter said that other fellow came down with a whole team of lawyers and fancy experts."

Doug smiled thinly. It was a legitimate concern. Given his youth, spartan office, and lack of extensive staff, he was surprised more prospective clients didn't ask the question.

"I won't lie to you. This will likely be a complicated and expensive case to investigate and try. I will need to hire some more help even though Bonnie here can do the work of ten. I may even want to associate another lawyer to assist me with the case. But all of that will be my worry, not yours." He looked directly at Kate. "I have an ethical duty to decline the case if I don't think I can effectively represent you, Mrs. Crouch. And what I'm saying is that if you choose to hire me, we will be up to the challenge."

"That's good enough for me," Kate replied while looking at her mother, who was also indicating her approval. "But you have to promise me one thing."

"What's that?"

"That you won't associate, or whatever you call it, with that other lawyer. I just have a strong feeling he's corrupt or something. I don't want anything to do with him."

Bonnie grinned and waited for Doug's response.

"I will be your attorney, not Paul Ravich. It may end up that his and my theory of the case turn out to be the same. If so, we might find a way to cooperate. If not, we will go our own way. But I give you my word that he will not call the shots for you. Only you and I will make decisions together. Fair enough?"

"That's all I ask."

The next few minutes were occupied with administrative details and going over the contingency fee agreement. When asked about charging a fee for processing the workers comp death benefits, Doug was surprised as Kate informed him that Ravich had boasted it was a service he magnanimously offered for free. Kate's suspicions about Ravich seemed vindicated when Doug replied he didn't know of any lawyer that charged, or claimed special credit, for doing something so simple.

The rest of the two-hour meeting was spent talking about Dan. Bonnie took a few notes but the primary purpose was to give their new client an opportunity to reflect upon what she had just lost. In her eyes, Dan was still a husband, not a lawsuit. Failing to understand that basic fact was the biggest mistake Ravich had made. Doug actually cared about what Kate Crouch had to say, and both she and her mother seemed to know it. They felt some degree of comfort as they cathartically shared memories with someone who was trying to help.

Doug Stevens may have lacked the experience, resources, or wealth of the uber-attorney for the other victims, but he possessed a skill that Paul Ravich had long ago carelessly discarded in his zeal for fame — just *listening* was sometimes the most important thing a lawyer could do for a client.

—∞∞—

It was not the kind of week Rob Finnegan was used to. Even when the plant was operating around the clock, the President of SeaCoast Chemical still had it pretty easy. From his comfortable office in the detached business building, he would leisurely read production reports and supply requisitions. He occasionally drafted inter-company memos. He regularly delegated his more unpleasant chores to others. He would make short daily calls to the company's other and smaller chemical plants, primarily to tell those managers he was on top of things. Every now and again, there were meetings downtown at One Thornton Plaza. The remainder of his light schedule consisted of strutting around the flagship plant, making the occasional hiring and firing decision, and taking corporate buyers out for golf or long lunches. It was hardly a high stress job. He snuck out every Wednesday afternoon to play non-customer golf with his buddies at the country club.

SeaCoast had six other production facilities in the United States. Three were polymer plants while two produced elastomers. The sixth was a much smaller AN plant in the Midwest whose production, until this week, had always been dwarfed by the much larger facility that now lay outside Finnegan's office in ruins.

The company also operated two *maquiladoras* — border factories in Mexico — where labor costs consisted of starvation wages and where safety standards were far more lax than their American counterpart. Those facilities made pesticides and solvents. The profit margins from the Mexican factories were much higher than the American plants. Finnegan feared it was only a matter of time before Thornton Industries moved all or most of its other operations down there. They didn't care about American jobs; they cared about cash. The explosion would give them an excuse to rebuild SeaCoast's flagship fertilizer plant in Mexico, a prospect that Finnegan dreaded. If he kept his job, he faced the possibility of trading a comfortable suburban home in the US for a life inside a guarded compound, where he would have to keep himself safe from disgruntled workers, opportunistic kidnappers, and the drug-cartel thugs that had taken over the Mexican border states.

But he didn't have to wait for a move to a foreign country to see things go bad. His job was never going to be the same. He was barely halfway through the worst week imaginable: Monday had ended watching his plant and workers burn. Tuesday had been filled with the aftershocks of Charles Thornton's wrath and Ken Slator's resignation. Now, on Wednesday morning, he was scheduled to walk through the debris with initial lead investigators from both the EPA and OSHA. Al Harris would be at his side to answer routine inquiries about how the plant operated. Bruce Waltman would be there to handle any liability-suggestive questions that might be asked. There would be no golf today.

So far, no one had discovered any hint of his direct role in causing the disaster. Finnegan expected they never would, although his conversation with Slator the day before still had him worried.

With Dave Phillips dead and Slator gone, Al Harris was now the most senior and knowledgeable plant employee, so Finnegan had him perform a critical peace-of-mind errand after Slator's threatening words and dismissive hang-up. On Tuesday afternoon, Harris was told to scour the burnt control room. He reported back that the fire destroyed all operations records and that no computer files were salvageable. Relieved by the news but careful not to show it, Rob Finnegan felt safer having verified there was no trail — human, paper, or electronic — that might reveal his nighttime order to bypass the safety system. His name would be kept out of things, leaving it to the company's lawyers to come up with a plausible explanation for the explosion, one that might quickly appease the government investigators and end further inquiry.

Bruce Waltman arrived at Finnegan's barely scorched office around nine-thirty and got straight to business.

"Rob, these investigators are due here in about a half-hour. Like I said on the phone yesterday, if you're asked any question, pause long enough to give me a chance to interrupt. If I think the inquiry might be incriminating to the company, I'll respond. If I deem it benign, I'll say nothing and you or Al Harris can answer."

"Got it."

As the two men pulled jumpsuits over their business attire in preparation for the site walk, Finnegan decided to start his own investigation.

"So, do we think it was lightning?"

Waltman shook his head dismissively.

"Our legal department contacted the National Weather Service yesterday. Their Doppler radar showed the rainstorm passing only marginally over the plant. Area lightning detectors also recorded minimal electrical activity within the storm. It's highly unlikely, but we aren't going to concede that. We'll make the government and the plaintiffs' lawyer prove what happened."

Finnegan nodded his head in agreement. "What about that guy who came out here yesterday with a cameraman and some engineer? What was he doing? The lawyer from your department didn't want me to go around with him."

"That was Paul Ravich and his crew. He's the lawyer for the victims. Don't ask me how he got to them so fast. He's going to be a problem. He's tough and good."

"What scum," Finnegan replied. "There haven't even been funerals yet and their spouses are already treasure-hunting."

Waltman recalled the similar insult that Charles Thornton had made regarding the workers' families. Executives seemed to share a hatred for tort claims, regardless of case merits or company conduct. Waltman was a company officer himself but his law degree allowed him to see things differently. Legal Departments existed, in part, because companies sometimes do things that give rise to legitimate claims being made against them. This wasn't war where you *had* to hate your enemies. It was just the law.

"Speaking of that, the first funerals are tomorrow," Waltman informed. "I think for Evans and Phillips. The company expects you to attend all of them on our behalf. Make yourself seen, offer condolences, then leave."

"Those people are pretty upset with us," Finnegan said. He was hoping to avoid any further uncomfortable contact. "You sure it's a good idea for me to be there?"

"It looks worse if you're not. So buck up and go. Check in the paper for the obits. The time and place for all the services will be listed."

As they put on work boots and hard hats, Al Harris came in to say that the plans were ready for review. The original blueprints and schematics for the plant had been stored at the back of the business offices. Harris located and laid them out on a table in the reception area of the small building. They bore a musty smell from both age and the fire's smoke, but were otherwise intact.

As the three men walked the short distance from Finnegan's office to review the documents, Waltman's cell phone rang. One of his department lawyers was calling to report that Paul Ravich had just held a press conference. He listened with growing rage as his staff attorney advised that the media wanted to know if SeaCoast cared to comment.

"Fellows, I need to finish this call," he said with exasperation in his voice. "I'm going to use your office, Rob. Come get me if the investigators arrive before I'm done."

While Waltman busied himself with the latest Ravich-caused crisis, Harris tried to explain the blueprints to Finnegan. He pointed to the drawing of the neutralizer tank, saying it was the location of the largest blast crater. Finnegan listened and looked at the lines and circles on the paper. The images helped him recall the general layout but he still didn't fully understand the role that each line, valve, and vessel played in the process of making ammonium nitrate. *I should have known more*, he thought, as Harris kept describing what once was where. Then he recalled the strategy that came to him the day before, sitting alone in his office. He needed to focus on something more pressing. He needed to find out what others knew and what they could prove.

"So, Al, what do you think happened?"

Harris looked up from the blueprints.

"I won't say this to them OSHA and EPA boys, but you know we were running full out all month long. I was taxing the equipment on my shifts and I'm sure Dave Phillips was too that night."

"Yeah, but…"

"All I'm saying is that when you operate at higher temps and with bigger loads, things get a little spooky. It looks to me like the N-Tank blew up first and started a chain reaction. What I don't get is why the DCSS didn't kick in before the trouble started."

"You mean the safety system?"

"Exactly. It should have warned Dave and automatically shut everything down long before anything like this could happen."

Finnegan braced himself. It was time to go fishing. "Do you think it might have malfunctioned?"

"What, the DCSS?"

"Yeah."

"It never had with me. Ken trusted that system. So I kinda doubt it."

"Guess we'll never know for sure, huh?"

Al Harris thought about the question before answering.

"All them process records were electronic. The computers would've told us exactly what was happening during that evening shift but they all got blowed up."

Then he recalled something and offered it as an afterthought.

"Unless maybe Ken still has some of the data."

Finnegan looked askance. *What is he talking about?* Slator wasn't even on duty.

"What data?" he asked anxiously.

"I don't know what he got or how it worked, but I remember calling Ken at home a time or two with a question when I was after-hours shift head. He could look at his computer to see the same things I was seeing on the control room monitors and he would talk me through whatever problem I had."

Finnegan froze. He felt flush. He didn't want Al to notice his sudden discomfort. He asked another question, fervently hoping not to hear the answer he now suspected.

"How could he possibly do that?"

"He had some sort of relay tied into the controls. Dave never thought anything about it but it kinda kept me on my toes. You know, thinking the boss might be at home watching what I'm doin'."

"And this information came into his home computer?"

"Guess so. I mean, I've never been to his place, but he damn sure could verify everything I was doing at the plant from the other end of the phone. It was almost creepy."

Al Harris noticed that the company president seemed uneasy and lost in thought. He tried a guess at what he was thinking.

"You think maybe his computer could show us what happened?"

Finnegan had to think quick. He had to be firm. He needed to act like he was in charge and he wanted this discussion kept between them.

"I'll look into it. You know, of course, that Slator's off for a while dealing with the death of his daughter."

"Yeah, you mentioned that. That's a shame too. How old was his girl anyway? I think she must have only been around…"

Finnegan cut him off. He needed Al Harris to pay attention.

"Listen, Al, I'll get with Ken and find out what he knows. Until then, let's keep this relay thing between us. If you mention it to the General Counsel, he may have to tell the government people and then they'll be all over it before we have a chance to review it ourselves."

"Okay."

"I mean it. When you're out walking around with those people today, don't say a word about Slator or his data access. And that goes for anyone else, even after today. Far as you know, no such thing exists. Are we clear?"

"Crystal clear, boss."

Finnegan redirected the discussion back to the blueprints. With their agreement of silence firmly in place, he wanted Harris to return to the task at hand. As his employee resumed an explanation of the plant's equipment layout, Finnegan's mind stirred. *Whatever Ken knows is on his computer. Is that why he sounded threatening? Does it show the safety system was overridden? Even if it did, how could he trace that to me?*

Bruce Waltman returned to the reception area and broke Finnegan's guilt-filled analysis.

"Sorry, men, I had to deal with another thorny issue. Now remember, OSHA is coming here today looking for evidence of workplace safety violations while the EPA will be trying to determine the cause of the explosion so it can make future operating recommendations. It's not our job to make theirs easy. They haven't asked for any business records yet and we won't volunteer anything either. Understood?"

The two men nodded their heads affirmatively. Al Harris gave a knowing look to Finnegan. Senior management had now given him the same advice twice: "Shut up and say nothing." His lips were sealed.

As Harris began a blueprint orientation for Waltman, Rob Finnegan pretended to be attentive but his mind was clearly elsewhere. His own special investigation was now all that mattered to him. And suddenly, it was specific and targeted. He needed to confirm what was in the head of his former plant manager and, even more importantly, on his computer.

Melanie Egan took the call from Doug.

She and her fellow associate, Dustin Kirkland, suddenly had a big dilemma on their hands. At the union hall, they had been tasked with getting signed client contracts from each of the SeaCoast explosion plaintiffs. All but one of the claimants had immediately signed on after their boss left that morning. The young lawyers had assured Ravich in a follow-up phone call that the lone holdout would not be a problem, that the widow was simply too distraught to sign papers so soon after the accident. They planned to make a polite call to Kate Crouch after a few days and offer to answer any additional questions she might have. They would have a signed contract from her soon. They were sure of it.

Ravich had voiced no concerns about the unsigned widow. In fact, he seemed pleased with their efforts, especially since Dustin had also managed to get Derron Lucas's wife to sign an employment contract early Tuesday afternoon. After leaving the union hall, Dustin had gone to the hospital where the surviving burn victim was being treated. Stu Mitchell had called to tell Derron's wife that everyone else was going with Ravich and that she should too. The exhausted and fretful Mrs. Lucas signed on behalf of herself and her husband, who was still unconscious and in very critical condition.

Ravich either forgot the precise details of his conversation with his associates or took them at their word that no client complications existed. Regardless of the reason, both Melanie and Dustin knew it would never be Ravich's fault when he misspoke at the hastily called press conference held in his office on Wednesday morning.

Ravich had stood before two print reporters and three television news crews to proudly announce he was now the attorney-of-record for *all* the victims' families. He stared intently into the cameras and said his already vigorous investigation into the cause of the disaster would soon lead to lawsuits against the companies responsible for so much tragedy. Behind him, on easels, were three large posters. Two were blowups of scene photos taken the day before by Jeff Eastman. Ravich had picked the images he felt most closely resembled the devastation of Hiroshima. The third poster displayed the faces and names of the five dead and one injured, their head-shots enlarged from copies of union IDs furnished by the ever-helpful Stu Mitchell.

Kate Crouch was alone on her sofa, a blanket wrapped around her as she drifted in and out of the fog that a sudden death shrouds around a survivor. Her mother had spent the night and didn't want to leave but Kate had insisted. Her mom had already missed a day of work, and Kate realized her solitary life would have to start sometime. The living room television was on to provide false companionship or distraction and was failing miserably at both. She had not focused on the local noon-news broadcast until the pretty news anchor said something that seized her attention:

"In the wake of yesterday's explosion and fire at the fertilizer plant owned by SeaCoast Chemical, investigations and lawsuits already appear to be underway. Government agencies are scheduled to meet with company officials today, while an attorney for the victims spoke this morning from his downtown law office to our own Kevin Dobbs."

Kate leaned forward to see the man she so disliked declare his representation of all the families. Behind him, she could see Dan's picture arranged among the others, their faces bordered by a tableau of destruction. A news banner identified the speaker as *"Paul Ravich - Lawyer for the Victims."* He was working the camera the same way he had worked the families at the union hall. His look was pensive and his words were confidently delivered. He was acting, another performance. Her dislike turned instantly to hate.

She leapt from the sofa and called her lawyer: the real one, not the one claiming to be.

Doug was at his office doing online research, attempting to discover details about SeaCoast Chemical from the required corporate filings maintained on the state's website, when Bonnie patched the call through. He quickly assured his angrily excited client that he had kept his promise not to refer the case to Ravich and that the man had no authority to claim, on television or elsewhere, any right to speak for her. He calmed Kate down by saying that he would call the egomaniacal lawyer and straighten him out just as soon as they hung up.

Bonnie overheard the surprise in Doug's voice and rushed into his office as he got off the phone.

"What was that all about?"

"Paul Ravich is on television saying he represents everybody, including the Crouch family."

Bonnie fumed. "I knew that S.O.B. could run cases before the bodies even got cold but I can't believe he's cocky enough to try and steal clients on TV."

As she vented, Doug did a quick Google search for the firm's phone number. "I'm calling them now," he said, picking up the receiver.

"Chew him out good, and tell him you're going to call the press and state bar next," Bonnie advised, as she remained leaning against the office door to better listen in on the fireworks.

The receptionist who answered followed standing orders to never put an unknown caller directly through to Ravich so, after explaining the subject matter of his call, Doug was routed to one of the associates handling the *Seacoast* matter.

Melanie sat at her desk, the color quickly draining from her face as Doug sternly pointed out both his representation of Kate Crouch and the public misrepresentation of that fact by Ravich. She nervously assured the angry voice on the other end of the line that she would immediately look into what "was surely just an innocent mix-up" and would call him right back.

"If I don't hear from Paul Ravich directly in the next fifteen minutes, I'll make my introduction to him in the form of my own press release and letter to the bar's grievance committee, neither of which will be flattering to your firm."

"Yes, sir, Mr. Stevens. Let me get your number and I'll get right on this."

Melanie hung up and walked into Dustin Kirkland's adjacent office, her pale complexion an obvious sign of trouble. He too grew ashen as she related the call. There wasn't enough time to make this right or mitigate the damage. They talked of drawing straws but decided against it. They were friends. Neither wanted to watch the other march down the long hallway and incur the wrath alone. They would face their boss together. They would stand side-by-side and listen to him scream how it was their failure and not his own impulsiveness that was to blame. They would apologize profusely in the hope their jobs might be saved by repentant attitudes.

They had never heard of Douglas H. Stevens before and were certain Ravich would not have either. As they stood outside his closed office door, telling Jan they needed to go in to speak to him, each was hoping their boss, once he calmed down, would find a way to bring this nobody-lawyer and his trouble-making client into the fold.

They had agreed a simple service at the funeral home would be best. Melissa didn't have many real friends and they doubted any of her drug-enabling acquaintances would care enough to pay last respects. The relatives, on both sides, were far distant family to Joan and Ken Slator. A few had called to say how sad they were but none was planning to make the long trip to attend the funeral.

They delivered a colorful sundress to the mortician. Joan handed it over, saying her daughter had always seemed happiest in the summer. The funeral director guided them through the cruel choices of expensive or cheap caskets, then discussed with well-practiced solemnity the other costs associated with sending a child away for eternity. He told them a tasteful obituary, incorporating the phrase they had given him the day before, was to be published in today's paper along with the time of the memorial service on Friday.

Driving back to Joan's home, where he had been allowed to stay since it happened, Ken Slator felt they had dwelt long enough for one day on the horror of their daughter's death. He could tell that Joan needed a break too. But it seemed wrong, almost offensive, to talk of mundane things like the weather or items needed from the grocery store. So he decided to talk about the most important thing imaginable.

"Joan, I realize this should not have changed anything between us but, for me, it has."

She looked over at him, trying to read his meaning. He wished his eyes didn't have to be kept primarily on the road.

"I know that, Ken," she responded softly. "It's been good having you with me the past few days. I don't know that I could have coped with this if you weren't."

He stared straight ahead. This was hard. But he pressed on.

"I just see things differently now. Life is different. What you mean to

130

me now is more important than it ever was, even back when our times together were good."

She reached over and took his right hand.

"You're going through a lot right now, Ken."

He had told her the night before about the plant explosion and his decision to quit. He had not burdened her with any details, only that it was enough to make him never go back.

"Joan, this isn't because of work or even about Melissa. It's just, I can see now how much we belong together and I realize how badly I took that for granted."

"We both made mistakes, Ken. But right now is not the best time for either of us to try and correct that."

He turned to glance at her. "Could there ever be such a time?"

"Perhaps." She smiled sweetly. "Let's just help each other through this first."

He nodded in agreement. He drove another mile before speaking again.

"It was never a lack of love. I want you to understand that. It was only my inability to show it."

His ex-wife was genuinely moved. She had never before heard her engineer husband speak so clearly from his heart.

"No, dear," she said, clutching his hand tighter. "Just like it was for our little Melissa, the problems we had are nobody's fault. It just happened."

The blue sedan continued along a direct course while the thoughts of its occupants veered back and forth in separate and silent reflection. They still had their grief. But now there was something else, something very important, they also needed to consider.

Compatibility — the potential for a harmonious relationship — faintly glimmered like a soft ray of light warming their ocean of sadness.

He could run hot or cold. Depending on wants or needs, Paul Ravich could be instantly charming and soft-spoken, or mean and maniacal. In most professions, such capriciousness is not a trait to be admired. It makes people uncomfortable. In social contexts, those who exhibit an unpredictable duality usually find themselves shunned. It's prudent to avoid both Jekyll *and* Hyde if you don't know who will show up. But to a plaintiff's lawyer, the ability to quickly change one's personality had its advantages. Clients often need to be handled gently, the way a kindly country doctor would treat a sick neighbor. But an adversary's defense strategy might instead require a demeanor more akin to an alpha wolf protecting the pack. A smile in one context becomes a menacing growl in the next. The skill of rapid transformation is especially helpful in the courtroom. Juries must perceive you as a reliable friend but the lawyer on the other side needs to be constantly afraid.

Ravich had mastered the art of keeping people either assured or unbalanced depending on whether they were friend or foe at any particular moment. There were no absolutes, other than judges and juries, who had to be treated with kid gloves and kindness at all times. Occasionally, a client had to be scolded by the wolf. At times, a defense lawyer got courted with kindness, especially in those cases where more dollars could be realized by ganging up together against an unsuspecting co-defendant.

It paid to guess right and be ready when Paul Ravich unleashed one of his competing personalties on you. The two Ravich associates saw both sides of their complex boss when they informed him that Kate Crouch had hired a different lawyer.

His anger was immediate. He belittled them as incompetents. They cowered as he stomped and shouted. Both Melanie and Dustin knew the failure to sign up all the SeaCoast claimants could be a firing offense. Their friend, Trey, had been tossed out of the firm two days earlier for a much less grievous offense. They assumed they were doomed.

But Ravich possessed another considerable skill prized by successful tort lawyers. He always knew when he had to compromise.

The *SeaCoast* case would occupy much of his time and the firm's resources. A large docket of older cases also still had to be handled. Ravich couldn't afford to dump two more lawyers at such a critical time. And Melanie and Dustin were two of his best despite this blunder. So, to the happy surprise of the lawyers standing before him, Ravich abandoned his vengeful personality and suddenly forgave them. Even more shocking, he admitted mildly that he should have checked back with them before making broad statements at his press conference.

Who knows why a hunter decides not to shoot the prey directly in their gun-sight? These young lawyers only knew they had been spared. It was now someone else's turn to be targeted.

When handed Doug's number and told of his demand that Ravich call back immediately, the super-lawyer leaned back in his leather chair and laughed.

"Well, let's call him then, shall we? I wouldn't want to make an enemy of someone as powerful as Douglas 'Who-the-Fuck-are-You' Stevens."

His sarcastic tone evidenced a complete lack of concern. He was actually looking forward to swatting this fly. Ravich motioned for his associates to have a seat as he dialed the number. He grinned widely as he thought of what best to say to the no-name lawyer who had now screwed up the perfect game he thought had been pitched down at the union hall.

Bonnie answered the call and put him on hold. She ran into Doug's office. "Paul Ravich, calling for you. Can I stay and listen?"

Doug laughed and said sure. Bonnie Rogers was no disinterested employee.

He picked up the phone. "This is Doug Stevens."

"Mr. Stevens; Paul Ravich. I understand that an unfortunate miscommunication here at my office has you upset with me. Now, I don't want any fellow plaintiff counsel thinking poorly of me, so I first want to apologize."

"Okay."

"And second, I want to confirm directly with you that you have, in fact, been formally retained by ah…, the nice lady, I'm sorry…"

"Her name is Kate Crouch, she's the widow of Dan Crouch. And yes, she signed a contract with me yesterday."

"That's it, her name just slipped my mind. We've been really busy, as you probably are, getting this case started in earnest."

Ravich made a mocking face towards his associates. He wanted them to realize that both his civility and respect toward the other lawyer was being feigned. He continued the ploy.

"Since we clearly have compatible interests, Mr. Stevens, I was wondering if you might be willing to stop by my office this Friday, at your convenience of course, to talk about things. I'll be more than happy to share with you what we have already learned from our expert's site visit. It's the least I could do after stepping on your toes like I did."

Doug listened quietly, then decided to fake his own spirit of camaraderie.

"That might be a good idea. How about eleven o'clock?"

"Perfect. May I call you Doug?"

"Sure."

"Great, from now on I'm just Paul to you. Listen, Doug, after our meeting I will be happy to call your client, with you here obviously, to personally apologize for my *faux pas*."

"I'm sure that won't be necessary. I'll see you Friday, Paul."

"Look forward to it, Doug. Bye now."

Ravich hung up, pleased with himself, and looked at his two lawyers.

"Dougie will join us Friday at eleven for a joint-strategy conference," he announced, laughing at the thought of so ridiculous a notion. "Let's make sure he gets the full show. His case needs to be mine."

Melanie and Dustin rose to leave. They knew what to do.

In a far more austere office a few miles away, another employee anxiously waited for a full report.

"He wants to cooperate with us," Doug informed Bonnie.

"Bullshit!" was her only reply.

Chapter 10
Cause and Effect

The guilt was a cancer cell that anxiety had grown into a tumor.

Rob Finnegan sat alone in his den on Wednesday evening, pondering the possible outcomes. If he did nothing, this problem would consume him as surely as any real and ravaging disease. His physical life may not be at stake but his way of life most certainly was.

He had trouble sleeping the night before but in the morning realized the ghosts of dead workers weren't real. The nightmares he was having were just transitory punishments, self-condemnation delivered through the specters of burned men. The carting away of the ashes and twisted metal from the plant had already begun. In time, the ghosts would also disappear.

But his fear of discovery was real. It would mean, at a minimum, the loss of his job. He was almost sixty, with a huge mortgage and the steadily high expenses of a comfortable suburban life. The bank might foreclose. He would be sued personally by the victims. *I could be left with nothing,* he kept thinking. That might not even be the worst of it. *What if I were charged criminally?* He thought about the ship captain who got blamed for that big oil spill in Alaska. They prosecuted him. *Could my order to turn off a safety system also be a crime? That man killed birds and fish. I killed people.*

During the day, the ghosts left him alone but thoughts of becoming destitute or imprisoned dominated. He had to do something to protect himself, his family, his things. Desperate times; desperate measures. It wasn't a cliché to the President of SeaCoast Chemical.

The idea struck him while looking at the newspaper's obituary page. He had been trying to confirm the location and times of the workers' funerals when he saw something unexpected. Centered above a three-sentence death announcement was an underlined name that grabbed his attention:

"*Slator.*" The first line read: "*A Memorial Service for Melissa Slator will be held Friday at two p.m. at Laurelwood Funeral Home.*" The address was then listed. The short paragraph ended with: "*The twenty-one year old passed away in her sleep and is survived by her parents Joan and Ken Slator.*" He closed the paper and stared up at the ceiling of the richly paneled room. His demons spoke to him.

At first, he dismissed the thought as insane. Slator might still be willing to meet and talk, to reveal what he did or didn't know. Obviously, with the death of his daughter, the man had far more personal things on his mind right now. Maybe he just needed to be left alone for a week or two. With time, his attitude toward his former bosses might even change. After all, Slator was also a middle-aged man with a now uncertain future. He had quit his job in an impulsive reaction to Charles Thornton's harsh insensitivity. Jobs in this economy were hard to find. Slator might soon regret his decision and want back in. Only the President of SeaCoast Chemical could make that happen. A bargain could be struck: Slator would forget whatever he knew in exchange for a guarantee of re-employment. Practicalities would overcome any desire for vengeance.

There was no need to do anything rash or stupid, Finnegan decided. He went to bed and battled the ghosts again.

He changed his mind after attending the Thursday funerals for Dave Phillips and Bill Evans. At both services, he was treated like a pariah. The families refused to shake his hand. They had no evidence against him, he was merely the embodiment of the company that took their loved one away. That's all it was. Their bitterness should have been understandable. But to Rob Finnegan's worried mind, it carried another message. It served to confirm that some people can never forgive or forget. It made him suspect that even if some arrangement were made with Slator, the man might one day change his mind and decide that bringing his boss down was more important than a steady paycheck.

He had to find out what Slator could prove and needed to get rid of the evidence. A guilty man who relies upon an innocent one to maintain a conspiracy of silence is a fool. The blameless might later decide to blackmail. And even if financial gain never became a motive for Slator, a mere change of heart could prove just as disastrous. Either way, if the beans were spilled, a rehired Slator would only lose the job he already abandoned once before. *But the consequence to me would be far greater. I could lose everything,* thought Finnegan.

After the Evans funeral, Rob Finnegan returned to the plant's business building and located Ken Slator's personnel file. He saw a home address change and recalled Ken mentioning a divorce some time back. That would explain why there was also an apartment number listed. His ex-wife probably got the house. He typed the new address into his cell phone and left.

After returning home, he thought about the timing. The funeral for another worker, Hector Ruiz, was scheduled at one the next day and was on the west side of town. He googled Slator's new address. It was no more than fifteen minutes from where the Ruiz funeral mass would be held. He could extend his sympathies there, make himself seen, then retreat to the back of the church for a quiet and early exit. No one would recall the exact time he left. Everyone's attention would be directed forward, with eyes on the casket or heads bowed in prayer. It would give him a plausible alibi were it to be needed.

Slator would be at his daughter's memorial service. That was a certainty. The probabilities were that he would leave his apartment no later than a half hour before it started at two. Even if that service was short, and Slator drove straight home afterwards, it still gave him enough time to pull it off.

Rob Finnegan went to bed late Thursday night only to find his sleep more fitful than ever. This time, however, it wasn't from apparitions of the dead. There were no recurring nightmares of scorched hands and screams emanating from a wall of fire. His dreams that night were different but no less troubling. Twice he bolted awake, his body shaking so hard he was sure it would wake his wife. But she stayed sleeping and never saw lying next to her what he had seen in tonight's dreams: a scared and desperate man who was about to cross a line.

———— ∞∞∞ ————

It was a Hero Wall.

Doug stared across at the framed images lining the hallway. They were neatly arranged on either side of an oversized entry to a large conference room. The soaring glass doors that interrupted the rows of frames were identical to and symmetrically aligned with the firm's entry on the opposite side of the cavernously large reception area where he sat waiting for his meeting with Paul Ravich.

He had arrived a few minutes early, unaware that it was Ravich's habit to make others wait beyond their scheduled appointment time. It was a less than subtle way to imply that his time was more valuable. It also suggested he might be busy with far more pressing matters. Most importantly, the delay gave waiting lawyers a chance to walk over and peruse the framed shrine he had erected to himself.

"Are you sure I can't offer you something to drink, Mr. Stevens?"

The remarkably beautiful receptionist tried to placate him with a second offer of coffee or soda. She had learned the art of distracting waiting lawyers who repeatedly looked at their watches.

"No, I'm fine, thanks," he replied while standing. "I'll just stretch my legs."

Doug Stevens fell into the trap. His curiosity was no different from the others. The receptionist smiled as Doug walked slowly to the wall. He was just like all the rest.

There were dozens of photos of Ravich with prominent people. In one, he was shaking hands with the President. It was no doubt a small souvenir for a large campaign contribution. In another, he stood smiling between the Governor and Mayor. There were also numerous magazine and newspaper articles about him, carefully preserved behind richly matted frames and scattered among other pictures of Ravich with members of the State Senate and Supreme Court. There were plaques evidencing his membership in the most prestigious and exclusive trial lawyer organizations, and certificates of appreciation from numerous charities. He even had framed copies of his biggest court judgments in the garish display.

Doug stepped closer to examine those in more detail. One documented a thirty-four million dollar verdict against a Big-Three automaker in a design-defect case. Another described a fifty-two million dollar punitive damage award recovered against a major oil company. There were others on the opposite side of the conference room doors. He was walking over to look at them when he heard his name.

"You must be Doug."

Doug turned to see the man in all the photos stride toward him, his hand extended for a handshake.

"It's good to meet you. I'm Paul Ravich. Let's talk in here."

They entered the conference room. Ravich's staff had reassembled the SeaCoast scene posters on easels and stacked the other investigative photos on the table. A glass screen, mounted into a wall with a rear projector obviously somewhere behind, was displaying the site video recorded the day after the fire. Melanie and Dustin sat at one end of the conference table, a pile of documents before them.

"Doug, meet my associates: Melanie Egan, whom I think you spoke with yesterday, and this is Dustin Kirkland. They will be part of our *SeaCoast* litigation team."

They rose, exchanging brief pleasantries, followed by Ravich suggesting they all take a seat.

"So, tell us, Doug, how did Kate Crouch come to be your client?"

Melanie held her pen above a legal pad as if his explanation was something she might need to notate.

"Very simply, actually. I previously represented her mother in a relatively small matter. She evidently thought well enough of me to recommend that her daughter come in and talk."

"Ah, well, there's nothing better than a referral from a former client, is there?"

Ravich smiled broadly and paused. Doug responded to the awkward silence with a simple shrug.

"Now, we don't know much about your shop," Ravich continued. "Tell us about your firm and the type of cases you typically handle."

Doug knew he was being sized up. "It's a solo practice right now. Exclusively plaintiff's work, primarily injury cases but also a small amount of business disputes."

"Well, that's great," Ravich said, maintaining his hard-to-read smile. "You must have a lot of support help if it's just you?"

"No, just one. A very talented and experienced assistant who wears more hats than she should."

Ravich furrowed his brow. He wanted to convey an expression of concern and surprise. "I see. Have you ever been involved in a mass disaster case like this? They can be real bears."

"I'm sure," was Doug's only reply.

"I've successfully tried or settled a good many. Sometimes they end up being straightforward but most often not. When an industrial facility like this goes up in flames, we routinely find multiple defendants involved. Complex product-liability theories get raised. Damages like these, to say nothing of the public spectacle, cause the defendants to circle the wagons pretty tight. They spend lots of money trying to stall and defeat our claims."

Doug listened without comment.

"For example, we concluded a difficult case a few years back where a rig explosion suit ended up with eleven defendants. It cost this firm a fortune in advanced expenses to get that case trial-ready. What was that figure, Dustin, do you remember?"

"Six-hundred thousand."

"That's right," he said, his eyes growing wide as he looked at Doug. "Can you imagine that much invested money? It took an in-house staff of seven and a team of expensive experts to bring that baby in."

Ravich shook his head dramatically as if recalling an ordeal of epic proportions. Then he got to the point.

"It sounds like your firm is not fully equipped for that kind of war. Now, obviously, we're happy to help. We can share our investigative product. You see some of it here already. I'm also certainly willing to act as lead counsel, given the number of claimants I represent compared to your one."

Ravich shifted his tone to one of deep gravity. "But we clearly can't front your share of the expected large case expense, and it's only fair to ask that you contribute almost all of your time and more than one person as additional support personnel if we are going to joint-venture this case."

"I'm listening," Doug said, sounding flatly noncommittal.

"Unless, of course, you would consider simply making a referral of the *Crouch* claim to us. We would gladly pay you the customary third of any fee derived from her recovery. Doing it that way, you could avoid having to make *any* financial contribution as the joint case expenses are being incurred. It would also allow you to continue a focus on your existing docket while doing both yourself and your newest client a lot of good."

Doug made direct eye contact with Ravich as he gave his reply. "I certainly appreciate the offer but my client insists that I prosecute her case."

Ravich was unfazed.

"I get that, believe me. Look, we would be more than willing to have you assist to the extent you can. Maybe attend some of the depositions and motion hearings. Even occupy a seat at counsel table if we go to trial. As long as it's still a referral and we call the shots, it might be a great way for us to get know each other better, and for you to gain some valuable experience. Do as much or as little as you like. What do you think?"

"Again, my client hired me to handle her case. I'm sure we'll have common interests but it's important that I retain a certain independence."

Ravich pretended to be confused. "I don't really understand what that means."

"It means I intend to remain her attorney-of-record. I can't refer it to you."

Ravich tried a different tack. "Now, Doug, I don't mean to suggest improper motives on your part but surely you're aware that your client obligations are more important than a chance to earn a little more fee. You should do what's in her best interest, not yours."

Doug tensed. He didn't like the implication. "She made herself quite clear on this point. She doesn't want you as her lawyer."

The two Ravich associates looked at each other uncomfortably. They doubted their boss would stay conciliatory much longer.

"Did I do something to offend her?" Ravich feigned hurt feelings. "I mean, I may have misspoken to the press yesterday but that's hardly a hanging offense, wouldn't you agree?"

Doug felt the need to assert himself.

"Paul, you have a history of getting results and you obviously have the assets to prosecute your case on behalf of the other victims. I have just the one client and far fewer resources, but it's going to remain my case unless that client fires me."

"She might do that if she were made fully aware of your obvious limitations. And then you would be left with no fee at all."

The gauntlet had been thrown. As he made his veiled threat, Ravich stared at the young turk who was resisting his offer.

Doug thought carefully about his response before speaking.

"I see. Of course, surely *you're* aware that if you or anyone with your office were to directly contact my client for any purpose, especially to lobby her against my continued representation, I would have no choice but to report that kind of improper conduct to the state bar." Doug gave a thin smile as he paused for emphasis. "You see, Paul, I actually do understand my professional obligations. And yours."

Melanie Egan squirmed in her seat. No one talked to Paul Ravich that way, especially not in his own office.

The smile on her boss's face vanished as he began a soft but strangely sinister chuckle. He stood up to tower over Doug, who raised his head to maintain eye contact.

"Son, nobody rides my coattails for free. If you think you can come in here, insult me, then attach yourself to my reputation or work product whenever you want — like some little sucking remora catching a free ride on a big shark — you are very badly mistaken."

"I never said that I …"

"Let me finish," Ravich barked.

The cold water had been turned off. He was running hot.

"If you don't do the right thing and refer your case, I'll go to great lengths to see that your lawsuit is never consolidated with mine and that my experts and evidence are kept unavailable to you. I can guarantee that any documents turned over to me in the discovery process will get sealed under a protective order to keep you from using them. You'll be all alone, Doug, with only your one little assistant and an increasingly disgruntled client. I'll see to it that any settlements I negotiate with the defendants exclude your claim. I can make that an express condition to even entertaining an offer from them. And don't think I won't."

Doug didn't cower or beg for mercy. He suspected that was the reaction Ravich was looking for.

"Well, we have both made ourselves clear then. I'm glad we had this talk." Doug rose from his seat, then decided to toss a barb of his own. "I'm sorry you find my client and me to be an irritant. It certainly doesn't have to be that way. There are enough people damaged by this disaster to keep more than one firm busy. Our respective goals shouldn't be adversarial. We both want our clients to be fairly compensated for the injustice done to them."

Ravich interrupted. "I don't need some young lawyer to come in here to tell me..."

"Wait, you let *me* finish now," Doug snapped back.

Melanie and Dustin leaned back in their chairs as their boss angrily narrowed his gaze at the insolent lawyer who had just cut him off.

"I don't have as many clients as you. That's true generally and as regards the *SeaCoast* case. I also don't have your money or an office wall touting my connections and accomplishments. But I'm pretty good at what I do. Maybe, just maybe, I could have helped your case too, not just the other way around."

Ravich stood silent, his face tightly drawn, as he tried to decide whether huge balls or no brains were responsible for the speech he was hearing.

Doug continued. "But you'd have to be willing to work with others to find out something like that. From your comments, the name you chose for your firm, and all those pictures of yourself out there on that wall, I get the feeling you don't like to share much of anything."

Ravich's face now displayed a demonic ire. Doug delivered one last blow, as he looked over at the two associates.

"That's a shame for you, Melanie and Dustin. If I had to guess, some of those framed judgments out there were probably the result of your efforts too." He turned to leave. "Nice meeting you all."

Doug walked out of the conference room and paused only to say goodbye to the sweet receptionist as he exited the devil's lair.

Ravich shot a fiery glance at his employees. From the corner of his eye, he thought he had seen them smile at the last remark made by the smart-mouth kid now walking out of his office.

"You two mark my words," he vowed. "That boy will be my bitch before this is done."

———— ⟨∞⟩ ————

"So, that went well," Doug announced.

Bonnie watched as her young boss re-entered their office and slung his suit coat over a chair and loosened his tie. He looked drained. She raised an eyebrow.

"He insisted that I refer the case to him," Doug added.

"You had to expect that," she said, unsurprised.

"I didn't say 'asked.' I said 'insisted.' When I told him we were keeping the case, he threatened me."

"Oh, come on, what could he do?"

"For starters, he said he would fight consolidation of the cases, get his discovery sealed so I couldn't use it, and torpedo my settlement chances with the defendants."

"That sorry mother-fucker."

Doug laughed. It helped the smarting he still felt.

"Aren't you the little lady?" he teased.

"Well, I'm sorry, but that's just not right. He's already got every other claimant. It's not like he needs the money."

"Maybe you should go talk to him."

Bonnie smiled. She would have relished the opportunity.

"So what did you say to him?"

"Guess."

"You told him to kiss your ass?"

"Pretty much. I don't think we parted as friends."

Bonnie beamed. She liked that her young cub had stood up to the swaggering old lion. But she was also worried. They were outmanned and ill-equipped. She knew her history. It was the same with the Texans who defended the Alamo. And they all got killed.

"We gotta get us some help," she declared.

"I was thinking that very thing on the way back over," Doug said. "Come on in. We'll kick around my idea."

She followed him into his office, a confident and happy smile on her face. *Great minds think alike,* she told herself as she sat down, eager to hear his strategy.

❧

There is an adrenaline surge that comes when committing a crime, especially for a rank amateur. The pulse races faster and the senses are heightened. You are "in the moment" because you have to be. The extraneous pulls of ordinary life are set aside and concentration must remain laser-focused on only two things: getting what you want and not getting caught.

Rob Finnegan pulled into the parking lot of the apartment complex. It was early afternoon on a Friday and there were lots of spaces. He decided to park close to, but not directly in front of, the leasing office. His car could not be seen from the manager's windows. But if someone observed him walking around and asked what he was doing, he would claim he was just surveying the grounds before inquiring at the office about the rent. He wore a business suit because he had come from the Ruiz funeral. But he reasoned it also made for a clever disguise. No burglar wore a coat and tie.

He turned off the ignition and took a deep breath. *What am I doing?* He sat in the now silent car contemplating the absurdity of his planned actions. A corporate executive whose "rap sheet" consisted of only two traffic tickets in the past twenty-five years was about to commit a Class-A felony. *How had it come to this?* Maybe with more time he would have seen the stupidity of what he was about to do and smartly backed out. But it was already 2:05. There could be no second-guessing now. He needed to get it done.

He exited his car carrying a briefcase. In it was a small crowbar, hammer, and towel. His eyes darted left and right as he entered the courtyard. If he weren't so scared, it would have felt exciting. He was like a spy holding a bag full of alarming secrets, surveying the territory while trying to appear inconspicuous. Just like they did in the movies.

He saw no one. No one saw him. He took comfort in the fact that it was a workday. This was a low-end complex built for the working-class, in a neighborhood that lazy college students and bored retirees would choose to avoid. The odds were in his favor that few people were home.

It took a couple of minutes to locate Slator's unit. While it was no mega-complex, the four buildings were arranged at perpendicular angles and the numbering system was illogical, especially for a nervous man. As he approached the last building his heart froze. He saw a flash of movement. Someone had turned the corner between the buildings and was coming towards him! *What do I do now?* He lowered his head and kept walking. The man passed. Finnegan turned around to look. It was a UPS man, the ubiquitous brown shirt and shorts a dead giveaway. The worker's hands were empty except for the small device used to record signatures and drops. The package must have been delivered and he was on his way back to the truck. Finnegan breathed normally again. To the UPS man, he would just be a white-collar tenant coming home early on a Friday afternoon. Nothing to remember. His goal of staying unnoticed was still intact.

Slator's ground floor apartment was at the corner of Building 4, the front door facing a small, side parking lot. Finnegan quickly discovered a setback. There was a sturdy-looking deadbolt above the locked knob. Even if the door itself was poorly constructed, prying past two separate locks would be time-consuming and loud. The crowbar was useless now. He walked around to the opposite side of the apartment and saw an opportunity. It was probably a bathroom window, opaque and smaller than the others but large enough to squeeze through. He placed his briefcase down and turned around, facing an open and empty field. He was lucky that Slator had chosen a unit in the last building. There were no windows across the way for a stay-at-home witness to peer from and observe a breaking-and-entering in progress.

His heart began pounding as he extracted the other items from the briefcase. He pressed the towel against the glass to muffle the sound and tapped lightly against it with the hammer. His first attempts were too gentle. The terry cloth barrier required a firmer strike. He took a bigger swing and the glass cracked. If the towel dampened the noise, he didn't think by much. It was no more than a mild, shattering crunch but to his guilty ears it sounded like a loud explosion. Finnegan paused to look around again. Nothing. He used the towel to brush aside the broken glass, then returned it and the hammer to the briefcase, tossing the closed case through the broken window. He then lifted himself up and through.

Once inside, he looked at his watch. It was 2:15. He had planned to be driving away no later than 2:30. He needed to work fast. He reached into his pant pocket to pull out a pair of latex gloves and put them on. Every crime show he had ever seen featured a gloved intruder so he thought it best to pick up a pair at the hardware store. He was unaware that big city police departments rarely dust for fingerprints in a routine apartment burglary. They simply fill out a stolen property report and call it a day.

His search would be swift and methodical. He wasn't, after all, looking for cash or jewelry. The objects of his attention would not be secreted away in drawers or under beds. A computer, even a laptop, would be open and obvious. If there were a landline telephone, he would check around for a message machine. He knew there was little chance of also finding Slator's cell phone. He would probably have that with him. But still he would look.

The computer was the most important item. If Al Harris was right about the data relay, it would have recorded the plant's operating problems on the night of the explosion. It most likely documented any manual override of the safety system. If he could get his hands on that evidence it would be gone forever, exactly like the computer it cloned from, which was now just control room trash being driven to a landfill.

The concern over phone messages came to him in the second of the previous night's dreams. It had startled him awake and left him with cold sweats. He spent the rest of the night with eyes wide open, intuitively testing the hypothesis. Nothing in any computer data would directly bear his name or reveal his involvement. *So why were Slator's comments so personally accusatory?* He could come up with just three explanations:

The first didn't concern him. Perhaps Slator's harsh words meant only that he blamed management for pushing the plant so hard. If that was all there was to it, he could fade that heat. The huge increase in production was, after all, Thornton Industries' fault, not his.

Another possibility was that Dave Phillips talked directly with Slator after ten p.m. to speak about the override order and who gave it. But that made no sense. Slator wasn't taking any calls that night. Phillips said so, and his own failed efforts to reach Ken after the explosion suggested that such a conversation was highly unlikely. Logic also ruled it out. If Slator had timely heard such an idea from Phillips he would have told him to ignore the order. He would also have called his boss immediately to say "butt out."

It was the third explanation that was reason enough to break into a man's apartment. If Phillips left Slator a voicemail or message detailing the override conversation, and Slator played it back after the explosion, then there existed a recorded indictment. Slator would not have erased such a message. Like the computer data, it would be valuable evidence against the President of SeaCoast.

Finnegan's plan was not to sit down and examine the hard drive or play back any messages. He would simply steal the equipment, making it appear like an ordinary break-in. As long as the computer and answering machine were gone, he figured he was in the clear. Especially if he also found the cell phone.

The apartment was small but yielded no treasure. There was no computer sitting out. He looked everywhere a laptop might be stored. Each drawer was examined and left open. The tiny closet was upended. The television was pulled aside. He found no landline telephone, no answering machine. He panicked. It was now 2:25. He started tossing cushions and pillows in hopes of discovering a carelessly left cell phone. He rooted through the bathroom medicine cabinet, under the bed, and between the mattresses. There were no other places to look.

Had he been a more observant criminal, he might have found the lack of underwear and socks in the dresser drawers to be curious. The absence of a razor or toothbrush in the bathroom should have raised a suspicion. Had he not been in such a rush, he would have noticed that only a couple of items of clothing still hung in the closet. He also never considered the clear improbability of a man taking his computer to a funeral. Clues were all around but his quest was far too focused. It didn't register with him that there was no trash in the bin, no perishables in the kitchen, no suitcase anywhere.

He stood in the middle of the ransacked apartment, shaking. His devious and risky plan had netted him nothing. It was almost 2:45. He had to leave. There was no time for a second look. He turned the deadbolt with his still gloved hand, then twisted the knob below to release its lock. He peeked outside and saw no one. He stepped out, closed the door, took off his gloves and walked briskly back to his car.

He drove away, thankful he had not been caught but frustrated by the futility of his crime. To console his sense of failure, he kept telling himself that the whole foolish enterprise had been unnecessary. He rationalized that both his worst fears of incriminating evidence and his darkest suspicions about Slator would each have to be fully realized in order to make any kind of case against him. The odds were against that. He had been worried over nothing. His anxiety lifted somewhat as he pulled into his driveway, happy to begin a weekend at home instead of in jail for burglary.

A short time later, sitting in his favorite chair with a strong whiskey in his hand, he replayed the burglary in his head. His technique had been flawless. It wasn't his fault the goods weren't there. He had been careful. He left no trace. He took a sip of his drink. Then a thought struck him. The anxiety returned. His hand starting trembling and he lost his grip. The cocktail glass bounced off the Persian carpet, ice and amber liquor spilling at his feet and onto the expensive rug.

He had left his briefcase in the apartment bathroom! It was still sitting exactly where it landed after being tossed in through the broken window. *Stupid, idiotic mistake!* He knelt down to clean up the mess on the floor while rapidly assessing the greater damage left across town. *No name or initials had been engraved on the case. There was no monogram on the cheap towel that laid inside on top of the hammer and crowbar. The tools were as generic as a loaf of bread.*

Dumb, but not disastrous. He decided it was no big deal. He would lose no sleep over that. Even so, it would be another difficult night. The ghosts of burnt men would be back.

They were spent. Saying goodbye to someone so young, a daughter they loved so much, was both emotionally and physically exhausting. Joan and Ken Slator returned to the house and collapsed in the master-bedroom bed. Fully clothed, they embraced and fell asleep. It marked a change but they were too tired to comment on it. He had been sleeping in the guest room since Tuesday when she first asked him to stay.

It had just gotten dark outside when his cell phone rang at six. They were both still napping. He scrambled to reach for it on the nightstand. It was the resident manager of his apartment complex, calling to say they had discovered a broken window and unlocked front door. The manager had gone inside. She said it looked like somebody had trashed the apartment. She wanted to know if she should call the police. Slator told her no, that he would be right over. He hung up and rose from the bed.

The call woke Joan as well and she sat up.

"What is it, Ken?"

"Some trouble back at my apartment. I should run over there."

"Can I help? Do you want me to go with you?"

He leaned over and kissed her forehead.

"No, stay here. Try to nap some more. I'll bring back something for dinner."

She nodded as he remained close. He kissed her mouth. She kissed back.

Driving to his apartment, he made a quick mental inventory of its contents: there was a cheap, outdated television and a crappy mini-sound system that played a single CD and which he had never used. Those were the "valuable" items. The used furniture wasn't worth stealing. The rest of the personal property would probably fit in two boxes and carry a value at Goodwill of less than three-hundred dollars. There would be no need to involve the police. Whoever chose to rob his apartment was probably the most disappointed thief in history.

This was no real crisis considering the week he was having. He would straighten the place up, then meet with the manager and offer to pay for the window. He would use the opportunity to give notice. He wasn't planning on moving back in. Joan's kiss had conveyed a new commitment.

Entering the small apartment, he was struck by the oddity of the crime scene. The TV and sound system were still there. Sofa cushions were thrown on the floor, and kitchen cabinet doors and drawers were all left opened. In the bedroom, the top mattress partially hung off the box springs, and sheets and pillows were hurled in all directions. Nothing appeared to have been taken.

He deduced that the burglar was probably an addict looking for cash or drugs. The thought pained him. *How could anyone let their life descend so badly? Had Melissa resorted to such desperation in her final weeks?* He walked into the bathroom to check the small medicine cabinet. He knew he hadn't left behind any prescription medicine but the mirrored front was opened, a bottle of aspirin and a roll of antacids still on the shelf where he had left them. He turned and saw the broken window. It was obviously the point of entry. Glass shards lay scattered on the floor. A brown briefcase laid flat near the tub.

It wasn't his. He knew that. He knelt down and opened it. He removed the tools and towel from the bottom compartment. The inside top of the case had an expandable file separator for sorting papers. He felt inside. There was nothing in there. On the front side of the separator was a stitched pocket for holding pens and a calculator. Next to it was a smaller stitched pouch for storing business cards.

He saw a tiny corner of white protruding barely above the top line of the smaller pocket. He reached in and removed the single card which had been inserted backwards. It was crumpled and apparently long forgotten. He turned the blank side over and stared at the print in disbelief. It read:

Robert E. Finnegan

President

SeaCoast Chemical Corporation

—⬗—

It was a Friday night. Doug decided to forget about Paul Ravich and the *Crouch* case, at least for the evening. Tonight, he was going to honor a promise made to himself on Monday: to become a real friend to the court clerk, Sarah Ash. It was just a casual dinner, a small way to say thanks for her kindnesses over his short career. But, as things turned out, she was once again helping him. After a trying week, he badly needed to relax with someone pleasant.

She had seemed surprised — or was she happy? — when he called midweek at the courthouse and asked her out for dinner on Friday. She had teased "Is this a date?" He responded with "It's two friends having a meal. But we'll be drinking, so who knows?" It was pretty weak banter, he now realized, but she had accepted. He supposed that attractive court clerks were used to lame talk from lawyers.

Doug hadn't been involved in a serious relationship for the last six years and wasn't looking to begin one. His law school girlfriend had been his last committed relationship. A few years after graduation, they decided their individual careers left none of the time that true couples need. Since that breakup, he found himself too busy at work to bother looking for "the right one." The occasional date or hookup led to a couple of short-term casual relationships. His professional life was complicated enough. He tried to keep his social life simple. This date with Sarah was not an effort to change that. It was just going to be a nice evening with a nice person.

Sarah had ditched her conservative clerk wardrobe in favor of a sleek black cocktail dress. It was her Friday night too. Clothes may make the man, but her outfit made men notice. She was stunning, her look transformative. The businesslike clerk became the carefree single girl with only a few yards of black silk and a pair of high-heel pumps.

They talked and laughed over drinks and sushi. There were none of the usual first date hesitations. They knew each other. Still, they spent time initially talking shop, trading stories about lawyers and trials. Nothing too personal was discussed. No revelations shared. Doug was enjoying the light conversation and she was too.

Eventually, a sense of comfort took over — aided by the warm saki and cold Japanese beer — and they ended up sounding more like a couple on a date rather than two people at a legal convention. He complimented her looks. She said she liked his eyes. They told each other what music they listened to and chatted about other favorite things. When she said she enjoyed dancing, he took that as a cue. They left the restaurant in search of a club.

They danced like it was a high-school prom. As the night progressed, hands that were joined on the dance floor stayed clasped as they sat at their table. They began to flirt more and dance less. She had a great body and was smart and pretty. He was a handsome gentleman who liked to have fun. They were both very pleased with the way things were going.

When it came time, they left the club arm-in-arm. When he walked her to her condominium door, they both knew. There was no need for frat boy lines. He kissed her. She didn't engage in any coy, schoolgirl retreat. She kissed him back. They were both in their thirties. They no longer had to play games.

"Would you like to come in?" she asked, as she opened her door.

"Do you think I should?" he demurely replied, a sly grin betraying his words.

"I think you'd better," she said, almost as an order, while pulling him across the threshold.

"Thank God you weren't there."

Joan reacted to her ex-husband's account of the apartment break-in. She was worried for him; about him. He took it as a telling expression of concern. She cared once again.

He didn't provide all the details when he returned to the house Friday night. He said only that someone had broken a window and entered the place, apparently searching for cash or drugs. He didn't burden her with the ominous clue he had discovered. Rob Finnegan's briefcase was left outside in his car's trunk.

"These things happen, especially in neighborhoods like that."

He spoke as if it were a minor episode, hoping to conceal his greater concerns. Joan already had enough to worry about.

She reached across the kitchen table, ignoring the take-out Chinese he brought back for dinner, and took his hand.

"Ken, I want you to stay here. With me. And not just because it's unsafe over there."

He looked into her eyes.

"I don't know what I'm feeling right now," she continued. "You don't either. I just know that I need your support, your kindness, and I'm grateful that you're here for me."

He felt tears form but fought them back. He wanted to remain strong for her.

"So I'll give it a try," she said smiling, "if you want that as well."

He squeezed her hand gently and softly nodded as a single tear escaped. She saw it and squeezed back harder, returning a look of happy wonder. He was not the stoic and distant man she had divorced. He was again the man she married. Words were no longer necessary. Through touch and gaze, they silently renewed their vows.

He woke up late in a much too comfortable bed. Sarah Ash was standing beside it, wearing a delicate bathrobe and a conspiratorial smile. She held out a fresh cup of great-smelling coffee and raised her eyebrows suggestively when he looked at her.

"Good morning, counselor."

He sat up in bed, tugging the sheet around his naked chest. The Saturday sunlight brought with it the modesty that had been tossed aside the night before. He took the cup and grinned.

"Thanks."

"For what?" she teased.

He laughed. "I appreciate the coffee too."

She sat down beside him. "I don't normally do things like that," she began, with a complete lack of remorse. She lightly brushed at his hair with her fingers. "I'm just a shy court clerk by day."

"And Wonder-Woman by night. What got into us?"

She ran her fingers across his chest. "I found your closing argument to be persuasive."

He played along. "You were quite eloquent yourself."

She responded with a devious grin. "Well, that could explain why there was so much rebuttal."

They both laughed hard, each glad that humor had diffused that awkward first-time, morning-after moment.

Doug took a sip of coffee and looked at his watch. It was almost ten.

"I haven't slept this late in years."

"You only got five hours sleep." She rose from the bed. "I keep track of what lawyers do. It's my job."

He nodded appreciatively.

She spun and headed for the bathroom, talking as she disappeared. "You need to get up and sneak out of here. I have a reputation to maintain with my neighbors."

He laughed again as he swung his feet to the floor. He stood and reached for his clothes piled on a nearby chair and began dressing. While buttoning his shirt, he heard water running and the sound of teeth being brushed behind the closed door. As he put on his shoes, he continued their conversation with a raised voice.

"Hey, if I'm seen leaving, I'll just say I'm your brother paying a visit."

The water stopped and the door opened. She leaned against one side of the door casing with a playful smile and pointed her toothbrush at him for emphasis.

"Considering the noise we made last night, that should confuse them pretty good."

He walked over and put his arms around her waist. "I really had a great time," he said, shifting to a more serious tone.

"Me too."

He pulled her closer and they kissed with passion. He then took a step away. Otherwise, they were headed back to the bed. He smiled and looked into her eyes.

"Um, minty-fresh."

"You might want to try some yourself," she joked, as she lightly pushed him away. "I'll let you show yourself out."

Her sense of humor and easy-going attitude were even more refreshing than her breath. Sarah Ash, the docile court clerk, was indeed full of pleasant surprises. He turned to say one more thing.

"I'd like to see you again."

She gave him an impish look as he instantly realized how trite those words probably sounded. He tried to salvage things.

"I mean, maybe next time we could even talk more."

"And sleep?" she teased.

"Whatever you'd like to do."

She flashed a radiant smile.

"I'll keep you at the top of my docket, Counselor."

———— ∞ ————

He was home. It was not a statement of location, but of mind. Sitting at the small kitchen table, finishing a simple breakfast of cereal and fruit, Ken Slator felt comforted by the bond he had with this house. Even with the redecorating she had done, its familiar walls, furniture, and feel provided the much-needed reassurance that a few good things remained in his life. The old house was welcoming. Living here again was a reunion with a close friend.

His second chance with Joan meant even more. United, they might find a new life. Committed, they could rediscover a love misplaced by neglect but never really gone. Together, they would survive Melissa's death.

No parent ever gets over the grief. A child's death remains an emotional tattoo, permanent and indelible. Even so, life went on. It had to. They wanted it to. It was far too early for anything big, but they took their small first steps. Joan left early for a Saturday morning exercise class. Her motivation was greater than a desire for fitness, she had told him. Melissa was gone but he was back. She needed to at least try to start living again. Her daughter would have wanted it and her husband now merited that from her. He had kissed her goodbye when she left. It felt good.

He stared out the kitchen bay window and reflected on the past week. The glass panes diffused the light of the morning sun, casting a warm glow. But his mind sought another form of illumination. A lifetime of life-altering events had occurred in the span of a single workweek. It was all too much to process and much too hard to understand. Still, he needed to try to unravel the chaos. *Why had it all happened?*

His engineering training took over. He began to think about cause and effect. In chemistry, direct links are easily drawn between the two. In life, he was now discovering, the connections were seldom as neatly linear.

Melissa's death had been caused by what was lacking. She lacked the ability to control her own life but perhaps that fatal shortcoming was also the consequence of his own deficiencies. *Had I been more active in her life, would it have had any positive effect?* Both he and Joan failed to adequately intervene. He lacked the time while she lacked the courage. If their marriage had been salvageable earlier, maybe it would have made a difference for their daughter. *Could their happiness have affected hers?*

He didn't have easy answers to those questions. He realized he never would. He did, however, know with certainty that her death caused him to change. The effect, incongruous yet welcome, was a renewed relationship with Joan. *Would it ever have happened otherwise? And could they in time, or ever, be able to admit that a good thing resulted from something so bad?* He thought about how strange their reconciliation was. *Is it even possible for love to tangle its way out of so much despair and finally last?* He didn't know. Experiments with the human heart were different from those in science. The interplay between cause and effect could not be so easily predicted.

Slator got up, taking the morning paper with him, and walked into the home study where his laptop and cell phone laid side-by-side. He glanced at them, knowing the evidence each contained. Causation and consequence were much clearer in the other tragedy from the past week. Greed caused the death of five decent men as definitively as chemistry caused the explosion. Straight lines: Cause and Effect.

He thought about Derron Lucas as well. The new kid. Hired only five weeks before because of the plant's ramp-up in production. He now lay in a hospital fighting for his life because his employer wanted a few more dollars. Eighty-five percent body-surface burns, that's what the news had reported. The effects of such injury were too great. Vital organs other than skin would also suffer, then shut down. Derron would likely soon become the sixth fatality. Slator knew enough biology to know that much.

SeaCoast's post-explosion conduct disgusted him even more. *The company cared very little about cause and a lot about effect.* Why the disaster happened was not nearly as important to them as minimizing its harmful consequences — to both image and balance sheet. Thornton's corporate lawyer had come to the plant, for the first time, to publicly speculate that the weather caused everything. To the media, SeaCoast pledged support for the victims and cooperation with government authorities. *It was pure grandstanding.* Behind the scenes, they would frustrate and hamper any attempt to get to the truth. The truth would make them look bad. It might affect their bottom line.

Share-price, not safety, dictated everything they did. That was true before the explosion and remained true after. *How else can you explain the company's long delay and cost-concerns over purchasing a safety system the plant needed? And what motivation, other than money, could possibly compel management to ever order an employee to turn it off once it was finally installed?*

Slator's anger rose. He sat down and unfolded the Saturday paper. He needed to let other events, different thoughts, calm him down. He directed his eyes to the headlines but the copy went unread. His mind could not be distracted. *What should be front page news,* he kept thinking, *was the arrogance and stupidity of his corporate superiors.*

Charles Thornton was an incredibly rich man at the helm of a vast and lucrative conglomerate. SeaCoast Chemical was but a single spoke in his large moneymaking wheel. Destroyed equipment and dead men were a temporary business interruption, not a tragedy, to him. Slator began grinding his teeth. *Watching the plant burn on television was probably the first time the jerk had even seen his asset,* he thought, with growing rage. He felt an uncomfortable hatred toward the man he had never met, a man who possessed the temerity to demand a father return to work on the morning after his daughter died, an ogre that, to use his words, didn't "give a good goddamn" about anyone's problems other than his own.

Rob Finnegan was no better. In a way, he was worse. *He had always cared more about keeping his position than keeping things safe.* The focus of the SeaCoast President was constantly on pleasing the men above him, not protecting the men downline. Slator thought back over the years, recounting the numerous times that had been true. He had grown to accept and deal with Finnegan's shortcomings. A perpetual ass-kisser could be tolerated. But a man who would do anything to save his own ass could not.

The apartment break-in was simple cause and effect. Slator had spent much of the previous night thinking about the bizarre criminal act and came to a single conclusion: Finnegan had learned, somehow, about the DCSS data backup. His boss feared that his role in causing the explosion might be revealed and knew it would cost him his job. The effect was panic — that basic fearful reaction to adversity that seldom leads to sound action.

What did Finnegan think he would gain? Even if his boss had found and stolen the computer, the details and numbers had already been seen. Surely testimony would still be allowed. And Dave Phillips' last voicemail would prove the override order and direct link to Finnegan. *But there was no way Finnegan could know about that call.* Then again, he had looked in places too small to hold a laptop. *Was he searching for my phone?* Maybe he correctly suspected that Phillips left messages about the crisis at the plant. If so, then Finnegan's deductive skills were far better than his burglary prowess. Slator doubted he was that smart. *What thief leaves behind his business card?* That was incredibly sloppy, even for a man with a deserved reputation for not paying attention to details.

The ignored newspaper remained on his lap. He placed it aside on the sofa, then balled his hand into a fist as another troubling aspect of the burglary struck him. *The bastard didn't find what he came for.* If so, it would only be a matter of time before he discovered he had simply gone to the wrong place. *Would he try again here? What if Joan were home alone? What would happen if he were holding another hammer or crowbar and came face-to-face with me?*

Slator now grasped that he had a serious problem. He was dealing with more than a stupid ex-boss. Job preservation and desperation had turned Rob Finnegan into a dangerous man, one who would surely be willing to commit other crimes in furtherance of his cover-up. The madness had to be stopped. *But how?*

An impulsive man might have gotten off the couch to personally confront the culprit. A practical man might have dialed the police with a burglary report and a solid evidence lead. But Ken Slator was an engineer.

The only impulsive thing he had ever done in his life was quit his job. As for being practical, he had always done the safe thing and it had gotten him nowhere.

He recalled the second vow made to himself while driving back from the hospital on Tuesday morning. He was already honoring the first: he was taking care of Joan. It was now time to honor the second: to make them pay.

He sat thinking. There had to be a way. Both Rob Finnegan and Charles Thornton owed a debt to the victims and to him. Both executives, and their companies, deserved harsh punishment. It took awhile but an idea finally struck him, one that might actually gain both a benefit for him and justice for his coworkers. He deliberated slowly, looking for any possible weakness in the plan. He analyzed and dismissed the alternatives. He weighed the risks and consequences. He was being an engineer: a professional trained to study cause and effect while tasked to turn it into something productive.

It would work, he finally told himself. He rose from the sofa. Joan would be back soon. He felt good knowing that what he was about to do would make them more secure, in more ways than one.

But in devising his careful plan for opportunity and vengeance, he forgot the most important engineering lesson of all: things can still go wrong. He should have remembered that past scientific minds were similarly confident in their detailed calculations only to later see their bridges collapse or space shuttles explode. The elements could be studied, predicted, and often successfully manipulated. But nature can never be completely controlled.

It is precisely the same with people.

Chapter 11
Teams

"Kinda dumb to start a war against a nuclear power when all you've got is a bow and arrow."

Doug Stevens sipped his coffee and smiled as Bill Gaston gave his folksy take on the situation. Their Sunday morning meeting at Starbucks was the first step toward finding some help with the *Crouch* case. Doug's friend and law school classmate had listened attentively as the Friday showdown with Ravich was recounted, interrupting Doug's tale at least twice with: "You're shittin' me!" It was Gaston's favorite phrase of incredulity.

"He left me no choice," Doug told him. "I can't refer him the case. My client hates the man."

"You always get the smart plaintiffs. My clients can't tell a good lawyer from a bad one. That's how I get so much business."

Doug laughed. He never got tired of Gaston's self-deprecations.

"So, what do you think I should do?" Doug asked.

Bill Gaston tossed aside the straw and took a last gulp of his frappuccino, wiping the whipped cream from his mouth with a shirt sleeve. He looked up at the ceiling, closed one eye, then contorted his face like Popeye.

Doug knew what the goofy look meant. He had seen it many times. It was the same expression Gaston made back in law school whenever a professor called on him to explain a difficult case or legal principle to the rest of the class. It meant Gaston was thinking. Doug sat silently, knowing a brilliant mind was churning behind the cartoonish pose. It was always worth the wait to hear what Bill Gaston had to say.

When his musing was finished, Gaston returned with a confident look, nodding his head up and down, while rubbing his chin in affirmation. You might disagree with Bill Gaston's thoughts but at least you knew he had fully considered them before they were shared.

"Okay, here's the deal," he began.

He held up a clinched hand and unfurled a finger with each point he made. He would have made a great teacher.

"First, Paul Ravich has every other case but yours, so if you end up consolidated he gets to call all the shots anyway, which is bad news for your client since he no longer gives a damn about you or her."

Doug grinned. Gaston always could cut to the chase.

"Second, make sure your lawsuit contains at least one alternative, and preferably inconsistent, theory of liability to whatever is in Ravich's pleadings. Even better, try to sue some defendants he doesn't name. That makes your case far less likely to be joined with his if he later decides that's the best way to screw you. Think of that as shark repellent."

Doug interrupted. "But he made clear he would fight any merging of the cases. To punish me."

Gaston rolled his eyes, expressing disappointment at such naiveté. He held his hand closer to Doug's face and unfurled the third finger.

"All right, son, point number three. Never believe a word that turd says. Look, I heard Ravich has a peculiar way of getting his big lawsuits in front of his favorite judicial lackeys. You and I both know that new cases are supposed to be randomly assigned among the courts, but where there's a will there's a way, and that man has figured out a surefire and probably illegal way to get his blockbusters in the courtrooms of his fishing buddies, if you get my drift."

Doug was glad he had invited his old pal for Sunday coffee. The man was a walking encyclopedia of inside information.

"So, let's pretend that happens," Gaston continued. "Now, all of a sudden, Ravich's *SeaCoast* cases are being administered by a judge who will do anything Ravich wants. That includes screwing you, maybe with a consolidation followed by other procedural orders that benefit Ravich and harm you. Now, why do you suppose he would do that?"

Gaston was playing the role of law school professor, Socratic method and all, where a student learns by coming up with his own answer.

Doug said he didn't know. The professor was disappointed. Exasperated, he provided the explanation.

"So that, *eventually,* your client decides with that smart brain of hers that the only way she can win is by ditching you and hiring him. Duh!"

Doug nodded appreciatively. He wasn't going to interrupt the professor again.

"Numero quatro," he drawled, as he added a fourth up-stretched finger. "Get yourself a legal team that can help you fly this bird. You're smart enough to go solo but it's too long a trip, the case is too big, and you could use extra pilots on board who, unlike Ravich, aren't trying to crash your plane."

Doug smiled. He loved the way Bill Gaston could paint pictures with words.

"Got anybody in mind?"

His lanky buddy raised his hand to his brow in a four-finger salute.

"Lieutenant Lawyer Gaston, reporting for duty, sir!"

Doug laughed. "Welcome aboard, airman."

"You just pay me more than an enlisted man and less than a mercenary when it's all said and done."

"Deal," Doug replied. "But what about the rest of your docket? I know you stay pretty busy."

"Like my hero, Willie Nelson, sings: 'You got the money, honey, I got the time.'"

Doug grinned widely. With Gaston on his side, he was in for a lot of laughs and the defendants were in for a lot of trouble.

"Are you finished with your PowerPoint presentation?" Doug quipped.

Gaston chuckled, getting the double entendre. He re-curled his four fingers and made a "thumbs up" gesture at Doug.

"Not quite. Point number five. And it's a big one." He leaned forward as if to let Doug in on a secret. "We're a couple of young and brilliant trial lawyers. One of us is even handsome, but don't let that get you down. We're like that *Top Gun* movie. I'll be Maverick, you're Goose. We're both pretty good pilots, right? At least when flying our tiny jets."

Doug shook his head in amazement. No analogy, metaphor, or simile was ever safe from Bill Gaston. His buddy never broke stride.

"But what we're clearly not is rich enough or experienced enough to handle this 747 of a case you've got. We need another airman. One with a lot of flight hours who might be willing to invest his time and money in a possible dogfight with Paul Ravich."

"You got a name?"

"Go you one better, Goose. I'll get us an appointment with him tomorrow."

⁂

Ken Slator didn't attend his coworkers' funerals. Burying his daughter and helping his wife through the ordeal required all his time and attention. The widows of his fellow employees didn't need to be told what they surely understood from the events of the past week: family came first.

The lost men had been Slator's friends in only the workplace sense.

While they all got along and saw each other more than their real families, the camaraderie never extended beyond the plant's parking lot. A closer relationship was neither expected nor sought. That was especially true for Slator. He had also been their boss. A certain distance is required when you're in charge. He had always been courteous to and supportive of the men he supervised but he readily accepted that his role meant he could never be "just one of the boys."

Their deaths, however, affected him deeply. They were all hardworking men who had trusted their boss to keep them safe in a dangerous work environment. He had failed them in that regard. It didn't matter that others had caused the explosion. A sense of personal responsibility remained. A real leader lacks the capacity for self-absolution when things go wrong. A general finds no comfort in being told it was someone else's mistake that killed his men.

Ken Slator converted those pangs of guilt into a continuing sense of duty. That commitment formed the genesis for his plan. Getting even with his former employer had to also help the families of the dead and injured. Without recompense to the victims, he would be no different from the men he wanted to hurt. After all, the action he was about to take would intentionally and directly benefit him. That was precisely the type of self-centered conduct that Charles Thornton and Rob Finnegan had engaged in and that he was trying to punish. *It has to be done this way,* he reasoned, *so that the victims can also gain.* Otherwise, he would be a man motivated only by money, making deals with the devil.

He got the name from Dave Phillips' widow. He called her on Sunday to offer condolences and explain his absence at Dave's service. She was shocked by the news of Melissa's death and expressed sympathies of her own. She said she appreciated his call and that Dave had always spoken highly of him. She sounded puzzled when he told her he quit his job with SeaCoast, but she seemed relieved by his assurance that he would do all he could to help the families get to the truth.

That's when he asked. The name she provided sounded familiar but he couldn't recall why.

On Monday morning, he was ready to take the next step but hesitated before dialing the number. Uncertainty entered his mind. *Are you really sure this is the best way?* He never imagined being capable of inflicting so much damage on the people who signed his paycheck. But that was the old Ken Slator. He was gone for good, just like five decent men. He pushed aside any last-second doubts and dialed.

A perky voice answered.

"Law Office of Paul Ravich and Associates. How may I help you?"

———⚬⚬⚬———

The contrast between new and old could not have been greater. The offices were located inside a modern glass-tower, chrome and granite gleaming everywhere until you entered the twenty-seventh floor lobby of Greenbaum & Walker. It was like stepping back in time.

There was brown shag carpeting on the floors of the office suite. A starving artist oil painting hung above the scuffed and dated sofa. The chairs were ancient and cheap-looking, as was every other piece of furniture in the reception area. If a film crew ever needed a set for a seventies-era struggling law office, this was the place to come. The high, bulky reception desk concealed all but the head of the firm's greeter, an older woman whose out-of-style bouffant was in complete harmony with the office's nostalgic theme. A betting man would wager that an old phone with a rotary-dial was hidden behind the tall front panel of the receptionist's station.

Doug sat smiling, across from Bill Gaston who was busy glancing around comically, making faces and pointing, pretending to be impressed by all the grandeur. Gaston had been in the offices before. Several years back, he had a companion case with Greenbaum and had watched the old man shine. That was why he wanted Doug to consider adding Harry to their team. He knew what the man could do. He also knew how ridiculously quaint the office was but kept that fact a secret. He figured it would be a fun surprise for his co-counsel.

Doug thought back to his first encounter with Harry Greenbaum only a week before, when he watched the rumpled old fox best a young big-firm defense lawyer in a minor discovery hearing before Judge Hinojosa. He recalled initially mistaking him for a broke and burned-out lawyer based upon his old and mismatched clothes. Now Doug more fully understood the man. Greenbaum's office, like his wardrobe, were simply carefully crafted tools: lures to fool the unsuspecting into underestimating him. He was looking forward to this meeting.

The disheveled old war-horse suddenly appeared from down the hallway. He greeted them with a tone worthy of royalty.

"Gentlemen, welcome, and thank you so much for coming over here to talk with me this fine afternoon."

He introduced himself to Doug and gave him a surprisingly vigorous handshake considering his age, which had to be over seventy.

"How have you been, Billy?" he then asked, as he turned to shake hands with Gaston.

"Doing great, Harry. How about you?"

"Can't complain," he shrugged, arms partially extended with palms up-stretched, making himself resemble an old deli owner being asked about the lunch business.

Doug took the whole show in. Greenbaum wore an unstarched and wrinkled white shirt with a collar the size of Travolta's disco outfit in *Saturday Night Fever.* A wide baby-blue tie had been loosened and pulled down to the second button of his shirt. A set of brown suspenders held up a pair of corduroy pants the color of old mustard.

"Let's go back to my office and talk." He motioned with his arm. "Right this way, boys."

As Doug walked down the hallway another contrast struck. There was no hero wall here. Greenbaum had successfully practiced plaintiff's trial law for nearly half a century yet no mementos or self-aggrandizing records hung anywhere. Instead, there were a few inexpensive wildlife prints hung between the prefabricated bookcases that were crammed full with dusty volumes of case reporters.

They passed a number of offices along the way, each occupied by a diligently working lawyer or paralegal; Doug couldn't tell which. Each person sat behind a standard issue metal desk, the kind you would expect to find only in the military or wherever low-level bureaucrats work. If you didn't know better, you could mistake the offices of Greenbaum & Walker for a small operation that had fallen on hard times. But Doug had already figured things out. He wasn't taking the bait.

Bill Gaston had explained on the way over that despite the firm's name, it was all Harry's show. The other named partner, Stan Walker, was now listed on the firm's letterhead as "Of Counsel," a legal euphemism for "essentially retired." For years, Walker had handled mostly small business litigation while Harry tackled the big injury cases. They had been partners from the start. Greenbaum brought in most of the money but, according to Gaston, they split everything fifty-fifty. If that were true, it said a lot about Harry. *Maybe it isn't just a show,* Doug thought as he entered Harry's office. *Money may not be the most important thing to him.*

"Sit down, sit down," Harry directed, pointing to an old upholstered sofa that would not look out of place on a curb waiting for trash pickup.

Harry stepped behind his desk, a simple oak table with an antique roll-top behind it serving as a credenza. He pushed his high-back wooden desk chair, which was on wheels, across the room to face the sofa. He plopped himself down and smiled.

"So, what can I do for you lads?"

"We'd like your input on this SeaCoast explosion case," Gaston began.

"Such a tragedy," Harry commented, having read about the accident in the paper. "How many again were killed?"

"Five," Doug replied. "Another victim has severe burns and may not live."

"Such a shame." Harry grimaced and shook his head sadly. "And who do you represent?"

"The widow of one of the victims. Her name is Kate Crouch."

"How old was her husband, may I ask?"

"Only twenty-four."

Harry looked up at the ceiling. "My, oh my. So young. Any children of this brief marriage?"

"No," replied Doug.

"Well, that's probably for the best."

Bill Gaston redirected the conversation. "Paul Ravich has all the other cases."

"Yes, I think I read something about that." Greenbaum paused. "And then I saw it on the TV." He smiled knowingly. "And I'm sure it was on the radio too."

Gaston understood the point he was making. "He's a media whore, that's for sure. He got his clients signed up the morning after and held a press conference the following day."

"That's Paul," Greenbaum replied nonchalantly. "Did you know he once worked for me?"

Doug and Gaston were both taken aback. Their surprise apparently showed.

"It's true. I hired him when he first got out of law school. He was a bright little fellow and very ambitious. I'm sure he learned a few things from me but I can assure you that blowing one's horn was not one of them."

Doug was intrigued. "How long was he with you?"

"Not long. After a couple of years, he was thoroughly convinced he knew everything. Said I should make him a partner, that he deserved better offices and bigger cases."

Gaston laughed. "And what did you say?"

"I wished him nothing but success and showed him the door. From his subsequent press releases, I assume he has done pretty well for himself."

"Then you already know how difficult he can be," Doug said.

Harry responded with a sly grin. "I presume, gentlemen, that's the very reason you are here."

Doug was smitten. The old hobo still had it: that remarkable intuition possessed by every great trial lawyer. Gaston once described it as "always having your antennae up." It meant that you missed nothing, read things correctly, and stayed one jump ahead. The description fit. The wily

Mr. Greenbaum was a walking cell tower.

"I met with Ravich last week," Doug explained. "He essentially said he would wreck my case if I didn't refer it to him."

"Now, I thought I raised him better than that," Harry said sarcastically. "And you said what in reply?"

"That my client wants me, not him."

Greenbaum smiled. "So Mr. Ravich is going to take all his marbles and go home. That leaves you where?"

"Needing help," answered Doug.

"Am I to be the third Musketeer?"

Gaston spoke up. "You kiddin' me? You're friggin' D'Artagnan!"

They all laughed. Had there been swords, this was the moment they would have been drawn in unity.

They spent time discussing what they knew about the explosion — which wasn't much — followed by what Doug had discovered about SeaCoast Chemical. He informed Harry that SeaCoast was a subsidiary of Thornton Industries.

"I knew that," Harry said, without sounding patronizing. "You may discover that Charles Thornton keeps very close tabs on all his companies. At least he used to." The observation hinted that he had done battle with the corporate giant. "I wouldn't be the least bit surprised to find his greedy paw prints somewhere close to our disaster site," Greenbaum added.

"We'd like you to come on board with us," Doug offered. "We both know how to try a case but, unlike your former associate, we don't presume to know everything. We could use your help."

"I am honored by your request, Mr. Stevens." He paused, twiddling his fingers. "How does this sound? I will formally associate with you fellows on the case and we can all take a third of its eventual fee. If you need help financing the litigation, I can front our expenses on the condition that I be fully reimbursed, off the top, before we divvy up our respective fee shares. Is that fair?"

Doug was startled by the offer. "It's more than fair. But why would you want to make that deal?"

Greenbaum barely hesitated. "Mr. Gaston's literary imagery was a bit off, Mr. Stevens. You see, I consider myself more of a Don Quixote. I like fighting windmills, or perhaps in this particular case, windbags."

Doug beamed. He was charmed by the old buzzard. "So, where should we begin?"

The old man rose from his chair and walked over to his roll-top desk. He raised the curved wood cover along its tracks and reached inside. He returned with identical gifts for the two young lawyers seated on his velour sofa. Tossing one to each, he smiled and said: "Boys, take some notes. I'm going to outline how to win a case the old-fashioned way."

Doug and Bill reached for their pens, then curled back the covers on their new Big Chief writing tablets.

⎯⎯⎯⎯ ⊶⊷⊶ ⎯⎯⎯⎯

Owning your own jet gives you flexibility.

Paul Ravich was in Chicago to speak at a conference sponsored by the National Alliance of Trial Lawyers. His address to the attendees would be on the topic of "Effective Jury Argument." The convention's flyer billed him and six other scheduled speakers as: "The Giants of Civil Litigation." Ravich thought the seminar's title was far too flattering to the other presenters. He didn't believe any lawyer sharing the dais could hold a candle to him.

The occasional seminar lecture was Ravich's least favorite type of marketing. To him, that's all it really was. If you were claiming to be the best trial lawyer in the nation, you had to act like it. Standing before a large group of attorneys and pontificating about your courtroom conquests under the guise of "practice tips" was the equivalent of a one-hour commercial. Such appearances served to bolster a larger-than-life image among his colleagues. Plus, it occasionally yielded good case referrals. It was enough of a "win-win" to justify the time and expense of making four or five trips a year to speak to various trial lawyer groups.

The midmorning speaker was halfway through a depressing speech entitled "Surviving the Trends in Tort Reform" when Ravich's iPhone began to vibrate vigorously. He extracted the device from his suit pocket and read the text message from his associate, Dustin Kirkland: "*Urgent! SeaCoast case. Call ASAP.*" He rose from the dais to slip out a nearby back door of the hotel ballroom. He understood it was rude to do so but balanced the breach of etiquette against the importance of his newest big case. Besides, anyone who noticed his exit might get the positive impression that he was just too damn busy and important to sit around all day listening to others talk. Once outside, he placed the call. His receptionist patched him through quickly.

"What is it, Dustin?"

"Sorry to interrupt the conference but this sounds pretty big. I just got off the phone with a guy who said he was the head of operations at the SeaCoast plant. He claims to have very strong evidence of what happened out there and wants to work with us."

"His company won't let him, you know that."

"No, here's the deal. He said he quit over the explosion. He sounded

165

like he had a score to settle."

"Then you know what to do. Take Ron with you and get a signed statement. Lock him down on his story. I'll be back on Wednesday and we can decide then how best to use what he has to say."

"I already suggested that to him. He said he would only talk directly with you and it had to be now. He also told me what he has will blow the doors off SeaCoast."

Ravich chuckled. "Sounds like my kind of guy. And you think he's for real?"

"I do. He was very cagey and deliberate. Wouldn't even give me a hint of what he knows. The guy sounded smart."

"All right, I'll head home right after I make my speech. That actually saves me from hanging around here for a bunch of needless glad-handing. Call my pilots and tell them the change in schedule. I want the plane ready for wheels-up at three-thirty. Then, call this witness back and set up a meet at our offices for eight tonight. You need to stick around for that. Meanwhile, try and get background on him. Call Stu Mitchell at the union. Find out if he's ever heard of the guy."

"I can do all that but there's one wrinkle."

"Yeah?"

"He said he would only meet with you, alone, at a place of his choosing."

Ravich laughed. "Fine. Call 'Deep Throat' back and set it up. No earlier than seven-thirty. We might hit some weather flying home. Text me with the time and location."

"Why do you think he's being so cloak-and-dagger about this?" Dustin asked.

Ravich had already considered the question.

"One of two reasons: he's really got the goods or he's seen too many movies. Either way, I'll know how to handle him."

Paul Ravich hung up the phone, feeling smug about himself and stronger about his case. Except for one flippant young lawyer, it seemed that everyone wanted to be on his team.

Bill Gaston came back to Doug's office after their meeting with Harry Greenbaum. It had been a true education. Harry spent almost two hours outlining his initial strategy thoughts while assigning each of them very specific tasks that required immediate attention. The old man spoke with the confidence of a war-experienced field commander. It was obvious from that single session that Greenbaum's maladroit courtroom persona was pure schtick. There was no actual "bumbling" going on inside that man's brain.

They walked in carrying their writing tablets, looking like two boys coming home from school. Bonnie looked up at them and giggled.

"Whatcha got there, kids?"

"Homework," replied Doug.

She smiled. "So you're both 'Wild about Harry' now?"

Gaston chuckled. "I think ole Forrest Gump might actually be Stephen Hawking."

"So he signed on?" she asked.

"Yep," Doug answered.

Bonnie was wearing her bookkeeper hat. She thought of a concern.

"How are you splitting the fee?"

Doug explained the arrangement.

"Well, Harry's sure worth his third." She looked straight at Gaston. "You, on the other hand, are going to have to prove your merit to me."

Gaston didn't know how to react until the other two started laughing. Doug came to his friend's defense.

"He's deceptively smart, Bonnie. Trust me."

"You say so," she teased back.

She stared at the writing pad tucked under Doug's arm. The Native-American in full headdress on its bright red cover evoked old classroom memories.

"Are those Big Chief tablets?"

"Yes, ma'am," replied Bill Gaston. "Compliments of Harry Greenbaum. He claims they have magical powers in a courtroom."

"Y'all know they quit making those years ago?"

Doug smiled and explained.

"Maybe so, but our co-counsel bought their last bulk order. As we were leaving, he proudly showed us a supply room full of them."

"My God, I do love that man," Bonnie said in admiration.

"You know much about him?" asked Gaston.

"Bonnie knows everything about everybody," Doug prefaced.

She glowed as she related the story, a fun memory recalled. "I sat in a trial twenty-three years ago and watched my old boss get his ass handed to him by Harry. It was better entertainment than going to the movies. Harry plodded around that courtroom like a damn fool. When it was all over, the jury gave him everything he wanted and I wanted to give him a standing ovation. I'll never forget it."

"He was probably wearing the same outfit he had on today," Doug joked.

They all laughed.

Doug suddenly remembered one of the items on Harry's to-do list.

"Bonnie, see if you can reach the landlord. Tell him his favorite tenant would like to rent some additional space."

"What for?" she asked.

"A war room," he replied.

———— ∞∞ ————

Carter picked him up at the airport and drove straight to the meeting location. It was ten after eight when the Bentley pulled into the parking lot. The corner strip mall housed the type storefronts found in low rent suburban complexes: a tanning salon, liquor store, a haircut place that catered to walk-in traffic. Next to a mailbox and shipping store stood the little soup-and-salad cafe. *Hell of a place for a rendezvous,* thought Paul Ravich.

His driver was even more surprised. He couldn't imagine why his boss wanted to come so far to eat at such a dive-looking place. Ravich bounded out of the car and instructed his driver to wait on the far side of the parking lot. *I'll never figure that man out,* Carter thought to himself, as he pulled away.

When Ravich entered the restaurant, he immediately realized it was the perfect spot for a discreet meeting. A single employee, a high school kid, stood behind the counter, bored to death with a job that consisted of handing out plates and bowls in exchange for an all-you-can-eat $5.95. The salad bar and soup station looked as if they were seldom serviced. Food scraps littered the floor. Cleaning up apparently wasn't in the kid's job description. Neither was paying attention. He never looked up from his mobile phone, too busy texting some girl to notice Ravich's entrance. You couldn't blame the kid. There wasn't much business to monitor. A single customer sat in the back corner booth sipping an iced tea. It had to be him.

Ken Slator saw the suited man approach and tensed. *How do I handle this?* He was in over his head. *What do I say?* His anxiety dissipated only slightly when the man extended his hand and gave a friendly smile.

"I'm Paul Ravich. Sorry I'm a few minutes late."

Slator made a gesture for him to sit but said nothing. Ravich could tell the man was nervous.

"I didn't catch your name?"

He cleared his throat. "Ken Slator."

"All right, Ken, nice to meet you. I understand you want to talk with me about the SeaCoast explosion?"

"Yes, I think I do. But first, who do you represent?"

Ravich saw no need to answer the question precisely. It would take too much time. "All the victims," he replied.

"And Derron, how's he doing?"

"Looks bad. Doctors tell us he probably won't make it."

Slator lowered his head. "He was a good kid."

Ravich studied the body language and expression. *He has something heavy on his mind.* "So, Ken, how can I help you?"

Before answering, Slator glanced around cautiously, verifying that no one was within earshot. He had nothing to worry about. The kid's sexting must have worked. The disinterested young cashier was now talking on his phone, his flirting obvious.

Slator began his story and Ravich never interrupted. He spelled it all out, in succinct detail, like the engineer he was.

Over the years, Ravich had obtained his fair share of outcome-determinative witnesses and "smoking gun" evidence, mostly through good investigative efforts. Some people had to be paid to tell what they knew and a few got paid even more to make their testimony fit. His chief investigator, Ron, was good at finding evidence and purchasing it when necessary. Once in a while, the altruistic witness just came forward, asking for nothing more than a chance to perform their civic duty. Ravich used them, of course, but had no respect for such people. They were too stupid to realize that something of value should never be given away. He wasn't sure about Ken Slator's motives but could tell the man wasn't dumb. He would probably have to be paid something but it would be well worth the price. Ravich's excitement had grown as he learned about the revealing plant data and voicemails but he kept any elation carefully concealed.

"So that's it," Slator concluded. "That's what I can prove."

"Do you have the computer and cell phone with you now?"

"No, but they're both in a very secure place."

"You seem concerned. Why?"

Slator told him about the break-in and how he tied it to his boss.

"That's incredible," Ravich said, sincerely amazed by the brazenness and ineptitude of Rob Finnegan.

Ravich thought quickly. Maybe he could use that to create an unbreakable bond with this superstar witness.

"That man, and his company, will obviously do anything they can. I mean *anything*. I've been handling cases like this for years, Ken. They want their hands on that evidence. If it's destroyed, nobody can prove gross negligence. But also know this, if that evidence is gone, they will simply make you the fall guy."

Slator shifted uncomfortably in his seat. "How could this be my fault?"

"Without your evidence, corporate could claim they had no idea how careless *you* had been in running this plant. They'll argue this happened only because you weren't on top of things. You see, that would only be conceding a case of simple negligence on the part of a SeaCoast employee, and the employer doesn't get tagged for that when other employees get killed. They'll say you were the man in charge, the man who couldn't be reached in time of crisis, the man who quit the day after out of guilt. The best thing that would happen is you get drug through the mud."

Slator was concerned. "And what's the worst thing?"

"We already know they want that evidence pretty badly. They have proven your property is in danger. Your life may be too."

The dread on Slator's face signified he had not contemplated such extremes.

"I know it sounds ridiculous but think about it. This evidence and your testimony could cost them untold millions. From what you've just said about how they ran things, it's not much of a stretch to say they care deeply about money. People will do bad things for that kind of dough."

Slator nodded in agreement.

"So let me help you. Have you backed this data up? Made a copy of the voicemails?"

"No."

"Then allow me to take possession of the devices. I'll make duplicates, secure the originals for trial, and return copies to you. You'll get back a new laptop with the same files and a new and better cell phone."

"Why should I get the replacements?"

"Because the originals will have to be used in evidence. You'll have to authenticate them and I'll have to prove a proper chain of custody. They need to be under my control. It's the only way we can get the truth in front of a jury."

"I understand." Slator replied.

He clearly didn't. What Ravich had said was total horse shit. He just wanted to get his hands on the evidence in case the witness changed his mind.

"Let me ask you, why are willing to give this information to me?"

Slator hesitated. He wasn't quite sure how to bring it up.

"Because, I guess, it's the right thing to do," he said, stalling.

"That it is, and you should be commended."

Ravich couldn't believe his ears. *This moron might give away the gold for free.*

"And because I want to hurt them. SeaCoast doesn't care about me and they never cared about those men. Both it and the parent company care only about maximizing profits and cutting losses regardless of the consequences. They need to be taught a lesson."

Ravich played along. The man was a fiddle in his hands.

"I give you my guarantee that, with your help, we will send those companies to school. A very expensive one, in fact."

The reference to money caused Slator to speak up. Now was the time.

"And I want something for me."

Ravich leaned back. He should have guessed it was too good to be true.

"Like what?"

"Some financial security. I lost my job over this. I'm almost fifty-seven. There aren't many jobs out there for people like me. I've been screwed over long enough. This time, I want to be paid for what I bring to the table."

Ravich sighed deeply, telegraphing he now had a problem. It was all part of the act.

"Now, of course, you can't be paid for your testimony unless you're acting as an expert witness. Luckily, you do qualify as one. Perhaps by casting you in that role I can allow you to bill me for your time."

"What can that earn me?"

Ravich had to be careful. He wasn't ready to offer full price and needed to find out what the seller was thinking.

"Oh, I don't know. Depending on how long this drags on, maybe you pocket forty, fifty-grand — all completely legitimate."

The *new* Ken Slator made an appearance.

"Legitimacy has gotten me nowhere. You stand to make millions with this evidence and maybe nothing without it. I should get something more."

"I can't share fees with a non-lawyer. It's against the law." Ravich delivered the line with indignation, proving to himself how good an actor he was.

"I don't care what you have to call it," Slator persisted. "Unless I'm taken care of, the evidence stays with me."

Ravich was not yet ready to give up the charade.

"Look, I understand your anger and position but don't take it out on me. You need to realize that either side can simply subpoena you to testify and produce the evidence. You'd then be forced to give it all away for nothing. At least I'm trying to make something work for you."

Slator took a deep breath. This was so unlike him. He had to be firm. There was nothing left but this opportunity. He had to make it work somehow.

"I'm sorry, but this is my only chance to start a new life." He played his ace. "If anyone tries to get me or the evidence for free they'll find my memory has suddenly failed me and that my things are gone."

Ravich was surprised but also a little impressed. Even the amateurs were beginning to figure out the con. *How do I best deal with this?* He began thinking.

An unlikely ally appeared, giving him a few more seconds to come up with a plan.

"Dudes, we close in like fifteen minutes."

The lazy employee had summoned the initiative to walk over and announce the end of his shift, hoping that his big-spending iced tea customer and the other guy would take the hint and leave.

"We're just wrapping up," Slator assured.

"Whatever," mumbled the young man, as he sauntered away.

"Look," Ravich began, "this is highly unorthodox and I'm reluctant to offer this because it violates my own high ethical standards, but here's what I'm willing to do."

He kept from laughing at his own words and leaned across the table, lowering his voice. He wasn't worried about the kid, he simply wanted the witness to think he was bending over backwards for him.

"I'll see to it that you're given a check, which won't be drawn on my firm's account, in exchange for turning the computer and phone over to me. I will still perform the necessary duplication, return a new phone and computer to you, and also formally retain you as a high-billing expert for the duration of the case. In short, I'll do everything I've already promised but will sweeten the deal with, let's call it a 'signing bonus.'"

"How much?"

"A hundred-grand. Anything more would be hard to explain to the IRS, don't you think?"

Slator knew it was a negotiation but was afraid to counter with a higher number. The comment about traceable income also worried him. He hadn't thought of that.

"Why not pay me in cash then?" He couldn't believe his own words. The events of the past week had him talking like a gangster.

"I can do that, but I have to know that the actual evidence confirms everything you just said. I mean, I can't just hand you a bag full of money and hope."

Ravich's mind was quick. He thought of a clever trick.

"So let's do this. Tomorrow, I'll send my most-trusted investigator, Ron, around to your house. He'll have a sealed envelope for you. Inside will be a check from one of my investment companies."

Slator looked confused.

"Don't worry, it's just a temporary safeguard for me. The check will be for one-hundred thousand dollars, payable to you. It will be postdated for Wednesday. You then give Ron the evidence and I'll have a chance to review and copy it on Tuesday. If it's not what you say, I will cancel the check. If it is — and I'm certain that it will be — Ron will return to your home Wednesday morning with your new laptop and phone, along with cash to replace the still undeposited check. We're then square and no paper record will exist of any unusual payment. I'll follow up with a letter of engagement hiring you as my expert witness. From that point on, you get to legitimately bill me for every second you spend on this case."

The transaction sounded funny but Slator's nerves were already frazzled. He didn't know why, but neither the man nor his proposal made him feel comfortable.

Ravich could sense such things. He had, after all, been reading the minds of reluctant jurors for years.

"Unless, of course, you want to show me the evidence tonight. I could follow you home or wherever you have it. We do it now and Ron will have cash for you in the morning when he takes possession. We wouldn't have to mess with a holding check."

"I don't want to make that kind of fuss. It's locked up in our home safe. My wife is at home and she's been through a lot recently. Our daughter recently died. We can wait and do it the other way tomorrow. She has an exercise class at noon. Maybe your guy can come around 12:30?"

"That's good thinking."

Ravich patted his palms down on the table, signaling that the deal was done, then thought of something else.

"One more important thing: should anyone contact you about the case, for any reason, put them off. Tell them nothing, especially don't mention this evidence or me. Let's protect things first before we take any of this public. All right?"

Slator nodded in agreement.

"Obviously, Ken, I'm on your side. Both you and your evidence will be safe with me. I need your testimony and the devices if I'm to see justice done. After all, that's really our primary motivation, right?"

Slator nodded again. But he was already beginning to wonder.

Harry Greenbaum sat in his office on Tuesday morning, busily thinking outside the box. It was something he had done exceptionally well for nearly fifty years. He ruminated over his newest case, trying to decide how best to begin the important task he had assigned to himself.

He had delegated the routine things to the young lawyers. They would get the lawsuit filed by close of business today. The initial pleading only had to be short and sweet, stating a gross negligence claim against SeaCoast and requesting service of process on the company's registered agent. The boys could handle that.

He had a bigger challenge: finding out what actually happened. Somebody screwed up. Someone was negligent. That much was certain. Old lawyers like him still used the phrase: *res ipsa loquitur,* Latin for "the thing speaks for itself." It was a commonsense and common law doctrine that inferred the breach of a legal duty by the *very nature* of the accident. In the absence of negligence, planes don't ordinarily fall from the sky and manufacturing plants don't just blow up.

But this was a much thornier case. Because SeaCoast was Dan Crouch's employer, he had to prove *more* than simple negligence. He had to show a wanton and reckless disregard for safety. It wasn't impossible — he had won gross negligence cases before — but it was damn hard to do without someone on the inside telling the jury how little the company cared.

Harry believed that most young trial lawyers relied too much on the rules of discovery to make their cases. They file suit, then send out a bunch of written discovery requests to the other side, trying to get a list of everyone who worked for the defendant and might possibly know anything. Next came the ridiculously time-wasting task of deposing every person named. Not surprisingly, those young by-the-book lawyers almost never learned much of anything helpful. By the time depositions started, the company lawyers had "wood-shedded" all their witnesses. That was Harry's descriptive phrase for pulling someone aside and telling them what to say and how to behave.

In the good old days, you just knocked on doors, smiled and asked questions, while hoping to stumble across a witness who could make your case. That was still the best way to do it, Harry figured. Other types of dinosaurs may be extinct, but this one wasn't. Harry Greenbaum was still winning cases the old way.

Ordinarily, Harry would have started with a visit to the union hall. They were often cooperative sources, willing to provide a list of employees who worked at a given site once they learned you were on the side of the worker victim. But he knew better this time. The only way Ravich could have gotten all those other cases so fast is with some organized help. He assumed it was from organized labor. If the union was in Ravich's pocket, he would get nowhere that route.

The old chess player was far from checkmated, however. It had already been a week since the explosion. He figured the government agency charged with enforcing employee-safety had begun an investigation. So he decided to call OSHA. He asked for an old friend.

"This is Bob," the voice answered, after the call was transferred to his extension.

"*The* Bob Edison, *the* champion of the working man and most-dedicated bureaucrat I know?"

He instantly recognized the silly flattery and distinctive voice. "Harry Greenbaum! To what do I owe this pleasure?"

"Well, my friend, I was considering retiring from this troubling business but unfortunately, like that movie gangster said: 'They keep pulling me back in.'"

Bob laughed. Like anyone who spent time around Greenbaum, it was hard not to like the man. And they had spent lots of time together. Bob Edison had been with the local OSHA office for almost twenty years, during which time Harry handled numerous cases arising out of workplace accidents that Edison had initially investigated. He had always appreciated the fact that Harry was the kind of lawyer who didn't just ask for information; many times, he also voluntarily shared the fruits of his own investigation to help the government conclude its statutory responsibilities. It was a small thing — reciprocity — but Edison had grown accustomed to, and weary of, the one-way street view held by most of the fancy plaintiff lawyers. Harry, on the other hand, never treated him like a government valet. Instead, the man went out of his way to show cooperative respect and admiration for the work that OSHA did.

"So, who is in trouble this time?" Edison asked.

"I have been requested to share my limited expertise as co-counsel for one of the tragic SeaCoast Chemical plant victims. I suspect your office is already on top of things?"

"Yeah, we've been out there for initial inspection along with the EPA. Not me personally. Like you, I'm getting too old to get my shoes dirty. But my guys report to me on the big ones. I'll be in charge of the final report and fine-assessments on that one."

"As it should be," Harry replied. "There's no better public official."

Edison chuckled. He never got tired of the old lawyer's style.

"Okay, I'm fully buttered and basted. What do you need?"

"Well, I was thinking that a highly competent government investigation would begin with acquiring an employee directory for that plant since it would constitute an inclusive list of everyone still alive who might know something about why this horrible event took place."

"We haven't asked for that but we could. Then again, so could you, right?"

"Well, yes and no. These tortfeasors for some reason don't like to voluntarily cooperate with me in my efforts to stick it to them. I'd have to file suit and send a formal request for production. Could take months. I'm old, Bob. Might not be around that long."

Edison laughed again. "You'll outlive us all. Only the good die young," he teased.

"Such words give me comfort in my twilight years, old friend. So, how about making that directory request for us today? Perhaps you could tell SeaCoast it's a routine item of production and that its prompt delivery might help expedite what otherwise could turn out to be a long and protracted government interference with their affairs."

"Maybe I'll just say I want it."

"Even better. A man of few words is wise."

"I'm looking at the schedule right now. One of my field men is supposed to go over there this morning to get copies of whatever shift and production records they still have left. I'm sure he's dealing with a company secretary or file clerk. They never show us much respect. I'll add your item to the request."

"So, I might be able to come over to your office and examine such document as early as this afternoon?"

"I'll get him back here by noon. Buy me lunch, and a copy is yours."

"Well, that would be swell," Greenbaum replied, sounding like someone from a fifties sitcom. "You are both a generous and efficient servant of the people, Bob. Why is it, you think, that so many citizens mistakenly believe our government isn't doing a good job?"

"They're the same folks who think lawyers like you are just in it for the money."

"True, so true. How are we to ever convince them otherwise? It's a tremendous cross to bear."

"I'll see you in a few hours, Harry. I'm in the mood for Chinese."

"Then let us hope our fortune cookies read: 'You will soon discover the unknown.'"

Bob Edison chucked and said goodbye. He loved that man.

———— ✺ ————

He had never used a Mac before, but it didn't take long to figure things out. Transferring files over a home network wasn't difficult for a man who had written a complex data relay program in his spare time. On

Tuesday, Ken Slator sat in the small study and joined the home wireless network with his PC laptop. It instantly showed up as a shared device on Joan's iMac. He compressed the DCSS relay program and all of its data into a zip file on his laptop, then copied it over to her desktop computer.

That left the phone and its voicemails. He looked at the tiny camera embedded at the top of the iMac. He knew it was used for video-chats. *Could it also make a video recording?* He did an internet search for a tutorial and quickly learned it would be amazingly simple.

He followed the clear online directions he found. Launching the Mac's QuickTime Player application, he selected *"New Movie Recording"* from its File Menu. The built-in camera came on and a window popped open. It displayed his face staring back at him in high-definition. A large red *Record* button sat at the bottom of the window. He clicked it with the mouse, then spoke: "Test, one, two, three." He clicked the *Stop* button, then played it back. It worked! The audio and video were crystal clear. He knew then what he wanted to do. He got up to retrieve another item he wanted to record.

He returned and repeated the steps, this time for keeps. He pressed *Record* and outlined the whole story — everything he knew. He spoke of the plant's stressed capacity, the pressure the company had placed on him and the men. He opened his laptop and adjusted the monitor on the iMac to video-capture the laptop's screen. He played back the DCSS data while narrating the significance of every entry.

He then held up his cell phone, turned up its volume keys, and played back all the messages he had saved from the night of the explosion, carefully displaying the date and time from the phone's message screen.

He concluded by detailing Finnegan's botched burglary, holding up the briefcase and its tools that he had fetched from his trunk. He ended by displaying for the camera the crumpled business card that was left inside.

He clicked on the *Stop* button. He pulled down the File Menu and selected *"Save As."* He thought about what to call the file. He named it *"Just In Case."* The title seemed appropriate.

He dragged the copied zip file and the digital movie into a folder he created within Joan's Home Folder on her iMac. He named that new folder *"Melissa."* Should anything happen to him, it would be a place she would eventually look. He added a small text file to the folder, which summarized the contents and their significance. Those old Apple commercials were right. The damn thing was incredibly easy to use.

He looked at his watch. Ravich's man with a check would be stopping by in a half hour for the laptop and phone.

Ken Slator felt a little silly for having gone to the trouble of backing things up. After all, Paul Ravich would want and need the evidence preserved even more than him. There would be plenty of duplicates by this time tomorrow.

He also didn't really fear for his personal safety. That had been subtle paranoia planted in his head by a crafty plaintiff's lawyer in order to make a deal. He was confident that Joan would never have to stumble upon the "*Melissa*" folder to get the story out.

But a lifetime of careful habits, combined with a recently acquired suspicion of everyone and everything, made it seem like the right thing to do. He left the study and placed the two devices on the table in the entry foyer. They were ready for delivery. All he had to do now was wait.

———— ∞∞∞ ————

They beat Ravich to the courthouse. Bill Gaston checked the county's computerized filing records before handing the suit papers and filing fee to the intake clerk. There had been no recent cases filed against SeaCoast or Thornton Industries. In *Crouch v. SeaCoast Chemical Corporation*, Doug was listed as the attorney-in-charge with Gaston and Greenbaum as co-counsel. The suit alleged gross negligence and sought punitive damages.

The clerk took the pleading and date stamped the first page: "*3:48 p.m. - Tuesday, October 22.*" Theirs would be the first-filed case. It was a tactical move.

Clever old Harry Greenbaum explained the strategy in yesterday's meeting. According to long-standing practice, whenever multiple cases involving the same incident landed in different courts, the judge with the earliest filed case was given the responsibility to rule on all motions to consolidate. If the motion was granted, the later-filed cases would then be transferred to that court.

Neither Doug nor Bill had ever heard of such rule, which was understandable. It wasn't written down anywhere, it was just the way things were done. According to Harry, it was a simple rule of comity worked out among the county's judges decades ago to prevent intramural squabbles over which judge was best qualified to preside over merged cases. The current occupiers of the bench followed the obscure rule only out of respect for tradition. "Judges are like that," Harry had explained, as if describing the known traits of a particular breed of dog.

Of course, there was no guarantee they would draw a friendly judge by simply filing first. But it was at least a proactive attempt to avoid winding up in a court that was clearly in Ravich's pocket. Harry had named off four judges he called "crooks who would do anything for Paul Ravich." His warning was clear: "He owns Judges Roberts, Carlton, Lewis, and

Fegan. We better hope we draw someone else."

Gaston had discussed his earlier idea of pleading the case with odd legal theories to make any consolidation less likely. Harry summarily dismissed the notion, calling it "peeing into the prevailing wind" if Ravich beat them to the courthouse and drew one of his cronies. "And he *will* draw one of his black-robed devils," Harry had warned, "because he owns the intake clerk too. She's driving a car won at one of his Christmas parties." The insight the old man had was priceless. It was worth more than a third of any fee.

The intake clerk punched the F10 key on her keyboard to bring up a computer-randomized court for assignment. *The way it's done for everyone but Ravich,* thought Gaston, as he watched the process. She then grabbed a rubber stamp and slammed it down on the blank line in the case caption, the place where the court's number would now be typed on all subsequent papers filed in the case.

"127th District - The Honorable Robert Hinojosa," she blandly announced with all the enthusiasm one would expect from a constantly bored file clerk.

Gaston smiled. They had dodged the first bullet.

⸎

As power-plays go, this one was pretty big. Charles Thornton, looking irritated, sat beside his General Counsel in the lobby of Paul Ravich & Associates. The wealthiest man in the city had left the skyscraper that bore his name to attend a meeting on the other side of downtown with someone he considered an ambulance-chaser.

Ravich had assured Bruce Waltman that the Wednesday morning session was critically important and would be well worth their time. He also insisted it take place at his office. He blamed his overbooked schedule but that wasn't the real reason. What Ravich intended to propose required a room he knew was secure. The fact that Waltman agreed to the location was evidence that they were scared. The fact that Thornton didn't throw a fit was the first indication of possible interest.

Ravich went against pattern this time. He didn't make them wait. Marching from his office and entering the office lobby, he greeted his guests enthusiastically. "I'm Paul Ravich. Thank you both for coming."

Tentative handshakes were made. He planned to take them back to his private meeting room, adjacent to his office. Unlike the main conference room, it had no audiovisual equipment built into the walls. He needed Thornton to feel comfortable he wasn't being recorded.

There was also a second reason for meeting back there. It gave both invitees a full opportunity to survey his long wall of framed accomplishments and connections. Ravich intentionally stopped in the middle of the hallway.

"I'm sorry, did my receptionist offer you gentlemen some coffee?"

He noticed Waltman glancing at the framed judgments. Charles Thornton was pretending to be unimpressed. In truth, he was making a mental note: *It might be good to have a few more self-tributes hanging outside my place.* The two magazine covers that flanked Thornton's office now seemed inadequate.

"We're fine, thanks," replied Waltman.

Ravich played a second card.

"I see you were looking at the Judgment in the *Carlyle* case. It was only for twenty-eight million but paying that award eventually bankrupted that little company." He looked directly at Charles Thornton. "I can't imagine one of my verdicts toppling a much bigger corporation, like yours, but you never know."

Waltman rolled his eyes. Thornton showed no reaction but appreciated the chutzpah. *The man's got balls,* he thought.

"So, anyway, please follow me."

They soon settled into the comfortable leather chairs of Ravich's private conference room, the two visitors trying to appear disinterested. Ravich always got a kick out of seeing the poker faces of his opponents. It was all part of the game: never come to a meeting looking anxious to make a deal.

"First, I appreciate your coming over here, Mr. Thornton. As I told your General Counsel, I would not have suggested it unless I was absolutely certain you would have a direct interest in what I'm about to tell you."

"Then get to it," Thornton snapped back.

Ravich was unfazed. But he was about to unsettle Bruce Waltman completely.

"Very well. But it would be best if I discussed this with you alone."

Waltman became apoplectic, as expected.

"Are you insane?" he shouted. "He's not going to talk or listen without his counsel present. What's wrong with you?"

"Look, Bruce — if I may call you by your first name? — I don't mean any disrespect to you. But what I intend to propose is a *business* deal. It has certain aspects which you're better off not being privy to, as Mr. Thornton will clearly attest once he has heard me out. It's for your own good."

Waltman turned to his boss. "Charles, this is madness. I'm not leaving you alone to talk to this jackal."

He was just doing his job. Protecting his client; his company. But something about Waltman's tone struck Charles Thornton wrong. He didn't need any employee to safeguard him or provide instruction on what he could or couldn't say. Thornton was also intrigued by Ravich. *A cocky son-of-a-bitch*, just like him, who was cool as a cucumber while his company's head lawyer was coming unglued.

"Calm down, Bruce," Thornton directed. "I'll give him ten minutes of my time." He glared at Ravich. "And it had better be worth it." He looked back at his GC. "Now, go on outside and look at all his pictures. See if you can count all the famous people this shyster knows."

Ravich grinned. He wasn't insulted at all. The gambit had worked. He gave an innocent shrug to Bruce Waltman, a gesture saying: "What can you do?" It was meant to imply sympathy for the General Counsel's plight. Everyone has to deal with stubborn clients once in a while.

Waltman felt demeaned. He also didn't trust Ravich any more than he would a coiled cobra. "Charles, this is a huge mistake, we should…"

"Leave, Bruce. I can handle this guy."

Waltman knew he had no choice. He got up. Men like Charles Thornton occasionally follow advice but they never follow direction.

"I'll be right outside," he said, defeated. He decided to exit like a lawyer instead of a whipping boy. As he stood holding the door, he pointed a finger at Ravich. "I'll allow this only if you promise you will not seek any statement or evidence from this man regarding the incident. Not one question."

Ravich raised three fingers of his right hand in salute.

"Scout's honor," he replied, with a toothy grin.

The door slammed and he was gone.

"You're not going to intimidate me, so don't try," Thornton cautioned, when they were finally alone.

"I understand that, sir. Believe me, that's not my intent. Since you have limited our time, let me get straight to the point. I now have in my possession direct and irrefutable evidence that proves what happened at your fertilizer plant last week."

Thornton's facial expression remained fixed.

"Computer records, Mr. Thornton, which conclusively prove that someone employed by SeaCoast Chemical intentionally turned off the facility's automatic safety system at a time when the plant was in a highly dangerous state. And they did it due to pressures from management to increase production."

"No computers survived that explosion. Bruce confirmed that to me last Wednesday. And, as I understand it, both you and those government idiots have already been out there and seen the destruction. So don't waste my time."

He got up to leave.

"You might want to give me my remaining nine minutes."

"You're bluffing," he huffed.

"I can bluff, sure. But good trial lawyers and executives, like great poker players, never bluff when they don't have to. I have a source that can both authenticate and explain these records which were generated daily as a data backup for the plant. They're more than a smoking gun, sir, and they will be marked as 'Plaintiffs' Exhibit 1' unless we come to an understanding."

Thornton was furious. He wasn't used to being the victim of a shakedown.

"I won't be blackmailed, you little prick."

"Sir, blackmail is when someone attempts to extort money for their gain to another's detriment. If you'll just sit down and hear me out, I'm about to propose something entirely different: a gain-gain, a win-win, for each of us. Mr. Thornton, this isn't blackmail, it's a business proposal."

Thornton returned to the table but didn't sit down. Instead, he rested his burly hands on the top of the leather chair and leaned over to dominate the trial lawyer sitting across from him.

"So what? Even if you prove that some plant flunky screwed up and killed a bunch of workers, you can't hurt us. I've learned a good bit about your type of law this past week. As their employer, SeaCoast has immunity from suit."

"Very good! That's exactly true. Unless, of course, you're guilty of gross negligence. Which ordinarily is very hard to prove. I mean, what company just up and says: 'I don't give a damn, kill 'em if you have to,' right?"

Thornton didn't blink.

"Which brings me to 'Plaintiffs' Exhibit 2.' I also have a voicemail documenting a troubling order from company management to the man in the control room that night. This will be hard to explain away, Mr. Thornton. It turns out that the SeaCoast President himself gave the directive to override the safety system which left the plant running out-of-control. The explosion happened a little more than an hour later."

"Bullshit! Even that numb-nuts isn't that stupid."

"One would think. But again, I can fully prove and authenticate that the conversation took place."

"Then why haven't you already sued us? Gone on TV to read the indictment or whatever you bastards call it? I understand you like publicity. So why all this private disclosure? Did you actually think I'd come in here and dump a sack of money on the table just because you stumbled onto some helpful evidence?"

"No, sir. I'm interested in someone else's money."

Ravich paused for a moment to let the seemingly absurd statement soak in. Thornton's anger-flushed face changed to a look of surprise.

"Now, please, if you'll just sit back down, I would like to outline a very nice way for both you and me to make money off this unfortunate event."

That got his attention. Thornton pulled out a chair and flopped into it. "You have another five minutes."

"Thank you. The reason I asked your counsel to step outside is because my plan is — Oh, how should I put this? — let's just say my idea is *novel*. And maybe a wee bit outside what most lawyers might consider proper. But that's why other lawyers struggle and I don't."

Ravich placed his elbows on the table and pressed his palms together, forming an arrow with his index fingers which he now pointed at the corporate titan.

"You see, Mr. Thornton, I have no interest in pursuing SeaCoast on a gross negligence claim. The burden of proof is way too high and the law only allows me to recover a punitive damage award on such a theory. I'd get a big verdict for sure with this evidence, but thirty or forty million is about all your bought-and-paid-for, right-wing state supreme court would ever let me keep on appeal. My third of that would be a nice payday but nothing to write home about. Of course, handling it that way would also mean your company gets trashed in court and in the media for their very stupid and bad behavior. Even worse, you have to write that check. You ask me, neither one of us ends up all that happy."

Charles Thornton wasn't showing it but he was starting to appreciate the man's style.

"You ever gone elk hunting, Mr. Thornton?"

He suddenly changed his mind. The fool was now getting off-topic. Thornton shook his head no and made a face indicating he wasn't interested in small talk.

"I bring it up because we're like a couple of elk bulls, you and I. You see, when mating season comes, the DNA of a male elk compels him to attack any other bull that comes sniffing around his herd of ladies. The two bulls end up locking horns, wasting a lot of time and energy that could've been better spent in cooperation. If they only had the capacity to think things over, it might dawn on them that since the herd of females is so damn large, they could both have more fun than either could possibly handle. But the bulls just can't make that agreement because of their DNA."

He paused to emphasize his point.

"Of course, my trial lawyer DNA makes me to want to charge at you. And you, with your corporate DNA, would obviously like to see plaintiff lawyers like me gored. But we're both thinking men, Mr. Thornton, not dumb animals. We can act like the elk or we can be smarter, and both get satiated."

Thornton raised an eyebrow and Paul Ravich noticed. He missed nothing. He knew at that moment he had an interested party sitting across from him. Another couple of minutes and he would have his co-conspirator.

A knock on the door was immediately followed by the head of Bruce Waltman, interrupting to make sure things were all right.

"Get out," Thornton barked, and the door closed again.

Ravich smiled. He had found an aggressive elk bull that, for once, was maybe willing to share.

In a far less impressive-looking office, far more legitimate maneuvers were also taking place. Harry Greenbaum sat at his desk, working the SeaCoast plant directory like a telemarketer. Bob Edison had given him the copy yesterday at lunch. It was easily worth the cost of the House-Special Lo Mein they had shared.

Harry made some calls the night before but hadn't gotten far. He only reached a couple of men, calling their home numbers listed in the employee directory. One worker said he didn't have shift duty that day and the only thing he could say for sure was "the plant had been going full tilt and harder than ever." The second worker he reached said he hated his employer but would still have to clear it with his bosses before talking to anybody. Harry was always amazed by such loyalty. Even a dog will quit licking you if you mistreat it enough.

He continued his logical selection method with his Wednesday morning calls. He had obviously crossed off the names of the victims. He would also skip the company president and the man whose title was "Head of Process Engineering." Those with the highest-ranking jobs were always the least likely to be a cooperative witness for the other side. Instead, he called the employees who — at least based on the job descriptions — had the entry level positions. Those people were usually the most junior and most willing to talk.

Most calls went unanswered. Maybe SeaCoast had put them back to work sweeping up the mess. Regardless of the reason, he knew better than to leave a daytime message on any answering machines. The best way to catch important facts is from an unguarded witness who wasn't prepared to hear from you.

He did finally speak to a man named Wally Brinkman, who said he had worked the day shift on the date of the explosion. Mr. Brinkman was Harry's type of guy. The only question he cared to ask before spilling his beans had been: "Who's you client?" Once he was told that it was Dan Crouch's widow, Wally became a little chatterbox.

"Dan was good people," he began.

The country compliment told Greenbaum they had been friends.

Wally gave the complete rundown. He told Harry how the plant was "bustin' at the seams" trying to complete a huge order for export. He described the hazards associated with making ammonium nitrate fertilizer and said it was left up to the head man, Ken Slator, to see that things ran safe.

"Well, it looks like Mr. Slator wasn't there when it happened or he would have also been a victim, I guess?" Harry said, hoping to coax further details.

"That's right. He was strictly a day shift man. Dave Phillips and Al Harris were his other supervisors. Dave was working the evening shift that night. Had the thing blown up an hour later, it would have been Harris killed instead of Dave."

"So Mr. Harris and Mr. Slator seem like the boys who might know best what could have gone wrong?"

"Yep, I guess so. Al's good people too. He'll probably talk to you."

"I guess Mr. Slator would be too much the management type to want to speak to somebody like me, huh?"

"Maybe not. My wife and me took a casserole over to Dave Phillips' house day before yesterday. You know, just trying to help the widow out some. She said she talked to Slator last Sunday and he told her he up and quit. He don't work for SeaCoast anymore."

Harry felt a rush of excitement course through his tired old veins. If a man in charge quits so soon after so devastating an event, he probably had a good reason. More importantly, he would probably be willing to talk about it.

Harry quickly wrapped up with the very helpful Mr. Brinkman.

"I want to thank you, sir, for your kindness in talking with me today. I'll see that Mrs. Crouch is told what a good friend Dan had in you."

"You don't have to do nothing like that, but I appreciate it, and good luck with whatever you have to do."

Harry thanked him again and said he would be back in touch at a later time. He hung up, reaching for a well-worn copy of the White Pages he kept inside his roll top desk. Harry wasn't too keen on using "the Internets," as he referred to the technology that changed the world for everyone but him. The phone book was several years old but served him just fine. He figured most folks don't move too often so there wasn't much need for a current volume. He found a listing for a Ken and Joan Slator, although the phone number didn't match the man's listing in the SeaCoast directory. It didn't matter. He was looking for a home address anyway, not some number to call.

Now and again, you need to put the boat in the water, as Harry liked to say. When you want to catch a big fish, you have to be willing to row yourself out to his hole.

The details were as explicit as they were illegal. Paul Ravich continued his private meeting with Charles Thornton, explaining it all to an attentive listener. It was a complex scheme, with lots of moving parts. It was the kind of deal that Thornton loved. Ravich outlined it precisely, without hesitation, pausing only to answer Thornton's entirely appropriate questions.

First, acting as the business agent for, and not as the lawyer of, the witness who owned all the damning evidence, Ravich would accept a wire transfer on the man's behalf into a Ravich-controlled Swiss account. The amount: six-million dollars. Thornton's payment — which he could paper any way he needed to disguise its real purpose — would assure that the witness would never testify in any trial or investigation and would guarantee that the real evidence would never be seen.

"Who is this witness?" Thornton asked.

"I can't reveal that for obvious reasons."

"I could probably figure it out."

"That's probably true," Ravich countered. "But it wouldn't make any difference."

"I'd have to see this evidence first."

"Fine, but know that if you do, you might have to testify later that you never did. Can you do that?"

"I could swear to anything if it makes or saves me money."

Ravich grinned. The man was, as he had guessed, a corruptible tyrant — just like him.

"Fair enough."

Ravich reached under the table and pulled out the laptop. He launched the program and played back the recorded data, explaining its significance as Slator had detailed it to him. Thornton may not have understood all the entries and figures but he quickly recognized it for what it was: an incredibly precise record of his company screwing up.

"What about this voicemail evidence?"

Ravich pulled from his suit jacket a small digital voice recorder that contained a copy of Dave Phillips' last message to Slator. He hit play, knowing that the recipient's name was never mentioned. Thornton listened as a now dead SeaCoast employee related the order from his subsidiary's president to turn off the safety system. He curled his lip in disgust. *Rob Finnegan was indeed an idiot.*

Charles Thornton, however, was not.

"So, let's say I agree it's in my interest to do this deal. I give you the money. Then what? There's nothing that keeps your witness, or you, from just taking the cash and still releasing the evidence afterwards. No offense, counsel, but I don't trust you or your mystery man."

"Excellent observations. As for the witness, I will provide you with irrefutable proof, within forty-eight hours of my receipt of funds, that he will never renege on the deal. I won't explain how I will do that, but if you don't find the proof sufficient you can have the money back."

"Which means again I have to trust. And I don't. What keeps *you* from breaking the deal? You could steal my money and still sue me, since I assume we're not putting any of this in writing."

"But I'm a man of my word. I would never do that," Ravich assured him, smiling.

Thornton scoffed. "I'm going to need a hell of a lot more than *your* promise."

"Which brings me to the next part of our arrangement," Ravich responded, eager to pitch the larger prize. "The only way to absolutely protect yourself against my later deciding to harm you is to completely align our interests."

"I don't follow."

"Bear with me, please. It's really pretty simple. I become *your* lawyer in this case."

Thornton sneered. "You might have a little bit of a conflict there, counsel."

"Right now I do but in a few days I won't. You see, once you buy this evidence, you have only purchased protection from an adverse judgment. That's a good thing, of course, but it hardly recoups anything for you. But what if this evidence could also be *changed*? Imagine what might happen if this computer record was altered to prove something altogether different. Do you know how much better the outcome could be for you if this data revealed the safety system *malfunctioned* as opposed to having been intentionally bypassed?"

"What difference would that make? My people or my equipment. Either way, I get the blame."

"No, you don't. This safety system was designed, installed, and sold to SeaCoast eighteen months ago by another company. A company that owed a legal duty to provide a non-defective product. A company that I have already looked into. Ever heard of Integrated Sentry, Inc?"

"Nope."

"Me either. But I learned they are a wholly owned subsidiary of VyStream Corporation. Heard of them?"

Thornton's ears perked up. VyStream was huge, with a market cap close to GE.

"I'm listening," he said, gleaning a sense of where things were going but unsure of the details. "But I don't understand why you want to go to the trouble of altering evidence. Why commit fraud if you don't have to?"

Ravich was happy to provide the answer.

"Let's assume for the sake of argument that we met here today so I could tell you that evidence was discovered proving that a third-party vendor was responsible for blowing up your plant and killing your people. That I, and only I, could prove it wasn't your fault at all. What would a man like you say in response to that?"

"Thanks, I guess."

Ravich laughed. "No, here's what you would say and do. You would hold a press conference, when I say the time is right, to announce that a joint investigation by your company and the counsel for the victims has revealed the cause of the disaster, and the true culprit was a faulty and defective safety system that SeaCoast recently purchased from another company."

"Okay, so?"

"Wait, you're not done talking. You would also say at this press conference that even though SeaCoast was not responsible for their deaths, the families of your dear employee-victims need help now, which is why you're announcing a voluntary payment of ten-million dollars to be divided equally among my clients. Since the payment is nothing more than a gratuitous and compassionate gesture, the families will still have both their workers compensation claim rights as well as the power to seek full compensation from the third-party company now responsible. Of course, you won't need to mention that SeaCoast received full releases from my clients protecting you against any future gross negligence or other liability claim they might have otherwise asserted."

"So far, all I hear is *you* making money. What's in it for me?"

"Ah, the best part," Ravich beamed. "Guess who'll be standing next to you at that press conference?"

Thornton was tired of playing twenty questions.

"Why don't you just tell me?"

"Me! When you get done, I look into the camera and say that because I agree that SeaCoast isn't at fault, and since your company is making such a noble effort to provide temporary help to my desperately hurting clients, I will not take a single penny of fee from your money that has been so graciously volunteered to them."

"And you'll do that because?"

"Because it helps my 'good-guy' image. And because you still have one last thing you need to say."

Ravich leaned forward.

"You're also going to announce that in recognition of his investigative efforts and desire to pursue only those truly responsible, you have decided to retain Paul Ravich to represent SeaCoast in its own and separate claim against the defective product maker, where damages for your destroyed plant, lost inventory, and profits will be sought."

"It's still all about you."

"No, sir, quite the contrary. You stand to recoup all your losses which my expert, who visited the site, estimates will easily be between three-hundred and five-hundred million dollars. Think about it. Instead of *paying* out a big damage award, you get to *earn* a huge one. For the small upfront investment of sixteen million — ten to my clients and six more to my witness — you get to be the biggest victim, reaping the biggest windfall. Oh, and of course, I should mention that I will receive, on the back-end, a fee payment of twenty percent of whatever I recover for you from Integrated Sentry and VyStream. Do the math, Mr. Thornton. It's a no-brainer for both of us."

"And you also get to make money off the victims' claims against this VyStream company?"

Ravich nodded yes with a sly smile and widened eyes.

"You're a greedy little bastard, I'll give you that."

"I prefer to say I'm just an opportunistic elk bull, like you."

Ravich wanted to make sure his potential partner understood the high stakes.

"Look, outside that door are file cabinets full of decent cases, each of them making me a million here, a million there, off individual human tragedy. But a life is worth only so much, Mr. Thornton, and no death or injury case is as lucrative as a big property damage claim that involves rebuilding a chemical plant and recouping its lost profits."

He stared at Thornton with stony eyes, knowing that what he was about to say would make sense to a business mogul with a reputation for playing hardball when it came to money.

"I'm not willing to commit a crime for six or even ten-million dollars, sir. But if we do this deal, I stand to make in fee at least that much from the victims' cases against Integrated Sentry, and another hundred million from your property damage claim. At that price, I think a few rules can be broken."

"You can't represent us and the victims, can you? Isn't that a direct conflict?"

"Not once we all agree there's only one target. Everyone's interests will then be identical. We all have the same common goal of making our new deep-pocket defendant pay for what they did to all of us. My clients will sign off. They obviously will be told nothing other than what the press hears. I'll be their hero and you won't be very far behind. We'll all just march together, singing *Kumbaya*, holding hands, seeking the same justice."

Thornton was impressed. *This goddamn ambulance-chaser is as smart and devious as me.* He made a face to indicate he was mulling it over but he liked it. It could work.

Ravich surveyed the man's expressions and felt certain he had won another important argument. But just to make sure, he put his hand on Slator's now closed laptop.

"I probably don't even need to add this point, but I will. At the beginning, you expressed concern about my possibly betraying you later with what's inside this incredible machine. Those fears are now neatly overcome by our little deal don't you think? After all, it would be very much against my own large financial interest to ever let the *real* evidence see the light of day, wouldn't it?"

"How are you going to pull that off? Change the records, reinvent the facts?"

"That, kind sir, is not your worry. But it is my specialty. Like the Good Book says: 'Thy will be done.'"

Thornton nodded. He admired a cocky willingness to do whatever is necessary. It was, after all, how he had made his money. But he still had a question. "How much can Waltman know?"

He was already talking to Ravich as if he was his lawyer. That was a good sign.

"What we discussed here today is obviously criminal. I'd go to jail and lose my license. If that happens, you're going to be my cellmate. Waltman is just an employee of yours. As a lawyer, he also has an ethical obligation to report any evidence alteration or false testimony that he knows about. I can't tell you how to run your business, Mr. Thornton, but I would think it's in our mutual best interest to keep him in the dark."

"That's why you wanted him to leave."

"Precisely. The initial wire-transfer payment from you to me has to be completely outside your company. No trace, no record for Waltman to find. Everything else you ought to be able to publicly spin as reasonable actions that you alone decided are good for both your company and the people who were harmed. Is convincing your General Counsel of that going to be a problem?"

"If it is, I'll fire his ass."

Ravich slid over a piece of paper with five lines of information.

"Good, here's the routing information you need."

Thornton folded it and tucked the paper away in his coat pocket.

"When my foreign bank confirms receipt of the six million, I'll know we have a contract. Today is best, Thursday at the latest. I'll then start on my promises. If you change your mind, this conversation never happened. I'll then be left with no choice but to file suit against SeaCoast and, using the real evidence, make your life as uncomfortable as I possibly can. Of course, I would also testify that I spent all our time alone here today trying to get you to settle but that you were just too damn stubborn. Now that we're friends, I would hate to do and say things like that."

Thornton smirked. *This bastard could be my twin,* he thought. "One last question: How do you make sure this witness of yours never flips and tells the truth?"

"On that point, Mr. Thornton, you now have something in common with your in-house lawyer standing outside that door. There are just some things you can't be told."

Chapter 12
Crossing Lines

The rules don't apply to me.

It takes time for the mind to accept such a bold premise. Except in the case of the sociopathic criminal, where such conceit instinctively drives bad behavior, it requires years of not being punished before such a delusion becomes an accepted truth.

But Paul Ravich believed it for a reason. A career of manipulated triumph without reprimand was proof enough. He had gotten everything he wanted — fame, wealth, reputation — by bending, breaking, and ignoring rules that stood in his way.

The sad irony was he didn't have to. His natural talents alone were guarantors of success. A person with a pleasant smile and razor-sharp brain, who can read and influence people while waging intellectual war with ruthless determination, is destined to be a great trial lawyer. He could have won his cases by playing it straight. But he saw no fun in doing what any talented and hardworking lawyer could also do. He was different. He was special. He was better. The egotism that made him bold became the flaw that made him reckless.

If there were two ways of doing something, easy and correct or devious and difficult, he would often choose the latter. It was more of a sport playing dirty, requiring extra effort to achieve a goal in ways that others could not. It had always been that way for him. Although he was inevitably the smartest kid in the class, he cheated on tests in both high school and college that could have been easily passed with little study. In law school, he paid another student to research and write his article for the school's prestigious Law Review. He never got caught and so the thought became fact: *the rules don't apply to me.*

In the practice of law, there are countless opportunities to game the system if you're so disposed and Paul Ravich certainly was. Case-running, evidence fabrication, bought witnesses and judges were all examples. You had to be clever to get away with things like that. The law is an institution grounded in principles of fairness and order. Those who make the laws go to great lengths creating safeguards that protect the system from manipulation. The people who make the rules are bright. You have to be brilliant to break them without getting caught.

Crimes that go unpunished embolden the wrongdoer. If you cheat a little on your taxes without consequence, pretty soon you don't pay any at all. If you can shoplift without getting caught, why not go for the cash register next time? Prisons are full of dumb convicts who didn't know when to stop, whose escalating crimes finally became their downfall. But Paul Ravich wasn't dumb. His dishonest schemes, like his ego, grew exponentially along with his reputation and bank account. By the time he got the *SeaCoast* cases, he was certain he could get away with anything. *The rules don't apply to me.*

But this was clearly the next level. Fraud, bribery, and other financial crimes — hidden deep within a bustling law practice — had made him rich. They were all felonies, just like the one he was now contemplating. Yet this crime was worse.

He once paid a potential defense witness two-hundred thousand dollars to change his name and disappear for awhile. It made his case. Deprived of key testimony, the other side had to fold. The resulting settlement netted him over a million dollars in fee, even after subtracting that large and nondeductible case expense. Now, he needed another witness to disappear. It was just another crime, but the dividend this time was much greater. So much so he couldn't trust this latest witness to just go away until the coast was clear. For a million bucks, he had accepted that kind of risk. For a hundred-million dollars, give or take, there was no way he could.

The scheme he hatched and sold to Charles Thornton would easily make him that kind of money. It would be a record verdict or settlement and, like the explosion itself, it would be heard for miles and talked about forever. All it required was a little manipulation of the facts.

The plant had to blow up due to third-party equipment malfunction instead of first-party stupidity. It had to be the fault of Integrated Sentry instead of SeaCoast Chemical. His I.T. employee, a computer geek with connections, had already put his trusted investigator Ron in touch with independent computer programmers in India. The geek didn't have to be told why. The foreign programmers could alter Slator's DCSS data to prove what Ravich needed. Everyone over there would be told they were only altering a backup copy, not the actual original. They would accept the cover story that the program's owner wanted to illustrate a DCSS design failure so it could be used for training purposes. A realistic doomsday simulator, if you will, to show future plant operators what a major safety system malfunction would look like. The contracted programmers would buy the ruse. It sounded like something an American company would waste money doing. They would enjoy the challenge and appreciate the cash money. Most importantly, the tech-guys in Mumbai would remain far outside the jurisdiction and subpoena power of the court where *SeaCoast Chemical v. Integrated Sentry* would be tried. That part of the equation was going to be easy. Making a computer say what you want isn't really all that hard.

The harder part was the breathing witness. Ken Slator wanted revenge on SeaCoast. He made that point emphatically clear. He would never go along with a scheme making his former employer the ultimate beneficiary of the disaster. He also didn't strike Ravich as the kind of guy whose false testimony could be bought. Perjury has its price but some people just aren't in the market. Instead of being the all-knowing hero who could explain what happened, Ken Slator was now the knows-too-much witness gumming up his master plan.

It was only a slight escalation of criminality in his mind. To a lawyer who once relocated a damaging witness without repercussion, it was a short leap to send another one away for good. Both were necessary acts for the good of a case. Both were felonies. It didn't really matter if one was bribery and one was murder.

After all, the rules didn't apply to him.

Ravich's lead investigator, Ron Carroll, was used to performing unusual and questionable tasks for his boss. He served as the coordinator of the firm's illegal case-running program. He was also the bag man when someone had to be paid off. His talents were many. He knew how to get a witness to sign a false statement. He could make physical evidence appear or disappear, depending on need. His years as a detective gave him long tentacles within law enforcement. He could access police records and confidential files when necessary. He was, in short, the buffer between Ravich's sinister ideas and their execution.

A man like that is valuable and Ravich knew when to pay full price. Ron earned a lawyer's salary as base compensation and large bonuses were frequent, especially whenever his questionable conduct produced a favorable result. Ravich treated him with both generosity and respect, and was repaid with the kind of loyalty you would expect from a former officer in Delta Force, where taking care of your own at any cost is rule number one. Ron would do anything for him. In his mind, they were fellow soldiers but in a different kind of war: Ravich against the world.

Ron's assignment this Wednesday afternoon was to go back to the home of Ken Slator, the place where he had been the day before to pick up the man's computer and cell phone. He now had three things to return: a different phone, a replacement computer, and cash.

The new phone came with a new number. He was to tell Slator that was necessary to make sure no one accidentally erased the critical voicemails still on the original now in Ravich's safe.

The new computer was a nice one, and Ron was told to sit down and demonstrate to Slator's satisfaction that all his files had been copied to it from the original, including the very important DCSS data. What Ron would not be saying is that the shiny new laptop's hard drive also contained a worm program that would launch itself in forty-eight hours and begin a secure erase of every single byte and bit that wasn't part of the laptop's basic operating software. The firm's I.T. guy installed it after being told it was a necessary security measure to assure compliance with a court's protective order in a case where confidential documents produced by a defendant could be examined, but not kept, by the plaintiff's expert. Ron had come up with that jewel of a lie. It had sounded reasonable to the geek and he was never told the name of the fictitious case or the identity of the made-up expert.

The cash was one-hundred thousand dollars in non-sequential hundreds. Ron had specific instructions for that too. He was to hand it over only after first retrieving the envelope and check left by him the day before. Next, he was to tell Slator to not deposit the money in a lump sum or even large increments to avoid questions arising as to its source. He was to suggest that Slator put it, for now, in his home safe and keep it there for a few weeks before spending any. Just to be sure.

As black-op missions go, this one was pretty tame. It went off without a hitch. Ken Slator was a nice guy the day before and again today, even though he appeared a little nervous at first. He seemed to understand the necessity of a new mobile phone number and appeared satisfied with his inspection of the new laptop, saying it looked like "everything was still there." He was, by that time, so foolishly trusting that he didn't even care as Ron watched him open his little safe in the floor of the study cabinet and deposit the money inside.

As Ron started to leave, he carried out another of Ravich's instructions. "Oh, Mr. Slator, I nearly forgot. My boss needs you to come down to his office tomorrow evening if you can. Unfortunately, it has to be pretty late.

He's traveling on another case and won't get back in town until almost eleven."

Slator was caught off-guard. *Why do I have to come in, and why then?* "I don't understand" he said.

"I'm not a lawyer, but the way Mr. Ravich explained it to me was he needs to obtain a sworn videotaped statement from you about the computer to authenticate its contents. All you have to do is answer a few questions to establish that the plant data is accurate and was kept by you in the regular course of your business with SeaCoast. It's one of those evidence-technicality things, I guess."

"Then why can't it wait until another time? That's pretty late at night, you know."

"I know, believe me, I do. Mr. Ravich said he was very sorry to ask you to do this but he needs that taped statement and a signed affidavit right away so he can use them in some motion he wants to file on Friday morning to make sure that both the evidence and you stay protected."

"I guess I could," Slator responded, with confused hesitation. "If he thinks it's really necessary."

"He does. Also, he wanted me to stress that until we have everything nailed down, you have to keep all this just between us. I don't just mean the money. Don't let anyone know about the evidence or the time, place, or purpose of this upcoming meeting. We don't want to give the other side any chance to connect the dots and prevent our efforts to protect you. You understand?"

Slator nodded. Were it not for Finnegan's burglary, he would have seen no need for such secrecy or urgency. But now he couldn't be sure. These guys obviously knew best.

"If you could arrive at 11:30, he should be back and waiting for you," Ron added, before giving him the firm's address and describing the downtown tower.

Slator knew the building. It was a signature tower in the city's skyline, one of the tallest downtown.

"How do I get in? I'm sure the building's locked up by that time of night."

Ron handed him a magnetic key card.

"Here, use this. I can get another. It's my employee access card. It will get you into the parking lot and through the building entry doors. It also activates the elevators after-hours. Just take the one that goes to the sixty-third floor and you step right out into our offices. We'll see you from the conference room. The meeting should only take an hour or so."

"Will anyone from SeaCoast be there?"

"No, of course not. I think that's why he wants to do this, so you won't have to confront them in person for a while."

Slator once again accepted at face value whatever Ron said.

"Anyway, Mr. Ravich wanted me to apologize for putting you out like this, and to tell you he wouldn't have asked for so late a meeting if it could have been avoided."

"Okay, I'll be there."

Ron started to turn and leave, then remembered one last detail. "Oh, by the way, Mr. Slator, I'm supposed to take back that envelope I left with you yesterday."

Slator reached in his back pocket and handed over the "holding check" that had now been replaced with cash, just as Ravich had promised. Ron tucked the envelope into his jacket, before offering some parting words.

"Hey, I know it's none of my business, but Mr. Ravich also mentioned to me that you just lost a daughter. I just want to say how sorry I am for you and your wife."

"Thanks," Slator replied, as he opened the front door for the investigator. "It's been rough."

"I can only imagine. Just know that if there's anything we can do, please let us help."

Slator nodded his head and watched Ron exit down the front porch steps. The man's last comments settled his anxiety somewhat. That fellow, and his boss, appeared to have genuine concern for him.

He could not have been more wrong.

Harry Greenbaum slowly shuffled up the sidewalk, ascended the three porch steps, and rang the doorbell. It was Wednesday evening, a quarter after six; a time, he figured, when most decent folks were at home getting ready for supper. Harry always knew how to increase his chances of success. Besides, it was practically on his way home from downtown. The Slators lived in a pleasant and unpretentious neighborhood, just like he did. *My kind of people,* he thought.

A nice lady answered the door.

"Good evening, madam. I hope I'm not here at a bad time."

Taking a look at the disheveled old man standing on the porch, Joan assumed he was a down on his luck door-to-door salesman.

"I'm sorry, we're not interested in anything right now."

"Oh, no ma'am, I'm not selling anything, although I did peddle a few Fuller Brushes back in the day. My name's Harry Greenbaum, and I was wondering if I might have a word with Mr. Slator."

She still wasn't convinced. He was an odd-looking little man.

"Regarding?"

"It's about his old job with SeaCoast. I'm looking into what happened out there."

"Are you a reporter?"

Harry laughed. "No ma'am, I make an honest living. I'm a lawyer!" he said with a big smile.

She glanced up and down at him, trying to square his wardrobe with the claimed profession. Something wasn't quite right but he seemed harmless.

"Just a moment, please."

She partially closed the door, leaving Harry standing outside. A few seconds later, Ken Slator appeared, giving his own concerned look to the man standing in front of him.

Greenbaum extended his hand. "Mr. Slator, nice to meet you. Name's Harry Greenbaum. I'm a lawyer for one of your fellow workers killed at the plant last week."

Slator shook his hand warily. He doubted that the slick attorney he'd been dealing with would have someone like this on his staff.

"You work for Ravich & Associates?"

Harry raised an eyebrow. *So, the bad guys got here first,* he thought, before answering the question.

"Lord, no, I couldn't imagine a worse job!" Harry chuckled at the joke that was lost on Slator. "I've got my own little law shop, and we represent the widow of Dan Crouch."

"But Mr. Ravich said he represented all the victims."

"Well, now, you should know that man once worked for me. I had to let him go. You can't always believe everything he says."

Slator's brow was furrowed. He appeared confused.

"I can assure you, Mr. Slator, I am who I say." He handed him a business card as confirmation. "I was just hoping to talk with you for a minute about the explosion."

Slator decided the man was probably legitimate but that changed nothing. Ravich had told him two nights before that if contacted by *anyone* he should "put them off, tell them nothing." He had also been warned three hours before — while accepting a huge sum of cash from Ravich's investigator — to "keep things just between us." The kindly old man standing at his door was probably no enemy but Slator decided to play it safe.

"I'm sorry, I can't speak to you about that."

Harry wasn't dissuaded. "Really? I was hoping you could. I'm just trying to help Mrs. Crouch, not get anyone in trouble."

Slator said nothing.

"You see, I'd completely understand if your employer told you not to talk to the families' lawyers, but I spoke earlier today to one of your coworkers — Wally Brinkman, nice fellow — and he said you quit SeaCoast. That means the company can't tell you what to do anymore."

Slator was caught off-guard. He fumbled for an excuse. "I'm sorry, this isn't a good time. We're just sitting down for dinner."

Greenbaum gave a thin smile in response. He smelled no food and another keen sense called intuition told him he was being stonewalled. Harry knew not to push a reluctant witness, but he saw no harm in prodding just a little.

"I sure get that. I'm getting hungry myself. I'll let you go, but please give me a call at your convenience tomorrow, if you could. I've been told you were in charge out there — probably for a long time I'll bet — and one thing I've learned in my many years is that career folks like us don't just up and quit unless we feel we have to. Now I don't know what SeaCoast did to cause this explosion, or for you to quit, but I reckon it's one hell of a story and you're the man to tell it. I'm a darn good listener."

Slator stood expressionless. The old man was clearly both plainspoken and smart.

Harry turned slightly away from the door. Then he stopped suddenly, as if remembering an important detail.

"Oh, Mr. Slator, one last thing I've learned in my old age. I wouldn't trust Paul Ravich any further than I could throw Charles Thornton. You've got my card. Call me before people like that start telling you what's best for you."

Slator looked into the old man's eyes. He couldn't say why but they conveyed trust to him.

Greenbaum again extended his hand for a shake. "Have a good evening, Mr. Slator. I look forward to hearing from you soon. Tomorrow, maybe, if it's not too much trouble?"

"Let me think about it," Slator replied.

Harry nodded his head in agreement. That sounded much better than "No." He decided to plant one last seed.

"Please do. I'll bet once you search your conscience, you'll do the right thing. My home and office numbers are on that little card there. You call me anytime once you've made up your mind."

Harry Greenbaum turned and waddled down the steps. Slator watched as the elderly lawyer walked with bowed legs and a slow gait toward his old Plymouth parked alongside the curb.

That man is the key to the case, thought Harry, as he reached for his car door.

Ken Slator saw the old-timer get in and start the clunker up. He grinned as the rumpled lawyer gave a friendly wave goodbye before pulling away. Then suddenly, his thoughts turned more serious. The man's last comment involving Ravich and Thornton made him recall something his mother had always told him: "*Good people do the right thing. Bad people don't.*"

He stared down at the business card he'd been given. It read:

Harry Greenbaum

Honest Lawyer

Greenbaum & Walker, P.C.

Ken Slator closed the door. He had a lot to think about.

⸺ ❧ ⸺

He had done it before, in service to his country.

Ron Carroll had been hand-picked for the assignment a year and a half after the 1983 bombing in Beirut that killed 241 American servicemen in their barracks. It was a long time ago but you never forget.

By that time, he had already compiled a distinguished four-year service record as a member of the Army's elite Delta Force unit. Because he was a small explosives expert, he got assigned to assist the CIA's Special Operations Group in an important covert mission. The job was described to him as "tactical counter-terrorism." But everyone involved knew what it really was: Revenge.

The CIA had identified one of the central plotters of the barracks bombing and decided to eliminate him. Politics required that things look like an accident. Ron never really understood that part. He thought then, and still believed today, that public retaliation was the best way to send the bastards a message. But he was just a soldier. He didn't make policy, he made bombs.

The target's car had been parked near his home along a rubble-filled street in central Beirut. The Agency didn't want a Mafia-like car bomb exploding everything when the ignition was turned. That would be clear evidence of murder. They needed, for whatever reason, deniability. So Ron devised a very small explosive charge with a timed detonator and, under cover of darkness, attached it to the right front axle of the doomed sedan. A clever ruse, involving a local CIA asset, assured that the car's owner left by nine the next morning in a hurry to make a hastily arranged but important meeting.

The plan worked flawlessly. The charge blew as the car sped down the highway towards Syria, splitting the axle and separating the right wheel hub. The sedan rolled four times, crushing the man inside, before it came to a stop in a rock-filled ditch. Ron's CIA contact confirmed the kill; a tracking satellite had recorded "the accident." Ron was told it looked exactly like an old, poorly maintained, middle-east Mercedes was simply traveling too fast and fell apart, killing somebody. Happens all the time.

Ron hadn't thought about that mission for years. He left the Army in 1988 and returned home to begin his police career. He put in twenty-years, fifteen as a detective, before Paul Ravich talked him into leaving the department to become the firm's primary investigator. The pay at the firm was incredible and the rare "black-ops" activity that Ravich asked him to do paled easily in comparison to what his own government had once required of him.

Until now.

Dressing as Santa and pulling a rigged raffle ticket was child's play. Paying off witnesses and even the occasional judge was nothing. Training and controlling case-runners was no big thing. But *killing* someone was a completely different matter.

As he laid in bed on Wednesday night, Ron focused his eyes at a spot on the ceiling and thought back to what was said. The meeting with his boss, only hours before, had answered most questions but one still remained. *Would I do it?*

The case was huge. Ron understood that. As Ravich explained things, the deal he struck with the owner of the destroyed plant would net the firm one hundred-million if all went well. Only one man could mess everything up and that person, unlike Ron, couldn't be trusted to play ball. "He needs to be out of the case" were the words his boss had carefully used.

Ravich was good at lawyer word games. He knew how to communicate a criminal message without expressly incriminating himself. The bright trial lawyer always found a way to obfuscate when giving any illicit order. Initially, Ron had been offended by such lack of directness, thinking it a sign that his boss didn't fully trust him and was therefore guarding his speech for fear of a hidden wire. But he came to realize it was just how the man operated. Ravich liked the sneakiness and playing coy. He obviously enjoyed the fruits of his criminal acts but he seemed to relish the crime's conception and cover-up even more.

His boss didn't have to expressly outline the entire scheme anyway. Ron wasn't dumb. It was obvious from the data alteration assignment he'd been given that Ravich didn't like what was on Ken Slator's computer. *It didn't fit his theory,* Ron surmised. Giving Slator back a computer that would erase itself was telling as well. It suggested the witness wasn't in on the deal. Which, in turn, meant he could be a real problem. Those kind of deductions were easy for a retired police detective.

Ron couldn't sleep. He continued to stare up at the ceiling, filling his vision with flat, shadowy white. It served as a movie screen for the mind, his memory the flickering reel. The "bonus discussion" — held after everyone else had gone home for the evening — replayed in his head.

"Ron, this will be my biggest case by far. But it requires some *special services* on your part; things that may sound crazy until you consider the prize. So, I think it's only fair to make sure you're amply rewarded for your unique efforts in getting this case on the right track."

"What do you need?"

From his desk, Ravich picked up the envelope and check that Ron had retrieved from Slator that afternoon. He lit the corner of the envelope with his cigar lighter and dropped the flaming paper into the empty metal trash bucket behind his desk. He talked while the evidence disappeared into smoke.

"First of all, the cash you delivered today in exchange for those ashes behind me is now yours. All you have to do is go get it. I'm sure the man placed it in the home safe he told me about when we first met and which I instructed you to suggest he use. That is also where he'll likely store the new computer you just gave him. Sometime after Friday, you should make an 'unannounced visit' and see if you can't fetch those things. I don't want to see either that cash or hardware ever again. I assume you will figure out a nice way to dispose of both."

Ravich smiled, knowing he didn't have to explain to Ron how to handle and hide large sums of cash. His investigator had been doing that very thing for years. Case-runners don't take checks.

"That little program we installed on his new laptop was just insurance in case you run into a problem and can't get your hands on it. I assume you glanced around when you were at his house?"

"Of course. I even saw him put the money in his safe. It's a cheap little home model. Keypad entry. I was standing right next to him when he opened it. I think the code is '2-6-1-8' but it won't matter. I could pry that thing out of the cabinet in three-seconds."

Ravich grinned. His man was worth every penny.

"Did you notice any other computers around the house?"

"Yeah, there was one in the study where the safe was."

"Good. Make sure you also erase its hard drive. That should be easy. It's just another way to protect ourselves in case our man lied to me and made a backup."

Ron was amused by how Ravich didn't mention Slator or the case by name. It was all part of his silly, overly cautious attempt to be vague — in case the walls had ears.

"You can ask the firm's tech boy how to do something like that. Just tell him you need to erase an old computer of yours before giving it to charity or some such crap."

Ron nodded and filed another task in his memory. This was not the kind of discussion where you were allowed to take notes or make a to-do list.

"Okay, but what about the witness? He still knows what he knows and probably isn't going to be real happy to find his money and stuff gone."

"Good point," Ravich said, as if he hadn't thought about that.

Ron shook his head slightly as Ravich resumed speaking. It was all part of the game.

"Once he comes here tomorrow night and gives an affidavit proving up what will soon be the 'corrected' computer record, he really is of no use anymore. Actually, the more I think about it, I would be happy if I never saw him again."

Ron shifted uncomfortably in his seat. The more Ravich talked in code, the more heinous the crime being contemplated.

"Sometimes people have accidents on their way home. Get in wrecks and things," Ravich observed, as if he were simply talking in the abstract.

Ron suddenly recalled the time, five years earlier, when he got drunk on a fishing trip with Ravich and told him stories from his military days. *He can't possibly be thinking that,* Ron wondered to himself.

He didn't have to wonder long.

Ravich leaned back in his chair and spoke as if he were speculating out loud. "I suppose someone who really knew what they were doing could find something wrong with that old car of his in under an hour?"

Recalling that precise moment in their conversation, Ron closed his eyes briefly and punched the mattress in frustration. It marked the point at which he could have — should have — said: "Forget it. It's too dangerous." But he didn't. Instead of putting the clamps on it then and there, he had allowed Ravich to continue.

"That's about how long he'll be here. If 'the mechanic' needs more time, I could always arrive a little later from my 'out-of-town trip.'"

203

More code. Ron knew his boss wasn't scheduled to travel on Thursday. But now he understood why he had been instructed to tell Slator otherwise. Ravich wanted easy access to the car while no one was around. The late night meeting at the office suddenly made sense.

"I don't know. This is very risky stuff. Especially for me."

"I understand that, Ron. Which is why you need to be adequately compensated for your expertise."

He slid a document across the desk.

"That's a quitclaim deed to my Florida condo. It transfers full ownership to you. When it's done, I'll see that it gets filed. No one has to know, except my accountants, who'll be told it was a generous gift to a dedicated employee. The condo is very nice and worth well over two million. A great place to finally retire."

Ron stared at the deed. He knew it would be the only thing connected to the scheme that would ever have Ravich's name on it. And he already had come up with an innocent explanation for why it existed.

"That's generous of you. But do you understand what we're talking about here?"

"Oh, that reminds me," Ravich replied, as if he were not finished making his offer. "The taxes on that place are incredibly high. And what's the point of living in Florida if you don't have a boat? You'll have lots of new lifestyle expenses pretty soon so I thought of a way to get you some additional spending cash."

Ron listened in amazement.

"I'm coming into some pretty big money tomorrow. Cash in an offshore bank from another business deal. It's very simple to have my Swiss banker open an account in your name. I'll have him transfer half of what I'm getting to your own private account. Your share equals one-million dollars. It will be yours to spend discreetly, however you wish."

Ron exhaled deeply and kicked the sheet off his body as he reached that point in his recollection. The dollars discussed became a mental intermission. His mind stepped briefly out of its ceiling theater and paid a visit to the concession stand. He laid in bed contemplating all the things such money could buy. Just as in the actual meeting, the distraction of cash was once again keeping him in the dark over things his boss didn't want him to know.

Unbeknownst to Ron, Ravich had been pleased with himself at that point in their conversation. While his investigator sat across the desk, quietly considering the huge windfall, the lawyer's giant ego fed self-congratulations for coming up with so clever a plan.

   Charles Thornton had agreed that day to all material terms of the proposed crooked deal. In a quick phone call acceptance only hours after their meeting, Thornton first made empty threats of retaliation if things didn't go as planned but finally concluded with: "Okay, let's do it." Ravich never expected any other decision. Thornton had too much to gain and that was all that matters to a man like that. The old tyrant's six-million dollars would be in Ravich's Swiss bank by close of business Thursday. Ron didn't have to know the source of funds or the exact amount.

   It was the kind of beautifully complex and criminal scheme that only Ravich's devious mind could have come up with. Everyone except him was getting screwed in some way: Slator would never see a penny of the money falsely negotiated "on his behalf" from Thornton; Ron would think he was getting half of a big deposit when, in fact, it was only a small part of the huge theft from Thornton; that payment, along with the other cash and condo, would easily push Ron over the edge and get him to take care of Slator; and all of it meant that Paul Ravich, the brilliant manipulator, would be left with a cool five-million in instant profit and a clear path to greater riches with the only witness who could hurt him gone forever.

   Ron's bedtime money-thoughts disappeared. His mind returned to the meeting movie. He laid there recalling how Ravich had persisted in speaking only in riddles while he had sat listening, mulling over the difference between murder for money and killing for country.

   "Who knows why old cars fall apart on the freeway? Thank God, some accidents occur late at night when other people aren't likely to be involved. You hate to see tragedy compounded."

   Ravich persisted in the charade.

   "I've handled a lot of car wreck cases, Ron. Sometimes the damage is so great, it's impossible to tell exactly what happened. Can you imagine?"

   Ron said nothing in reply. His silence told Ravich that the instructions were being understood.

   "So, it will be good having all this behind us after tomorrow night, don't you think? When you went back over there, did you get the make and model like I asked you?"

   "Yeah. It was in the driveway. 01' or 02' Blue Ford Taurus. "

   "Then it's done. Do your research, then your magic."

   Ravich outlined the schedule, then ended their clandestine talk with a bone-chilling statement.

   "Tomorrow night, when you call from the downstairs garage, I'll know it's time to let our friend drive home."

Ron laid wide awake, still staring at a dot on the ceiling as his memory reached the end of its movie. He remembered every single word, every little detail, of their fateful meeting and discussion. *Why wouldn't I?* he thought, as he finally rolled over to go to sleep. *It's not every day that someone asks you to commit murder.*

⎯⎯ ⠿ ⎯⎯

He didn't want her to worry.

It wasn't yet time to sit down with Joan and explain what he was doing. He wasn't even sure he fully knew at this point. Selling your testimony to hurt a company that employed you for twenty-two years? Becoming the star witness for a rich plaintiff's lawyer who only wants to make more millions off the deaths of your fellow workers? Accepting a hundred-thousand dollars in cash like some drug dealer? How do you explain that to anyone, much less your wife?

Why he said what he did, he supposed, was as much out of shame as it was an attempt not to cause her concern. Joan had been doing better, crying less, smiling more. The sadness of Melissa's death was still with them of course. It would never leave. But there were small rays of light. She held him close at night. They talked more than they ever had before. She looked forward to sitting down and sharing meals. Over dinner on Thursday evening, because he loved her and because he didn't like the truth, he told her a lie.

"I have to go down to the plant late tonight."

That made no sense to her. "Why? You don't work for them anymore."

"I know, but I did tell them I'd assist in their investigation when they needed me."

"But tonight? Why so late?"

It was a reasonable question. He expected it to be asked. He had come up with a plausible excuse. The shame that caused him to create the lie grew worse as he looked into her trusting eyes.

"The company's flying in an engineer of some kind — I think he's a reconstruction expert — to advise them during an inspection by the government tomorrow. He lands at ten tonight and the inspection is first thing in the morning. They want me to go over the plant schematics with him and help him get oriented."

She accepted the explanation but not his willingness. "You don't owe them anything, Ken."

"I know, but I said I'd help. I'll only be a few hours. I'll try not to wake

206

you when I get back."

She nodded, then thought of something else to ask. "What do you think happened out there?"

He was tired of lying but not ready to tell her the whole truth. "Mistakes were made," was all he said.

Joan took that to mean he didn't want to discuss the tragedy further. She understood. Not dwelling so much on death was a new rule they had made together. She picked her fork back up and resumed eating.

Slator reached across the table and took her other hand. He gave her an appreciative smile. She deserved more. She was owed his honesty.

As they finished their meal, he thought about the timing. Once this late-night meeting with Paul Ravich was over he would reassess things. He wasn't sure about his current plan. Something didn't feel right. Maybe it was the money locked away in the next room. It made him too ashamed to share any details with the woman he loved. He lectured himself silently: *That should tell you something.* He decided, right then, that tomorrow he would call that other lawyer, the old gentleman with the trusting eyes who seemed to have a motive other than money. He could at least listen to what the other lawyer had to say. Then he would sit down with Joan and tell her everything.

∞∞∞

Doug and Sarah also dined together that night. It was a violation of "man-law" — that unspoken code of male conduct — which requires waiting at least a week after the first date before asking a girl out again. But he didn't care. Sarah Ash was fun and exciting. He felt good about her and his week. He now had a great team of co-counsel, both of whom were smart and talented. The *Crouch* case had been filed, beating Ravich to the courthouse. Things were going well at work. Why not allow good fortune to continue into his personal life?

Doug had accompanied Bill Gaston on the Tuesday afternoon trip to the courthouse. While Bill was on the first floor filing their suit against SeaCoast, Doug went up to Judge Thompkins' court to say hello to Sarah. She was back in her tiny office, busy with the mundane tasks of a court clerk, and she welcomed the visit. When he suggested a Thursday night casual dinner, she smiled and teased him, revealing more of the wit he remembered fondly from their first date.

"*Casual?* What does that mean? You're done trying to impress me?"

He laughed. "I meant only that you don't have to wear that sexy black dress again. It does things to me."

"So, it's the clothes you're attracted to?"

He knew she wouldn't stop. "Just say yes. I can't possibly keep this banter up."

"Okay, but we both have to work on Friday, so no staying up past two this time."

"Darn. That was the best part," he joked suggestively.

She understood the meaning and gave him a naughty grin. "Then let's have our *casual* dinner earlier. That way we could get to the 'best part' before nine."

He took her at her word and on Thursday evening they found themselves sitting among the other early birders at a little Mexican restaurant, munching on fish tacos before the sun had fully set. The conversation was again easy. Her smarts and smile were as appealing to him as her body and the talents she possessed with it.

Shoptalk dominated. They were both okay with that. Put two people together who make their livings at the courthouse and it's inevitable. The law, with all its drama and absurdities, makes for good dinner-theater. He told her about his latest case and she seemed impressed. He described his bad experience with Ravich and she said she wasn't surprised.

"I've seen him in trial a lot," she explained. "When I was Judge Lewis' clerk, he was in there all the time. They're pretty tight."

Doug remembered what Harry had said. Lewis was one of Ravich's gang of four.

"And let me tell you, Paul Ravich can be a real jerk," she added. "Oh, he's sweet as saccharine if the jury's in the box or the judge is on the bench. But when they're not around, you're just a dog there to fetch his slippers. He can look right through you while asking you to do something for him, like he shouldn't even have to bother."

"That sounds like him," Doug agreed.

"If he didn't throw that Christmas party of his, he'd be on the shit-list of every county employee, trust me."

Doug knew nothing about the annual party. Sarah filled him in as he sat shaking his head in amazement, now realizing what Harry had meant about the intake clerk owning a "Christmas car."

"Well, Ms. Ash, if I could ever give away a car to a deserving clerk, I want you to know you are most definitely in the running."

"That's very nice of you, kind sir, but you've already proven you can get me in bed for a lot less."

They both laughed. But the joke, for some reason, also reminded Doug of another sexual episode, this one actually serious. He recalled Sarah's story about Judge Lewis' improper advances. It was, after all, his tactless discounting of that shared secret that made him want to treat Sarah more as a friend. At least in that respect, some good had come out of the old fool's harassment.

"Hey, I've been meaning to ask you. Has there been any fallout since you transferred up to Judge Thompkins? I mean, do other people know why you moved out of Lewis' court?"

She rolled her eyes in disgust. "He avoids me like the plague now. Which is good news for me. The other day, Judge Lewis came walking down the hall. He looked up and saw me, then spun around like a ballerina and went the other way. He's a sick old perv."

"You don't want to file a complaint? Not even a letter to the Judicial Ethics Commission?"

"What good would it do? It becomes a he said, she said. And *he's* a prominent judge; *she's* a lowly clerk."

"That's a pretty cynical take on the system, you know."

She gave Doug a dismissive look. "And how long have you been practicing law?"

He got the point. She *would* face an uphill battle.

"Still, it's not right," he added.

"I know, and he'll keep doing it. You know Jane, his court reporter?"

Doug nodded.

"Well, evidently, she's his latest target. She told me he came into her office last week when no one else was around and just started rubbing her shoulders and back. He told her she needed a good pat down."

Doug wrinkled his nose at the odious thought.

"He needs to be strung up by his judicial balls," he said.

"Yeah, well, I'd settle for just smacking them pretty hard with his gavel."

Doug smiled thinly.

"Hey!" she chirped suddenly. "How about some flan for dessert?"

She asked the question enthusiastically and then took the last sip of her margarita. It was a clear signal to drop the subject. She obviously didn't want to discuss Judge Lewis any further on their date. But Doug knew that no woman — especially one as bright and sweet as Sarah — could ever casually toss aside something as demeaning and offensive as overt sexual harassment. She was simply downplaying it for now. She wanted the rest of their time to be about them. She didn't want to burden him with her problems. She just wanted him to have fun and feel happy.

Her selfless attentions brought to mind something he told himself that busy Monday morning, now almost two weeks ago, as she helped him juggle his court schedule. He thought it then. He knew it now.

She is a good person.

—∞∞∞—

His new cell phone rang at ten-fifteen. Ken Slator was in the bathroom brushing his teeth, having put on a clean shirt in preparation for his upcoming session with Ravich. Joan was already in bed reading and assumed the call had something to do with the ridiculously late night plant meeting her husband had agreed to attend.

He ran to the study to answer it. It had to be them. No one else had been given the new number. Maybe the downtown meeting at eleven-thirty was being called off. If so, that would be welcome news. The doubts about everything he was doing had continued to grow.

"Hello," he answered warily.

"Mr. Slator, it's Ron. I'm calling to confirm our meeting. I just heard from Mr. Ravich. His flight's on time and he should be at the office pretty close to our arranged schedule. You still remember how to get in?"

"Yes, I have your card key."

"Good. I'm already down here. The parking garage here is huge and of course it will be empty. Drive up to Level Three. Just look for my black Suburban and park right next to it. You'll see the glass entry doors to the building on that level. Just wave that card on top of the sensor beside the doors and they'll unlock."

"Okay."

"Remember, our offices are on the sixty-third floor. Mr Ravich said to tell you he really appreciates it and he'll try to have you out of here as quick as he can."

Slator felt somewhat reassured by the helpful follow up and pleasant comments.

"All right, I'll see you there."

He hung up and remained in the study, deep in thought. If this videotaped statement or affidavit could somehow keep him protected from Rob Finnegan and SeaCoast, he guessed the late-night trip was worth it. Maybe he would ask Paul Ravich about the other lawyer who came to see him. The old man said they knew each other. *Ravich shouldn't care if I call the man back and speak to him.* They were both lawyers for the victims. *But why did Ravich say he represented all of them?* Slator clearly recalled him making that statement at the soup-and-salad place. Maybe he had simply misspoke. It could easily be cleared up. *Why are you so worried about things?* he asked himself scoldingly.

Standing in the study, he looked down at the cabinet doors and found the answer to his unease. Behind the alder panels was a safe loaded with cash, money a lawyer had secretly given him so he would give evidence against his former employer, cash from a lawyer that preferred meeting only at night, a lawyer who obviously loved money and apparently had plenty to throw anyone's way.

He realized Joan would be going to sleep soon. He sat down in the study and pressed the space key on the iMac's keyboard, springing it awake.

He navigated to the "Melissa Folder" created two days before and double-clicked on the movie file he had recorded. He turned the computer volume down slightly, thinking it could not be heard in the next room, and sat watching. It felt eerie, seeing himself on screen, pointing at his laptop data, carefully detailing the accident and its causes. He assumed he would soon be doing it all over again in depositions and at a trial. As he watched, he realized his testimony would be ironclad and accurate. It helped a little watching the movie file. What he had to say was valuable. *It was worth something.*

When it ended, he closed the file and put the computer back to sleep. He went into the kitchen for a bottle of water and to grab his keys. By the time he needed to leave, the lights were off in the bedroom. Quietly, he walked in and kissed Joan softly on the forehead. She was barely asleep.

She kept her eyes closed as she whispered: "Be careful."

He looked at her resting comfortably and smiled.

"I love you," he said.

Her eyes still shut, she made a small grin of satisfaction and rolled over.

Then he turned and walked away, headed for his car.

The drive into downtown was easy. There was not much traffic inbound at eleven at night. He found the building and parking garage entrance without problem. He drove up to the third level as instructed. He saw the glass doors and the big Suburban in the space closest to the entrance. He parked his car beside Ron's SUV. He entered the building by swiping the same access card used to enter the garage. As he rode the elevator up to the penthouse office, he thought about how alone he was. He had seen no one — not even a security guard — inside the garage. Then again, it was almost eleven-thirty. Nobody in their right mind, except for Paul Ravich, would be working at this time of night.

The elevator doors opened and, as Ron had said, he stood facing the ornate entry of Paul Ravich & Associates. The glass doors to the suite were unlocked. He entered and took two steps before he heard footsteps coming down the hall.

"Mr. Slator, you made it! Thanks for coming."

It was Ron, wearing black jeans and a black shirt, a friendly smile contrasting his dark appearance.

"Come on into the conference room. Mr. Ravich just landed. He called to say he'd be here in twenty minutes at the latest. Can I get you some coffee or something?"

"No, I'm fine, thanks."

They settled into chairs. Ravich had instructed Ron to set a video camera on a tripod at one end of the table. On the other side of the room, Ron was told to bring in all the scene photos that had been taken the morning after the explosion. They would be used as a time-wasting distraction.

"I need to run down to my office to grab some files for tomorrow," Ron said apologetically. "They stuck me down on sixty-two in some far crappier-looking space," he explained.

He pointed toward the stack of photos. "I've laid out the *SeaCoast* evidence we have so far. Thought you might want to take a look at it while you wait. Just make yourself at home. Mr. Ravich will probably beat me back here. But I'll try and come back up to say goodnight."

He held out his hand and Slator, still seated, shook it.

"You're by yourself for a couple of minutes, so don't steal anything," Ron said laughingly, patting the man on the back.

Then he disappeared out the front doors.

That's odd, thought Slator, but then he realized everything about this was strange: the claimed importance of the meeting, the lateness of the hour, the absence of any other law firm staff, and now, being left alone — it all seemed peculiar. He looked around. The offices were certainly elegant. Paul Ravich and his people might be eccentric but they evidently were successful at what they did.

He got up and went over to the photo evidence. It was exactly what they calculated he would do. They figured Slator could easily spend fifteen or twenty minutes with the pictures of his destroyed plant before he would start getting fidgety. That's all the extra time they needed. Ravich would then make his appearance and waste more time getting the authentication evidence he wanted while Ron did what he needed to do.

Ken Slator began studying the horrific images of destruction that were stacked almost a foot high. To most people, the piles of ash and twisted metal in each photograph would look pretty much the same. But he recognized all the collapsed vessels and each piece of mangled pipe. Every picture was different to him, and he laid them out in order atop the conference room table as if rebuilding his old facility. It was the place he had helped design. It was the place he had worked for twenty-two years. It was still a complex canvas that he understood better than anyone. But now that canvas was cloaked in black.

Just like Ravich's investigator.

There were no offices on the sixty-second floor, at least not ones belonging to Paul Ravich & Associates. Ron left Ken Slator and entered the elevator, pressing the button for Level 3 of the parking garage. He was back in his Suburban when he heard Ravich's Bentley round the corner. The lawyer parked his three-hundred thousand dollar car on the opposite side of the virtually worthless old Ford and stepped out. He smiled at his investigator, slumped down in the driver's seat of the black SUV. It was exactly as they had planned. There was now a wall of metal on either side of Slator's blue Taurus.

Without exchanging words, Paul Ravich strode into the building. He had his part to play, the "mechanic" had his.

The vehicles on either side provided essential protection in case a security patrol came circling through the garage. Ron had checked their schedule earlier in the day with a call to building security. They did hourly patrols of the garage commencing on the half hour. Unless there was a glitch, he would be just fine. His only risk of discovery was from a "rent-a-cop" driving around early who decided, for once, to be extra-observant. Compared to working on a terrorist-filled street in Beirut, he liked his chances. He wouldn't be seen. Even the security camera mounted above the Level 3 entry doors couldn't make out the cars right below it. Ron had shorted it out when he left the office earlier that evening to run home for a few hours. The camera above the parking garage's main entrance and exit had also been similarly put out of commission for tonight's event. There would be no video record of their comings and goings.

Ron slipped out of the Suburban, a small toolbox and two jacks in his hands. He crouched down and quickly disappeared beneath the front end of Slator's car. Ron now wore a tiny flashlight attached to an elastic strap around his head. He stared up at the car's undercarriage. The light illuminated his target. He had researched the steering system for this model and a quick visual inspection confirmed the site of vulnerability.

He pulled himself back out and slid a scissor jack under the right front end. Cranking its handle, he quickly elevated the right front tire off the ground. He then slid a stronger jack stand beneath the undercarriage to secure things before removing the tire. Disappearing back beneath the car, he began a deadly alteration of the tie-rod end.

The tie-rod is a relatively small but critically important part of the steering linkage. It is all that connects the wheel to the rest of the steering components. If it breaks, the wheel can move in any direction. If it breaks at high speeds, the results can be devastating.

Using a simple torque wrench, Ron loosened the jam-nut on the inner side of the tie-rod end, then did the same with the nut that secured the opposite side to the steering knuckle. The car could still be driven, although an attentive driver might feel some loss of alignment and slight looseness. It wouldn't be enough to cause the ordinary person to pull over and stop, especially if they had a relatively short drive home. But it made for a slightly weakened joint that another tool would snap in two when the time was right.

That other "tool" was a small object, no more than four inches wide, with the soft texture of modeling clay. It could be mistaken for white Play-Doh but there was nothing childlike about it. It was C4, a plastic explosive commonly used by the military. From his years as an explosive expert with Delta Force, Ron knew how to use it in very uncommon ways.

He also knew how to secure it. Army demolition specialists stay connected. A request for a small quantity "to blast out some stubborn rocks on my ranch land" was easily accommodated. After a quick drive to the local armory — and a few back slaps and war stories later — he left with more than he needed. It wasn't legal to hand the stuff out but Ron was a special forces hero, not some terrorist. The National Guard ordinance officer knew that much. Besides, he didn't give him enough to do much damage. *Those rocks must be pretty small*, the officer had thought, when Ron informed him a single mini-brick would be more than enough.

Ron kneaded and packed the pliable C4 tightly around the tie-rod end. He used just enough that it could blow apart the mechanical joint but not so much as to leave obvious evidence that a bomb went off at the wheel hub. If all went as planned, it would look like ordinary part failure, with fatal consequences. If the Beirut job were any indicator, nobody would ever notice the strangely disintegrated steering linkage on one side. There would be plenty of other physical damage and broken parts after the car spun out of control and crashed. It would be impossible to tell what broke or fell apart first.

The trick would be the detonation. C4 is very stable in the absence of an explosive charge. So much so that Ron and his Delta Force commandos used it in the field as a heat source, lighting bricks of it to cook their rations. Only when subjected to extreme heat *and* shock would it explode. To do that, you needed a trigger.

Ron carefully inserted a small electrical firing circuit into the glob of C4 that was now encapsulating the tie-rod end. He then secured a small disposable cell phone to the adjacent steering knuckle with a single plastic zip tie. He had already modified the phone, using the same technique the terrorist bastards do to remotely set off their IEDs. It was stupidly simple. The vibration feature in a cell phone consists of a tiny motor connected to an irregularly shaped knob which "shakes" the phone when activated. By connecting the firing circuit to the vibrating knob, a phone call will trigger the circuit which, in turn, detonates the C4. The phone would be blown apart, the zip tie disintegrated. To find any bomb trace-evidence, you would first have to know what to look for and then get lucky to find it. Highway patrol officers aren't bomb experts. This would look like nothing more than a car that lost control and crashed. Even a close-looking mechanic would only be able to say that the steering system failed.

Ron tipped his head down to shine the flashlight's spot of light on his watch. It was 12:18. Another five minutes and he'd be done. He pulled himself out from under the Taurus and replaced the right front tire. He kept those lugs nuts loose to increase the chances it would fly off when the charge exploded. It's hard enough to maintain control at freeway speed with a front wheel you cannot steer. One that's missing its tire is even tougher.

He removed the jack stand, then released the scissor jack. The car's right front end settled softly back down to the ground, its mortal injury safely hidden from view. He threw his tools back into the Suburban, then called Ravich's cell phone.

"Hello?"

"It's done," Ron stated flatly before hanging up.

Inside the conference room, Ravich began a pretense for the benefit of Slator, sitting across from him.

"No, Ron, no need to come back up."

He paused as if listening to further conversation.

"No, that's okay. I'm glad you stayed and finished up that scene report. I'll need it tomorrow. Lock up your office and go home. We're almost done here. I can show Mr. Slator out." He paused again. "I'll tell him. Goodnight, Ron."

Ravich hung up and looked at Slator.

"Ron said to tell you thanks for coming and he's sorry he didn't make it back up."

Slator nodded.

"So, we're done with the videotape. Let me just run to my office and get the affidavit for you to sign."

He left the conference room, returning in a matter of seconds with the single page document, which he handed to his witness.

Slator read it quickly. Like Ravich had said, it contained the exact same language they had used in the video Q & A. It was simply his attestation that the laptop data was a reliable business record, maintained in the ordinary course of his job as SeaCoast's head of process engineering, and that it was a true and accurate copy of the data recorded by the plant on the night of the explosion. Slator signed it and Ravich assured him that an assistant would notarize it in the morning.

They talked a few minutes more, then got up to leave. Slator still didn't understand why the sworn statement was needed but Ravich had firmly declared that without it, they would never be able to get the protective order he would seek in the morning. It sounded like legal i-dotting so Slator didn't question it further. Ravich loved that. Laypersons were so easy to dupe.

They rode the elevator down together. Sixty-three floors is a long way to go without speaking.

"Do you know a man named Harry Greenbaum?" Slator asked, breaking the silence.

Ravich looked as if he were stung by a bee but quickly regained his composure. "Sure. What about him?"

"He came by my house yesterday evening and wanted to talk about the explosion. He said he represented Dan Crouch's widow."

Ravich bit his lip. *That punk lawyer found some firepower to help him.*

"What did you tell him?"

"Nothing. I said I didn't want to talk about it. I thought I'd check with you first."

"You did the right thing, Ken. I appreciate your caution, I really do. But Harry's an old and trusted friend. I keep no secrets from him. We'll all be working together on this soon enough. If you want to talk with him tomorrow about what you know, you have my blessing. But let's try and keep the money thing between us, okay?"

Slator nodded in agreement.

The building elevator doors opened at garage Level 3. Slator felt better knowing that Ravich was close to, and willing to work with, the trust-inspiring old lawyer that paid a visit to his home.

Ravich also felt good. He knew that Ken Slator would not be talking to anyone ever again.

———— ⊶∞⊷ ————

Ron left the garage well ahead of Ravich and Slator. He quickly drove the black Suburban to a surface-parking lot three blocks away. He pulled up next to a parked gray sedan, the only other vehicle in the outside pay lot. He got out, locked the Suburban, and jumped into the rented Chevy Malibu.

He pulled out of the lot and stopped where he could see, from that distance, the cars emerge from the garage exit of their building. He sat in the nondescript car, its engine idling, and waited.

Ravich's Bentley was the first to exit and he turned left, the opposite direction from where Ron was waiting in his rented car. Ravich was headed home where, Ron suspected, he would sleep like a baby.

The blue Ford came chugging out soon after and made the same left. Ron knew the route Slator would take. He had twice made the same drive to Slator's home over the past several days. Ron still had the skills of a good police detective. He knew how to follow a suspect without being noticed. He pulled away from the curb, trailing at least two blocks behind, paying careful attention to the way the car in front of him was handling the road. He saw no excessive tire wobble, nothing that would cause Slator concern. He watched from a safe distance as the Taurus climbed up the freeway entrance ramp and he dropped back to follow a quarter mile behind.

Fifteen minutes later, the Taurus was traveling at freeway speed, the road virtually deserted except for them. Slator would soon be approaching a sharp curve where the elevated freeway descended slightly and bent to the east. The bend was just past Exit 182, which Ron took, steering his rent car down the ramp and onto the parallel feeder road below the freeway. He accelerated down the access road and pulled out his phone. He had programmed the speed dial. He pressed "1" and four seconds later he heard an explosion followed by the unmistakable sounds of impact and crushing metal scraping down the roadway above him. He turned right at the next traffic light, where the access road intersected Richland Road.

In less than a minute, he was a considerable distance from the accident site. By the time emergency responders arrived, he would be many miles away.

Ron had been an aural witness only. His ears confirmed the crash. Nobody had seen him and he had witnessed nothing with his own eyes, including the old rusty Buick that had come flying up the freeway entrance just after he had exited.

He looked at his watch. 1:20 a.m. It was now Friday, October 25th . The date would be forever seared in his mind.

You never forget the days you kill a man.

Part III

---⦿⦿⦿---

Fictions and Facts

Chapter 13
Questions

He never changed his drivers license after the divorce. The card now in the officer's hand — like the feelings that last filled the dead man's heart — said this was home.

It wasn't usually done this way but the location was close and the cop decided it would be better than a phone call. He wouldn't have made the trip for a drunk but there was no odor of alcohol on either victim, unusual for a fatal collision at that time of night. Wherever this man had been, whatever he was out doing, he didn't deserve to die.

The highway patrolman stood on the porch at five in the morning and rang the doorbell. The residence was only three miles from the accident site. The victim had been traveling toward, not away from, this address. *He almost made it home*, the officer thought, as he rang a second time. Inside the house, a light came on and the trooper braced himself. Traffic stops, arrests, even high-speed chases were easy compared to this.

A porch light illuminated and the door opened slightly. A woman in a robe peered through the crack, her eyes filled with confusion.

"Are you Mrs. Ken Slator?" the officer asked.

"Yes," came the meek reply.

"Ma'am, your husband was involved in a serious vehicle crash."

She opened the door wider and held tightly onto the door's handle, bracing herself for support.

"I'm sorry to have to tell you this, but he did not survive the collision."

She fell to her knees, her left arm stretched upward as her fingers stayed frozen around the door handle. Her head leaned against the door frame. She was too shocked to cry out.

The trooper bent down and raised her gently.

"Let me help you. May I come inside?"

She said nothing but her body went limp again. He didn't wait for permission. He led her to the living room sofa where she collapsed. The suddenness that had frozen her emotions started to thaw. The tears began.

He stood and waited in silence. She would have questions and he would try to provide answers in the softest possible way. He had questions as well, but decided for now to ask only the most important ones.

"Is there anyone else here?"

She shook her head no.

"Is there someone I can call for you?"

She glanced up at him with a look of abject terror. The question hit her hard.

She had *nobody* now. Her only child had been buried the week before. Now the only man in her life was also dead. *What kind of vengeful God would do this?*

She looked up at the ceiling and cried out two anguished questions. They were not the ones he expected.

"What...did I do? Why...do I deserve this?"

The trooper looked on in pain. He knew she wasn't talking to him.

Her tearful challenges went unanswered. *If there is a God*, she thought, *he has abandoned me.*

The young trooper took her by the hand. All she could now do was repeat the word "No."

He had seen plenty of death. So much so that the corpses in wrecked cars were now just "scene evidence" to him. Unless it was a child he never let it get to him anymore. But seeing this sweet woman emotionally dismantle before his eyes was more aching than anything he had witnessed in uniform. It was woefully uncomfortable to watch. It made him realize his decision to ignore protocol had been the right one. Had he simply placed a call, she would be all alone — like this.

Car wrecks were daily occurrences. Fatalities were all too frequent. He thought about the latest two names he had written into yet another accident report. They were traffic statistics, sure. But they were also family to someone. Watching this woman shed tears and contemplate her loss made him think about how incredibly fragile all life and love is. *Two people, gone in an instant, for no good reason.*

Joan Slator, inconsolable, was thinking the exact same thing.

———— ᙏᙢᙢᙎ ————

Paul Ravich called at seven that morning. It was all part of being careful. The call record, at that time of day, would not be out of the ordinary. He frequently phoned staff early, including his chief investigator, to issue assignments for the day. He had specifically instructed Ron that no calls or messages be left for him in the middle of the night.

"It's confirmed," Ron said, when he saw the name and answered his cell. He knew his boss was not calling to invite him to breakfast.

"How do you know?"

"Had my police scanner with me. Heard the code announced within fifteen minutes. '10-45D.' It means 'condition-dead.'" He paused, then added: "But there's a wrinkle."

Ravich said nothing. The hint of a complication made him more circumspect.

"Trooper called it in as multiple vehicle. Two victims."

"The road was supposed to be empty," Ravich barked, forgetting his own discipline.

"It was when I exited. It's not like I could direct traffic. Who knows?"

"Okay, do the follow-up. Get the report when you can and track down the man's car. Make sure it's gone."

"I will."

"And come in this morning. Let staff see you working on routine shit. Just another day. Understand?"

"All right. Anything else?"

"Yeah, don't forget you have some things to pick up at somebody's house."

Ron shook his head. Again, speaking in code — no names. His boss would never change.

"I'll take care of it."

"Good," replied Ravich.

The lawyer stood confidently in his gym, knowing that Ron now had a vested interest in making sure everything else fell into place. He thought of the silly line they say at the end of every Super Bowl, realizing it disguised his intended message pretty well. He couldn't resist reminding his murder co-conspirator that huge rewards, including a nice place in Florida, now awaited him.

"Nice work, Mr. M.V.P., looks like you're going to DisneyWorld!"

Charles Thornton was at his desk on Friday morning, going over the week-ending briefing memos from each of his companies. Every subsidiary of Thornton Industries reported by end of day each Thursday. Thornton wanted it that way for a reason. Good reports meant his Fridays were pleasant. Bad ones meant he had time to ruin the weekends of poor-performing division presidents.

It had been a good week for every subsidiary except SeaCoast Chemical. His healthcare company oozed millions in profits regardless of what Congress did to change the law. Thornton Financial was also posting record earnings, as more and more businesses looked to floor-planning and other methods of inventory financing to stay afloat. His shopping center business continued to thrive because he could pay cash for distressed properties in tough economic times. His domestic oil company was riding the wave of high-barrel prices caused by the continual unrest in the middle-east. His controlling interest in a high-risk, high-return hedge fund was paying like a slot machine that someone forgot to limit. Diversification was the key to success. Men like Charles Thornton never kept their eggs in one basket.

He studied the SeaCoast report. The numbers were pitiful. With the main plant gone, it looked as if someone had moved the total sales decimal point in the wrong direction. Ordinarily, he would have been furious. But today he smiled. This report would one day be courtroom evidence: proof of recoverable damages, along with the formal estimates of rebuild costs and lost inventory he had been furnished the day before. The grand was easily going to be around a half-billion. Last week, he thought of litigation as a business nuisance. Now suddenly, this clever lawsuit invented by that sleazy lawyer was shaping up to become a decent little accounts receivable for him.

It better, he thought. Yesterday, he paid six-million dollars in hard-to-trace cash for an opportunity to spin Paul Ravich's crooked wheel of justice. The wire to a Swiss bank didn't surprise Thornton's personal banker. The man had moved much more money offshore before. Now all Thornton had to do was wait. Ravich had only days to confirm the damaging evidence was gone, replaced with believable proof that a VyStream subsidiary had blown up his plant. If the slick attorney could do both, he would gladly remit the second installment of ten-million dollars in the form of payments to Ravich's clients. *Very clever,* he thought, sitting at his desk. *I get to look like a generous, caring employer and he gets credit for waiving his fee.* Thornton chuckled to himself. He never cared much for partners, but this guy was truly deserving. Anyone that duplicitous was worthy of his respect.

It had been a hard sell to his General Counsel. Bruce Waltman had asked far too many questions about the deal. He was understandably not told about the wire transfer since it was purchase-money for false evidence. Not being aware of that key fact made it harder for Waltman to fathom why Thornton Industries would *voluntarily* pay money to employee victims who couldn't win a case against them in court. After all, "it's the right thing to do" wasn't something that Charles Thornton ever said. Recalling that he had actually uttered those words, Thornton shook his head in disbelief. *I can't blame Bruce for thinking there was more to it.* But he knew his GC wouldn't dare question that decision further. He wanted to stay inside the loop. If Waltman persisted with objections, Thornton could just send him out in the hall again. To his chief lawyer, that would be a greater punishment than not being privy to the whole truth.

Waltman also raised concerns about the hiring of Ravich to handle SeaCoast's damage claim; in fact, he had made some very insightful comments. While agreeing that a proposed contingency fee of twenty percent was reasonable in the abstract, Waltman wondered aloud if it was even necessary in this particular case. As he explained it, if Ravich had the goods on a third-party, he was going to use that evidence anyway to get even more money for his clients. Once disclosed, the liability evidence could then be used by anyone — including SeaCoast through its General Counsel. Waltman had asked the obvious question: "Why not just let me ride his coattails?" He correctly observed that by doing so the company would collect 100% of its damages instead of a net 80%. It was a good point, which is why he was chosen to be General Counsel. The man was smart.

The actual reason why Ravich was hired to represent Seacoast, of course, couldn't be disclosed to Waltman. Thornton knew that Ravich was only willing to *create* the necessary evidence *if* he also benefited from *all* of its use. He got that. If the shoe were on the other foot, and Charles Thornton were dictating the terms, it would have been exactly the same.

Thornton also remembered another thing that Ravich had said. Waltman was just an employee and basically an honest lawyer. He couldn't be told the evidence was fabricated. He could never know the fee was just another way of compensating Ravich for his most-helpful fraud. His in-house lawyer would have to be told something else, something he might not agree with, but something he could accept as a proper motivation for hiring the enemy: a plaintiff's lawyer.

Charles Thornton had never been reluctant to insult the people around him but Waltman was almost a friend. Still, he had to be told something credible. Thornton recalled what he had said to his General Counsel on Wednesday afternoon. It seemed to fit, and was holding up:

"Bruce, you're a transactional guy. He's a trial lawyer. He obviously knows what he's doing in a courtroom and you don't. Besides, I need you concentrating on my other interests. This SeaCoast thing may be a large pimple but it's still just a pimple on my ass. He'll handle it for us, so we can take care of more important things."

When Waltman tried to protest further, Thornton shut him down with a favorite phrase, one he rarely used when talking about himself:

"Quit worrying about the twenty-percent, Bruce. Pigs get fed and hogs get slaughtered."

———— ❦ ————

There's a fine line between follow-up and hounding. Harry Greenbaum knew how to walk it.

He fully expected to hear from the ex-plant manager the day following his evening visit to Ken Slator's home. Instincts told him the man had something he wanted to share. But Thursday came and went with no contact.

On Friday afternoon, the old trial lawyer decided there could be only three reasons why he hadn't called. Perhaps SeaCoast had secured his silence. But that was highly unlikely since he quit his job right after the explosion. A more innocent explanation was the man was still making reasonable inquiries before volunteering information to a stranger. That made sense. Harry knew that engineers are overly cautious types. The third explanation, however, was deeply troubling. Without intending to do so, Ken Slator revealed in their doorstep conversation that Paul Ravich had already spoken to him. Ordinarily, a willingness to talk with one plaintiff's lawyer signaled a cooperative attitude toward all the victims' counsel. But Harry knew better in this instance. Ravich was competitive and devious. It would not be out of character for Ravich to tell a witness to trust only him. Especially if he were trying to teach the young Doug Stevens a lesson.

Such pettiness was an intrinsic part of his former associate's character. Harry recalled Ravich's first jury verdict as a young lawyer with Greenbaum & Walker. He had been "second-chair" to a more experienced associate at the firm, which meant he was a copilot and not the lawyer in charge. When the twosome won their case for a surprising amount of money, a reporter called up the next day asking for details. Paul Ravich provided everything except the name of his co-counsel, the man who actually rowed the laboring oar. It was to be the first time Ravich would see his name in print and he didn't like the idea of shared billing. Of course, he later lied when confronted with the oversight, telling everyone at the office he had insisted that the reporter include *both* their names. Harry knew the reporter personally and made a quiet call to verify the claim. It was the first of many confirmations that Paul Ravich was only in the game for himself.

Harry stared at his phone. He had options.

One was to call Ravich and inform him that his old boss was now a part of the *Crouch* case team. They would exchange false pleasantries and reminisce briefly about old times. When it came time to discuss business, Ravich would no doubt pledge full cooperation while intending just the opposite. He may or may not tell him the truth about what Ken Slator knew. It would all depend on Ravich's master plan. Harry knew that dealing with Paul Ravich was like playing with a python. Sometimes, they wrap themselves around you for fun. Other times, the coils are intended to squeeze the life out of you. Although he could be a wily snake-charmer, Harry preferred avoiding serpents all together whenever possible.

A second option made more sense. He picked up the phone and dialed the number listed in the SeaCoast employee directory. Ken Slator's old cell phone, now turned off and safely tucked inside Paul Ravich's office safe, returned the message: "*The cellular customer you are trying to reach is not available.*" It did not roll over to voicemail.

Harry reached again for his trusty White Pages and called the home number listed for Ken and Joan Slator. An answering machine picked up after the fourth ring. Harry hated the damn things. If the person you were trying to reach didn't return the call, you had no idea whether you were being ignored or they simply hadn't checked the playback. That's why he preferred in-person contacts with important witnesses. But he also knew better than to become a pest. People can also quickly learn how to not answer their door. So he decided to leave a message, trusting that the witness would eventually get back to him. Ken Slator seemed to be a decent fellow. Harry felt he had treated him with decency when they first met. The man would come around if given a chance instead of a push.

"*Mr. Slator, this is Harry Greenbaum calling. It's Friday afternoon, around two o'clock. You may recall I stopped by your house the other day. I'm the lawyer for Dan Crouch's family and it's just awfully important that I talk with you about things down at that plant. I know we both have questions, and I assure you I'm only looking to give and get honest answers. Please do call at your convenience. I gave you my card. Help me get to the truth as only you know it. We both know it's the right thing to do. Thank you, sir.*"

Joan Slator stood in the hallway listening to the gentle and sincere voice record a polite request for help. She could have picked up the phone but didn't think it possible to discuss her husband's death with another person today. It was just too hard.

After the state trooper left, she had sat accompanied by only her tears, never moving from the living room sofa until the city morgue called at nine, requesting that she come down to identify the body. The harsh words brought her again to her knees and to the realization she could never get through this alone.

She then called her sister, who agreed to fly in for a few days despite the great distance between them in terms of both relationship and miles. They had not seen each other in years. Still, her sister was now the closest family she had left.

After another hour of crying, she made a difficult call to the same funeral home that handled Melissa's service exactly one week before. The considerable skills of the funeral director were fully tested as he once again tried to sound consoling. But he knew that words of comfort sounded empty when repeated this quickly.

Joan somehow managed to make one more call after that, concluding her last conversation only minutes before Greenbaum left his message. That was another reason she didn't feel like talking to anyone else. She was still trying to sort out what she had just been told. It left her as perplexed as she was anguished.

She had called SeaCoast to find out what she could about her husband's last moments: what he had done, who he had spoken to, what time he left for his fateful drive home. She was patched through to Rob Finnegan who was finishing up another week of anxious days at the office, still awaiting further repercussions from either Charles Thornton or Ken Slator.

When told of Ken's death, Rob Finnegan sounded oddly energized. "You're kidding!" is not the response she had expected. It was not only the surprise in his voice — that part was understandable — but his tone sounded almost relieved in some strange way. Joan had only been around the SeaCoast President a few times and knew he had never been close to her husband. Still, his quick and enthusiastic questions about the wreck — "When? Where? How?" — struck her as macabre and unsettling.

Even more disturbing was his apparent confusion over her husband's late-night trip to the plant. "What meeting?" he had asked. When she explained what Ken had told her, he sounded completely flummoxed. "There was no meeting here last night," he had stammered. "I would have known about it. We haven't flown in any experts and there are no government inspectors here today."

When she pressed the point, asking if he were sure, he had replied: "I don't know what Ken was up to but nobody here has seen him since the day he quit."

Tears once again filled her eyes as she leaned against the hallway wall recalling the denials of Rob Finnegan. She remembered vividly what her husband had said to her: "I have to go down to the plant late tonight." *Could it be his last words to me were all lies?* It made no sense. Even when they had their worst marital problems, deception was never part of the equation.

"Where were you going?"

She cried out the words to an empty house knowing that it, like the person to whom the question was directed, could provide no answer. She walked into the home study, collapsed into the desk chair, and played back the voicemail.

"...I'm only looking to give and get honest answers....Help me get to the truth as only you know it...."

The words resonated. She decided then that the voice speaking to her dead husband deserved a return call. She was, after all, looking for the same thing.

His card was still sitting where her husband had tossed it: on top of the desk, next to the vase of flowers. She picked it up and read the raised lettering.

Harry Greenbaum never intended the phrase "Honest Lawyer" to be anything more than a humorous alternative to the pretentious "Esquire" or "Attorney & Counselor at Law" that adorned the business cards of most of his peers. But Joan Slator, filled with understandable despair and confusion, read it differently. She saw the words as a needed promise from a friendly man that only two days earlier she had mistaken for a completely different kind of solicitor.

As Joan Slator reached for the telephone, Harry Greenbaum sat in his office thinking about a possible next move in the *SeaCoast* inquiry. He was far too experienced to become frustrated by the lack of investigative progress. He knew that some cases reveal themselves quickly while others take time. Breaks come when they want to, sometimes in ways you never expect. But in his wildest imagination there was no way he could ever have expected this.

Two silly words, engraved on a business card, would soon be responsible for taking him down the most dangerous path of his career.

⊗⊗⊗

A defendant in a civil case must receive formal notice of suit. Papers are delivered by a process server or through certified mail. Corporations designate an individual to receive such notices. For Thornton Industries and its related companies, including SeaCoast Chemical, the registered agent for service of process was Bruce Waltman.

The Legal Department receptionist signed the certified mail receipt and placed the thick envelope from the District Clerk's office into a company mail pouch marked "Urgent." It would be on his desk within minutes.

The General Counsel was in his office working on a first draft of remarks to be made by Charles Thornton at the joint press conference with Paul Ravich. It had not yet been scheduled but Waltman wanted to be ahead of the game. He needed to make sure his boss was not caught in any trap of words. It was tricky business declaring a voluntary payment of ten-million dollars to victims while simultaneously revealing the company was also hiring the victims' lawyer to pursue a third-party defendant for its own damages. It was not the type of thing that is ordinarily done. Waltman assumed if *he* had trouble wrapping his head around the concept, so might the press. But as the company's chief lawyer, it was his job to implement Charles Thornton's strategy decisions even when they sounded questionable.

The mail clerk dropped two pouches on top of the inbox that sat on a small table just inside the door of Waltman's office. The corporate lawyer looked up to see the delivery and decided to take a short break. Drafting language to make his boss sound generous, caring, and wise was proving harder than he had imagined. Fiction writing wasn't easy. He walked over and carried the "Urgent" pouch back to his desk. The routine mail could wait but this daily delivery of motions, pleadings, and notices from courts had to be reviewed timely. It was an important chore only he could perform. He would make notes and assign priorities, then promptly delegate response tasks among his team of in-house lawyers.

He opened the envelope from the District Clerk and began reading the summons and pleading in *Crouch v. SeaCoast Chemical*. It made no sense. *They're suing us for gross negligence!* That was in direct violation of the deal Thornton said he struck with Ravich. The Company's upcoming payment to the victims was supposed to be in exchange for a binding release of exactly this type claim. Waltman grew furious. He knew better than to trust a plaintiff's lawyer. *Why didn't I stand up to Thornton and talk him out of this deal?*

He turned to the last page of the pleading and saw names he didn't recognize. *Who is Douglas H. Stevens? Who are these listed co-counsel: Harry Greenbaum and Bill Gaston? Where is Ravich's name? He said he represented all the victims.*

"What the hell?" he shouted in an angry voice that caused his assistant to leave her desk and enter the office to check on things. "Call Marlene and ask if Thornton is available," he barked. "I need to see him right away."

"Yes, sir," she replied, disappearing back to her desk.

Bruce Waltman didn't wait. He got up and hurriedly put on his suit jacket, then gathered up the betraying papers and walked towards his door. As he exited, his assistant hung up the phone at her desk.

"Mr. Thornton is in his office. He can see you now."

She got no reply. Waltman was already striding for the elevator.

Some very bad shit was about to hit the fan.

⎯⎯⎯◦∞◦⎯⎯⎯

"Hello, my name is Joan. I'm returning your call to my husband, Ken Slator."

Harry Greenbaum leaned back in his high-back wooden chair, pleased by the prompt reply to his voicemail but curious about the need for an intermediary.

"Yes, ma'am, I believe we met at your doorstep last Wednesday evening. You mistook me for a door-to-door salesman!"

"I'm very sorry about that…"

"Please, don't be," he interrupted with a chuckle. "I assure you I've been accused of worse."

His attempt at humor was greeted with an ominous response. "Yes, well…I have some terrible news."

Harry's brow furrowed. He could hear the stress as the woman's voice cracked.

"My husband was…killed…in a car accident late last night. I don't know why it happened."

Harry bolted upright in his chair.

"Oh, my dear, Mrs. Slator. This is tragic. I don't know what to say." The shock in his tone matched the sadness in hers. "I am so sorry for your loss. Please accept my deepest sympathies."

"Thank you."

An uncomfortable silence followed. He could make out her faint crying. He waited a moment before speaking again.

"Mrs. Slator, I greatly appreciate being informed, but surely you have more pressing needs right now beyond returning my call. Is there anything I can do to help?"

Joan collected herself, a little. "I was…hoping you could."

"I am at you service," he immediately replied. It sounded sincere because it was.

"You came by to talk with him about the explosion. Maybe you can help me understand. He said he had to go down to the plant last night to meet with people but today I learned there was no meeting." Her uncertainty was unmistakable. "I don't know where he went or what is going on," she added.

Harry was equally puzzled but instantly knew what he wanted to ask. "Has he met recently with anyone else concerning the SeaCoast incident?"

"Not here at the house," she replied. "He had some phone conversations with people at his work, I know that much."

"Do you know with whom?"

"I can't say for sure. But he quit his job, so I'm sure it was his boss."

231

Then she thought of something else. "And he missed dinner this past Monday night. He said he was going to talk with someone about work, and then was planning to stop by his old apartment for his remaining things. He came back home with stuff in the car so I didn't bother to ask questions. We've had a lot going on lately."

Harry was confused. *Talks with the boss? Meetings at night? Old apartment? Other distractions?* Her answer raised only more questions but he was smart enough not to press for details. Now was not the time.

"How might I be of some help?"

"I don't know. Your message said you wanted to get to the truth. So do I."

She realized suddenly that what she had been describing could be misconstrued.

"Mr. Greenbaum, you have to believe me, my husband is…was…a good man. Whatever he was doing, wherever he went last night and the Monday before, it could only have been something to do with his work. I just don't know why he couldn't tell me. I was hoping maybe you could help me find out."

"I am confident, ma'am, that he was a good man and a good husband. I will do all in my power to get you the answers you seek."

"Thank you." She paused, still sniffling. "I didn't even think to ask this first. Who are you the lawyer for?"

"I represent the wife of a young man killed in the explosion. Like you, she is a now a widow who needs to find out what happened to her husband."

"Can you?" she asked. "Find out, I mean."

"It's what I have been doing for almost fifty years. I don't always succeed but I have never stopped trying."

"This is so hard for me. Our daughter passed away ten days ago. I feel lost. I probably shouldn't have called but I don't know where to turn."

He could hear the pain. *A daughter gone too?* The poor woman was on the brink.

"Mrs. Slator, I am honored that you have turned to me. I give you my pledge that I will help you as best I can."

"I'll need to pay you something for your time, I gather? I know lawyers don't work for free."

"The young ones don't but I am anything but."

"I'm sorry?"

"What I mean, madam, is that I'm an old man who wants only answers. The truth, whatever it is, will be more than adequate compensation for me."

"I see. Well, thank you for that. Then what do you need from me?"

"Let me stop by and visit with you when you are ready. Maybe by talking face-to-face we can get ourselves on the right track."

"Okay."

"But Mrs. Slator, I know your thoughts right now are understandably with your husband and loss, as they should be. I don't want to intrude. You just tell me when you think you might be ready to talk."

"I have to go to…the coroner's office tomorrow," she said haltingly.

"Oh, dear me, that is so very unpleasant. Do you have someone to take you?"

"No, my sister isn't flying in until Sunday."

"Would you like me to accompany you?"

"That's kind of you, but…"

"No buts, please. The mark of a friendship is made in times of crisis. You have already asked me to help you in one important task and I said I would. That means we are already friends. So I would not have it any other way. What time shall I pick you up?"

"Are you sure? You don't need to do that."

"I understand. But I *want* to. If you feel like talking about these other things while we drive, that's fine. If not, it can wait for as long as you need. Either way, it would be my privilege to escort you tomorrow."

Joan paused to consider the offer. Imposing upon a stranger was not part of her general makeup but this very nice lawyer seemed willing to assist her through what she knew would be a painful ordeal. Like a soothing balm, his courtly charm and reassuring manner had already managed to bring her some temporary solace. So she decided to say yes.

"Is ten o'clock too early?"

"Of course not. For a man my age, the day is already half over by then. I will be in your driveway at the appointed hour."

"Thank you, Mr. Greenbaum."

"Friends call me Harry. Now, if you need anything at all between now and then, you have my number, all right?"

"All right. Thank you."

She hung up, relieved she had made the call. Like the thousand jurors who had also been charmed by the man over the years, she instinctively trusted this attorney's motivations. She truly believed he wanted to help. *Perhaps there is an "Honest Lawyer,"* she sat thinking, as she stared at the flowers on the desk that no longer held any beauty for her.

Downtown, Harry Greenbaum leaned back once more in his chair, this time in deep reflection as he rubbed his hand through his thinning hair.

Was it even an accident? Maybe Ken Slator had secrets. Personal torments he couldn't handle. The timeline fit. The plant he ran killed so many. He quit his job right after. *Was guilt the reason?* He kept an apartment and went to late night meetings. *Was his life complicated by someone else?* He lost a daughter recently; she had to be young. *The depression had to be great.*

People can choose to surrender when their lives spin out of control. Harry had seen it happen. He thought of a long-dead friend, a strong and talented lawyer who took his own life when financial and professional pressures became too much for him to bear. No one had seen it coming. Then it was too late.

Could I do more harm than good? Harry sat in his office, concerned he might discover facts that would bring the poor Mrs. Slator only more hurt. He also knew his inquiries might reveal nothing of value for the *Crouch* case. Still, he had given his word. He honored his commitments. He would make the effort.

Things happen for a reason, he reminded himself, while contemplating the strange circumstances involving the man who most certainly would have been the key witness in the *SeaCoast* case. Although Harry Greenbaum was a man of faith, the thought lacked any trace of religiosity this Friday afternoon. The phrase did not come to him as a philosophical explanation for tragedy. Instead, it was a purely secular and legalistic statement.

Things happen for a reason.

He was now more determined than ever to find out what those reasons were.

Charles Thornton listened with growing irritation. He tapped his stubby fingers angrily on the desk as his General Counsel reported that SeaCoast Chemical had been sued for gross negligence.

"Ravich did this?" he asked.

"Well, it's a different firm on the pleadings but as you know he claims to represent all the potential plaintiffs." Bruce Waltman held up the document he had been served with, shaking it for emphasis. "Regardless of who filed this, it's in direct contravention of the agreement Ravich said he was making with us."

"He doesn't know who he's screwing with," Thornton huffed, picking up the phone. "Leave that with me," he said, pointing to the pleading still in Waltman's hand.

"Don't you want me to talk to him?" Waltman asked, still smarting from his lack of involvement in the previous negotiations with Ravich.

"No, let me handle this Bruce. Close the door on your way out."

Waltman surrendered the papers and shook his head in dismay. *What's the point of having a General Counsel you don't use?* A man who represents himself has a fool for a client, the saying went. *He deserves getting screwed,* Waltman thought treasonously, as he walked out of Thornton's office in a sullen mood, shutting the door behind him.

Paul Ravich was seated comfortably behind his desk, pretending it was just another routine day at the office. There was always mail to read and a few important phone calls to return. When not in court, not much else got done on a typical Friday afternoon and he was determined to make this particular day look as typical as possible. Fifteen hours ago he had intentionally sent a man to his death. Now was not the time to do anything unusual.

Jan's voice came over the intercom. "Charles Thornton of Thornton Industries is holding on Line 3 for you."

Ravich straightened up in his chair and reached for the phone. He wasn't surprised by the call. Yesterday, the man had sent him six-million dollars with absolutely nothing in writing to protect that investment. It was the kind of transaction that can make a businessman a little antsy.

"Hello, Charles, how are you today?"

The chirpy tone only stoked the ire of the man on the other end of the line.

"Listen to me, you slimy bastard! What's going on here? I don't know what you're trying to pull but you won't get away with it!"

Ravich lifted the receiver away from his ear as the words were being shouted. He had no idea what Thornton was talking about but did know the man was a bully. *How childish,* he thought. It would take more than a little screaming to faze him.

"Well, good afternoon to you, too. Now let's start over and act like partners. What exactly has you upset?"

"You promised there would be no lawsuits against SeaCoast."

"And I've kept that promise."

"Then why am I holding papers that say I have twenty days to file a response to this claim of gross negligence against the company?"

At first, Ravich remained confused. Then it struck him. He clinched his teeth, angry with himself for not taking care of all loose ends. *That little smart-ass lawyer!*

"Was the suit filed by a Doug Stevens?"

"How the hell should I know?" Thornton shouted back.

It was time to take control. His "partner" was losing it.

"Charles, calm down. We have too much at stake here to go flying off the handle. Just turn to the last page of the pleading and tell me the name of the attorney who signed the damn thing."

He could hear the papers rustling.

"It's signed by a Douglas H. Stevens. And it lists some other lawyers below his name."

"That's what I thought. Who are the others?"

"It says: Bill Gaston and Harry Greenbaum."

Ravich winced. Slator had asked about Greenbaum in the elevator last night. He knew then that his old boss was helping the young lawyer. He should have made some calls already. But he had been too busy today trying not to look busy.

"All right, that explains it then. That case is from a rogue claimant, a widow of one of the victims who decided to have a family friend-lawyer handle her claim instead of me. I'll take care of it."

"How?"

"I know the lawyers involved. They can't learn about our 'arrangement' but I can convince them it's not in their interest to pursue SeaCoast. Just give me some time. Meanwhile, have your General Counsel answer the lawsuit. All he has to do is file what is called a 'General Denial.' Nothing else has to happen for a month or so. This little problem will go away once our suit gets filed against Integrated Sentry, if not sooner."

"But you said you represented everybody."

"I do, everyone except this one silly woman. It's a very small wrinkle and I've already said I'd take care of the ironing. Now, if you're through yelling, would you like to be briefed on some other truly important developments?"

Thornton was still mad but had six million reasons to hear the man out.

"They'd better be good ones," he warned.

"Oh, they are. Is anyone else listening?"

"I'm not on speaker. There's nobody in my office."

"No recording devices?"

"Of course not."

"Good."

Despite the assurances, Ravich knew better than to directly outline certain details over a phone. Careless men — including a President of the United States — had seen their downfall brought about by overheard or recorded words. He needed to disguise his true message in deniable ambiguity and hope the tempestuous fool on the phone would catch his drift.

"First of all, I want to acknowledge receipt of your favorable response yesterday to our proposed course of action."

Thornton recognized that he was talking about the wire transfer and appreciated the fact that Ravich was talking in code. Being careful. *He's just like me*, Thornton thought.

Ravich was even more guarded in his next words.

"Second, I just received some startling news from one my SeaCoast clients. I guess they must have heard about this from his family or something. Your former plant manager died in a car accident last night. You remember, the man I told you about? I met with him at the start of this week and he gave me his computer records. You know, the records that show how Integrated Sentry's safety system malfunctioned and caused the explosion?"

Charles Thornton's jaw dropped. *The man that hung up on him the day after the plant blew up?* He couldn't recall the name. *He's dead?*

Silence followed as Thornton quickly made some panicked but accurate deductions. *The manager was the secret witness.* The six-million dollars was supposed to buy his silence. *But an accident?* He didn't know he was paying for a hit. *Who gets that money now?* The cash was already sitting in Ravich's Swiss account. *That was a stupid thought.* Thornton's mind was swirling. *My God, this lawyer will do anything.*

"Isn't that awful?" Ravich finally added, trying to resume their coded conversation.

"Well…yes…that's terrible news."

Thornton stumbled his words, realizing he was now at the mercy of this devious attorney. The wire transfer could be evidence of a solicitation of *murder*, if that's what actually happened.

"It is sad," Ravich replied, continuing the pretense. "He was a good man, and he so wanted the truth to come out. Luckily for us, from a legal standpoint, we can still have the benefit of his evidence. My office got testimony from him that will allow those critical records to be admitted at trial. Thank God we were diligent and acted quickly."

Ravich spoke with a smugness that even Charles Thornton found disconcerting. *This man is pure evil.* Then he grasped another important fact: Ravich had undeniably delivered his end of the first part of their deal. The witness could never flip and expose their scam. *Could he manage the rest of it?*

"So, what's next?" Thornton asked warily.

"I have experts tentatively scheduled for next week. They'll review the computer records and form some initial opinions about the cause of your plant's destruction. Assuming they verify what I think they will, I believe you will have a very strong case against the third-party maker of that defective safety system."

He paused to let his biggest client soak it all in.

"Next week, huh?" Thornton asked, surprised by the fast pace.

"That's right, two weeks at the latest. Which means I might have a lawsuit ready to file on your behalf and for the victims by, let's say, ten days from today if all goes well? How does that sound?"

"I'll let you decide the timing," Thornton responded, his anger now gone.

"Which brings me to ask a small favor of you," Ravich replied.

"Haven't I done enough already?"

"Yes, you've been very cooperative," Ravich laughed. "But this new request will cost you nothing and would help expedite our little timetable."

Ravich had already begun the next step in his intricate plan. The programmers Ron had retained in Mumbai were standing by, reportedly thrilled to be offered high compensation for something so simple as creating a believable computer simulation of a system failure. All they needed was the original program and data to be uploaded to their server, along with detailed instructions of what should be changed.

"What is it you want?" Thornton asked.

"I need the plant's schematics delivered to me along with any documents SeaCoast might still have from Integrated Sentry; specifically, any operations manual and diagrams of the DCSS safety system which that company supplied at the time of their installation."

"I'm not your errand boy, counselor."

"Yes, yes, I realize that, Charles. But you are now my partner in *all* of this, don't you see?"

Thornton shifted uncomfortably in his chair. Ravich placed extra emphasis on the word "all." The implication was sinister.

"So, if you could get me those things by tomorrow, I should be able to complete our next important step over the weekend."

"Which is?" Thornton asked, almost afraid of the answer.

"Well, I need to have a consulting expert look over those documents to help me better understand how this irresponsible company caused you so much damage. The 'malfunction' we both know occurred has to be explained and revealed very carefully as I'm sure you can understand."

Thornton knew what Ravich's coded words meant. They were about as subtle as his earlier threat. The fake computer records had to pass the smell test. You can't have a computer showing component failure if you don't have a clue what the parts were supposed to do in the first place.

"I'll make a call to the idiot that runs SeaCoast," Thornton pledged. "If we still have copies, they'll be on my desk in two hours. My office will then call you. You can send someone by to pick them up here."

"Excellent!"

Ravich was pleased by the promise of prompt action and was equally satisfied that Thornton now understood he no longer had a choice about whether or not to cooperate fully. Ravich knew if he got those documents today, he could have his consulting expert at his office on Saturday or Sunday for a very private working session. A "script" for the Indian programmers could be ready as early as Monday or Tuesday.

"Is there anything else I can do for you?" Thornton asked sarcastically.

Even though he was justifiably apprehensive, considering the shocking things he had just learned, the corporate magnate wanted to make clear that his quick acquiescence was not a sign of weakness. He was still Charles Thornton.

Ravich couldn't resist tweaking him some more.

"We'll plan on holding our joint press conference right after the suit gets filed. I'm going to prepare a fee agreement between us along the lines we previously discussed. When my man stops by to pick up those documents, he will deliver the agreement to you for your signature, along with a separate letter confirming your pledge to make the voluntary payment of ten-million dollars to my clients. In that letter, I'll say the deadline for payment is in two weeks. Fair enough?"

Thornton didn't like having terms dictated to him. That had always been his province. But now he recognized that things were very different. You don't have much bargaining power when dealing with a murderer. "All right," was all he could manage to say.

"Very good. Now, let me get back to work. I'll get started on neutralizing that other little lawsuit that has you so upset. You have nothing to worry about there. As I told you before, I'm a man of my word. I won't let anything stand in our way."

Thornton's curiosity, or perhaps his fear, got the better of him. "What happened to that man? I mean, what do you know about his accident?"

"I know absolutely nothing," Ravich said with a feigned sense of indignation. His next sentence, spoken sternly, would also carry another hint of threat: "The same as you."

Ravich grinned broadly as he imagined Thornton's reaction on the other end of the line.

He would have loved to have seen it.

Behind a massive desk, in an office the size of an airplane hanger, on an upper floor of a tall skyscraper named after him, sat an arrogant tycoon who was now trembling in his chair, a cold sweat breaking across his brow.

Charles Thornton had just committed the mistake every good trial lawyer knew never to make. He had asked one question too many.

Chapter 14
Hide and Seek

The rented Malibu was put to good use. The same car used to tail Ken Slator on his fatal drive home was now parked two blocks away from the dead man's house.

The location was perfect for a Saturday morning stakeout: a small neighborhood park, a place for local residents to picnic or for kids to roll around in the grass. The sedan parked alongside the curb would not seem out of place. It obviously belonged to the man sitting on a bench enjoying the fresh air. An obedient Labrador sat calmly nearby waiting to play yet another game of fetch whenever his master was ready. A man and his dog spending a leisurely autumn morning in such a tranquil place would not appear suspicious to anyone.

Ron first noticed the quiet little park while driving through the neighborhood the night before. In hindsight, it was foolish to think it could have been done then. The chance of the widow venturing outside in the first twenty-four hours following the accident was a long shot at best. She would still be paralyzed by shock and grief. Lights inside the house on Friday night confirmed someone was there. But an accidental death eventually brings chores for the surviving spouse. A body has to be claimed and funeral arrangements have to be made. Ron assumed Mrs. Slator would begin to attend to such things the following day and he wanted to be nearby if she left the house.

The key to daylight surveillance is blending in with your surroundings. Ron also knew that his dog, Ranger, wouldn't mind being used as a prop. He must have thrown Ranger's tennis ball a hundred times, clapping his hands whenever the Lab came bounding back with his slobbered fetch. Even if a person was watching their every move — which clearly no one was — he and his dog would seem odd only in their steady compulsiveness. Just one person came down the sidewalk during that first hour: a young woman pushing her baby in a stroller. She waved and Ron smiled, saying "good morning" to her as she passed by without concern. He and Ranger were passing the test.

From the park bench, Ron could peer down the straight residential street and see the house in the distance. A few minutes before ten, he saw an old car amble up the street and turn into the Slator's driveway. An elderly man got out and walked to the door. A minute later, the man escorted a woman down the steps and into the waiting vehicle. He watched carefully as the car backed out and headed back in the direction of the park. Ron glanced as the car glided past. The old male driver never looked his way. Neither did the woman, mid-fifties, in the passenger seat. The Plymouth continued down the street for several more blocks before turning right at a larger four-way stop intersection.

"C'mon boy, let's go," Ron called out, as he patted his leg. Ranger knew the signal and heeled beside his master as they walked back to the rented Malibu.

Most criminals rely on stealth but in broad daylight that is seldom an option. In such circumstances, acting like you have nothing to hide can sometimes be the best cover. Ron pulled his rented car directly into the Slator driveway and parked in front of the closed garage situated at the back of the house. He cracked open a car window and told Ranger to "Stay." He was a smart dog. He would sit quietly in the back seat and wait for his master's return; that is, unless someone else suddenly approached the car, in which case he would bark loudly. It made him the perfect lookout.

Ron got out of the car, carrying a large grocery bag. Inside was a bakery box containing a fresh lemon coffee cake. On top of the cake and sticking out of the bag were some flowers. If someone else was in the house, or should a neighbor come outside and ask, his story would be he was a fellow worker from the plant who had learned of Ken's death and was just stopping by with a few things as an act of kindness to the widow.

A wood privacy fence connected the back of the house to the garage behind and beside it. Once through the fence's gate and into the backyard, he couldn't be seen by even a nosey neighbor. He stepped to the back door of the house and knocked. There was no answer. He then tried the door handle. It was locked. He sat the grocery bag down and reached inside his windbreaker to extract a set of burglar's tools. Picking a household lock was no real challenge. He was inside the kitchen within a minute. He placed the bag down on the table and headed for the study. Once there, he reached in his jacket pocket again, pulling out a disc and a folded piece of paper.

The firm's I.T. employee had prepared a memo explaining how to erase a Macintosh hard drive and furnished an operating system disc that could do so. The kid readily accepted Ron's story that he was donating his old home computer to charity and had agreed it was a good idea to erase the contents before giving it away. Ron unfolded the helpful memo, sat down at the small desk and carefully followed the steps.

He woke the iMac from sleep mode by pressing the keyboard's spacebar. He inserted the disc into the computer's DVD slot and selected *"Restart"* from the Apple Menu. When the startup chime sounded, he pressed and held the *"C"* key until the computer booted up from the spinning disc. He then opened the *"Disc Utility"* application from the Installer Menu on the software disc. He clicked on the image of the hard drive that appeared in the application window and selected *"Erase,"* making sure to pick the option for *"7 Pass Erase."* The firm's computer geek explained that option would take several hours to complete but it would write over all data sufficiently to make everything irretrievable forever. Ron then wadded up the instruction memo and put it back in his jacket pocket.

While the disc ran its destructive program, Ron turned his attention to the cabinet safe. Three days before, Ken Slator had carelessly let Ron see its location and didn't object as he stood over Slator's knelt body, watching him key in the combination. Ron had been trained by both the military and the police to pay attention to the smallest of details. He opened the lower cabinet doors and bent down to the safe. He typed the number sequence he recalled: "2-6-1-8." The door sprang open. Ron smiled, self-congratulating his acute observational skills. Now he wouldn't have to make a mess. If his memory of the combination had proven to be incorrect, he was prepared to steal the whole thing by prying the safe up and cutting the bolt securing it to the cabinet floor. The necessary tools, which were laying in the car's trunk, would now not be needed.

Inside the open safe was the one-hundred thousand in cash. Next to it was the new laptop, exactly as Ravich had predicted. Ron took both, disregarding the personal papers that appeared to be a deed, a divorce decree, and some insurance policies. He closed both the safe and cabinet doors.

He quickly retreated back to the kitchen where he tossed the laptop and cash into the grocery sack before making a quick pass through the rest of the house to verify no computers were in the other rooms. He left the way he came in and was greeted by Ranger, eagerly wagging his tail. Ron tossed the grocery bag into the front seat, got in, and started the car.

"Good boy," Ron whispered, reaching back to scratch his dog's head as a reward for being so helpful. He then backed out the driveway and drove safely out of the neighborhood. The lemon cake, partially smashed by the new weight of a laptop and so much cash, smelled even better than it had before. It would now become a nice treat for a job well done. Ranger might even get a piece. Rolling down his window to allow some brisk autumn air to blow through the cabin of the handy rental, which could now be returned, Ron grinned with satisfaction. *I can have my cake and eat it too.* He laughed at the thought.

The entire operation — not counting the wait in the park — had taken only eleven minutes. For that, he had earned a hundred-grand and would soon gain even more praise from his boss. Not bad for less than two total hours of his time on a Saturday morning.

He had to walk the dog anyway.

⸎

In a cover-up, the law itself can be a useful tool. Paul Ravich figured out a way to use the legitimate rules of discovery to perpetuate his fraudulent evidence scheme.

Prior to trial, each litigant in a civil suit must formally identify those experts who will be called as witnesses. The other side then has an opportunity to discover an expert's opinions through reports and depositions before walking into the courtroom. However, "consulting experts" — those specialists who assist the attorney but will never be used as witnesses — don't have to be named. The law considers such consultants to be part of the attorney's "work product" which makes their identity and advice privileged from disclosure.

On Saturday morning — while his investigator was committing a burglary — Paul Ravich sat listening to a very important "consulting expert" in his private conference room, the same place where he and Charles Thornton held their fateful meeting four days earlier. Dr. Peter Garrison was a specialist in Industrial Safety. He was one of the show horses that Ravich maintained in his stable of experts. Garrison was smart and would have made a great testifying expert in the *SeaCoast* case. But Ravich needed him for a different task, one that meant Garrison's name would never appear on any witness disclosure list.

Ravich stood over the blueprints that Thornton had furnished on Friday, describing what his other expert had speculated to be the cause of the explosion.

"Dr. Norman Clark went with me the morning after the explosion. We obtained access to the scene and he thought the explosive pattern made things pretty clear. You know Norman, don't you?" Ravich asked.

"Of course, we've had cases together," Garrison replied.

243

"Well, he shares your specialty but he's also a chemical process engineer, which is why I have chosen him as our principal testifying expert in this case. Juries hate redundancy, as you know. I hope you aren't offended by my relegating you to a purely consulting role this time?"

"Of course not. The pay's the same."

Both men laughed.

"As you can imagine, this case is going to be huge. Therefore, I wanted to get a second opinion, to make sure we're on the right track."

Ravich tossed one of the scene photographs across the table.

"That crater is where the mixing vessel once stood, what this blueprint lists as a neutralizer tank," Ravich said, pointing to the spot on the plant diagram. "Dr. Clark is convinced this was the point of ignition and told me there was only one thing that would cause that vessel to explode from the inside."

"A self-sustaining decomposition of the ammonium nitrate," Garrison answered with authority.

"Precisely. Now, the circumstantial evidence is strong as to the cause of the explosion but what's most troubling is: Why didn't the plant's safety system detect this dangerous condition before it got out of hand?"

Ravich slid over the rest of the package that had been frantically copied by Rob Finnegan and raced over to Charles Thornton. It was a copy of Integrated Sentry's detailed schematic of the DCSS system along with its operation manual. SeaCoast had been furnished two copies of the manual at the time of purchase. One was kept in the control room and was destroyed in the fire; the other was spared by its location in the business office.

"This is the safety system that should have prevented the disaster. As you can see on that schematic, there were over fifty different sensors that supplied readings and measurements to the plant's control room."

Ravich saw his consultant pick up and leaf through the manual. He continued his set-up.

"That document makes clear that the company which sold and installed the system understood the importance of controlling temperatures and volatility in that mixing tank. There's an entire chapter in there describing what each sensor does and when abnormal activity inside the neutralizer tank will trigger a safety shutdown."

Dr. Garrison was used to being led by Paul Ravich. "So the system failed, is that what you're getting at?"

"It sure looks that way to me and Dr. Clark. Otherwise, the explosion doesn't happen."

His consultant nodded in agreement.

"But here's the tricky part. All the sensor data and process operations logs were destroyed in the blast and subsequent fire. Therefore, at least for now, we have to build a circumstantial case from that schematic and manual."

Ravich then made his main point.

"I need you to look for the weakest links in that safety system, come up with a scientific explanation for its failure, and assure me that such a failure scenario could have led to this explosion. Can you do that?"

"Well, I can certainly review and critique the system. Most times, when something like this occurs, you find inadequate fail-safes in the system design."

"That's what I need you looking for here."

"I can obviously identify vulnerable spots in their design that could lead to catastrophe but how are you ever going to prove that's what *actually* happened?"

Dr. Garrison was a seasoned veteran of the courtroom. He knew that expert speculation is not the same as admissible evidence.

"Let me worry about that. We haven't even filed suit yet. I expect, through discovery, we will come across additional evidence to confirm our theories. Right now, I just need a plausible failure mode so that I can make a more directed search for the truth."

Ravich was lying masterfully. Everything he had said so far made perfect sense to his consultant. Dr. Garrison would, of course, never be told that any eventual *theory* he came up with would become *fact* once the programmers in India got finished with Slator's computer records.

It was a brilliant circular insulating of the fraud. His consultant would feel proud when told after the verdict or settlement that his initial theory had been borne out by later discovered "facts." Meanwhile, his testifying expert, Dr. Clark, would discover the "facts" only after reviewing computer records that had been secretly altered in accordance with Dr. Garrison's theory. The two experts would never be in the same room. The target defendant, Integrated Sentry, would never learn of Dr. Garrison's role in "creating" the liability theory since he was a mere "consulting" expert. Nobody except Ravich, Thornton, and Ron would ever realize that the chicken came before the egg. In most cases, *evidence* leads to liability on someone's part. Here, a liability theory would lead to *evidence creation*.

"Can I take this home with me?" Garrison asked, gesturing to the documents before him.

"Of course, but I need you to be constantly on the clock. I would really like to have the benefit of your analysis by Monday afternoon, if possible."

"Whew," Dr. Garrison loudly huffed, intending to communicate that

Ravich was asking for the impossible. "Why so quick?"

Ravich lied. "For strategic reasons I need to get a suit filed next week. And I don't want to sue this company if you tell me their safety system could not have possibly malfunctioned. You know, I have an ethical duty to only assert claims that have some valid basis in fact."

"I see," the expert replied, not realizing Ravich's incredible misstatement of intent. "This is going to cost you, Paul," Garrison chuckled. "It's the weekend you know."

"Then bill me double-time. I don't care. Just give me a detailed report outlining what could have gone wrong. Make sure you specifically identify the potential failed sensors or actions, using ISI's terminology as stated in their DCSS manual. Tell me how that safety system might have malfunctioned and why it might have lulled the plant operator into a false sense of security. Without that kind of detail, I wouldn't even know where to begin with my discovery."

"I'll do my best."

Dr. Garrison got up to leave and began gathering the documents into a stack. He thought of a question.

"Say, would it be all right if I run some of my thoughts or impressions by Norman as well? Two heads are better than one."

"No, absolutely don't do that," Ravich instructed harshly.

His consulting expert looked askance and Ravich, always fast on his feet, came up with a credible though false excuse for the directive.

"I need Dr. Clark to remain truly independent of you. You know how these damn defense lawyers are, Peter. If Clark has to testify that he spoke to you, or relied upon your theories or opinions in any way, they will claim the right to depose you too. And you know what happens then. They will concoct the foolish argument that your theories were made up out of whole cloth without any advance evidence in support. I need your *ideas* to be my privileged work product — part of my investigative theory — so that I can probe later for *real evidence* which Dr. Clark can rely upon in forming his opinions."

Dr. Garrison nodded in agreement. But Ravich wanted to make the point clear.

"You're a pro, Doc. You know how these things can get twisted around. That's why you will remain a consulting expert only. Let's maintain an *honest* wall between you and the people I ask to testify. All right?"

Ravich smiled at the word he had emphasized. *This guy has no idea how funny that sounds.*

"I understand completely, Paul. You know, most lawyers aren't as concerned as you about doing the right thing."

"I know," Ravich said, continuing the ironic charade.

Signaling the meeting was over, he shook the hand of his completely unaware conspirator and concluded with a statement that only his dishonest mind could deliver with a straight face:

"Other lawyers can and do skirt the rules," Ravich said. "But I built my reputation upon integrity. No case is worth throwing that away."

———⊗⊗⊗———

Both women expected an uneasy reunion. They had not seen each other in years. They spoke rarely by phone, always briefly and superficially, primarily at Christmas, occasionally on birthdays. Growing up, the sisters had been inseparable yet in their adult lives they had grown inexplicably apart. Neither could say why the closeness disappeared. There was no specific event that caused an estrangement. Life had simply gotten in the way. After college, both moved to cities in distant states, got married, and started families of their own. In time, each had similar but unshared burdens of marital discord and troubled children. Priorities understandably began to revolve around their most immediate relationships. It left little time to focus on those from childhood. Theirs was not an unusual transformation: two siblings growing up to lead their own and different lives. It was a common story. Time and outside pressures can stretch the familial bond as if it were a rubber band, growing thinner and thinner until it suddenly snaps in two and loses all purpose.

As Joan Slator sat in her idling car outside of baggage claim, she wondered if she would even recognize her sister Nicole. *Had she grown fat? Would her hair now have streaks of gray, like mine?* Beyond the problem of identification at a busy airport, none of that mattered. The important things were that Nicole wanted to come and that Joan needed her here. Maybe that meant their bond was not broken but merely misplaced. Joan desperately hoped so. She wretched in emotional pain as she waited for her sister's arrival, thinking how badly she needed family — any family — after being so unfairly robbed of both her daughter and husband in the span of less than two weeks. Even if broken, she reached for that rubber band to help hold her life together. It was all she had left.

The day before, she had borne the torture of standing in a stark room as a sheet was slowly pulled back to reveal the lifeless face of her husband, her precious Ken, whose sudden personality change after Melissa's death had brought for them the promise of a second chance. At the morgue, she had slumped into the arms of a lawyer that days earlier had been a complete stranger. The kindnesses which Harry Greenbaum showed her that day would never be forgotten. The old gentleman might not be family but he had offered his own form of badly needed reassurance in the promise that he wouldn't rest until they both understood why all this had happened.

Amid the flow of passengers exiting through the automatic doors she saw a familiar face. Perhaps it was a little rounder. Maybe a bit more wrinkled. But it was Nicole. Joan rolled down the window and called out. Her older sister, pulling a small roller bag behind her, waved enthusiastically and quickened her pace. Joan sprang out of the car as she approached. They hugged tightly and simultaneously burst into tears. Their embrace lasted for almost a minute. For that moment, time and distance evaporated. They were two little girls again, sitting atop twin beds in a shared room, each glad the other was there. It felt good at a time when absolutely nothing else did. When they separated, their eyes met, silently saying what both needed to hear: *"I'm so sorry for you, sis." "I'm so grateful that you came."*

Nicole held her sister's right hand as they drove back to the house. The tragic events of recent days and the recurring years of short meaningless phone calls made conversation difficult. But somehow they struggled with words and, in so doing, the bond between them slowly grew once again.

"I should have been here when Melissa passed," Nicole apologized. "There's no excuse. I'm sorry."

"It's okay. Ken was with me."

Saying those words made her start to weep again. Nicole squeezed her hand tighter.

"Well, I'm here now. We're going to get through this together, all right?"

Joan nodded in appreciation.

"Sis, I know we haven't been very close lately, but that's going to change. I can stay for as long as you need. Carl and the kids understand and they send their love."

Joan smiled faintly. "How is everyone?" she asked.

"You know how it is," Nicole replied, with a brief shrug. "Things could always be better. But when I see what you're going through, I realize it could also be much worse. So I have no right to complain."

Joan nodded and stared vacantly at the road ahead. For some time they said nothing. Finding the silence awkward, Nicole sought to discover details about the accident.

"Did Ken suffer at all?"

"No, the coroner said he died instantly, that he wasn't in any pain. But that's also what the doctors told me about Melissa. How can they possibly know?"

"Let's just choose to believe they're right. Do they know what caused his accident?"

Joan clenched her lips and shook her head no.

"Well, it's not important, I guess. What matters most is to remember that both Ken and Melissa left this world loving you."

Joan's face showed no expression as she navigated the freeway exit ramp and turned toward her neighborhood. But she was deep in thought about her sister's last comment. While it was clearly meant to comfort, she couldn't disagree more.

No, what really matters most is: Why?

For that, she still had no answers.

You could always count on Dr. Garrison. He was an expert who could find a defect in a handmade Swiss timepiece. Paul Ravich grinned widely as he reached the end of the five-page report his "consulting expert" dropped off at noon on Monday, together with a return of the materials he had been asked to review.

Garrison had evidently worked long hours through the weekend, devouring the documents Ravich had allowed him to take home. The expert obviously became deeply versed in the minutiae of the DCSS operating manual and had quickly educated himself, using the plant drawings and safety system schematics, on how the system was supposed to work. More importantly, he had identified potential weaknesses in Integrated Sentry's design for the SeaCoast plant. As an industrial safety expert with impeccable credentials, Dr. Garrison probably found the entire task easier than following assembly instructions for Ikea furniture.

The report read beautifully. It outlined two distinct problems that might lead to the safety system's failure to diagnose, report, and respond to an emergency occurring in the plant's neutralizer tank. Dr. Garrison believed he was only presenting *potential* explanations that would require extensive investigation. He had no idea, and would never learn, that his words would soon be on a programmer's desk halfway around the world, serving as a blueprint for what Slator's computer data needed to show:

"The DCSS, overall, was a sophisticated plant control system, its design integrating multiple fail-safe components and automated response mechanisms. Through an intricate network of electronic sensors, it was intended to eliminate or minimize human error input in two important respects: first, by providing accurate and quantitative information to the plant operator via real time measurements of critical process variants like temperatures and liquid or gas volumes; and second, by automatically initiating appropriate responses to conditions falling outside of safe operating

parameters."

Ravich was used to reading expert reports filled with technical and verbose language. It was, after all, his job to translate such gobbledygook into understandable themes for appreciative juries. That introductory paragraph was actually pretty easy to distill. Garrison was simply making the point that Integrated Sentry's design was *supposed* to report and correct *anything* that might be going wrong. Enough said. The fact that something did go horribly wrong was a clear indication that the design was flawed. Ravich had already decided that clever syllogism would be his main case theme.

However, the law also requires proof of a specific design defect. Dr. Garrison certainly understood that as well, as he made clear in later paragraphs of his detailed report which Ravich enthusiastically underlined with a yellow marker:

"The device intended to measure and calibrate volume levels in the neutralizer tank [identified in both schematic and manual as 'Sensor V18'] is a single pressure-sensitive monitor energized through electrical current supplied from Control Box D22, which is an auxiliary power panel. All other sensors in the system are energized through Control Box D14 which, in turn, relies upon Control Box D17 for emergency power in the event of any power interruption at D14."

"The existence of backup electrical supply to D14 is clear evidence that Integrated Sentry properly recognized the importance of providing reserve power to all its measuring sensors. However, panel D14 was two circuits shy of accommodating all ISI leads, which is probably why the ISI installers connected Sensor V18 and another less critical steam flow sensor [S42] to the auxiliary panel D22. [see schematic, page 3, items F&G.]"

"In short, it appears that ISI ran out of room in its primary electrical panel and decided to install power for a critical neutralizer component [V18] in an electrical panel that had no backup. Consequently, in the event of fuse or panel failure in D22, Sensor V18 would be unable to transmit any actual changes in the neutralizer's volume level, resulting in a continuous and erroneous control room display of its last powered reading."

"A self-sustaining decomposition of ammonium nitrate, which most likely caused the initial explosion within the neutralizer tank, would have been easily detected by a properly powered Sensor V18, since dramatic and rapid changes in volume occur as AN turns itself into deadly volatile gases. The fact that such volume changes were not detected, and no shutdown sequence was thereafter initiated, is strong circumstantial evidence that Sensor V18 failed to operate as intended. A constant volume reading in the neutralizer, at or near the time of the explosion, would be the most direct

evidence of component V18 failure. The failure to provide supplemental power to ALL critical measuring sensors would constitute both negligent and defective design."

It would be easy to explain, in plain language, what Dr. Garrison meant. The ISI designers and installers had simply cut a corner, leaving their system vulnerable at the *very* place where the initial explosion occurred. Ravich could barely contain his glee. He had his first alteration requirement. The programmers in India would be told to make any data reading from Sensor V18 constant and within normal limits. Ravich made a quick note to call and ask Dr. Garrison what a *normal* number should be. He then continued reading:

"A most interesting feature of this DCSS design is that it actually contemplates scenarios wherein an individual system component might fail to perform its intended purpose. In such instances, the system is designed to self-activate from its normal operating mode (Automatic) to a procedure described by Integrated Sentry as 'Cascade Mode.' The electronics will then try to isolate the problem by triggering sequenced responses that take the troublemaker out of the equation, while directing the remaining components to pick up the slack, so to speak. In theory, Cascade Mode allows process operations to continue only if a single sensor failure is involved. If multiple failures or abnormalities are reported, the system will always default to a full process shutdown."

"However, in the event of an electrical problem with Sensor V18, there is one particular scenario where the DCSS computer, acting in Cascade Mode, might allow operations to continue even in the face of impending disaster."

Ravich reached again for his yellow marker. As he underlined the key lines at the end Dr. Garrison's report, he smiled, thinking that the distinctive odor of the highlighter's ink smelled a lot like fresh money:

"The neutralizer's auto-shutdown procedure is triggered by a combination of sensor readings. The DCSS looks for both elevated temperatures and abnormal volume readings before it gives the electronic command to turn things off. But if the volume sensor is not making new readings due to a power loss, as outlined above, it fools the system into thinking everything's fine on the volume end. Now, when temperature readings begin to rapidly rise, and there being no volume abnormality to confirm an imminent problem, the DCSS kicks into Cascade Mode where it might potentially misdiagnose the problem as being a malfunctioning temperature sensor. The computer could, in turn, bypass that properly functioning warning device and let the dangerous mixing process continue."

"Said simply, the DCSS might have been electronically fooled into allowing the bomb inside the tank to keep forming. Cascade Mode could be

tricked by a power loss into trusting the dead volume sensor, causing it to ignore the accurate temperature sensor. Since that could happen, the Cascade Mode programming is defective and unreasonably dangerous on its face. If that is what happened, you have a perfectly clean explanation for why no one saw the explosion coming. The DCSS was, in effect, lying to the controller — assuring him that volume activity was normal when it wasn't, and telling him to disregard temperature readings that were, in fact, ominous."

"I caution these are simply theories based upon how the system was constructed and designed to work. But if you can prove that the plant was operating in Cascade Mode during the last hour or so before the explosion, and that the neutralizer's temp sensor was in fact bypassed by the system, you will have bolstered your proof of a power failure to Sensor V18 while also demonstrating the disastrous effects of poor programming design."

Paul Ravich laid the confidential report down on his desk, ecstatic with its contents. He picked up the phone and called his newest hero, Dr. Peter Garrison. After thanking him for his Herculean efforts, Ravich asked a few more questions. He scribbled notes on his legal pad as his consultant spoke. When he was done, he knew exactly what the altered computer records needed to show.

"Doc, you're the best. Again, I really appreciate your hard work on this. It's a shame I can't use you at trial."

"I understand. Norman Clark will do a fine job for you, I'm sure," Garrison replied. "Although without the physical evidence, he's got his work cut out for him on the witness stand. Obviously, none of the actual components will be available for inspection based upon those damage photos I saw. If you only had that DCSS data, you could prove or disprove my theory in five minutes."

"I hear you," Ravich responded with false exasperation. "Maybe we'll get lucky and a backup copy will turn up somewhere in the case discovery. At least now, with this report of yours, I will know what to ask and look for."

"Glad to be of help."

"By the way, Doc, I didn't see a bill for your time."

"I'm in no rush. I'll get something out to you in the next couple of days."

"Fine. I'll see that you're promptly paid. I can tell the work you put into this. Don't hesitate to bill me in full."

"You are a rare treat among lawyers, Paul. Most of my time is spent arguing over my fees and collecting my invoices."

"That will never be a problem with me," Ravich assured the expert, as he said goodbye.

Using the underlined report and his notes, the lawyer sat at his office computer and prepared detailed instructions that Ron would upload that evening to the programmers in India, along with Slator's original DCSS file. All the hired programmers would have to do was read and follow the script, transforming the actual DCSS output into a new one that fit Garrison's theory. Ordinarily, Ravich dictated all his memos which his assistant Jan would then type up and distribute. But this was not the kind of document that an honest employee could have anything to do with. It was a template for believable fraud. *It was worth one-hundred million dollars in fee.*

That thought reminded him of something important. Using the office's instant-messaging system, he typed something he *could* share with his assistant: *"Jan, when Dr. Garrison's bill comes in on the SeaCoast case, pay him three times more than he charges."*

The two sisters spent time catching up on lost years. With glasses of wine and surrounded by old photo albums, they reminisced about far happier days: growing up, attending college together, their weddings and children. Nicole reasoned the best therapy she could provide her sister was to talk about anything other than death. Joan appreciated the diversion and her sister's company but her mind was never free of the pain.

As they flipped through pages of her wedding album, Joan was struck by how circular her life with Ken had been. In the fading glossies, Ken posed happily, his arm around his bride. In each picture he bore the same expression as in their last week together: that of a caring husband in love with his wife. They next browsed through baby photos of Melissa. She was so vulnerable, so young. *Another full circle*, thought Joan, for that was also how she died. The memories were all so bittersweet. Every picture brought smiles then sadness.

Nicole detailed the travails of her own marriage and family while Joan listened politely but her thoughts were always somewhere else. Joan kept repeating "Really?" in response to her sister's stories but the next day she wouldn't recall much of anything she had been told. They went to bed early on Sunday. Nicole was tired from the long flight and Joan was emotionally fatigued.

The next morning, as Joan cleared the dishes from their light breakfast, her sister went into the study to check for email from home. She sat at the desk and pressed the keyboard on Joan's iMac. The screen lit up and displayed a flashing folder bearing a question mark. No keystroke or mouse click could make it go away.

"Sis, what's the deal with your Mac?" Nicole shouted from her chair.

Joan had not touched the computer since learning of Ken's death. She had little reason or desire to. This was hardly the time for online shopping or surfing the Internet for news and celebrity gossip. What few emails she got were retrieved from her smart phone. Had her sister not sat down to use it, the erased hard drive on her home computer might have gone undetected for weeks. Joan walked into the study, still drying her hands with a kitchen towel. She peered over her sister's shoulder with a confused look.

"I have no idea. I've never seen it act like that before. It usually just comes on."

"Maybe if we turn it off, then back on," Nicole suggested.

"There's a power button on the other side," Joan replied. "Press that and see what happens."

The restart button cycled the computer but soon the ghostly blinking question mark folder reappeared.

"I don't know what's wrong with it," Joan said apologetically.

"That's okay," replied Nicole, not wanting to add even this small amount of stress to her sister's burdens. "I'll call Kevin and get him to help."

Nicole got up to fetch her cell phone. Looking at her watch, she realized her youngest son, now twenty-eight and working as a securities analyst on the West coast, would probably still be in the middle of his Monday morning commute. Kevin was into technology and used Macs exclusively. He would know what to do. She reached him on his mobile number and he tried to guide his mother through the steps of a proper startup sequence.

Joan returned to the kitchen while Nicole spoke to her son. She wasn't concerned that her rarely used computer was acting odd. She had far bigger things to deal with. She was still standing in the kitchen, drying and putting away the coffee cups, when Nicole reappeared in the doorway, a worried look on her face.

"Joanie, how old is your computer?"

"I got it right after the divorce. Why?"

"Kevin says your hard drive has failed, or else it has been erased."

As she heard that last word, a clean coffee cup slipped from her grip, smashing to pieces on the kitchen tile floor. Joan stood trembling as her puzzled sister ran over to her.

"What's wrong, sweetie?" Nicole pleaded.

Joan gave no reply. Her head was spinning. *Erased?* She frantically thought about the last time the device had been used. *It was just before he left for his claimed late-night trip to the plant.* He had gone to the study to answer his cell phone. She had been in bed but remembered hearing Ken talking to someone, followed by what sounded like keystrokes and something being played back on the computer. Afterwards, he had come in to say goodnight and leave. The plant meeting had been a lie. *Was there something else he was trying to keep from me?*

Her suspicions fused with sadness and her already fragile composure shattered as completely as the coffee cup on the floor. Nicole held her sister tightly as Joan violently convulsed with tears. While trying to calm her with comforting whispers that everything would be all right, Nicole immediately decided on a course of action: *I have to get her out of this place.*

It was a simple loose-end to check.

Even though the state highway patrol worked the wreck, a copy of the official accident report would be filed with the local police department since the incident occurred within city limits. That made things nice and easy.

One of Ravich's case-runners had the connection. For years, that runner exchanged an envelope of cash each week for a fresh stack of accident records. He had trained the clerk at the accident division to copy for him only those reports involving serious injuries or deaths. The minimum-wage clerk was more than happy to accommodate. She needed the money.

The runner then used the reports as leads. They were a treasure-trove of information. The home addresses of drivers were always listed, most times with phone numbers. A brief description of the severity of injuries was included, along with the name of the hospital where the victims had been transported. Even more helpful, the investigating officer had to complete a section detailing what happened and assigning fault when possible. That meant all the runner had to do was read the damn thing to find out who had the civil claim for damages. He would ignore the driver who caused the wreck and find some excuse for contacting the innocent victim. He averaged three decent case signups per month for Ravich with his little scheme, which made the two hundred bucks he paid weekly to a city records clerk a very smart investment. Ron had paid the runner over a hundred-grand in cash last year for the cases he steered to Ravich.

For reasons unknown to the case runner, Ron wanted to personally examine the most recent batch of reports on Tuesday afternoon. The runner would have gladly furnished them for free but when his handler offered to pay him for his trouble he promptly drove them over to the convenience store parking lot where Ron had suggested they meet.

Ron leafed through the stack. There were sixteen reports from the past week, reminding him how dangerous it was to drive in this city. He quickly found the incident involving Slator and extracted it along with one other.

"We've already signed up these two," Ron lied to his case-runner. "That's why I needed to go through them," he added, handing the others back. "My boss didn't want you bothering these people. Apparently, they're friends of his or something."

The runner couldn't care less. He still had plenty to work on and now had a little drinking money too thanks to the hundred dollar bill Ron had palmed over to him. He smiled and drove off.

Ron took the irrelevant report and crumpled it into a ball, tossing it from his open car window into the trash bin behind the store. He had pulled the second record only to deflect attention from the true object of his desire.

He sat reading the officer's notations from the Slator wreck:

"Unwitnessed incident. Gouge and skid mark measurements indicate Vehicle 1 lost control while traveling southbound in Lane 3, overturning into Lane 4 where struck by Vehicle 2. Distance from point-of-impact to point-of-rest = 419 feet. Cause of incident: Failure to control speed - Vehicle 1."

Ron grinned. The cop had done the bare minimum and wrote it up, just as he expected. He continued reading.

"Drivers dead at scene. No passengers either vehicle."

Ron looked at the identity record for the unintended victim. A forty-seven year old Hispanic woman, driving an old Buick. *Collateral damage,* he thought to himself. He looked on the back side of the report. They hadn't changed the form since he was a young cop. At the bottom was the information he needed most:

"Disposition of Vehicles: Vehicle 1 - Towed by Sammy's Wrecker & Salvage."

A phone number was listed. He pulled out his cell phone and dialed.

"Sammy's," a gruff female voice answered.

Ron assumed a believable and false identity.

"Yes, this is Mel Johnson with Allstate Insurance. We need to confirm a vehicle towed to your yard on October 25th.

"You got a plate number or VIN?"

"Sure," Ron replied, reading off the information from the police report still in his lap.

"Hang on," the terse woman said.

He could hear the sound of typing on a keyboard.

"Yeah, 02' Ford Taurus. We got it listed as full-totaled. You need us to put a hold on it?"

"No, won't be necessary. That's what the accident report shows as well.

We can adjust the loss on cars this old without an inspection."

"I hear ya," she replied.

Ron maintained the ruse, hoping to learn more.

"By the way, just curious, how do you dispose of vehicles like that?"

"After ten days, unless you guys or the cops put a hold on it, we assign it to scrap or salvage."

"What does that mean if you don't mind my asking?"

"Pretty simple. If it's a total, we throw it in the crusher and sell it as scrap metal. If its got decent salvageable parts, we'll keep it out in the general yard for the scavenger buyers."

"And you say this one's listed as a total?"

"Yep. She'll be flat as a pancake and on a scrap truck this time next week."

As he mentally checked another cover-up item off his list, Ron thanked the woman who had been most informative.

"I appreciate your time," he said sincerely.

"Not a problem," the salvage yard employee replied.

Ron smiled. He couldn't have said it better himself.

⸾⸾⸾

"Mr. Greenbaum, there's a Joan Slator here to see you."

The announcement over his desk intercom surprised the old lawyer. He swiveled around in his oak chair to inspect the calendar entries for this morning.

Did I forget an appointment?

It wouldn't be the first time. Despite a still sharp mind, advancing age occasionally confounded the seventy-four year-old litigator. Fortunately, long before his senior years, his crafted persona had been that of a bumbler, which now came in handy whenever there was an actual lapse of memory. Most times only he knew for certain that a forgotten fact, name, or appointment was no longer part of the act.

This time, however, the fault was not his. His Wednesday morning calendar showed no scheduled meetings. But even had his calendar been full, he would have made time for this poor widow. Never mind that her deceased husband was the central witness in the *SeaCoast* case. Her pain and need for answers had touched him deeply when he accompanied her to the morgue. Wanting to help people like her was why he had become a plaintiff's lawyer and why he still loved the practice after so many decades.

He rose from his desk and ambled down the hall toward the reception area. Harry Greenbaum was not the kind of professional who barked "show them back" to his staff. He liked greeting clients and witnesses promptly and personally, even if they had no appointment. He thought all attorneys should do the same. It was, in his mind, a simple act that elevated lawyers above doctors. Every physician he knew seemed to take pride in making their patients wait to be seen. Harry believed that no one who needed him should ever have to sit and linger.

"Mrs. Slator, what a pleasant surprise," he said cheerfully, greeting Joan as she rose from the same weathered sofa where Bill Gaston had sat nine days earlier, laughing with Doug over the law firm's cheap decor.

"I'm so sorry to drop by like this. I know you must be busy."

"Madam, my days are easy compared to yours right now." He extended his arm to escort her. "Won't you please come back to my office so that we may visit?"

He spoke with a genteel quality that was equal parts antiquated and pleasant. It made Joan smile for the first time in days.

"Thank you. I promise not to take up much of your time." She continued talking as they started down the hall. "But I thought it was important to see you before I left."

Harry was confused by the last remark but decided not to show it as they reached the door of his office. "If you think it might be important, then it is. Please sit down and tell me where you're going. But first, may I have some tea or something brought in for you?"

"No, thank you."

She took her seat and nervously brushed at the wrinkles in her skirt. She sighed and looked into the lawyer's attentive eyes.

"Mr Greenbaum…"

"It's Harry," he interrupted. "Remember, we're friends."

She made a small but appreciative grin. He *had* been a real friend to her on Saturday. Not only did he help her endure the emotional trauma of identifying her dead husband, he had also spoken at length about the case he was handling and how it could lead to answers they were both looking for.

"All right. Harry, I've decided to go and stay with my sister and her family for a while, a few months perhaps, maybe longer. I'm leaving tomorrow."

"Didn't you tell me she was coming here to see you?"

"Yes, she arrived on Sunday. And it's been good having her here. But she's made the case I might be better off away from the house and all its memories for the time being."

"That sounds reasonable. But weren't you having a memorial service for Ken on Thursday?" He turned to look at his calendar again. "Yes, here it is. I was planning to attend."

"Oh, I'm sorry. I thought I called everyone. Only a few were planning to come. No, I decided yesterday to cancel the service. I'm taking his ashes with me to Florida where my sister lives. Ken and I had our honeymoon nearby. I thought I would spread his remains there, along the beach."

"Well, that's a fine idea. You should both return to a happier place."

"Yes, well, I just wanted you to know I'm not abandoning you. I promised my cooperation to help you find the information you need about the explosion and Ken's involvement. And I'll be available if and when you need me."

"You've already been a tremendous help," he assured her. "That talk we had on Saturday about Ken, I now feel like I knew him personally. I realize from your stories he was not the type man who would ever compromise someone's safety, that he was a careful person. That makes both the plant disaster and his car accident so puzzling to me. And it makes me want to work hard to solve those mysteries."

"I appreciate that," she replied, pausing to collect her thoughts. "Which is the other reason I'm here. I first wanted to thank you for your kindness but I also need to tell you something disturbing I recently discovered. Maybe it's nothing, but under the circumstances, I thought you should know."

Harry nodded and maintained direct eye contact. He was listening.

"I think Ken was hiding something. I already told you how he didn't tell me the truth about where he was going on the night he died. Well, two days ago I also discovered he may have erased the computer at the house."

"Why do you think that?" Harry said with surprise.

"The hard drive has been scrubbed clean. My sister and I found a software disc inside the slot of the computer that can be used to blank out everything. At least that's how her son explained it to us."

"Did Ken use this computer for work?"

"No, at least I don't think so. I bought it after we divorced. Once we decided to get back together he was only in the house for a week before his accident. But maybe he put something on there during that time and decided later he didn't want me to see it. I know he took a call and was working on the computer just before he left that night."

Harry tapped his hands together as he sat thinking. *Ken Slator was trying to hide something he was ashamed or afraid of.* Maybe he received emails that proved a dalliance, or hinted at problems with gambling, drugs, or financial difficulties. *Everyone has secrets,* he thought only to himself, not wanting to speculate out loud in front of a woman who had already been through enough. But whatever his secret, destroying a computer was a pretty drastic measure. A man who was trying to erase all tracks might also be prone to suicide. Harry's intuition returned to the same premise he initially considered after that first phone call from Joan. *Or maybe, just maybe, it was something else.* Something that also related to work. Harry had been a trial lawyer long enough to know that, until all the evidence was in, one should never march blindly down a single rabbit trail.

"Let me ask you. Did Ken also keep a work computer? A laptop perhaps?"

"Yes, he did. It's funny you should ask. Nicole and I spent all day yesterday looking for it around the house. We thought maybe it could tell us something. He always had that thing with him. I never saw him use it for anything other than his job."

"But you say it's gone?"

"He must have had it with him. I didn't think to ask the policeman who came to the house if there was anything found in the car. Wouldn't they ordinarily tell you things like that?"

"Sometimes they do, assuming they actually retrieve something."

"That's what I thought. Harry, I'm sorry to bother you with this. It's bad enough losing Ken but to think he was involved in something he couldn't share with me — something that had him out late at night and not paying attention on the highway — it just tears me to pieces. I can't imagine it has anything to do with what happened at that plant but I thought at least you should know."

He stood up and walked over to her.

"I very much appreciate your coming over here this morning to tell me this. Why don't you give me some time to look into it for you? Would that be all right?"

"Of course, whatever you think best."

A thought suddenly entered his mind. "Did anyone else have access to your home computer? Somebody that came over to the house maybe?"

"No. Other than the highway patrolman and my sister, no one has been by."

"And there's nothing else missing around the place? No sign that someone broke in?"

Joan was shocked by the question. "Why no. Do you think someone else could have done this?"

She was suddenly fearful, and Harry regretted mentioning so remote a possibility.

"Of course not," he said to reassure her. "Sometimes my old foggy head just gets filled with crazy ideas. Forget I even said that."

"Maybe it's a good thing I'm leaving town."

"Oh, no, please, I didn't mean to alarm you. You don't have to leave for your safety, my dear. But it may be good for your grief. You'll be in good care with your sister, I'm sure."

He took her by the hand as she rose to leave. "Is there anything I can do to help you with the empty house? Or assist you in preparing for your trip?"

Joan's anxiety lessened, which was his intent. She pulled from her purse a piece of paper on which she had scribbled her sister's address and phone number.

"No, but thank you for asking. If you find out anything, or want to speak with me, here's where I can be reached. I'll return home anytime you need me."

Harry took the information and tucked it into the one pant pocket that wasn't already partially sticking out.

As he started to escort her back to the reception area, she withdrew her hand and smiled at the courtly lawyer.

"I can show myself out, Harry. Thank you for what you're doing and for being there for me."

She leaned over and gave him a friendly kiss on the cheek. It was just a soft peck, but the old warhorse, who wasn't thrown off by much, blushed like a schoolboy.

He stood at the doorway of his office watching the sweet and damaged widow walk slowly down the hall. *She deserves to know what happened,* he thought with determination. The same was true for the other woman he recently committed himself to help: Kate Crouch. She and Joan Slator were the purest of victims. Both were just looking for the truth.

He worried he might not bring them what they were seeking. As a veteran trial lawyer, he knew that things don't always work out. Doors can remain closed, secrets can go unrevealed, justice is sometimes denied. His mind and experience warned him, once again, that his efforts might be futile, that the outcome could be bad. But his heart and compassion would invigorate him to take action anyway. It always did. Throughout his long career, he had been a sucker for "stray dogs and lost causes" as his partner, Stan Walker, often referred to the impossibly tough cases Harry took on for no reason other than he felt sorry for someone. Of course, he somehow managed to win those cases too. His skills made him a lot of money but, unlike the buck-chasing case hustlers, Harry remained in the business for a higher purpose: to help people in need.

Walking back over to his desk, he resolved to work harder, to unravel this Gordian Knot of unexplained events and increasingly mysterious facts that somehow linked Ken Slator's strange behavior with the SeaCoast plant disaster. *Let the young lawyers, Doug and Bill, fiddle with the law. I'll get to looking under some rugs.*

He now knew the first place he wanted to go.

———⊗⊗⊗———

Everyone had done their jobs.

Paul Ravich sat at his desk on Thursday, scrolling through the altered DCSS data on Slator's old computer. It was a work of art, a piece of believable fiction. Gone was any evidence of Dave Phillips' manual bypass of the DCSS, the real facts erased faster than wiping a chalkboard clean. The truth was replaced with entries that fit Dr. Garrison's failure theory like a soft leather glove on a tender hand. As the new chronology and sensor readings passed before his eyes, the man who had conceived and executed the plan smiled with self-satisfaction.

The complex jumble of fabricated information remained as confusing to a layperson's eyes as the original plant data Ken Slator had brought to him. Expert testimony would be needed to translate the output to a jury. But Ravich was no longer concerned. *Now those experts would be reading from my script.* The lines of new data would be parsed by his paid witnesses, using just enough technical language to impress his jury of dupes. His job in the courtroom would be to distill those scientific explanations into plain talk, to give the jury a clear picture of what happened. The figures on the computer screen might seem indecipherable now but when he was done no one would doubt what they revealed: a faulty safety system — designed, sold and installed by Integrated Sentry Inc. — was responsible for blowing up the SeaCoast plant and killing all those good men.

Ravich closed the laptop with a confident smugness. He had managed to cobble together an assembly line of dedicated workers who had, each unknowingly, produced an impressive piece of false evidence. *I'm the Henry Ford of fraud,* he laughed to himself. The raw materials had been supplied by the honest plant manager who, conveniently before his death, swore that any data appearing on this computer was accurate and true. The designer, Dr. Garrison, had come up with a failure scenario that placed responsibility squarely on Integrated Sentry, having no idea that his theory had become fact in less than three days, thanks to the efforts of two Indian computer programmers who had diligently followed the clear instructions given to them. The file they returned was guaranteed to have no trace of alteration. The programmers innocently still believed they had created a realistic simulation for company training purposes. With a wire transfer from his personal account, Ron had paid the workers in India less than a Detroit autoworker earns in a week.

Ravich complimented himself on a job well done. *No one else could have pulled this off,* he thought, as he sat reflecting on his crimes, twiddling his fingers on the computer case. He had bent the facts to his needs using unwitting experts and technicians. He had eliminated the only witness who could derail his plan. He had talked a greedy businessman into joining his conspiracy by dangling the prospect of riches before him. Ravich understood people and what motivates them. Offer a fat man food. Offer a wealthy man the opportunity for more money. The voracious Charles Thornton was so focused on his own promised buffet of riches that he didn't care if he was tossing a scrap to a plaintiff's lawyer: a one-hundred million dollar scrap in the form of a lawyer's fee.

Like any good assembly line product, final inspection was all that was left to do. If the altered program passed the smell test, he was home free. Ravich turned to his office computer and scanned his database of experts which was neatly organized by area of specialty. Like a seasoned casting director, he had lots of talent to choose from. Over the years, Ravich had amassed an impressive list of credentialed experts, each willing to consult or testify when needed. Every name on his list was a veteran of a previous successful case for the firm. Only those experts who understood how to play the game remained on the roster. The few who didn't care who was paying them, and the several who were poor courtroom performers, were quickly pruned from Ravich's always growing list of persons with testimony for sale.

He found the man he was looking for: Dr. Stephen F. Sandt, professor of computer science at the local university and a recognized authority in the field of computer forensics. He had first hired Sandt two years before in a case where the defendant sought to exclude from evidence a series of incriminating corporate emails by claiming their authenticity could not be proved. Dr. Sandt had demonstrated to the court's satisfaction that the records in question were indeed original and unaltered, paving the way for their admission into evidence. Ravich thereafter used the damning emails to gore the defendant before the jury.

If Dr. Sandt could be fooled by the Indian programmers' work, then Ravich was certain the lawyers and experts eventually hired by Integrated Sentry would also find nothing to challenge in the new version of Slator's records. While his name appeared under the heading of "Computer Forensics" in Ravich's database, Dr. Sandt was actually being hired in the *SeaCoast* case to be Ravich's "Quality-Assurance" consultant. And, like both Dr. Garrison and the programmers, he would never be told the truth.

Ravich got up and walked over to close the door to his office. Returning to his desk, he picked up the phone and made the call.

"Department of Information Technology. How may I direct your call?"

Ravich responded and within a minute he heard a familiar voice on the other end of the line.

"This is Steve Sandt."

"Stephen, how the hell are you? Paul Ravich here."

"Paul, good to hear from you again."

The professor's statement was more than simple pleasantry. Dr. Sandt remembered being handsomely paid by Ravich for his previous work and assumed he was being tapped again for another lucrative assignment. Even tenured professors don't make enough salary to forget the windfalls they can earn through litigation consulting.

"I'm happy to say I need your help once more, Stephen. Are you available to look something over for me this afternoon or tomorrow?"

"I'll try. What have you got?"

"Well, it's a pretty simple task I think, at least for you. I have a pending matter where I've come into possession of some important computer evidence that might be outcome-determinative in the case. The computer's owner has sworn that the pertinent data is authentic and I have no reason to doubt him. However, I asked this witness if he would permit a forensic inspection of the computer to verify there's no funny business."

"So you want me to check file origination dates, look for modification markers, that sort of thing?"

"Precisely. I just want some level of confidence that the records haven't been doctored. It's a self-designed PC program intended to monitor a chemical plant's operations. This laptop, where the program resides, is running Windows XP. Pretty basic looking stuff. I just need a short report documenting what tests you ran along with your conclusions."

"Sure, I'll be happy to run some diagnostics. When can you get it over here to me?"

"How about now? I can have my office courier bring it to you in the next hour or so."

"And when do you need my report?"

"Sooner the better. If you pass the data as authentic, I'd like to get my lawsuit filed this coming Monday."

"That's a pretty quick turnaround, but for you I'm willing to do it."

Ravich smiled. Once again, he was being rewarded for his habit of overpaying his experts. "You're the best, Dr. S. Obviously, you'll be examining the original record so no destructive testing, and please take great care handling this evidence because it's potentially very valuable."

"I understand. I'll maintain a clean chain-of-custody record and will document everything I do. You remember from the last case that none of the tests we run actually affects the underlying core data."

"That I do, which is why you were the only man to call on this. Listen, Stephen, I doubt you'll have to testify in this case but, regardless, I'll see that you are reasonably compensated."

"I have no doubts about that," the professor said. "Unless I hit a snag I'll email a draft report to you by early afternoon Friday and your messenger can then come by to reclaim the computer. How's that?"

"All I could ask for," Ravich laughingly replied, before concluding the call with a pleasant goodbye.

If the altered records could fake out Dr. Sandt, the rest would be easy. The lawsuit would be filed and the splashy press conference with Thornton could be held. Ravich could then look forward to the panicked response of Integrated Sentry and await the pleadings filed by whichever law firm was chosen to defend the target defendant. It didn't matter who the company retained. No defense firm, even the really good ones, would be able to save ISI's bacon once these computer records were introduced in evidence. And his best testifying safety and engineering expert would be right behind that offer of proof, rubbing the defendant's nose in it. His courtroom experts always knew what they needed to say. In this case, the evidence was now going to be as clear as it was false: Integrated Sentry's DCSS system malfunctioned and caused disaster.

Paul Ravich leaned back in his comfortable leather chair and splayed his arms behind his head, relaxing like a man who had just eaten a satisfying meal. His assembly line was about to turn out a very fine product to be sold for a half-billion or more, with twenty percent going to him as a sales commission. With an egotism that could rival Donald Trump, Ravich thought to himself: *Henry Ford was a hack. He had to build thousands of his product to get super rich. I only need one.*

Next week, Paul Ravich was finally going to unveil to the world his Ferrari of fraud.

———————

Great trial lawyers are good detectives. Harry Greenbaum was no exception. His astute mind, masked behind a bungling demeanor, made him a real-life Columbo. Like the fictional character from the old television series, Harry's self-deprecating and slovenly style made people lower their guard and underestimate his prowess. The clothes he wore on Friday for his planned errands perpetuated the ruse. A pair of baggy jeans contrasted strikingly with an ill-fitting, medium-sized golf shirt that stretched tightly around his size-large torso. An old barbecue sauce stain on the left side of the shirt formed a sort of hillbilly logo at the exact place where the names of country clubs are usually sewn in. The ensemble was topped off with a tacky and well-worn baseball cap that read: *I'd Rather Be Fishin.*

His first stop was to the records division of the city police department. He gave the clerk the required information, paid his four dollars, and left with a copy of the official accident report from Ken Slator's wreck. Like Ron had done three days before, he perused the document for details and found the name and number for the wrecker yard where the vehicles had been towed. Unlike Ravich's investigator, however, Harry was planning to pay a visit rather than simply make a call. *"You get more done in person"* was his credo.

Besides, he was looking forward to it. Harry was an old car nut, having grown up in an age where kids actually worked on their rides and knew what made them run. He loved going to salvage yards as a teen, scrambling around the wrecks to find cheap replacement parts. To him, the oily smell and grime of such places was like walking through a meadow of fragrant flowers. He just hoped he wouldn't get his nice clothes too messy.

Sammy's Wrecker & Salvage was located on the outskirts of town, along an industrial road lined with other similarly dirty businesses. Harry pulled through the open chain-linked gate and into the gravel lot. He got out and adjusted his cap's bill slightly upward. He didn't want to look too fancy.

"Howdy-do?" Harry chimed, as he entered the trailer home that had been converted to an office for the salvage yard.

An obese and tough woman looked up from her magazine and removed the cigarette from her lips. She was Sammy's wife and her lack of charm played well with the drab surroundings.

"You lookin' for somethin'?" she asked in a gravelly voice that bore testament to her decades-long nicotine habit.

"Indeed I am, madam," Harry replied, pulling the rolled-up accident report from his back pocket and laying it on the counter. "I'd like to see this car here," he said, pointing at the Slator vehicle, identified by plate number and VIN.

"You don't look like no insurance man. You the owner?"

"No, ma'am, just a family friend. They wanted me to come down and see if any personal items were left behind."

"Well, if they were, they're still in there. We don't steal nothin'."

"Of that, I have no doubt," he assured her with a smile.

She read from the report and typed in the information, using a keyboard that had evidently never been cleaned. The equally dirty monitor displayed the location.

"It's on Row 8, section 4. That'll be on the right side. If you take something out of that car, stop by here before you leave and let me make a list. If you take any parts off, I'll have to charge you."

"That all sounds perfectly reasonable." He raised his cap while tipping his head in thanks. "You've been most helpful."

"You say so," she muttered, before quickly returning to her magazine.

Harry soon found the heavily damaged blue Ford and shook his head in amazement. No one could have survived this kind of impact. The roof was crushed, the frame was bent. The driver's side door had been cut away by the emergency responders. There were blood stains on the steering wheel.

He squeezed himself into the small pocket of space between the front seat and crumpled roof, feeling around. He was looking for a laptop computer. He reached under the seats and felt nothing. The glove box was empty except for a now useless owner's manual and registration papers. He struggled to pull himself out of the front seat and repeated the sequence for the back. He found no computer. The only thing he managed to retrieve from the interior compartment was a white plastic card found lying partially under the driver's seat. It had no markings, only a magnetic strip along the top of one side. It looked like an access card. He put it in his pocket.

Once he exited from the crushed metal interior, he walked around to the trunk. The rear end of the car was deformed and the accident forces had broken the trunk latch. He carefully raised the lid, avoiding its now sharp edges. He peered inside and his heart raced. There, cramped against the spare tire well, was a brown briefcase. He removed it and laid the attaché on top of the car. *Please be in here,* he whispered, as he clicked open its latches.

Inside was a hammer, crowbar, and towel. *What the hell? Did this even belong to Slator?* Harry thought maybe the tow truck driver left it behind in error. *But what kind of tow man carries his tools in a briefcase?* He reached in the case's compartments — just as Ken Slator had done two weeks earlier to the day — and found the crumpled business card of "Robert Finnegan; President, SeaCoast Chemical Corporation." Harry closed the briefcase and sat it down on the ground. He would be taking it with him.

Disappointed by his failure to find a laptop, Harry decided to look under the hood. The accident report said that Slator's vehicle had lost control. He thought he might as well check to see if the car itself played any role. It would have to be open and obvious: there was so much damage and it had been years since he had worked on any car. To him, a 2002 Ford Taurus was a modern marvel. He had earned his mechanic chops as a teenager tinkering with a 1952 Chevy.

There was nothing other than crushed and broken parts in the engine compartment. He walked around the car. One thing seemed odd. There was no tire on the right front wheel. The hub was scuffed and bent. He got on his knees and peered into the wheel well. The steering linkage was broken. There were so many busted parts he couldn't decide if it had happened before or because of the accident. He looked on the other side. The linkage was intact.

Dusting himself off, he walked back to the office, the briefcase in his hand. As he entered, the spring-loaded door of the trailer snapped closed and Sammy's wife looked up, again irritated by the interruption of her quiet time.

"Find sumthin'?"

"Just this in the trunk," Harry replied, holding up the briefcase. "Has some of his tools inside. Thought I'd return it to the family."

Who keeps tools in a briefcase? she quickly thought. "Let's see," she said with suspicion.

Harry laid the case on the counter and opened it for inspection.

"Well, I'll be damned," she huffed. "Fool ought to get his self a tool box."

"I'll be sure to pass that suggestion along." Harry said with a smile. "Would you like to make a list of the contents?"

"Hell no! That piddlin' crap ain't worth me making no inventory. Take it with you."

"I appreciate it," Harry replied. "Say, I noticed the right front tire was missing."

"That's got nothin' to do with us," the woman snapped defensively. "If there's no tire, then that's the way we towed it."

"Of course, I didn't mean to imply anything sinister." Harry quickly changed the subject. "By the way, if I wanted to have that car looked at by my mechanic, you think he could come down here?"

"He'd better hurry. That car there is a total. It's gonna get crushed and sold in a few days."

"Well, I'll be," Harry responded. "We might not get to it in time. Let me think here a second." He paused, then snapped his fingers as if struck by a great idea. "What would it cost to buy the thing as junk?"

The woman stared at him quizzically. "You're kiddin', right?"

"No, ma'am, I'd like to buy it."

The large woman huffed and walked over to grab a bulky, soft-bound book that laid on a shelf alongside used alternators, batteries, and other auto parts. The book reminded Harry of his trusty phone directory, only slightly smaller. She thumbed through the pages and announced a figure.

"02' Ford Taurus. Scrap value is $470. That's how much the recycler would pay us."

Harry reached in his back pocket and pulled out his wallet.

"Let's call it an even $500 then, how's that?"

He pulled out hundred dollar bills and asked for a receipt.

The woman cast a wary gaze. "You got to come and get it. We ain't truckin' it nowhere for you."

"That will be fine. I'll make arrangements over the weekend and have someone come fetch it on Monday."

She handed him his copy of the sales slip, retaining a carbon copy. She made sure to advise it would be his claim ticket when he came back for the car.

"You gonna make an insurance claim on it? Cause if so, you didn't have to buy the damn thang."

"No, ma'am."

"Then why on earth do you want it?"

"That's an excellent question, madam. Right now, I haven't a clue."

The woman shook her head, thinking the old coot must have lost his mind. It wasn't her problem. *Money is money.*

"Have a wonderful day and a nice weekend," Harry called out jocularly, lifting his cap as he made his way toward the door.

The large woman just stood there watching him leave, still shaking her head. *That man is crazy as a loon,* she thought to herself.

Crazy like a fox was more like it.

⊶∞⊷

The report from the computer forensics expert was attached with an email to Ravich on Friday afternoon. Dr. Sandt first listed his credentials, then described the test protocols he had followed in examining the DCSS computer relay program on Slator's laptop. Ravich glossed over those sections, focusing instead on the last two paragraphs of the two page report which told him all he needed to know:

"The subject program — a data recording application titled 'DCSS Relay,' authored by Ken Slator — was subjected to and successfully passed a battery of diagnostics tests designed to ensure the integrity of all data on the device and to identify any latent alteration. These tests included: a parity check algorithm of the programs contents, a cross survey of file creation times with log file checksums, and the National Institute of Standards & Technology's Secure Hash Algorithm 256 survey."

"While the evidential significance of the data is beyond the scope of my investigation, I can state as both a founder and current board member of the International Association of Computer Investigation Specialists — the organization charged with establishing standards and practices for computer forensics — that it is my opinion and certification that the subject computer

data is genuine and has not been altered or compromised in any way."

Ravich was euphoric. A foremost and unimpeachable expert in the field of discovering doctored computer records had, in effect, given an unknowing A+ to a couple of foreign programmers for their ability to hide what they had done. If the defense lawyers for Integrated Sentry tried to challenge the legitimacy of the data — which they would certainly consider since the computer records hung their client — Dr. Sandt could come down to the courthouse and testify that "any alteration claim lacks scientific or verifiable merit." The best part was that the good professor would actually think he was telling the truth. His testimony, along with Slator's affidavit that the records were authentic, put Ravich in the clear. All that would be left to prove, through someone from Ravich's firm, was the fact that the evidence had been locked away in a secure place since Slator surrendered it.

Ravich happily tossed the report on his desk, then summoned a paralegal to retrieve the computer from the university along with the signed original of Dr. Sandt's report. As he watched his employee exit his office, a chain-of-custody receipt in his hand, Paul Ravich beamed in amazement. He had pulled it off.

He sat back and grinned as he thought about his future jury argument on this point; how he would say with indignation that: "any claim of tampering is nothing more than a despicable red herring, invented by desperate lawyers who will try anything to rescue their careless client from responsibility for its errors." He might even use an old standby, a surefire and homey phrase, whose effectiveness in argument was often augmented by a pounding of his fists on the jury box rail: "They are trying to throw a skunk in this jury box, in a ridiculous effort to throw you off the scent of truth."

He couldn't wait for that moment. The excitement of advancing his crimes into a forum he owned — the courtroom — filled him with the kind of gleeful anticipation that children exhibit when being told they are going on vacation. Nothing could stop him now. It was simply a matter of time.

He picked up his voice recorder and began drafting the pleading that would sue Integrated Sentry. His individual clients and SeaCoast Chemical would be joint plaintiffs. The collective damages sought would be so large the dollar figure would have to be typed in words only; otherwise, all those zeros would overwhelm the page. He would also name Integrated Sentry's parent company, VyStream Corporation, as a defendant. You could allege anything in an initial pleading. He would claim that VyStream controlled all actions of their subsidiary and was therefore equally liable for this horrendous incident. He knew such a charge was probably frivolous but adding one of the world's biggest companies to the lawsuit guaranteed greater press coverage of the case. And this case wasn't *just* about the money. It was also about securing his name forever in the pantheon of the greatest trial lawyers that ever lived.

He ended his dictation with an instruction for Jan to prepare the accompanying filing documents and service requests, and to have the entire package on his desk before she left for the day. Next week, he would personally hand-file the suit to make sure the intake clerk understood it was time for her to make a car payment. She was, after all, an adult. Surely, she realized there was no Santa Claus, even if a jolly man in a white beard and red suit had given her the keys to a free car four years ago. *SeaCoast Chemical Corporation, et al, v. Integrated Sentry, et al* had to be assigned to one of his most-trusted courts, where his bought-and-paid-for judge could help him control the inevitable outcome.

Ravich next summoned his associates and, without telling them why, instructed Melanie and Dustin to round up all the *SeaCoast* clients for an important Monday morning meeting at the office. Ravich looked forward to telling his trusting clients about the important evidence discovery he had made and the magnificent deal he had already struck for them. He was certain the fools would be blinded by the big money he had talked SeaCoast into voluntarily paying, and they would be dripping with appreciation over his not taking a cut as a fee. He would explain in simple terms how another company had killed the workers and what he was going to do about it. He would describe their upcoming claim against Integrated Sentry as "another bite at the apple" that would get him paid while making them even more money. Getting the clients to sign off on his dual representation of both them and SeaCoast Chemical, while securing their release of any claim against the employer they once hated but would now feel sorry for, was going to be a cakewalk. *Nobody but me could have lined up the stars this way*, he thought pridefully, as he watched his associates scramble out of his office to contact the plaintiffs.

That left two more agenda items before he could leave for the weekend.

He still needed to get Doug Stevens into the fold. He couldn't stand the thought of groveling before the upstart young lawyer who had stood up to him. *Maybe there was a better way.* Ravich decided to call Harry Greenbaum and invite the old man to a lunch meeting on Monday. He would charm his crazy ex-boss, then lobby him to convince young Doug and that other lawyer, whose name he had already forgotten, that the three of them should join the fast-moving Ravich train to riches. Even an eccentric like Harry was smart enough to know when to take the easy way out. Greenbaum would surely tell his two young compatriots to take the deal he was going to propose, especially once Harry learned about the open-and-shut evidence that had been recently "uncovered."

"Jan, get Harry Greenbaum on the phone," Ravich barked.

"Yes, sir, right away," she calmly replied.

A minute later, the two men were connected. Harry was back from the salvage yard, sitting at his desk, having not bothered to stop by his house to change into cleaner and more lawyer-like clothes. No one at his office said a word when he walked in after lunch looking like a redneck mechanic. They were past being surprised by anything the old man wore.

"Harry, a little bird told me you were now involved in this *SeaCoast* case," Ravich began cheerfully. "On behalf of a widow named…"

Harry interrupted with the name, knowing that Ravich seldom recalled anything that wasn't of use to him. "Kate Crouch is her name, Paul, and yes, I've been asked to help a couple of fine lawyers on her behalf."

"Well, that's just great, Harry. I always hoped we could handle another case together before you decided to retire. You know I represent all the other victims?"

"Yes, I did know, and I'll bet it was the same little birdie that told me that," Harry quickly replied.

"So, I was thinking the two of us ought to have lunch, catch up, and discuss the case. You free on Monday?" Ravich asked.

"I guess I could do that."

"Perfect. How about noon at the Barrister's Club?"

Ravich knew that Harry frequently dined at the private restaurant located across from the courthouse. It was a small place where lawyers and judges could dine, drink, and visit without fear of being watched or overheard by jurors and the public. It was an "exclusive club" only in that you had to be a member of the local bar association to join. Ravich hated the food and considered it a dump but realized that Harry was most comfortable there.

"Fine," Harry responded. "Would you like me to bring my two co-counsel?"

"No, I see no need to bore the children," Ravich said insultingly. "Let's just have us two old heads visit, what do you say?"

Harry smiled. He knew he was being set up.

"Fine and dandy. Just you and me, like on a date. Do you promise a kiss before you try to fornicate me?"

Ravich laughed heartily. The old fool was an original.

"Come on, Harry," Ravich joked back, "you know we can make beautiful love on this case. The best kind: where we both get rich."

"Hmm. I know how important that is to you, Paul. I shall look forward to seeing you."

"Thanks, Harry. See you Monday. Bye now."

Ravich hung up, having no doubt he was a mere bad salad away from getting the *Crouch* case referred to him.

All that was left to do this Friday afternoon was to make a call to Charles Thornton and give him the good news. By day's end on Monday, Ravich would have all his ducks in a row. Then it would be showtime. He and Thornton could stand side-by-side and reveal to the world who caused the SeaCoast disaster and what should be done about it. They would hold their press conference on Tuesday, November 5th. That was also election day, which meant more people than usual would be tuning in to the news that night. Everybody in the city would soon be singing his praises and saluting his genius.

He could hardly wait.

Chapter 15
Discussions

Derron Lucas died on Sunday. The lone survivor of the plant explosion succumbed to his burn injuries after nineteen gruelingly painful days. His doctors were privately surprised he made it that long. He was only twenty-seven.

His widow phoned Dustin Kirkland at home to tell him the news. Like the rest of Ravich's clients, her principal contact was now with the firm's associates. She had never even met the man who was her "attorney-of-record." The other plaintiffs, who saw their celebrity lawyer just once at the union hall signup, were now also entirely shepherded by either Melanie or Dustin. That's the way Ravich liked it. Shake hands with the clients twice: first, when they sign on; and last, when their case is tried or settled. He considered every point in between both boring and beneath him. Therefore, pretrial client-tasks were delegated to his staff of lawyers. They processed the workers compensation claims. They sat with the clients through their monotonous depositions. They answered the naive questions that tort clients ask in anxious phone calls, things like: "How much longer will it take?" Ravich disdainfully referred to such client relations as "hand-holding." He was far too important for that. His associates were paid well to be the client babysitter. He had other things to do.

Dustin quickly texted the news of the death to his boss. Ravich, reading the message, was quietly pleased by this latest development. He wasn't sure what, if anything, Derron Lucas might have recalled about the explosion or the events leading up to it. The young man had never been fully debriefed. Since arriving at the hospital he was either unconscious, sedated, or in too much pain to talk. Had he recovered, who knows? Perhaps he knew things, truthful things, that would be inconsistent with the newly invented theory of what occurred out there. *We're better off with him dead,* Ravich coldly thought, as he phoned his associate with new instructions.

"Dustin, I got your message. I need you and Melanie to get up to the office today. You don't mind, do you?"

"No, of course not," Dustin said dutifully.

It wasn't really a question. A Ravich associate was always on call. That was made clear the day they were hired. His boss didn't cared if it was a weekend or holiday; he never hesitated even when you were on vacation or if it was the middle of the night. If he called and told his attorneys to get to work, they did. Dustin wouldn't dare mention to his boss that he had buddies over this Sunday afternoon to watch the big game. He would just ask his friends to lock up when they left, then get to the office as fast as possible.

"I can be there in a half hour. What would you like us to do?"

"First, confirm Monday's meeting at 10:30 with the *SeaCoast* plaintiffs. Were you able to contact all of them on Friday?"

"Everyone will be there. They all asked Melanie and me what the meeting was about. We said we didn't know but told them we were certain you had something important to tell them."

"Good," Ravich replied. "That's great."

He had intentionally kept his associates in the dark about the deal. He wanted to be the one to inform the clients they would be millionaires before even taking a step into a courtroom. He didn't want anyone spoiling that nice surprise.

"Next, we need to change the pleading that's going to be filed. I dictated the lawsuit on Friday and it should be on my desk. Change the Lucas injury claim to a death action but make sure you retain the claim for his pain and suffering prior to death."

"I understand," Dustin replied.

"Also, get me some binding releases typed up for the clients to sign on Monday. Make sure the document fully releases Thornton Industries and SeaCoast Chemical from any and all claims, including gross negligence. You don't have to specify the dollars they're paying us, just recite that there is 'adequate consideration' for making the release. Oh, and add a sentence stating that each of them has given their express consent to our firm's dual representation of SeaCoast Chemical."

"Okay," Dustin said hesitatingly.

Ravich now took the time to explain some things to him: how the evidence pointed to Integrated Sentry; that they and its parent company were the only entities he was going to sue; how he had bluffed SeaCoast into making a ten-million dollar voluntary payment to the victims; and about his finagling Thornton Industries into hiring him to pursue the company's huge property damage claim against ISI. The dollar figures were staggering. All that Ravich omitted from his summary was that murder and fraud were also involved.

"Wow!" was all that his young associate could manage to say.

"That means on Monday I'll be telling our clients that each family will receive almost $1.7 million, free of any fee, before we even get started. You think that will make them happy?"

"I'm sure it will," Dustin replied. But then he did the math in his head. "You mean two million though, right?"

"No, we have to assume the ten million will be divided by six. I'm pretty sure by the time we get SeaCoast's voluntary payment, we'll have all six victims instead of five."

"Really? That lawyer is going to refer the *Crouch* claim to us?"

"If he has any sense he will. So let's tell our five families on Monday that she'll get a share too. If Crouch's lawyers stupidly decide not to participate, then the extra money will make another nice surprise for our folks."

"Man, that's fantastic. And the case against the third-party defendant is really that solid?"

"Ironclad," Ravich replied. "You call Melanie and fill her in. I want everything ready when I arrive at the office tomorrow morning. You two get on it."

"Yes, sir," Dustin said excitedly. He was about to go to work on a half-billion dollar case. That made it easier to forget the football game and the party with his friends. He rushed to the office for his weekend sudden-duty.

Ravich hung up and retreated to his own luxurious den to watch the game himself. He could afford to kick off his shoes for a while. Things were ticking off like clockwork.

Harry had called the boys on Friday afternoon to schedule a Monday morning meeting of his own. He didn't give Doug or Bill any details, saying only that it was time for a "team powwow." Doug offered to come to Greenbaum's office but Harry wanted to see the new war room his co-counsel had set up.

He arrived at Doug's office on Monday a little before ten, dressed for success.

Bonnie looked up from her station as the squatty old man entered the reception area. He had on pinstripe pants, but his suit jacket was of a glen-plaid pattern. Both were almost the same shade of blue. *Somewhere in that man's closest hangs an exactly opposite mismatched suit,* she deduced. His festive tie featured green Christmas trees stamped randomly across bright red silk. He liked to wear it regardless of the season. He capped things off with a gray fedora that featured a three-inch cardinal's tail feather in the band.

"My word, if it isn't the ever-lovely Miss Bonnie," he said with eyes beaming. He bowed slightly while removing his hat with a flourish, as if she were royalty.

Bonnie laughed and rose to greet him.

"Mr. Greenbaum, it's so nice to see you again. But I'm pretty sure you don't really remember me. It's been a long time."

"Nineteen hundred and ninety, I believe it was. The trial was *Hunter v. Kaygill.* Your boss might have beat me in that case had he let you sit with him at counsel table. Your beauty was distracting enough from the back row."

Bonnie blushed and grinned. The old fart was a charmer and he kept pouring it on.

"You haven't changed one iota, I might add."

"Nor have you, Mr. Greenbaum," she said, admiring his recall and glancing again at his funny wardrobe.

"I do so wish that were true. Unlike you, my dear, I have grown old and tiresome." He paused and looked around. "Where might the younger lads be?"

She walked over to the front door.

"Follow me, they're waiting for you in the suite next door. We rented it to make room for the *Crouch* case. We've done gone big time," she teased.

Harry looked around at Doug's reception furniture which looked positively fancy and modern compared to his.

"That I can see," he stated, as if impressed.

Bonnie couldn't control herself. She stopped and gave the old man a warm hug.

"It's so good having you in this case with us."

"Oh my!" he exclaimed happily, his cheeks turning as rosy as the feather in his hat.

They walked into the common hall and entered the unmarked door to the left. Doug and Bill Gaston were seated on folding chairs at a long table placed in the center of a single large room. A rolling blackboard, some file boxes, and a coffee maker that shared space on a small table with a single telephone made up the rest of the war room's decor. The room was largely devoid of paper but that would soon change once the process of pretrial discovery began. Cases like *Crouch v SeaCoast* generate enough documents to fell a forest of trees. The now empty file boxes would be stuffed full of paper before it was all over.

"Harry, thanks for coming," Doug said, as he and Bill rose to greet their new mentor.

"Nice digs, fellows," Harry complimented.

"We'll buy some artwork and cushions for the chairs once we collect our fee from this case," Gaston joked.

"If y'all need anything, I'll be next door," Bonnie offered, as she turned to leave.

"Nonsense!" Harry blurted. "You stay right here. You are an integral part of this team."

Doug and Bill exchanged surprised glances as Harry pulled out an empty chair for Bonnie and escorted her by the hand to the table. He then walked over to the chalkboard as if to begin a lecture. He clapped his hands together. It was time to get to work. "So, get me up to speed and then I'll tell you what I've been up to."

"Well," Doug began, "I received SeaCoast's pleading late on Friday. It's just a General Denial, as we expected."

"And who filed the Answer on their behalf?"

"It was done in-house," Doug replied. "Signed by Bruce Waltman, their General Counsel."

"Ah, then, that's our first sign they are self-insured," Greenbaum said matter-of-factly. "Otherwise, insurance-defense counsel would have made the filing. And you say the case fell into Hinojosa's court?"

"That's right. We all better synchronize our watches," Gaston joked.

"I'd rather have a judge who can't tell time than one who won't follow the rules," Harry remarked. "Thank God, we didn't land in the courtroom of one of Ravich's cronies."

"Aren't you friends with Judge Hinojosa?" Bonnie asked.

"We have known one another for years," Greenbaum answered. "I'd like to believe he has a kind ear for my unusual style."

"That's good, because we're going to need all the help we can get," Gaston said, standing up to hand Harry a photocopy of a case he had uncovered in his legal research. "Take a look at this decision from our esteemed supreme court. It's their latest opinion rendered in an employer gross negligence case."

Harry squinted at the stapled pages, filled with passages that Gaston had covered in yellow highlights. "I didn't bring my reading glasses so fill me in like the good law student you were, William," Harry requested.

"All right." He pointed at the case decision still in Harry's hands. "Facts of that case are: a paper mill worker goes to take a crap in a new bathroom they added on the third floor of the mill; it's a one-holer they relocated inside a tiny cramped closet."

Doug and Bonnie looked at each other like Gaston was crazy as he continued his case recitation.

"Unbeknownst to the worker, the paper company decided it could save some plumbing costs by tying the new toilet to the main mill sewer instead of connecting it to the sanitary sewer system. They also forgot to install a pea trap; you know, that little u-shaped bend in the pipe. It's designed to catch gasses."

Gaston raised his eyebrows. The stupidity of the defendant seemed obvious but he continued his explanation.

"A natural byproduct of paper production is hydrogen sulfide, which percolates along in the mill's sealed sewer pipes along with other wastes of manufacture. I bet you bright people already know that H2S gas is plenty deadly when breathed. You would expect a paper company that deals everyday with the poison to know that too. But guess what? They didn't give a shit, pardon the pun. This poor employee does his business, goes to flush the john, and a big ole bubble of H2S gas comes shooting up the pipe and kills him dead before he can even pull up his pants. His widow sues the company for gross negligence and wins a verdict at trial. Jury finds the paper company recklessly disregarded the safety of its employees."

"And our state supreme court disagreed, I'm guessing?" Harry offered.

"That's correct. They voted eight to one that intentionally linking the toilet to a source of deadly gas was 'legally insufficient evidence' of gross negligence. I guess they felt it was just an unfortunate accident. 'Shit happens,' if you will. Again, pardon the pun."

"I'm not surprised," Harry added. "Boys, these gross negligence cases are tough ones. We not only have to prove that SeaCoast was stupid, we also have to show that at the highest level of their corporate hierarchy they couldn't care less."

"So, how do you propose we begin?" asked Doug.

"Well, I think we start by deposing a fellow named Al Harris. He was a relief supervisor doing the same job as the man-in-charge who was killed that night. We'll ask Harris: What was going on at the plant? How hard were they working? Were any corners were being cut? We probably won't get much but maybe we can find out who the real decision-makers were. Then, we take the deposition of the company president, a fellow named Rob Finnegan, and see if we can extract a confession of stupidity for something."

Doug and Bill made notes in their Big Chief tablets as Harry looked on in satisfaction.

"Meanwhile, I'm trying to track down info on the man who would know best what happened out there: the plant's process engineer, Ken Slator."

"Why don't we depose him too?" Gaston asked.

"Because he's dead," Greenbaum replied to three stunned faces. "Died in a car wreck ten days after the plant exploded. His widow — now a friend of mine — thinks something funny was going on. I aim to find out if her suspicions are correct."

Doug stared at his veteran co-counsel in amazement. *How did he already know who to depose? How did he become friends with the widow of a key witness in so short a time?*

Harry continued his remarks.

"Now, I'm not much for seeing a conspiracy around every corner. You might be surprised to learn I still believe only Oswald killed Kennedy. But there seems to be something fishy going on in this *SeaCoast* matter and I'd like to focus on that while you young turks hammer out interrogatories, send requests for production, and schedule depositions. In short, you get busy being lawyers and I'll stay busy playing detective."

"What exactly are you looking for?" Bonnie asked.

That's a darn good question, Harry suddenly realized. So far, everything he had learned about Ken Slator — either through his widow or on his own — seemed peculiar: his daughter dies on the same night the plant explodes; he quits his job right after; he moves out of an apartment and reconciles with his wife; he goes on nighttime missions and lies to her; computers get lost or erased; he refuses to talk but has spoken to Ravich; the man dies in an oddly wrecked car; inside the trunk is a briefcase of tools with the card of the SeaCoast President inside. All that in the span of just ten days. Those strange and seemingly unrelated facts remained frustratingly scattered in his mind like pieces from multiple jigsaw puzzles: *What fit where? Were these things even connected or just coincidence?* Harry decided he couldn't possibly outline to others what he didn't fully understand himself. So he answered Bonnie's question in a short yet truthful way:

"I'm searching for a snake in the grass."

"Where do you start?" Doug replied.

"My next stop is the Barrister's Club. I'm having lunch today with Paul Ravich."

———— ⊗⊗⊗ ————

As his clients trickled in for their Monday morning meeting, each was given an ample opportunity to survey the hero wall outside the firm's large conference room. Paul Ravich wanted to remind them that their lawyer was someone special. Once assembled around the massive conference table, and while waiting for their attorney to enter the room, each family began sharing how they had been coping with their loss. Everyone made an effort to comfort Derron Lucas' widow, who was still in shock over her husband's passing the day before.

Melanie and Doug entered through the glass doors first, papers tucked in files under their arms. Ravich came in five minutes later. He was the headliner. A solo entrance was therefore in order.

He commenced the role of caring counsel with deft skill. He immediately walked over to introduce himself to, and hug, the still-crying Pam Lucas, promising her softly that Derron's death would be avenged. He then walked slowly around the table, greeting the others and asking everyone how they were holding up.

The clients were impressed. Paul Ravich had met them only once but, like an old friend, he addressed them all by first name.

It was a simple parlor trick but the clients would never know. Melanie had earlier stood in a corner of the reception area, looking through the glass panels of the conference room doors, making a seating chart for her boss. On a sheet of paper, she had drawn an oval to represent the table, then wrote the seated clients' names around it, like numbers on a clock face. She took the diagram to Ravich's office, handed it over, and left to make her own entrance. That gave her boss the few minutes he needed to memorize the names and seat positions.

"Thank you all for coming down here this morning," Ravich began. "Before I forget, please make sure that Missy in reception validates your parking garage tickets when you leave. I don't want this meeting costing you anything."

He smiled, then turned serious.

"As I promised when we first met down at the union hall, I have been working tirelessly to find out what happened at that plant. Through extensive investigation, and with the help of some very prominent experts, we now know *exactly* what caused that explosion."

The clients sat up straight in their chairs as Ravich outlined the evidence against Integrated Sentry Inc. "It's an airtight case," he explained, while assuring that the maker of the malfunctioning safety system "was going to pay dearly for their faulty design that led to the deaths of your loved ones."

He told them the suit would be filed tomorrow. He said that "justice takes time" and it might be months, even a year, before he could get the case against ISI settled or tried. He promised he would continue to work hard for them every day until it was over.

Ravich looked around at his attentive audience. *They're convinced I'm their guardian angel,* he decided. It was time to turn up the volume.

"Melanie and Doug advised me that everyone's claim for workers compensation death benefits has already been filed. Is that right?"

Heads nodded affirmatively around the table.

"Good. Those checks don't amount to much but they'll start coming soon. And like I promised, this firm is not taking one red cent of that money as a fee."

His clients smiled appreciatively.

"Now, I want to talk with you about another victim in this case: SeaCoast Chemical."

A few skeptical looks followed, along with an audible "What?" In the minds of the families, SeaCoast was still a bad guy.

"Please, hear me out. Just as your men had no idea this safety system was letting them down, their employer also had no clue it had been sold a defective product. That's what my investigation has revealed and it just makes sense. No company would allow a plant like that to operate if it had any reason to suspect that the expensive monitoring system it purchased to keep the plant safe was, in fact, a death trap. Think about it."

Ravich surveyed the table. He could see some doubts thawing.

"In short, there is no evidence here that SeaCoast was negligent, much less grossly negligent, which is what we would have to prove if we sue them. Still, I went to company management and demanded they do something good for you folks in exchange for my discovering this evidence that would exonerate them from liability. I pleaded with them to do the right thing. I convinced them that these token insurance benefits were simply inadequate for the loss you all have suffered."

"And they told you to go to hell, didn't they?" blurted Bill Evans' father.

It was the same weathered voice that had helped Ravich persuade the others to sign up at the union hall.

"Just the opposite, Roy," Ravich replied. "I talked them into making a voluntary payment to us of ten-million dollars, to be divided equally among the families."

The look of surprise on his clients' faces was priceless. He wished he could bottle moments like these.

"What you all need to understand and appreciate is they didn't *have* to do anything. Most times, money like this only gets paid when a company is absolutely legally responsible for the accident. Here, they absolutely aren't at fault. I've tried many cases and can honestly say there is no way we could win against SeaCoast. But they are making this payment out of a sense of duty to the families of their hardworking employees, knowing that each of you needs financial support beyond these workers comp benefits. This money will go a long way to tying you over until we collect all that is owed from Integrated Sentry."

"And how much will we get from *them*?" asked the always vocal Roy Evans.

"That will be up to the jury. But I will be asking for at least five million per family. The jury will then have to consider each family's situation and make individual awards to each of you."

"And that's in addition to what we're getting from SeaCoast?"

The question came from Dave Phillips' widow.

"Yes, ma'am, that's correct. We will argue that this voluntary, non-litigated payment from SeaCoast does not constitute a legal settlement that might otherwise give rise to a claim of offset or credit by the defendant that is truly responsible."

Ravich noticed some confused looks. He knew such technical talk would be over their heads, so he turned to a topic his clients would clearly understand.

"I want you to know that even though I proposed and negotiated this payment to you, I have decided to waive my contractual right to any fee on the money that SeaCoast is paying. That means each family will be getting just under $1.7 million dollars right at the start. It's all yours."

Applause broke out. To these clients, the term "hero wall" would not be a derisive comment about Ravich's egotistical hallway display. Instead, it would be an apt description. In their minds, the man in all those framed pictures outside was a hero.

Ravich could sense he had won them over. Even Pam Lucas had stopped crying amid the sudden euphoria and statements of thanks coming from the others. It was time to drop the other shoe.

"I waived my fee for the same reason that SeaCoast decided to make this payment: because it was the right thing to do. And the more we got to talking, the more both of us realized that Integrated Sentry owes not only you good people fair compensation for your loss, it also owes SeaCoast money for the destruction of the plant and its inventory. Since the facts SeaCoast would have to prove are the same I will need to prove on your behalf, they asked if I would also represent them, along with you, in one common lawsuit against this third-party defendant. I said I would — again, it's the right thing to do — but I first wanted to get your approval." Ravich cast a sincere-looking gaze around the room. "After all, you people are my primary concern."

"Will it help or hurt our case?" one woman smartly asked.

"Judy, that's the same question I asked myself and the answer is there is strength in numbers. The cost to rebuild that plant will be huge. It makes the dollar amounts we are talking about for your family seem small by comparison. It may actually cause the jury to give you everything we ask for."

"Then I have no problem with it," Tom Benson's widow replied.

Her decision led the others. The issue passed by acclamation.

"Fine; all that's left to do is for each of you to sign these forms that Melanie and Dustin are now going to pass around. It's got a bunch of legalese in it but here's the bottom line: it says that in exchange for getting this money from SeaCoast, we're not going to sue them. It also says everyone is okay with the idea of us all working together, SeaCoast included, with me as everyone's lawyer."

The documents were placed in front of them.

"Just sign on the line above your name. Then you are free to go."

While they sat executing the releases and consents, Ravich continued talking.

"One more thing: I want everybody to watch the evening news tomorrow. There might be some coverage of our case on there. We'll call you when the SeaCoast money arrives and your checks are ready. Are there any more questions?"

He looked around the room before turning to leave. As he made his way to the glass doors of the conference room, Roy Evans called out.

"Mr. Ravich, we appreciate what you've done here. But how are you gonna get paid?"

"Don't you worry about me. Like I said when I first met you, I will take my fee out of the money we collect against the third-party. I can wait for my payday from Integrated Sentry. You folks need help right now. I'm just glad I was able to find some for you."

With that, the maestro exited, leaving behind an orchestra of contented clients. *They were eating out of my hand,* he thought with amusement, as he headed toward his office to grab his keys and leave.

His next sales pitch was in twenty minutes and would be much tougher. He now had to convince a smarter and more skeptical audience of one.

Harry arrived at the private restaurant shortly before noon. He waited at a corner table, sipping his iced tea and munching on the butter crackers stacked in a wicker basket on the table. Lawyers and judges stopped by his table to shake his hand and exchange pleasantries as they passed. He was a regular. Everyone liked Harry.

Paul Ravich, true to form, was fifteen minutes late. He entered the Barrister's Club like a whirlwind. He extended his hand and shook Harry's vigorously.

"It's good to see you," he said. "Thanks for joining me."

Making no excuse for his tardiness, he plopped down at the table and picked up the menu, glancing at it quickly then tossing it aside.

"You eat here a lot don't you, Harry?"

"Tis' a home away from home for me," Harry replied.

"Then what they say about high-fat foods can't be true. That's all they serve here and you still look half your age."

"I've already had my fill of butter, thank you," Harry said, brushing the cracker crumbs off his side of the table. "You don't have to slather any more on me."

Ravich laughed as the uniformed waiter approached.

"Do you gentleman know what you'll be having today?" The experienced server spoke quietly, with a courtly manner consistent with the club's surroundings.

"The chicken caesar salad, hold the dressing, and no cheese," Ravich immediately demanded, making no eye contact with the waiter — who was just another nobody to him — as he handed back the filled water glass in front of him as if it were spoiled. "And bring me some fresh water. How about you, Harry?"

Greenbaum looked up at the waiter with raised eyebrows and a quick shrug, a silent message of apology for the gruff behavior of his dining companion.

"Just the gumbo please, Thomas, and maybe a couple of those tasty corn muffins."

"Yes, sir, Mr. Greenbaum."

Harry gently handed the menu back. "How's the family, Thomas? Your granddaughter ought to be starting college soon, I suspect."

The old waiter smiled appreciatively. "Why, yes sir, she is. Whole family's doing just fine, thank you for asking."

"When she graduates from high school, you let me know. I'll have a card with a nice surprise in it for her."

"Yes, sir, thank you sir."

Thomas retreated to the kitchen, wondering how two men in the same profession could be so entirely different.

"So, let's talk about this *SeaCoast* matter," Ravich began. "I've got all the other cases and you fellows have just the one widow. I'm about to hit a home run and would prefer to have you guys on base with my team."

"Which requires we all be running in the same direction, doesn't it?" Harry replied cutely.

"Indeed it does." Ravich leaned over and whispered in a hushed tone.

"Harry, I've got the goods on a third-party defendant that unquestionably caused this disaster. I'm filing my suit tomorrow and announcing it all in a press conference afterwards."

"Now, why am I not surprised by that?" Greenbaum said with some derision.

"Not surprised by what? My ability to quickly secure the facts?"

"No, by your desire to publicize it."

"Oh, that's right, Harry, I forgot. You're a behind-the-scenes kind of guy. Speak softly and never carry a big stick. Maybe that's why everyone has heard of me and you're only famous in this place."

Harry smiled at his former associate. "It's not only *who* knows you, Paul. It's equally important *what* people think of you."

Ravich expected some such remark. Harry was a judgmental old clown in his opinion.

"Different strokes, my friend," he said defensively. "But back to my point. I've come into possession of evidence that proves a safety system malfunction at that plant, and my experts have already determined that the company which sold that system to SeaCoast dropped the ball."

"So, you're not suing the employer for gross negligence?"

"No, I'm not. As a matter of fact, I think I can prove the company was victimized as much as the men who were killed. That's why SeaCoast has asked me to also prosecute their property damage claim. The value of that destroyed plant and product, as you can imagine, is pretty significant."

Harry absorbed the unusual news with a calculating mind. "Which means your death clients must be willing to release any claims against the employer. Otherwise, you can't represent both them and SeaCoast."

"That's right, Harry. But here's the sweet part. I managed to scare SeaCoast into making a voluntary payment to the victims. I made that a condition to my representation of the company."

"So, they fear you but want you?" Harry's question was filled with skepticism. "And just how much are they willing to pay as a result of these confused emotions?"

Ravich lowered his voice further, guarding the secret that tomorrow everyone would know.

"Ten million, to be divided equally among the clients. I have five families, you make six. Refer your case to me now and your little widow gets just under $1.7 mil, free of any fee, within two weeks. Then we stick it to the third-party defendant for another nice payday for her, and us."

"So Kate Crouch only gets to participate in this voluntary payment — which by the way is legally a settlement if exchanged for a release — if she becomes your client?"

"Don't you think that's fair? I mean, your kid lawyer, what's his name again?"

"Douglas Stephens."

"Yeah, that's right: Dougie. No way he could extract that kind of money from a company that has no gross negligence liability, much less be generous enough to give it all to his client. I'm willing to do all that for her but she has to release SeaCoast and let me handle her third-party case."

"So I'm out of the equation?"

"Of course not, Harry. You stay in. We'll have a ball trying the case against the real bad guy. I get to call the shots but we can split the *Crouch* fee fifty-fifty."

"You want us to refer the case, stay on for the third-party trial, and give up half our fee? Have I got that right?"

"Yeah, it's a helluva deal. For both you and your client."

Thomas returned with a fresh glass of water for Ravich and a basket of corn muffins for Harry.

"There's just one fly in the soup, Paul. Our client doesn't like you. She won't sign on to your representation."

Ravich huffed in surprise. "Come on! What did I ever do to her? For a guaranteed amount of almost two million, and a chance for greater riches, she can put up with me for a while. Especially now that you, her friendly old grandpa, can stay by her side."

Harry grinned at the insulting comment. "You're a fine trial lawyer, Paul. I knew you would be when I first hired you. So take no offense in what I'm about to say. You can rub people the wrong way, especially those you consider to be the 'little people,' like Kate Crouch."

"What are you talking about?" Ravich said.

"Look at the way you treated our waiter here today." He reached over and lifted the warm napkin off the bread basket. "Notice how hot and fresh my muffins are? Maybe that's quality service or maybe it's a repayment of simple kindness. Maybe there's spit in your fresh water. Do you catch my drift?"

"You're saying I'm a jerk because I don't give a damn about some waiter's family?"

"No, what I'm saying is that Kate Crouch is smart enough to know you don't give a damn about her."

"Look, Miss Manners, I appreciate the etiquette lesson but we're talking about something much larger here. Huge money for her; big money for us."

"I understand the stakes," Harry replied. "But to her, and me, there's something even more important than that: Justice. She wants to know why her husband was killed. She wants to make sure the truly responsible parties are held accountable."

Ravich scoffed. "Please, Harry, save that shit for closing argument. I'm offering you an opportunity to make that stupid woman financially secure before the end of this month, as well as a chance to be a part of something big."

Harry shook his head in disappointment. Ravich, as usual, wasn't heeding advice on how to deal with people.

"Why are you so sure that liability rests with a third-party?" Harry asked pointedly.

"Because I have conclusive evidence of their negligence. Computer records were given to me that show a system sold to SeaCoast malfunctioned and led to the explosion."

Harry instantly made the connection. It had to be the plant manager's missing laptop.

"And these computer records were furnished by a Ken Slator, I may presume?"

Ravich was startled by Greenbaum's mention of the name but managed to maintain a stoic face.

"That's right. He contacted me after learning my firm represented the families. He showed me the proof from his own computer, a laptop he was using as a data backup."

"And now that man is dead," Harry replied, in a tone that was difficult for Ravich to decipher.

This time, Ravich's poker face disappeared. *Was the old man stating a fact or an accusation?* As Ravich tensed, Greenbaum observed the "tell" and thought the reaction was odd. He had meant nothing by it.

"Yeah, how did you know that?" Ravich asked as nonchalantly as he could.

"It seems I have been following in your footsteps. I first spoke to the man shortly after you did."

Ravich could feel his heart rate increase. He knew he had to remain cool.

The waiter returned with the salad and soup.

"Thank you," Ravich said nervously, as Thomas set the salad before him.

Harry knew at that moment that something had thrown his lunch companion off his game. People act differently under pressure. In his sudden panic, Ravich had forgotten to be rude.

Something very important was now on Ravich's mind. He needed to find out if Slator had told Harry the truth before it got changed. "Then you probably know what I know: that his computer tells the whole story."

"No, actually, I don't know much of anything," Harry responded. He held out the muffin basket in an effort to keep Ravich off-balance. "Try one of these. They're delicious."

"No thanks, I'm fine."

"You don't know what you're missing," Harry teased, as he bit into the muffin, spilling yellow crumbs down his shirt.

Ravich gave a thin smile and waited. He knew Greenbaum was stalling.

"The man was reluctant to talk to me," Harry then offered. "I went by his house to ask a few questions and he brushed me off. I just assumed you told him not to cooperate."

"Why would I do something like that?" Ravich replied, still fishing.

"Because that's the way you are, Paul. Again, no offense intended."

He didn't care that he had been insulted once again. Inside, Ravich was relieved. Greenbaum knew nothing.

"That man would have been our star witness, Harry. His death could have tanked the case but fortunately for us he turned the evidence over to me and authenticated it before the car wreck."

"Authenticated it? How?"

"I had him come in and sign an affidavit at the same time he turned over custody of the computer to me."

"And when was that?"

"Hell, I can't remember. A few days before he died, I guess," Ravich lied.

"Why go to the trouble of getting a sworn affidavit?" Harry asked. "He could have authenticated his records in a deposition or on the witness stand when the time came."

"I realize that. But you know how it is, Harry. You've been in the game longer than me. Witnesses sometimes change their minds. Alliances get altered. I wanted to make sure we had this important evidence locked down."

Harry nodded in understanding. "So, you were just being careful?"

"Exactly."

"How did you know he died in a car wreck?" Harry then asked.

"One of my associates told me," Ravich quickly said. "I guess they got a call from somebody at the plant. Or maybe one of my clients had heard about it."

Harry nodded again. "Such a tragedy, don't you agree?" Harry said, before slurping a spoonful of his gumbo.

"Absolutely. I obviously would have preferred to have that man's live testimony."

"Yes, yes," Harry replied, still slowly eating. "Sometimes, we just can't have what we want."

Ravich stabbed at his salad. He knew his old boss well enough to realize he had intended a double meaning.

"So, will you consider my offer?"

"I'll discuss it with my co-counsel and client."

"Good, I'd like to have your commitment before my press conference tomorrow afternoon."

"I'll try and get back to you before then."

"That's all I ask."

Ravich took a bite of a chicken strip that laid atop his greens and frowned. *The food here is terrible,* he thought, as he put his fork down and pushed aside the plate. He decided to press his sales pitch.

"What alternative do you really have, Harry? If you continue to pursue your gross negligence case against SeaCoast, our interests become antagonistic. Neither of us wants that."

"I said we will consider your proposal," Harry responded patiently. "But you need to be aware that we have to weigh all our options."

"What options?"

"Oh, I don't know right now, but surely there has to be some viable alternative."

"Like what? Pursuing an impossibly hard gross negligence theory against the employer? Where the evidence is clearly against you?"

"Paul, you're so much smarter than me. I just need some time to think, to see if there is some other kind of plan for us."

"You're joking, right?"

"No, Paul, I'm deadly serious. Prudent people always take time to look into everything."

The waiter passed by to ask if they wanted anything else. Ravich nodded no, then gestured for the check that Thomas handed to him. This meal was going to be his treat. In the sudden distraction, the super-lawyer forgot about the cleverness of his former boss and completely failed to digest the last words his lunch companion had spoken.

Harry Greenbaum once again intended a double meaning.

———— ◦◦◦ ————

Doug, Bonnie, and Bill had lunch at a place that was the polar opposite of the Barrister's Club. It was a warm day by early November standards so they decided to sit on the outdoor benches at Rudy's, a barbecue dive in a seedy neighborhood south of downtown that served the best smoked brisket sandwich in the city. It was the kind of place where crowds came for the great food and customers sat together at the long wooden picnic tables.

Between bites, the trio discussed the morning session with Harry, speculating on the things he had said and the purpose of his lunch with Ravich.

"That was one strange meeting, don't you think?" Gaston said, as he dribbled more hot sauce on his sandwich. "In less than an hour, that man filled me with a day's worth of follow-up questions."

"I postponed two hearings in other cases so that we could meet," Doug complained. "I'm not sure it was worth it."

"Hey, never regret anything that keeps you out of the courthouse on Motion Mondays, my brother," Gaston replied.

"How can the man already know which employees of the defendant we should depose?" Doug wondered aloud. "We haven't even sent out interrogatories calling for the identity of persons with knowledge of relevant facts. We've yet to ask for production of documents. It's like he's months ahead of us."

"Get used to that boys," Bonnie cautioned. "Harry Greenbaum always stays one step ahead, which is mighty hard to do considering he also pretends to be stumbling."

The two young lawyers nodded their heads in agreement.

"And what do you think about this dead witness?" Doug asked. "What was the man's title?"

"Head Process Engineer," Gaston replied. "The Big Kahuna."

"Yeah, a key defense witness dies ten days after the explosion and Harry is already pals with the widow?" Doug raised his eyebrows. "How does that happen?"

Bonnie piped in. "You fellows aren't listening to me. I tell ya, that cuddly old fool has been out pounding the pavement, trying to make a case, while Mr. Egghead here is in the law library finding court decisions that say we can't win." She looked at Bill Gaston with contempt. "You and your shit case."

"I'll have you know that decision from our state supreme court is the controlling legal authority in employer gross negligence cases. I can't help it if the facts are offensive to you."

"Fine," she countered. "But while you're busy citing *Poop v. Paper Mill* maybe the rest of us should be out helping Harry."

Doug changed the subject. "So, what are he and Ravich talking about right now?"

"That's easy," Bill replied. "Ravich is saying what a smart-ass you are and that Harry should wash his hands of you."

"There's probably more truth to that than you can imagine," Doug confessed.

"Why hasn't Ravich filed his suit?" Bonnie asked. "What's he waiting for?"

"Could be he's waiting to identify every third-party company that supplied a nut or bolt to that plant," Doug speculated. "He's the type to take the scattergun approach: sue everybody and sort things out later."

Gaston agreed. "Unlike us, Ravich is smart enough to know you can't win against the employer, so he's probably out there lining up defendants with deep pockets to pick."

"Would Harry sell us out?" Doug asked, still focused on the Barrister's Club meeting.

The looks from Bonnie and Bill made him instantly regret the question.

"No way," Gaston assured him. "Greenbaum is a rock. He would never accept Ravich's involvement in our case. He distrusts that man more than anybody."

Bill Gaston had a bad habit of talking while chewing. Even though what he was saying was true, it lost much of its import as Bonnie caught repeated glimpses of masticated beef being tossed around between words.

"Would you please close your mouth when eating?" she entreated.

"Hey, this is Rudy's. Classy conduct is strictly prohibited here."

"Still, it's disgusting."

"Fine. But if manners trump my erudite insights, you won't learn as much."

Doug became the referee. "Come on, kids, let's play nice. We really do have a lot of work to do."

Bonnie turned her attention to Harry's earlier comments. "He said something 'funny' or 'fishy' was going on in the *SeaCoast* case. That he was playing detective. What could he possibly be talking about?"

Doug shrugged his shoulders. He had no idea.

Gaston swallowed hard and took a sip of water, swishing it back and forth, before addressing Bonnie's question. He was trying to behave.

"The man's an enigma," Gaston suggested. "His means and methods are puzzling to us normal humans. We are as confused by his genius as he is baffled by fashion."

Bonnie and Doug burst into laughter.

Gaston smiled and, in a spooky voice, adapted the quote from an old radio drama to make his point: "Who knows what evil lurks in the hearts of men? The Shadow Greenbaum knows!"

It was a funny moment on a serious day. All three cracked up, unaware that a fundamental rule of comedy applied: The very best laughs are always grounded in truth.

———◦◦◦◦———

When Harry returned from lunch with Paul Ravich, his receptionist handed him a stack of pink phone messages. He reviewed them while walking slowly back to his office, rearranging the slips in order of callback priority.

People who wanted to speak with Harry Greenbaum understood he was old school. He was good about returning calls but if you expected an immediate response you were out of luck. He carried no cell phone. He found the buttons too small, and the idea of something ringing in his pants was disconcerting. In Harry's opinion, mobile technology made communications too instantaneous. Even worse, it destroyed the simple joy of being "out of the office." He believed that brief periods of unavailability were essential to maintaining one's sanity. He didn't have to be "on call" at all hours of the day and night. He was a lawyer, for God's sake, not an ER doctor.

One message immediately caught his eye: a call from Rickey Deaton, his longtime friend and auto mechanic. Below the call back number, the words read: "Call me, you dumb bastard." Harry smiled. His old buddy knew that the office receptionist would scrawl, verbatim, any message a caller left.

Harry decided to reward Rickey for his concise and colorful choice of words. He settled into his desk chair and dialed the number. The other messages could wait. Besides, he was very much interested in what Rickey had to say.

"R.D. Auto Repair," the familiar voice answered.

"This is the 'dumb bastard,' returning your call."

A coughing laugh erupted on the other end of the line. Rickey loved Harry Greenbaum.

"Is that what she put down?" Rickey said with false surprise. "Cause I did not say that. I called you a 'stupid mother-fucker.'"

Harry laughed.

"I understand. She sometimes has trouble writing out hyphenated words." Harry paused while Rickey chuckled, then got down to business. "So, what can you tell me?"

"Well, I went down to that salvage yard this morning to pick up your wrecked Ford, and you were right. We had to hoist it up on a flatbed. There's no way that thing would roll down the street attached to a hook. And you were also correct in telling me to take your pay receipt. That fat ole bitch in the front office was mean as hell. Told me I was taking advantage of a senile old man."

"And what did you say in reply?"

"I says: 'Tell me somethin' I don't know.' She didn't even crack a smile."

"Yes, I found the charming woman to be very serious about her work," Harry commented.

"So, anyhows, I got this stinking hulk of metal in one of my service bays right now. What exactly do you want me to do with it? Cause it ain't gonna be drivable."

"R.D., you're the only man I would trust with this assignment. A friend of mine was killed driving that car. The police report says he lost control. I was wondering if you could determine what might have caused that?"

"Most often it's a liquor bottle," the mechanic said.

"I understand, but not in this case. Just give it the once-over with all your practical expertise and let me know if you discover anything odd."

"You have some reason to suspect the car acted up?"

"I don't have a clue. That's why I'm seeking help from the smartest automotive technician I have ever met."

"Harry, you don't have to blow smoke up my ass. I grant you that keeping your old Plymouth running makes me a certified magician in your eyes but I'm just an average grease monkey that you once turned into an expert witness."

Harry smiled fondly. He would never forget the trial where Rickey Deaton bested a team of high-priced mechanical engineers the defense had retained in a trailer-brake failure case. Harry's client had been badly injured when the surge brakes on a rented trailer failed to activate, causing a loss of control. The rental company's experts came into court with an expensive 3D computer simulation to demonstrate how surge brakes *always* worked effectively if the towing vehicle was being safely driven. The defendant also brought in company representatives to testify that their fleet of trailers underwent rigorous and frequent brake inspections.

Harry then called Rickey as a rebuttal witness. His "good ole boy" mechanic came into court wearing greasy overalls and rolling a large work cart. On top of the cart was a blue tarp, concealing some obviously big mechanical parts. After qualifying Rickey as an expert mechanic, Harry asked the question that was on the mind of everyone in the courtroom: "What's under that tarp?" Rickey tugged the cover off with the flair of a matador, revealing two surge brake assemblies he had carefully removed from trailers rented from the defendant company the day before. He then used a common screwdriver to simulate a braking force on each surge coupler. Both master cylinders began to leak fluid on the courtroom floor. As Harry apologized to the Judge for the mess, Rickey explained to the jury that these components from randomly rented trailers were poorly maintained and would soon fail on the road, just like the one that Harry's client rented. The jury was out for less than an hour before ruling for the plaintiff.

Courtroom memories like that helped fuel Harry's continuing passion for his job. Now he had another case for the colorful mechanic to work on.

"Rickey, just do your best and inspect the darned thing. If you find anything unusual with that Taurus, let me know."

"And if I don't?"

"Then take it to a crusher-recycler. I hear they'll give you $470 for the thing."

"And supposin' I find something funny?"

"Then you might have to wash those overalls of yours and pay another visit to the courthouse someday."

"I wouldn't want to jeopardize my perfect batting record down there," Rickey teased. "I sure hope I find somethin' that's easy to prove."

"Me too, R.D.," Harry replied, knowing the odds of that were long at best. He thanked his friend and hung up, realizing he was probably wasting both time and money.

Playing long shots is always a risky proposition but occasionally it pays dividends. When someone tries to box you in, you have to think outside the box. With the help of his old mechanic, Harry once taught those very lessons to an arrogant trailer company that was certain it couldn't lose. He now hoped another lesson from that long ago case would apply again here — Sometimes the truth can be discovered by simply scavenging around.

Chapter 16
Election Day

The car radio was tuned to a local news-talk station. It was the first Tuesday in November which meant "topic A" was today's election. The polls had been open for little more than an hour, yet predictions were already airing that the Mayor would be reelected by a large margin. The other races looked similarly certain. It was a non-presidential year, with incumbent state legislators and a longtime member of Congress going through the perfunctory motions of getting their two-year tickets punched. Foregone conclusions made for record low voter turnouts.

Even Doug, who considered himself a political junkie, wasn't sure he would make it by his precinct today. His thoughts were preoccupied with a very different election, one far more life affecting. He turned down the volume as he accelerated north, heading away from downtown in the opposite direction of morning traffic. His front seat companion took it as a cue for conversation.

"Isn't this a lovely autumn morning?" Harry remarked, with a lively sense of wonder in his cheerful voice. He wore an old but matching brown suit. He also knew that today was important.

Doug glanced in the rear view mirror and saw Bonnie smiling in the back seat. The old man's moods could be infectious.

"A fine day for a road trip," she added.

Doug wasn't sure if his passengers were actually enthused by the weather or if they were simply trying to defuse his worries. Everyone realized this meeting with Kate Crouch was a red-letter day in the case. What they needed to discuss with their client was far too important to handle by phone. Besides, Harry felt this kind of decision was best made by a client in the comfort of their own home. Doug decided to follow Harry's advice, even to the point of not questioning his insistence that Bonnie come along. *The man works in mysterious ways*, as Bill Gaston had pointed out repeatedly.

The day before, Harry had made an afternoon call to Doug and Bill to outline the lunch proposal made by Paul Ravich. It was, like most settlement offers, a decidedly mixed bag. Kate Crouch could receive almost two-million dollars in a matter of weeks, but at a price: she had to release SeaCoast — which meant their previously filed suit would be dismissed — and she would have to allow Ravich to act as her lead lawyer in the case against the third-party defendants. Economically, for her, it was a no-brainer: she should take the money and do the deal. Professionally, for them, it was disastrous. The "Three Musketeers" would have to surrender control of the case, leaving behind half their fee and most of their pride. Worst of all, there was little time for any of them to fully consider the consequences. Ravich made clear they had to be "in or out" by noon today.

After Harry's call, Doug and Bill had spent time debating the pros and cons before finally realizing there was no clear answer. Harry assumed his young charges were smart enough to know that; after all, he had ended his short phone briefing with a clear statement of the obvious: "It's up to her."

When Doug called Kate late Monday afternoon to schedule the meeting, he told her only that they wanted to come by to discuss some important case developments. She didn't press for details. It had to be big. She was pretty sure lawyers don't routinely make house calls. She asked if her mother should also be there and Doug said it would be fine. He promised to be at her place on Tuesday morning around nine. She didn't know whether to be scared or relieved by the prospect of an in-home meeting so she focused on something entirely different: *I need to straighten this place up.*

The GPS in Doug's car directed them off the freeway and into what a realtor's brochure might spin as a modest, quiet neighborhood. In actuality, it was more a hodgepodge of small and inexpensive tract homes, built almost thirty years ago, most showing their age through peeling coats of paint and deteriorating roofs. When originally constructed, the subdivision was probably marketed with pride to the "middle class." Time and changing economies had transformed the neighborhood to labels of "working class," then "underclass." Unkept yards and old cars in the driveway told the story: this was where the silent masses lived; these were the houses of people barely getting by.

Harry looked out the window. "I'm glad we drove up here. I think it's important to see where and how your client lives."

Doug and Bonnie nodded in agreement as they glanced around with dread. *How could anyone who struggles like this possibly turn down millions?*

Both knew that Kate Crouch was strong-willed. She had to be to resist Ravich's initial advances. But they also knew she wasn't stupid. She could be out of this bleak neighborhood by the end of the month if she accepted the deal.

"You have reached your destination," the car's computerized-female voice announced. Doug pulled into the short driveway and turned off the engine. He turned to his co-counsel who was reaching for his door handle.

"Harry, let me introduce you first. Then, you can outline the proposal to her and give your thoughts. I'll fill in afterwards if she or her mother has questions. Is that okay?"

"That will be fine. But never hesitate to ask for the ball if I begin to dribble too much."

The comment made both Doug and Bonnie smile. Harry Greenbaum was a master at relaxing people.

Kate heard their arrival and opened the front door before they had a chance to knock. She escorted them inside to the small living room where her mother was seated on the couch. Although the furniture was old and cheap, the room was clean and fresh-smelling. On a tiny coffee table sat a pot of fresh coffee and some blueberry scones, which were offered after short greetings were exchanged. Kate and her mom were trying hard to be gracious hosts. It reminded all three guests that dignity exists even where wealth is absent.

While Bonnie and Doug declined a scone, Harry accepted one with enthusiasm. He stood devouring the treat as Doug explained his role.

"Like I told you the day you hired me, Bonnie and I knew we would need some help on your case."

"These things are delicious!" Harry suddenly interrupted, as a few crumbs fell from his mouth to the floor.

Kate looked on in surprised amusement.

"Thank you, I made them myself," Kate's mom replied.

"Each bite is a gift from heaven," Harry effusively added. "Ma'am, I want you to know that."

Jackie Baker glowed and smiled toward her daughter.

"Anyway," Doug continued, "Mr. Greenbaum here is a living legal legend who has agreed to work with us, and…"

"Please, everyone call me Harry," he interrupted again, as he swallowed another bite of his treat.

Doug smiled at the uninhibited old lawyer. "I know this might not be your first impression, but there is no finer or more honest trial lawyer in this town."

Harry blushed slightly and waved his free hand in modesty.

Bonnie could tell the women might need convincing. "What we're saying is: 'Don't judge the book by its cover.'"

Everyone, including Harry, laughed. The ice was broken.

Doug went on to detail Harry's career accomplishments. He also lauded Bill Gaston, explaining their remaining team member was attending depositions in another case and therefore could not make the drive up. He ended with a short outline of what they had done so far: filing the suit, landing a fair judge, preparing initial discovery. Kate and her mother listened closely. He then turned things over to Harry.

"Ladies, first of all, I want to compliment you on your choice of counsel. Mrs. Crouch, I know you had an opportunity to hire Paul Ravich but chose instead to go with young Doug here. I also understand that you, Mrs. Baker, were once ably represented by this man. Now, I realize you don't know me from Adam and you shouldn't actually believe all those nice things that Doug just said about me. But he did get one thing right: I try to be a straight-shooter. And I would say this same thing under oath: Douglas H. Stevens and his ever-competent assistant Bonnie are two of the finest legal minds operating today. And this Gaston fellow is one smart cookie too. The only things I have over any of them is age and experience. I once thought such attributes were grossly overrated, until I grew old and wise."

Doug and Bonnie watched on with amazement. He was charming his way into trust. Kate and her mother were no different from jurors. Everyone, eventually, loves Harry.

"So, enough about how great we all are," Harry said, with a dismissive flourish of his hand. "The only reason to bring up our modest talents is to hopefully assure you that we're here today for just one purpose: to help you make a very important decision."

His tone became less casual as he began to outline in precise detail the terms of Ravich's proposal. He was all business now and Kate Crouch listened to his words intently. She said nothing, but reacted with predictable body language: she seemed overwhelmed by the enormity of the proposed voluntary payment from SeaCoast; she seemed leery of the company's motivations; and she appeared disgusted at the prospect of becoming a referral to Ravich.

Harry, sensing her conflict, spared her the chore of asking the obvious questions.

"Now, the first thing you're probably thinking is: Why would Dan's employer pay you and the other victims so much money without even making you fight for it?"

Kate and her mother both nodded. It didn't make sense.

"Well, the answer is: It makes no sense."

Both women were taken aback. Harry Greenbaum had read their minds.

"I'm here to tell you that in almost fifty years of handling litigation, I have never seen a defendant toss out a huge sack of money before their liability has even been partially revealed through discovery or trial. It just doesn't happen. So either they are more charitable than Mother Teresa or they have something to hide, something that might cost them even more if it were ever found out."

Harry scratched his head as if working through the puzzling dilemma.

"Now which is it? A good deed or a bad deal? I could be wrong, but I know the man who owns SeaCoast Chemical Corporation and I can tell you he ain't no saint. So there's that to consider."

Jackie Baker started to ask a question but Kate placed her hand gently on her mother's arm, signaling that she should wait.

"Another reasonable question is: Why would Paul Ravich negotiate such a quick deal with SeaCoast and not charge a dime in fee? He's contractually entitled to take a cut, at least from the folks he signed up on the morning after the explosion. Now you two don't know this, but I've been around that man since he got his law license and the only thing Paul Ravich loves more than himself is the almighty dollar. So unless he found religion, you have to assume his motivations aren't charitable either."

Bonnie sat across the room in a naugahyde recliner, enraptured by Greenbaum's clear and logical observations as the old man continued talking.

"Maybe the reason he wants everyone to accept this 'voluntary payment,' and the reason he's willing to waive his fee, is because doing so will bring him even greater monetary reward down the line. That might just explain why SeaCoast is hiring him to represent them in their own lawsuit. He stands to make tons more money as a lawyer for busted steel than he could ever earn representing lost souls. Call me crazy, but it seems to me that if a man would rather get rich protecting property instead of people, that man ain't much of a people person. A client ought to think about his or her lawyer's priorities is all I'm saying."

Kate Crouch slowly nodded her head.

"One more thing to think about: How can Paul Ravich be so cocksure he knows what really happened out there? He's going to file a lawsuit today against an outfit that allegedly sold a defective product to SeaCoast, which he says caused the plant to explode. Could that be true? Sure. Is it true? Who the heck knows? Not one deposition has been taken, not one fact has been put up for challenge in a court proceeding. All he's going on is some evidence he claims he got days after the explosion from a plant manager that has now turned up dead."

Both Kate and her mother appeared shocked by that revelation. They didn't know what to make of it but it sounded sinister. Which is precisely the point that Harry was trying to make.

"Ladies, I'm willing to accept God's promise of an afterlife. I do so on faith, without any actual proof of heaven's existence. But, as I have already pointed out, Paul Ravich is a far cry from a deity and therefore I can't in good conscience just also take him at his word."

Harry looked directly at Kate with unblinking eyes.

"Taking his deal means you blindly accept his explanation for your husband's death. Will that bring you financial security? Yes, it probably will. Will that bring you and Dan justice? I honestly can't say that. It's just too early to tell."

With that, Harry held up his arms in a shrug.

"So, there you go. That's all I know. I'm sorry that Mr. Ravich has given you so short a deadline but you must now make a decision."

Kate looked over at her mother, whose face shared her daughter's angst. She next glanced at both Doug and Bonnie. They knew better than to say anything else. Harry had fully laid the cards on the table.

"What do you think I should do?" she finally asked, looking directly at Harry.

"If you need the money, take the deal. If you want justice, turn it down. There is no right or wrong here, madam. No one, especially me, will judge you for the choice you make."

"I just don't know," she muttered in frustration.

"I understand," Harry said. "It's a difficult decision. Please realize, Mrs. Crouch, that our civil justice system can only compensate your loss with money. We can't bring Dan back. We can't give you your old life back. Ravich's deal brings you money now and will likely bring you even more from this company he's about to sue. So there is no shame in accepting his proposal. If you turn it down we will press on. We will work hard to win your case. Again, if we do, all you'll receive is money but, hopefully, you will also have answers. However, if we don't prove what really happened, we will lose your case and you will come back here with nothing. It's as simple as that."

Kate nodded in understanding and straightened her jaw. It was her time to speak.

"The day Dan died we had nothing. We lived paycheck to paycheck. We tried to stay happy but it's hard when there's so little good in your life. Our marriage was far from perfect but it was ours. Somebody took that away from us. He didn't deserve to die."

Harry knelt beside the couch and patted Kate's hand. He could see the tears forming in her eyes.

"Money isn't going to change anything," she continued. "I never had much growing up and neither did Dan. But we fell in love. We got by. He did honest work for honest pay. I think I owe him honest answers."

Doug and Bonnie looked on with deep empathy. It was hard not to be moved by her words.

"I hired Mr. Stevens because he's honest." She looked directly into Harry's eyes. "He hired you for the same reason. That other lawyer doesn't care about Dan or me. I doubt he even knows what honesty is. And you've made it pretty clear he's not interested in finding honest answers for me."

She glanced over at Doug.

"My mom always says: 'People want what they can't have.' You tell me I can have a lot of money but that's not what I want. I want to know the truth, and that other lawyer can't give that to me. I just know in my heart that he can't."

She looked back at Harry. The election was made.

"So tell him to go to hell."

Only a person of deep character could make such a Hobson's choice without reservation. Harry stared at the young woman's face and saw an unwavering sense of commitment. Turns out, they never had any risk of losing her as a client. Like the Mayor today, Harry and his team were destined to win by a landslide.

Doug breathed a quiet sigh of relief. Bonnie nodded her head in respectful admiration. Kate's mother gripped her daughter's hand, proud that she had brought up so strong a child. Harry continued to pat her other hand and gave her a look of solemn purpose. She had turned down a certain fortune to see that justice was done. That took courage and integrity.

Harry felt a deep and heavy responsibility towards his brave client. *Let the tort reformers call people like this 'money-grubbers,'* he thought. He knew better. The Kate Crouch's of the world were why he had become a plaintiff's lawyer. The fact that decent people would always need help and answers is the reason he could never retire. He was proud of her. He was proud of his profession.

And he was looking forward to his phone call to Paul Ravich.

His public relations people were under the gun. Paul Ravich wanted maximum exposure for this press conference. That was asking a lot. Media outlets were already geared up for their "special coverage" of the elections.

Although the contests lacked suspense, news stations had assigned most of their reporters to the biannual tasks of conducting exit polls with voters and videotaping candidates casting ballots for themselves. It was hard to convince them that a civil case filing was newsworthy enough to warrant coverage on this particular day.

The PR firm, however, wasn't about to lose a client like Paul Ravich. They had billed him almost three-hundred thousand dollars so far this year and knew the next contract renewal would be dependent upon their success in meeting his current need. So they coaxed and cajoled. They played up the importance of Ravich's announcement and dangled the intriguing element of Charles Thornton's participation. They downplayed the public's interest in the election, telling each news director the obvious: nobody really cared about the predictable outcomes anyway.

To Ravich, getting reporters to the party was a problem for the party-planners. He had issues of his own. The old clown and the young punk lawyer had, an hour before, flatly rejected his proposal. Greenbaum called to say they weren't referring the *Crouch* case. When he asked how the widow could turn down so much cash, his former boss muttered some crap about "money not being everything." *What were they and that stupid bitch possibly thinking?* No client in her right mind would say no to almost two-million dollars in an immediate cash payment, *especially when it also meant losing the services of the greatest trial lawyer who ever lived.* Only *he* could get her bigger money down the road. *Either Kate Crouch was crazy or her lawyers were unwilling to let go of some of their fee.* Never once did he consider that she and her attorneys simply distrusted him. In his mind, *what was there not to like?*

Ravich was livid over their rejection of him. Doug Stevens and his little troupe had ceased being a fly in the ointment. They were now a buzzing mosquito, a persistent irritant spoiling his planned picnic. *But not for long,* he thought vengefully. He now had a judge who would gladly point bug spray in any direction he was told.

Only hours before the press conference, Paul Ravich had handed the intake clerk the original pleading in *SeaCoast Chemical Corporation v. Integrated Sentry.* He intentionally planned the case filing for lunchtime, knowing that fewer clerks would be in the district clerk's office to watch the system being manipulated.

"Why hello, Janet, it's good to see you again," he began with a smile.

The intake clerk looked up, surprised to see a lawyer as rich and powerful as Paul Ravich doing routine court filings. Her bewilderment was quickly addressed.

"How's that Escalade running?"

The reference to the Cadillac she had "won" at Ravich's Christmas party four years earlier wasn't intended as small talk.

"Just great! I still can't thank you enough," she said innocently.

"Well, perhaps you can," he replied, handing over the lawsuit. "This one is pretty important to me, Janet; let's see if we can't get it to land in one of the less busy courts — perhaps Judge Lewis?"

His serious look communicated that he was issuing an instruction rather than a request. Janet tensed and looked around conspiratorially. She knew she could get in big trouble for this. It was a clear violation of policy to do what he was asking. It was a firing offense and a free car does you little good if you don't have a job. Still, she owed him this much. *What difference does it really make anyway?* she rationalized. His case had a one-in-fourteen chance of falling in Lewis' court using the computer randomization system. All she was being asked to do was tinker a bit with the odds. She hit the F10 key and didn't see the right name. She quickly punched it a second time and the wrong judge came up again. It took four more nervous keystrokes before they hit the jackpot. Janet breathed a sigh of relief. Her supervisor walked by at that precise moment, on her way out for lunch. The intake clerk reached for the rubber stamp that matched the court assignment now on her computer screen. Paul Ravich looked on with glee as he saw the biggest case of his career formally assigned to his biggest lackey. Judge Lewis would know how to kill mosquitos when the time came.

"Thanks, Janet," he said, as she handed him the filing receipt. "It's really good seeing you again."

"Same here," she demurely replied, hoping that her unspoken debt had now been fully paid.

"You take care of that SUV, hear?" he added, as he happily turned to walk away.

Once again, Paul Ravich had gotten his way.

The rules don't apply to me.

Charles Thornton sat in the passenger seat of Bruce Waltman's car, reviewing the script his General Counsel had written for him to deliver at the press conference. His chief lawyer was clever with words. The phrasing was excellent. Bruce was a smart man. So was Paul Ravich for having suggested that Waltman be kept in the dark about the illegality that gave rise to their planned announcement. The company's head lawyer still didn't know the sinister details behind the deal. And he never would if Thornton and Ravich had anything to do with it.

As they pulled up to the courthouse, Charles Thornton dropped the script on his lap and looked out the window, smiling. They were about to unleash unholy hell on an unsuspecting company that would soon be forced to reimburse his losses. The SeaCoast plant explosion would end up costing him next to nothing after Ravich got through jiggering-up the numbers. At the same time, his voluntary payment to the families would make him look like a philanthropic bleeding-heart. The whole world would think of him as a tycoon with a soft side. *That could come in handy in future business negotiations,* he mused. A wolf in sheep's clothing finds steady meals.

The only downside of today's affair was that he had to share the stage with Paul Ravich. *A goddamn trial lawyer was going to get just as much favorable press as me.* To Thornton's ego, that didn't seem fair but considering a future recoupment of hundreds of millions he supposed he could go halves on the spotlight just this once.

Charles Thornton was confident things would go smoothy. He had a lot at stake but Ravich had even more. The lawyer was playing for more than a big fee. He also had crimes — including an apparent murder — that had to be kept concealed. *All I have to do is read this sappy crap in front of the cameras,* he smirked to himself, as he walked to the front of the courthouse where a press podium had been placed and several news crews had gathered. *Paul Ravich will take care of everything else.* Thornton clutched his script in his chunky but well-manicured hands. *At least, he'd better.*

⸙

"Damnedest thing I've ever seen," Rickey Deaton blurted, as his lawyer buddy walked inside the small grimy office of R.D. Auto Repair.

Harry Greenbaum returned a look of keen interest. He rushed over on Tuesday afternoon after his everyman auto expert called to say he "found something very interesting with that Ford Taurus of yours."

"I wouldn't ordinarily drag you over here, but I can't begin to describe this crazy thing over the phone," R.D. continued, as he leaned back in his swivel chair.

Harry nodded in understanding. "I'm an in-person man myself," he reminded him.

The mechanic leaned forward and rose from his cluttered desk, starting toward the side door behind him. It led to the three bay garage where he made a decent living repairing cars at prices far below what dealership service departments charge.

"Follow me. I've got her hoisted out here on a lift."

Harry trailed his friend. Once through the door, he saw the blue

Taurus elevated in the most distant bay. Greenbaum silently pondered how they managed to drag the badly damaged sedan into position over the hydraulic lift. Approaching the wrecked car, they passed two mechanics who were busy under the hood of a minivan in the first bay.

"Hey," R.D. called out. "You two take a ten-minute break. I need some quiet time with this man here."

The two employees stopped what they were doing. Like synchronized swimmers, they simultaneously reached for their respective packs of cigarettes stuffed in the top pocket of their garage overalls. As they made their way out for a smoke break, R.D. grabbed the youngest looking one by the arm.

"Donny, this here's Harry Greenbaum, the best damn lawyer ever born. Harry, this here's my youngest boy, Donny."

Harry reached out for a handshake with the son. Most people would eschew a palm so dirty but Harry wasn't like most people. These people were his people. He vigorously pumped the young boy's hand.

"I can see you are a master apprentice, Donny. For the safety of the traveling public, I only hope your senile old dad let's you handle all the hard stuff."

Donny seemed puzzled by the funny-talking lawyer dressed in an old suit. He gave him a quizzical look, like a kid at the zoo seeing a giraffe for the first time and not quite knowing what to make of it.

"Yeah, nice to meet you," he replied dismissively, before reaching for the lighter in his pants pocket and heading quickly out the open bay door.

"He's a good boy," R.D. explained, as they continued walking towards the Taurus. He looked over his shoulder and added: "Dumb as a stump but handy with a wrench."

Harry nodded with a smile, then looked up at the wrecked car draped atop the X-shaped hoist arms.

R.D. gestured him toward the front of the undercarriage. "Take a look at this," he said, pointing to the steering linkage at the right front wheel. "Ever seen anything like that?"

Greenbaum glanced up at the dangling tie-rod assembly that seemed as if it were manufactured one foot too short. Its sheared-clean end extended outward but didn't reach the mushroomed-flat steering knuckle to which it should have been attached. The partially amputated metal arm hung in mechanical frustration, no longer a sufficient length to make the connection necessary to turn the wheel hub. Harry remembered the badly scraped hub. It was the one missing its tire at the salvage yard.

Meanwhile, R.D. answered his own question as he pointed up at the tie-rod remnant. "I'll tell you one damn thing: I sure as hell haven't. That part sheared off like someone took to it with a blowtorch. Metal can bend, crack, and break. But it don't just disappear like that."

Harry looked on with a mix of curiosity and unease. He didn't like what he was seeing or hearing.

"Another thing that ain't right," R.D. continued. "To do this kind of damage to the steering assembly up under here, you would also expect to see this wheel well all tore up. But except for that scraped hub and clean broken tie-rod there's not a lick of any other contact damage in this area."

Harry played the good direct-examiner. He didn't lead his witness. "So what does that tell you?"

"It suggests to me that something other than impact forces broke this thing."

Harry tensed. He had honestly hoped his crazy suspicions were simply those of a doddering old man.

"Like what?" Harry asked cautiously.

"Well, that's exactly what I asked myself this mornin'," the mechanic replied.

Rickey Deaton reached for the lever that controlled the hoist. He lowered it slightly to bring the wheel well closer to eye level. He pointed at what appeared to be dirt imbedded into the front side of the hard plastic wheel well liner. The liner was a dull gray color. The specks were much darker and had pitted the plastic in a spray pattern. In the center of the pattern, a one inch square of the plastic liner was missing.

"See them specks? It ain't mud."

"What is it then?"

"Hell if I know. That's why I cut out a piece of liner to give to you."

He walked over to a tool bench along the back wall and retrieved a sealed glass jar the size of a baby food container. Inside was the extracted square of plastic.

"Did you photograph the wheel well before you did that?"

"Before, during, and after," Rickey replied, in a tone of voice that feigned irritation at being questioned about his evidence collection techniques.

He unscrewed the cap and held it under Harry's nose. It had a chemical smell, a faint oily odor.

"Maybe some oil or transmission fluid got sprayed up there?" Harry suggested.

"Could be, if the Ford Motor Company was stupid enough to put their crank case or transmission assembly inside a sealed wheel well. But they're not. There's nothing in that wheel area that would make a spray pattern like that. And oil and transmission fluid wouldn't imbed that deep in plastic. The stuff in this jar is what you fancy lawyers might call a 'foreign substance.'"

"Like what?"

"Goddamn, Harry, do I have to do everything for you? I'm not a chemist but I bet you could find one. Have this shit tested. Somebody, or something, put this stuff in that tire well."

He handed the tiny jar to his lawyer buddy. "I thought this little square would be enough to analyze," he added. "I figured it was best to leave the rest where it is to preserve the evidence."

Harry smiled. Although Rickey Deaton looked like a back-alley mechanic, he had the brains of a magnificent courtroom expert. And he was not yet done with his report.

"And while we're on the subject of interesting and unusual shit, don't you think it odd that three out of four wheels remained attached to their hubs while this one just blew right off?"

R.D. stood with his hands on his hips, a look of incredulity on his face.

"Guess that could happen though, right?" Harry ventured.

"Well, sure, and you could win the lotto today. But it ain't likely. I checked the lugs on them other wheels. They're all torqued tight like they should be. Them others weren't coming off if a bus had hit that car. But this one sure did, yet the right front end was no more busted up than any other section of the car. There's only one explanation for that missing wheel. Its lug nuts were loose."

R.D. delivered his conclusion with an ominous tone before returning to his theory.

"Now listen, I've known some stupid mechanics in my day. A lazy dumb kid might forget to tighten all four wheels when he installs new tires. But them other three tires aren't new. The treads are all pretty wore down as you can see. That means they've been driven on for a while. An owner might not notice a loose tire right away but it's not the kind of thing you're gonna miss over some four or five thousand miles."

"So, what are you saying?"

"Just a wild-assed guess here, Harry: If we assume the missing front tire was put on at the same time as them others, then you have to conclude that someone loosened the lugs on that particular wheel shortly before the accident. How else can you explain it going missing during the wreck? We know it did; otherwise, that hub wouldn't have been all gouged up."

It was a valid point, concise and logical. Harry could think of no innocent explanation.

"And you say this is exactly how the car was delivered to that salvage yard?" Deaton asked, seeking confirmation.

Harry shook his head yes. He realized the missing tire and lug nuts were probably swept away and long discarded, along with the broken glass, plastic, and other detritus that had littered the freeway.

He had heard enough. He knew what needed to be done. The first thing was to protect his witness and friend.

"R.D., I really appreciate your thorough inspection. I'm going to take this residue for further study. In the meantime, I want you to wrap this wheel well in plastic or something to keep it as intact as you possibly can. Next, take this car down to one of those monthly storage facilities. Rent a stall and lock it up good in there. Send me a bill for everything. I'll be back in touch as soon as I know something."

The mechanic looked at his old friend. Harry's usual comic demeanor had disappeared, replaced by a grim look and a quick litany of instructions that made him sound like Jack Webb talking on the old *Dragnet* television series. R.D. knew they had stumbled onto something very unsettling. He had never seen Greenbaum act this way.

"What's this all about, Harry?"

Greenbaum held up the glass jar in his hand and squinted at its tiny contents. "I hope I'm wrong, pal. I honestly do. But I could be getting in over my head on this."

Rickey Deaton laughed uneasily. The notion that anything could vex the old lawyer was strange to him. He had seen the man in court. Harry Greenbaum could handle anything.

"What's there to worry about?" he asked out of concern.

Greenbaum thought about the question. He wasn't sure exactly, but it seemed there was now a sinister force compelling yet another election this day.

"R.D., I'm just a sore-back lawyer. Been an accident attorney all my career. I'm probably too old to be getting into something new."

"Like what?" his friend said.

Harry looked at him with a worried expression, then replied: "Criminal law."

"We appreciate your continuing interest in this important story."

Paul Ravich began his remarks looking out at the assembled press. He concealed his inner rage with a purposeful stare into the cameras. The turnout was less than he expected: only two of the four local television affiliates sent crews and he didn't recognize the reporter from the paper or the young kid sent by the leading news-radio station. His press conference was being treated like a publicity stunt — which it was — but he didn't like being given short shrift. He would have a long talk with his PR people later. Right now, he needed to sell soap.

"Only three weeks ago, an unexplained tragedy claimed the lives of decent hardworking men and destroyed a valuable cog in our city's economic engine: the flagship manufacturing plant of SeaCoast Chemical Corporation. When first hired by the victims' families to investigate this disaster, I made two promises: first, that I would work tirelessly to determine the cause of that devastating explosion; and second, that I would bring the responsible party or parties to justice for the harm they inflicted."

He looked over at Charles Thornton, standing to his right.

"With the extraordinary cooperation of the owner of this chemical plant, I am pleased to announce today that our diligent efforts have uncovered both the cause and the culprit behind this tragedy. An hour ago I filed suit against Integrated Sentry, Inc., which is a wholly owned subsidiary of the well-known VyStream Corporation, also named as a defendant in the lawsuit. These companies sold this plant a defective safety system which they alone designed, manufactured, and installed. That system malfunctioned on the night of the explosion and directly led to the deaths of six fine men and the complete destruction of a profitable and expensive chemical plant facility."

Ravich fixed his jaw and gazed with certainty into the cameras.

"There is no question about the defendants' responsibility. My firm does not file frivolous lawsuits. The evidence we have already uncovered conclusively proves the allegations made in the pleadings just filed. We acted promptly to find answers. We intend to move just as quickly to get this case to trial in order to make these defendants answer for their misdeeds."

He turned to his new partner.

"And now, I would ask Mr. Charles Thornton, who is known throughout this city, state, and country as a prominent business leader, to say a few words. His company, Thornton Industries, owned the SeaCoast Chemical plant that was destroyed by the defendants' carelessness and defective product. Mr. Thornton?"

The executive walked over and centered himself behind the array of microphones atop the podium. Ravich, ever the media professional, stepped behind him and to his left but took great care to remain in the camera shot. He was willing to *share* the spotlight, not give it up.

Thornton, unlike Ravich, was not used to such appearances. In his mind, this media circus was the realm of showboating lawyers and executives, and he had little use for the Gloria Allreds and Donald Trumps of the world. He preferred to make his mark in closed-door business negotiations. Like a grand puppeteer, he wanted to pull his strings unseen.

His unease showed. A gusting wind kept blowing up the corners of his prepared statement as he tried to hold the pages down from view of the cameras with his meaty right hand. Thornton started in a flat monotone, sounding more like a grade-schooler reading from a textbook than a sophisticated businessman who meant what he was saying.

"The SeaCoast family was forever changed by the events of October 14th. Our fertilizer business was destroyed but, most importantly, we also lost six dedicated, hardworking men who were the real reason for any success we may have had."

He then read off the names of the victims. He had to. He had never learned their names. When he said "Dan Crouch," Ravich winced slightly. He hadn't yet informed Thornton or his General Counsel about his earlier conversation with Harry Greenbaum.

"Our Company decided, on day one, to fully cooperate with government investigators and this lawyer for the families. We too wanted answers. Through our efforts, and those of Mr. Ravich, we came to learn that SeaCoast Chemical is a victim as well. Our plant and people were lost because a vendor we hired to improve safety at our facility didn't do its job. Instead of selling us a reliable safety system, it sold us a ticking time bomb. That system fooled our people into thinking it had their backs when, in fact, its design and malfunction caused their deaths."

He looked down at the first line of his next paragraph. At least one sentence in the damn press release was true.

"As a business owner, I don't care much for lawsuits and lawyers. But in law, as in business, it is only fair that those responsible for grave mistakes be held accountable. That is why SeaCoast Chemical Corporation joins Mr. Ravich in his efforts to right the wrong done to our workers, and it is why we have chosen to participate in this suit against Integrated Sentry and VyStream. Our business losses have already exceeded a half-billion dollars. We have therefore decided to also retain the services of Mr. Ravich's firm to pursue our company's claim for damages, on the express condition that our involvement not slow, in any way, his additional efforts to gain fair compensation for the victims' families."

He was almost to the end of his script. Waltman had decided they should finish with the best.

"We know that despite Mr. Ravich's hard efforts, the wheels of justice sometime turn slowly. We also know that the families of our workers need our help and support now. And that is why I am announcing today that SeaCoast Chemical is voluntarily contributing a total of ten-million dollars to be distributed to the victims; not because we have any liability to do so, but simply because we care about them."

That line was hard to deliver. Anyone who had ever crossed paths with Charles Thornton knew he actually cared about only two things: money and himself.

It was Ravich's cue. For the cameras, he moved forward to shake Thornton's hand, then resumed his position front and center. Like a good schoolboy, Charles Thornton took his paper with him and retreated from view.

"I first want to thank Thornton Industries and SeaCoast Chemical for being such responsive corporate citizens. If more companies cared this deeply about their employees there would be far fewer lawsuits, I assure you. In light of their charitable generosity, I would also like to announce that my firm will assess no fees against any monies paid by them to my clients. I feel that is the right thing to do."

Ravich made for much better soundbites. The reporters all smiled as he passionately delivered his last line. The man was a performer.

"We will, of course, keep you informed as this important litigation progresses. But make no mistake, justice will be done. Now, if there are any questions?"

A reporter from the CBS affiliate spoke up. "What specific evidence do you have against the companies you have sued?"

"The courtroom will be the place to discuss specifics," Ravich replied, with the dexterity of a seasoned presidential press secretary. "But we would not be standing here today making these statements if not absolutely sure these named defendants are truly responsible for this horrible explosion."

He pointed quickly to another reporter's raised hand. He was in his element.

"How much is SeaCoast paying you to represent them?" the woman asked pointedly.

Ravich should have expected such a question from the beat reporter from the NBC station. She considered herself to be a local Mike Wallace.

"Far less than my normal fee," he said, with a tone that made clear it was all he was going to say. He looked around. "Anyone else?"

The young reporter from the news-radio station seemed the most professional as he asked his questions. "Which court is the case filed inp[and do you have copies of the suit to distribute to us?"

Ravich gestured to Melanie Egan, who was standing off-camera.

"My associate here will immediately provide a copy of the lawsuit to any of you that request it. To answer your other question, I have been informed that the case was assigned to Judge Lewis of the 89th District

Court. I understand him to be an experienced and fair jurist. I trust that my clients and the defendants will all receive a fair trial."

He looked around again. There were no other questions but Ravich couldn't resist making one last statement. He was attracted to the lights of news cameras like a moth to a flame.

"It's worth noting that this suit was coincidentally filed on an election day. While we all know that true democracy depends on free and fair elections, it's also important to remember that true justice depends on full and unfettered access to our courts for a redress of civil wrongs. I am proud today to be a citizen of this great city and nation. I am also proud, yet humbled, to be an attorney for the victims of this tragedy. Thank you all for coming here today. If you have any further questions, please feel free to contact my office."

Ravich turned and walked away, hoping his last remarks would be aired somewhere tonight. There was nothing better for business than draping yourself in the Constitution or flag.

Charles Thornton briskly headed back to Bruce Waltman's waiting car. *People will do anything for money*, he thought pejoratively, as he mentally graded Ravich's over-the-top performance. The irony of his disgust instantly struck him. He was truly no different from the lawyer he disdained. He too was a willing participant in the show — and conspiracy. The thought marked an epiphany for him. The law, which he loathed, was the same as business, which he loved. In both, power and manipulation could get you what you want. You just had to be strong and smart enough to cheat the levers. In his own egotistical and twisted view of the world, the symmetry between the courtroom and boardroom was suddenly comforting: *People will do anything for money.*

Chapter 17
Adverse Parties

The reporter from the news-radio station called seeking comment on the recently filed suit. The same young man who demonstrated his professionalism at Ravich's press conference was again showing his chops. To assure a quote from a high-ranking source, he told the VyStream Corporation operator that he was airing a story on pending litigation and the allegations were big enough to affect the stock value of the publicly traded behemoth. That got the operator's attention, but the mention of share price caused the late afternoon call to be misrouted to the Investor Relations Department. The reporter was soon lateraled on to Public Affairs while the confusion continued. Eventually, he was patched through to the Legal Department where an in-house attorney listened, with only modest interest, to the report of a tort claim filed against the company in another state. He was about to say "no comment" when he heard the suit sought damages in excess of a half-billion dollars for a chemical plant explosion that killed six.

"I have no knowledge of any such claim," the lawyer quickly sputtered. "Where did you say this suit was filed and when?"

The reporter supplied the details.

"Today? Well, obviously, we haven't been served with any suit papers yet. We clearly can't respond until we've seen the allegations."

"Would you like me to email the plaintiffs' pleading? I have a PDF copy."

The lawyer accepted the reporter's offer and provided his email address before thinking to ask a follow-up question. "And who other than VyStream was named as a defendant?"

"Integrated Sentry, a company the plaintiffs' lawyer said is your subsidiary. He claims they and you made a faulty safety system that should have prevented the accident."

"Look, this is the first we've heard about any of this. In exchange for sending over the pleading, I'll get back to you once we've reviewed it. But I doubt we'll say anything other than 'we deny the allegations' until we're in court."

"I understand that," the reporter said, "but we prefer some form of reply before we start broadcasting the story this evening."

"I'll do what I can," the lawyer promised before ending the call.

A minute later, the email showed up. He opened the attached PDF file and read in disbelief before printing a copy. He then ran down the hall, only to discover his boss was in a closed-door meeting. Some things could wait; this could not. With a brief tap on the door, he entered and apologized for the interruption.

"I'm sorry, sir, but I think you'd better see this right away."

Jack Trenton, the General Counsel of VyStream Corporation, accepted the papers from his staff attorney with a glare that said: *"This better be important."* Before he finished scanning the first page, he could tell that it was. He turned to the two men in his office and, offering his own apologies, advised them that something urgent had come up. They quickly left, leaving VyStream's head lawyer standing in his office, reading the remainder of Ravich's pleading. He reached the end of the factual allegations against the company and its subsidiary.

"Fuck!"

The staff attorney nodded his head. He had been right to rush in with the alarming news. He stood watching as the veins on his boss's neck tensed and protruded as he kept reading. A moment later, there was another outburst.

"What the Fuck?"

Trenton had just seen the damage figures being sought. No other expletive seemed appropriate.

Multinational companies like VyStream are sued every day. It's a routine cost of doing business and the job of any General Counsel is to manage such costs. But a tort claim in excess of a half-billion dollars was far from routine. The reaction of the otherwise reserved corporate attorney was proof of that.

"I told the reporter who gave us the heads-up we would provide a comment," the staff attorney said meekly.

His boss looked up in further disgust. "Really? You promised a reply?"

"Yes, sir, I did," the attorney said softly, looking down at his feet.

"Call him back and say this is all *bullshit!*" he shouted, still incapable of regaining his composure. Then, just as suddenly, the General Counsel recalled why he held the title. It was his job to orchestrate and execute the legal affairs of one of the world's largest companies. The position didn't call for a hot head. "No, wait, tell him *exactly* this: These allegations are not only blatantly false but irresponsible as well. Neither VyStream nor Integrated Sentry did anything wrong and we will fully prove that in court if these frivolous claims are not dismissed immediately." He looked at his lawyer who was frantically jotting the quote on his legal pad. "Got that?"

"Yes, sir, got it. Anything else?"

"Yeah, get the President of ISI on the phone and brief him. His name is Mike Beasley. Tell Mike I'm instructing that no one from his company should make any comment to anyone. All inquiries about this case should be directed to my office. Let him know I'll call first thing in the morning expecting to be informed accurately about what their company did or didn't do inside that plant."

"Do you want me to also notify our insurance carriers?"

"Not yet. We haven't been properly served. I'm calling Dean Schiller in on this one. He'll be in charge of managing this litigation."

The staff attorney knew the name. It was another hint of exasperation from his boss, a milder version of shouting the f-word. Dean Schiller was VyStream's special outside trial counsel, used only when the stakes were extraordinarily high. He last represented the company's interests when its aircraft engine division got hit with a string of product liability claims after its defective turbines caused the crash of two commercial airliners. VyStream and its aviation division paid out almost two-billion in eventual settlement dollars to the involved airlines and victims. But it could have been even worse. Dean Schiller was credited with minimizing the massive financial exposure.

The young gstaff attorney stood holding his notes and realized something startling: he hadn't even heard of Integrated Sentry, Inc. before today. VyStream Corporation was that big. It had subsidiaries and divisions around the globe, selling all manner of goods and services. No one within the company, except maybe its CEO and General Counsel, could begin to name them all. While the in-house lawyer had no idea how large or capitalized ISI was, he was certain of one thing: if Dean Schiller was being called in to defend that subsidiary against a half-billion dollar claim, it was probably a "bet-the-company" case.

Harry had growing suspicions but was keeping them to himself for now. People who go flying off the handle with far-fetched conspiracy theories are too easily classified as fools. He thought about the "Truthers," "Birthers," and "Moon Landing Deniers." No one took *them* seriously. He reasoned that if an old man like him came up with a similarly crazy scenario, it might signal both stupidity and dementia to his trial team. Before sharing his concerns with Doug, Bill, or Bonnie, he decided he would get his ducks in a row.

He reached for his old-fashioned Rolodex that was stuffed with well-worn cards, a testament to almost a half century of trial lawyer networking. He found the name and dialed another old friend. It was only 8:15 in the morning but Harry expected that Roland Winters would be in his office; that is, unless he had already headed out to court or to the jailhouse.

A familiar husky voice answered on the second ring. It was too early for Roland's receptionist to be there. However, a good criminal defense lawyer is never afraid to pick up his own phone at any hour of the day.

"Lordy, Mr. Winters, I'm in a heap of trouble," Harry began, in a fake tone of desperation. "I may have killed my wife."

Despite Harry's effort to conceal his distinctive voice, his old buddy instantly recognized the prankster and decided to play along. "May have? You're not sure if she's dead?"

Harry snickered. "She must be because she hasn't said a word to me for the past twenty years."

The two lawyers erupted in laughter. Silly banter was the natural byproduct of a long and lasting friendship between the two accomplished litigators.

"Our defense, then, will be suicide. I can convince a jury that ending her own life would be preferable to living with you." As his caller laughed some more, Roland decided to end the schtick. "So, what can I do for you this morning, Harry? It's been awhile."

"Yes, I know Roland. With you practicing over at the criminal justice center and me toiling away at the civil courts building, we have, I'm afraid, become two ships passing in the night."

"Sad, but true, my friend. Hey, how'd you like that election yesterday?"

"As predictable as a Roland Winters' acquittal. I didn't give it much thought."

"Me either. Although I expect to pick up a couple of DUI cases from the Mayor's celebration party once her supporters get sprung from jail."

"Only the truly needy come to you. Which brings me to ask a favor."

"Shoot."

"I'm in need of a good forensics expert. One that can test some trace evidence."

"What kind of trace?"

"Don't know exactly. Could be explosive."

"You mean that literally or figuratively?"

"Literally, although if this stuff turns out to be bomb residue, that statement is figuratively true as well."

"What's a sore back lawyer doing handling a bomb case?"

"Roland, I'll be honest with you, I have no idea right now what kind of case this will turn out to be. But I need a good chemical analysis of a sample."

"I've got the guy. He's in Virginia, former FBI Crime Lab specialist, now has his own forensic consulting shop. Criminal defense lawyers like me use him all the time. Top shelf expert, calls true balls and strikes. He's no witness whore."

"Perfect. I'm not looking for molded testimony. Actually, I hope he finds nothing because if he confirms my hypothesis it only means more work for me."

"Well, I know better than to ask any more questions. You can't disclose your work product and I sure as hell don't need a bomb thrower coming after me too."

"Well put. Then I'm ready to transcribe the name and number," Harry replied, pen in hand.

Roland provided the contact information. The remainder of their conversation involved the usual mutual promises of getting together soon for a drink or dinner. While each knew that would not likely happen, both were content that something far more important had just occurred: they were always there for each other, professionally, anytime. Good trial lawyers — on both the civil and criminal side — never took support like that for granted.

After hanging up, Harry sat at his desk thinking about the strange turns his newest case kept presenting. He glanced across the room at the brown briefcase resting high on the top shelf of his office bookcase. It had been there since he retrieved it from the trunk of Ken Slator's car down at the wrecker yard. Inside it sat unexplained items: hand tools and the business card of the SeaCoast president, along with a card key that Harry had found under the seat of Slator's crushed car. Those items were as random as the tiny plastic square tucked inside the glass jar Rickey Deaton had furnished the day before. He couldn't fathom how any of those objects could possibly be connected. *I'm just collecting trash,* he told himself, unconvincingly. *Even if they were somehow tied together, who held the common thread?* SeaCoast management? Ravich? Someone else that Slator was meeting with at night?

From the corner of his desk, he grabbed the jar containing the wheel liner cutout. Tapping it gently on his Big Chief tablet, where he had written the name of Roland Winter's expert, Harry knew that the road, however winding, would begin with this piece of evidence. He reached again for the phone.

The jar would soon be encased in bubble wrap and tucked safely in a FedEx package on its way to Virginia. He had no idea how long the testing would take or what the results would be, but was certain of one thing: if it came back positive for explosive residue, *Crouch v. SeaCoast* would no longer be just a civil claim for money damages. It would also become a murder investigation.

⸎

Dean Schiller sat in his Manhattan office and grinned. He had just gotten off the phone with his favorite type of corporate client: scared and rich. VyStream was again being sued for a bunch of money and they again wanted him. Unlike his previous case for their well-known aircraft engine division, Schiller had never heard of VyStreams' latest subsidiary to be hauled into court for millions. Integrated Sentry, Inc, *a catchy name*, he thought, for a technology company that designed custom control systems for manufacturing plants.

VyStream's General Counsel had explained that ISI was a relatively small division but it produced steady revenues and had never been the victim of any serious liability claims. Now they were being charged with destroying a chemical plant with six men inside. The size of the plaintiffs' claims were large enough to make Schiller's retainer of three-hundred thousand dollars, and his thousand dollar hourly rate, seem like chump change.

You can charge whatever you want when you have a reputation like his. Dean Schiller was one of those few lawyers in America whose case files stretched across borders. His New York City firm quarterbacked litigation everywhere. He had made appearances in thirty-one of the fifty state courts. He had argued before the US Supreme Court. He had even represented multinational corporations in the courts of foreign countries, heading the defense of international deforesters and polluters.

He was smart but also practical. No lawyer knows the legal nuances of every jurisdiction. That's why each state has its own bar exam. And that's also why Dean Schiller always hired the best local counsel he could find. They reported to him; he reported to the client. If things went well, the client got told the result was the product of his careful and deliberative case coordination. If things went badly, they were told it was either because of mistakes of local counsel or one of those rare occasions where the defendant got served a dose of "home cooking" in some backwater county where the plaintiff lawyer and judge were old buddies.

In short, being a national trial counsel to large corporate clients meant three things: too much travel, great pay, and a lack of final accountability. Two out of three ain't bad, as the saying went. Dean Schiller loved the gig.

The defense of Integrated Sentry and VyStream would be easy, Schiller thought. Despite the size of the damage claim it remained a basic tort case: pure products liability law. As intellectual exercise, such cases were not as rigorous as his usual docket of antitrust and securities fraud defense. All he would have to do is find the right defense lawyer to handle things locally while he sat back and advised strategy, which included recommending a settlement when and if necessary. *Nice work if you can get it*, he thought to himself, as he began to look over the suit that VyStream's legal department had forwarded by email.

The name of the plaintiffs' counsel sounded familiar. *Paul Ravich?* Schiller wasn't certain, but the fact that he had even vaguely heard the name meant Ravich was probably a prominent lawyer. He wanted information quickly on both the counsel and the main plaintiff, SeaCoast Chemical.

Schiller summoned two younger partners into his office and handed out assignments. One was to research the plaintiff company and immediately report back about its ownership, activities, and prior litigation involvement. The other was tasked with preparing a quick dossier on Paul Ravich: education, career, significant verdicts and settlements. Schiller also wanted specifics about Ravich's last five jury verdicts: where they were, the type case, the amounts pled for and awarded, along with the names and phone numbers of the defense counsel in each case. Dean Schiller considered Sun Tzu's *The Art of War* to be a litigation treatise. "Know your enemies" was standard operating procedure for him.

He wasn't surprised when his partners' memos were turned in later that afternoon. Computerized public records made the requested information easy to obtain.

He read that SeaCoast Chemical was a subsidiary of Thornton Industries. *Interesting*, Schiller thought, as he contemplated two corporate giants doing battle through their respective pawns. VyStream would be pulling the strings for Integrated Sentry while Thornton Industries dictated SeaCoast's maneuvers. In his view, the only downside was that his most common litigation tactic would be lost in this case: given the size of Thornton Industries' pocketbook, Schiller would not be able to outspend the other side into submission.

He turned his attention to the memo on Paul Ravich. Schiller's partner had attached copies of media reports pulled from the Internet about the plaintiffs' counsel. The most commonly used descriptor was: "super-lawyer." *No wonder the name sounded familiar. The man is a media hog.* Also attached to the memo were copies of the website pages for Paul Ravich & Associates. One page conveniently listed all of Ravich's big verdicts and settlements. Schiller understood that most successful tort lawyers believe their track record makes for an impressive marketing tool. Dean Schiller looked down the list. *The man was a player,* he said to himself, noting the multiple results in the eight-figure range. Schiller surveyed the remainder of the attachments, then returned to the memo itself. It read that Ravich's latest verdict was a simple traffic case where the jury awarded three-million in damages. Schiller laughed. *He was still handling car wrecks?* That fact gave him some comfort. Despite a formidable record, a lawyer who was still trying fender-benders would clearly be no match for a Wall Street litigator who had argued before the Supreme Court.

He decided to make a call to the defense lawyer in Ravich's most recent trial. *You're only as good as your last performance,* Schiller reasoned, and he assumed that attorney would be willing to share his insights on Ravich. He googled the man's name and learned he was an experienced partner at the third biggest firm in that city. *A big fish in a small pond.* Then again, everyplace was a small pond compared to New York.

Schiller would need local counsel. Perhaps if this lawyer impressed him over the phone he might consider retaining him, or maybe not. *How good could you possibly be if you were still defending auto cases?* Then again, a man who had just lost a case to Ravich would surely like another shot, aided by a powerhouse trial team at his back. *Revenge can be a powerful motivator.* Sun Tzu may not have said that but Schiller knew it was true.

Ben Argent was in his office and took the call. The two defense lawyers spoke for almost an hour and hit it off. Despite the occasional small case, Schiller was impressed with Argent's trial background, and the competent-sounding defense lawyer was clearly familiar with Ravich's tricks and traps. Those facts, together with Argent's partnership in a prominent law firm, meant he would soon get the job as local counsel for Integrated Sentry and VyStream. It would result in big billable hours for Argent but it also meant something else, something equally important to him: he would again face the jerk who had arrogantly rubbed-it-in with an obnoxious post-verdict grin in Judge Peterson's court. The *Clayton* trial had been almost two months ago but Ravich's cocky look remained seared in Agent's mind. And it still stung.

It was Answer Day. The rules of procedure gave SeaCoast twenty days after being served to file its responsive pleading in the *Crouch* case. The company waited until the deadline before submitting a short one sentence general denial of the gross negligence allegations. The filing was the legal equivalent of a child shouting: "Did not!" The pleading's designation — "Answer" — is actually a misnomer. A defendant's initial filing rarely provides any factual rebuttal. Instead, it simply marks the true beginning of the litigation contest, the time when all the horses are finally in the starting gate.

For Doug Stevens, the only surprising part of the SeaCoast Answer were the signatures of the attorneys who would be representing the Defendant. He shook his head in disgust when he opened his mail-delivered copy and saw the pleading had been signed by both SeaCoast's General Counsel *and* Paul Ravich. Litigation makes for strange bedfellows but Doug had never seen anything like this. Ravich was now part of the defense team that would fight to deny Kate Crouch compensation. At the same time, he would seek compensation in another court for the families of Dan Crouch's coworkers. Only greed or pettiness could explain such inconsistency of purpose. It was just like Harry had told him: "Ravich needs us to lose so he can win." A line was now drawn in the sand. There was no turning back. The man who had once extended a self-serving olive branch was now determined to beat Kate Crouch's lawyers over the head with it.

If this was to be Ravich's opening salvo, they were ready to fire back. Now that SeaCoast Chemical had entered a plea, discovery could begin. Bill Gaston had already prepared a thick packet of discovery requests, compelling SeaCoast to produce documents ranging from production records to personnel files. He asked for over thirty distinct categories of records including: safety meeting minutes, plant maintenance records, prior OSHA safety violations, and all on-the-job injury reports. In a gross negligence case, such documents were either relevant or could lead to the discovery of relevant evidence. Gaston's Requests for Production were so detailed that if the defendant complied in full — which they seldom did without the Court's intervention — Doug's war room would soon be filled with boxes of SeaCoast paper. Harry had suggested that the discovery requests be hand-delivered to the defendant on the same day their Answer was filed. It would signal to them that this plaintiff was serious about quickly prosecuting her case. For reasons that went unexplained, he had also specifically instructed that Gaston include a request calling for production of: "all computer-generated records that detail or evidence plant operations or events on the date of the incident." Harry knew it would force the defendant's hand. It would require Ravich and SeaCoast to reveal precisely what was in Slator's laptop. Paul Ravich's bragging about such evidence at their Barrister's Club lunch was something Harry didn't forget.

Doug also had formal deposition notices ready to file. Again, following Harry's instruction, dates were set to obtain sworn testimony from Al Harris and Rob Finnegan. Ordinarily, witness depositions are arranged informally, with plaintiff and defense counsel cooperating to schedule convenient dates for everyone. But Doug didn't have to be told by Harry that such courtesies made no sense in this case. Paul Ravich and SeaCoast weren't interested in cooperation or convenience anymore. They would only stall and stonewall. So the decision was made to just "notice them up." It was Doug's signal that he too could play rough.

Bonnie bundled the large stack of discovery papers and called for a courthouse courier service. On the same day they filed their Answer, SeaCoast would be getting a hand-delivered mountain of homework. Doug's team was staying one step ahead of the competition.

Or so they thought.

⸎

Bruce Waltman called, wanting to know what Ravich intended to do about the *Crouch* case. Both he and Ravich's office had just received the mounds of discovery requests and multiple deposition notices signed by Doug Stevens in the *Crouch* case. Ravich had promised to take care of this renegade claimant. The question now was: When?

"I said I'd handle it and I will," Ravich explained, with exasperation in his voice. He didn't like being pushed around by a lawyer who never saw the inside of a courtroom. He told the General Counsel to relax.

"I'll relax when you do what you said you'd do. This kid seems serious about pressing a claim against us. He turned down our cash offer. If he makes any headway in a gross negligence case against us, it will clearly harm our case against Integrated Sentry."

Ravich listened with an unsympathetic ear. He wasn't worried about a thing but wasn't about to tell Waltman why.

"Look, Bruce, we need to get clear on something. I don't panic or need to consult you just because some discovery gets filed in that *Crouch* case. I expect to have it under control in the next couple of weeks."

"How?" the General Counsel asked, still sounding flushed.

"It'll be a one-two punch they can't do anything about. I don't have time to go into the details. Just look for the Motions. They'll be filed soon."

Waltman liked what he heard but didn't care for being kept outside the loop. Ravich's disassociation of him had started the day he was thrown out of the initial meeting with Charles Thornton. It was now continuing with the litigation strategy.

"Fine, but my name is on those pleadings too. As one of the attorneys for SeaCoast, I think I'm entitled to participate in these decisions."

"Well, you're not," Ravich curtly replied. "If you have a problem with the chain-of-command, take it up with Charles. I'm pretty sure he won't stand in my way."

Waltman felt trumped by the threat. Ravich had some mysterious hold over Thornton yet Waltman couldn't figure out what it was. He decided for now it was better to stay somewhat informed than being cut out of the case entirely.

"I'll wait to see what you file. I just wish you'd hurry."

Ravich knew then that Thornton's in-house lawyer had no real appetite for any fight. *Typical,* he thought. To Ravich, corporate lawyers like Bruce Waltman were akin to the ancient Roman spectators at the Coliseum: meek observers who enjoyed seeing blood so long as it wasn't theirs. Conversely, trial lawyers like him were the true gladiators facing the lions.

"Haste makes waste," Ravich teased back, in response to Waltman's demand for prompt action. "Bye now."

He hung up, satisfied that Bruce Waltman had been put in his proper place. Now he could concentrate on what needed to be done.

It would soon be time to unleash those lions on Doug and Harry.

———— ∞ ————

"Does this make us a couple?" Sarah asked, walking over to the sofa with a sly grin.

It was the third night in a row that Doug had come to her place for dinner. She liked cooking for him and he enjoyed both the meals and the way they were beginning to "play house." Over the past month, their relationship had grown from noncommittal dates to seeing each other exclusively on a regular basis. Now, it was evolving into pleasant domestic routines. He had cleared the dishes, kissed her cheek, and headed to the couch with his glass of wine. They didn't technically live together — Doug still had his place — but everything else looked and felt like a comfortable couple relaxing after a hard day's work.

"It makes us...happy," he replied, handing over the wine glass to share as she sat and snuggled next to him.

She took a sip and twirled his hair with her other hand.

"So it does," she said softly. Then, realizing that perhaps her question had sounded pressuring, she turned comical. "So, what now, honey?

Wanna watch some TV?"

Doug laughed. They had, over their short relationship, done a lot of things. But watching television wasn't one of them.

"Only after we're married," he said, proving he had caught the joke.

She liked the fact that their senses of humor were so closely aligned. In fact, she liked everything about the evening, and about him.

"You look tired. Want to spend the night?"

"Yeah, that sounds great," he replied, leaning back and briefly closing his eyes. Then he reopened them and smiled. "Although when does going upstairs translate into rest?"

"Take the night off if you want. Lots of bored couples do that."

"I'm not bored." He offered assurance by pulling her close and kissing her passionately.

"Me either," Sarah said breathlessly, once the kiss was over.

The moment morphed into another pleasant routine. She sat the wine glass on the sofa table and they walked, hand-in-hand, up the stairs.

Dean Schiller convinced his clients that an Answer to Ravich's suit should be filed immediately. Plaintiffs' counsel had wasted no time in exploiting the press with his lawsuit. A prompt denial in court and issuance of a strongly worded press release were the only appropriate responses. Once the VyStream General Counsel sought and obtained the necessary counsel-approval from its insurance carriers, the defense of Integrated Sentry and its parent company was turned over to the capable hands of Schiller and his local counsel.

Paul Ravich pounded his fists in excitement when he received his copy of the pleading and saw that Ben Argent had been retained. He considered Argent talented, for a defense lawyer, but his performance in the recent *Clayton* trial was rote and predictable. Ravich believed his opponent was no match for the onslaught that was about to be unleashed. The signature of Dean Schiller, appearing as co-counsel, also pleased Ravich. Schiller was a big national name, used only in high-profile cases. It meant the defendants were taking the claims of SeaCoast and his dead victims very seriously.

They'd better, Ravich thought, smirking to himself. He pondered how best to play his hand. Ben Argent would call soon and make inquiries. *"What, if anything, do you have on my clients?"* the defense lawyer would probably begin, feigning a spirit of cooperation and willingness to work informally on the messy tasks of case discovery. Ravich smiled at the prospect of responding to a question like that. He would say: *"Ben, your clients are dead-in-the-water on this one. Unlike that Clayton case, the evidence here is indisputable and the damages are astronomic."* Ravich grinned, knowing that Ben Argent would only press for more details.

Such entreaties would have to be put off initially. Phone disclosures are never dramatic enough. Ravich had better ways of revealing his cards to the other side: he could either make the defendants slowly extract the liability and damage proof through formal discovery or he could offer them a startling "peek under the kimono" in the form of an in-office presentation that would make them rush to commence settlement negotiations.

Ravich preferred the latter method for this case. He could use his impressive conference room and its audiovisual tools to display the computer records that now showed the explosion to be ISI's fault. He might play a video soundbite from his testifying chemical safety expert, Dr. Clark; a short explanation tying the DCSS data to ISI's negligence. He could then pound them with a series of damage projections: first, for the victims' families and then for SeaCoast. It would be fun watching Schiller and Argent pretending to be unimpressed while their company reps squirmed with anxiety in their seats. Ravich laughed out loud as he imagined their timid exit. Maybe they would even stop and reflect upon his huge judgments against other big companies that dotted the hero wall.

Ravich knew his case against Integrated Sentry and VyStream was the perfect candidate for a quick and substantial settlement. After all, he had invented the perfect case against them from the rubble of SeaCoast's own folly. He had killed to get to this point. It would soon be time to make his killing.

But first things first, he decided, shelving further daydreams of how he would introduce the defendants to the depth of their dilemma. He knew he would scare the defendants with the strength of his case but was also certain he could elevate their fear if they first witnessed the depth of his connections.

He reached for his voice recorder. An important motion needed to be filed. He recorded it along with instructions to Jan, informing his assistant to schedule the first available hearing date with Judge Lewis. He wanted to demonstrate to Dean Schiller what he assumed Ben Argent already suspected: that *this* judge was willing to do almost anything Paul Ravich asked. The hearing would also mark the beginning of the end for Doug Stevens' irritating little *Crouch* case.

It's brilliant, Ravich egotistically thought, as he contemplated his plan. *There aren't many lawyers crafty enough to kill two birds with one stone.*

326

———∞∞∞———

Harry had other cases that also required his attention. Depositions and an expected discovery dump in *Crouch v SeaCoast* would soon have him spending more time with Doug, Bill and the always lovely Bonnie. But this particular week he was scheduled for trial in one of his oil field injury cases.

His client, a young roustabout, had been pinned and crushed against the pipe rack by a subcontractor's delivery truck. The driver had simply failed to see the rig worker who was standing with his back turned, taking an inventory of the stacked tubular. Neither the reversing cab nor its trailer was equipped with an industry-standard backup alarm that could have alerted the young man of the approaching danger.

Although far less intriguing than an exploding chemical plant or a suspicious car wreck death, Harry's client in this case was equally deserving as Kate Crouch. The twenty-eight year old man had suffered severe internal injuries and was in the hospital for over two months. His right arm had to be amputated. His career in the oil field was finished and his life had changed forever.

Harry told the jury in opening statement that the driver's conduct was clearly negligent but his employer had been even more careless for not equipping the tractor-trailer rig with a common backup alarm which would have prevented the accident. The trucking company countered that the plaintiff was where he shouldn't have been, wasn't paying attention to his surroundings, and that choosing not to install the expensive alarm is both reasonable and non-negligent because the sound of beeping devices are so commonplace at a worksite that workers routinely ignore them.

Harry loved poking holes in that kind of defense strategy. It always reminded him of the old joke about defending a dog bite case. First, you say you don't own a dog. If the plaintiff proves otherwise, you claim your dog doesn't bite. When the ferociousness of the animal is demonstrated you take a different tack: "That's not my dog." Why the defendants in this case would choose to argue such similarly absurd positions was beyond Harry but not beyond his abilities to ridicule them for it. With his folksy charm, he made quick work of the liability case and then artfully focused the jury's attention on the suffering and loss sustained by his client. He rested his case on Wednesday afternoon, confident the jury was with him. The defense would commence the following morning. Harry was looking forward to attacking their hodgepodge theories of non-liability.

The defense lawyers, perhaps realizing they had little else to argue, brought in a flashy human-factors expert from California. Their witness spent almost two hours on direct exam, condescendingly explaining the principle of "attenuation" to Harry's twelve newest friends sitting in the jury box. The arrogant expert likened a truck's backup alarm to other commonly ignored alert systems, telling the jury: "How many times have you heard a car or house alarm go off in middle of the night? And how many times did any of you call the police?" He explained that people simply become numb to such sounds — "attenuated" in the scientific parlance — and that such alarms rarely produce the intended response of prompt action by the listener.

Harry pretended to be bored by the expert's testimony and made sure the jury could see him doodling in his Big Chief tablet while the witness droned on. The defense finally passed the witness and the judge broke for lunch, informing the jury that cross-examination would commence when they resumed at 1:30.

That was all the time Harry needed. He excused himself from sharing a noon meal with his client, explaining he had to attend to some important business. He then quickly scampered over to the Barrister's Club, the same place where he had listened to Paul Ravich's referral and settlement proposal in the *Crouch* case. The private restaurant was perfectly convenient, being situated on the adjacent corner to the courthouse. But Harry wasn't hungry. He was on a mission. He entered and asked if he could go back in the kitchen for a brief word with Ted, the restaurant manager. All the staff, including Ted, knew Harry well and liked him. He was escorted through the kitchen's swinging doors and shown to the manager's tiny office near the back.

"What can I do for you, Mr. Greenbaum?" the surprised manager asked, extending his hand for a warm handshake.

"Ted, I need a favor. When does that Sysco truck make its food deliveries to you?"

The question sounded odd but Harry Greenbaum was a nice man so Ted answered willingly. "Usual deliveries are on Mondays, in the morning, but sometimes we order up special deliveries when we're short of something."

"And how fast can they deliver a special order?"

"Their warehouse is downtown, so I get things here quickly when I need them. Why do you ask?"

"Because I badly need you to need a special delivery at precisely two p.m. today. I don't care what you order, just make sure it's delivered on one of their big refrigerated trucks. Put whatever they bring on my club bill. Order up some lobsters or steaks, I don't care. Just make sure they hotshot that delivery over to you at *exactly* two o'clock."

Ted looked at the old lawyer as if dementia had claimed him. "Mr.

Greenbaum, I don't understand."

"No time to explain. Just consider it a huge favor to me and a gift to your food-cost budget for the week."

"I guess we could stock some additional cheeses and butter, things like that, but…"

"Terrific, and get them to deliver a side of beef while you're at it. I might be bringing a crowd over in the next day or two for a post-verdict celebration lunch."

"You're talking about a lot of money there, sir."

"Ted, my boy, money is not the object. But time *is* of the essence. Whatever you order, just please make sure it gets dropped off at that loading dock of yours at two today; no sooner, no later." Harry smiled warmly. "It would just mean the world to me."

"I'll do what I can for you, Mr. Greenbaum. I'll give our purveyor a call right now."

"Excellent! Trust me, my lad, there is method to my madness. I just can't go into it right now."

"I understand," Ted replied, although clearly he didn't. "Will you be joining us for lunch right now?"

"Not today, Ted. I've got a big fish-fry this afternoon."

With that, Harry bolted for the door and returned to the now empty courtroom. With everyone at lunch, he was alone with his thoughts. He rose to make sure that all the street-facing windows were pulled open to allow the soft autumn breeze to blow into the courtroom during the afternoon session.

They don't teach this in law school, he giggled to himself, returning to his seat at the counsel table and silently waiting for court to resume.

———⚬⚭⚬———

"I'm sorry, Mr. Greenbaum is still in trial. May I take a message and have him get back to you this evening?"

In his panic, Doug had forgotten about Harry's trial schedule this week. He stood at his desk, with Ravich's surprising Motion and Hearing Notice in his hand, while Bonnie looked on with concern.

"Yes, uh, just let him know that Doug Stevens called regarding a sudden development in the *Crouch* case. Please ask him to call back as soon as he can."

"I'll make certain he calls you when he returns from court." The receptionist could sense the urgency in his voice. "But it will most likely be around five o'clock."

Doug understood that when one is in trial, no other matters take precedence. It was a cardinal rule for successful litigators.

"That will be fine," he replied, trying to temper his anxiety. He didn't want the receptionist reporting to Harry that his co-counsel was having fits. "Have a nice day," he offered before hanging up.

Bonnie knew her boss better than Harry's receptionist ever could. She could see he was still shaken by Ravich's latest legal maneuver.

"He won't get away with it, you know that," she assured him. "Even if he owns Judge Lewis."

"He does," replied Doug dejectedly. "That's the problem."

The door to the war room opened and a lanky Bill Gaston charged in. Bonnie had called him at his office a half hour earlier with the news and he immediately cancelled an afternoon client meeting to attend to the crisis.

"I guess this suite is appropriately named after all," Gaston joked, as he entered. "I hear that Rat Ravich has now fired the first shot over Fort Sumter."

Doug handed him Ravich's devastating motion as Bonnie confirmed the inevitable. In her characteristically concise way she replied: "It's gonna be a civil war all right."

As Doug and Bill sat contemplating their response to Ravich's Motion, Harry settled in for his afternoon cross-examination of the defendant's human-factors expert.

"You may proceed, Mr. Greenbaum," said the judge, after everyone returned to their seats. Several jurors leaned forward in their chairs. It was obvious they liked hearing what the plaintiff lawyer had to say.

"Good afternoon, Dr. Hudson. I hope you had a most excellent lunch in our little town."

"I did, thank you. It's always a pleasure to travel here to your fine city."

The expert turned his head and smiled smugly at the jury, thinking he was ingratiating himself.

"I trust your meal wasn't disturbed by any alarms going off?"

Several jurors, and the judge, laughed.

"If they did, I certainly didn't pay attention to them. Just like everyone else."

"So you say. And you tell us there's good science to back the proposition that the more we hear alarms, the less we pay attention. Have I got that right?" Harry flipped to a blank page in his Big Chief tablet. "I think that's what I wrote down from your testimony this morning."

"Well, I said a great deal more than that, but I think you got the gist."

"So, here's something I can't square with that notion," Harry said in feigned earnest. "All of us in this room have been listening to police and firetruck sirens our whole lives and yet we still pull over when we hear that sound coming up behind us. How come we haven't all been afflicted with that 'attenuation' you talk so much about?"

"A-ha! That's a very fine distinction, you see."

The witness pursed his lips in satisfaction with his performance and at least one juror noticed it. The expert was delighted by Harry's question. *He's throwing me a softball.* He couldn't believe his good fortune. *This plaintiff lawyer is a rube,* he thought to himself as he began his explanation.

"There is a stark difference between what we in the human-factors business designate as 'emergency signals' and 'alert signals.' We are all socialized to accept that an emergency signal, like a police siren, is something we cannot ignore without consequence, so we pay closer attention and react appropriately when we hear one. Contrast that with a neighbor's car alarm going off. That's considered an alert type signal. It could signify a car break-in but more likely it's just the wind or something bumping lightly against the alarmed vehicle. We don't immediately hop out of bed and investigate. For most of us, we wait for the silly thing to turn itself off. For many of us, who live in urban areas, the sound becomes so commonplace we simply ignore it. For some, we get to where we don't even hear it."

"Well, doggone, I guess that is a big difference," Harry confessed, acting as though his best point had been batted down.

"Exactly," the expert replied smugly, looking over at his defense counsel to make sure they were appreciating his smooth handling of this idiot's questions.

"So things like backup alarms on trucks, I mean, we hear stuff like that all the time, right?"

"That's correct."

"And those would be what you experts say is an 'alert signal' that, for whatever reason, most people choose to ignore?"

"Precisely."

"So, you're telling this jury that more likely than not, had one of those alarms been installed on the defendant's truck that day, my client would be just like the rest of us citizens and choose to ignore the silly thing?"

"That's what the science teaches. In fact, as I've said, people who are around such sounds regularly become so attenuated they actually stop hearing the sound at all."

"That's amazing," Harry responded, with carefully scripted surprise.

"The sound is clearly audible but nobody hears it, right?"

"Experiments in the field have borne this out repeatedly," the witness assured the jury.

"Then why on earth would any company even buy these foolish backup alarms? Or for that matter, why would companies make and sell them if they don't work?"

"In answer to your first question, it's a bit of a pack mentality that drives the market. Trucking companies reason that since some competitors purchase them, we will too."

"We're all just a bunch of sheep, you're saying?"

"Something like that. In answer to your second question, lots of companies make and sell things that don't work like they're supposed to. Ever bought a computer?"

The expert witness laughed at his own cleverness but the joke fell flat in the courtroom. He wasn't aware that his haughty manner had turned everyone off. The jury had already grown attenuated to his pomposity.

"Actually, sir, I'm probably the last lawyer standing that doesn't own a computer. I can barely keep up with this little writing tablet here." Harry tapped on the Big Chief notebook sitting in front of him while several jurors giggled. Comedy is easier when the comic is likable.

He really is a fool, the expert thought. "The point I'm making is still the same," the witness hurled back.

Harry looked up at the courtroom clock. It was ten till two.

"All right. Let's make sure we've got this straight. If a firetruck were to come roaring down the street outside this courtroom, its siren blazing, all of our ears would perk up, but if a car alarm or backup alarm went off we would do the same thing you say my client would have done, which is either ignore it or not hear it at all?"

"Couldn't have said it better myself," the expert confidently replied.

Harry needed to keep the jackass talking for a few more minutes. He decided to violate a fundamental rule of cross-examination and ask a big open-ended question.

"This is fascinating, Doctor Hudson. Can you give us some more examples in the real world where attenuation makes us forget what we are hearing?"

"Of course. I'd be happy to." He again glanced over to defense counsel. They too couldn't believe that a seasoned pro like Harry Greenbaum was being so lackadaisical.

The witness began expounding on the phenomena of busy office workers who fail to notice phones ringing at nearby desks, and of construction workers who learn to tune out the pounding of a jackhammer.

Meanwhile, Harry patiently eyed the clock on the wall.

It began with three minutes to spare. Two stories below, a mere two-hundred feet from the open courtroom windows, a food delivery truck slowly backed into the loading dock of the Barristers Club. Its backup alarm was beeping loudly enough to be clearly heard over the instantly growing laughter of both the jury and the judge. Dr. Hudson blushed heavily and stopped talking, looking first toward the open windows and then back toward the lawyers that had hired him. They could offer their witness no sanctuary from the bleating truck.

Harry stood up and scratched his head.

"One last question, Your Honor. Anyone hear *that*?"

It was a simple Motion to Consolidate, seeking to combine the two separately filed cases that arose out of the SeaCoast plant disaster. Procedurally, there was nothing to it; the rules reasonably permit the joinder of claims that arise out of the same occurrence. Consolidation saves precious judicial resources and eliminates the risk of two different juries, in two different courts, arriving at inconsistent verdicts over the same facts. In many cases, combining such claims benefits everyone.

But Paul Ravich's motion had nothing to do with judicial economy or mutual benefit to the parties. He filed it solely as a first step towards inflicting maximum harm on Kate Crouch and her lawyers. If anyone had doubts about his motivations, they only had to look at the court number where the Motion was filed: the 89th District Court, Judge Lewis presiding.

Harry Greenbaum, fresh off his win in the backup alarm case two weeks earlier, headed to the courthouse along with his two young co-counsel to fight the consolidation. Their grounds of opposition were solid. Because the *Crouch* case was filed first in Judge Hinojosa's court, it was his court, not Judge Lewis', that should rule on any motion to consolidate. Such was the long-standing custom and practice of the local civil courts. Alternatively, they would argue that the theory of liability in the *Crouch* case was entirely opposite from the allegations being advanced by Ravich in his cases. There would be distinctly different avenues of discovery. Combining the cases wouldn't streamline anything; it would only muddle both cases.

But Doug, Harry, and Bill realized that valid legal grounds for denying the motion wouldn't matter. Paul Ravich knew the local rules as well as they did, and so did Judge Lewis. The fact that Ravich's Motion wasn't properly filed in Judge Hinojosa's court was not, they knew, a product of oversight. It was a sure sign the fix was in.

There were other clues of Judge Lewis' favoritism toward Ravich. Despite a Monday morning docket of over thirty hearings, many of which had been scheduled for far longer, the Judge had instructed his clerk to give Ravich the number one setting. Friends don't make friends wait.

While pretrial motions were normally the responsibility of Ravich's associates, this case was obviously different. Ravich would argue the motion himself to underscore its importance to Judge Lewis. Not that he needed to. The night before, the two of them had shared a couple of scotches in the Judge's backyard, just two old pals catching up. Ravich talked benignly about the pleasant fall weather and the recent elections before carefully weaving in reminiscences from the many hunting trips he had treated the Judge to in the past. Before the ice in the second cocktail had melted, Judge Lewis curiously asked about the hearing Ravich had scheduled for the next day. Discussing a pending case without other counsel present violates both attorney and judicial ethics. But neither man cared that their conversation about the case was an improper *ex parte* communication. They considered it no different from sitting around a campfire, talking about the trophy buck that the Judge always seemed to bag during Ravich's all-expense-paid trips.

True to form, Ravich entered the courtroom at the precise moment that Judge Lewis took the bench. He walked straight up to the bench, never acknowledging the presence of any other lawyer, especially his motion adversaries, who stood to advance when the case was immediately called. He also said nothing to Ben Argent, who was making his first appearance in the case on behalf of VyStream and Integrated Sentry.

"Good morning, gentlemen," the Judge began. "I have read the Motion to Consolidate and the Response in opposition filed by the plaintiff in the related case." He turned to Ben Argent. "Do the defendants in the case filed in my Court have any opposition to this consolidation?"

"No, Your Honor," Argent replied. "The *Crouch* plaintiff has not yet sued my clients, although I suspect her lawyers will eventually amend her pleadings to assert claims similar to those being advanced by Mr. Ravich's clients. If they do, it makes sense to litigate all claims in the same case. If they don't sue us, then I'd still like to have them here since my defense will be the same as their current position, which is that it was the employer's fault."

Argent wasn't trying to help Ravich. He was simply stating the best interests of his new clients. The Judge nodded in understanding.

"Well, I'm inclined to grant the relief requested." He looked down at Harry Greenbaum who was standing in front of Doug Stevens and Bill Gaston. "Is there any reason why I should not?"

Harry smiled widely, telegraphing to the Judge that he was not surprised by the Court's leanings.

"I suppose, Your Honor, the best reason is that standard practice in our courts demands that any consolidation motion be ruled upon by the court in which the first case was filed. That court, in this case, is not yours." Harry turned around to survey the courtroom packed with lawyers waiting for their hearings. "I would think a court as busy as yours should welcome the chance to have another judge decide this motion, and consequently try both cases if such consolidation is granted. Why, you could wipe an entire case off your docket in a matter of minutes by simply following that long-standing policy."

"Of course, you know, Mr. Greenbaum, that is not a formal rule of procedure," Judge Lewis replied, parroting the words that Paul Ravich had used the night before. "A Court may clearly exercise its discretion in deciding whether or not to defer to such antiquated traditions."

"Well, sure," Harry said, adding with characteristic aplomb: "that robe permits you to do a lot of things. We're just asking you to do the *right* thing."

"If I may," Ravich interrupted. "Judge, the case in your court involves five death claims. Mr. Greenbaum's lone client is the widow of the sixth victim. Also pending in your court is the substantial property damage claim of SeaCoast Chemical. All the other plaintiffs in this case have consented that their cases should be tried together with SeaCoast's in the interest of judicial economy. It just makes sense for you to combine this one small case from another court into the far-bigger one that properly landed in your court. Everyone else is already here. Why move the mountain when just one more plaintiff has to make the climb?"

Despite Doug's unease and desire for Harry to make further argument, the old lawyer could tell what was happening. It was as obvious as a blaring backup alarm. Nothing he could say would sway Judge Lewis' decision. He had earlier warned his young co-counsel to be prepared to accept the inevitable. And a ruling on this pretrial matter was not appealable.

Judge Lewis was ready to announce his ruling. His mind had been made up the night before. "I hereby grant the Motion to Consolidate and order that *Crouch v. SeaCoast* be transferred immediately from the 127th District Court into this Court for disposition or trial. Anything else, gentlemen?"

Paul Ravich jumped at the opportunity. When a friend is handing out candy, it never hurts to asks for more. "In light of your ruling, there is another matter that requires immediate attention. The *Crouch* plaintiff has already propounded discovery and deposition notices to SeaCoast. We would ask that those initial discovery requests filed in the 127th be quashed. They can obviously reissue them here in the 89th now that all parties are before this Court. It just makes sense; after all, the defendants I have sued will also want to attend those depositions and they are clearly entitled to full notice and use of any discovery."

"Do you agree, Mr Argent?" the Judge asked.

"This is the first I've heard about any depositions being noticed or discovery requests being sent so, yes, I think it makes sense to just start over here so we can also be involved."

Harry knew better than to resist.

The Judge announced: "Then I hereby quash any currently pending discovery in the 127th, without prejudice to the right of the plaintiff to re-propound them here. I trust that you excellent trial lawyers will cooperate fully with one another and avoid this Court's involvement in your pretrial discovery efforts. Good day, gentlemen."

Ravich spun around and headed for the door. He got what he came for and more. Doug Stevens would now have to refile his voluminous discovery requests in the *consolidated* case, starting a new timetable for responses. It was an important victory. It meant that Ravich would now have more than thirty days before he had to produce any SeaCoast employees for depositions. That, he figured, would be more than enough time to scare the checkbook out of VyStream and Integrated Sentry with his presentation of the DCSS computer evidence. He could get his settlement talks rolling before Harry and his cubs even got started.

Of course, even if he quickly concluded a settlement with the third-party defendants, Kate Crouch would still be left hanging around, trying to prove things differently and stirring up trouble. Ravich grinned as he walked out of Judge Lewis' courtroom. *Not for long,* he thought to himself, as he contemplated the next pretrial motion he would file the minute initial discovery was completed.

Since he had seen to the elimination of any evidence that SeaCoast was grossly negligent, it would only be a matter of time before he could file a Motion for Summary Judgment on behalf of his corporate client against the claim of Kate Crouch. A summary judgment is a court-ordered end to civil litigation in those rare cases where no pretrial evidence is uncovered that could legally support a verdict on the plaintiff's claim. Ravich was confident he would win that motion as well, considering that the gross negligence case against SeaCoast died along with Ken Slator and the original DCSS computer records. All the evidence he had fraudulently created pointed only to those defendants that Doug Stevens *hadn't* sued. As

Ravich left the courthouse, he thought smugly: *Either Dougie and his team will come to their senses and align their focus with me, or they will soon be left with nothing.*

Judge Lewis would certainly see to that. It was, after all, hunting season again.

Chapter 18
Forms of Discovery

"You've got yourself a bomb."

Harry Greenbaum appreciated experts who got to the point but found himself startled by the suddenness of these words. The crime lab consultant in Virginia had completed his forensic analysis of the substance found in the wheel liner of Ken Slator's car and was calling in the results. After a brief apology for taking so long — the expert had been tied up in a lengthy criminal trial — he pronounced his five-word judgment with a certainty that sent chills down Harry's back.

Harry gritted his teeth as he held the phone tightly to his ear. Suspicions were one thing, proof is another. A hunch can be discounted but evidence can't be ignored. Ken Slator didn't just die, he was killed. The implications were huge: his intended death had something to do with the plant explosion. It had to. No one randomly murders a chemical engineer with a car bomb. The questions now became: Who? and Why? But first, Harry needed more details.

"How can you be sure?"

"I submitted your sample to mass spectrometry along with a chromatographic separation analysis. These are state-of-the-art laboratory methods used to detect explosive residue. I assure you the results are scientifically valid and would hold up in court. The FBI uses these same analytical techniques in their bomb investigations. Your sample is contaminated with RDX."

"Which is what?" Harry asked.

"RDX is the explosive constituent in plastic explosives. It accounts for over ninety percent of its weight. The rest is simply a plasticizer and a binder. When the polymer is destroyed in a blast, traces of RDX are usually left behind, most commonly imbedding itself in objects at or near the point

338

of detonation. Your letter that accompanied this sample stated it was a piece of wheel liner from a car?"

"That's correct," Harry confirmed. "Right front wheel of a Ford Taurus. The steering tie-rod was found cleanly sheared in two and the wheel detached. But neither appear to be caused by impact damage. Our mechanic found this substance pitted into the adjacent liner."

"And the car itself was not blown to bits?"

"No, but it was heavily damaged in the ensuing crash after the driver lost control."

"Those wheel components were blown apart with C4, a rather small quantity, I suspect, if they were the only front end components directly affected by the blast. That's tricky work, trying to hide an explosion behind wreck damage."

Harry felt the hairs on the back of his neck tingle.

"C4? The stuff the Army uses?"

"That's right. In fact, your C4 came from a military installation."

"How can you tell?"

"It isn't widely publicized, but government manufactured C4 is tainted with a very specific chemical tracer — what we call a detection taggant — that remains behind in the explosive residue. I tested for its presence. Whoever planted this bomb got their material from a government armory."

"As opposed to..."

The expert interrupted Harry's question. "As opposed to making it themselves. I'm sorry to say, but recipes for homemade plastic explosives are as readily available on the Internet as porn. But your bomber didn't mix his C4 up in a sink. He's either military-connected or he broke into an armory and stole it."

Harry shuddered at the revelation. *How high did this conspiracy go?* He remained lost in thought until the expert filled the silence.

"I have to ask this, Mr. Greenbaum. Is there a criminal case pending on this? Because, if not, you and I have a duty to report this."

"I'm well aware of our obligations," Harry replied. "If you will permit me some time, I may be able to turn over to the DA both the bomb evidence and the bomber."

"So, you're not a criminal defense lawyer?"

"No, sir, just an old personal injury lawyer. But it seems my little car wreck case now has some very sinister undertones."

"That's putting it mildly," the expert countered. "Look, whoever planted this bomb knew what they were doing. A controlled and limited detonation of C4 is the work of a talented expert, someone who knows how to kill. You and your client had better be careful."

"No truer words have ever been spoken, my friend," Harry smartly replied. Ending the call, he thanked his consultant and again offered assurances that he would do the right thing once he had more answers.

Placing the receiver back down, Harry stared out his office window, deep in thought. *Will tracking this crime get answers for Joan Slator? For Kate Crouch? Or will it get us all killed too?* He was certain of only one thing: the murder of Ken Slator was connected to the SeaCoast disaster. Which meant his civil case now involved stakes higher than money.

The real question was: *What do I do now?* Harry opened his Big Chief tablet and began jotting down strategy thoughts. Thinking outside the box had served him well over a long career. He won his cases by surprising opponents in unorthodox ways while they slept comfortably in their own arrogance. But this time, he was pulling double-duty. He had to prove what destroyed a chemical plant at the same time he was chasing a killer.

Two mysteries. *Or was it?* Harry's instincts told him that a solution to either unsolved case would lead inexorably to answers in the other. The trick, he knew, would be to keep the culprits feeling safe for as long as he could. Whoever they were, they couldn't know he was searching them out. If they caught him kicking over some rocks, he would just pretend to be stubbing his toes. In short, he would need to *be* smart and *play* dumb. A career of doing just that, he realized, might be the only thing that would keep him and his case alive.

———— ✖✖✖ ————

Sarah listened patiently as Doug vented growing frustrations with his biggest case. Their relationship was continuing to grow; so much so that he now freely discussed his work troubles over dinner with her. She didn't mind. As a court clerk, she understood what he was talking about. More importantly, it meant he was willing to confide in her. People who are just "casually dating" don't do that sort of thing. While she wasn't looking for a commitment this early, it was a positive sign. So was the fact that he was now staying at her place more than his.

"We're members of the same club," Doug concluded, after telling her about the ruling on Ravich's Motion to Consolidate. "Judge Lewis has now tried to screw us both."

The comment, intended as a joke, made Sarah think back to the harassment by her former boss. The man was a pig. She knew that. She wasn't surprised that Lewis was also a whore for Ravich. She was glad she had been transferred up to Judge Thompkins' courtroom.

"So what more can he do to you?" she asked, with a tone intended to downplay her boyfriend's anxiety.

"I'm not sure, but if Paul Ravich can think of any way to hurt my case, I'm betting the Judge will go along."

"But if Ravich wins, you win, right? You're suing the same parties."

"Not yet, but probably soon. The thorn is, we can't drop the case against SeaCoast until we know for sure who caused that explosion. It's either the third-parties Ravich sued or it's SeaCoast. We're not willing to take Ravich's word that he knows what really happened."

"I'd say that's pretty smart of you. Why didn't Judge Hinojosa throw a fit over Lewis' ruling? His Court should have gotten the consolidated cases if you filed there first." Like most court clerks, Sarah knew procedure better than most lawyers.

"You know how Judge Hinojosa is," Doug replied. "He's too busy forgetting what time it is to care about another judge stealing control of his case."

"I could try and make an internal stink out of it if you'd like," Sarah offered, as she stood to clear the dishes from their dinner. "Maybe by mentioning the issue directly with the District Clerk. She wouldn't be happy to learn that a certain judge wasn't following the county's own rules for her files."

"Thanks, but there's no point. The order's not appealable. All that would happen is Judge Hinojosa might get mad at Judge Lewis for a minute. That doesn't help me. I'll still be stuck in Lewis' court, waiting to be gored by that trained bull whenever Ravich says 'Charge!'"

Sarah realized Doug was right. There was nothing he could do. But that didn't mean that nothing could be done. She kissed his forehead on the way to the kitchen, where she began thinking.

The pretrial discovery process is about avoiding surprises. All parties in a civil action get to take depositions, obtain their opponent's documents, secure reports from the other side's experts, and force admissions or denials of facts relevant to the case. Full disclosure is intended by the Rules of Civil Procedure. In theory, by the time of trial, the litigants are supposed to already know every card in the other player's hand.

In actual practice, though, discovery is a game. You win by exhausting your opponent with depositions and discovery requests, while resisting meaningful disclosure of your case. Like a selfish child, the goal is to ask for everything and share very little.

Gamesmanship trumps the fair exchange of information. Parties ask for extensions of time to file their responses, then make objections on the new deadline to delay things further. Lawyers jockey to depose an opponent's witnesses before they produce their own for cross-examination. It's considered a strategic advantage to know what the other side will say first.

Word games are commonplace. An evidence-seeking Request for Production might specify, for example: "Accident Reports." Yet the other side will fail to produce the contemplated records because the caption on their responsive documents reads instead: "Incident Record." Therefore, good lawyers keep a good thesaurus close by, and a simple request to produce records of prior accidents might end up reading like a sentence filled with barbs:

"Produce within thirty days any and all records, minutes, recordings (whether audio or video) and/or any other form of written or electronic history that in whole or in part documents, summarizes, describes, depicts or discusses a workplace injury, claimed injury, accident or incident (including those accidents or incidents not involving a physical injury or claimed injury) for the period of ten years preceding the incident that forms the basis of this suit, regardless of the caption or title assigned to such document or record."

It takes talent to draft such all-encompassing language. It takes even more skill for the other side to find the loophole that keeps the information sought from being turned over. The discovery process becomes a game of Three-Card Monty, with clever lawyers quickly moving words and evidence around to keep their opponents off balance.

Depositions are no different. Although the client or witness takes the same oath they would give in a courtroom, they are customarily coached to "answer only the question that is being asked" and to "never volunteer anything." The goal of being tightlipped is to make the other lawyer work hard to get any useful information. If you're lucky, the cross-examiner will eventually grow weary of your witness's laconic style and forget to ask a truly important question.

Word games, obfuscations, objections, and efforts to overwhelm the other side are the sad products of a process that is supposed to reveal facts rather than conceal them. But since "everyone does it," everyone does it. And so it goes.

Paul Ravich enjoyed such games more than most lawyers. He made sure that no documents of any real value were turned over to Kate Crouch after first buying himself some additional time to stall, thanks to Judge Lewis' order that Doug's discovery requests be resubmitted in his court. Despite Bill Gaston's artful and thorough wording in the numerous requests, the SeaCoast papers that would finally get delivered to Doug Steven's office would all fit comfortably in one small file box.

It required some careful editing. Waltman's in-house lawyers had been tasked with initiating a search of the company's files and they simply provided a list of requested items to Rob Finnegan. Not wanting to disappoint his bosses again, Finnegan diligently complied. He turned over a mountain of relevant and requested documents, including production records that revealed how badly the plant was being pushed in its final days. *Idiots,* Ravich thought, when he saw the fourteen boxes of documents that got transferred over to him for final review.

Ravich made quick work of segregating any documents that contained even a hint of negligence. *What had Bruce Waltman been thinking?* Ravich's disdain for the non-litigator General Counsel grew as he moved through the piles of paper. *Did he really believe we were going to turn this stuff over?* By the time Ravich was finished, thirteen boxes of potentially incriminating records would be locked tightly away in his office storeroom. All that would be disclosed were innocuous memos, routine safety-meeting minutes, and plant schematics — nothing that could come close to proving a claim of gross negligence against SeaCoast Chemical.

He changed many of Waltman's draft responses from: "See Documents Attached" to: "Requested Documents Destroyed by Plant Fire." Ravich wasn't going to give Doug, Harry, and Bill even an inch of rope to fashion a noose around his client. Anything suggesting that SeaCoast Chemical might have been careless was clearly inconsistent with Ravich's fraudulently created theory that it was all Integrated Sentry's fault.

Even honest trial lawyers struggle with the dilemma of producing records harmful to their case. That's why word games and delaying tactics are so prevalent. But hiding or destroying evidence remains the exclusive province of crooked lawyers. And Paul Ravich was crooked beyond repair. A lawyer who is willing to order the killing of a witness certainly has no problem lying about the existence of records.

Ravich was also intent on punishing Kate Crouch and her lawyers for not getting on board with him. If they weren't willing to refer their case, he saw no good reason to turn over to them his custom-made evidence of third-party liability. Instead of producing a copy of his criminally manufactured computer records that now showed Integrated Sentry was at fault, Ravich decided to respond to their specifically worded request for plant computer records with a false excuse for its non-production: *"Item 28 cannot be copied or reproduced without risk of altering or damaging the original. Accordingly, such computer records will only be made available for review at a future time and place convenient to the parties."*

Ravich smiled at the wording. *That day, for you, Doug Stevens, will never come,* he thought, as he mulled over his eventual plan to make them pay for flying solo. He would present his fake evidence to VyStream and Integrated Sentry in a private meeting that Doug and his team would not be invited to attend. His shocking presentation of Integrated Sentry's clear liability would surely lead to a quick settlement for SeaCoast and his death clients. Ravich would then insist that the resulting Settlement Agreement contain a few unusual but express conditions: first, the *Crouch* claim could not be included in their settlement; and second, upon his receipt of their payment, Ravich would relinquish custody of the key evidence — Slator's computer — to VyStream's counsel.

He wouldn't tell the third-party defendants that once their money was paid and releases exchanged, he was planning to destroy the payment-inducing computer contents. He would first fry the hard drive with a strong electrical surge, then blame the overnight package company for "somehow damaging it in transit."

Ravich loved his plan. *It was perfect.* It would allow him to forever erase any future chance that his computer alteration could be uncovered while at the same time denying to Doug Stevens the very evidence used to secure a fortune for his own clients. Ravich thought about it in his usual arrogant way: *Like God, that which I create I can also destroy.*

He completed his remaining revised responses to the discovery requests and chuckled at the results. If the *Crouch* lawyers were expecting him to give them any ammunition to shoot at SeaCoast, they were going to be sorely disappointed.

⸚⸚⸚

"They've given us nothing," Bill Gaston said with exasperation, as he and Doug read through the smattering of useless records that were eventually delivered from Ravich's office.

"You're right," Doug replied, tossing another irrelevant memo into a pile after scanning its contents. "Isn't it strange the fire destroyed only those documents that could prove what happened?"

"An arsonist couldn't be prouder that so little was left behind," Gaston offered in his usual cheeky way. "These guys are dirty, Doug. Any defendant with nothing to hide would have at least buried us with paper."

"I agree. This document production will all fit in my little office. Renting this space for a war room warehouse seems kind of foolish now."

"We can always turn it into a gym," Gaston teased. "We need to get in better shape. SeaCoast and Ravich are going to make us run in constant circles to find out anything."

"Maybe Harry will uncover something useful. He warned us not to expect much from this formal discovery."

"Yeah, I know. That old buzzard thinks nothing good ever comes from doing things the standard way." Bill stood up from the table and walked

344

over to look out the window. "What do you think Harry's up to? He hasn't shared much with us."

"Who knows?" Doug replied. "He's been in trial in other cases this past month so I haven't bugged him for details."

Gaston spun back around.

"Yeah, can you believe he tagged a company for four-million over not putting a backup alarm on a truck?" Gaston shook his head in admiration. "His guy lets a slow-backing semi run him down and Harry convinces a jury that the plaintiff had no fault at all."

"Let's just hope he can find magic like that in *this* case," Doug offered, as he threw aside another meaningless SeaCoast document. "You don't think the old man might be losing it, do you?" he added, almost apologetically. "I mean, Harry can obviously still win trials but I've yet to hear him explain what good can be done in our case by his running around secretly behind the scenes."

"Have faith, my friend," Gaston counseled.

"Oh, I do," Doug said, pointing at the pile of discovery responses. "Because right now, between this useless crap and Ravich owning Judge Lewis, that's pretty much all we've got."

———∽∾∾∽———

"Mr. Greenbaum, so nice of you to call."

Joan Slator, now settled in at her sister's house in Florida, was both fretful and pleased to hear from the gentle lawyer who had helped her in the initial days following Ken's death. *Perhaps he found out something. Or maybe he was simply calling to be kind.*

"It's supposed to be just 'Harry,' remember?"

"Of course. How are you Harry?"

"Well, to be honest, I'm quite troubled. I've learned some very distressing news about your husband's accident."

Her pulse raced as she sat down beside the phone table, bracing herself. But even her wildest imagination could not have predicted the words that followed.

"I'm afraid it wasn't an accident at all. We have found evidence that his car was tampered with to make it lose control."

She flushed with a combination of anger and fear. It felt as if her face had been blasted with hot air. "I don't…understand," she began haltingly.

"Nor do I, at least not yet. But I promised I would get you some answers and that's what I'm going to do."

She was still absorbing the impact. Her mind searched quickly to make sense of the news and she came up with nothing. "But why? Why would anyone want to kill Ken?" she finally asked.

"I was hoping you could help me there." Harry paused. "Did he have or make any recent enemies at work?"

"At work? No, not that I was aware of. He didn't talk much about the plant or even about the explosion or why he quit. Harry, to be honest, his former preoccupation with the job was a big factor in why we once grew apart. After our daughter's death, I really think he was trying hard to act differently."

"I see."

She suddenly realized the implication of Harry's question. *Why had he mentioned only work?*

"You suspect someone from SeaCoast caused his death?"

Her question sounded filled with either incredulity or shock, perhaps both.

"Only because of the timing and his prominent position there. An expensive chemical plant got destroyed and a lot of people died out there. Millions of dollars are at stake in the upcoming lawsuits."

"But what difference should that make? I know Ken couldn't have been responsible for any of that. He had his faults, but being unsafe wasn't one of them."

"Well then, were there any other faults that might help explain this?" Harry probed gently. "A gambling problem? Womanizing? Hanging out with the wrong crowds?"

"Oh, my God, no!" Joan replied emphatically. "Ken was the opposite of a wild man. He never cared anything about betting or hanging out with the boys. I never saw him rowdy or drunk or flirtatious. He didn't even experience a mid-life crisis. Only I did — I thought my life was missing something — which is why I filed for divorce."

"Then it must have something to do with his job," Harry concluded for the both of them. "You spoke of unusual nighttime meetings about work, both before and on the night he died. And then there's the mystery of lost and erased computers."

"So you never recovered his laptop?" she asked.

"I'm afraid not. It wasn't in his car after the wreck. I went down to the salvage yard myself to look for it."

Harry had later learned, at his Barrister's Club lunch, that Paul Ravich had it. But he saw no reason to get into that now with her. He did, however, want to find out what, if anything, she knew about the other lawyer.

"Did your husband ever mention the name of any attorney following the explosion?"

"No, not that I recall."

"And I take it I was the only lawyer you ever saw drop by the house?"

"Yes, why?"

"Just curious if he was talking to anyone outside the company about what he knew."

"I have no idea. Could that have been what those nighttime meetings were about?"

Harry was impressed with her intuition but thought it would do her no good to share his as yet unconfirmed suspicions.

"I will certainly be looking into that for us." A different thought suddenly popped into his head. "Is that erased computer still at your home by any chance?"

"Yes, of course. I just locked up the house and left with my sister. Why? Do you think you can recover something from it?"

"Madam, I must confess that I would be the last to know if it's even humanly possible. But I can ask around."

Joan quickly thought about how she could best help the investigation. A decision was made.

"Harry, I've been thinking about coming back after the holidays. My sister has been gracious but I can't stay here forever. When I return, I could let you or your people into the house to look at it. But if you feel it's urgent, I could certainly fly home sooner."

"Oh, no, please, spend this important time with your family. You have been through so much. A little chore like that can wait. It's probably a waste of time anyway. It was just a random thought I had."

"Well, if you change your mind, just call. Otherwise, I'll phone you up immediately when I get back."

"I shall look forward to seeing you again, madam," Harry replied, with his characteristic charm. "In the meantime, I have plenty of other leads to pursue."

Joan paused to consider all that the man had already done for her, without charge, for no apparent reason other than he was kind.

"Harry, I can't thank you enough for what you're doing." She didn't know what else to say.

"I'm merely keeping a small promise," Harry assured her. "It's nothing."

"No, if someone killed Ken, then you're risking your own safety by looking into this for me. There's nothing small about that."

No truer words, he thought to himself, recalling what he had said the day before in response to a similar warning from the crime lab consultant. But he didn't want to cause any fear for Joan Slator.

"Whoever did this isn't after you or me. They don't even know that we're now looking for them," Harry said, to ease her concern.

"I hope you can keep it that way," she said warily.

No truer words, he thought again.

———— ❧ ————

The first depositions taken in the consolidated SeaCoast disaster cases were of two technicians from Integrated Sentry. They were the men who had actually installed and tested the automated safety system now being blamed for the explosion.

As is tradition, the session took place at the office of the lawyer producing the witnesses for questioning; in this case, Ben Argent, the local counsel for ISI and VyStream. Dean Schiller, their national trial counsel, did not attend but expected prompt reports once the proceedings were completed.

Paul Ravich was the lead questioner. His presence signified the importance of their testimony. Unlike what he routinely did in other cases, he wasn't about to trust these cross-examinations to any of his associates. For a hundred-million dollars in potential fee, he figured he should participate in the pretrial discovery a little.

Doug Stevens attended on behalf of Kate Crouch. Even though she hadn't yet sued Integrated Sentry or VyStream, Judge Lewis' order of consolidation gave him a seat at this table. As others shook hands and exchanged pleasantries before the depositions began, Ravich pointedly snubbed Doug, ignoring him as if he wasn't there. Ravich thought vengefully: *Given my future plans, he soon won't be.*

Witness depositions are often long and dull, filled with background questions and minutiae. But there is an old truism among seasoned trial lawyers: the more experienced the attorney, the shorter the depo. Paul Ravich, while short on manners, was long on experience. He quickly got to the point with the first of the ISI employees.

"Now, it's true, is it not, that your company alone was responsible for the design implementation and installation of the DCSS hardware and software at the SeaCoast facility?"

"Yes, although their head guy gave us some very specific criteria for the controls."

"You're speaking of Ken Slator, the plant process manager?"

"That's correct."

"And you found that man and the data he maintained to be very reliable, didn't you?"

"I suppose."

Ravich smiled thinly as he thought about how nicely that concession

348

would sound when he finally revealed Slator's laptop data from the night of the explosion.

It was now time to set the traps. Ravich had spent the night before re-reading the report of Dr. Garrison, the consulting expert who came up with the failure theory that ultimately became fact after Slator's computer was altered. Certain key points had to be established.

"Did Mr. Slator tell you to power your sensor number V18 by connecting it to the plant's auxiliary power panel instead of to the main electrical supply?"

Ravich then showed the witness ISI's own schematic that confirmed such connection.

"No sir, he did not. But we had to supply power to it from somewhere. The main panel was all used up."

"Did you know that the auxiliary panel had no emergency backup power?"

"No."

"Did you even think to ask if it did before connecting that sensor of yours to it?"

"I don't think so."

"So in the event of a fuse or auxiliary panel failure, your safety system might not provide proper volume level detection in the neutralizer tank, which is what sensor V18 detects, isn't that possible?"

"Possible, but I can't imagine that actually happening," the technician defended.

"Volume level inside that tank is a critical safety measurement, true?"

"True."

"And if that sensor lost power, all that would be shown on your system's control monitors is its last powered reading, correct?"

"I guess so."

"You don't even know?" Ravich said sarcastically.

"I never thought about it."

"Exactly," Ravich said, having scored a key point.

Since he had not yet revealed his tampered computer data to anyone, only Ravich knew that his prey had stepped, unaware, into his snare. He made quick work of getting the technician to admit other key facts consistent with Dr. Garrison's original musings about what could have possibly gone wrong.

Ravich gained even more helpful concessions from the second technician witness. He got him to admit that the DCSS's Cascade Mode feature could potentially misinterpret a non-powered volume sensor as normal and that glitch might, in-turn, cause the ISI computer to bypass or ignore a properly functioning temperature sensor. The witness also had to agree that such a scenario could produce inaccurate and confusing information for a plant operator. He further admitted that unless the system accurately reported both volume level and temperature inside the tank, no one could possibly know for sure if the ammonium nitrate was getting out-of-control.

Ben Argent objected to the entire line of questioning, calling it "purely hypothetical" and "the product of random conjecture."

Ravich ignored such interruptions. In a deposition, there's no judge to rule on any objections and they are made primarily to slow down your opponent when he's scoring points.

What Argent and the technicians didn't know — but would soon learn — is that Slator's laptop would reveal that such hypotheticals were *exactly* what happened in the moments before the blast; thanks, of course, to the assistance from some programmers in India.

Ravich was delighted when he finished with both witnesses. They had walked headfirst into his buzz saw of fabricated liability.

When it came time for Doug to question the witnesses, he probed only for evidence to indicate that SeaCoast ran a shoddy or unsafe workplace. Neither employee of Integrated Sentry said anything bad about the plant conditions or operation.

As Doug struggled and came up with nothing, Ravich beamed. At the appropriate time, Ravich could use some of that very testimony to support his Motion for Summary Judgment on the gross negligence claim that Kate Crouch was asserting against SeaCoast. Testimony that Doug elicited himself would later be used against him.

What a rookie mistake, Ravich thought, as he stared down the young lawyer who once had the nerve to lecture him. *Everything is going exactly as planned.*

Harry Greenbuam was old-school but he kept up with changes in the law. Like him, the legal system was old but never stagnant. With recent case decisions or legislation came new ways to do old things — like conduct good case investigation.

He called one of his youngest lawyers into his office and, before asking his question, handed him the SeaCoast employee directory that his friend, Bob Edison, the OSHA administrator, had turned over during a long-ago lunch at a Chinese restaurant. It was the same directory Harry had first used to call up plant employees looking for leads. Now it would come in handy again.

"Sam, have you ever done a Freedom of Information Act Request before?"

"No, sir," the associate replied. "But I can quickly research what needs to be filed."

"Good. I'm fairly certain that particular law will allow us to access some military service information without the veteran's authorization. I need you to run the twenty-two names in that directory for a check of prior military service. See what you can find out and report back ASAP."

"Yes, sir, I'll get on this today."

"Good man. And while you're at it, add these names to your list."

Harry handed over a memo that his assistant had prepared. It listed every staffer whose name appeared anywhere on the website of Paul Ravich & Associates. Since Ravich considered his large-scale operation to be another good marketing point, his website helpfully identified all of his employees and described their position at the firm.

The associate looked at the list, which had the big man's name at the top. "Is this is a firm roster for Paul Ravich?"

"That it is, lad. I'm just curious to find out if he or any of his people have dutifully served their country."

Sam looked puzzled but accepted the unusual assignment and rose to leave.

"I'm on it."

"Carry on, soldier," Harry said with a smile as he gave a silly salute.

Sam smiled back and exited. Working for Harry often involved strange projects. It made the firm of Greenbaum & Walker an interesting place to work.

Harry now sat alone in his office, satisfied he was looking in the right places. His mind could still process a complicated syllogism to it's most logical conclusion: Only someone who might benefit greatly from Ken Slator's death would go to such incredible lengths. Killing the man who knew the most about the destroyed plant with a sinister plot involving a hard to detect car bomb had to be the work of those who could gain the most by silencing this insider. Only SeaCoast and its lawyer stood to make hundreds of millions if their version of what happened got accepted in the end. *Perhaps this humble plant manager wouldn't go along with their plan for riches?* Ravich admitted he met with Ken Slator and obtained vital evidence from him in the days immediately before his death. *What was that evidence?* Did Ravich keep the good and destroy the bad? A dead plant manager with an erased computer was certainly not inconsistent with that crazy notion. Harry knew it was a far-fetched theory, *but what was a better one?*

Another syllogism made equal sense to him: If the killer obtained C4 through military contacts, and he killed on behalf of the most probable suspects, then wasn't it plausible that a veteran with explosives training would turn up with a close connection to either SeaCoast or Ravich?

It took only seconds of online research for Sam to discover what a properly filed request under the Freedom of Information Act could reveal: a veteran's dates of service; the branch of the military served; geographical locations and assignments; military education level; as well as final rank and duty status. Why his boss would want or need such information on SeaCoast employees and the Ravich firm was a mystery to him but the task wasn't going to be difficult. He compiled form requests for each name in the SeaCoast directory, then turned his attention to the memo.

One name from Ravich's firm immediately caught his attention: Trey Galloway. Sam and Trey had gone to law school together and remained friends. He knew that Trey no longer worked there. In fact, he remembered being told by his buddy how Ravich had fired him for merely talking to a reporter. He also knew that Trey was never in the service. They were the same age. Both had gone straight from high school to college, then law school.

Sam walked back down to Harry's office to point out that the memo list was out-of-date. Ravich's failure to update his website would turn out to be a fortuitous oversight. Harry took an immediate interest in Trey's departure from the firm.

"So, your friend was fired. And what was the reason?"

Sam related the circumstances that Trey had told him.

"That sounds like Paul Ravich. He can be a bully. I don't suppose your pal has any remaining loyalty to that firm?"

"None at all. He hates Ravich. He still hasn't found a full-time position. He's working right now as an hourly contract lawyer for the City."

"Is he a good and honest attorney?" Harry asked.

"Solid as they come," Sam replied.

"Then get him on the phone for me. Maybe young Trey can help us and we can help him."

Later that afternoon, equal good fortune would shine on the two men sitting across from each other as an impromptu job interview progressed.

Trey Galloway impressed Harry with his personality and work record, especially his many pretrial responsibilities while serving as a Ravich associate. Harry offered him a job on the spot, then picked his brain about his former employer.

"So, Trey, I know that Paul Ravich has a lot of people working for him.

Did you get to know most of them pretty well?"

"I knew some folks better than others, but yeah, I worked there for almost three years."

"I'm just curious, being a veteran myself. Anybody over there have any special military skills or prior service history that you know of?"

Trey thought the question was odd but Sam had briefed him to expect the unexpected when it came to talking with Harry.

"I'm sure there's some others, but the only one I can think of for sure would be Ron Carroll. He's Ravich's senior investigator. He was a policeman for a long time and I heard he was once a Navy Seal or something like that."

Harry's ears perked up.

"Wow! A commando and a cop, huh?" he said, as he reached for his trusty tablet and wrote down the name.

"I don't know Ron's history in any detail," Trey quickly added. "But he looked the part. He could be a scary guy."

"I see. Well, forget I even asked. I don't know why I get off on such tangents sometimes. Product of age, I suppose."

Harry redirected the conversation back to Trey's accomplishments, hoping the young man would soon forget their brief conversational sidetrack.

Trey seemed delighted by the prospect of working for Harry Greenbaum. Every trial lawyer in town, even the young ones like Trey, knew that the old man was a talented and kind plaintiff's lawyer. It would be a welcome change from his prior experience with Ravich.

Harry was delighted too. Not only was he gaining a new and competent lawyer — one who had personal insight into Ravich's operation — but Harry had also gained an important lead. After Trey left, he summoned Sam back into his office.

"Sam, I hired your friend. I only hope he turns out to be as valuable an addition as you."

"Thank you, sir. That's great news."

"And here's some more happy news for you. I've decided to trim down that assignment I just gave you. Just get me the military records on the SeaCoast employees and anyone who is listed as an investigator on Ravich's website. You can disregard the rest of the firm's employees." Harry looked down at the notes he had taken during his interview with Trey Galloway. "In fact, I'd start first with his main investigator — a fellow named Ron Carroll."

———⊙⊛⊙———

Even in those ordinary cases where you have every intention of settling, an agreement can take a long time to conclude. Paul Ravich knew that, but this was no ordinary case and his master plan wouldn't allow the *SeaCoast* litigation to take its normal lengthy course. Although well-over ninety percent of all civil claims settle out of court, the majority of those require at least the real threat of actually starting a trial to get a good deal done. Unless and until the defendant is scared, a plaintiff's desire for meaningful settlement talks is much the same as a child's longing to move up Christmas to July: no matter how much you want it to happen, it won't.

But for Ravich, there was a compelling reason to press here for early settlement. He needed to reduce the risk of his crimes being discovered. A settlement with the third-party defendants would bring finality to their investigation, leaving only Doug Stevens' client standing in his way. Once the big case was out of the way, he could easily take care of that gnat *Crouch* claim. After both cases were dismissed — his by settlement agreement, the *Crouch* case by summary judgment — he was home free. It was therefore essential that he accelerate the process of making VyStream and Integrated Sentry crater. It would require finesse but he was up to the challenge.

He phoned Ben Argent. Despite his many efforts to humiliate Argent in the recently tried *Clayton* case, Ravich now needed his cooperation. He wanted his former enemy to now become his friend. Such is often the case in the strange world of civil litigation. A different lawsuit with the same lawyers may demand different approaches. Facts are fickle. Trial lawyers must be too.

Argent took the call and Ravich began his conversation with false praise for his repeat adversary: "Ben, I don't want to press my luck down at the courthouse, trying to beat a lawyer as good as you two times in a row."

Like any compliment Paul Ravich ever gave, it sounded plainly backhanded. Ben Argent listened patiently for his caller to get to the point. He knew the only reason Ravich would be calling was because he wanted something badly.

"I'd like to get your people in for a strictly informal sit-down at my office," Ravich suddenly announced.

Ben Argent was confused by the proposal. "Are you suggesting we mediate the thing this early?"

"No, like I said, this will be informal. We don't need a mediator and nothing has to be binding. But I know what kind of case I've got and I think if I provide you and Dean Schiller with a detailed outline of my evidence we might save both sides a lot of time."

"And a lot of money?" Argent pointedly asked.

"I can't promise that, but I can predict that if you bring along your company decision-makers, we might end this thing earlier rather than later. And later, as you know, is always more expensive in the end."

"This isn't like you, Paul, offering early cooperation and wanting to avoid the courtroom. Why should I think this is anything other than a trick of some kind?"

"You should reserve your concerns until after our meeting. I guarantee it will be enlightening even if we can't agree on what needs to be done."

"I'll check with Schiller and get back to you. How soon do you want to do this?"

"Next week, if possible. Before I start taking any more depositions," Ravich added confidently.

"Can we also use some of this meeting time to hammer out a full discovery schedule?"

"Sure, but that won't be necessary if I first convince you to settle."

"Come on, Paul, you know any settlement this early is highly unlikely."

"Don't be so sure, Ben. I wouldn't be willing to show my hand this quickly if it weren't so strong."

"Okay. Whatever. But what about the other claimant? That *Crouch* case; I see that her lawyers have just sent out notices to depose several of the SeaCoast employees. My people may want to postpone any meetings with you until after those are concluded."

"Why?" Ravich asked indignantly.

"That plaintiff believes the explosion was SeaCoast's fault, not ours. Maybe they know something you and I don't."

"I'm going to say this once, Ben. Only I know what really happened out at that plant, and only I have the evidence to prove it. I'm willing to show you that proof at our meeting if you'll get it set up. The fact that the *Crouch* lawyers haven't amended their suit to add claims against your clients is a sure sign they're clueless."

"I don't know much about this Doug Stevens or that other co-counsel, but Harry Greenbaum's certainly no slouch. He must have his reasons for taking a different tack than you."

"Harry's practically senile. And those other two lawyers couldn't pour piss out of a boot. They were in diapers when I made my first million. What makes you think either of them knows how to plead, much less try, a case like this one?"

"I'm not sure I agree with your assessment of those people or of the case."

Ravich knew what Argent was trying to do. He was being intentionally elusive in an attempt to get his caller to reveal more details. Ravich hated asking again, but he needed to get this meeting held.

"Look, Ben, I wouldn't worry about the *Crouch* lawyers. They have nothing to do with what we need to talk about. So let's have this sit-down and talk."

"Are they also being asked to participate in this meeting?"

"No reason for them to." Ravich was now weary of Argent's preoccupation with Doug Stevens and his silly gang. "For God's sake, Ben, they haven't sued your clients."

"But they will. You know that, Paul. Why wouldn't they?"

"Because they're stupid. Right now, they want to only go after SeaCoast. Maybe it's because I haven't shown them what I'm willing to show you. Come to this meeting and perhaps they'll never learn why such a strong case exists against your clients."

"So you're going to cut them out, is that what you're saying?"

"No, you said that," Ravich quickly replied. "But if a benefit flows to your clients and it doesn't harm mine, why not keep them in the dark?"

"If you wanted them out of your loop, then why did you move to consolidate their case with yours?"

Ravich knew then that Argent would not relent until he was told something he didn't already know.

"Because once you see the light and persuade your clients to settle, I believe Judge Lewis might view with some favor SeaCoast's Motion for Summary Judgment on their claim against my corporate client."

Argent wasn't surprised that Ravich was thinking two steps ahead. He had seen it before. "What did that other plaintiff do to piss you off?" Argent asked, only half-kidding.

"They wouldn't listen to me when I offered to cooperate with them," Ravich responded. "Don't you make that same mistake, Ben."

Typical, Argent thought. Ravich was a master at flattering his opponents in the instant before he began intimidating them.

"All right. I'll recommend the meeting. But you'd better have the goods. This Schiller guy can't be bluffed. Believe it or not, he thinks he's a bigger name than you."

Argent intended the remark to be biting but Ravich didn't take the bait.

"Good. If he's that talented, we may have a peace accord before Christmas. Smart lawyers, like you and him, always know when to fold 'em."

"That must be a big smoking gun you've got if you think you can extract a half-billion from us on the basis of a single meeting."

"Gun?" Ravich laughed heartily. "Think bigger, Ben. Think nuclear."

"All right." Argent realized he lacked both the ego and time to keep verbally sparring with Ravich. "I'll call Dean Schiller but let me warn you, Paul, you're not going to get far with him by just pounding your chest and making threats."

"Why, Ben, that's never been my style," Ravich protested, with a mocking tone.

"Just a word of advice," Argent said, knowing it would be ignored.

After their call ended, Argent realized, once again, that telling Paul Ravich anything he didn't want to hear was a waste of time. He also expected that an early settlement meeting with the egomaniac would be exactly the same.

———— ⬤ ————

If the war room wasn't going to be filled with case documents, at least it could be used for meetings. Doug and Bill sat anxiously waiting for Harry's arrival while Bonnie brewed a fresh pot of coffee. The dejected mood of everyone matched the bleak temporary furniture they had gathered for the space.

"If Harry's got any magic to dispense, now would be a good time," Gaston said, as they waited for their senior co-counsel to arrive.

"Perk up, boys," Bonnie shouted over her shoulder. "It could always be worse."

"How's that?" Doug asked.

"I could quit and go to work for some lawyers that aren't as pouty," she threatened in jest.

Doug and Bill both smiled. The comment made them realize they were feeling sorry for themselves. It served as a gentle reminder for them to act like trial lawyers: unfazed and confident.

"Please don't quit," Bill Gaston falsely pleaded. "Who could we ever find to file all these papers?"

Everyone cracked up as they looked down at the meager SeaCoast documents Ravich had turned over.

Harry Greenbuam entered the room to find them all laughing. "What's so funny?" he asked, as he tossed his fedora on the table.

"We just realized we don't have to buy a bunch of exhibit stickers for this case," Gaston replied. "We've got no evidence to introduce."

Harry glanced at the small pile of production documents. "I wouldn't worry. That's more than I expected Paul Ravich would send over. So, tell us, Doug, how did those depositions of the third-party technicians turn out?"

Doug's sour mood returned. "They had nothing but nice things to say about SeaCoast. I didn't make a dent."

"Did Ravich?" Harry asked.

357

"Who knows? He certainly acted like he was laying a predicate for other evidence he has against Integrated Sentry. But he never revealed to anyone what it was."

"That's the mark of a good lawyer, gentlemen. Score your points before you show the other side where the end zone is." He turned to Bonnie. "May I have a cup of your spectacular Joe?"

Bonnie grinned. "Cream and sugar?"

"No, thanks, you're sweet enough."

Doug shook his head at the corny remark while Gaston pondered the dinosaur they were relying upon so heavily. *Who still calls coffee a 'cup of Joe'?* he thought briefly. *For that matter, who still wears a fedora?*

"Thank you so much," Harry politely said, as Bonnie handed him the warm cup. "Now, let's get down to business."

The two younger lawyers sat up straighter in their seats, like students trying to impress a teacher. Bonnie pulled up a chair and sat down as well. She wasn't about to miss out on a lesson plan from Harry Greenbaum.

"First, I have never found any deposition witness who even knows what gross negligence is; and second, you will never get any defendant to confess to such conduct anyway."

Harry, still standing, stopped talking and gave everyone a look that his point had been made. Three sets of eyes stared back confused.

"All I'm saying is, quit worrying about the lack of useful deposition testimony or the inadequcy of produced documents."

"Okay," ventured Bill. "But we can't get a verdict without *some* evidence. So where do you propose we find a little?"

"In places they don't expect us to look."

"Such as?" Doug asked the question with a slight tone of irritation. *Is he going to make us guess?*

"Does anybody know if you can get stuff off an erased computer?"

There were more looks of confusion. Even Bonnie thought the comment was off-the-wall.

Doug spoke up. He was comfortable around technology. "It all depends on whether the data was simply deleted or if the hard drive was written over and scrubbed. It's a fifty-fifty proposition."

"Well, I have no idea. How can we tell?"

"We first get the hard drive," Doug explained. "There are data recovery companies that do this sort of thing."

"Excellent," Harry replied. "Then let's see if..."

"Wait a minute," Bill Gaston interrupted. "What computer?"

Harry explained. "You remember my telling you about that SeaCoast plant manager who died a short time ago? Well, turns out he had a home computer that got erased and his widow thinks it might have something to do with work."

"Who erased it?" Bonnie asked.

"Probably he did, although it could have been someone else."

To Bill Gaston, it sounded like a highly tenuous link to proving anything. "Harry, why do you believe this computer ever contained anything relevant to the plant explosion?"

"Just a hunch," the old man replied.

Doug raised his hands in resignation. He liked Harry, but was hoping to hear something more concrete. A hunch was no better than the useless SeaCoast documents in front of him.

Harry saw the frustration on the young lawyer's face and decided it was time.

"Oh, and there's the fact that the man was killed by a car bomb."

Three jaws dropped simultaneously. Harry took a sip of coffee and waited for the impact to subside. He expected immediate questions but everyone was too dumbfounded to ask one.

Harry sat down, placing his coffee cup on the table before adding: "Call me crazy, but I think we should focus on that and see where it leads."

Chapter 19
Thrust and Parry

The requested military records arrived in Harry's office. The Freedom of Information Act Requests his associate submitted were considered routine by the National Military Personnel Records Center and ended up being processed in reasonably short order, especially considering the federal government was involved.

Like percentages in the general population, very few of the submitted names had ever served their nation in uniform. There were only four veterans out of the twenty-two persons listed in the directory for the destroyed SeaCoast plant. One was Tom Benson, who was killed in the explosion. The other three were honorably discharged at low ranks and had no specialized training. Harry noted with interest that Rob Finnegan — the SeaCoast President whose business card was found in a briefcase of tools inside the wrecked car's trunk — had no prior military service. Unless Finnegan had an Army friend with access to and experience with C4, and that friend was stupid enough to kill for him and leave behind proof of Finnegan's involvement, it appeared doubtful that any employee at SeaCoast was a probable suspect in the highly technical car-bombing that killed Ken Slator.

That left Ravich's three investigators. The only one with a military record was Ron Carroll, the man who Trey Galloway had talked about. Looking over Ron's service history, Harry knew instantly that Ravich's senior investigator deserved further scrutiny.

He was indeed a former elite commando. Assigned to the Army's Delta Force unit, Carroll had served in various duty-stations that were political hot-beds during his eight years of service. His last Military Occupational Specialty Code was listed as "MOS 18C - Special Forces Engineer Sergeant." Harry summoned his associate, Sam, back into his office and asked him to check for a public record definition of that military job title. When Sam returned ten minutes later with a page printed from the Army's public website, Harry stared at the description as his increasingly shaking fingers caused the words to practically leap up at him:

"*MOSC 18C30: Performs and teaches tasks in demolitions, explosives, improvised munitions, US and foreign land mines, mine/counter-mine operations, construction, field fortification, bridging, rigging, electrical wiring, reconnaissance, target analysis and civil action projects....Plans, teaches and performs sabotage operations with standard, nonstandard and improvised munitions and explosives.*"

Harry knew from his own stint in the Marines that military jargon can often be purposefully vague or even indecipherable. But here, the text could not be clearer, nor its meaning more certain.

Ron Carroll, and by extension, Paul Ravich, were now his prime suspects.

It was going to be the ultimate "dog-and-pony show."

Paul Ravich routinely used such phrase to describe any presentation intended to dazzle. Most often, it meant the display of persuasive visual evidence in a courtroom. But today, the stirring evidence was cued up on his conference room AV system, ready to scare the pants off four guests who had just arrived in his lobby.

Ben Argent identified his entourage to the receptionist while Dean Schiller, fresh off a flight from New York aboard a VyStream private jet, stood next to him, looking around. Schiller was impressed by Ravich's ornate law office. It was nicer than his. The General Counsel for VyStream stood behind the two trial lawyers as did the President of Integrated Sentry. They were all there to hear what Ravich had to say and to learn about the promised "smoking gun" which the plaintiffs' lawyer was so certain would cause them to surrender.

The pretty receptionist spoke into the phone system's intercom.

"Mr. Ravich, a Mr. Argent and his party are here to see you."

"Thank you, Missy," Ravich replied from his office, smiling at her word choice. This was going to be a party, all right, at least for him.

For a half-billion, he wouldn't make these people wait long in the lobby. The *SeaCoast* case was bigger than all the others. His pattern could therefore change. Besides, there would be plenty of opportunity after the meeting to show Dean Schiller and his crew the hero wall — if it was even necessary. Once his presentation was over, the third-party defendants would likely need no further convincing that Paul Ravich knew what he was doing. He practically danced down the long corridor toward the reception area and strode into the lobby with enthusiasm.

"Hello, gentlemen," he began with a smile, that false look of warmth and sincerity that had conned so many juries in the past.

But these were not jurors. They were defense lawyers and company executives. They shook his hand tepidly and acknowledged him coldly. He was a wolf out to bite them. There was no reason to pretend they weren't wary.

"Please, follow me into our conference room. I know your time is valuable so we'll get started right away. We have some refreshments set up in there, if you'd like."

Ben Argent was amused by the gracious host routine. His experience with Paul Ravich told him the man was only pleasant to the other side when he truly wanted something from them.

As they made their way through the glass doors of the conference room, Ravich tried to engage Schiller. "Dean, it's good to finally meet you. Like many, I'm well aware of your career. It's quite impressive."

"As is yours," the New Yorker replied flatly.

His audience took their seats. It was time to start the show.

"Gentleman, as I'm sure Ben has already told you, I don't usually invite over the defendants I've sued for a session like this. I've found through years of experience that, typically, the best way to get your opponent to see eye-to-eye with you is by first blackening theirs with some hard punches delivered in court."

Argent looked up at the ceiling in disgust. When he called to confirm the meeting, he had specifically asked Ravich not to rooster-crow about his skills. *The man can't help himself,* he thought.

"But this case is too big, the stakes are too high for all of us, and the evidence I'm about to show you doesn't need to be accompanied by any arm twisting," Ravich continued.

"Then let's get on with it," Schiller interrupted, intending to make known his role as quarterback.

"I agree," Ravich quickly replied, with a smug grin. He then picked up a remote control from the table and pressed "Power," then "Play." The interior left wall of the conference room, a large section of opaque glass in its center, suddenly came alive. Through the glass, the rear projector in the adjacent AV room displayed aerial pictures of the SeaCoast plant: first before, then after, the explosion. It was a shocking montage of total destruction.

"This is what happened. The consequences really can't be disputed much."

Ravich then turned to the credenza below the screen and retrieved four sets of leather-bound thick files for each of his attendees. He walked over and handed them out.

"I'm not going to make any damage argument today. The numbers are in these. You will find detailed spreadsheets and estimates that document the cost to rebuild this plant. There is also an independent appraisal for the value of its lost inventory, and a statement of our business interruption losses. We might end up quibbling over a few million here and there but the proof before you shows a *minimum* price tag of $460 million in property damage alone."

He watched as the four men leafed through the booklets, trying to appear calm.

"If you'll turn to page thirty-seven, you'll see a summary of the wrongful death damage claims for my five client families. Each worker's prior earnings are documented and the loss of future earnings is calculated. I don't want to insult you with emotional verbiage about the loss suffered by the victims' survivors, so I have prepared a single chart that reflects my best estimate of what a jury in this city might award for their loss of companionship. There is also a reasonable estimation of fair compensation for the victims' suffering prior to death."

Ravich couldn't resist making a dig.

"Ben Argent knows firsthand what juries will do with the evidence I present to them on the intangible elements of damage. I believe, on the way back to your offices, he can confirm that my figure of $7.5 million per family is not an exaggerated verdict estimate."

All three men looked over at Argent. He simply stared at Ravich in disgust.

"So, the bottom line is, I have a collective damage case worth, on the low side, a half-billion dollars. The high side? Who knows what a willing jury might award? The real issue is who should pay?"

"Maybe the answer to that is no one," Schiller said confidently. "We think your client's own operational negligence caused this. Which means your families get only comp death benefits and SeaCoast gets nothing."

"That's what I thought initially as well," Ravich quickly replied. "Until I saw this."

He pressed the "Forward" button on his presentation remote. The projector began displaying screenshots from Ken Slator's laptop.

"Fellows, what you are looking at here is a real-time backup of your company's DCSS data in the two hours before the explosion."

"Where did that come from?" Argent asked. "It's our understanding that all the equipment, including the DCSS computers, got destroyed in the fire."

"They were, and but for the ingenuity of a very dedicated plant manager none of us would have ever known what really happened. But you see, that manager kept a laptop which contained a program that streamed plant data to him at home so he could stay on top of things even when he wasn't there."

The President of ISI gave a panicked look to VyStream's General Counsel.

"Can you imagine that kind of employee commitment?" Ravich said, with mock praise. "We should all wish to have those kind of people working for us."

Although he was enjoying holding his audience in suspense, it was time to get to the point.

"What this data stream you're now looking at proves, as I'm sure your own engineers will soon attest, is that due to a nonfunctioning volume sensor, your DCSS program kicked into a programmed reaction — what ISI calls 'Cascade Mode' — causing it to foolishly trust the dead sensor's last reading. That, in turn, caused your computer program to disregard and bypass a properly functioning temperature sensor that could have alerted the man at the control panel that something seriously wrong was occurring inside the mixing tank. But, because your installers stupidly connected one of your sensors to a power source with no emergency backup, and because your computer programmers didn't consider that an installer could ever be that dumb, the volatile ammonium nitrate in that tank spun out of control without anyone knowing."

Ravich pressed his remote again and a closeup image of the crater where the neutralizer tank once sat was displayed.

"This is the direct result of your company's negligence and faulty design."

"Why should we believe those records are accurate?" the General Counsel of VyStream remarked.

Dean Schiller looked at him crossly. Jack Trenton was supposed to sit and listen, not talk.

"The laptop, with its original record, is in my possession. It will be Plaintiffs' Exhibit 1. The plant manager has authenticated it, and your own engineers will have to concede that it accurately depicts the DCSS program not working as intended due to your poor design."

"We've already talked to the OSHA and EPA investigators," Ben Argent countered. "They didn't know anything about this backup record."

"Does that surprise you, Ben? All they had to do was ask us for it and we'd have given it to them. After all, SeaCoast isn't worried about any fines or penalties from those agencies. This whole accident is your fault."

Schiller spoke up. It was time to punch holes in Ravich's thick armor.

"I'm sure reasonable minds could differ on what that data actually shows and what should have been done by SeaCoast employees in response to it."

"I suppose you're talking about hiring experts to minimize the meaning of this record. Before you do, let me show you mine."

He pressed the "Forward" button again. The image of an intelligent-looking, middle-aged man sitting at his desk with engineering volumes behind him appeared in freeze-frame. Ravich reached back to the credenza and pulled copies of his expert's C.V. and handed them over.

"This is Dr. Norman Clark, a preeminent expert in Chemical Process Engineering and a specialist in Industrial Safety. He's been to the accident site, analyzed your system design, studied this computer data, and … well, let him give you a brief summary."

He pressed the "Play" button. In a carefully rehearsed video, Dr. Clark outlined in understandable terms the problems he had found with Integrated Sentry's safety system and its installation, while making specific references to Slator's computer data to back up his opinions as to the cause of the explosion. He concluded with words that Argent and Schiller knew would also be the last things spoken on direct exam if the case went to trial:

"This DCSS program was defective in its design, and the employees of Integrated Sentry were negligent in its installation. Both factors led directly to this horrific explosion. The SeaCoast personnel were fooled by this faulty system into believing they were not at risk when, in fact, their deaths were imminent. There can be no doubt about this. ISI's own data proves that's what happened."

Paul Ravich pressed "Off" on his remote. The projector in the next room shut down. The glass panel returned to its cloudy-white appearance.

"So, gentleman, that's all I have for today. Ben Argent can remind you that two ISI technicians have already made damning depositions admissions which are consistent with this other evidence." He paused, then walked over to the glass doors and opened one. "I have too much respect for you fellows to ask that you stay around and give me your reactions. Why don't I let you go and talk? Ben or Dean, call me later if you'd like to discuss ending this before it gets worse for your people."

The four men stood to leave, taking their leather-bound volumes with them. Ravich, who notices everything, observed the ISI President tightly squeezing his jaw. The strain on his face was visible. The eyes of the VyStream General Counsel darted back and forth, as if he didn't know where to walk or what to do next. Argent and Schiller, equally stunned, were far better at concealing their surprise. They were, after all, trial lawyers. They were used to taking a hit and pretending it was a puff of wind.

"Have a good day, boys," Ravich said, as they walked past.

The four men beat a hasty retreat out the reception doors, no doubt eager to reach the elevator where they could commiserate with one another. They didn't even glance at the hero wall on their way out.

Ravich didn't care. Its purpose had already been served through different methods. He knew his opponents had been overwhelmed and scared senseless.

Harry's startling revelation about the death of the SeaCoast plant manager turned their morning war room strategy meeting into an all-day think session. While Ravich was downtown, peddling a settlement proposal based upon lies, Kate Crouch's trial team sat in Doug's austere building three miles away and talked about how they could get at the truth.

Harry detailed all he knew so far. Doug, Bill, and Bonnie sat spellbound as he explained how his suspicions began as a result of conversations with Joan Slator; why they grew once he tracked down the wrecked car; and when they turned deeply sinister after the trace evidence found in the wheel liner was analyzed. They were in awe of the deductive reasoning that led Harry to the conclusion that only Ravich or someone at SeaCoast could benefit by Slator's death. They were impressed by his quick work that identified Ravich's chief investigator as a person who was capable of planting such a sophisticated car bomb. They were eager to hear what he thought should be done next. But first, Doug had a question.

"Why didn't you tell us any of this before today?"

Harry shrugged. "Forgive me, won't you? Men my age can't go around expressing strange ideas. It makes friends and family question their mental fitness. I didn't want to disclose any of this until I was sure."

"And you're *sure* that Paul Ravich would order a hit on someone?" Bill Gaston asked, incredulously. "Over a civil case?"

"I'll admit it makes no sense to a decent person. But Paul is indecent. Indecent men always have their price, a point at which they will do anything to get what they want."

Doug also needed further convincing.

"Okay, let's say his investigator did this at Ravich's instruction. What does that get him? The absence of the plant manager doesn't prove Ravich's case against the third-parties he sued. Why would he risk so much for so little?"

"Exactly," Harry remarked, proud that his young co-counsel had asked the operative question. "Admittedly, the half-billion he's suing for would make him rich beyond his current comfortable status but that, standing alone, is not reason enough to kill. Ravich could still win his case and make a huge fee by simply discrediting any witness who came forward with adverse testimony. We all know how easy that is to do. So that tells us this poor dead man knew things that were unimpeachable, things that would destroy Ravich's claims in an instant. And what, pray tell, does that in turn suggest to us?"

It was a test. Harry wanted to see who could think most logically.

"It means that whatever the plant manager knew would absolutely prove it wasn't Integrated Sentry's fault, which means it was probably SeaCoast's. He had the goods on them."

Harry beamed as he complimented his star pupil. "That's precisely correct, my dear Bonnie. I guess the boys have their heads filled with too much law. I am delighted that yours still has room for deep thinking."

Bonnie gave a satisfied look to suggest it had been easy. Both she and Harry enjoyed the moment.

"As the fair Bonnie has pointed out," Harry continued, "if Ken Slator knew facts that were inconsistent with Ravich's third-party theory, then those facts might well be very consistent with our theory of Seacoast's gross negligence. No other companies are candidates for culpability. It's an either/or."

Doug appreciated the logic, but spotted a hole. "If this guy Slator was the man-in-charge out there, why would he want to come forward with evidence that proves he or his company was grossly negligent?"

"A-Ha! Welcome back, Doug, to our think tank. You are now asking the right question. Either Mr. Slator was guilt-ridden and wanted to do the right thing or this plant disaster was caused by decisions made over his head, by higher management. If it's the latter, it means what?"

Bill Gaston was determined not to be the only dumb guy in the class. He spoke up. "It means it might rise to the level of gross negligence! The court opinions have said the carelessness of an average coworker isn't enough. There has to be indifference or recklessness at the highest management levels to win against your employer."

"Bravo," Harry said, clapping his hands. "So you see, it's as simple as this: what Ken Slator knew, and that which Ravich wants to keep a secret, may very well be the key to victory in the case we have pled."

Everyone looked at each and nodded in agreement. It was a defining moment in the case and in their relationship. That powerful consensus carried them through the remainder of their daylong meeting as they collectively mapped a strategy that would help them unravel the mystery at the core of their case.

The dedicated foursome in that spartan office were now a true team, each contributing something of value, all working as one toward a common goal. Alexandre Dumas would have been proud. More than a hundred-fifty years after he first dreamt them up, the spirit of his fictional D'Artagnan and the Three Musketeers still existed in the real world.

Personal injury victims are typically people with little, if any, prior experience with the legal system. Their questions about litigation are understandable and expected. A court case is something new to them and more than a little frightening.

Corporate clients are supposed to be different. It is presumed that big companies, with in-house lawyers and sophisticated management, are less apprehensive when a claim is made against them.

But clients are clients. The harsh reality of what can happen inside a courtroom is a great equalizer when it comes to dosing out trepidation. Even smart executives and their clever corporate counsel become weak at the knees when there is a lot at stake. Gambling big in the casino known as the civil justice system is not for the faint of heart. It can get scary regardless of whether you are a Fortune 500 company or a person with only $500 to your name.

No one knew that better than Dean Schiller. He was, after all, the man companies called when they panicked the most. After the meeting in Paul Ravich's office, it was fair to describe both VyStream's General Counsel and the President of Integrated Sentry as some very panicked clients indeed.

The defense team had retreated back to Ben Argent's office for a private discussion of the bombshell liability disclosures. The ride down Ravich's elevator and the two block walk back over to Argent's building had been telling by the lack of words spoken. VyStream's chief lawyer had seemed lost in deep and troubling thought while the ISI President bore the countenance of a shell-shocked soldier. Argent's conference room, far less extravagant than Ravich's, soon became the triage ward where the two defense lawyers would try to treat the sudden wounds of their corporate clients. It would not be easy. The General Counsel sat mumbling in a conference room chair as he stared at the damage numbers in Ravich's leather-bound book of horrors. The President of Integrated Sentry paced slowly around the room before stopping in mid-stride to lose what little remained of his composure.

"What do we do now?" he frantically asked his trial counsel, using the same tone of voice as someone whose home had just been blown away by a tornado. "This case will put me out of business. If that jerk is right about what happened, ISI is toast."

Schiller rolled his eyes. "Relax, Mike. Your company has multiple layers of insurance coverage, and your parent company isn't going to let you go under."

The nervous ISI president turned to VyStream's General Counsel. "Is that true, Jack?"

"We'll see," was Jack Trenton's lawyerly reply.

Ben Argent privately thought such a noncommittal statement of support was a poor way to treat a subsidiary, and a friend in distress, but he said nothing. He wouldn't have been heard anyway.

"What?" the ISI President immediately shouted.

Trenton only shrugged.

Dean Schiller stepped in to defuse the tension.

"All right, gentlemen, let's not discuss the funeral until we're dead. Just because the plaintiffs' counsel says it's so, doesn't make it true. He has to prove everything he claims and the job of Mr. Argent here is to poke holes in the plaintiffs' story."

The sudden delegation was not lost upon Argent. As local trial counsel, he realized that the more their ship began to list, the greater likelihood he would be made its captain. Schiller would make sure of that.

"What's our defense?" the increasingly anxious executive asked. "That my people didn't hook up that sensor to a power supply with no backup? That my software designers couldn't be expected to foresee this type of system failure? I won't be in a position to say either. We're fucked."

Argent decided to do a little hand-holding. "Mike, I know it looks bad. And it is bad. But we haven't taken any depositions yet of the SeaCoast people. We might score some points. It was their plant. They were there everyday. Your people weren't. SeaCoast had some responsibility to maintain and control the system they bought."

"Oh, that's great," the ISI chief replied. "So my company defends itself like an automaker? A defect in my product gets identified and my answer is you're a bad driver? How does that strategy work out for them?"

"All Ben is saying is give him some time," Schiller counseled. "A slow drip of water can erode the hardest rock. We'll find a weak spot in their case and work it."

Jack Trenton, who was ignoring the meltdown of his subsidiary president, looked up from the SeaCoast damage estimates and appraisals he had been reviewing. His shock was wearing off. It was time to get back to business.

"These property damage numbers don't appear to be inflated. They're big, but like that asshole said, it may just be a few million here and there that's going to be worth arguing about." He glanced over to Argent. "Now, I have no idea about the value of these death claims. Ben?"

Argent hated giving verdict predictions. But if he were going to be put on the spot, he damn sure wasn't going to sugarcoat things.

"I've seen good death cases bring five to ten million. It all depends on what the deceased could have earned over his lifetime and whether the jury considers the survivors to be quality people who deserve a lot of money for their tears."

"So a demand of $7.5 million per claim is not outrageous on its face?" Trenton asked with disgust.

With a bit of intended irony, and with the same noncommittal tone the General Counsel had used earlier, Argent replied: "We'll see."

The callback to his cavalier comment about ISI's future stung. Jack Trenton was not amused. He turned to Dean Schiller for less judgmental answers. "So, what's the next step?"

"Like I said, Ben here will kick some tires through discovery. I'm sure he'll want to hire consulting experts to look over that computer data and the plant schematics. Maybe they'll come up with an interpretation that differs from Ravich's theory."

"And if they don't?" Mike Beasley asked.

"Then we have to consider a controlled and dignified surrender."

"You mean a settlement? This soon?" The President of ISI couldn't believe what he was hearing and it showed in his voice.

"Time does not dictate the decision to settle," Schiller calmly replied. "The facts do."

Ben Argent knew at that moment what the outcome would be. Ravich's little show had shaken the powerful New York City litigator, even though he was experienced enough not to show it. *This case will never be tried*, Argent thought to himself, as he listened to Dean Schiller outline the steps necessary to fold their tent.

"When I return to my office, I'll contact both the primary and excess insurance carriers for Integrated Sentry. They consented to my representation in lieu of their usual insurance-defense counsel because they trust my skills and judgement, and because they knew this might be a big case. I'll submit a detailed report to them along with our written demand that both insurance companies tender their liability policy limits to me now with full authority to settle."

"But those combined limits total only $150 million," Jack Trenton interrupted. "That plaintiffs' lawyer is never going to accept that amount against a half-billion dollar claim."

"You're probably right, but the size of his claim is the main reason those insurance companies will likely tender their limits. If they refuse and we take the full hit at trial, the law puts the insurance companies on the hook for placing your companies at risk of such a large excess judgment. We could actually sue them back to pay the difference between their policy limits and what the jury awards."

The ISI President shook his head in disgust. The attorneys were contemplating a second lawsuit before the first was finished. *No wonder people hate lawyers.*

The VyStream General Counsel had other thoughts. "If the insurance carriers tender their money and we decide not to risk a verdict, where does the extra money come from?"

"Come on, Jack," Schiller replied. "You know the answer to that."

Panic retook the ISI President. *Were they talking about him?*

"Integrated Sentry has minimal liquid assets," Mike Beasely protested. "We couldn't possibly contribute enough cash to make a dent in this demand."

Schiller turned to his other client. "Then that leaves VyStream to take up the slack."

Jack Trenton did indeed know that was the answer. While ISI was technically a separate corporation and the only company that dealt directly with SeaCoast, its parent company was not going to let it go under because of a tort claim. In that sense, VyStream Corporation was no different from the parents of an adult child in financial trouble: although having no legal liability for their kid's debts, and despite the fact that no one can make them provide support, mom and dad always seem to come to the rescue anyway. In the human context, it's out of love. In the corporate context, it's to preserve the parent company's image as the strong owner of quality subsidiaries.

"Fuck," Jack Trenton unprofessionally blurted, not recalling how that same word had been uttered repeatedly when he first saw the suit papers in this case. It was fast becoming his most-used phrase when discussing the SeaCoast disaster.

"Feed a man breakfast and he's yours for the day," Harry said, as he stirred his coffee and looked at his watch. "He should be here any minute."

Doug Stevens loved the way Harry's mind worked. The two of them sat in the coffee shop, waiting for the witness to arrive. It was the first step in a long walk mapped out in the war room four days earlier.

They needed an insider, someone who worked in the SeaCoast plant and was on the floor in the days leading up to the explosion. A defendant-company usually instructs its employees not to meet or talk with a plaintiff's lawyer. But they can't control an ex-employee. Harry correctly guessed that with the workplace destroyed many of the jobs would go too. He was right, and he was looking forward to speaking again with the very cooperative Wally Brinkman.

Back during Harry's initial cold calls, as he worked his way through the SeaCoast directory looking for leads, Wally Brinkman was one of the few workers who spoke with him. Harry explained to Doug that Brinkman was the talkative floor hand who first informed him that Ken Slator had quit the day after the fire. It was that revelation that started the wheels of their current investigation in motion. Harry thought it wise to spin those wheels back around to see what else Mr. Brinkman might know.

A pudgy man wearing boots, jeans, and a denim shirt walked into the restaurant and glanced around. When scheduling the meeting, Harry had told the witness to simply look for a frumpy old man sitting next to a good-looking young one. Brinkman spotted two likely suspects and approached their booth. Harry rose and extended his hand.

"Mr. Brinkman, I presume?"

"Call me Wally."

"Then it's Harry for me and this here is Doug. Please, sit down."

Brinkman shook their hands and in his simple country accent, said: "How ya doin'?" as he slid into the booth to face them.

An attentive waitress came over to attend to her new arrival. Like any good morning server, a pot of coffee seemed permanently attached to her hand. "Coffee?"

"Thanks," Wally replied, sliding over the white mug that was already atop the paper placemat in front of him.

She poured while asking: "What else can I get you?"

Wally looked over at the two lawyers. "You fellows having sumthin'?"

"Do I look like I miss any meals?" Harry joked, tapping his stomach. "We were just waiting for you. Order up."

Although eating can sometimes be an impediment to important conversation, Harry knew that treating a potential witness to a restaurant meal was smart strategy. Not only does it assure adequate time to conduct an interview, but buying someone's meal is somehow subliminally comforting to them and makes a person more willing to talk. Nothing was ever lost on Harry Greenbaum.

After the men placed their orders, Harry got down to business.

"So, Wally, they laid you and everybody off?" he began.

"Not everybody. They kept Al Harris on, who's an assistant plant manager. I can't see why, there's no plant to run. All the peons like me, of course, got the pink slip."

"That's no way to treat people," Harry replied.

Doug sat listening and learning. He assumed Harry would try and forge an early alliance. He just didn't know how he would go about it.

"Guess it's better than killing me, which is what they did to poor Dan. I'm only sittin' here with you today because that Crouch kid was a nice boy."

"We appreciate that," Doug responded. "We're only trying to help his widow."

"I hear that. It's tough losing that paycheck, believe you me."

Harry leaned forward slightly, drawing himself closer to the witness sitting across from him in the booth.

"Wally, we need to know what was going on down at that plant in the days or weeks before this happened. We hope maybe you can help us out a little."

The witness took a sip of coffee, then sat the mug down.

"Sure. It's like I told you when you called me up that first time. That place was being pushed to the max in the month before it got blowed up. We were even asked to work double-shifts. Now, don't get me wrong, I liked the extra money but sixteen hours will leave you hangdog tired. Everyone was bushed and stressed out at the same time."

"Do you think that might have affected safety out there?" Doug asked.

"Could have. I mean, whenever Ken Slator was in the control room, things ran smooth as crap through a goose. That man stayed on top of things. But Slator left at four every day. I worked the mornin' shift the day it happened, along with Dave Phillips. By the grace of God, I wasn't assigned to pull a double shift that day. But Dave was. I guaran-damn-tee you, Phillips was probably half-asleep and fully exhausted by the time that plant exploded that night. They was grinding us hard."

"And Phillips would have been at the controls, is that right?" Doug asked in follow-up.

"Yep."

Harry wanted to ask his helpful insider an open-ended question. "So, Wally, what do you think happened out there that night?"

"From what I know about how we made that shit, the neutralizer tank got out of control and the melt heated up too much, then exploded. Now once you get a fire going in that plant, there's enough methane, chemicals, and fertilizer around to keep it roarin' for days. I'm amazed they got it put out so fast."

It was time to focus the inquiry so Harry guided the discussion. "Wasn't there a safety system out there, a computer controlled program of some kind, to keep all that from happening?"

"Oh yeah, they called it a DCSS. Damn thing was like a robot. If any equipment sneezed on that floor, the computer knew it and brought it a hanky. Once that thing was installed, all we really had to do was sit around and watch it work. Only thing it couldn't do automatically was tote the finished bags of fertilizer into storage. That's what my dumb-ass was for."

"So why didn't it detect that tank in trouble?"

"Maybe it did and Dave was too tired to notice. Hell, I don't know. All I can say for sure is them computer-controlled sensors and valves always worked fine when I was around 'em."

Harry decided to test the statement Ravich had made to him at their Barrister's Club lunch meeting. "Did your boss, Mr. Slator, ever tell you he kept a computer backup of the DCSS data at home?"

"Not to me directly, no. But I wouldn't be surprised. That fellow was a 'company man' if you get my drift. I never heard him talk about nothin' other than work. The assistant managers thought he had hidden cameras around or somethin' like that, because both Dave Phillips and Al Harris said to me on different occasions that Slator knew what was going on even when he wasn't there."

Doug looked over at Harry and nodded. They were on the right track.

"Did Mr. Slator call the shots or were there other SeaCoast folks over him?"

Harry knew the answer but wanted to get Wally Brinkman's take on the chain-of-command. Before he had time to answer, the waitress returned with their food.

"Now, who had the eggs-over-easy?"

Doug raised his hand quickly, regretting her bad timing.

"And the waffle?" she said, raising the next plate off her tray.

"That's me," Wally offered, as he reached up to grab his order.

"Then that must leave the oatmeal for this nice gentleman," she cooed, in a childlike tone of voice that some people insist on using when speaking to old people.

Harry smiled anyway. "Your powers of deduction are remarkable, madam. Thank you."

She looked at him warily, unsure if the old geezer intended that as a compliment or insult. After offering them more coffee, she left and allowed the discussion to continue.

Harry reminded his guest of the pending question as Brinkman poured a full cup of maple syrup over his breakfast. "Now, who again was the big boss out there?"

"Well, if you're askin' who knew the most about making fertilizer, that was Ken Slator. If you're askin' who the straw boss was, the person who ran the place and had shit-for-brains, that would be Rob Finnegan." Brinkman took a big bite of waffle and continued talking with his mouth half full. It reminded Doug of Bonnie's lecture to Bill Gaston for doing the same thing. "He's the President of the whole damn company. All I ever saw him do is parade around like a banty rooster while telling all of us how far behind we were on this big order."

"So it was Rob Finnegan who was pushing things to the breaking point?" Harry pointedly asked.

"Yes, sir. All that man needed was a bullwhip to make him a slave master. Of course, he had bosses too, I guess. When someone came down from the parent company, he would escort `em around the plant, his nose up their ass like a scent hound."

"So you had people from Thornton Industries actually come on site?"

"From time to time."

"How about during that last month, when things were obviously running in such high gear?"

"Sure. I seen Finnegan and a couple of men in suits come through one mornin' about a week before the fire. I was dead tired because I'd already worked the graveyard shift and was starting my double-header. As pooped as I was, I still had more on-the-ball than those jackasses. Two of `em had their hard hats on backwards."

"Cream always curdles before it rises to the top, doesn't it?" Harry said, knowing that working men universally held management in low light.

"You got that right," Wally said with a laugh that caused a small piece of bacon to come flying out of his mouth. *Bonnie would be on him by now,* thought Doug.

"Well, you've been most helpful to us," Harry said, concluding the interview. "Thank you, Wally. What say we just sit and enjoy the rest of our breakfast?"

"Glad to help. Like I said, Dan was good people."

Wally Brinkman reached for the second slice of bacon on his plate. Before devouring it, he thought of something else. He waived the brown pork strip in front of him for emphasis.

"Oh, let me tell you this. It'll give you a better idea about how squirrely that Finnegan is. A month after the explosion, I drive down there to pick up my final paycheck and he was still sittin' behind the desk in that business office like nothin' had happened. Crazy. The place was filled with moving boxes so I asked if he was headed someplace else. He said no, that those boxes were just records he was fixin' to deliver to the company's lawyers. He sat right there and told me he was gonna keep reporting to that empty office till they made him hit the road."

Brinkman shook his head back and forth to signify he thought Finnegan had gone mad. As their witness finally chomped down on the bacon he had been using as a pointer, Doug looked over at Harrry and raised his eyebrows. *Boxes of records.* That's certainly more than the discovery turned over to them. Wally Brinkman had just confirmed Doug's suspicion that evidence was being withheld.

Both Harry and Doug knew better than to interrupt with questions. They each made faces to indicate they were fascinated by what Wally had to say. It worked. The talkative witness offered up something else.

"So, anyway, we get to talkin' about things and Finnegan tells me that Ken got killed in a car wreck. First I'd heard about it and it threw me for a loop. I mean, we wasn't good friends or nothin' but he was a decent fellow. I said somethin' like: 'that's a damn shame,' and Finnegan just sat there with a shit-eatin' grin on his face. I tell you, that man is squirrely."

Harry thought again about the briefcase of tools with the curious business card found in Slator's wrecked trunk. *Coincidence or Conspiracy?* This productive session with Wally Brinkman provided tidbits of information and a hearty breakfast. It also gave Harry Greenbaum food for thought.

The deposition of Robert Finnegan was already scheduled for the following week. Harry now had a few more questions to ask the President of SeaCoast Chemical Corporation.

⸺ ❧ ⸺

The news wasn't good.

Ben Argent had been tasked with getting a quick but thorough analysis of the DCSS record that Ravich had provided to the third-party defendants. The programmers from Integrated Sentry confirmed that the data backup appeared to reveal their system had misread a nonfunctioning volume sensor as normal, causing Cascade Mode to ignore the temperature readings that would have otherwise sounded the alert.

"This isn't the way it was supposed to work," one of the ISI employees had confessed.

No shit, Argent remembered thinking when it was said.

The independent consultant that Argent retained was similarly unhelpful. The highly paid expert reviewed the plant schematics and ISI's control system in detail before announcing his verdict. While praising the DCSS program as "a good general effort," he conceded that in this specific instance it had not performed as intended.

"Great, thanks for nothing," Argent recalled saying to himself as he left the expert's office.

When Dean Schiller got those updates he knew what to tell his local counsel. "Ben, let's get the families deposed quickly. Hire an economist and a construction expert to evaluate and trim some fat off the SeaCoast property damage claim."

"So you're saying…"

Schiller interrupted. There could be no doubt about what he was saying.

"We can't afford to try this case, Ben. If Ravich is half as good in the courtroom as his record indicates, we lose this liability case nine times out of ten. I know we could hire some testifying clowns to say that ISI wasn't negligent and their product wasn't defective, but Ravich will eat them alive on cross. We get a jury mad at us and a half-billion may become the *starting* point of their damage deliberations."

Argent listened without comment. He knew it was true. *But how do you quickly and quietly settle a case this big?* No good answer came to him. The numbers were astronomical. Ravich's insistence on a full recovery would be fueled by their easy surrender on the issue of fault. Argent recalled his failed settlement negotiations in the recently tried *Clayton* case. His opponent was hard to deal with then and Argent had at least a decent counter-argument in that case. Here, Ravich would be impossible to work with. He wasn't looking forward to again seeing Ravich's smug look once serious settlement talks commenced.

Ben Argent wanted to hear the New York mega-lawyer issue the directive. "So, we put down our weapons and start counting our losses?"

"Just do the best you can, Ben," Schiller replied. "I'll take care of communicating things to our clients."

Argent was an experienced defense attorney. He knew exactly what that meant. VyStream and Integrated Sentry would be told "his best" wouldn't be good enough. Dean Schiller would soon posture himself as the only man who could save ISI from a devastating jury verdict by insisting that it and the parent company step up to write their checks *now*. Any discount Ravich might give for prompt payment would be to Schiller's credit.

Like all of Dean Schiller's local counsel, Ben Argent would get credit for nothing. He knew that too. It wasn't his first rodeo.

Harry insisted on driving. He pulled his chugging Plymouth up to the front entrance of Doug's building. His two co-counsel, who had been waiting inside the small lobby, saw and heard him come to a stop. The squeaking brakes could be heard through the glass doors.

"My God! That car is as old as he is," Bill Gaston chortled, as he and Doug made their way out.

"But like its owner it probably gears up fast," Doug joked back.

"Good morning, fearless champions of justice!" Harry said with a smile, as the younger lawyers climbed into the still rumbling antique.

The man behind the wheel was in high spirits. Today was an important day in the *Crouch* case.

"Where'd you get this hotrod?" Gaston asked.

"It's been so long ago, I forgot," came the cheerful reply, as Harry accelerated away. As they made the short drive into downtown, Harry offered advice on the depositions of Al Harris and Rob Finnegan that would begin in a half hour.

"Boys, expect no admissions of liability today. Paul Ravich will have these witnesses wood-shedded to the point of no surprises. They've probably been rehearsing for hours. Remember though, *what* is said is not nearly as important as *how* they say it."

It was another of Harry's seemingly inane practice tips. However, both Doug and Bill had, by now, stopped questioning the old man's techniques. His instincts and methods were the marks of genius.

"Did you see that Ben Argent just noticed up the depositions of Ravich's families for next week?" Gaston wanted Harry's take. "Kinda early to be doing damage discovery, don't you think?"

"It's a sign that settlement considerations have already begun," Harry replied, without any concern.

Doug, however, did have worries. "We still haven't sued Integrated Sentry. Don't you think it's time? If Ravich already has them on the ropes, we could benefit too."

"We benefit most from the truth, fellows. If it turns out the third-party defendant is at fault, we will still have plenty of time to amend our pleadings and add them. But right now, we are the only ones taking a serious look at the conduct of SeaCoast. Let's see where these depositions today lead us before we start remaking our bed."

Gaston still needed convincing. "What are we going to grill these two about? We have no incriminating company memos, no production records, no *nada* to question them on. Ravich made sure of that."

"Then we will just have to sit down and visit, won't we?"

Doug smiled. Gaston wasn't going to faze the unflappable Harry Greenbaum.

They reached Ravich's office tower and Harry maneuvered his old relic into the guest-parking entrance lane in the building's attached garage. He took a ticket from the automated machine and looked around as the gate-barrier arm swung up. In minutes, they were parked and in the elevator, riding up to the sixty-third floor.

Doug noticed that Harry had brought along more than just a Big Chief tablet. He actually looked a bit more like a normal trial lawyer, toting a briefcase with a couple of books tucked under his arm.

"I see you're loaded for bear," Doug remarked.

Harry waived his free hand dismissively. "Please, these are mere props. Indicia of intelligence."

Gaston wondered silently why a similar thought wasn't given by the man to his wardrobe. His clothes this morning were particularly unlawyer-like. A fall tweed sport coat clashed mightily with summer plaid trousers.

"Lookin' sharp, Harry," he teased, with a wink.

Harry caught the joke. "One must try to look their best when going to an office as fancy as Paul's penthouse."

Doug and Bill smiled knowingly. Even if today's depositions failed to reveal any strong evidence against SeaCoast Chemical, with Harry asking the questions, it was at least going to be an enjoyable show.

⌾⌾⌾

Ron Carroll hooked another tarpon and basked in the moment. It was a beautiful South Florida morning and he was enjoying his vacation. He had already spent the first seven days settling into his new condo, trying not to think too much about what had been done to acquire it.

Paul Ravich had been true to his word. A week after Slator's wreck, a quitclaim deed was filed in Collier County making Ron the record-owner of a very nice place situated a mere block from a pleasant marina in Naples. It was something he could never have purchased on a policeman's retirement pay or even with the savings from his much higher salary at Ravich & Associates.

There was still no confirmation that a Swiss account had been opened in his name and funded with a million dollars as promised, but Ron wasn't worried. Ravich may be a crook but he wasn't a stupid one. His boss knew better than to betray the only man who could, with his testimony alone, convict him of murder. On that point, Ron reasoned, the two of them now had that much permanently in common. Such a bond — of mutual assured destruction — served to insure that secrets would remain safe. Neither man wanted to end up in jail.

Week two was all about fishing, and forgetting. Ron never lost sleep after the Beirut car bomb mission: then, he was a hero; there, the victim had been a rat-terrorist. But the killing of Ken Slator was different: that man had done nothing wrong other than meet Paul Ravich. He died so that Ravich and Ron could be rich, not in order to make the world a safer place. Ron's guilt over that was bad but manageable. He would soon have another million reasons, literally, to get over it.

When Ron left town, there was no discussion of when he'd be back. Ravich certainly wasn't going to protest if this became an extended vacation. The firm still had two other investigators. Neither knew anything about the case-running program that Ron handled but he assumed that didn't matter. Once Ravich collected his hundred-million in fee from the *SeaCoast* case, Ron presumed there would be little interest in continuing a scheme to obtain much smaller cases illegally.

The charter captain walked back to the stern of the boat and offered his customer a cigar. He was a good client: paid in cash and wanted to go back out again tomorrow. Ron accepted the gift as the captain commented on the joys of a lazy, warm Florida day on the water.

"There's worse places you could be, my friend," he said, as he handed over a lighter and cutter.

"Don't I know it," Ron casually replied, as he trimmed and lit the cigar, then took a puff. The Cuban tobacco tasted good. He exhaled and leaned back in the fishing chair, as all thoughts of crime and punishment curled up with the smoke and blew gently away in the Gulf breeze.

Just as Harry had deduced, Paul Ravich also equated Ben Argent's scheduling of damage depositions for the following week to be a sure sign that the third-party defendants were teetering. *Why wouldn't they settle?* Ravich thought, when he saw the notices to depose widows and family members come across his desk. After all, his conference room presentation to them had been overwhelming.

That same room would be used today for the depositions of Harris and Finnegan. But Ravich would not attend. He would continue to personally prosecute his made-up claim for riches but saw no need to engage in the daily defense of SeaCoast in the *Crouch* case. The foolish gross negligence claim being asserted by those *silly lawyers* was not worthy of his time. He would get involved again in that aspect of the case only when it came time to ask Judge Lewis to throw their claim out of court. In the meantime, he could return to his old habits of delegating pretrial matters to his associates. Dustin Kirkland would sit beside the witnesses today as *Doug or Harry or that other guy — hell, it didn't matter who — asked a bunch of questions that would get them nowhere.*

The three lawyers who Ravich held in such low-esteem entered his conference room to find Ben Argent already there. As defense counsel in the consolidated case, Argent had every right to attend.

"Gentle Ben, it's so good to be with you again," Harry said warmly as they shook hands. They had little opportunity to talk at the consolidation hearing.

"Likewise, Harry," Argent replied sincerely.

Argent had been involved in prior cases where Harry was on the other side. But unlike with Ravich, whose "take no prisoners" approach alienated most defense counsel, Ben and Harry could and did remain friends after their adversarial trials were over. Argent respected Greenbaum's talents and liked the man personally. Then again, it seemed almost everyone liked Harry.

Al Harris went first.

Rob Finnegan waited back in Dustin's office, reading a *Time* magazine and feeling relaxed. After all, his role in causing the plant explosion would never be discovered. He would deny ever talking to anyone at the plant the night it happened. Dave Phillips was dead. Ken Slator was also gone, although from the sound of things, it wouldn't have made any difference if he were still alive. Dustin had explained this morning that all the evidence, including Slator's computer backup records, proved that it was entirely Integrated Sentry's fault.

"Do you swear to tell the truth, the whole truth, so help you God?"

Al Harris looked directly at the court reporter and said "I do" before lowering his right hand.

"How ya doin'?" Harry began, recalling the phrase that Wally Brinkman had used to start their productive conversation in the coffee shop several days ago.

Dustin looked up from his legal pad in surprise. This was not the typical first question asked in a deposition.

"I'm good," Harris answered.

"That's great!" Harry enthusiastically replied. "I figured you might be a little bit tired, considering you've probably already been here for a couple of hours talking with this young man about what you're going to say, huh?"

Harry pointed a friendly finger toward Dustin as he asked the question.

"I object," Ravich's associate spat back. "You don't have to answer that, Mr. Harris."

"Relax, kid," Harry said with a smile. "I was just breaking the ice."

"Well, then chip away someplace else," Dustin countered.

"Okey-dokey. So Mr. Harris, how long had you worked for SeaCoast prior to this disaster?"

"Seven years."

"And you rose to the position of 'Assistant Operations Manager' in that time? Have I got that title right?"

"Yep."

"Had the plant not blown up, you would have been in charge of it from midnight till eight in the morning on October 15th, isn't that so?"

"Yep."

"And I understand the explosion took place less than an hour before your shift was scheduled to begin?"

"Yep."

"It was a busy time down there in the days before the explosion, wasn't it?"

"Yep."

"Things were going full tilt, round the clock?"

"Yep."

"Highest production level ever in the history of that facility, far as you know, correct?"

"Yep."

"Now, Mr. Harris, I understand your lawyer here has probably told you to keep your answers short and sweet, but feel free to vary the word every now and again."

Harry smiled and Harris smiled back.

Dustin Kirkland, however, was not amused. "I object."

"Oh, lighten up, young man, or you'll grow old before your time," Harry counseled back. He turned his attention back to the witness.

"Did you folks regularly keep records of what you produced, how fast you made it, where it was stored, and any problems you may have encountered during a shift?"

"Yes, sir, we did."

"Be careful, Al," Harry warned in jest, "You just said *four* words."

Harris grinned again. He liked this old buzzard.

Dustin decided Harry's teasing banter was causing no harm and stayed quiet.

"Where did you folks store those records?"

"In the business office."

"That's the building that was *not* burned in the fire, correct?"

"Correct."

Harry decided to ask something he didn't already know the answer to, but phrased the question to suggest otherwise. It was a common trick employed by good cross-examiners.

"And you were even asked to review some of those production and business records after the explosion, isn't that right?"

Harris didn't know how the old lawyer could possibly know such a thing but he wasn't going to lie.

"Yes, sir, I was."

"There were boxes and boxes of them, isn't that true?" Harry ventured.

"There was a good bit, yes, sir."

Doug and Bill nodded in appreciation. They now had sworn proof of discovery being withheld. Harry kept pressing ahead.

"Were you worried about safety in those weeks before the explosion, when things were going full tilt?"

"I was always worried about safety. That's my job."

"Touché. What I meant was: Were you even more worried in that month before?"

"To be honest, yeah."

"Oh, please be honest, Mr. Harris. There's no finer way to be." Harry glanced over at Doug and Bill. "What had you worried you so much?"

Dustin shifted uncomfortably in his seat.

"We were pushing the equipment, taxing the men. Some fellows were putting in sixteen hour days to get this Chinese order fulfilled. Things were hectic."

"Oh, my Lord. Why didn't you complain to management?"

"They're the ones that had us working like that. We were told we needed to push even more. So asking the boss if we could slow down didn't seem like it would get me too far."

"And who was that boss?"

"Mr. Finnegan."

"And who was his boss?"

"Thornton Industries, I suppose."

"Did you ever have any trouble with that DCSS system?"

"Never a day."

Argent quickly jotted down a note.

"Did you ever have any trouble with Mr. Finnegan?"

"Now you're trying to get me in hot water here," Harris replied reluctantly.

"To the contrary, I'm only trying to get to the truth. And you're under oath, remember?"

"Well, let's just say he wasn't very hands-on. He didn't care much about how it got done so long as it got done faster."

Again, Ben Argent appeared interested.

Harry kept at it for just under an hour. With delicate and folksy questions, he scored points while the goalie, Dustin Kirkland, slept at the net. When he was through, Al Harris thought the whole experience was no worse than a pleasant conversation.

Doug and Bill knew better. Through a series of increasingly pointed questions, Harris had unwittingly painted a picture of company management driving its workers to the brink, while asking them to disregard routine practices and safety considerations. It wasn't enough, standing alone, to prove gross negligence but it was a start.

Argent also got to question the witness, whose understanding of the DCSS was too basic to give the ISI attorney anything concrete to work with.

Dustin Kirkland, like any other lawyer producing his own party's witness for deposition, merely announced when it was his turn: "We reserve our questions for time of trial." It was an unnecessary statement, but lawyers, for some reason, liked saying that.

Harry rose to shake Al Harris' hand and wish him luck. He liked the fellow and thought the assistant operations manager had been fairly cooperative once he got thawed out.

But the real test was coming. Harry would need a blow torch to melt the next witness.

Rob Finnegan would give his deposition after their short lunch break.

———— ✕✕✕ ————

Sarah Ash had lunch that same day with a small group of women. One was a court reporter; another, like her, a court clerk. The fourth woman had been invited to listen to the stories of the three county employees. They dined on salads and sandwiches at a small deli near the courthouse.

Sarah had arranged the noon meeting, unsure of what to expect. Her county coworkers were both friends but the conversation today would not be the run-of-the-mill exchange of work gossip, rumors, and tales of government inefficiency. The discussion instead would be focused on one subject: Judge Lewis. The fourth woman was a trial lawyer, active in feminist causes and a specialist in a field of law that developed due to men like this judge: the sexual harassment case.

Each of the county employees described their experiences with Judge Lewis. While the time periods were different and the extent varied, there were common themes: inappropriate touching, sexually suggestive remarks, and warnings to keep quiet about his advances. The lawyer listened with growing rage but waited until the three women were finished speaking. It took courage to even consider confronting a powerful officeholder and she wasn't going to interrupt these brave civil servants. When they were done, she began.

"There's no question it's actionable harassment, and your collective testimony would show a consistent pattern of abuse. He won't be able to slander all of you and he'll have a hard time suggesting that these interactions were consensual. I've appeared in that pig's court many times. All it will take is one look at him and another at you three for a jury to decide that he forced himself on you."

"Will we lose our jobs if we go forward with a claim?" asked Jane, the court reporter, who was still working in Lewis' court and had grown weary of the Judge's frequent gropes.

"No, the County may be dumb but it's not stupid. You'll be transferred, no doubt, and you other two will also be told to avoid the Judge, which you are probably already doing."

Sarah had a different concern. "What do you think he will do if we file suit?"

"You can expect strong denials and perhaps some mud thrown back at you. The press will pick up the story — they love any salacious accusations about a public official — and the Judge will have to face the political and public heat."

"And we can recover damages from him for this? Doesn't he get 'judicial immunity' or something?" the other clerk wanted to know.

"Yes, you can and no, he doesn't," the lawyer replied.

"Can we have some time to think this over?"

"Of course, Sarah, take whatever time you need. I'll keep our discussion confidential, of course, so the only way this thing goes public is if and when you three say so. But let me urge each of you: Do this. Shrinking away out of fear only empowers abusers like Judge Lewis to commit more abuse."

The two other women nodded their heads and looked over at Sarah. She had suggested the meeting. It would be up to her to decide.

Sarah had not mentioned her thoughts to Doug and, at least for now, decided it best to keep this lunch session a secret from him. He had other things on his plate. This was primarily about her and her fellow workers. She would take her time and come to the right decision. But if her boyfriend ended up benefitting from something she should do anyway, *wouldn't that be nice?*

———— ∞ ————

Stupid men are often the most arrogant. Rob Finnegan was a prime example. He sat confidently across from Harry Greenbaum, waiting for the deposition to begin. He took in the wardrobe and "aw-shucks" demeanor of his adversary as they met and shook hands. He wasn't the least bit worried about sparring with someone he mistook for an old clown.

Harry wrestled lightly at first, extracting meaningful but seemingly benign concessions from the President of SeaCoast Chemical:

"Yes, I'm considered senior management; and yes, I'm in charge of all decisions at all our plants," Finnegan had bragged.

"It's true I received guidance from the parent company, Thornton Industries, and that they had the power to increase or limit my authority at anytime," he had also conceded.

Harry questioned him at length about the unusual level of production that was taxing the plant in the days and weeks before the explosion.

Finnegan responded with carefully rehearsed answers, minimizing the chaotic picture of his plant that Harry was trying to paint. *He hasn't laid a glove on me*, Finnegan thought, as he continued to deny that SeaCoast or the parent company ever put profits ahead of safety.

Finally, Harry had heard enough. It was time to see if he could get the pompous witness off script a little.

"Now, Mr. Finnegan, you wouldn't be fudging your testimony here today just to make yourself and SeaCoast look good, would you?"

"I object," Dustin Kirkland barked. "If you want to accuse this man of perjury, do so in your closing arguments in court. If you get that far."

Harry smiled.

Rob Finnegan chose to answer the question anyway. "Why would I? I have nothing to hide."

Now was the moment. Harry reached under the table where the items he had brought with him had been concealed. The books could stay. They were mere diversions. He grabbed the brown briefcase — the one he had found in Slator's car — and placed it down on the table between him and the witness.

Rob Finnegan's cocky attitude evaporated the instant he recognized it. The last time he was this close to that case was when it was tossed through the bathroom window he had shattered to gain access to Slator's apartment.

What the hell! Finnegan eyes were locked on his recovered property.

He could have just as easily said what he was thinking. The words were written all over his shocked face. Everyone in the room could tell that the placement of the innocuous briefcase on the table had suddenly affected the deponent.

He looked up from the incriminating object and saw Harry Greenbaum staring knowingly into his eyes. Finnegan began sweating profusely and wildly fidgeting in his seat.

"Nothing to hide? Are you sure about that?" Harry asked.

Dustin Kirkland quickly became more interested. Until now, there had been no major fireworks. He didn't know what Greenbaum was up to but decided to pay closer attention.

Finnegan had to regroup, and fast. "What? I don't know what you're talking about."

"Should we look inside this case, Mr. Finnegan, or would you like to tell the rest of the people in this room what you already know is in there?"

"I, uh, I ... must have left that somewhere."

"Well, that solves one mystery for me," Harry cheerfully said. "I wasn't sure until just now that this even belonged to you."

Finnegan realized he had blundered. "I don't know what's in it; I mean, what you may have put in there."

Harry placed his fingers on the case's clasps. "Oh, I haven't put anything in here, sir. Shall we open her up and take a look?"

"Whatever," Finnegan tried to say as if he didn't care. His cracking voice betrayed him.

"I've got a better idea. Why don't you tell me why your briefcase and its unusual contents were found in the trunk of your dead plant manager's wrecked car?"

"I don't know anything about that."

Dustin furrowed his brow. He knew nothing about Ravich's scheme or about how Slator died. He was trying to process it all and determine where the plaintiff's lawyer was headed. He couldn't figure it out.

Doug and Bill were similarly confused. Although Harry had detailed most of his findings and suspicions during their war room strategy session the week before, he had failed to mention Finnegan's briefcase. Like Dustin, they were both eager to see where all this was going.

"Well, then, let's talk about the things you do know. What did you say to Ken Slator on the day of the explosion, before it occurred?"

"I never spoke to him that day," Finnegan shot back quickly and confidently, hoping to regain his equilibrium.

"Then what did you say to his assistant, Dave Phillips?"

Harry had no idea if the two men had talked. He was just playing hunches.

Finnegan raised his hand and covered his mouth. Shock had caused the reaction. He didn't even realize he had done it. He would have made a terrible poker player.

"I, uh, I....can't recall."

"So you admit you spoke with Philips before the explosion, you just can't remember what you said?"

"Did I say that?"

"Yes, sir, I believe you just did. What time was it when you last talked with him that day?"

Harry was firing randomly. He had no idea what he was shooting at but he also knew that Finnegan didn't know that.

Finnegan's head was pounding. *Did they get phone records? Did Dave talk to Ken? Did Ken speak with this lawyer before he died?* So many thoughts were running through Finnegan's mind that he failed to answer the question. He seemed lost in panicked confusion.

Harry leaned forward. "Excuse me, Mr, Finnegan, could you rejoin us please?"

Lying is hard. Lying under pressure is harder. Rob Finnegan felt cornered. He had to say something. "He called me for advice. I simply told him to do what's best."

"My question was, what time was that?"

"I don't know, sometime during the evening shift."

"Now why was he seeking advice from you? Were there problems at the plant?"

"I can't remember."

"What did you tell him?"

"I can't recall."

"Do you even know *how* to run that plant?"

"Well, I…"

"I'll remind you you're under oath."

"Not really."

"So the man in charge of controlling the plant — a facility running at full capacity — calls you up, knowing you don't know much, and he wants your advice on some trouble he's having?"

"I can't remember what he wanted."

"He must have been desperate to call someone that couldn't help."

"I object; calls for speculation," Dustin interjected.

"Mr. Finnegan," Harry replied, "I'm going to keep speculating until either you tell the truth or I find out on my own. Is that clear?"

"I guess the DCSS malfunctioned," Finnegan volunteered. The witness caught his breath. *That was good*, he thought quickly, recognizing that the reply was consistent with his company's case-theory against Integrated Sentry.

"Now, Mr. Finnegan, you see the man at the opposite end of this table? That's Mr. Argent, the lawyer for the company that made the DCSS, and he told me at the lunch break that the SeaCoast lawyers have evidence showing that computer system went on the fritz sometime after nine p.m., a mere two hours before the explosion. Are you telling us that you spoke to the control room during that critical time?"

"I don't recall the time."

"Well, were you down there?"

388

"No."

"So you were at home?"

"Yes."

"So your home phone records will reveal the time of any calls between you and the plant, won't they?"

Finnegan was trapped. "I suppose."

"Come clean, Mr. Finnegan. If you don't, it will only get worse for you and your company."

Finnegan exhaled deeply. He was punched hard but not yet down. He needed some time to think. *I need this goddamn deposition to end.* "I don't have anything else to say. I don't remember anything more."

"Fine," Harry said, surprising the witness. "Then I'll have to start digging around someplace else. You have made a mistake here today, sir; perhaps bigger than the one you are attempting to conceal."

"I don't know what…"

Harry held up his hand. Finnegan had blown his chance.

"Please, we're through for today, but know this: I'm not through with you. I pass the witness."

"What the hell was that?" Gaston gleefully said, once his trial team was alone in the elevator, riding back down to the garage. Neither he nor Doug had ever seen a witness self-destruct so badly in a routine deposition.

"I had to determine if the President of SeaCoast was involved somehow in this sordid business. I now know that he is. Either he knows more than he's saying about the explosion or he was a conspirator in Mr. Slator's death. Either way, we are on the right track."

"So, what do we do next?" Doug asked.

"We leave, and continue to look for clues."

The two young lawyers looked at each other and shrugged. *Let the adventure continue.* Harry would only keep them guessing. It was his style.

They were soon back in Harry's Plymouth and approaching the parking garage's exit. Both passengers noticed when Harry swerved into the contract-parking lane intended for tenant use. He should have been in the visitor's lane which led to a booth and cashier.

"Harry, you're in the wrong lane," Doug warned, but it was too late. A concrete curb between the two exits now had the vehicle committed.

"So I am," Harry replied, with no distress in his voice.

He pulled up to the metal post on the driver's side of the lane. He extracted a white plastic card from the top pocket of his sport coat and pressed the magnetic strip against the sensor pad. The gate barrier arm swung open.

Harry drove out into the sunlight of the street and turned back towards Doug's office.

"Where'd you get that?" Gaston asked.

"It was in Ken Slator's car the night he died. I think we have just proved he paid Paul Ravich a visit sometime before."

Dustin walked down the hall to give his boss a report on the depositions just concluded. Ravich was in his office, playing around with spreadsheets of SeaCoast's damage projections. He was composing alternative ways to get to, and past, a half-billion. He assumed he would need to be fully number-ready soon. Settlement with Integrated Sentry and VyStream couldn't be far off.

He glanced up and saw Dustin approach. "How'd it go?" Ravich asked, before looking back down at his calculations.

"Okay, I guess," his associate replied. "The assistant manager made a few slips but nothing that truly hurts us. The company president, that Finnegan guy, was a piece of work though. He practically broke down."

Ravich looked up from his papers. "Over what?"

"I honestly can't say. And neither did he. It was the craziest thing I ever saw. He was breezing along, just like we practiced in the depo prep, and all of a sudden Harry Greenbaum pulls out a beat-up old briefcase he claims belongs to Finnegan, sits it in front of him, and our witness starts sweating bullets."

"What was in the case?"

"I don't know. Greenbaum never opened it."

"And you didn't ask?"

"Once he moved on, I thought it best to let it slide."

"What do you think was in it?" Ravich pressed.

"I have no idea, but Greenbaum said he found it in the trunk of a wrecked car belonging to the plant manager."

Unlike Finnegan, Paul Ravich *was* a good poker player. The mention of Slator's car hit him as hard as the briefcase had affected the SeaCoast President. But Ravich didn't show it. He couldn't show it. Not to Dustin, not to anyone.

It suddenly came back to him. Paul Ravich's skills as a trial lawyer were based in part upon his keen ability to recall even the smallest of details drawn from a witness. At their initial meeting at the soup-and-salad cafe, Slator had told him about a break-in at his apartment; how he had found Finnegan's briefcase of tools on his bathroom floor. The fact that the

SeaCoast President was shocked to see it again at his deposition wasn't surprising. The shocking surprise for Ravich was that it had been retrieved by Harry Greenbaum from a car that was supposed to no longer exist. It took all his skills at maintaining false appearances to keep his cool.

"Okay, you can go. Nice job." He watched as his associate turned to leave. "Hey, please close my doors on your way out. I've got to concentrate on these damage figures."

"Sure, boss."

Once Dustin had complied, and was well down the hall, Ravich picked up his cell phone and frantically dialed a number. He noticed his hand was shaking. *Goddamnit.*

A mobile phone rang atop a teak bar in an open air restaurant overlooking the Florida bay. Its owner put down his beer and answered it.

"This is Ron."

Ravich held the phone closely to his mouth and whispered a directive in a cold and exacting tone before quickly hanging up.

"Get back here. We have a problem."

Part IV

Remedy and Reward

Chapter 20
Emergency Landing

In one respect, a criminal enterprise is no different from a marriage: when things start to unravel, distrust and blame enter the picture.

The two conspirators sat across from each other in Paul Ravich's home study on Saturday afternoon. Ron flew back from Florida on a last-minute booked flight. No return was purchased. He wouldn't be fishing again until this crisis — whatever it was — had passed. The cryptic phone call from his boss, devoid of any detail, suggested it might be a serious one.

Ravich was increasing security. The housekeeper was given the afternoon off. His wife was out shopping. There would be no chance of any eavesdropping. There could be no more mistakes.

"I thought you told me the car was destroyed," Ravich immediately began, once they settled in their chairs. The circumstances offered no time for the usual "how was your flight?" banter.

Ron was thrown off by the statement and didn't like its tone. "It was, or at least that's what I was told."

"Told? By whom?"

"The woman at the wrecker yard confirmed for me that the vehicle was totaled and would be crushed and sold for scrap."

"Would be?" Ravich almost screamed the question. "Not had been?"

"She said it was only a matter of days. That was months ago."

"And you did no follow-up? No confirmation?"

Ron's silence provided the answer.

"Nice work," Ravich said sarcastically, before shifting into a shout. "One big piece of potentially incriminating evidence is out there and you decide to make a huge assumption about it?"

"Settle down," Ron barked back. The sternness of his voice was enough to silence his outraged boss. Once Ravich bit his lip, Ron added calmly:

"Okay, now tell me what this is all about."

Ravich outlined Greenbaum's deposition reveal of Finnegan's briefcase, what it meant and where it had been found. Ron listened closely, then summarized things.

"Look, let's think this through. That other lawyer probably went by Slator's house after he died as part of a routine witness-locate in his case. The widow informs him about the wreck, so this Greenbaum lawyer tracks down the car to see if maybe something was left inside that might explain Slator's whereabouts that night. Hats off to him, but all he manages to find is a briefcase belonging to this SeaCoast idiot. There's no connection to us."

As Ron continued talking, Ravich listened closely, trying hard to spot any weakness in his assessment.

"Worst thing that could happen is this Finnegan fool ultimately confesses to a break-in and admits he was looking for Slator's laptop out of fear it contained evidence damaging to his company. So what? *We* have that laptop. Slator turned it over to us for *safekeeping*. And it clearly proves — at least it does now — that the plant fire wasn't even SeaCoast's fault. So Finnegan's stupid paranoia turns out to be unjustified, which only makes sense because, once again, he's an idiot. End of story."

"But Greenbaum also saw the car," Ravich countered, still thinking of Harry and recalling his many skills. "Maybe he examined it, maybe he found evidence of tampering."

"Come on, Paul. If that was the case, don't you think that deposition would have involved something more than just flashing a briefcase?"

Ravich took some comfort in Ron's analysis but it wasn't enough. He barked an order to his investigator.

"This time, use your feet instead of the phone. Go down to that salvage yard and find out what ultimately happened to that car. If it got crushed and sold after Greenbaum retrieved the briefcase, maybe I'll sleep a little better."

"All right. Anything *else* I can do for you?"

Ron asked the question in a way to suggest his boss had overreacted; that his hasty return from his new Florida condo had been unnecessary. Ravich caught the snideness in the remark and wasn't pleased.

"You listen to me, Ron. I've got my case on the brink of settlement and Greenbaum's on the brink of dismissal. I can't afford any wrinkles. Until both cases have ended, our adversaries have the right to ask questions. I don't need the lawyers for the third-party defendants or Harry Greenbaum digging around for any dirt."

Ron nodded. He agreed it paid to be careful. Privately, he cussed himself for being so lazy regarding the car's disposal. But things were still going as planned. In his mind, they had dodged a stray bullet. *Let's move on,* he thought.

Thinking of "the plan" reminded Ron of another slight deviation from the way things were supposed to go. He decided to bring it up. It was important to make clear to his boss that, as regards this conspiracy, he was actually Ravich's partner, not his employee.

"Different subject: I still haven't received confirmation about my one-million. I expected by now that it would be in that Swiss account you agreed to set up for me."

Ravich was no fool. His investigator was saying: *"Don't screw with me."*

"I've been a little busy while you've been on vacation. I haven't forgotten. Do you think I would actually try to renege on something that petty when so much is at stake?"

"I'm not saying you're doing that. Just saying my priorities may be a little different from yours."

Ravich understood the point being made. It was a bold and cocky thing for Ron to say but it takes someone who's both to think they can get away with murder. Ron was solicited because of those attributes. Ravich couldn't now begrudge his mean dog for continuing to show some teeth.

"I'll take care of my end," Ravich announced. "You take care of yours, properly this time."

Their conversation ended with irritation on both sides. Like in a discordant marriage, both would go to sleep that night a little angry.

⸎

The free parking Harry received — thanks to the access card he discovered beneath the crushed driver's seat of Slator's car — focused their investigation further. The plant manager, at some point, had most likely used it just as Harry did following the depositions at Ravich's office. The card's existence in the dead man's vehicle hinted of a prearranged meeting that took place sometime before the wreck in a building occupied by their prime suspects.

Doug, Bonnie, and Bill sat in the war room on Monday morning listening with rapt attention as Harry made his case.

"Why else would Mr. Slator be in possession of an access card to Ravich's building?" As he spoke, Harry held the innocuous looking square of white plastic as if it had magically opened more than just an exit gate. "This was obviously given to him by a tenant in that building. Now, I realize it's a big office tower, filled with possible providers, but the fact that the building houses the offices of Paul Ravich & Associates is a bit too coincidental don't you think?"

397

Three distinct elements serve to establish a suspect's probable role in the commission of a crime: motive, means, and opportunity. Harry wanted his team to understand that all three legs of the stool were seemingly present.

"This access card, if it proves what I think it will, establishes that Ravich and his investigator may have had an ample and secluded opportunity to tamper with that car. Think about it. Slator's widow told me her husband went out for a late night meeting on the night he was killed. We know he didn't go down to his destroyed plant as he told his wife. So where did he go?"

Harry tapped the access card on the folding table, as if collecting his thoughts.

"We know he gave Paul Ravich his computer. Ravich told me himself that Slator came by his office to turn it over and authenticate its contents. I remember now that, during our lunch, Paul was inexact about when such meeting occurred. Maybe his memory was intentionally vague to avoid placing himself at a crime scene."

Once again, Doug and Bill sat staring at their senior co-counsel, amazed by how fluidly Harry's brain worked.

"So, how does one gain entrance to a downtown building and its parking garage after hours?"

Harry answered his own question with a flourish of the access card.

"Through simple logic, we have already established that Ravich had possible motives for getting rid of this witness. From our facts, we made the educated guess that Mr. Slator might have stood between him and obscene millions in fee. Through simple investigation, we have learned that Ravich's senior investigator is a military-trained explosives expert, and we know that military-supplied plastic explosives were planted expertly in Slator's car. Thus, we have motive and means, although we still lack sufficient connected proof of those particular elements to go to the police."

"So, what do we do?" asked Bonnie.

"We get more unimpeachable proof of 'opportunity' first. Let's subpoena the security-camera tapes and after-hour access records from Ravich's building for the night in question. Perhaps a seeing-eye or all-knowing computer logged our culprits and victim entering and exiting that garage. If we can put the three of them in close proximity during the hours just prior to Mr. Slator's tragic death, we are well on our way to solving this crime which — I shall remind you all once again — may very well lead to further truths and proof of our case against SeaCoast."

"But we can't just send out a subpoena in the *Crouch* case for that stuff," Bill Gaston smartly pointed out. "Our cases are consolidated now.

Ravich would get a copy of the subpoena. All parties do. We tip our hand and we're dead, figuratively if not literally."

"That's true," Harry conceded. "I guess I hadn't thought it through completely," he added in embarrassment.

"Don't be so hard on yourself; you've done most of our thinking so far," Gaston said with a smile. "You're entitled to be off-base occasionally."

Harry grinned appreciatively.

Doug was suddenly thunderstruck with an idea.

"Hey! How about this? Let's subpoena those building records through an unrelated case. Only the involved parties are entitled to notice and an opportunity to object to the relevancy of a subpoena for evidence, right? So let's use a case where Ravich isn't involved."

"That's it!" Bill exclaimed, as he clapped his hands, applauding Doug's clever idea. "I've got just the one. A really good buddy is on the other side of one of my pending cases. It's a simple contract dispute that's going to settle soon anyway. Now, of course, neither party in that suit has offices in Ravich's building. But so what?"

Harry began to smile. His young cubs were starting to think outside-the-box. They might turn out to be great trial lawyers after all.

Gaston outlined the plan. "I can tell my buddy the truth but not the whole truth. I simply say I want to use his and my case as a sham, as a method to acquire records by subpoena so my opponent in the real case won't find out what I'm up to. My buddy owes me — I refer him defense cases — and he won't care as long as I guarantee it can't hurt him in our little contract case. He'll go along. He likes sneaky shit like that."

Bonnie looked at Gaston with a grudging acceptance. The man might be goofy but he wasn't dumb.

"Excellent boys," Harry proclaimed. "I'll let you handle the details. But get on this right away. If we can get some proof that Ravich and Ron Carroll were with Ken Slator the night he died, I think we can take the next step."

"Which is?" Doug asked.

Harry paused to ponder, then simply announced: "Tighten the noose."

That same morning, Ravich's young lawyers were busy with settlement tasks in the *SeaCoast* case. Dustin Kirkland and Melanie Egan were sharing typical associate duty. Dustin sat in his office, prepping the next client in line, while Melanie sat in the large conference room beside the current plaintiff in the hot seat. Ben Argent, following Dean Schiller's directive to get the case ready for settlement evaluation, was busy conducting back-to-back depositions of Ravich's death-claim clients. It would be a daylong marathon, as each plaintiff gave their separate sworn testimony about the death of their loved one in the plant disaster. The stories varied slightly but the themes were always the same: *my world was destroyed; he was a good husband and father; I will never get over it.*

It was a depressing day for all involved. The family members had to lay bare unhealed emotional wounds that could only be treated, ineffectively, by a large money poultice. Ben Argent also hated the experience. These were good people who had done nothing wrong. Deposing them was a waste of time. Argent knew what they would say before they began and he had no evidence to contradict their statements of love and loss. The two Ravich associates found their clients' tears painful to watch. Melanie and Dustin actually cared about these individuals.

Their empathy was in stark contrast to their boss. Paul Ravich's primary concern now was the far-larger property damage claim of his corporate client, SeaCoast Chemical. He didn't even bother to come out of his office to say hello to his human clients as they paraded sadly in and out of the conference room.

Doug, Harry, and Bill all agreed they didn't need to attend these depositions. None of the family members represented by Ravich knew anything firsthand about what caused the accident, and the lawyers for Kate Crouch clearly held no animosity toward the people sharing the same ordeal as their client.

Their growing differences and suspicions were limited solely to *the lawyer* those unfortunate people had been corralled into hiring.

Ron Carroll also had a busy day. He arrived at Sammy's Wrecker & Salvage wearing a shirt with a button-down collar, a blue blazer, cheap slacks and some sensible shoes. He was dressed to play a part. His police badge would complete the costume. He pulled out the folding leather case from his sport coat and flashed the tin star inside.

For reasons just like this, police are required to surrender their badges at the time they retire. But Ron knew the credential might come in handy during his next profession as a private investigator. The badge in his hand was his original detective issue. Its replacement — the one he did turn back in — had been conveniently obtained by falsely claiming, two years before he left the force, that the first one got lost in a scuffle with a suspect.

"I'm Detective Johnson, with Metro PD," he said quickly, giving the large woman behind the counter little time to study the badge or retain the name. "We're trying to ascertain the disposition of a vehicle that was

400

brought into your facility at the end of last October."

Ron intentionally spoke like a cop on the witness stand. It was all a part of his cover.

"Yes, sir, Officer," replied Sammy's usually gruff wife. Like most people, she cowered in front of the police. "If you've got a VIN or plate, I should be able to track it down."

Ron smiled and gave her the information. She pulled up the history on her still dingy computer and announced: "Sold to a private party on November 1st."

"Private party? You mean a scrap company or something?"

"No, our crush and scraps are coded in as bulk sales. This one got bought by an individual."

Ron tensed. "We need to know who, ma'am."

"We ain't in no trouble for selling it, are we? Because I had no idea it was part of some police thang."

"No, ma'am, you did nothing wrong. I'm just following leads."

"Let me go get my receipt book then. It should have some record."

The fat woman waddled over to a filthy desk behind the counter and retrieved an equally dirty sales book from the top drawer. It was the type of record pad sold at office supply stores, about the size of an envelope, and now filled with the carbons of torn receipts handed out to customers. Apparently exhausted by the effort of her short walk, she placed the pad down on the front counter and paused to light a cigarette.

Ron waited patiently. The less he said, the less she would likely remember about him.

"All-righty," she began, after exhaling a large puff, "let's see what we've got." She flipped through the chronological carbons looking for those from November 1st. By the time she located it, her cigarette was half gone. "Here we go."

She saw the name and the price paid. It jogged her memory. She offered an explanation as she slid the receipt book in front of Ron, pointing at the information that was only faintly visible on the carbon paper.

"Man's name was Greenbaum. I remember him too, an old nut-job. He come in here wantin' to buy the thang. I told him it was scheduled for crush and he said he'd pay full scrap value and come fetch it later."

"And did he?" Ron asked.

"He sent somebody down here to get it. A mechanic or tow truck driver. They had to hoist it on a flatbed, I remember that. That goddamn thang already looked crushed to me. Stupidest purchase I ever saw."

"Did you happen to record the name of the man or his company that came for it?"

"I did not. But I made him show me the receipt I gave that old jackass. I run a proper place here, officer. I don't just let people come on site and drag shit away."

"I'm sure you don't, ma'am. Well, thank you for your time, you've been most helpful."

"Was that old buzzard a criminal? Because he didn't match the profile if you get my drift."

"Well, you know how it is," Ron replied, with a twinge of irony that was lost on Sammy's unsuspecting wife. "People aren't always what they seem."

⚛⚛⚛

Paul Ravich did not take the news well.

Ron waited until the end of a long day, almost 6:30, before slowly walking down the hall to knock on Ravich's door. Ben Argent and the last of the *SeaCoast* plaintiffs had left an hour before. Ron watched them exit, then lingered in the firm's library until the last of the firm's associates, assistants, and staff members decided to call it quits for the evening. Ravich was expecting an update on the car. When the offices were empty, they could talk. Ron knew his boss wasn't going anywhere until they spoke.

"Greenbaum's got the car," Ron said, getting directly to the point as he entered Ravich's office. He was a firm believer in the notion that bad news grows worse when buried under bullshit.

Ravich didn't even try to hide his shock. He closed his eyes tightly and squeezed his facial muscles so taut he looked like the victim of a bad facelift. He pounded his fists on his cherry-wood desk and began taking deep breaths, almost to the point of hyperventilating. The man who could handle anything and anybody looked like he was about to cry.

Pussy, thought Ron. *He wouldn't have lasted a day in Delta Force.*

Finally, Ravich got a loose grip on himself, sighed one more time, then asked: "What do we do now?"

"There's not much we can do except have faith in my work. The demolition appears to have gone as planned. If so, it didn't leave a trace. He can't prove anything with that car except that it was in a very bad wreck."

"Then why did he acquire it?" Ravich began raising his voice and his final words were practically shouted as he stood up from his desk and marched around the room. "Maybe he was just looking for a fixer-upper, is that what you're going to tell me next?"

Ravich was coming unglued. *Stupid*, Ron thought. The cleaning people would be in soon. He needed to keep his voice down.

"He probably just wanted someone to take a look, to try and determine why the driver lost control. Maybe he suspected Finnegan used that

402

crowbar in his briefcase to monkey with things. Bottom line, there's nothing to tie that car to us. So chill out."

Ravich looked at his investigator demonically and took two steps toward him.

"Did you just tell *me* to chill out?" he said, as if scolding a back-talking child.

"Yeah, chill-the-fuck-out." Ron enunciated each word slowly and calmly, making clear he was in control. "Grace under fire keeps you alive. Panic gets you killed."

Ravich scoffed. "Spare me your commando catch-phrases, asshole. The only reason anyone's upset is because you didn't do your job."

Ron covered the remaining distance between them with three menacing steps toward his boss. He was angry at the remark and Ravich knew it. The big tough lawyer leaned back submissively when Ron got in his face.

Ron jabbed his index finger in Ravich's chest. "Then do yours," was all he said, punctuating the three words with taps of his finger against Ravich's sternum.

Paul Ravich wasn't sure what his investigator meant by those words but he needed to regain the upper hand. He wasn't going to do it with physicality or rants. He decided instead to rely upon his best weapon: his brain.

"Okay, look Ron, I'm sorry. But this screwup could blow everything. We have to come up with a plan."

Ron backed off. He had made his point. Ravich could remain a bully to others but no longer to him.

"That's my plan," Ron replied calmly. "Do - Your - Job. Get this *SeaCoast* case settled and all the other questions melt away. Give that Greenbaum guy and his client some of the money if you have to. Pay me first what you still owe me, then buy them off. Put us all to bed, Paul. People whose problems have been addressed don't keep knocking on doors looking for answers. It's just that simple."

"Look, I'll have your additional money to you by midweek. This isn't about my trying to hang on to cash. It's about our trying to stay out of jail."

Ron nodded in agreement.

"I'll have a settlement with Integrated Sentry and VyStream within thirty days." Ravich assured. "I know exactly what I need to do to make that happen."

"Good," Ron replied. He was glad to see that his boss was thinking clearly again.

"The problem will be with Harry. He's a fool but a tenacious one. If he thinks he's on to something, he might be harder to buy off."

"We all have our price. You and I have already proved that in this case. Find his number and pay it."

Ron turned to leave.

Ravich called out to his back.

"Okay, but in the meantime, can you do anything to quietly find out what he does and doesn't know?"

Ron stopped in his tracks and turned back around.

"I already know he doesn't know shit," he replied, matter-of-factly.

"How can you be so sure?" Ravich asked, hoping to hear something comforting.

Ron smirked. "Because we're not in handcuffs right now. Goodnight, Paul."

With that, the man who was not afraid of him — the murderous commando, the mistake-making investigator, the threatening co-conspirator — disappeared quickly down the unlit hall, leaving Paul Ravich alone with his thoughts and fears.

———— ⟨∞⟩ ————

Bonnie dubbed the document summons, served in the unrelated case, "the sneaky subpoena." Three days after he issued it, Bill Gaston received a call from the Office of Building Security at the sixty-three story tower where the law offices of Paul Ravich & Associates were located.

An assistant security manager held the legal document in his hand. It called for the immediate production of very specific records but he had both questions and concerns. He didn't want to get himself or his building owner in any trouble with some court.

"Mr. Gaston, I've been assigned to comply with this subpoena we got served with, but first will you tell us why you need this information?"

"Sure." Being a fast-thinker came in handy. Gaston decided to freewheel. "It's just a routine civil case, a squabble between a couple of companies over a claim of exchanging trade secrets. We need those specific enumerated records from your security files to rule out or confirm a late night meeting that allegedly took place on the evening of October 24th at your building. We don't know if this meeting even took place or, if it did, in which tenant space. We're just going on a reliable tip. So, it's really no big deal and certainly not anything that puts you or your security team in any hot water."

"Okay, I understand," the man responded, although Gaston's vague explanation was intended to stifle full comprehension. The security man next sought clarification. "Now this subpoena only seeks access records and surveillance photos for the time period from 9:00 p.m. on the night of October 24th to 3:00 a.m. on the 25th . Is that correct?"

"Precisely," Gaston confirmed. "That six hour window is when our tipster said this meeting might have occurred," he added with a liar's flourish.

In truth, the time frame was derived through a quick call by Harry to Joan Slator to get her best recollection of when her husband left the house that night, and by applying the time noted on the fatal accident report. Those sources revealed that the true window of opportunity was actually from 11 p.m. to 1:00 a.m. but Gaston added extra padding on each side just to be safe.

"All right," the helpful security man said. "Well, I've reviewed our security camera archives for that time period. We have digital cameras above all our building entrances and also at the garage entry-exit. During the day, we monitor a continuous video feed at the security desk, looking for signs of trouble. After regular business hours, these things are strictly motion activated to record images of any person entering the building and of any vehicles entering or leaving the garage at night."

"Sounds good," Gaston replied.

"Well, here's the problem: our building entrance cameras show no pedestrian entry activity during your time frame except by our security personnel. We also have four levels of tower entry from within the parking garage, each equipped with a similar camera. Three out of those four show no entries."

"What about the fourth?" Bill said, asking the obvious question.

"That's what's strange," the security director replied. "The camera stationed at the building entrance on Level 3 stopped transmitting signals sometime after six-thirty that night. The garage entry-exit camera also malfunctioned around that time, so we have no photos of any vehicles that might have come through the garage during your time period. We didn't discover these problems until the following day. Our service technicians found that both cameras had shorted out and we got them back online fairly quickly. But because of the power glitch, I've got no pictures during your requested time to show if someone entered our garage or came into our building through Level 3 of the parking structure. I'm sorry."

Gaston absorbed it all with a clear sense of suspicion, bred from the continuing chain of curious events surrounding Ken Slator.

"Maybe someone tampered with those cameras," Gaston ventured. "Do their last recorded images show anyone standing nearby?"

"No, I checked."

"Could someone get at the camera wires without stepping into the lens' range of vision?"

"I hadn't thought about that but I guess it could be done. The work order, though, shows no wires were cut. The service team wrote it up as a strong power surge so I doubt anyone was messing with them."

The assistant security manager was starting to enjoy this subpoena assignment. "But if somebody intentionally put those things out of commission, your trade secrets must be pretty important."

"Yeah, life and death to some of us," Bill said with his usual wit.

"I was able, however, to print out our access card log for that night. I see that you also asked for that. Most people don't even know that we can generate those."

The talkative security man obviously wanted to help or perhaps he thought he had no choice. Gaston was amazed by the effect a subpoena sometimes had on laypersons. Even a camouflaged subpoena, issued in a random case that had nothing at all to do with trade secrets or the *SeaCoast* matter, was yielding clues.

"Now these cards are identifiable only by tenant, not by individual employees. But, falling within your search times, we did have some very limited activity at the garage entrance and exit sensors, and also at the Level 3 building-entrance swipe pad."

Gaston's pulse quickened. "Well, that's pretty interesting. What can you tell from that log?"

"Three different cards were used to gain ingress and egress from the garage and the building between the hours of 10:05 p.m. and 1:25 a.m. on the night in question."

"I see," Gaston replied, barely able to remain calm.

"Do you think your trade secrets meeting might have taken place in a lawyer's office?" the security man asked.

"That would certainly make sense," Gaston answered, realizing his quickly imagined explanation for the subpoena was holding up nicely.

"Because all three cards, based upon their registered and unique ID numbers, were assigned to our penthouse tenant, the law firm of Paul Ravich & Associates."

Gaston barely held on to the phone.

The caller's confusion about the process for responding to a subpoena continued to show.

"So, do you need copies of these records? And, if so, do you want to pick them up or am I supposed to file them with the court that's listed on this paper? I really don't know how any of this is supposed to work. We've never gotten a request like this before."

"I'll stop by this afternoon for a copy of those log records. I don't want you to go to any more trouble than you already have."

"It's no trouble. Just tell the security desk at the main lobby to radio me. My name's Charles Wooten. I'll bring the records down to you."

"Thanks. You're a prince, Charles," Gaston remarked, his corny sense of humor lost on his caller.

"No problem. I'm learning a lot from this. I actually once thought about going to law school myself. Sounds like you get some pretty interesting cases, huh?"

"If you only knew," Gaston replied, now glad to be speaking honestly to the helpful man.

"Would you like me to make some inquiries with that particular tenant? Maybe they could help you with the identities of those access card holders."

"No!" Gaston almost shouted, before quickly regaining his cool. "No, that's nice of you, but it won't be necessary." Gaston scrambled for an excuse and came up with a doozy. "That firm is actually working on our side of this case. We'll just talk to them directly about it. More I think about it now, our tipster sounded a little bit flakey. Now that I know he was only referring to our colleagues, I realize there's probably nothing to worry about."

"Well, that's good. See you this afternoon."

"You got it. And thanks again for your help."

Bill Gaston hung up the phone, his heart racing. He had ended his mostly deceptive conversation by telling the biggest lie of all.

In truth, there was *plenty* to worry about it. The "sneaky subpoena" had just confirmed that two people from Ravich's office — most likely the man himself and his bomb-making investigator — had the opportunity, along with both motive and means, to commit murder.

―――∞――

Late in the day, back in the war room, Bill Gaston sat at the table with a copy of the access card log records in front of him.

"So we have to conclude that Ron Carroll planted the bomb while Slator's car was parked in the garage," he explained, pointing to the three entrance and exit times reflected in the log.

The entire team was present and everyone was now convinced that Ravich's investigator had committed the crime. It all fit: the garage entries, the conveniently disabled security cameras, a cleverly disguised car bomb, his bomb-making skills, the time chronology. The clues were simply not consistent with any claim of innocence on his part.

"And obviously, Mr. Slator couldn't be allowed to stand around and watch his car being tampered with," Doug added. "So he needed to be kept inside the building for a sufficient length of time. We know that three people entered and exited at that Level 3 building entrance. Slator is clearly one of those three."

"And where did he go?" Harry asked, knowing the answer but wanting to keep the logic string unfurling.

"To Ravich's offices," Bonnie responded. "It had to be. The security guy at the ground floor lobby never saw him or there would have been a record. So Mr. Slator went *up* the building elevators from Level 3, not down."

"Good point," Harry replied, giving Bonnie credit for the deduction. "And up, of course, is where Ravich's offices are. The third access card used that night also belonged to his firm. There would need to be someone in those offices to keep Mr. Slator occupied, someone who was coordinating somehow with Ron Carroll down in the garage. So, who was our mystery babysitter?" Harry held up his index finger as a *voila* gesture. "Who else but Ravich could compel this witness to attend so late a meeting? Who else could be trusted to be a knowing diversionary while the bomb was being installed?"

The four looked at each other and paused. Everyone recognized the powerful impact of their analysis. Harry resumed the discussion.

"Logic tells us there is no other employee of that firm, other than Ravich himself, who would have the motive or temerity to participate in this sordid affair. But in a criminal prosecution, you must offer more than just logical conjecture. We need further evidence, people. Right now, with what we assembled, Paul Ravich would beat a murder conspiracy charge, if the DA could even be persuaded to bring charges."

"What's missing?" Bonnie asked.

"Several things," Harry replied. "For one, it would help if we could prove exactly what Mr. Slator knew that got him killed. Right now, we're only guessing it was evidence that Ravich didn't like. But if we can *prove* conclusively that it was something Ravich had to conceal, at any cost, in order to derive substantial benefit for himself, then we become solid accusers rather than mere speculators."

"Where do we get that information?" Doug asked.

"I'm still working on it," Harry said, before moving on to the next item in his thought process. "We could also use some direct evidence that places both murderers in that garage and building. Placing the victim there is easy. We still have the access card he used, and it's encoded number matches one of the three in the log record that we've obtained. But we don't have the cards belonging to the bad guys, nor do we have other *direct* proof of their presence. They apparently realized how critical such evidence would be.

They went to considerable lengths to make sure nobody saw them. Our case for their actual presence is weak and circumstantial."

Bonnie threw out a thought. "How about fingerprints on the door?"

"I'm afraid not," Harry replied gently, not wanting to hurt her feelings too much. "The Level 3 entrance door is touched by hundreds of tenants legitimately each day, perhaps even by Ravich and Ron. Both men's prints would also be properly present on the doors of their offices; after all, they pass through them routinely. And no print says when it was left."

"Somebody must have seen them driving up to the building or driving in," Doug remarked. "Even at that hour, a few people are still on the street downtown."

"True, but why would a passerby recall something as commonplace as a car entering a building garage?" Harry countered.

"What kind of cars do our suspects drive?" Gaston suddenly asked.

"I could ask a young lawyer at my office if he knows," Harry offered. "This fellow, Trey, who I recently hired, used to work for them."

Doug didn't see the purpose. "What good would that information do?"

Bill Gaston made his Popeye face. Doug knew what the comical, squinty look meant. He had seen it too many times. *Gaston was thinking, hard.*

After a few seconds, his friend reopened his eyes and relaxed his tightly drawn cheeks, only to make an announcement to his team.

"Harry, keep your man Trey on standby." He raised his eyebrows and made a coy smile. "I've got an idea."

The turbulence created by the revelation that Harry Greenbaum had custody of the death car rocked what was supposed to be a smooth flight to riches, causing the pilot to change course and fly faster. Paul Ravich was declaring an emergency and needed to get his half-billion dollar airplane safely on the ground before it broke apart in midair.

Ben Argent took the distress call.

"What can I do for you, Paul?" he asked.

"I'm filing a Motion for Preferential Setting today. I'm asking that the *Seacoast* case be tried the first week of February. Just calling to see if you have objections to my request."

"Are you kidding me? This case isn't near ready for trial and it won't be by then either. We have tons of discovery left to do."

"I thought you might say that. Haven't you defense lawyers ever heard that justice delayed is justice denied?"

"Come on, Paul. Even if this were a little case, it takes more than three months to get ready. The fact that it's a huge one means it will take far longer."

"That's where we disagree, Ben. It's not the number of zeros that matter, it's the facts in dispute. And you guys don't have a lot to argue."

"Well, we're opposed to your motion."

"That's too bad because I'm confident Judge Lewis won't be."

Ravich was flexing his muscles, displaying his strong connections. Argent knew that the Judge would give his rich plaintiff-lawyer pal anything he asked for.

"I gather this means you are no longer interested in a settlement of the case?" Argent asked, still curious about his opponent's sudden change of strategy.

Ravich smiled at the question. February might be too late. His request for a prompt trial setting was merely an attempt to force the third-party defendants to come to the bargaining table *now*.

"I'm always willing to talk. You know that, Ben. But at least now we can all assume that the time for talking is going to be short."

"I'll call Schiller and get his thoughts," Argent replied.

"You do that."

"Paul, our people have looked at this DCSS backup data of yours. I'd like to depose the plant manager who had custody of it. What's his name again?"

"It *was* Ken Slator."

"What?" Argent replied, confused.

"Mr. Slator was killed in a freeway wreck ten days or so after the plant disaster. He turned the evidence over to us some days before and we were planning, of course, to use him as our star witness. But what can you do?"

Argent suddenly remembered Harry's question at the deposition of Rob Finnegan; something about a wrecked car. He had forgotten to ask any follow-up questions when he had the chance.

"Then how are you going to prove those records up?"

"I have the man's sworn affidavit attesting that the laptop data was a proper *SeaCoast* business record. He gave it, obviously, prior to his unfortunate demise. I can assure you that Judge Lewis will have no problem admitting those records into evidence."

"And you're going to explain them solely through your retained experts?"

"Primarily. Of course, Al Harris, the surviving assistant manager, can also help the jury understand what poor Dave Phillips must have been going through when those confusing readings started to bounce across his screen."

410

"We already deposed Harris. He didn't appear to know all that much."

"Oh, he knows enough to swear that this data from Integrated Sentry's defective program would have also lulled him into thinking that nothing was wrong." Ravich paused to let Argent accept the certainty of that prediction. "That, and a little expert testimony, is all I'll need to sink your ship."

Argent knew that was true so he changed subjects. "How firm are you going to be in your settlement demand?"

Ravich leaned back in his chair, beaming. He had accomplished the phone call's mission. Settlement talks were about to begin in earnest.

"Firmer than Jello, softer than rock," Ravich teased cryptically. "Give me a call back soon and maybe I'll save your clients a little money and you the embarrassment of a record adverse verdict."

Argent hated the man. Everything was a game to Paul Ravich. Still, he owed a duty to his clients. He knew their ass was in a sling.

"I'll see if Schiller wants to talk. If so, you can do so directly with him."

"That will be fine. Thanks for your time today, Ben. Bye now."

The plaintiffs' lawyer hung up, suddenly feeling better about things. He might wrap up his case in one fell swoop and, by so doing, also put an end to Harry Greenbaum's dangerous inquiries. If he could get the third-party defendants to pay hundreds of millions and stop asking questions, he could easily get the *Crouch* lawyers to accept an undeserved small chunk of that and move on as well. It would have to be more money than was offered to Harry down at the Barrister's Club but surely not much more. Ron was right. He only needed to find Harry's number and pay it.

Ravich decided the *Crouch* lawyers might first need a strong incentive of their own to think about settling their case. He smiled. He had the legal equivalent of a cattle-prod. His Motion for Summary Judgment could be filed at any time and a prompt hearing on it could be requested. A fear of seeing their case against SeaCoast thrown summarily out of court would send Doug and Harry scrambling back to his bargaining table.

Things weren't so disastrous after all. Like that pilot who brought a wounded jet safely to a stop on the Hudson River, Paul Ravich was confident that, with his skills, he too could still make a big splash and a successful emergency landing with the biggest case of his career.

Chapter 21
Dispositions

In sumo wrestling, the competitors engage in a series of pre-match rituals. There is hand-clapping and leg-stomping. There is salt-throwing and stare-downs. The huge men assume menacing fixed positions while opening their hands wide to reveal they are fighting fairly. They spring from their crouch but almost never engage on the first occasion. They retreat from the ring for more mental preparation. They throw more salt, then step back into the ring. They crouch; they stare. They rise; they retreat again. The process repeats. When both sets of fists finally touch the mat at the same time, the wrestlers charge. They push; they shove. The actual physical contact often ends quickly. When it's over, the participants bow to each other, signifying respect.

Negotiating the settlement of a major civil case is a sumo match.

Parties and their lawyers toss out fixed positions as freely as flinging salt. It means nothing; it is just for show. Grandstanding follows: they too must stomp and sway. Each side tries to maintain an intractable countenance while speaking of compromise. They walk away from negotiations, then return. They repeat the process through phone calls, meetings, and mediations. At some point, the rituals cease and the parties engage. They make strategic pushes, shoves and, most times, an outcome is finally reached. A settlement agreement is signed. The case is dismissed and money is exchanged for a release and a meaningless mutual declaration in writing that no one is the victor. It is the legal equivalent of bowing to your opponent.

A fierce match was about to commence between two of the country's strongest legal-wrestlers. They would meet privately in Manhattan to discuss the *SeaCoast* case. Paul Ravich had accepted Dean Schiller's invitation to "fly up for the weekend, bring your wife, take in some shows;

then, let's you and I talk alone on Monday."

Behind closed doors, they could dispense with some of the pre-fight rituals. There would be no clients, no co-counsel, no insurance representatives, no general counsels, no mediator. Their match would have no audience. That way, they could get straight to the push and shove.

Their dohyo, the sumo ring, was a hospitality suite at the Waldorf-Astoria. Dean Schiller booked the room knowing that peace talks require a neutral setting. His office, like Ravich's, was no place to make a deal. Schiller sat at the table in the elegant suite and looked at his watch. Arriving late for the afternoon meeting would be a bad sign. They had promised each other no games would be played.

Ravich knocked on the door a mere three minutes after the appointed time. This was New York; that was considered punctual. Schiller rose to let him in. He hung a "Do Not Disturb" sign on the door as he closed it behind his guest.

"I'm having a drink before we get down to business," Schiller announced, as he made his way to a fully stocked bar sitting atop an antique credenza. "Want one?"

Ravich smiled. He was being spoken to like a call girl: *We can screw later, let's have a drink first.*

"Single malt, neat, would be great," Ravich replied.

Schiller fished among the bottles, finding an eighteen year-old Macallan. He reached for two cut-crystal lowball glasses, filled them unequally, then handed Ravich the more generous pour.

"Let's sit over here," he suggested, grabbing his glass and gesturing toward two large easy chairs that sat on either side of a coffee table adorned with burl-wood inlays. "If we get to the paper and pencil stage, we can move over to the conference table."

"Sounds good," Ravich replied, as he followed his host. He was being treated like the hooker in *Pretty Woman,* with class and respect. He almost burst out laughing.

"Are you enjoying the City?" Schiller asked after he sat, sounding like the hotel's concierge.

"I could take it or leave it," Ravich replied curtly, as he settled into his chair. He thought a noncommittal statement was a good way to begin their settlement conversation. He also wanted to make clear that New York, its fancy hotels, and especially its lawyers, weren't particularly impressive to him.

"Well, then, let's not keep you here too long," Schiller said, downing his scotch. It was a striking gulp. His lowball glass had been a third full. He sat the glass down, hard, on the expensive table. "We're prepared to make you an offer."

Ravich took a tiny sip of his drink. It was a signal that he had all the time in the world.

"I insisted we meet alone because I'm going to start off by saying something I couldn't say in the presence of clients: You're not going to accept this first offer but I have to present it anyway. *Capisce?*"

Ravich nodded with a grin. He was starting to like Dean Schiller's style, even finding his use of hokey mob dialogue to be an interesting way to imply they weren't going to be negotiating by the book.

"Integrated Sentry will make an immediate payment of one hundred fifty-million dollars — the limits of all their insurance — which you can apportion as you see fit, by and among your death claim clients and SeaCoast Chemical, in exchange for full releases from all."

Schiller recited the terms as if they were words to be quickly ignored, like the boilerplate in an apartment lease. He paused, waiting for the appropriate response.

"I hereby decline your offer," Ravich said, in the flat tone that Schiller was expecting. "Oh, and before we move past this perfunctory stuff, you need to know that I won't put myself in the conflict position of deciding how to split a cumulative offer between my people and SeaCoast. From here on out, you need to offer the death plaintiffs a set sum that is separate from any amount you put on the table for the property damage case."

Schiller was surprised to hear Ravich express a legitimate ethical concern. It was contrary to everything he had been told about the way this plaintiff lawyer operated.

"Fair enough. Why don't we just agree on a figure right now for the death cases and be done with it?"

"I've given you a fair demand: $7.5 million per family."

"Will you take less? Would you consider five?"

Ravich wrinkled his nose and took another sip of scotch. He twisted the upheld glass in his hand.

"Really, Dean? You want to horse-trade on the most insignificant part of this case? Would you like me to counter with seven and we haggle it to six? Because if we're going to do that shit on the little stuff, there's not enough scotch over there to get us through a similar back-and-forth on the much bigger claim of SeaCoast Chemical."

"Throw me a bone, Paul, and we'll move on to other things. I understand that SeaCoast has already paid those people a sizable amount voluntarily. If my information is correct, they got two-million per family, free and clear. Knock that dollar amount off your per-family demand and we have a deal. I will pay $5.5 million whereas Seacoast has already paid them two. That equals $7.5 in combined recovery for each of your families, which is *exactly* the amount of your verdict estimate and demand."

Ravich couldn't really argue with such logic except that he needed to; not for the families — he couldn't care less — but to preserve his image as someone who would not be easy to deal with later when it came to the big stuff.

He paused to consider how best to counter the newest offer. Schiller wouldn't have to wait long. Ravich's mind was quick. He suddenly realized there might be a way to squeeze a little more out of Schiller's clients while also aiding his plan to get rid of the *Crouch* case and its meddlesome lawyers.

Before he left for New York, Ravich instructed his staff to file, first thing this Monday morning, the summary judgment motion he had prepared. That meant Doug Stevens was probably reading the dismissal motion right now for the first time. With Judge Lewis making the ruling, the threat of seeing their case against SeaCoast thrown out for lack of evidence would be quite real to Harry's little band of lawyers. Ravich could now make another pitch to them which they would be fools to refuse. While he would like to see them get nothing — which was the original purpose of filing for summary judgment — the sudden appearance of Harry Greenbaum going through his garbage made an alternative disposition strategy worth considering. Like Ron had suggested, maybe it was better if the people on his trail were bought off and thereby freely abandoned their efforts. Maybe it was better to get them some money instead of giving them grief. If so, the cash might as well come from someone else's pocket.

"Tell you what," Ravich began, looking over at Schiller. "I need a little bone too. Make it six for my death-action clients, along with a contractual set-aside of five million for that Crouch widow who I don't represent. I'll get her lawyers to release you for that and then you're officially done with everyone."

"That plaintiff hasn't even sued us," Schiller said in dismay, as if Ravich had upped the ante with a ridiculous add-on. "Why would my clients pay her anything?"

Ravich now put his scotch glass down, hard, on the table.

"Goddamnit, Dean, we agreed not to jerk each other's chains here today. Don't ask me stupid questions when you already know the answer. The very second you pay my plaintiffs, the *Crouch* lawyers are going to amend their pleadings and add your companies as defendants. They'll have to. It would be malpractice if they didn't. I'm just trying to bring finality for everyone. And I'm discounting my people's cases in order to accomplish that for you."

Schiller privately respected the tactic. When negotiations begin to stall on money amounts, switching to other considerations is a good way to allow a lesser opponent to forget where his last offer stood. *But I'm not the lesser one here,* Schiller thought, his ego still not willing to give Paul Ravich equal billing. He sensed that perhaps Ravich wanted the *Crouch* case settled even more than he wanted to win this first settlement skirmish. So he tested the theory.

"I'll go five million across the board. Your five clients and the Crouch woman, thirty-million total. That's my final offer, but if you can't secure her release, your folks can still get their twenty-five."

Ravich realized then he was not dealing with the typical defense lawyer, someone he could manipulate at will. Schiller had called his bluff while also managing to take some previously tossed chips off the table. Ordinarily, Ravich would say: *"Go fuck yourself"* but he needed the *Crouch* case to go away.

Ron's carelessness and Harry's diligence had just cost him $2.5 million, maybe even twice that, that he could have held out for in the death cases. Considering a third of that lost money would have been his fee, that car of Slator's was getting pretty damn expensive.

He shook his head and bit his lip. He had no better option.

"It's a deal," he said, only to watch Dean Schiller make the kind of smirk that Ravich considered his own trademark.

In match number one, the New York sumo master had prevailed. Ravich briefly lost his grip, worrying about his crimes, and was tossed from the wrestling dohyo in defeat. But the bigger contest — how to settle the SeaCoast property damage case — remained. Paul Ravich was determined not to be pushed out of the ring on that one.

It was an earthquake masquerading as a five-page legal motion.

Doug sat reading Ravich's Motion for Summary Judgment, but his shock and anger blurred the key words:

"The pleadings, depositions, and discovery conclusively demonstrate there is no genuine issue of material fact that could support a verdict in favor of the plaintiff on a claim of gross negligence. Accordingly, defendant SeaCoast Chemical Corporation is entitled to summary judgment as a matter of law, and the plaintiff's case should be dismissed."

The pleading was hand-delivered on Monday morning to Kate Crouch's attorney-of-record. It was accompanied by a Notice of Hearing stating that Judge Lewis would hear oral argument in ten days on

SeaCoast's request to throw Kate Crouch out of court. With the Judge deeply in Ravich's pocket, the hearing would be a mere formality, the outcome certain: the good guys would lose.

In panic, Doug quickly considered what could be done. Bill Gaston was a scholarly writer; he could help draft an appropriate response and get it filed. Harry Greenbaum was an effective speaker in court; he could argue to Judge Lewis there was still discovery to be conducted and that gross negligence might still be provable. Doug would then be left to explain things to his client, including informing the poor widow that this particular judge would probably not bother to read, or listen to, anything coming from them. He was Ravich's bought-buddy, the Judge would do anything for him. The thought only made his panic worse.

When Doug called Harry with the news, his mentor counseled him to remain calm, pointing out that the deposition testimony of Al Harris, the defendant's employee, revealed that SeaCoast had withheld requested documents which might still prove their case. "Even Judge Lewis might be offended by that kind of discovery abuse," Harry had said. *Maybe not,* Doug recalled thinking pessimistically.

His subsequent conversations with Bill and Bonnie did little to alleviate his fear. Their assurances that Ravich "can't get away with this" were meant to comfort but Doug knew the phrase was hollow. It's the same thing people say when a bank forecloses on their home, and they're wrong too. Those with the power — whether obtained by mortgage contract or by bribing a judge — end up getting what they want.

Later that evening, Doug went over to Sarah's place for dinner but his mood was sullen, his appetite sparse. She could tell something was wrong. He really didn't want to talk about it. He had already spent the entire day feeling sorry for himself and for Kate Crouch. But Sarah pressed and he finally told her. Their relationship had grown to the point where his troubles were hers.

She listened with growing rage. She now hated Paul Ravich and everything about him, especially his arrogance and corrupt connections.

"He won't get away with it," Sarah said, stroking her boyfriend's forehead, trying to relax him.

That's what they all say, Doug thought to himself, choosing not to utter the words out loud. It would be wrong to belittle her attempt to comfort.

What he didn't realize in his defeated and depressed state was that her word of negation was slightly stronger, a little more certain, than what Bill and Bonnie had said back at the office. The word "won't" is subtly more definitive than "can't."

His troubles were hers. Hers would soon help his.

—∞∞—

"Shall we toast this fine accord on behalf of the deceased?" Dean Schiller asked, as he reached for his empty scotch glass.

"No, thanks, let's keep working."

Ravich was in no celebratory mood. He had been bested in the negotiations over the death claims. It wasn't much of a defeat, certainly not from a money standpoint, but he wasn't used to losing at anything, whether large or small. Harry Greenbaum, doing detective work, had weakened his hand and forced him to compromise. He now badly needed to reassert his strong bargaining position. *Forget Harry and the death plaintiffs,* he told himself. *This is about the Big Sell: your perfectly created case for SeaCoast.* Ravich could accept defeat in a small battle costing him less than a million or two in additional fee. But he was not about to lose his war for a one hundred-million dollar windfall. He would be firm in his demand on the SeaCoast property damage case.

Dean Schiller, a veteran of large case negotiations, realized that landing the first punch seldom meant a knockout. A fighter like Ravich, a lawyer who rarely lost in court and to whom a few million was throw-around money, was not going down easy. If anything, Schiller's quick trimming of millions off the settlement demand in the death cases would probably mean that Ravich would come back swinging wildly. This second round of negotiations would not be a sumo match, it would be a bar fight.

Schiller clapped his hands together. "Okay then, let's keep rolling. Why don't we move over there?"

He rose from his easy chair and began walking to the small conference table at the back of the hospitality suite. Ravich followed. The shift carried symbolism. A bigger battle requires a larger battlefield.

Schiller chose a very specific chair. Pulling it out from the table revealed two notebooks resting on its seat. He picked them up and tossed both on the conference table before sitting down. Ravich sat across from him, leaning back. His posture was saying: *Bring it on.*

Schiller slid one of the notebooks across to him.

"Paul, these are analyses of SeaCoast's property damage claims. They were compiled by our factory construction experts and our forensic accountants. You will find them quite detailed."

Ravich leaned forward and began thumbing through the number-filled pages.

"While we intend to contest the liability vigorously, and believe we can convince a jury that we owe nothing, I had this work-up prepared to demonstrate to you that even if things go your way on fault, your damage projections are nowhere near accurate."

Ravich closed the notebook. He wasn't about to appear concerned.

"Look, Dean, let's you and I continue talking to each other like a couple of pros, all right? First of all, you have no intention of trying this case. Our just concluded settlement of the death claims makes that clear. Second, if you did foolishly choose to go to trial on only the SeaCoast damage claim, the liability evidence is so strong that by the time my jury gets to a consideration of damages they are not going to be inclined to even look at, much less accept, your numbers."

Schiller returned a perplexed look. He didn't see the point that Ravich was trying to make.

"Ever try a red-light case, Dean?"

Schiller smirked at the off-topic question and shook his head no.

"Well, they're instructive here. You see, when you have an eyewitness testify he saw the defendant run the red light and hit the plaintiff's car at high speed, the jury makes up their mind pretty quick that the defendant should pay. They don't seem to like it much when the wrongdoer spends time in court arguing: 'no big deal, you're not hurt too bad.' For some reason — let's call it a basic shared sense that folks should accept responsibility for their actions — juries tend to award more, not less, when a defendant tries to minimize the consequences of their bad conduct."

Schiller grinned.

"Thanks for that practice tip, Paul. If I ever go back to trying petty car wreck cases, I'll keep that in mind. But this is something different. Average people aren't used to seeing somebody hold their hand out for a half-billion dollars. Most people don't even know how many zeros are in that number. It's an absurdly huge figure. And when those hands are big companies like SeaCoast and Thornton Industries it can even appear offensive to those 'little people' that you like to put on your juries."

Ravich smiled back.

"If that will be your damage control strategy, I need to leave now and buy a bigger private jet to fly home on. I guarantee that your argument along the lines of *we did so much harm you can't add up the numbers* will fall on deaf ears in that courtroom and only make me mega-rich."

Schiller decided not to volley back. They could both keep at this for hours. It's what good trial lawyers do. When negotiating, it's important to point out that nothing the other side says ever makes any sense.

"Why don't we just look at the numbers?" Schiller suggested. "See how far apart we are."

"Why don't you just tell me?" Ravich shot back, intending to maintain a stubborn tone.

"If you prefer," Schiller calmly replied.

He then proceeded to outline various evaluation differences — the depreciated values, the cost of replacement and rebuild, the value of unsold inventory, the speculative nature of future lost contracts — before concluding that the real damage figure was more in the neighborhood of $350 million.

"Is that what you're prepared to offer my corporate client?" Ravich asked, when Schiller stopped talking.

"Well, no, I think that's the figure we should attempt to negotiate from."

Ravich stood up to leave. "Thanks for the drink, then. I'll see you at trial in February. If you want to take back our death claims settlement, you can do that too. Nothing's in writing yet."

It was the biggest bluff of his career. Ravich started walking toward the door.

"Paul, sit back down." Schiller called out his request in a tone that was halfway between "you're being silly" and "we still have things to discuss."

Ravich stopped and turned around.

Schiller needed to make a point. "Look, I'm sure there are some defense counsel in your little town that shake in their boots when you threaten to try your case, but I'm not one of those and you know that. Did you really think I would simply sit here and pay your demand in full?"

Ravich broke character and laughed. "That's what I'd do if I was in your boots," he replied, drawing a similar chuckle from his opponent.

The laughter diffused the tension and negated the need to call the bluff.

"Let's talk some more and see where the gap really is," Schiller proposed.

If it were a smaller case, if he didn't have crimes to conceal, he would have said "no thanks" and left. But this was his biggest case and it was built upon bigger fiction. More time for others to investigate is never the ally of a criminal. Only a binding settlement and payments to the plaintiffs, including Kate Crouch, would end all searches for the truth.

He sat back down.

Schiller wasted no time. "We can offer $300 million for a release from SeaCoast and Thornton."

"Can't do it," Ravich responded without hesitation. "And you wouldn't either if you had my case."

"Paul, this isn't strictly about wanting to beat you up, although I'd like to. Integrated Sentry has no liquid assets to speak of. They can only contribute five million or so from their books to this settlement. The rest has to come from VyStream. They, of course, have the money but their large size is actually your nemesis here. It seems their Board of Directors would rather pay my outrageous fees and risk five hundred-million at trial as opposed to rolling over and paying something higher than four."

The new number was not lost on Paul Ravich. He also knew that Dean Schiller was too savvy to have let it accidentally slip.

"Okay, how's this? I'll recommend that SeaCoast accept your immediate cash payment of four hundred million, provided VyStream also makes additional guaranteed payments of ten million per year for ten years, with the first installment due one year after our settlement agreement is executed."

"That's no compromise at all," Schiller replied. "You're still getting five hundred-million in the end."

"Time is money, my friend. The VyStream Board knows that. Investment return on the parceled hundred million will generate those additional payments without reducing the principal I saved you. In short, it's no sweat off them. Plus, to VyStream, a ten-million dollar annual check is equivalent to you and me paying a monthly utility bill. It won't affect their operations or share price."

"Structuring payments over time as part of this settlement gets tricky, though," Schiller remarked, somewhat intrigued by the idea. "For instance, how do you account for your fee?"

"It's kind of you to think of me, Dean. I appreciate it. Again, time is money. A simple actuarial calculation will show the present value of your future payments. Seacoast will either pay me my cut of that present value out of their cash up front, or maybe I decide to get my twenty percent from those annual checks when they arrive. Pay me now or pay me later, I don't care. Later might even be better. It's always good to have some 'mailbox money' coming in as you grow older."

Schiller hadn't known the details of Ravich's contingent fee contract with Thornton Industries and SeaCoast.

"You got them to pay you twenty percent? Nice going. Maybe you and I should become partners after this case is over," he teased.

"It would never work out," Ravich joked back. "When two people are exactly alike, no marriage can survive."

They both laughed, appreciating the decision to meet privately. Complimenting one another on how much money they were extracting from this litigation was not a conversation that could be had if their clients were in the room.

"I need another bone," Schiller said suddenly, returning to a more serious tone.

"You're an awfully hungry dog, Dean."

"I have to earn my high fee too. You told us during that flashy case presentation in your office that the property damage claim was worth a minimum of $460 million, if my memory serves correctly. I'm pretty sure that's the figure you pointed out in that pretty leather booklet you distributed to us."

"That's right, that's the *minimum* damage calculation. I will give the jury that number along with a middle and high estimate. Guess which one they'll pick? Juries always want to appear reasonable. They like taking the middle ground. The middle number, Dean, is way north of a half-billion."

"But we're trying to *avoid* trial here, Paul. So let's accept the premise that you, not a jury, will be content with the minimum number. I'll recommend that my clients pay SeaCoast $360 million up front, with an additional hundred structured over fifteen years instead of ten. Investment returns aren't what they used to be."

Ravich rose again from the table, but this time not in feigned anger.

"I'll think about it. Check with your people and see if they'll sign on."

"I don't need to. What I recommend is what they'll do. Believe it or not, they have listened to me in cases even bigger than yours. I'm not going to them with your 'maybe.' So, do we have a deal or not?"

Paul Ravich made him wait, at least for twenty-seconds or so. He wanted to bask in his victory. His ego told him to pause and appreciate his genius. He had invented a case, manufactured the proof, convinced a greedy corporate titan to hire him; and now, he had scared a couple of fault-free companies into paying him more than he had ever earned from a single case. Charles Thornton would be ecstatic. His death clients would rejoice for having hired him. He would make millions from fraud and get away with it. *The rules don't apply to me.*

"We have a deal," he finally said. "Draw up a proposed settlement agreement and forward it to me by the end of the week."

"Do I include that Crouch woman in our papers?"

Ravich, in his euphoria, had forgotten about the loose-end. "Yeah, but let me handle pitching the deal to her lawyers. You can assume they'll sign."

The mention of the *Crouch* claim had been a downer. *Harry Greenbaum, with all his self-righteous purpose and stupid clothes, was still out there probing in dangerous places, looking for the truth.* Ravich knew he needed to meet with *that bumbling fool* as soon as he got back home.

But first things first. Right now, like a victorious sumo wrestler, he needed to bow in respect to his defeated opponent. He extended his felonious hand for a handshake with another duped victim.

"Nice working with you, Dean; what say you and I have that second drink now?"

———— ⚬⚬⚬ ————

Two days after returning from New York, and one week before his Summary Judgment Motion would be heard by Judge Lewis, Paul Ravich decided to give Harry Greenbaum a call. The timing was perfect. The pending threat of Judge Lewis' dismissal of their case would make the old man and his young co-counsel scramble for any decent resolution of their case. They were fools in the first place to have ever asserted a gross negligence claim against Seacoast: the burden of proof was too high. And Harry's unorthodox investigation to uncover dirt against his client, or against him, had obviously stalled. Like Ron had assured, they would both be under arrest if Harry had turned up any evidence at all about the truth. Both empty-handed and scared of getting nothing, the *Crouch* lawyers would be delighted to learn he had negotiated a settlement for them from the third-party defendants. He wouldn't even charge them a fee. He was just being a nice guy.

"Harry, thanks for taking my call. I hope you're not too busy to talk."

"Well, I am in the middle of preparing a vigorous defense against your motion to dismiss our claim. So perhaps you can be brief."

Harry spoke with no charm in his voice. He saw no point in being gregarious with a killer.

"I'm just representing my client that you wrongly sued. Don't take it personally."

"What can I do for you, Paul?" Harry tersely replied.

"I think we should meet before the hearing next week. Before it's too late for you."

"And what would be the purpose of this meeting?"

"We're old friends, Harry. I don't want to see you come away with nothing, even though that's what your little friend, Doug Stevens, deserves. I have a plan that permits your team to save face and do your client some good."

"Is this another attempt to gain a referral of the claim? Because that won't work. I'm afraid you have made yourself an enemy to my client and my co-counsel."

Ravich wasn't going to detail his third-party settlement over the phone. He needed the element of surprise. It would make Harry more inclined to accept his five million on the spot.

"I assure you I have no interest in any of your client's, or your, money. But if you would just sit down with me, I think it would be worth your while."

"Should we meet during the day? Or do you prefer meetings at night?"

Ravich grimaced. *What was that supposed to mean?* "You pick," he replied flatly.

Harry wanted to put him off as long as possible. They were still gathering evidence.

"I have some time next Tuesday afternoon."

"But that's the day before the summary judgment hearing. Why wait that long?"

"I'm afraid I'm keeping myself very busy until then."

"Doing what?"

"Seeking justice for all. It's a burden some of us must bear."

Typical Greenbaum, Ravich thought. *Always spouting off his silly phrases.*

He looked at his calendar. "Four o'clock Tuesday. My office okay?"

"Will you validate my parking?" Harry asked.

Ravich shook his head at the mention of so small a concern. *He really is an old fool.* "Of course, Harry. It's on me."

"That's what I was thinking," replied the double-meaning lawyer, who was listening hard for a reaction from his suspect. "Is there any particular level in that garage of yours where I should park?"

Ravich tensed and his three-second delay spoke volumes. "Wherever you like. Look forward to our visit, Harry. Bye now."

Both men hung up with sudden questions in their heads.

Paul Ravich sat at his desk with a mild sense of worry: *Did he mean something by that last remark?*

Harry Greenbaum sat nervously in his chair: *Will he commit other crimes to keep me quiet?*

Harry called his co-counsel. Bill Gaston and Doug were busy in the war room, putting the final touches on their written response to the summary judgment motion. Doug and Bill listened on speakerphone as Harry informed them of Ravich's odd request for a meeting before the hearing next week.

"Why does he want to talk?" Doug asked.

"He was intentionally nonspecific," Harry replied. "But he promised it would be worth my while."

"Well, don't go alone *mi amigo.* Bad things could happen," Gaston joked.

"That's probably good advice," Harry said, only half-laughingly.

"Hey! Wait a minute." Bill Gaston's voice sounded excited. "Was Ravich at his building just now when he called you?"

"I believe so, why?"

"Because his office would never confirm that for me. I've tried every ruse I could think of. I made calls saying I had a personal delivery for him; next try, I said I was a judge; last time, I told the girl I was his bookie. Each call, I simply asked if he was in. Every time, his receptionist gave me that "he's not available" line, which didn't tell me what I needed to know."

"Which is?" Doug asked, looking at his strange friend as Gaston leaned over the speakerphone.

"I need to know that he's there and now I do. Harry, is your man Trey in the office this afternoon?"

"Yes, Bill, I think he is. Would you like to speak with him?"

"No," Gaston replied, as he sprung up from his chair. "Just tell him to be downstairs in front of your building in ten minutes. I'm on my way."

Gaston had no time to explain himself. The lanky lawyer flew out of the war room as if he were fleeing a fire. Harry could hear the door slam over the phone.

"What is this all about?" Harry asked.

"He's getting more and more like you," Doug replied. "I have no idea."

When Gaston pulled up to Harry's building, he saw a young man in a suit standing curbside, looking around. He lowered his window and called out.

"You Trey?"

Trey Galloway approached. "Yes, sir."

"Get in."

Trey entered the car and it sped away. Harry had said nothing more than: "Run outside, meet Mr. Gaston who's on his way, and do whatever he says." The newest employee of Greenbaum & Walker thought the assignment was odd but his friend and now fellow worker, Sam, had told him at the start to expect the unexpected when working for Harry.

As Gaston drove quickly through the downtown traffic, he extended his hand. "I'm Bill Gaston, nice to meet you."

"Same here," Trey said nervously, as he watched the erratic driving. "What's this all about, Mr. Gaston?"

"We're almost there," was his only reply.

A minute later, Gaston pulled into the parking garage at Ravich's building, taking a ticket and driving through the gate.

"What kind of car does Paul Ravich drive?" he asked his passenger.

Trey looked at him funny. "He uses a personal driver most of the time. But his car's a Bentley, a dark blue sedan."

"You're sure?"

"Yeah, I mean that's what he drove around in when I worked over here.

425

I assume he's still got it."

"But he knows how to drive himself, right? I mean, he doesn't always have that chauffeur with him, does he?"

The questions were odd. Trey was starting to worry about the man who was driving him.

"Of course he can drive. He just likes other people doing his work for him, like I used to do when I was his associate."

"Yeah, I hear he's a real people person," Gaston said sarcastically.

As they drove up to Level 1, he made clear their purpose. "When you see Ravich's car, point it out."

"Seriously, what's this all about?"

"Sorry, my friend, that information is on a need to know basis. I'm sure your boss will agree with me, you don't need to know. You look to the right, I'll look left."

Gaston began scanning the parked cars, making his way slowly around the first two corners of the garage as it wound upward.

"Hey, just go up to Level 3," Trey directed. "That's where the firm's reserved spaces are. If he's in the office, his car will be parked right by the building entrance up there."

Level 3. Interesting, Gaston thought to himself.

Sure enough, it was exactly where Trey had said. Gaston rolled down his window and, using his mobile phone's camera, snapped two pictures: one of Ravich's car; another a closeup of its license plate. He tossed his phone back in the center console and asked Trey another question.

"Do you know what kind of car Ron Carroll, that investigator of his, drives?"

Trey was now utterly confused but also knew this guy wasn't going to clear things up for him.

"The three investigators all drive black Suburbans. The firm owns them." He pointed at a parked vehicle that was on his side of Gaston's idling car. "There, that looks like one of them."

"Gaston backed up slightly and used the window control buttons on his driver side to lower Trey's window. He reached again for his phone, leaned over his confused passenger and took two more photos.

"Can you tell if that particular one is assigned to Carroll?"

Trey shook his head no. "They all look alike."

"Dude, considering the color, that's pretty racist," Gaston joked.

Trey Galloway didn't think the line was funny, nor did he like what was going on.

"Look, I've got no love for my old firm but why are you spying on these two?"

"If I told you, I'd have to kill you," Gaston teased with a serious voice.

Trey leaned back and tensed.

Bill Gaston slapped his chest with a hearty laugh. "I'm just fucking with you, kid. Relax."

He circled his car around and headed back down to the exit. As the cashier took his ticket, Gaston looked over in the opposite lane and smiled. He stared in appreciation at the access card reader, the device that had already yielded an important clue. It was the impetus for his current bizarre behavior. The log records told him what time three cars had entered and exited the garage. Now he knew what kind of cars to look for. There was only one more thing to do.

While Trey looked on in confusion, Bill Gaston blew the card reader a kiss with his hand as he exited the garage. *Using that thing wasn't Ravich's first mistake,* Gaston thought to himself as he contemplated his next move against the lawyer and his henchman. *But it was a pretty big one.*

⸺ ⋙⋘ ⸺

Everyone, it seemed, was watching the local evening news on Wednesday. The lead story was that three female county employees had filed suit against a prominent district judge for sexual harassment.

A lawyer was shown announcing that her clients, who she did not identify by name, had been the victims of a consistent pattern of harassment, including the commission of acts that constituted sexual assault. She ended by stating that Judge Tom Lewis would now face the consequences for his deplorable conduct. The broadcast then cut to video of the Judge fleeing two camera crews, shouting "no comment" in a most injudicious manner.

What the hell? Paul Ravich sat in his den, watching in stunned silence, as the jurist-in-his-pocket tried to shield his face from the media like a suspect on a perp walk.

"Well, well, well, what have we here?" Harry Greenbaum exclaimed in glee, as he sat at home in front of the TV slurping his evening meal, a bowl of soup.

At the same time, eight miles away, his co-counsel caught a glimpse of things on the screen and exclaimed.

"Oh, my God, Sarah, look at this."

Doug Stevens would have spilled his drink had it been in his hand at that precise moment. They were seated at the bar of a downtown restaurant, having a glass of wine after work and before dinner.

"Yeah, I know," Sarah said quietly, staring down at her Chardonnay.

It struck him. He looked at her, back up at the television above the bar,

427

then back down to her.

"Wait a minute. You did this? You're one of the plaintiff employees?"

She looked at him with a blend of mischievousness and pride, then nodded.

"Oh, my God!" Doug repeated, as he processed the shock. "He's finished! Even if he fights the charges, the Regional Presiding Judge will ask Lewis to take administrative leave until this gets resolved."

"That's what I figured," she replied, before taking a small gulp of her wine.

"Hold on," he blurted, having finally pieced the puzzle. "You did this for me?"

"No, I did it for me. The timing was for you."

"But everyone at the courthouse knows we're dating, right? Ravich or Lewis could put two and two together."

"Relax. First of all, they're not that smart. Second, unless you've been running around bragging about your conquest of me, no one really knows. I've kept our relationship quite discreet at my place of employment."

"Oh, my God," he said again, suddenly realizing that the very pretty and sweet Sarah Ash, the kind court clerk who had come to his rescue before, had done so once again — this time in a devilishly clever way.

He stood, leaning her back over the bar stool, and kissed her with flair, looking like that iconic photo of the sailor in Times Square celebrating the end of World War II by dipping a passing nurse for a smooch.

"Hey, now *everybody* knows about us," she teased. "This is a public place."

"I don't care. I *love* you!"

His always witty girlfriend couldn't resist the dig.

"I was wondering what I had to do to get you to say that."

Chapter 22
Recovery

Joan Slator arrived back at her home on Sunday night to find that it had changed. Everything physically was as she left it, but in her mind the house now felt foreboding and cold. Reminders of Melissa and Ken were around every corner: the tea cup her daughter favored when dropping by for a visit; his toothbrush, with its bristles dried hard, still in the holder. Dozens of inanimate objects that belonged to or were touched by her lost family lurked in places, waiting to torture her with memories. They were gone forever yet their presence was still there.

The home offered no sanctuary when she needed it most. The news that Ken had been murdered made the house feel watched. The people who had tampered with her husband's car could surely, with greater ease, come straight through the door. *Perhaps they already had.* She thought back to Harry's questions about her erased computer: *"Did anyone else have access?" "Any sign that someone broke in?"* The thought made her shake. She had no one to protect her. She tried to dismiss as silly her now justifiable fears but the more she thought about it, the more it made sense. Ken was never the type to destroy things. Even had he wanted to delete something on her computer, he could have done so without also wiping away all her personal files. *Couldn't he?*

The following morning, she walked into her study where the lobotomized computer still sat. She remembered that Harry wanted to have someone examine it when she got back home. She sat down at the small desk and pulled out its single center drawer, where she remembered placing his business card. She found it and smiled again at the "Honest Lawyer" inscription below his name. She now knew the man well enough to take comfort in the words. She reached for the phone and called his office.

The old lawyer sounded thrilled to hear her voice, as if they were lifelong friends. He asked how her holidays had been and how she was holding up. His kind voice was supportive but she kept thinking as he spoke: *What can he do to protect me? What answers can he possibly find?* She mentioned the computer and Harry politely asked if he and a colleague could stop by the house. There was some urgency in his voice. She said "of course," and he said "we're on our way."

While waiting, she reached out and touched the useless keyboard in front of her. She ran her fingers across the keys, like a planchette being slid over its Ouija Board. *What can you tell me?*

Joan was a novice computer user. She bought the iMac when she and Ken divorced. She had given Melissa her credit card and asked her to buy whatever she thought would be best. Her daughter had done the shopping, then set it up for her and configured a wireless network so her mom could surf the Internet and find new avenues of interest. Joan rarely used the computer and couldn't begin to tell you how everything worked. But she occasionally would sit and browse the web. More often than not, though, she would simply look at the pictures her daughter had placed on the computer's photo program. They included copies of Melissa's art work and photos of the three of them in happier times, before drugs got the best of Melissa and before Joan grew tired of Ken's distance. She missed those digital images now. Like her family, they had inexplicably vanished. She stared at the empty screen and saw her new life.

She remained lost in thought, surrounded by loneliness until they arrived.

The doorbell rang and when she opened the front door, her sadness temporarily vanished. Harry Greenbaum stood at the door, his felt hat in his hand, wearing a broad smile and a loud tie. To his side was a neatly dressed and handsome young man.

"My dear Joan Slator, the Florida sunshine has made you more beautiful!" Harry said cheerfully in greeting.

"It's good to see you again, Mr. Greenba...Harry," she replied, correcting herself as he started to raise a mock-scolding finger at her for trying to address him formally. She smiled. "Please come inside."

She held the door open and the two men entered. Harry made the introduction.

"This is my co-counsel, Douglas Stevens. He's working diligently with me to help find you answers."

"How are you?" Doug politely asked as he extended his hand. The words were spoken as a sincere question of concern, not merely as a casual greeting.

"I'm doing better, thank you."

Harry looked on as if he were a proud father. This young lawyer knew how to treat people in need. Harry equally admired Joan Slator's emotional fortitude. He was amazed that any person could survive the nearly simultaneous deaths of a child and spouse with such dignity and strength.

"I know you wanted to see the erased computer," she said, directing them into the study. "Are you a computer expert, Mr. Stevens?"

They entered and Doug saw the iMac atop the desk.

"No, ma'am, just someone who's pretty familiar with Mac."

"That's a good thing, I suppose," Harry added. "Because I don't know who Mac is."

Joan laughed and Doug smiled knowingly. The man was a master at relaxing people with his folksy-innocence.

Doug reached for the desk chair. He wanted to get started.

"May I?"

"Yes, of course, please," Joan said. "Take all the time you need." It dawned on her that she had not been a proper host. "Oh, I'm sorry. Would either of you like some coffee or tea? Something to drink?"

Harry seized the opportunity.

"I would love an energizing product, madam. Caffeine may be the only thing that keeps an old man like me going. Let me join you in the kitchen while our young wizard works. We can use the time to catch up."

"Something for you, Mr. Stevens?" she asked.

"Whatever you two are having, and please, call me Doug."

She smiled and turned toward the kitchen. Harry followed. As Doug pressed the Power button on the back of the display, he could hear her in the next room ask: "So, what have you learned?" Harry could keep her occupied for days answering that one but Doug doubted that his partner was ready to reveal the names of his prime suspects to anyone, not even to the victim's wife. Still, he expected Harry would diplomatically handle the question and keep her, like he was keeping him, encouraged that the truth would eventually come out.

But if any truth was ever inside this iMac, it appeared gone forever. Doug knew from the non-advancing startup screen that the hard drive couldn't mount. He got up and went into the kitchen to ask a question.

"Mrs. Slator, do you by any chance still have the software disc that came with your computer?"

She stepped away from the now brewing coffee maker and returned to the study with Doug. Harry shuffled over to stand at the open doorway, filled with curiosity.

She reached again for the center drawer of her desk and pulled out a silver round object.

"My sister found this in that CD slot or whatever you call it. Is this what you need?"

She handed it to Doug. It was indeed a system software DVD, the same one Ron Carroll had used to erase the hard drive. Doug examined it in surprise. He knew it wasn't originally supplied with this desktop computer. The label made clear it was an installation disc for a different model.

"Do you or did Mr. Slator also own a Mac laptop?"

"No, that's the only Apple computer we have. He had some kind of PC laptop he used for work. I can't remember the brand."

Harry could see that Doug was perplexed. But, like Joan, he didn't know enough about these things to realize Doug had found a clue.

"Okay, thanks," Doug said, "let me see if this helps."

He quickly shot a troubled glance at Harry. His partner got the message.

"I smell coffee!" Harry exclaimed, holding his hand out to his host. "Let the young lad toil while we enjoy a cup of Joe."

After they disappeared back into the kitchen, Doug rebooted the computer from the disc that didn't belong in this house. Doug knew what he was doing. He and an old Mac laptop had been constant companions in law school and he continued to use Apple's newer devices in his law practice. He was no stranger to troubleshooting these machines on those rare occasions when trouble came up. He understood that this software installation disc from a laptop model could be used to view the hard drive on this iMac. When he did, he saw it had nothing on it. If Joan Slator's computer ever worked before, and he had been told that it had, the absence of any system files or data inside the internal mechanism was conclusive proof: the hard drive had been erased. He also knew something else, something even more alarming: the same disc he was using to learn that disturbing fact could have also been used to initiate a clean scrub of a computer's files. If the software disc currently spinning away inside the computer's slot didn't belong to her, then someone else had brought it in to do damage.

Doug was now playing detective. It had to be either Ken Slator or the bad guys. Regardless of who used it, an intentional effort was made to delete files. By now, Doug was a veteran of Harry's logic sessions. He could decipher on his own that those deleted files, more likely than not, had something to do with his case.

Joan reappeared with a cup of coffee for Doug. He thanked her as he powered down the computer.

"Did you find anything on it?" she asked, hopefully.

Doug shook his head no, then took a sip of coffee.

She seemed dejected.

"But I'd like to take it and this disc you gave me back for further study," he said, putting his cup back down. "Would that be all right?"

"Of course. Take whatever you need."

Harry came in. "Can the doctor cure the patient?"

"Not here," Doug replied. "Maybe a data recovery service can find files on the drive. But there's no guarantee."

Doug got up to unplug the machine and gather up the cord. He tucked the mouse in one hand, the keyboard under his arm, and lifted the computer from the desk.

"Do you want to take everything?" Joan asked.

"This is all there is," Doug replied.

"No, there's also that little thing," she said as she turned around, pointing to the cabinet and bookshelves behind her.

It was the same piece of built-in furniture that concealed, at its bottom, the safe that Ken Slator had used, unsuccessfully, to guard his cash and new computer from theft. At its top, on the highest bookshelf, sat the device she was pointing to.

"That thing up here, it's part of the computer I'm pretty sure. My daughter installed it and set everything up. She said that white box does stuff. I think it allows me to get on the Internet without wires."

Joan then pulled the desk chair over. She started to stand on it to retrieve the small plastic box that was tucked back and just barely visible on the shelf.

"Let me help you with that," Doug said, as he returned the computer to the desk and coaxed her back down.

He then stood on the chair and saw what it was: one of Apple's wireless base stations. An ethernet cable was attached to it, providing Internet signal to the device. The base station then broadcast that signal wirelessly to any computers in its range.

Doug wouldn't need to take it with him. He had his own wireless routers; besides, a computer with a fully erased hard drive can't access the Internet anyway. He started to get down.

Then it struck him. *Could it be?* He knew the two devices, after all, looked identical. He stood back up, holding his breath.

Apple sold two versions of its WI-FI device. One simply distributed an Internet signal. The other and more expensive product did that too, but was also equipped with an internal hard drive. Software preinstalled on every Mac can use that external drive to wirelessly backup a computer's contents. It does so on an hourly basis, behind the scenes, with no effort on the part of the user except to activate the program one time when the computer is first set up. The less expensive WI-FI model was marketed with the name "Airport." The more expensive version had its own unique name, a clever moniker that Apple came up with to highlight that product's backup features. Doug had owned both. The higher-end models now protected his data at both his office and home.

With nervous hands, he picked up the thin white square, its green power light still glowing on front. He turned it over to read the product identifying label on the bottom and found what he hoped he would see. The label read: "Time Capsule."

Doug looked down at Harry with the eyes of a treasure hunter who had just hit pay dirt. Harry didn't know what to make of it but Doug certainly did. If Joan's daughter had known what this was and how to use it, they might just have a chance.

Melissa Slator, the girl whose sad and short life left behind so many questions for her parents, might just have given her mother — and the lawyers trying to help — some answers they were looking for.

———— ⊶⊷ ————

The war room was abuzz with activity on Monday afternoon.

Doug sat in front of Joan Slator's computer, which now rested atop the office's table. Cabled to the iMac, and transferring its contents, was the retrieved little white box of possible secrets. He had been working for almost two hours: first, reinstalling system software on the brainless hard drive so that it could think once again; and now, commencing a restore of the last full backup made by the Time Capsule device before the computer was sabotaged.

All the while, Harry Greenbaum sat next to him, asking questions and looking on in amazement. He had never understood or trusted modern technology but was glad his young case partner did.

Bill Gaston suddenly burst into the room carrying a manilla folder. He saw Doug and Harry huddled next to each other with Bonnie standing, staring over their shoulders. They were all mesmerized by a desktop computer that had seemingly appeared from nowhere. *That wasn't here on Friday,* he thought. His colleagues looked like three kids sharing a video game. They barely acknowledged his entrance.

"What's up?" he finally asked.

Bonnie quickly filled him in as Doug continued to watch the restore process continue.

Gaston summarized, in his own inimitable way, the significance of what they were doing. "Holy shit! Back from the dead."

Harry grinned and said: "Hopefully, in more ways than one."

Gaston shared their excitement but now realized that the computer show would steal much of his thunder. He flapped the manilla folder in his hands. He had been looking forward to making a dramatic presentation of its contents.

"Hey, while you wait for that thing to speak, wanna see something *right now* that will knock your socks off?"

This time, all three of them looked up. *Now they're paying attention,* he thought.

Gaston pulled up a chair across from his team and laid the folder down on the table.

"Doug, you may remember that I represent Ravi Kapur, that nice Indian fellow who owns the Exxon station at the corner of Elm and Main downtown."

Doug wrinkled his brow. It was a *"so what"* look.

"I looked over his initial franchise agreement years ago and since then he's used me for other legal work. He also has other business interests. The guy's a go-getter."

"Does this story have a point?" Doug decided to ask. "We're kind of busy here."

"Trust me, it does. Poor Ravi, a few years back, started having a bunch of drive-offs; you know, where people get gas and don't pay. Guess high gas prices make desperadoes of some people. Anyway, I suggested he install security cameras on the corners of his building to tape the thieves getting away. He did, then turned a few people in, and the thefts dropped dramatically. But he kept the cameras up, figuring they were a good deterrent."

"That's a great little tale," Bonnie snidely offered.

"Bear with me. Anybody know what's two blocks from Kapur's station?"

Harry shrugged.

"The garage entrance to Paul Ravich's building. It's on Elm Street."

Joan's iMac instantly got second billing in the attention department.

"So, I go down and visit with my old client and the guy tells me he still leaves the recorder on every night, even after he closes, just in case someone comes by to vandalize the place or something. His cameras record movement in low resolution so the digital output doesn't take up much room on the storage drive he keeps back in the office. These video files show his gas pumps in the foreground and you can see the traffic on Elm in the background. Guess how far back his archives go?"

Doug smiled. "At least to October?"

"All the way back to August! Can you imagine? The little dude throws nothing away."

Gaston reached inside the manilla folder and pulled out a stack of ink jet printed photos. But he waited to pass them out. He was enjoying the moment too much.

"I spent an afternoon at Ravi's station, looking through the late night video captures for the night of October 24th, starting at eight p.m. and ending at two a.m. For obvious reasons, the video is time and date stamped. It doesn't do Ravi or the police any good if they don't know when a videotaped crime took place. Wanna see what I found?"

Doug, Harry, and Bonnie eagerly leaned forward.

He slid the first image across.

"Look closely in the background there. That's an old Ford Taurus headed north on Elm, passing the pumps at 11:12 p.m." He passed out the next photo. "Here's that same car headed in the opposite direction, southbound, at 1:03 a.m. I know, Harry, it looks quite a bit different after the wreck, but dimes-to-donuts that's Ken Slator's car."

"I can't make out the plate number," Bonnie remarked.

"Yeah, these are low-res, black-and-white images," Gaston reported. "But Ravi gave me the hard drive. Maybe we can enhance the video enough when the time comes."

He passed out four more images.

"That top picture is of Paul Ravich's Bentley parked in his office garage. I took it with my cell phone the day Trey Galloway and I went for a ride. Now, have a look at this next one which is a gas station shot. That looks to me like the same fancy car, headed north on Elm at 11:40, less than a half-hour after the Taurus passed by." He handed across another page. "And here it is again, this time southbound, passing the station exactly twenty-eight seconds before the Taurus comes following up behind."

Harry looked on with pride. These two young lawyers were indeed smart and creative in their investigative talents.

"Now, I was also looking for a black Suburban in these surveillance tapes because Trey said that's what Ron Carroll drives." He slid across another video-capture image. "This shows a dark Suburban going by at 10:05 p.m. So I'm thinking maybe Ron was asked to get up to the office early and meet with Slator before Ravich shows up."

"What time did that Suburban come back by?" Harry asked.

"Well, that's where my hole is. The only other vehicle that drives southbound on Elm immediately after Slator's car is this one."

Gaston slid over his last video image, which depicted a lightly shaded Chevrolet Malibu.

"This car comes past the station a half minute after the Taurus did."

"You think the investigator switched vehicles?" Doug said.

"Makes sense. The Bentley and this Chevy have Slator sandwiched in pretty tight in the time line. And believe me, at that time of night downtown, there were very few other cars on the road."

"And these back-and-forth cars, do those times all fit with the garage log records that tell us when Ravich's access cards were used?"

Once again, Bonnie had hit on the key question.

"Like a glove," Bill replied with a smile.

Harry stood up and reached over to vigorously shake Gaston's hand.

"Congratulations, sir, your diligence is exceeded only by your brilliance."

"It's nothing, really. I've got helpful clients all over this town," Gaston joked in reply. "People will do anything for me."

"Excellent thing to remember," Harry said with a laugh. Then he turned deadly serious. "And let us also not forget that some people will do anything, it seems, for money."

—————

"Where's your proposed settlement agreement?"

Paul Ravich barked the question into the phone at Dean Schiller. It was Monday. Schiller had promised a draft by the end of last week.

"It got tied up over at Jack Trenton's office. The General Counsel of VyStream wants to make a few changes."

"Fine, as long as the material terms aren't affected. Speaking of the most material one, when can we expect our money?"

"I'll have the draft agreement to you by Wednesday. We can fund upon receipt of your fully executed Releases and the contemporaneous filing of an Order of Dismissal at the courthouse."

"I won't dawdle on my end. If I get papers by Wednesday, you should plan to wire-in your payments to my client-trust account by this coming Friday."

"Did you get the Crouch widow to go along?"

"I'm meeting tomorrow with her lawyer. Won't be an issue."

"Good," Schiller replied, before changing the subject to gossip. "Ben Argent informs me that our assigned judge found himself in a bit of trouble?"

"Yeah, like a lot of stupid men he thinks too much with his dick."

Dean Schiller laughed. "Argent implied this scandal could have been a bad turn for you if we hadn't settled. He said this judge was your friend and he probably won't get to keep his bench."

"I have many friends, Dean. Judge Lewis just happens to be one. But I could have tried this case in front of your mother and won. That's why you're gathering up $385 million to send to me this Friday, with more to follow each year."

"Only for fifteen more years," Schiller corrected.

"That's right," Ravich said with a chuckle.

"I suppose Charles Thornton was pleased with your recovery on his behalf?"

"Like a kid getting a pony at Christmas. See you, Dean."

"Good talking with you, Paul."

Ravich hung up, thinking back to his meeting with Thornton the day after returning from New York with a settlement in hand. The arrogant tycoon first wanted to know why there had been any compromise at all. Only after it was explained to the fool that they both had "certain risks" to avoid did the greedy bastard become effusive in his praise. They had pulled it off. SeaCoast's reputation as a victim would be preserved and Thornton Industries was recouping much of its losses.

The only thing apparently painful for Charles Thornton was that Paul Ravich was getting paid so much. The tycoon whined for five minutes about the 20% contingency fee he would now have to pay. In that, Ravich thought Thornton was no different from his typical personal injury clients. The agreed percentage split always sounds reasonable before victory is achieved but never after. "No recovery, I don't pay anything? I like that." Then you win and they say: "Nice recovery, but why do I have to pay so much?" It didn't seem to matter if your fee was a million bucks or, like here, seventy-two million with another twenty-million dollars more to come from the annual installments. *Clients are clients*, Ravich thought disdainfully. *They all like to bitch.*

Shifting his thoughts to handling the final details and loose-ends, Ravich considered his meeting with Harry the next day. *That's one client who shouldn't be bitching at all,* he told himself. Kate Crouch would be getting a windfall, thanks to him, and no thanks to the attorneys she hired. Neither she nor her lawyers would make any waves.

As Paul Ravich sat comfortably in his office on Monday afternoon, he was confident he had navigated his ship of fraud safely into dock.

What he didn't know was that a tidal wave of truth had just appeared on a computer screen three miles away.

———— ∞ ————

Doug found it quickly after the computer backup was fully restored. It was three-thirty in the afternoon on Monday. The four of them would never forget the moment.

438

Once the hard drive contents were back in place, Doug had the iMac list its files in the order of most recent creation or modification date. That way, the files that were worked on last — before the hard drive was erased — would appear first. It took nothing more than a mouse click to set the sort order.

At the top of the list was a folder named *"Melissa"* that was created on October 22nd, less than three days before Ken Slator's death. Inside it was a zip file labeled *"DCSS,"* a small text file, and a sizable QuickTime movie file titled *"Just in Case."*

He clicked on the movie file and it began playing. The image of the deceased plant manager filled the screen. Doug hit the pause button and called his team over to watch along with him.

No one said a word as they viewed Ken Slator outlining everything. They stared with mouths agape as he held up his laptop while it displayed the *true* DCSS output and as he explained its significance. They looked at each other in shock when he played back the voicemail proving the safety system had been intentionally overridden by SeaCoast at the insistence of its President, Rob Finnegan. Harry nodded his head in understanding when Slator held up Finnegan's open briefcase and showed the tools and business card inside, while detailing how he came into possession of it. He ended by saying the zip file was an exact copy of what came across the plant's computer that night, and he pointed out the text file he had created which summarized everything a second time. The movie ended with his words: "That's it. That's all I know."

The presentation was as thorough as it was clear.

Doug, Harry, Bonnie, and Bill stood in the war room, silent, each of them reflecting on what they had just seen, processing what it all meant, amazed to discover that the reality was worse than even their darkest suspicions.

How close the wrongdoers had come to purging all trace of his truth. But truth is like a stubborn leak: it is hard to contain, even harder to eliminate. Secret meetings get revealed, trace evidence gets left behind, incriminating evidence survives even the best attempts to destroy it.

Their other investigative efforts had shown that Ravich and his investigator were behind the death of this honest man. But it was the victim's own conscientious act — his decision to memorialize everything — that would, in the end, prove *why* he was killed.

From the grave, Ken Slator answered all their questions:

Ravich's case against Integrated Sentry was based upon lies, a bold strategy of both evidence creation and destruction to maximize the corrupt lawyer's gain. They now had direct confirmation that what Slator turned over to Ravich was not what the lawyer was showing to the world.

They knew now there was a strong case of gross negligence against SeaCoast Chemical. They even had proof that company management had gone to criminal lengths to keep that fact from becoming known.

The now fully revealed scope of Ravich's deception made clear his need to alter and erase computers that would divulge what really happened. It also told them, with heartbreaking clarity, why Paul Ravich decided the plant manager had to die:

Ken Slator knew *the truth* and Paul Ravich simply wasn't interested in that.

There were still things to be done to strengthen their hand against Ravich. But reaching a consensus on what to do and when to do it had been difficult. Their newly discovered evidence was the subject of both debate and brainstorming that lasted well into the evening on Monday. The four didn't walk out of the war room until almost eight.

Doug had urged that they take their evidence to the police now. He argued this was a criminal matter, that they had no business waiting when they had such clear proof of a crime. Harry and Bill Gaston urged a slower tack. They wanted to shore up the case, to collect even more evidence to prove both the murder and fraud. "Let's have things play out," Harry had suggested, unconvinced that the conspiracy stopped at only Ravich and Ron. Bonnie's position was the easiest to understand: she was for anything that would make Paul Ravich suffer the most.

In the end, they decided to make a series of strategic moves that included, but wasn't limited to, going to the authorities. This had been, and was still, *their* case. They were a team that knew how to win trials. They knew that *some* evidence — even strong evidence — is not the same as *sufficient* evidence. They would not let haste or police or prosecutors screw this one up.

On Tuesday morning, they would commence their plan. Harry had even given it a name: "Operation Rat Trap."

It began with a simple phone call to Ben Argent. Harry wanted to ask the local lawyer for Integrated Sentry about a few things that were still unclear. The Tuesday morning conversation quickly revealed there was much they didn't yet know.

"Ben, my pleasant friend, how are you?"

The defense lawyer on the other end of the line grinned. There was something about the old man that just made people smile.

"I'm fine, Harry, and I'll bet you are too."

"What do you mean by that?"

"You're calling about the settlement, right?"

"What settlement?" Harry quickly replied.

"My lead counsel, Dean Schiller, called last week to say he and Ravich made a deal on the cases; a full settlement with SeaCoast and the death plaintiffs. He said the accord also includes your client's potential claim. I thought that was crazy, of course. I've never heard of paying money to someone who hasn't even sued you." Argent paused when he heard no response. "I'm sorry, Harry, I thought you already knew. I figured Ravich would have told you by now."

Harry now had a pretty good idea about the reason for his mysterious meeting with Ravich, scheduled for this afternoon.

"He tries to keep a lot of things from me, Ben. Have you seen these proposed settlement documents?"

"No, they are due in tomorrow."

"Do you know how much the kind Mr. Ravich negotiated for my client without my consent?"

"I think I was told it was five-million; the same as for his people."

Harry sat stunned in his chair. "Well, well, this case grows more strange by the minute," he finally replied.

"Tell me about it. When was the last time you saw defendants settle a multimillion dollar case in a matter of months?"

"Exactly never," Harry replied. "And, as you know, I've been around a long time."

Argent laughed again. "Yeah, maybe it's the New York way. Everything runs faster up there."

"Why am I always the last to learn anything?" Harry said, in mocking despair. "The deal-making Mr. Ravich has scheduled a meeting with me for four o'clock today. I now presume its purpose is to get me up to speed on the settlement."

"Yeah, you need to do that."

"Ben, just curious. What do your people do if I don't go along?"

"Schiller says we settle with Ravich's clients anyway. He just wants to wrap you up at the same time if he can."

"Imagine that, a New Yorker that is both generous and efficient."

Argent laughed out loud before shifting gears. "Hey, speaking of other surprising news, you've heard about Judge Lewis?"

"Of course," Harry replied. "I saw his unfortunate proclivities described on the news."

"No, I'm referring to the aftershock. One of the lawyers from my office returned from the courthouse yesterday to say the Judge has decided to go on immediate administrative leave until his scandal blows over, if it ever does."

"No, I hadn't heard that either," Harry replied.

"Yeah," Argent laughed, "I guess a few days of watching people glare at him in the halls prompted the need to hide out for the time being. Plus, I'm sure he was getting pressure from the county to step down, at least for the interim."

"It couldn't happen to a nicer fellow," Harry added. "So Ben, who do you think will be appointed to take his place?"

"Oh, you're going to love this. You remember Judge Louise Pavey? The old battle-axe who retired from the 215th three years ago?"

"Of course, she was a stern but fair jurist."

"Well, the Regional Presiding Judge has appointed her as a visiting judge until either Lewis comes back or he permanently resigns. My associate was told she starts in his court tomorrow."

"Well, that is good timing," Harry remarked. "The hearing on Mr. Ravich's motion for summary judgment is scheduled for then. Perhaps my argument for retaining the *Crouch* claim will now find a more receptive ear."

Argent chuckled again. He too knew of Ravich's close connections with the disgraced Judge. "She couldn't be any worse than the man she's replacing. But why are you guys still having that hearing anyway?"

"Informing me of a possible settlement of the *Crouch* claim doesn't make it so, Ben. Until Ravich says otherwise, I have to assume the hearing is still on."

"You two definitely need to talk. Schiller told me to stay out of all this, that Ravich was communicating directly with you."

"I harbor no ill will toward you, Ben, for my lack of notice. I'll do the necessary follow-up."

"Good."

Harry suddenly remembered the original purpose of his call. In the startling one-two punch of other news, he had almost forgotten about his need for specific information.

"Ben, since I didn't know a thing about any of this, I have been continuing my case investigation. I think I still want to. Could you do me a favor?"

"Sure, Harry, as long as it's not illegal."

"It's not. I'll leave that to others involved in our case. Did you ever get copies of that computer data which Ravich says proves your people messed up?"

"Of course, he shoved it down our throats early. I was given printouts in a nice leather-bound settlement brochure."

"Can you share those with me?"

"Absolutely. Again, I thought you were already in the loop on that. I'll have my assistant make you a copy. Send someone over here to pick them up in an hour or so."

"Thank you so much. I'll do just that. I'm curious, though. Did he ever explain to you how he was planning to authenticate those records?"

"Oh, you mean because of the death of the manager that kept them? Yeah, I asked that question, and Ravich gave me a copy of a business records authentication affidavit he obtained from the man before his accident."

"I was never furnished a copy of that either. Could you put your hands on it for me?"

"Right now?"

"If it's not too much trouble."

"Sure, hold on. It's in the case file. Let me get to my filing cabinet."

"You are most helpful," Harry said, before he heard Argent lay the phone down.

A short time later, the voice came back on the line. "Okay, I've got it right here. What do you want to know?"

"What is the date shown for that document's execution?"

"October 22nd. Why?"

"Just curious. I assume it's properly notarized?"

"Yeah, there's a notary seal. I can't make out the name. I'm sure it's one of Ravich's secretaries."

Harry knew then that both the date and seal were inaccurate. Ken Slator's tell-all movie file was made in his home on the 22nd. He still had his computer with him on that date. The misdated affidavit was an obvious attempt to further conceal the late night meeting on the 24th where Slator met with Ravich, then death.

"Could you add a copy of that to my stack of documents?" Harry asked.

"Sure. But what's the deal?"

"I'd just like to have it for my files. The subject could come up when Paul and I meet to discuss his wonderful efforts on my behalf."

Ben Argent had no idea what Harry was talking about, or how Ken Slator's affidavit proving up the DCSS backup could have anything to do now with the task of concluding a settlement. But Argent had tried cases against Harry before. He knew better than to ask. Harry Greenbaum marched to a different drummer.

"Your copies will be at the front desk under your name. Just have your messenger come in and ask for it."

"Will do."

"So I'm assuming you guys are going to wrap up your case too. Is that right?"

"That's what I'm hoping to determine: What is the right thing to do? Thanks so much for your help today, Ben. You have been a cornucopia of fascinating news."

"You're welcome. Goodbye, Harry."

Ben Argent hung up the phone, confused as always by the old lawyer's words and tactics.

Harry hung up and immediately called Doug. Operation Rat Trap needed to change slightly. He wanted another team meeting.

— ∞ —

"Paul Ravich, please. This is Harry Greenbaum calling."

"I'm sorry, Mr. Greenbaum," the receptionist replied. "He's not available at the moment. May I take a message?"

"That would be lovely. Please inform him that I am tied up in depositions in another matter and cannot make our four o'clock meeting today. I'll see him in court tomorrow and perhaps we can reschedule."

"May he phone you back if there's a problem?"

"I'm sorry, madam, but to use your phrase, I'm not available for the remainder of the day. Thank you and goodbye."

Harry hung up the phone and looked over at Doug and Bill. After learning about the settlement from Ben Argent, it was decided to postpone any meeting with Ravich.

Bill Gaston was having second thoughts. "Shouldn't we be just a *little* concerned about this hearing tomorrow? I appreciate that Judge Pavey is not Judge Lewis, but she is a *judge*. We all know what that means. You never know what one of them might do."

"I'm not concerned," Harry replied. "Ravich only wanted this meeting with me today so he could hang the threat of dismissal over my head and hopefully pressure us to sign off on his crooked settlement. We have clear grounds to defeat his summary judgment but even if Judge Pavey were to grant it, Ravich will still be eager to make a deal with us. Remember, he needs everyone to go away in order to get away with his crime. If we're thrown out of court against SeaCoast, we can come right back in against the third-party defendants. That reopens a can of worms that he's racing to snap tight."

"Good point," Doug said. Harry could always see both sides of any knife blade. "So, what's next?"

"We assure him tomorrow, regardless of the hearing's outcome, that we would still like to talk. He'll say let's do it now, in the courthouse halls, but I will make some excuse for needing to rush right out. We want to stall him until he can wait no longer. We want him to get antsy and demand his money from the third party defendants before we sign off. I would like to see him return his client's releases and receive a money transfer before we make our move."

"Why?" asked Bonnie.

"So that all elements of civil and criminal fraud are present," Harry explained. "The last element, as these two legal scholars here will attest, is a proof requirement that someone has been damaged. That is quite easy to prove when the victim has parted with hundreds of millions of dollars based upon misrepresentations and lies. His own death clients will similarly be victims of fraud when that money has to go back."

Doug and Bill nodded their heads in agreement.

"And that's important why?" Bonnie was still unclear on the strategy.

"To assure both criminal conviction of Ravich for fraud and the viability of future civil liability claims against him for his misdeeds."

"So, you want to put him away *and* take his money?"

Doug looked at Bonnie in surprise. "Do you think that's unfair?"

"No, guess not," she said. "Screw him."

Harry blushed. Everyone laughed.

"By the time he receives his money, we will be ready to move," Harry continued, resuming his outline and trying to restore a more dignified discussion. "I will then meet with him and play hard to get with regard to Kate Crouch's release. I'll act like that last property owner who holds out for extra when everyone else has already sold their land to the railroad. I'll make outrageous demands. I'll throw him off base. I'll get him so flustered he might just make some incriminating statements."

"So what?" Bonnie countered. "He'll just deny making them."

"That is why, my dear, before I have that fateful meeting with the devil, we will get the police involved."

Chapter 23
Rat Trap

"All Rise."

The bailiff of the 89th District Court called out the ceremonial order as the elderly woman appeared from the adjacent chambers and stepped up to the bench.

"Good morning, counsel, please be seated," she said, after settling into her chair. "I'm Louise Pavey, retired Judge of the 215th. I'll be serving here by temporary appointment in light of the sudden absence of Judge Lewis."

Doug liked her choice of words: *"sudden absence."* Had she known, she might have added: *"Thanks to Sarah Ash."*

While most motions are presented on Monday mornings, a court can and will schedule pretrial matters during the week, especially if no jury trial is ongoing. Judge Lewis, before his scandal broke, had kept his trial docket clear for this particular week. One reason, Doug and Harry both suspected, was because his pal Paul Ravich wanted to get this Motion for Summary Judgment heard quickly.

The courtroom this Wednesday morning was fairly empty. Only ten lawyers were present. Six were there on other matters. Harry and Bill sat next to Doug on the first row of the gallery's long bench seats. Their murderous opponent, true to form, arrived seconds before the session began and positioned himself at one of the counsel tables. Ravich glanced back over to the *Crouch* lawyers and briefly smiled.

His confident grin was not due to any faith in Judge Pavey but because of his need to begin the process of appeasement. With Judge Lewis gone, Ravich knew he couldn't count on a summary dismissal of the *Crouch* claim. He also realized his new strategy required making an agreement with his old enemies, an accord that would get them paid. *Fat, dumb, and happy,* he now knew, was the best way to make sure they wouldn't keep looking for the truth.

"Counsel," the Judge continued, "I see here that four hearings were previously scheduled for today. One is a simple motion to appoint an ad litem in a minor's case. I can hear that without knowing much about the case merits. Two others, according to the docket sheet, are requests to alter the discovery schedule previously issued by Judge Lewis. I can assume that the lawyers involved in those two cases can get me up to speed in order to make a ruling?"

Judge Pavey looked out and saw four heads nod yes. "Good. Then that leaves only one other matter, which I see is a Motion for Summary Judgment. Are all counsel in that case present?"

Doug's team and Ravich all stood. Harry answered quickly on behalf of all. "We are, Your Honor."

"Well, I want to apologize for making you come down here but, as you know, my appointment was very recent and I didn't have time to direct the clerk to call you. I know nothing at all about this case," she said, before looking down at the list to identify the name, "this consolidated matter of *SeaCoast Chemical v. Integrated Sentry.*"

She looked over at Harry, a familiar face. "Mr. Greenbaum, it's been sometime. Who do you represent in this matter?"

Harry had appeared before Judge Pavey dozens of times in her former court. She respected him, as everyone did, and was looking to him for information.

"Good morning, Judge. It's wonderful to see your wisdom gracing our County once again. I represent one of the plaintiffs, a lady named Kate Crouch. Mr. Ravich, over there, is seeking to have her claim for damages thrown out of court summarily."

Judge Pavey glanced over at Paul Ravich. She remembered him too and in a less favorable light.

"Well, gentlemen, here's the problem. I haven't had an opportunity to even read the motion and response, so oral argument won't do me much good. While I'm prepared to rule on these three other docketed cases which involve simple issues, I'm not inclined to rule in the dark on a motion to dismiss a claim entirely."

Doug and Bill looked at each other with smiles as the Judge continued speaking.

"A summary judgment is a harsh remedy. It deprives a party of their day in court and requires a judge who has carefully considered the evidence and arguments. I see no need to make any rulings on a dispositive motion until I have a chance to study the particular issues. I'm afraid your matter will have to be rescheduled. I suggest you lawyers get with the clerk and obtain a future hearing date."

Doug looked over at Ravich, expecting to see him disappointed. Instead, he appeared nonplused.

"We appreciate the Court's hesitancy, Your Honor," Harry then said. "May we then be excused?"

"By all means. And it is nice to see you still working, Mr. Greenbaum," the Judge remarked.

Harry bowed slightly, like a knight before his queen. "Not nearly as pleasant as welcoming you back to the bench, Judge Pavey," he said, before staring directly at Paul Ravich as he finished his thought. "Your much needed presence here will undoubtedly serve justice in the end."

––––––∞∞∞––––––

While they were at the courthouse, Bonnie was on the phone. With the blessing of her lawyers, she was dusting off an old contact. It felt a little awkward, calling an old beau she had not talked to in years but it was the least she could do.

Bonnie had only been married once and just briefly. Her no-nonsense personality and sharp mind did not blend well, matrimonially speaking, with the lazy man she once foolishly fell in love with thirty-five years ago. After that mistake was quickly corrected, she remained determinedly single. She dated a few men over the years, primarily people she met through her work contacts. One of those men was Lieutenant Charley Frain.

He accepted her call with surprise and pleasure. They had dated for about a year, almost ten years ago. Both had been committed to making no commitments and when they finally drifted apart it was without a nasty breakup or even a harsh word.

"Bonnie Rogers! A blast from my past," he said with a laugh. "Did you just figure out you couldn't live without me?"

"Charley, I reckon a decade can make a woman forget any man's faults. How the hell are you?"

"I'm the same. Just older."

"Aren't we all? Hey, I figured you'd be retired from police work by now. I was shocked when I called over and they said you were still there."

"The only cops who retire are the ones with smarts or a family. I've got neither," he said with a chuckle. "To what do I owe this pleasure?"

"I need a competent policeman. You were awful in bed," she teased, "but I heard you were a pretty good detective."

He laughed heartily. "Well, if you've got yourself in bad enough trouble maybe I'll get another chance to redeem myself."

"Play your cards right and we'll see. Look, Charley, no bullshit, I need to talk to somebody at the department about a big crime the lawyers I'm working for have found out about. We want to get the bad guys arrested."

"What did they do?"

"Murder, for one thing."

"You run with a tough crowd, Bonnie," Charley Frain began, but then decided her sudden serious words should mark an end to the silly banter. "We've got more than a few unexplained corpses in this town. Tell me the victim's name and I'll put you in touch with the detective working the case."

"That's the problem," she replied. "Nobody but us and the bad boys even know there was a murder. I need you to help finish the investigation with us."

"Why me? I'm just a bureaucrat now. I only supervise detectives over here. I don't even know where my service revolver is anymore."

"It has to be you. You're the only one I trust."

"Why's that?"

Bonnie thought about how to explain things to her old policeman-boyfriend. She decided, in her efficient way of speaking, to say the one concise thing that would assure a prompt visit by him to her office:

"Because one of our murder suspects used to work for you."

They exited the courtroom with deliberate speed. Even Harry, whose normal gait could only be flatteringly described as a slow shuffle, tried to pick up the pace. Their rush for the exit was designed as a test. They wanted to see how worried Paul Ravich actually was. As Doug and Bill reached the elevator, they got their answer.

Paul Ravich came bounding out the courtroom doors, calling to his former boss who was trailing behind his younger lawyers by several steps.

"Harry, hold on a minute. I was hoping we might talk."

Greenbaum stopped and turned around.

As Ravich approached, the elevator doors opened. Harry suggested to his co-counsel that they go on down and get the car, that he would be right with them. Bill and Doug complied but tried to appear reluctant to do so.

It was playing out exactly as Harry had predicted it would. Doug was beginning to believe the old man was clairvoyant.

Without saying a word to Ravich, both Doug and Bill entered the elevator and were soon gone.

"What can I do for you, Paul?" Harry finally said.

"We were supposed to have a meeting yesterday. You canceled," Ravich began.

449

"I assumed correctly that you weren't going to announce a withdrawal of today's motion, so I didn't see the point in coming."

"Look, this whole summary judgment thing was just a way to get your attention, to hopefully get you guys on the right track."

"And that track is for us to drop our claims against SeaCoast, I gather?"

"Of course. Listen, Harry, I've made significant headway against the third-party defendants. They're cratering. I can still get you in on the deal."

"Perhaps if Judge Lewis were still around, though, you might not be telling me this. Or am I wrong to assume that?"

"Think whatever you want. I'm just trying to help you."

Harry pressed the elevator call button. "We're doing just fine on our own, thanks. And next time you want to do me a favor, start by not trying to get my case thrown out."

"Come on, pal, cases are fluid things. You know that better than anybody. Changing circumstances require changes in strategy. As the lawyer for SeaCoast, I'll admit that, initially, I thought it would be advantageous to get your gross negligence claim dismissed. But that no longer even matters to me. I now have an opportunity to end the entire case for all of us and can do so in a way that benefits your client too. Why wouldn't you be interested in that?"

"I didn't say I wasn't. But you have badly alienated my client and co-counsel. They want no more to do with you."

The elevator arrived. Harry moved toward the opening doors.

"And what about you?" Ravich asked.

"I'm always open to suggestions, Paul. You know that." Harry stepped into the elevator. "But I can't talk here or now. My colleagues are downstairs waiting. My private phone, however, still rings."

He delivered the last sentence in a way that sounded slightly conspiratorial. He wanted to leave Ravich with an impression that a schism might be developing within the *Crouch* trial team.

Ravich took the bait. He put his hand against the door, temporarily preventing its closing. "So, when can I call? When can we visit alone?"

"I'm busy today and tomorrow. Perhaps Friday, Monday at the latest."

Ravich didn't want that kind of delay but he took any overture of cooperation as an indication that Harry still didn't have the goods on him. It was a positive sign. Until the old man could be sold on the settlement, the goal was simply to get him to stop looking.

"So, let me get this straight," he decided to ask pointedly, as the elevator door began to kick back in mechanical frustration against his hand. "You might be ready to make a deal?"

"I'm old, Paul. Putting an end to tiresome litigation always sounds attractive to me. Now, please, I must go. I can't have my co-counsel thinking I'm up here being courted by you."

"Okay," he replied, releasing his grip on the door and stepping back into the hallway. "Then let's you and I get together and do the right thing."

"I always do," called back the double-meaning Harry Greenbaum, as the door began to slam shut on Paul Ravich.

Charley Frain left the downtown precinct to make the short drive over to Bonnie's office which was only five minutes away. He told her he could be there around 11:00. He figured that would give him enough time to meet with her and her lawyers, hear their story, and then take his old flame out for lunch. He was looking forward to seeing her again. It had been so long he actually forgot why they had stopped dating. But he could still recall that she was damn smart and a lot of fun. Now, ten years older, those qualities in a woman seemed a little more important to him. Maybe a spark could be reignited. *Who knows?* He wasn't sure what this crime report was going to be about but it gave him an ulterior motive to see her again.

As instructed, he found the unmarked door to the left of Suite 302. He gave a brief knock, then let himself in. Behind a folding table, an old man in a cheap suit sat between two younger men dressed far better. The room was sparse. Even the precinct's break room was nicer. At least there was one thing worth looking at: Bonnie Rogers sprang from her corner of the table and walked over to give him a big hug.

"Charley, look at you! Not an ounce of fat and just a touch of gray."

As she pulled back, he kept his hands on both her arms and took her in.

"And you still look smokin.' Why did I ever lose your number?"

Bill Gaston glanced over at Doug and raised his eyebrows while making a face of surprise, imparting his silent joke: "*Don't you have the naughty secretary!*"

"You quit calling because you were a fool," Bonnie replied to his question. "Here's a chance to act differently." She walked over to her lawyers who were now standing to meet the detective. "Charley, this is my boss, Doug Stevens."

"Thanks for coming over," Doug said, as he shook hands.

Bonnie continued the introductions.

"And this here is Harry Greenbaum, lawyer extraordinaire; and that goofy thing next to him is Bill Gaston."

"Nice to meet you all," Charley Frain said.

"Pull up a chair," Harry suggested. "We have quite a story to share with you."

"Yeah, Bonnie tells me you have a case of unreported murder and it involves someone I might know."

"So, she didn't give you a name?" Doug asked.

"No. I think she was trying to be careful around me."

"That comes from my earlier experiences with you," Bonnie teased.

Harry got to the point. "How long have you been with the department, Lieutenant Frain?"

"Twenty-six years. Why?"

"One of our suspects was there for twenty before he retired. He now works in the private sector. We figure you know him. We fear you might be friends."

"If an ex-cop committed a murder, he's not my friend."

"Well, that's what I thought a dedicated professional like yourself might say. But can you keep the lid on things down at the station once we tell you what we know? I'm sure gossip could get out. We can't have this man receiving any notice that we're on to him. He's very dangerous."

"I share information only when I have to. I'm like a lawyer that way."

Everyone smiled.

"So, who's your bad man?" Frain asked.

"Ron Carroll."

Harry watched the detective's reaction. *He knows him all right.* Charley Frain looked shocked but stiffened his jaw.

"Yeah, I remember Ron. He was a good cop. A straight twenty-year man. As I recall, he went to work for some law firm after he threw down the badge."

"That's right, he did," Harry confirmed. "And that law firm is headed by his co-conspirator in this crime, Paul Ravich. Ever heard of him?"

"Name sounds familiar. He's one of those rich ambulance-chasers, right?"

Harry grinned. The insulting phrase directed at injury lawyers had become so commonplace that people felt comfortable using it even when talking to one.

"That he is," Harry replied, adding: "As are we three; except, of course, for the rich part, as you can tell by our offices here."

Bonnie smiled as she watched her old boyfriend roll his eyes in regret.

"Hey, I meant nothing by that."

"No offense taken, officer. How about a cup of coffee while I tell you our tale?"

"Sure."

Bonnie rose to pour him a cup. Charley Frain started to get up. "I can get it myself, Bonnie. Keep your seat."

Hanging out with Harry Greenbaum had taught her the joys of the double-entendre. "Oh, sit down, Charley. I can wait on you. I've waited for ten years."

As the detective laughed, Gaston shot another schoolboy glance at Doug.

By the time the coffee was delivered, Harry had begun talking.

By the time he was finished, no one — especially Lieutenant Charley Frain — was laughing anymore.

———— ∞∞ ————

On Thursday, Harry took the next step. He phoned Paul Ravich to make apologies for his schedule, informing him that he wouldn't be available to meet until late on Monday. Ravich sounded frustrated, so Harry made a proposal that was filled with surprises.

"Paul, look, I know my various schedule conflicts are holding things up for you. You see, I spoke with Ben Argent today and he told me about your pending settlement with Integrated Sentry. Congratulations, my good man, that's quite the accomplishment."

Ravich was thrown off by the comment. The purpose of their upcoming meeting was, after all, for *him* to inform Greenbaum about the deal.

"Ben even made mention that you held out in order to make some kind of provision for my client from your third-party defendants."

"Yeah, that's right," Ravich replied with hesitation, finding Harry's easy-going acceptance of the news to be encouraging yet unsettling at the same time. He had expected him to be a tougher sell. Harry's sudden change in attitude seemed odd.

"Now, Ben didn't give me any details about my end of this proposed deal, which I presume is what you want to meet and tell me about. But he did say you were busy trying to get your client's settlement money in before the weekend. Please don't let me stop you. We can either work our little part out on Monday or we don't. Either way, I don't want to stop the chance for you to get your clients' money in the bank."

Ravich didn't quite know what to make of such a conciliatory tone.

"Well, I appreciate that, Harry. I do already have the releases and settlement agreement signed by my clients, including SeaCoast. Integrated Sentry and VyStream are ready to fund the settlement once they get those returned to them."

"Then let me make this suggestion," Harry said. "You go ahead and close your deal so you can get the money into your client-trust account for distribution to your people at the earliest convenience. Leave me out of it. We'll talk on Monday evening and if the settlement makes sense to me we can simply call Ben Argent, or that New York lawyer that's heading things up, and add me on. I could then deal straight with them and be out of your hair."

Ravich liked what he was hearing. He needed to make sure it was the total package.

"But you understand, Harry, don't you, that accepting this settlement requires that Kate Crouch also release her claim against SeaCoast? I can't be helping you on the one hand and have you still trying to hurt me on the other."

"That sounds reasonable in the main, Paul. Let me think things over and we'll talk on Monday. Is six o'clock at your office too late? I have a deposition in another case that won't be over until after five."

"Sure," Ravich replied. "That will be fine."

"Excellent. Perhaps we can find common ground after all," Harry intimated.

"That would be good. But Harry, aren't you going to have problems with that cocky co-counsel of yours and maybe even his client?"

"I know how to handle them. Like you, I consider myself to be a problem-solver."

Ravich was so excited by the prospect of shutting down the *Crouch* case that he missed Harry's clever double-meaning.

"Well, then, I look forward to talking with you on Monday, Harry. I'm glad you want to see this thing end."

"I have no other motive," the wily old lawyer replied.

———— oⱥⱥo ————

With a few keystrokes, it was done. Near the close of business on Friday, wire transfers from two insurers and a VyStream operating account merged the mind-boggling sums into the client-trust account of Paul Ravich & Associates. His banker was used to seeing large amounts flow in and out of the successful law firm's accounts. Paul Ravich was, after all, a very big player handling very big cases. But these particular account credits were gigantic and he had been instructed to call and confirm their receipt.

Ravich took the call himself. He wanted to hear the words spoken.

"Mr. Ravich, the three transfers are confirmed. A total of $385 million has been wired-in and is now on deposit in your client-trust account."

"Thank you, Ethan," he happily replied before issuing further orders. "I'll probably make client distributions next Tuesday. But please go ahead and transfer $80.5 million of that total into my firm's money-market account today. I want to earn interest on my share over the weekend."

The banker on the other end of the line was dumbfounded. *Boy, did I go into the wrong profession,* he thought. "Yes, sir, Mr. Ravich. Have a great weekend."

"It's off to a good start. Thanks again, Ethan," he said cheerfully, as he hung up, breathing a deep sigh of relief.

It took effort to get the money in this quickly. The day before, Dean Schiller had told Ravich the funds would be withheld until the signed releases and settlement agreement were in his New York office. "Probably be Monday at the earliest," he had said, happy with any payment delay. Ravich wanted to demonstrate again that he was a man of action. He had Dustin Kirkland fly up on the private jet Thursday night, and the associate was standing outside Dean Schiller's lobby the next day. He hand-delivered the signed documents to the New York super-lawyer as he came strolling into his office at nine o'clock that morning. Dustin passed along Ravich's insistence that the failure to fund by five o'clock that day would be considered a material breach of their settlement agreement. *It pays not to screw with me,* Ravich had wanted to communicate to his fellow sumo-wrestler.

Ravich now leaned back in his chair and calculated the windfall. He made $72 million in fee off of the initial payment to SeaCoast of $360 million. Another $8.33 million represented a one-third cut of the $25 million collected for the families in his five death cases. He wasn't quite sure what his final reimbursable case expenses would end up totaling, so from the top of his head he picked the figure of a hundred seventy-five thousand dollars simply because it rounded nicely. None of his clients were going to question what he spent on depositions, experts, and flying his jet to New York to secure this amazingly quick settlement for them. If any client ungratefully did, he would find a way to adjust his case expense total further upward. *It pays not to sweat the small stuff when dealing with me,* he thought with a smile.

SeaCoast Chemical Corporation was one client that would not be lodging any complaints. Next week, Charles Thornton would recoup a net of $288 million for damages his own greed and stupid management had caused. And that wasn't all. A year from now, Thornton and Ravich would also be splitting, 80/20, a nice little anniversary check of $6.66 million, the first of fifteen such annual payments that would total another $100 million when all was said and done.

Paul Ravich left the question of *"What is one life worth?"* for the philosophers and theologians to debate. He already had his answer. The audacious murder of Ken Slator, and the manipulation of his evidence, had a clearly definable value and those figures were now gleefully bouncing around in Ravich's head.

He had pulled it off. It took crooked connections to get the initial cases. It required a crooked judge to help move things along. It entailed a brilliantly devious scheme to change the case facts to suit the needs. It even demanded that a few crimes be committed along the way. But there was now something tangible and fungible to show for it, something to inform the world he really was the best, the brightest, the baddest tort lawyer around. He had never doubted himself. Now, nobody could doubt the claim.

He thought about how he would spend the weekend celebrating. Maybe fly over to Aspen and ski, or perhaps go down to Mexico for a few rounds of golf. He could finally relax for a couple of days while looking forward to a fairly easy workweek to follow. All that was left to do in the biggest case of his career was one short meeting with Harry Greenbaum and then several happy sessions with appreciative clients stopping by to pick up their checks. After that, it would be a series of press appearances and interviews to make sure everyone got the news of his remarkable achievement.

The hard part was over. The rest would be easy. The money was now his. *What could possibly go wrong?*

———— ∞ ————

While their target relaxed out-of-town, his pursuers spent a busy weekend getting prepared. The final act of Operation Rat Trap required dress rehearsals. There was much discussion of the risks. There were logistics to consider. Contingency plans had to be considered in the event things didn't go as planned. The war room was originally intended to be the headquarters and storage facility for a large civil case. But it now served as the staging area for a team dedicated to exposing a massive criminal conspiracy and bringing the culprits to justice.

Bonnie's friend, Charley Frain, turned out to be a godsend. He understood what needed to be done and knew how to support the effort. The experienced policeman spent much of his weekend with them, helping to improve their chances of success. He had his own distinct motivations: they were decent people trying to right a wrong; he also might impress Bonnie and rekindle her interest in him; and perhaps most of all, he hated crooked cops. It came as no surprise to him that a lawyer would do anything for money. But it hurt his professional pride that one of his own had sold his integrity for some form of criminal reward.

Doug, Bill, and Bonnie traded watch over all the fretting. When he wasn't deep in thought, Harry spent most of his time defusing the tension with simple sayings meant to reassure:

"I know what I'm doing, relax."

"This will be easier than a jury summation"

"Who would mess with an old man like me?"

Perhaps all the cloak-and-dagger talk would have been thrilling, even fun, had the stakes not been so high. But a man had been murdered, justice had been brutally assaulted, companies had been badly robbed. So much evil had been done for so callous a purpose: so the rich could get richer. The purely mercenary purpose of the maniacal lawyer was hard to understand. But it was easy to see that it had to be stopped.

Bringing down Paul Ravich was a duty to them now. They owed it to the victims of his crimes: the dead workers, Kate Crouch, Ken Slator and his widow, the defrauded companies. They owed a debt to the truth that could only be paid by seeing Ravich, his henchman, and anyone else involved in the conspiracy held fully accountable. They owed it to the system itself. If the law could not catch its own rats, the institution was doomed. Society's strongest pillar of order could not be expected to shield others if it provided a safe hiding place for its own vermin.

To Harry Greenbaum, this was not about "winning" a case. To Doug Stevens and Bill Gaston, it was no longer about simply making a recovery for a client and earning a fee. To Bonnie, it meant more than wanting to see her lawyers succeed. To Charley Frain, it was different from just planning a few more arrests.

Everyone in the room that weekend felt something stronger. Everyone wanted to believe their efforts might fulfill a higher purpose. The corruption of the *SeaCoast* case had reminded them all of an important lesson, one that is too easily forgotten in the bustle and tumult of trying to make a living in and around the courts: the scales of justice are fragilely balanced and easily upset. Justice can only be dispensed when the truth is revealed, and the law is only as good as the people who take oaths to uphold it. It was now time for this small group of professionals — people who still believed that to be true — to show those who did not just how wrong they were.

Harry called Ben Argent at home on Sunday evening. He apologized profusely for his "horrible weekend intrusion" and for "disrupting a lawyer's sacred day of rest." Argent, thoroughly entertained by Greenbaum's dramatic prefaces, was happy to sit in his home study and talk.

"I was hoping to meet with you tomorrow, Ben. Do you have hearings in the morning?"

"Come on, Harry, you know better than that. Of course I do. But you're also aware I'm a partner in a big firm. I can have associates cover them for me if you and I need to sit down and talk."

"I believe we do."

"I'm assuming it's about the *SeaCoast* settlement?"

"Your intuition bears the hallmark of an accomplished litigator."

Argent laughed. "Sure, Harry, we can meet. But don't keep me in suspense. Have you and Ravich come to terms? Are you taking the deal he made for you?"

"We are discussing that possibility at his office tomorrow evening. But I have another deal I wish to discuss with you first."

"Is it one that is good for me and my clients?"

"To quote a Corleone, I'll make you an offer you can't refuse."

"Let's get Dean Schiller on the line."

Harry sat in Ben Argent's office, nodding his head.

The local counsel for Integrated Sentry and VyStream made the conference call suggestion after listening, spellbound, to the incredible proposal. If it were anyone else, he would have assumed it was some kind of scam. But he knew and trusted Harry Greenbaum. The fact that his story was fantastical didn't mean it wasn't true.

Their Monday morning meeting had, so far, gone according to Harry's plan. Argent first verified that Ravich had indeed received his settlement funds. Harry then proceeded to do what he did best: surprise the hell out of a defense lawyer. He told him just enough to keep Argent's jaw from hitting the top of his desk.

"This is incredible," Argent said, as he dialed the New York number and waited to be patched through. When Schiller answered, Argent switched over to speakerphone.

"Dean, I have in my office Harry Greenbaum, one of the lawyers representing the Crouch plaintiff in the *SeaCoast* explosion cases. I think it's important that you hear what he has to say."

"Good morning, Mr. Schiller," Harry spoke out, confirming his presence.

"Yes, hello to you. I don't think we've had a chance to meet. Now yours is the claim that remains unsettled, is that right?"

"That is true," Harry responded.

"Well, of course, you probably know we have already made payment to all of Paul Ravich's clients," Schiller began, as if he were the one with information to impart. "Mr. Ravich assured me he could and would obtain your client's release as well. In fact, he told me on Friday he thought that was going to happen sometime today."

"Yes, he assumes many things," Harry replied.

Schiller detected the meaning. "Are you calling to tell me you want to turn down our five-million dollar offer? That you don't want a bucket of money from defendants you haven't even sued yet?" Harry's cryptic statement already had the Manhattan lawyer in a rant. "Ben told me, Mr. Greenbaum, that your methods were unorthodox. He didn't tell me you were crazy."

Argent looked over at Harry and smiled, glad that his reaction could not be seen over a voice line. Dean Schiller was new to the Harry Greenbaum show and Argent was looking forward to how this conversation would progress.

Harry leaned closer to the speakerphone as he responded. "What if I were to tell you, Mr. Schiller, that five million is not a large enough reward."

"What?" Schiller barked. *Did he say reward?* The phone connection was clear. Argent had mentioned this lawyer was old. *Was he really so senile that he confuses the word "reward" with "award" when speaking of a judgment or settlement?*

"As I have previously asked Ben, thus prompting this call to you, what would it be worth if I could get back for you all the money just paid to Mr. Ravich?"

"What are you talking about?" Schiller snapped impatiently. "We made a contractually binding settlement with him. Money exchanged in return for releases and dismissal." Schiller decided to show his ugly side. "Is that not how they did things when you first started practicing law?"

Harry laughed at the impertinent remark. "No, Mr. Schiller, I first started before pen and paper were invented. Back then, we settled disputes with clubs and shields." Harry then made his point. "Sir, perhaps my age is an asset while youth is your liability. You see, in almost fifty years of practice, I can honestly say I have never been defrauded in a case like you have just been."

"What is this lunatic talking about, Ben?"

"Dean, you really should hear him out," Argent suggested.

"Mr. Ravich has perpetrated a fraud upon you and your clients," Harry continued. "I have conclusive proof of that fact. How I handle that proof could very well result in your clients getting all of their money returned. My question remains: Are such efforts worthy of some reward?"

It took several minutes for Dean Schiller to learn the art of listening. At first, he continued to interrupt and badger Harry with questions. Eventually, he realized the wisdom of just letting the old man talk. When

Harry was done, Dean Schiller was finally speechless.

"I can't...I can't believe this. Ben, is this...could this...be true?"

"If Harry says it's true, it is."

"How is it possible that a lawyer could conceal or destroy *all* the real facts?" Schiller sputtered. "I've heard of manipulating some evidence but you're accusing this man of *inventing* an entire case against us?"

"By tomorrow, provided you and Ben say nothing to anyone about our conversation today, I can demonstrate to your satisfaction that you have been conned out of hundreds of millions. For the next twenty-four hours, however, I must ask for your cooperation and silence, as I am about to embark upon the most dangerous part of exposing this criminal scheme. Can I have your agreement that neither of you will tip off Mr. Ravich that we are on to him?"

"Of course, Harry," Argent immediately offered on behalf of both. "We won't do anything to put you in peril."

"If you can prove what you say, then he has attempted to steal $485 million from us," Schiller added. "What am I saying, *attempted?* He already has all but a hundred of that."

"Precisely my point. Would my getting that money back for you be worth something from your people?"

Schiller now understood the question. "You're asking for a reward? Like a whistle-blower fee? Is that it?"

"No. I won't hold you or justice hostage for any amount. That would make me no better than the man I am about to punish. You must understand that, Mr. Schiller. I will do what I need to do regardless of what you and your clients decide. I don't want you to give me any of this stolen money. I only want your clients to hire me and my co-counsel to pursue a punitive damages case against the co-conspirators who devised this criminal enterprise."

"Who other than Ravich are you talking about?" Schiller asked.

"That's what I aim to find out today. But even Mr. Ravich, you see, has additional money over and above that which you just foolishly paid to him. In fact, I heard he was quite wealthy even before he stumbled upon your naiveté."

"So let me get this straight," Schiller began, wanting to make clear he understood the proposal. "You want no cash reward from us for exposing Ravich's scheme and recouping our prior payment?"

"That's correct."

"You simply want my clients to hire you to pursue a punitive damages case on their behalf against those that perpetrated this fraud?"

"Exactly. You know, Mr. Schiller, I've always heard you New York litigators were sharp. You catch on very quickly."

"Why would they want to hire you? They've got me."

"Oh, yes, the man who suggested his clients pay a king's ransom to settle a case of no liability would be the ideal candidate to lead these new efforts. Maybe I should be having this conversation with VyStream's General Counsel instead."

Argent smiled but didn't laugh out loud. He was enjoying listening to Schiller receive his comeuppance for so hasty a surrender to Ravich's settlement demands.

"What *precisely* are you proposing?" Schiller asked, knowing he had been checkmated.

"I want nothing more than your recommendation to your clients that they hire me and my co-counsel to represent them in a subsequent punitive damage claim against Ravich and his partners in crime, whoever they might be. I will seek punishment damages in civil court from the bad actors on your client's behalf. It seems only fair that my co-counsel and I should receive a small contingent fee for such work: oh, let's say, 25% of anything I am able to collect from the coffers of the bad people involved."

"Why do you think they'll follow my referral recommendation? They can do whatever they want and hire whoever they wish."

"I understand that, Mr. Schiller. But they obviously are willing to do anything you say. This very bad settlement you told them to make is proof enough of that. So, what do you say? Let's have you end up looking good by getting their money promptly recovered, and then you reward my most helpful efforts at maintaining your reputation by simply urging that I be in charge of any subsequent civil claim filed down here against the bad boys."

Schiller recalled a phrase he had used with Ravich only two weeks before at the Waldorf. "You want me to throw you a bone, is that all?"

"Woof, woof," Harry replied heartily.

Argent burst out laughing. He could no longer contain his amusement.

"All right," Schiller said, knowing it was time to relent. "We'll stay out of your way today and let this play out. If you call me tomorrow and tell me that Ravich has been stopped, I'll see to it that you get the job once our settlement money is returned."

"Thank you so much for that." Harry gave a wink to Ben Argent. "I knew we would probably see eye-to-eye. And now, if you gentlemen will excuse me, I'm off to slay a dragon."

"Good luck," Dean Schiller said, trying to repair his previous harsh words directed at the cagey old lawyer.

"Thank you, sir. But don't worry about me. You see, Mr. Schiller, I'm so old we actually had to battle the *real* thing when I was just a lad."

———&&&———

Harry dressed appropriately for his six o'clock meeting with Paul Ravich. While none of his suits were new, this gray polyester one was particularly tattered. The stitching on one of the lapels had begun to unravel, looking like an errant whisker growing out of a poorly shaved face. The shirt was so wrinkled it appeared slept in. The tie was as faded as the gray fedora he carried in his hand. The only splash of color in the whole ensemble was the cardinal tail feather in the hat band and the non-matching socks he wore. One sock was blue, the other brown. He was determined to look the part of a man that might need money.

The law office was closing up for the day and the last of the lawyers and staff were making their exit. That was the main reason Harry wanted the meeting to be at six; the fewer people that were there, the more likely Ravich would talk.

The receptionist had already left but Ravich's assistant, Jan, was sitting out front, waiting for the arrival of her boss's last appointment for the day. When she saw Harry Greenbaum come shuffling through the door she almost felt sorry for him. *So that's what a broke plaintiff lawyer looks like,* she thought. His greeting, however, seemed more lively than either his pace or wardrobe.

"Good evening, madam. I am here to see the incomparable Paul Ravich. Name's Greenbaum."

"Yes, sir," she said smiling, as she picked up the intercom. "Mr. Ravich, a Mr. Greenbaum is here to see you."

Harry could overhear him say: "I'll be right out." He looked up at Jan and smiled.

"I hope you can go home now. Surely, we're past your regular hours?"

"I'll be leaving in a couple of minutes. Would you like something to drink?"

"No, thank you, I'm fine."

Harry walked over to the hero wall and began browsing though all of Ravich's proud accomplishments and contacts. *Such a waste,* he thought to himself. He twiddled his hat in his hand.

"Harry, we finally get to have our meeting," Ravich called out, as he bounded down the hall. He gave the old lawyer the once over. He had seen homeless men dressed better. "Come back with me to my private meeting room. It's better than this huge, cold space here," he said, pointing to the firm's large conference room behind the glass double doors.

"Lead the way," Harry replied, extending his right arm outward, while keeping his left hand, which held his hat, at his side.

As he walked down the hall following his host, Harry counted the steps and calculated the distance. *Surely, it wouldn't be a problem.*

They arrived at the small ante room just to the side of Ravich's main office. It was the same room where two elk bulls had locked horns before deciding to cooperate. Harry had no idea when he entered the small study-like room that it was where the conspiracy had first been hatched. He only hoped it would be the room where it would all end.

"Please, sit down. Make yourself comfortable," Ravich implored.

Harry glanced behind him. The room was lined with beautiful built-in wall shelves that contained a few volumes of legal treatises but mainly displayed small treasures of art and mementos from Ravich's world travels and his active practice. The shelves were cluttered, but in that stylish way only interior decorators can seem to accomplish.

As he sat down in one of the leather chairs, Harry reached back and tossed his fedora on one of the lower shelves. It came to a rest next to an African tribal mask.

At the time, Paul Ravich was crossing to the other side of the table, taking the same seat where he had first pitched his plan for riches to Charles Thornton.

"So, Harry, you understand by now that I have settled my cases with the third-party defendants. Did Ben Argent provide all the details?"

"No, actually I was in a hurry, racing off to one of these other depositions that have kept me so busy the past few days, and I just got the broad outline from him."

"So, you don't know the numbers?"

"I'm sorry to say, I don't."

Ravich filled him in, tossing out the dollar figures as if they were Olympic records.

"I'd say that's a pretty fair result, Paul, for less than four months work."

Ravich smiled. His old boss was a master of understatement.

"But don't think I forgot about you, Harry. Look, I know there have been some differences in our approach to this case, but little of that conflict was really between you and me. Perhaps I got my feathers too ruffled when your young co-counsel, Doug Stevens, first came in here and tried to strong-arm me. It caused me to be a bit more antagonistic than usual. Maybe I shouldn't have taken it out on you and that Crouch woman. I hope you can forgive my excessively competitive streak."

"Why do I feel you would be less mollifying if Judge Lewis were still around?" Harry pointedly asked.

"You make too much of my friendship with him."

"You two were a bit close for my comfort."

"What can I say? He likes me. So I had one judge who thought well of me. And now he's gone. But everyone likes you. I hardly have any advantage there."

Ravich was not going to admit to any kind of wrongdoing in a casual back-in-forth. Harry realized he would have to push harder to trigger such responses.

"So, back to my point," Ravich continued. "When I negotiated this settlement on behalf of my victims and SeaCoast, I decided to raise your potential claim as something the third parties should consider resolving as well. Of course, they stomped and said you hadn't even sued them yet. But I convinced them that you would, eventually, and I told them they could only buy complete peace if it also included your client."

"How very kind."

"I thought so. Harry, I know you have some misgivings about me, some issues of trust. But the proof is in the pudding. VyStream and Integrated Sentry have offered your client five-million dollars to settle her case. That's the exact same amount — not one dime less — that each of my victim families are receiving from them. I could have sold you down the river but didn't. And the fact they're willing to extend such an offer to you should be proof of just how strong the case is against them."

"And how weak it is against your client, SeaCoast?"

"Of course. Come on, you've tried enough cases to know this: if a third-party product liability defendant concedes responsibility for killing an employer's workers, then it necessarily follows that the employer can't also be grossly negligent. The theories of liability are inconsistent. SeaCoast was either villain or victim. They can't be both. Third-party defendants don't pay hundreds of millions in settlement damages to villains."

It was time. Harry wasn't sure how long he had.

"But a villain can cast himself as a victim if he's clever enough, can't he?"

"What's that supposed to mean?" Ravich said, suddenly tensing.

"Paul, I'm not here to only accept a five-million dollar offer. Now understand this: I will take it, and my young co-counsel and our client will undoubtedly be thrilled with the result. You'll get your release of Seacoast Chemical at the same time they get that money. That's good enough for them. But I need something more and I'm pretty sure you'll be willing to pay it to me."

Ravich listened with a perplexed look. The words didn't sound like Harry Greenbaum. The old man always spoke in terms of client duty and "doing the right thing." *Now, for some reason, it was suddenly about him?* Paul Ravich understood self-dealing better than anyone. What he couldn't understand was why Greenbaum was also speaking in such terms.

"I don't know what you're talking about," Ravich decided to reply, sticking an unsuspecting toe into the muddy waters.

Harry returned a serious and knowing look.

"Oh, I think you do. You see, Paul, I know everything. While my co-counsel were busy running around acting like lawyers, counting trees instead of looking for the edge of the forest, I was busy trying to figure out how you managed to pull off this remarkable scam."

Ravich straightened in his chair. *"Scam?" "I know everything?"* He felt an immediate sense of panic that only years of courtroom acting could begin to conceal. It was important not to react. He also remembered the wisdom of not uttering something incriminating.

"What are you saying, Harry? You sound like a crazy man. Are you taking medication of some kind? You don't appear to be your normal self."

"I'm just fine, Paul, and if you quit playing games with me, you can stay that way too. If you're not willing to deal straight with me then I'm willing to go straight to the police."

This time the panic showed. His worst fears were realized. *Greenbaum knew! Or was he bluffing?* Ravich decided to shrug his shoulders in a claim of innocence and said nothing.

"Are you afraid to talk?" Harry taunted. "That's why I offered to come this late and to your office. Your walls surely have no ears. So, let's talk."

The comment reminded Ravich of his need to be careful. But he couldn't use coded words and innocent-sounding phrases if he had to discuss *this*. It was time to take charge.

"Listen to me, you old bastard. I don't know what you're trying to pull but you won't trick me into saying something that isn't true."

Harry laughed. "Paul, you haven't said anything that *is* true about this case. Do I have to name a few specifics to get your attention?"

Ravich shrugged again.

"Tampered computers and tinkered cars," Harry said slowly.

The words instantly dispelled any hope that Greenbaum was bluffing. Ravich began breathing hard. There would be no way to avoid the conversation now. But he had to do something first.

"Give me a second," he said, as he got up to walk over to the phone in the corner of the room. He lifted the receiver and punched three numbers. He stared at Harry with evil eyes.

Harry looked on with worry as Ravich waited for the phone to be answered.

"Good, you're still here. Ron, I need you in my private conference room, now."

As he spoke the name, he watched Harry carefully. He saw the old man tense. Like a lingering look from a judge about to announce a verdict, it told Paul Ravich what he needed to know: *He does know everything.* Ravich hung up the phone and glared.

No words were spoken as the two trial lawyers locked eyes in a staring contest. Each was thinking hard about their next move. Both knew they were in danger.

A knock was sounded on the closed door.

"Come in, Ron," Ravich called out.

The murdering investigator walked into the room, showing no expression other than stern attention to his boss. Ravich had informed him that morning of the scheduled meeting with Greenbaum. Ron had been told if the meeting went well they would be in the clear with no loose-ends. He knew if he was being summoned to participate in that meeting, things weren't going well at all.

"Stand up, Harry, and walk over to that door," Ravich demanded.

The old lawyer rose from his seat and complied. He thought maybe the four steps he took would be his last.

Ravich nodded to his investigator. "Pat him down good. We're looking for a wire."

Ron approached. *The man is a scary looking guy,* Harry thought. Trey Galloway had been accurate in his initial description.

"Turn around and spread your arms and legs." Ron's words were not a request but an order. Harry had no choice.

It was a thorough search. Ron even had Harry remove his shoes to feel along his mismatched socks. He covered his body twice, and found nothing.

"He's clean."

"Thank you, Ron. You can go now."

Ron didn't like what was going on. You don't look for hidden wires on someone who presents no issues.

"You sure?"

"Yes, but why don't you hang around in the main conference room until we're finished? Just in case something should come up."

Harry understood the less-than-veiled threat. Ron nodded and left, closing the door behind him.

Ravich returned to his chair. "Now that we've gotten that out of the way, you were saying?"

Harry breathed a sigh of short-term relief and also returned to his chair. Things were still as they needed to be. It was time to get back to the plan.

"I know everything," Harry said, as he tried to regain his composure.

Ravich didn't blink. "Prove it. Tell me a few things."

Harry wasted no time. He told him about the car bomb; how it had been planted by the man who had just frisked him. He connected all the dots, as Ravich looked on with a grudging acceptance that he had been found out. Then Harry revealed something that Ravich didn't already know.

"And I have sole custody of a backup of the *real* DCSS data from the night of the explosion. You tried to account for it but somebody slipped up. It proves that your 'authenticated' records are false; it reveals what really happened; and it explains why you, and your muscle, did what you did."

Ravich tried to control his fidgeting hands. Like so many others before him, he had badly underestimated the brains of his former boss, the man who played the part of a doddering old fool. Ravich also knew he wouldn't be hearing any of this if Harry hadn't already made provisions to protect himself.

"And who else knows all this?"

"From my end? Nobody. I can't exactly parlay this knowledge into a payday for me if others have also been told these shocking secrets. My co-counsel and client may correctly think of you as a jerk but they have no idea you're a killer."

Ravich grinned at the revelation that Harry was keeping things to himself. Harry took his smile as a threat.

"But, surely, you don't think I'm stupid enough to walk in here without some insurance that I can walk back out. Should anything happen to me the whole story will be revealed. Old men have to leave instructions to others about where to look for wills and things. You and Mr. Carroll couldn't begin to recover the many copies of the true DCSS data that will surprisingly turn up should I pass away unexpectedly. I'm not even sure how many backups I actually have out there. I think I lost count."

Ravich nodded in resignation. This old fool was smart. He was no Ken Slator.

Harry continued. "So again, from my end, it's just me. You see, I'm a bit more careful than you. From your end, I figure there's you, your goon, Rob Finnegan, and Charles Thornton. Have I missed anybody?"

Harry was only making an educated guess about the last two names. But Ravich didn't know that.

"Finnegan knows nothing. He's an idiot."

Harry now had the confirmation he wanted.

"Good, he would clearly be a weak link in your fragile chain." Harry next applied his searing logic skills to extract more information. "So how much does Thornton know?"

"Who said he knows anything?"

"I think you just did. That much was obvious anyway, Paul. There is no way Charles Thornton would have ever hired you to represent SeaCoast unless he had no choice. I know the man. He hates tort lawyers more than he loves money. His big settlement recovery will keep him quiet forever about his role in helping you create and hide evidence. But can you trust a man like that to maintain a murder conspiracy?"

Harry shook his head side-to-side with doubt.

"He doesn't know about the car bomb," Ravich countered. "He only knows I took care of any evidence adverse to our liability theory."

Harry now nodded his head up and down in happy acceptance. He wanted Ravich to believe he was now looking out for their mutual interests, that he was now part of the cover-up plan. But in truth, Harry was pleased for different reasons: he had just gotten Ravich to implicate Charles Thornton in the fraud, while confessing himself to both fraud *and* murder."

What about his in-house lawyers? Are any in the loop?"

"No. I can manage Thornton. You can't always manage lawyers."

"So you have just learned."

"Let's cut the crap, Harry. You have all this proof, you've pieced it all together, now what do you want? If your motives were pure, we'd all be under arrest by now. If you were trying to extract an evidentiary confession from me, you'd have been wearing a wire." Ravich raised his voice. "So, just what is it you want?"

"My little piece of your delicious pie. Give me something to keep me quiet. I'm sure your investigator didn't kill out of pure loyalty to you. How much did he get for his services and silence?"

"That's none of your business."

"Then let's go at it this way: how much would you and Charles Thornton pay to remain free? I would imagine it might be pretty much all you stole."

Ravich knew then it was a shakedown. He didn't like being shook. He preferred doing the shaking. His anger and anxiety both showed.

"Relax, Paul. I'm way too old to spend that much money. How about this? I'm sure you have untraceable money tucked away somewhere. I doubt your investigator got paid his cut with a firm check. Let's reward my investigative skills with an amount that will keep me comfortable and quiet. I'm thinking ten-million will do just fine."

"And what about the next time? You have no skin in the game. This is just blackmail. What keeps you from coming back and asking for more, issuing new threats of exposing us all?"

"Once I accept your money, I become a criminal too. I don't want to go to jail either. Plus, Paul, at my age, I probably won't outlive the ten-million. For me, it's one and done. If I were you, I would be more worried about that Ron fellow coming back for more."

"He's been paid well enough. I don't worry about him."

Harry gave a thin smile. It disguised his glee. Ravich had just confessed to a death penalty offense: murder-for-hire.

"Great," Harry replied. He stood to leave. "So here's how it can work. You get my money to me. It's easy, I have a Cayman Islands bank account. I'll then get my people to sign off on your third-party settlement. They can get their five-million from VyStream and Integrated Sentry, and we can all have our celebration party with the widow Crouch. Everyone lives happily ever after. Any questions?"

"Yeah, just one, Harry. Was it always an act? The clothes, the demeanor, the caring? All these years? I never saw even a trace that you were this smart or this devious."

Harry smiled.

"Good lawyers create their own opportunities, Paul. I think we have both proved that. There's just different ways to seize them."

He reached down with his left hand to retrieve his hat from the lower bookshelf. Ravich was still in shock and took no notice. The man he thought he knew, the man he considered his opposite, was just like him.

"I bid you goodnight," Harry said, opening the door with his free hand. "I'm so glad we finally had this talk."

Harry Greenbaum walked down the hall alone, reaching the hero wall where he paused to take a deep breath and put on his old fedora. Before he turned to exit the reception area, he looked over and through the glass doors of the conference room and saw Ron Carroll sitting nervously at the large table.

He tipped his hat to the man and walked out the door.

Chapter 24
Reverberations

Harry Greenbaum stepped into the elevator and pressed the button marked "62." When the doors closed shut, he finally felt safe.

The car dropped down one floor and the doors opened. He walked out and around to the building's emergency exit and opened the fire door. He entered the stairwell and climbed up the first flight of steps, stopping at the landing midway between the floors.

He was greeted with a hero's welcome. Two uniformed policemen gave the old lawyer high-fives. Lieutenant Charley Frain stood up from a folding chair and removed his headphones. He powered off the surveillance receiver-recorder resting on the floor. He smiled and shook Harry's hand.

"Damn, man, you were cooler than iced tea on a summer day in there. I'd have shit my pants when Ron Carroll walked in that room."

"Who's to say I didn't?"

Everyone laughed.

"Where was your hat the whole time?" Frain asked. "When I heard they were frisking you, I figured we were on our way in."

"I kept it at my side when I entered the room, then tossed it on a low shelf behind me when I sat down. I suppose Ravich never even noticed or quickly forgot. After all, who wears a hat these days?"

Harry handed over the gray fedora. Charley Frain gently pulled the cardinal feather from the band and began to remove the filament size wire that had been taped to the backside of the quill. The transmitting antennae had boosted the signal tremendously. The audio capture was crystal clear. He then reached inside the hat and removed the small listening device and transmitter from its hiding place beneath the hat's silk lining. As he pulled it out, the tiny wire followed behind through a pinhole that had been concealed by the hat's band.

"Did you get everything you wanted?" one of the uniformed officers asked.

"We already knew most of it," Harry replied, "but I have always found that, in a courtroom, admissions straight from the horse's mouth are particularly damning."

The three cops all nodded their heads.

"You were pretty convincing with that blackmail claim of yours," Frain noted with a grin. "It's a good thing I was briefed on what you intended to say; otherwise, I might have to charge you with actually trying to extort some money for yourself."

"Well, as I pointed out this past weekend, Paul Ravich would never make incriminating statements about his crimes unless he truly believed I was crooked too. That's why I had to play the role of a scoundrel. I'm just glad, Lieutenant, you were in on the ruse. I'm far too feeble to start a long prison sentence."

Charley Frain shook his head in amazement. Like so many others before him, he had come to admire the wisdom and wit of the clever old lawyer. Pulling out the arrest warrants from the inside pocket of his sport coat, Frain joked: "I don't have one here with your name on it, so I guess you're in the clear."

The warrants for Ravich and Ron Carroll had been secured earlier that day from a cooperative magistrate based solely upon the circumstantial evidence the *Crouch* lawyers had already furnished. Ravich's taped admissions were just gild for the lily. It was now time to make the busts.

Frain picked up his radio with the other hand. "Base to Backup. Come in."

"*Backup here.*"

"What's your 20?"

"*We're in the lobby, with a building security officer.*"

"Leave him down there. Have a rolling unit ready at the building's front door. The rest of you come up, get off on 62, and meet me half a flight up in the stairwell. We're going in."

"*10-4.*"

Frain turned to his elderly undercover agent, the man in the decidedly non-James Bond attire. "Again, nice work, Harry. You can go back down now and wait for us in the building lobby. We'll go in to make the arrests. I can't have you taking any more risks."

Harry smiled and put his no-worse-for-wear hat back on his head. He touched the brim in a salute to his helpers and walked away, thankful it was all over.

Riding back down the elevator, he regretted for the first time ever that he didn't carry a cell phone. It would have been nice to make a call right then to Doug, Bonnie, and Bill. But he would see them soon enough.

Back at the war room, the lights were still on. His Musketeers were waiting.

It was not the kind of press he wanted. The next day, the paper and local news began carrying detailed accounts of the arrest of prominent trial lawyer, Paul Ravich, on charges of murder, solicitation, criminal conspiracy, and fraud. Although Ravich had always craved being the big story, this was a negative headline he could not control. From his jail cell, he longed for the slight mention paid to his co-defendant, Ron Carroll, who was only identified in most reports as "one of the law firm's investigators."

Ravich retained the best criminal lawyer in the state but it would do him no good. Bail was not available in a capital case. The DA, having been provided the evidence that Harry and his team collected, was making it a death penalty case.

Equally shocking news was the subsequent arrest of business magnate Charles Thornton on charges of conspiracy and fraud related to the Ravich case.

Bruce Waltman was summoned to get his boss out of jail but he refused. *Let him find a lawyer he trusts*, the General Counsel of Thornton Industries decided before tendering his resignation. He now understood why he had been kept in the dark for so long by Ravich and Thornton. They could both rot in jail or hell; it didn't matter to him.

The assets of Paul Ravich & Associates were immediately frozen. None of the wrongdoers would ever reap their windfall. In a matter of weeks, the money stolen from VyStream, Integrated Sentry, and its insurers would all get returned. The associates and employees of Paul Ravich & Associates were each questioned. None knew anything about the scheme and no one else was charged. But the firm was finished. A lot of people would soon be looking for work.

Joan Slator finally learned the whole truth. Harry sat in her home and patiently answered all her questions. In the end, it brought her no peace. Her husband's death made no more sense than the sudden loss of her daughter. Both perished because things got beyond their control.

Harry informed her, with regret, that she could not sue the men who murdered Ken. Although the couple had reconciled in their hearts, they were still legally divorced at the time of his death — a fact which barred any claim by her for wrongful death damages. She took such news with a calm acceptance. She was only looking for answers anyway.

Despite the harsh nuance of law, and the painful truths he had revealed, she deeply appreciated the old lawyer's help. He would remain a trusted friend. She had lost everything else but he restored in her a belief that good can ultimately prevail. Harry's efforts and kindness comforted her with the realization that, in a world with so much cruelty, honest and caring people still exist.

— ❦ —

The outcomes of the criminal cases were forgone conclusions. Criminals, like dogs, tend to roll-over when something nasty lands on their backs.

Facing the death penalty, Ron Carroll decided to cooperate with prosecutors in exchange for a life sentence with the possibility of parole. He filled in the few gaps left in the evidence furnished by Harry and his team. He told the DA how he made the bomb and where he got his C4; he explained how he destroyed and created evidence at Ravich's direction; he even told how he came into possession of a nice condo in Florida.

Paul Ravich was left with few cards to play. Prosecutors informed him he would face life with no parole, but could avoid death by lethal injection only if he testified truthfully in the fraud and conspiracy case against Charles Thornton. It wasn't much of a deal, but Ravich didn't think much of Thornton either, so he accepted.

Charles Thornton, having no one left in the food chain to bite, eventually pled guilty after stonewalling the charges for almost a year with a team of high-priced criminal defense lawyers. His eleven-year sentence was far lighter solely because he had not been involved in the planning or execution of Slator's murder.

The Board of Thornton Industries, his longtime rubber stamp, found itself a rudderless ship after the arrest and conviction of the company's Chairman and CEO. To keep the business afloat, the Directors formally ousted their disgraced leader and reflagged the vessel. Thornton Industries was no longer a corporate name that conveyed trust. It became Dynesta Corporation. The granite panels above the entrances to "One Thornton Plaza" were changed.

—⊶⊷⊶—

Crouch v Seacoast was tried one year to the day after the suit was filed. Judge Pavey was still on the bench, following the permanent resignation of Judge Lewis. She gave the *Crouch* lawyers an option to transfer the matter back to Judge Hinojosa's court, where it belonged, but they decided to stay where Paul Ravich once thought he could corral them.

Kate Crouch, their brave client, sat on a long bench and watched the proceedings. This time, she was accompanied by more than just her mother. The other five families — Ravich's former clients — had all come to Doug, Harry, and Bill, now wanting to find real justice for their dead. They didn't have to be solicited this time. Each was smart enough to realize that the lawyers who had uncovered Ravich's elaborate fraud would also be able to prove what really happened to their loved ones.

The new defense lawyers for SeaCoast argued that the other families couldn't join the suit because of the releases they signed in exchange for the company's prior ten-million dollar payment. But Judge Pavey set aside the releases as being based upon fraud, ruling that the previously paid amount could only act as a credit against any larger verdict that might be rendered against SeaCoast in the gross negligence trial.

The evidence against SeaCoast Chemical Corporation was devastating. The records that Paul Ravich had secreted away in his firm's storage room were located in the initial police search of his office. The documents were used to show how badly the company had been pushing its employees and the plant facilities. The jury was allowed to be told that Seacoast, through its lawyer, had tried to hide the incriminating evidence.

Ken Slator's backup records and the voicemail from Dave Phillips proved that the former president of the company had doomed the men with his conscious disregard of safety. Rob Finnegan, since fired, confessed to everything, even his break-in of the murdered plant manager's apartment in a futile effort to conceal the truth.

There was no question in any juror's mind that the company's reckless disregard of human life and its callous desire to make money at any cost had resulted in the deaths of six good men. They decided SeaCoast Chemical Corporation deserved to be punished severely for that, and for their willingness to try and hide their responsibility.

It turned out to be the largest punitive damage verdict ever rendered in an employer gross negligence case. The jury awarded just under seventeen-million dollars per death victim, one-hundred million dollars total.

Even the conservative appellate courts would not disturb this verdict. If *this* defendant's conduct wasn't gross negligence, nothing was.

Kate Crouch cried and hugged her lawyers after the verdict was announced. It was never about the money but the money would certainly help. More importantly, she had fulfilled a personal pledge to her dead husband — she did what it took to discover the truth. He was still gone, but at least a jury had now declared that Dan's life had value and that it was wrongfully stolen by an uncaring employer. Because of that, no one could ever say that her lawsuit was frivolous. To her, it was the most important thing she had ever done.

After applying the credit for SeaCoast's prior payment to the other families, the Judgment entered was for ninety-million dollars. Doug, Bill, and Harry would end up splitting a thirty-million dollar fee three ways. Harry found it ironic that his fee share of the legitimate case turned out to be the exact same amount as the fabricated blackmail demand he had tossed out to Ravich in their taped meeting.

Like a lot of litigation, one case bred another.

Dean Schiller honored his verbal agreement, convincing VyStream, Integrated Sentry, and its insurers to retain Harry's trial team to pursue a civil case against Paul Ravich and Charles Thornton for their fraudulent attempt to make those companies the fall guys.

By the time that case was tried, the defendants had been convicted for their crimes. The civil jury heard all the sordid details and wanted to make sure that every penny the innocent companies had expended in their defense was returned to them. They also wanted to send a message to future lawyers and CEO's who might foolishly consider corrupting justice to make a buck. Their punitive damage award was intended to set an example.

Paul Ravich was hit with a twenty-four million dollar personal judgment; Thornton for half that. Assets of both men were located and used to satisfy the judgments. The 25% contingent fee Harry had negotiated for the case netted another nine million dollars in fee that he split equally with Doug and Bill. Harry then donated his three-million dollar share to Joan Slator. Once again, he stepped outside the box to do justice. If the law could not legally recognize her loss, at least he certainly could.

Sarah Ash and her two fellow county employees dropped their lawsuit after Judge Lewis permanently resigned. It was never about the money for any of them, especially Sarah.

Doug and Sarah discovered that his new financial success didn't change things for them. They were happy before; they remained happy after. Their relationship would continue to improve. The outcome would be inevitable. They were *both* good people.

—⊕⊕⊕—

Bonnie Rogers got an incredible bonus when the *SeaCoast* fees were finally collected: Doug gave her the equivalent of five years salary. She took a nice long vacation with her once flakey but now steady boyfriend, Lieutenant Charley Frain. He finally retired from the police department and, even more surprisingly, finally decided that a long-term commitment with a smart and sassy girl like Bonnie wasn't such a bad thing after all.

—⊕⊕⊕—

The favorable press and courthouse buzz from the *SeaCoast* cases paid future dividends as well.

Business began flowing to the three attorneys after a city magazine featured them on its cover with the title: "The Honest Lawyers." No PR firm had to be used. Their exploits were newsworthy and noble. Harry laughed out loud when he saw the issue. The silly inscription on his business card now carried the imprimatur of a respected publication.

Lawyers started calling Doug Stevens with good case referrals.

Integrated Sentry began using Bill Gaston for all its legal work.

Union reps and courthouse personnel began steering cases to all three, no strings attached. Great lawyers don't have to send anyone to Vegas or give away Christmas cars.

—⊕⊕⊕—

The tragic disaster that started it all was a singular event, unique in its facts and consequences. Yet for the people involved, when they paused to reflect, it would always be remembered as more than a plant explosion that killed six. The causes and casualties, the lessons and litigation, the triumph of integrity over deceit — all those things would leave an indelible mark in each of their lives.

In the civil justice system, people get hurt, others get sued, issues get contested, money gets paid.

In that process, contaminants creep in — greed, manipulation, gamesmanship — to occasionally stain the temples of justice.

But in the end, so long as there are decent and talented people standing nearby to do the hard job, the law's white pillars can always be washed clean.

Epilogue

He would have loved it.

Every lawyer in the city, it seemed, sat in the pews and listened, alternatively smiling and nodding their heads in affirmation, sometimes even laughing out loud as the man's remarkable personality and career were recalled.

Atop the closed casket sat a triangular-folded American flag, signifying his prior military service. Next to it rested an old gray fedora, its cardinal-tail feather adornment no longer quite as red as it was ten years earlier when used to conceal an antennae. Time fades everything except the memory of greatness.

Doug Stevens stood at the front of the synagogue to deliver the eulogy in a strong and loving voice. He too had changed in the decade since he and Harry Greenbaum first met. Now forty-four, his body had grown a little fuller and the hair at his temples revealed the first brush strokes of gray.

He would speak without notes. The man he was paying tribute to had become a part of him.

Less than a year after the last *SeaCoast* case concluded, they had joined forces permanently. Harry's previous partner passed away and the firm of Greenbaum & Walker became Greenbaum, Gaston, & Stevens. When the new firm was formed, Harry reluctantly suggested a move to new space. They could certainly afford it and his new young partners deserved a fresh look. "Nothing too fancy, though," he had counseled, not wanting to completely abandon the career-crafted image of frugality and understatement that had served him so well.

He didn't need to say it. A simple makeover of Harry's old office would more than suffice. Both Doug and Bill had learned that opulence was overrated. They never even considered renting the impressive penthouse space down the street that once served as the palace of Paul Ravich & Associates. Once that firm disbanded, the space became available. It would sit vacant for almost four years.

Paul Ravich would sit forever in a prison cell. His consecutive sentences on counts of murder, conspiracy, and fraud gave him a lifetime behind bars to contemplate the error in believing: "the rules don't apply to me."

Doug stared down at the casket as he began his remarks.

"Here lies a man whose love of people and love for the law were always intertwined. That perfect marriage served him and his clients equally well, and it leaves behind a legacy that every attorney should aspire to achieve."

Doug looked out at the packed assembly. Everyone loved Harry, and almost everyone came to pay last respects.

"How best to honor that legacy? I think it's pretty clear: Let others remain cynical of our profession. Let us hold up Harry's light to shine justice upon those who find themselves in the dark. Let motivations of greed become the exception and not the rule among lawyers. Let kindness and skill defeat those forces aligned against the truth."

The last sentence made more than a few think of Paul Ravich, although his name was never mentioned. Nor should it have been. The funeral of Harry Greenbaum was a celebration of honesty and integrity. Ravich had no place at such an event. He had already been much talked about when his evil was first exposed and his downfall remained, ten years later, a continuing morality lesson to the assembled trial lawyers: When avarice supplants the oath to protect your clients' interests, you cease being a lawyer.

Doug looked over at Bonnie and Bill Gaston. Their eyes were filled with tears, their hearts were filled with pride. To have worked with Harry was an exceptional experience. It had made them wealthy but even greater riches were found simply sharing time beside the man.

No one could ever replace him. The knowing smiles that Bonnie and Bill returned, as Doug continued to speak, communicated their common understanding: all they could do now was work harder and try to do good, which was all that Harry had ever asked of them.

"At eighty-five and in his sleep, after sixty years of faithfully serving clients on this Earth, God decided he needed an honest lawyer. I don't know what trouble The Creator found himself in, but Harry will undoubtedly serve and surprise his new client with talents not yet seen by even the all-knowing."

The audience laughed. Everyone had their own Harry Greenbaum story and Doug's comment evoked pleasant and humorous memories.

"He never ceased to amaze. Trial adversaries remained close friends with him outside the courtroom doors. His most hostile witnesses found themselves being charmed while being trapped by his cross-examinations. He fought modern technology and pretentiousness with equal vigor. His wardrobe remained cheap and confused while his intellect remained priceless and strong."

There were more smiles at the mention of his sartorial style. It was a closed-casket service, but no one doubted that Harry was being buried in a non-matching ensemble of ridiculous-looking clothes.

"He revealed both the law's absurdities and its attributes with the same self-deprecating manner. He taught us life's most important lessons through soft shuffles and silly laughs."

Doug shifted his gaze to his wife and six-year old daughter, seated next to Bill and Bonnie.

"There will never be another Harry Greenbaum, but there will soon be another Harry."

Sarah clutched little Katy's hand as both looked up at the man they loved. Sarah Ash became Sarah Stevens two years after the *SeaCoast* case. Like her husband, she had also changed slightly with time. While still maintaining her playful spirit and good looks, her outlook now was much more purposeful. No longer a county clerk, she devoted her time serving as the executive director of a shelter for abused and homeless women. She also had a family to raise: a daughter, and a son on the way. At seven months, her pregnancy was definitely showing.

Others knew now it was a boy and what his name would be. The announcement was meant to help the mourners understand something profoundly true at this sad time: Life goes on.

"Like our next child, our firm will also continue to bear his name. Who we are, what we do, and how we do it — we owe it all to him. His name above the door will serve to remind every lawyer and staff member who works with us that we did not create, but only inherited, a place where the rights of victims remain paramount."

Joan Slator, paying her respects to the man who fought for her need to know, sat four rows back, nodding her head in deep appreciation.

Kate Crouch and her mother were also in attendance but each thought the speaker was only being modest at that point. It was all of them, not just Harry, who brought justice for Dan and vindicated Kate's long ago decision to hire Doug.

The two hundred or more attorneys who sat among Harry's non-lawyer friends and past clients reacted reverentially to the continuation of the firm's name. Greenbaum, Gaston, & Stevens was now widely regarded as the preeminent plaintiff's shop in town. Harry would be badly missed but the firm's reputation was solidly firm in its own right. While it was fitting to honor the man who made that possible, their colleagues fully expected that Doug Stevens and Bill Gaston, together with the new lawyers they would train, would continue Harry's tradition of effective, colorful, and creative trial work.

Doug could have eulogized his old friend for hours but knew that to do so would have displeased Harry immensely. Like Bonnie's to-the-point style of speaking, his old partner also believed in the sanctity of brevity. "Words should not be wasted," Harry was fond of saying. That was especially true today, when nothing could possibly be said that would adequately convey the depth of their loss or the quality of the man being laid to rest.

"So let us now say goodbye. The law has lost a champion. We have lost a friend. But both it, and we, are better for having been touched by Harry Greenbaum. Whatever adventures await his unique soul in the beyond, we want to make sure we send him on his way fully prepared."

With that, Doug moved away from the pulpit and carried his final gift down the three steps of the altar to stand behind the casket.

"Godspeed, D'Artagnan," he spoke with a cracking voice, as he gently laid a Big Chief tablet between Harry's hat and the Stars and Stripes.

Author Note and Acknowledgments

Writing a novel is a long and solitary journey of plot outlining, character development, research, and writing sessions followed by inevitable hours of rewrites and edits: all necessary tasks to shape a story into something others will hopefully want to read. The fictional events in *Gamesmanship* take place primarily over the course of a single year. In reality, the writing and publishing of this book took far longer.

As a former trial lawyer, I can safely report that the book's central villain, Paul Ravich, is a grossly exaggerated example of the unethical attorney. In fact, my own encounters with real life rule skirters were surprisingly few, especially considering the vast amounts of money often at stake in civil litigation. Do sleazy lawyers exist? Of course they do, but I had to combine every offensive trait and all the devious practices I could imagine in order to create a character as devoid of character as Paul Ravich. Conversely, I am proud to say I do know trial lawyers who are as honest and creative as the fictional Harry Greenbaum, and I was fortunate enough to work with many attorneys who possess the same integrity and decency as the imaginary Doug Stevens and Bill Gaston.

Judicial favoritism, case running, discovery and rule abuses, witness and evidence manipulation all exist in the real world. But the law owns no monopoly on corruption. Sometimes, corporations engage in illegal or questionable practices, as do politicians and preachers. Wherever money, competition, or power are in play, there will always be players who try to game the system. While *Gamesmanship* is a story about law and lawyers, its central theme — the triumph of integrity over deceit — applies, at least in the aspirational sense, across all human endeavor.

The city in which the story takes place was intentionally left unidentified. Just as Ken Slator served as the book's "everyman," I wanted the reader to conclude the place of action could be "anywhere." No town has yet to corner a market on good or evil.

And no author has yet to write a book all by themselves. I owe profound gratitude to my proofreading friends and family, all of whom caught more than one spelling or grammatical error, with many offering substantive suggestions that found their way into the final manuscript. A second set of eyes is an indispensable asset; a team of caring eyes is an invaluable gift. Thanks go to my real life Bonnie, Jan Bond Kast, for her edits and for the inspiration she gave me when writing about a legal assistant who is smarter than most lawyers. My thanks also to Wendy Clark, Greg Clark, Jim McInnis, Mike Phillips, Jeff Edison, Jack Massimino, Linda Cahalan, Robert Scardino, Rick and Diane Ash, Colin King, Dave Garrison, Mike Worel, Judy Deaton, and Lucille Ash for their detailed feedback and valuable input. To all others who graciously read early drafts or portions of this book and offered encouragement, the omission of your name here is solely the product of my poor memory and not intended as a slight. Perhaps "drinks on me" can count as my atonement for any oversight.

Getting your story into the hands of others is, unquestionably, more difficult than getting the words on the page. Thanks to my publisher, SandLine Press, for all its many tasks. A tip of the hat to my copyeditor, Terry Moffitt of TLM Creative, for her diligent work. My gratitude to Margaret Leslie Davis and Tony Thomas for their kind reviews. A note of appreciation to Kit Foster, a Scottish artist of immense talent who brilliantly designed the book's cover.

General thanks to retailers like Amazon, Apple iBookStore, Barnes & Noble, Google, and Kobo for making the book widely available to consumers. Also, my gratitude to those brick and mortar, brave and struggling, independent booksellers still willing to make space on their shelves and tables for new writers to be discovered.

A special thank you to my mother, Georgie Thompson, for both saying she liked the book and for never saying no to my childhood dreams.

My most heartfelt thanks go to my wife, Tina, who enthusiastically read the manuscript multiple times and never protested the many late nights of writing which disrupted my ability to be a decent daytime husband. Your love and belief in me helped to make the words flow.

Lastly, I want to thank someone I haven't seen in years but who taught me lessons that have lasted a lifetime: my high school drama teacher, Dolores Arnold. She managed to convince an impressionable young boy that curiosity overcomes circumstance, that hard work accentuates any native talent, and that confidence can turn dreams into reality. I would never have become a lawyer without the benefit of those teachings. Anything else I strive to be — including a writer of books — constantly recalls those lessons. May every person have a teacher like that sometime in their life.

— David D Williams

About the Author

David D Williams is a former attorney who practiced civil trial law in his native state of Texas, where he held Board Certification as a Personal Injury Trial Specialist and participated in the successful prosecution of numerous serious injury and death claims, always representing the victim.

He retired from active law practice to pursue a writing career and other creative endeavors. He nows makes his home in Park City, Utah.

GAMESMANSHIP

is available for purchase at

SandLine Press

sandlinepress.com

(hardcover, trade paperback, and e-book)

Amazon.com

amazon.com

(trade paperback and e-book)

Apple iBooks Store

apple.com/ibooks

(e-book)

Barnes and Noble.com

barnesandnoble.com/nook

(e-book)

Google

play.google.com/store/books

(e-book)

Kobo

store.kobobooks.com

(e-book)

And Through Any Bookstore

Publisher Inquiries

info@sandlinepress.com

www.ingramcontent.com/pod-product-compliance
Lightning Source LLC
Chambersburg PA
CBHW020825030726
47496CB00001B/90